D1499881

# FROMMER'S
# DOLLARWISE GUIDE TO
# TEXAS

by Rena Bulkin

**1987-88 Edition**

Published by Prentice Hall Press
A Division of Simon & Schuster, Inc.
Gulf + Western Building
One Gulf + Western Plaza
New York, NY 10023

ISBN 0-671-60624-7

Manufactured in the United States of America

# CONTENTS

# MAPS

**INFLATION ALERT:** I don't have to tell you that inflation has hit Texas as it has everywhere else. In researching this book, I have made every effort to obtain up-to-the-minute prices, but even the most conscientious researcher cannot keep up with the current pace of inflation. As we go to press, I believe we have obtained the most reliable data possible. Nonetheless, in the lifetime of this edition—particularly its second year (1988)—the wise traveler will add 15% to 20% to the prices quoted throughout these pages.

**A DISCLAIMER:** Although every effort was made to ensure the accuracy of the prices and travel information appearing in this book, it should be kept in mind that prices can and do fluctuate in the course of time, and that information does change under the impact of the varied and volatile factors that affect the travel industry.

# A DOLLARWISE GUIDE TO TEXAS

TEXAS IS AS MUCH A STATE OF MIND as it is a state—one that has always gripped the popular imagination. Larger-than-life Texas stereotypes—cowboys and Indians, lawmen and desperados, cattlemen and oil-rich millionaires—have inspired hundreds, probably thousands, of movies and television dramas. A generation of Americans grew up with Gene Autry, groomed to embrace J. R. Ewing and the urban cowboy craze. To the nation, and to themselves, Texans represent the last frontier—a place where men are men, John Wayne is king, and rugged individualism is a way of life. Which is not to say that Texas doesn't have Yuppies and nouvelle cuisine. It does. But if you go to Texas expecting the Hollywood version, you won't be too disappointed. Texans do, in fact, live the legend.

**TEXAS BIG:** If Texas is anything, it's big. Covering 275,416 square miles, it totals 7% of the area of the United States. It's large enough to hold 15 of the 50 states within its boundaries and still have 1,000 square miles to spare! It's larger than any European nation. In East Texas, you're closer to Chicago than to El Paso.

Not only is Texas big, everything in it is big. The high heels on cowboy boots make Texans seem taller. A contest in Texas is always a world championship—even if it's a world championship muleshoe-pitching or corn-shucking contest. And every Texas town has its world record. Seguin, Texas, is "the home of the world's largest pecan"; the "world's largest fish fry" is held each year in Borger; and the "world's longest-running domino game" (ongoing since the 1930s) is in Buffalo Springs. Texas ranches are the world's biggest, too —like the King Ranch in South Texas, an 825,000-acre spread where 60,000 head of cattle graze and 2,730 oil wells supplement the family income. Robert Redford started his horse ranch with King stock. Texas even claims the biggest natural disaster ever experienced in the U.S.—the 1900 hurricane in Galveston that killed 6,000 people. Of course, some Texans think the disaster that occurred on January 3, 1959, was worse; that's when Alaska joined the Union, usurping Texas's position as the largest state.

**TEXAS PRIDE:** 'Cause one thing Texans are is chauvinistic. I mean, what other state could inspire a song like "When I Die, Let Me Go to Texas"? When

I die, let me go to New York? Michigan? Idaho? Nope, these just don't work.

Texans love Texas. They'll buy anything in the shape of the state from ice-cube trays to cow patties. If they leave—and it's considered bad form to do so—they "see Texas in their rear-view mirrors." Expatriate Texans can be spotted around the country here and there—ordering steaks in New York City restaurants, lamenting the impossibility of finding good barbecue, and scanning the local papers to see if *The Best Little Whorehouse in Texas* is playing anywhere.

Why all the chauvinism? Some say it's an attempt at cohesiveness in a state that measures ranches in R.I.s (an R.I. equals one Rhode Island). Others explain Texas pride as a holdover from frontier days; the pioneers fought so damned hard for the place, it must be worth a lot. And yet a third explanation points to Texas's early days as an independent nation. Who knows? Texans would be surprised that anybody'd wonder about it. Isn't it obvious that this is the best place in the world? Well-known Texas joke: "Don't ask someone if he's from Texas. If he's not you'll embarrass him; if he is, he'll say so."

**TEXAS FRIENDLY:** Compensating for Texas chauvinism—which *can* get on outsiders' nerves—is Texas friendliness. The state was named for an Indian word meaning "friends," and Texans are, well, what else—the world's friendliest people. There's no such thing as a stranger to a Texan. If you're from back east, when you meet a new person you nod, say "Hi," and go back to whatever you are doing. A Texan will grin from ear to ear and drawl, "Well, it's a pleasure to meet 'yew.' This is just so 'nahce,' " and then treat you like a long-lost brother or sister. Even if you're a Yankee (if you don't harp on it). Part of Texas friendliness is a total lack of reticence. *The Genuine Texas Handbook* describes it this way—"No divorce is too messy, no problem child too tempestuous, to be the focus of a Texan's conversation with a complete stranger." Don't be surprised if a casual conversation with a bank teller or the clerk at K-Mart elicits intimate details during the course of a simple transaction. To me it's one of the Texans' most endearing qualities.

**TEXAS HUMOR:** Another great Texan quality is a sense of humor. Texans love jokes and good times. You don't grow up overly serious in a state that has peach-seed-spitting and jalapeño-eating contests. The Texas creed is: any excuse for a party, any excuse to let loose, whether you're 8 or 80. The two major butts of Texas jokes are ostensibly dumb Aggies (students at Texas A&M) and Okies (Oklahomans). A catchall Aggie/Okie joke: "Did you hear what happened when they sent all the Aggies to Oklahoma? The I.Q. of both states went up ten points!"

**TEXAS HISTORY:** The earliest Texans were descendants of paleolithic Asians who migrated over a period of tens of thousands of years, working their way to the New World across what is now the Bering Strait and southward through North America. They settled in Texas, among other places, some 10,000 years ago and evolved into Indians.

Since Texas is vast, and transportation was nonexistent (they didn't even have horses), these early settlers formed diverse societies. When the first Europeans arrived in the 1500s, they found tribes ranging from primitive nomads to complex agricultural communities. Some were peaceful, some fierce and war-like, and some were actually cannibals.

## They Brought Horses, Didn't They?

The Spanish flag was the first of six to fly over Texas. Alonso Alvarez de Piñeda charted the Gulf Coast from Florida to Vera Cruz, Mexico, in 1519. But the first actual exploration—a reluctant one—was made by Cabeza de Vaca who, in 1528, along with about 80 men, was washed up on the Galveston coast in a shipwreck. Worse luck, Galveston was the part of Texas where the Indians, the fearsome Karankawa, were cannibals! The Spaniards were kept prisoner there for six years, but not harmed because de Vaca gained a reputation as a healer among the Indians, even performing surgery on one man to remove an arrow from his chest. The fact that one of the survivors was a Moorish black slave also intrigued the Indians and predisposed them to believe their captives had supernatural powers. Almost all of the "survivors" did perish of exposure, however, in the first year of captivity. De Vaca (along with the Moor and two others) eventually made his way back to Mexico in 1536. Though his stories of the Karankawa dampened enthusiasm for Gulf Coast explorations, other tales he had heard from the Indians about "the seven golden cities of Cibola" to the north encouraged future expeditions.

In 1540 Francisco Vazquez de Coronado set out in search of those cities of gold with 300 armed *conquistadores*. But the cities were never found. Some historians believe that the Indians purposely lied to Europeans about areas of magnificent wealth—always far away—in order to get them to move on. Eventually, explorations of Texas were abandoned because much more accessible wealth could be gleaned from Mexico's Aztec and Mayan kingdoms. Except for sporadic efforts—a foray here, a mission there—they didn't pick up again until the 1680s when the French, under La Salle, landed at Lavaca Bay (about 100 miles south of Galveston) and established Fort St. Louis. He and his men were looking for the mouth of the Mississippi but were blown into the Gulf by storms. They claimed the area as the western boundary of the Louisiana Territory. Hence, the second, and prettiest, flag (golden fleur-de-lis on a field of white) of Texas. But French efforts were plagued by disaster. La Salle was murdered by one of his own men, and hostile Indians, exposure, and disease also took their toll. In 1689 the Spanish, under Capt. Alonso de Léon, tracked down survivors of La Salle's ill-fated settlement, eliminating what was left of French rule by 1690. Father Damien Massanet traveled with de Léon and met the Tejas Indians of the region (who called themselves *thecas* or *tejas,* either pronunciation translating as "friends"). It is from this word that Texas is named. These Indians were actually of the Caddo Confederacy that controlled parts of what are now not only Texas but Oklahoma, Arkansas, and Louisiana. The most advanced of all Texas Indians, they farmed, had sophisticated judicial and diplomatic procedures, and worshipped one god. Anxious to trade with the Spanish and acquire guns and horses, they welcomed the newcomers and expressed a willingness to embrace Christianity. Missions soon sprang up, but the Tejas quickly met the fate that would befall most mission Indians. Lacking antibodies to European diseases, they soon perished in epidemics. Though the missions folded, the red, white, and gold Spanish flag was firmly planted.

As the 18th century dawned, perhaps the most important consequence of the Spanish influx thus far was the introduction of horses and cattle to the region. Some of these horses ran loose and multiplied, and they were tamed by the Comanches, who were fierce warriors and expert horsemen. Equine transportation allowed the Comanches to move westward, where they came into conflict with the Apaches, also formidable warriors, who moved to the lower Texas plains and harassed more peaceful tribes. The French and Spanish also got involved in these Indian wars, usually on opposite sides. Needless to say, loyalties were shifting and self-serving. Meanwhile, the Spanish continued to build missions, which the Apaches and Comanches raided regularly to obtain horses and cattle. Though the Indians never planted a flag, they fought fiercely for the land until the middle of the 19th century. Perhaps if they had united, they would not have lost the country.

In 1762 the Spanish-French hostilities ceased on the eastern border when France ceded the Louisiana Territory in return for Spain's help in the Seven Years' War. This period marked the apex of Spanish power in the New World. But under Charles IV, who assumed the throne of Spain in 1788, the quality of colonial administrators declined, and, consequently, relations with the Indians further deteriorated.

## Mexico Tells Spain "Adios"

When Napoleon Bonaparte came to power after the French Revolution in 1789, he regained the Louisiana Territory and betrayed Spain by selling it to the United States, whose leaders were much more interested in Spanish Texas than the French had ever been. Soon Anglo-Americans began pouring into eastern Texas, building settlements and capturing wild horses to bring back to the United States. The United States was an obvious threat to New Spain, a double-edged threat in that American revolutionary ideals were spreading to Mexico. In a bloody decade-long war against Spanish domination, marked by mass executions and other vicious reprisals against rebellion, Mexico finally ousted the Spanish in 1821. Spain's role as a power in the New World had come to an end. And Texas was under a new flag, the red, white, and green banner of Mexico.

## Enter the Anglos

Shortly before Mexico won its independence, Moses Austin, a Missouri miner, applied to Spain for a Texas land grant. His request to bring 300 families to Texas was approved, but he died before the move began. His eldest son, 27-year-old Stephen F. Austin, took up the claim, and between 1824 and 1828 he brought 300 colonists to San Felipe. He also obtained permission to settle another 900. Other colonists followed, and though Austin's settlement remained by far the largest, by 1830 there were some 15,000 settlers in Texas, and Anglo Texans outnumbered Mexican Texans four to one. Most started out as loyal Mexican citizens. Austin even helped quell an Anglo revolt in 1827—but trouble was brewing. Mexico forbade the importation of slaves after 1827, and after 1830, banned further Anglo immigration. Austin managed to flout both prohibitions, but in spite of this the colonists, accustomed to American freedoms, chafed at the Mexican-imposed rules. Texas pioneers were also expected to embrace the Roman Catholic church, another point of contention. In 1833 Austin went to Mexico with various petitions from the colonists, including an appeal for a more independent status as a separate state. (This wasn't really such a radical demand; eventual statehood had been promised to Texas in 1824.) But Mexico, always distrustful of the Anglos, became alarmed and threw Austin in jail for a year in Mexico City. His detention exacerbated anti-Mexican sentiment in Texas.

Released in 1834, Austin returned and counseled war against Mexico. When the Mexicans tried to retrieve a cannon that had been given the colonists to fight off Indians, they met with resistance and withdrew. Soon afterward Gen. Martín Perfecto de Cos was driven from San Antonio by rebels. The Texans thought the war was over. Mexico was beset by financial and internal political problems (coup followed coup in the new country, and the average government lasted only 7½ months), and it seemed unlikely they'd have the wherewithal to reenter Texas. But the rebels reckoned without Mexican President Santa Anna. Enraged by the defeat of Cos, he was determined to drive all Anglo-American settlers from Texas. He intended to finance their eviction with money made from confiscating Anglo property.

The debacle of the Alamo, in which all the defenders were slaughtered, and the subsequent retaliation at San Jacinto, leading to independence, are covered in detail in the San Antonio and Houston chapters of this book, respectively. Suffice it to say that Santa Anna won a Pyrrhic victory at the Alamo, a battle he fought for reasons more emotional than tactical. He lost his best soldiers, and the time wasted there on a relatively unimportant fight gave Sam Houston time to regroup the Texan army. The Alamo, and later the murder of 350 captured Texans at Goliad, only further inflamed the revolutionaries. Santa Anna's Alamo victory may have cost him Texas.

## From Lone Star Republic . . .

During the years 1836 to 1845 Texas was an independent republic flying its own flag—a lone star on a red, white, and blue field. You'll still see this flag waving over Texas schools, banks, and government buildings—even on oil derricks. San Jacinto hero Sam Houston was the first president, and the famed Texas Rangers were formed to protect the frontier.

These were proud but difficult years for Texas. The debt-ridden new nation suffered financial and frontier hardships. Though the war with Mexico was officially won, there were still volatile border clashes and raids. And Indian attacks continued. The great Texas hero, Stephen Austin, died in December of 1836, having given his all for Texas, putting patriotism before personal gain. He died with no more money than he had upon his arrival in Texas a dozen years earlier.

## . . . To Lone Star State

On December 29, 1845, Texas solved many of its problems by becoming the 28th state in the Union. American backing brought new immigrants and investors, who were confident that Texas would survive. Sam Houston served two terms as a U.S. senator and became governor of Texas in 1859. Railroads, windmills, and other industrial inventions brought progress and development. Then came the Civil War. Sam Houston, a Union supporter, was driven from office. The Confederate flag became the sixth to fly over Texas. Like the rest of the South, Texas suffered during the war and the years of Reconstruction, though the devastation was less than elsewhere. Only in a few instances did Union troops occupy Texas territory. And during it all the wild Texas longhorns flourished and multiplied.

After the war, though cotton remained the state's major industry, cattle round-ups, cattle raising, and cattle drives became more prevalent. In 1866 alone over 250,000 head of cattle were driven to northern markets. Yankees were introduced to steak.

The invention of barbed wire in the 1870s revolutionized the cattle industry. John W. ("Bet-a-Million") Gates made a fortune selling the new fencing, which he promoted as "lighter than air, stronger than whisky, and cheaper than dirt." He bet ranchers $100 against $10 that his fencing would hold against anything, then worked the cattle penned inside it into a stampede to prove his point. The wire held, and ranchers bought it. Its advent led to wars between fencers and open-range cattlemen. The former sometimes fenced off water sources; the latter, who called barbed wire "the devil's necklace," retaliated with wire clippers. But barbed wire prevailed, and the fencing of herds allowed for vast improvements in cattle breeding. It might sound trivial, but in Texas barbed wire is taken seriously. Whole museums are devoted to it.

## Gushin' Black Gold

Texans always knew there was oil in the state, but before the Industrial Revolution it was more of a curse than a blessing. Heck, it just ruined wells that had been dug for water. The Indians used it as a salve, and the Spanish caulked boats with the stuff, but when oil was discovered at Spindletop, three miles from Beaumont, in 1901, Texas entered the 20th century with a boom. In its first year of operation Spindletop produced 3.2 million barrels of oil. The conversion from coal had already begun and Henry Ford was about to introduce the Model T. Land values skyrocketed, and speculators and wildcatters descended on the state. Fortunes were made overnight. Barbed-wire king Gates was one of the first to cash in; he started the Texas Company that would eventually become Texaco. Other oil discoveries followed, leading to the formation of hundreds of companies and an economy afloat on a sea of oil.

Other innovations also changed life in Texas dramatically. Air conditioning made sultry summers bearable, and the airplane shortened the state's vast distances. In the 1930s large-scale irrigation projects ended the problems of drought that had long beset the area. By the end of World War II, Texas was for the first time more urban than rural. The 1960s brought integration to Texas schools and voting rights to blacks in the state. The decade saw the assassination of a president in Dallas and the accession to office of quintessential Texan Lyndon B. Johnson. By 1970 three Texas cities—Houston, Dallas, and San Antonio—were among the ten largest in the U.S.

## Texas Today

Though Texas has retained its frontier spirit, it is today the third most populous of the 50 states, and about 80% of that population is urban. Cities like Houston and Dallas are considered big time; the world thinks of them as major cosmopolitan centers, along with New York, Los Angeles, San Francisco, and Chicago. Or to put it in small-town Texas terms, "they're as bad as New York." In point of fact, Houston and Dallas are nothing like New York. They're more like Los Angeles—vast urban sprawls connected by a network of freeways and dotted with shopping malls. In the last decade or so, real-estate speculators have run wild, while urban planners must have been turned away at the border. They're not beautiful cities, but they are fun, offering a sophisticated mix of haute couture and haute cuisine, posh hotels, culture, counterculture, and, in place of Los Angeles glamor, Texas-style entertainments. Neiman-Marcus aside, a city that never has a rodeo, a livestock show, or a George Strait concert is just not a city in Texas.

The state's two other most important cities, San Antonio and Austin, are very different from Dallas and Houston, and from each other. San Antonio is ancient by Texas standards. The Alamo and other still-extant missions date to the early 1700s, and much of the city's 18th- and 19th-century architecture has been preserved as well. The feel is definitely Spanish, and a large Mexican population—much given to colorful plaza festivals—enhances that Hispanic flavor. Centered on the tree-lined Paseo del Río (River Walk), San Antonio is one of the prettiest cities in Texas. The other contender for that title is Austin, a charming university town (home to about 50,000 University of Texas students) on a beautiful lake in the lush (for Texas) hill country. It has over 100 parks. Capital city Austin is cosmopolitan in a very different way from Dallas or Houston. It's a bit like a combination of Washington, D.C., and Berkeley, California.

Texas's population may be largely urban, but its vast terrain isn't. Traveling across the state, you'll encounter the subtropical Rio Grande Valley, the mountain ranges of the Trans-Pecos region, the lush pine forests of East Texas, lively

Mexican border towns, West Texas desert, Panhandle plains, verdant ranchlands where cattle and horses graze, citrus groves and cotton fields, rivers, lakes (Texas is second only to Alaska in its volume of inland water), and Gulf Coast beaches.

It's all pulled together by the Texas mystique—a blend of country music and chicken-fried steak, Baptists and bull riders, football and fajitas. Oil wells, longhorns, and cowboys come into it too. Don't bother trying to understand it, just enjoy it. If you can believe dozens of country-and-western songs, even the most urban Texans are just country folk at heart. They're sure to give you a big Texas welcome. So hang up your saddle and stay awhile.

**PLANNING AN ITINERARY:** My feeling is that you don't come to Texas to see the Galleria. You come for those things that are intrinsically Texan—rodeos and football, chili cookoffs and country music, ranches and rattlesnake roundups, Billy Bob's and Gilley's, the stockyards in Fort Worth, and, of course, the Alamo. Plan your trip to include as many things of this sort as possible. It's not that Texas doesn't have good museums, sophisticated restaurants, notable theater and symphony orchestras. And it's not that you shouldn't enjoy them when you're here, but you can do those things in any big city. Only in Texas can you yell "hook 'em horns" at UT football games and spend the Fourth of July at a picnic with Willie Nelson.

If you have only one week here, consider spending part of it on a dude ranch in Kerrville or Bandera—real cowboy country—and a few days in San Antonio, just 46 miles away, to see the Alamo, the old Spanish missions, and the River Walk. For longer stays, your options might include at least one day in a Mexican border town (Nuevo Laredo is best for shopping; Juárez connects to the most interesting of the Tex-Mex towns, El Paso). Want to bask at the beach? Spend a few days in Galveston, Corpus Christi, or South Padre Island. Texas beaches are okay, but not spectacular; if you come from Hawaii or take frequent jaunts to the Caribbean, you won't be impressed.

Traveling with kids? Stay at a dude ranch and/or in cowtown Fort Worth and visit nearby theme parks in Arlington—Texas's answer to Anaheim. At night, leave the kids with a sitter and go out two-steppin' at Billy Bob's, the world's largest honky-tonk.

The thing about itinerary planning is that it's just not objective. A hundred different people will very likely have 100 different ideal itineraries. The best way to plan is to read each chapter and see what fires your imagination. Perhaps you're longing to see South Fork. Or the NASA Space Center. Or you want to come in spring and follow the wildflower trail out of Austin. Maybe you'd like to penetrate the wilderness of Padre Island or spend all your time hiking nature trails at wildlife refuges. Consider factors like the amount of time you have, how you're going to get from here to there, and interesting annual events, and come up with the best itinerary you can. One final word of advice: I always think it's better to experience one thing fully than to try to see and do everything.

If you need additional information on a particular subject that is not fully covered in the upcoming chapters (for example, I've mentioned areas that are popular for hunting or fishing, but have not provided full details on all the options), write to the local chambers of commerce or convention and visitors' bureaus, whose addresses are listed in each chapter.

**WHEN TO COME:** The main thing to keep in mind is that the summers are very hot. On the other hand, they're the most activity-filled times. If you do come in summer, just bring your lightest clothes and plan to sweat a bit. It's really not too terrible. August through October is hurricane season; listen to weather reports before traveling to the coastal areas. Fall and spring are delightful, especially early spring and late fall when temperatures are at their most moderate. Winter temperatures vary from 40° in the Panhandle to 61° in the Rio Grande Valley, and those averages generally include an occasional few days of cold snaps amid many balmy days when coats are not required.

**DRESSING FOR TEXAS:** Texas is a pretty casual place. Sure, at high-priced Dallas and Houston hotels and restaurants you'll see some of the world's best-dressed women (if your husband was an oil millionaire wouldn't you make regular pilgrimages to Neiman-Marcus?). Pack a few fancy duds for special occasions, but don't forget to throw in one or two pairs of jeans, a few T-shirts, and comfortable walking shoes to make it through the days of sightseeing (no one wants to traipse around the Alamo and through Mexican markets' cobbled streets in high heels). In summer, if you're able to (without becoming an object of derision), wear shorts, a T-shirt, and jogging shoes. When it's 100°, who cares about fashion? A bathing suit is almost a year-round necessity. And if you really want to fit in, make an early stop at a good western-wear store and purchase the appropriate gear—shirt, Stetson, belt buckle, boots, and bandanna. Your salesperson will be knowledgeable about styles and won't (I hope) be a practical joker. *N.B.:* Jeans are de rigueur at cookoffs, cowboy bars, country concerts, and rodeos.

I hope you'll visit some of the state's wildlife refuges and nature preserves. When you do, wear boots (there are rattlesnakes), jeans (not shorts—there's poison ivy), and a long-sleeved shirt (there are mosquitoes). Cover yourself head to toe with mosquito repellent and you should survive. Don't let my caveats daunt you; these wild areas are among the most fascinating places in Texas.

## The $25-a-Day Travel Club—How to Save Money on All Your Travels

In this book we'll be looking at how to get your money's worth in Texas, but there is a "device" for saving money and determining value on *all* your trips. It's the popular, international $25-a-Day Travel Club, now in its 24th successful year of operation. The Club was formed at the urging of numerous readers of the $$$-a-Day and Dollarwise Guides, who felt that such an organization could provide continuing travel information and a sense of community to value-minded travelers in all parts of the world. And so it does!

In keeping with the budget concept, the annual membership fee is low and is immediately exceeded by the value of your benefits. Upon receipt of $18 (U.S. residents), or $20 U.S. by check drawn on a U.S. bank or via international postal money order in U.S. funds (Canadian, Mexican, and other foreign residents) to cover one year's membership, we will send all new members the following items.

### (1) *Any two* of the following books

Please designate in your letter which two you wish to receive:

**Europe on $25 a Day**
**Australia on $25 a Day**
**Eastern Europe on $25 a Day**
**England on $35 a Day**
**Greece including Istanbul and Turkey's Aegean Coast on $25 a Day**

Hawaii on $45 a Day
India on $15 & $25 a Day
Ireland on $35 a Day
Israel on $30 & $35 a Day
Mexico on $20 a Day
New York on $45 a Day
New Zealand on $25 a Day
Scandinavia on $40 a Day
Scotland and Wales on $35 a Day
South America on $25 a Day
Spain and Morocco (plus the Canary Is.) on $35 a Day
Turkey on $25 a Day (avail. May '87)
Washington, D.C., on $40 a Day

Dollarwise Guide to Austria and Hungary
Dollarwise Guide to Benelux (Belgium, the Netherlands, and Luxembourg) (avail. June '87)
Dollarwise Guide to Bermuda and The Bahamas
Dollarwise Guide to Canada
Dollarwise Guide to the Caribbean
Dollarwise Guide to Egypt
Dollarwise Guide to England and Scotland
Dollarwise Guide to France
Dollarwise Guide to Germany
Dollarwise Guide to Italy
Dollarwise Guide to Japan and Hong Kong
Dollarwise Guide to Portugal, Madeira, and the Azores
Dollarwise Guide to Switzerland and Liechtenstein
Dollarwise Guide to Alaska (avail. April '87)
Dollarwise Guide to California and Las Vegas
Dollarwise Guide to Florida
Dollarwise Guide to New England
Dollarwise Guide to New York State (avail. May '87)
Dollarwise Guide to the Northwest
Dollarwise Guide to Skiing USA–East
Dollarwise Guide to Skiing USA–West
Dollarwise Guide to the Southeast and New Orleans
Dollarwise Guide to the South Pacific (avail. June '87)
Dollarwise Guide to the Southwest
Dollarwise Guide to Texas
(Dollarwise Guides discuss accommodations and facilities in all price ranges, with emphasis on the medium-priced.)

**A Guide for the Disabled Traveler**
(A guide to the best destinations for wheelchair travelers and other disabled vacationers in Europe, the United States, and Canada by an experienced wheelchair traveler. Includes detailed information about accommodations, restaurants, sights, transportation, and their accessibility.)

**A Shopper's Guide to Best Buys in England, Scotland, and Wales**
(Describes in detail hundreds of places to shop—department stores, factory outlets, street markets, and craft centers—for great quality British bargains.)

**A Shopper's Guide to the Caribbean**
(A guide to the best shopping in the islands. Includes full descriptions of what to look for and where to find it.)

**Bed & Breakfast—North America**
(This guide contains a directory of over 150 organizations that offer bed & breakfast referrals and reservations throughout North America. The scenic attractions, businesses, and major schools and universities near the homes of each are also listed.)

**Dollarwise Guide to Cruises**
(This complete guide covers all the basics of cruising—ports of call, costs, fly-cruise package bargains, cabin selection booking, embarkation and debarkation and describes in detail over 60 or so ships cruising the waters of Alaska, the Caribbean, Mexico, Hawaii, Panama, Canada, and the United States.)

**Dollarwise Guide to Skiing Europe**
(Describes top ski resorts in Austria, France, Italy, and Switzerland. Illustrated with maps of each resort area plus full-color trail maps.)

**Travel Diary and Record Book**
(A 96-page diary for personal travel notes plus a section for such vital data as passport and traveler's check numbers, itinerary, postcard list, special people and places to visit, and a reference section with temperature and conversion charts, and world maps with distance zones.)

**How to Beat the High Cost of Travel**
(This practical guide details how to save money on absolutely all travel items—accommodations, transportation, dining, sightseeing, shopping, taxes, and more. Includes special budget information for seniors, students, singles, and families.)

**Marilyn Wood's Wonderful Weekends**
(This very selective guide covers the best mini-vacation destinations within a 175-mile radius of New York City. It describes special country inns and other accommodations, restaurants, picnic spots, sights, and activities—all the information needed for a two- or three-day stay.)

**Museums in New York**
(A complete guide to all the museums, historic houses, gardens, zoos, and more in the five boroughs. Illustrated with over 200 photographs.)

**Swap and Go—Home Exchanging Made Easy**
(Two veteran home exchangers explain in detail all the money-saving benefits of a home exchange, and then describe precisely how to do it. Also includes information on home rentals and many tips on low-cost travel.)

**The Fast 'n' Easy Phrase Book**
(French, German, Spanish, and Italian—all in one convenient, easy-to-use phrase guide.)

**Motorist's Phrase Book**
(A practical phrase book in French, German, and Spanish designed specifically for the English-speaking motorist touring abroad.)

**The New York Urban Athlete**
(The ultimate guide to all the sports facilities in New York City for jocks and novices.)

**Where to Stay USA**
(By the Council on International Educational Exchange, this extraordinary guide is the first to list accommodations in all 50 states that cost anywhere from $3 to $30 per night.)

## (2) A one-year subscription to *The Wonderful World of Budget Travel*

This quarterly eight-page tabloid newspaper keeps you up to date on fast-breaking developments in low-cost travel in all parts of the world bringing you the latest money-saving information—the kind of information you'd have to pay $25 a year to obtain elsewhere. This consumer-conscious publication also features columns of special interest to readers: **Hospitality Exchange** (members all over the world who are willing to provide hospitality to other members as they pass through their home cities); **Share-a-Trip** (offers and requests from members for travel companions who can share costs and help avoid the burdensome single supplement); and **Readers Ask . . . Readers Reply** (travel questions from members to which other members reply with authentic firsthand information).

## (3) A copy of *Arthur Frommer's Guide to New York*

This is a pocket-size guide to hotels, restaurants, nightspots, and sightseeing attractions in all price ranges throughout the New York area.

## (4) Your personal membership card

Membership entitles you to purchase through the Club all Arthur Frommer publications for a third to a half off their regular retail prices during the term of your membership.

So why not join this hardy band of international budgeteers and participate in its exchange of travel information and hospitality? Simply send your name and address, together with your annual membership fee of $18 (U.S. residents) or $20 U.S. (Canadian, Mexican, and other foreign residents), by check drawn on a U.S. bank or via international postal money order in U.S. funds to: $25-a-Day Travel Club, Inc., Prentice Hall Press, Gulf + Western Building, One Gulf + Western Plaza, New York, NY 10023. And please remember to specify which *two* of the books in section (1) above you wish to receive in your initial package of members' benefits. Or, if you prefer, use the last page of this book, simply checking off the two books you select and enclosing $18 or $20 in U.S. currency.

Once you are a member, there is no obligation to buy additional books. No books will be mailed to you without your specific order.

*Chapter I*

# THINGS YOU NEED TO KNOW

### 1. Getting There, Getting Oriented, Getting Around
### 2. Traveling in Mexico
### 3. Texas Lodgings, Food, and Nightlife

WHETHER YOU COME TO TEXAS for a day or two, a week, two weeks or longer, there are many choices you'll need to make before leaving home. In the sections that follow, I tell you about the travel options available.

## 1. Getting There, Getting Oriented, Getting Around

**GETTING THERE:** Texans will tell you it's a lot easier to get here than to leave. Getting here *is* easy, but figuring out the cheapest fares can be a headache. For example, you might fly round trip for under $200 if you catch a good airline promotion, but a 15-day bus ticket for $249 might end up cheaper since you can use it to get around the state as well. Remember, though, that bus and train travel eat into your vacation time. Compute all factors and figure out your best deal. A travel agent can help. Good luck!

### By Air

If you live in or near any major American city—not to mention foreign cities like Frankfurt, Düsseldorf, Paris, London, Mexico City, and Montréal, among a few dozen others—chances are you can hop an **American Airlines** (tel. toll free 800/433-7300) flight to Texas. Dallas-based American has more flights into Texas than any other airline. It serves Amarillo, Austin, Corpus Christi, Dallas/Fort Worth, El Paso, Harlingen, Houston, Lubbock, Midland/Odessa, and San Antonio. And **American Eagle,** a feeder network to/from American's hub cities, expands service to include Abilene, Beaumont/Port Arthur, Laredo, Longview, San Angelo, Texarkana, Tyler, and Wichita Falls. Of course, you can also fly American within Texas. If American Airlines doesn't serve your departure city, call your travel agent to find out which airline does. If you do fly American, ask about their **AAdvantage Program,** a travel-awards promotion with bonuses for accumulated mileage including free flights, upgrades to first class, and discounted or complimentary car rentals and hotel rooms.

Also, call a few weeks in advance to take advantage of fabulous promotional fares. For example, at this writing there's a $99 one-way fare between New York and Houston, $89 between New York and Dallas!

Twenty to thirty domestic, international, and commuter airlines cover the vast airport network in Texas, among them Continental, Delta, Eastern, Piedmont, Republic, TWA, USAir, United, Air Canada, British Caledonian, and Air France. For local numbers, consult your directory. For added information for the Dallas/Fort Worth area, consult the *Official Airline Guide,* published monthly, for the most current schedules and information.

### By Bus

Both **Trailways** and **Greyhound** bus lines serve every major city and many less-than-major cities in their vast transportation networks (consult the Yellow Pages for local telephone numbers). Both charge the same fares. Depending on how you take to bus travel, and how many places you want to visit, Greyhound's **Ameripass** and Trailways' identical **Eagle Pass** can provide terrific savings. These passes offer unlimited travel between all route cities for a fixed price during a given time period: 7 days for $189, 15 days for $249, 30 days for $349. The most you'd pay from any point in the U.S. to any city in Texas is, at this writing, $119 one way, $238 round trip. Even better for most people is a plan offering 15 days of bus travel during a 30-day period for just $150. Inquire about any special fares when you call; promotions come and go.

### By Train

**Amtrak** (tel. toll free 800/USA-RAIL) has fairly frequent service (three times a week) from various parts of the country to Houston, San Antonio, Austin, and El Paso. Amtrak has a slightly complicated fare structure. For instance, at this writing the one-way fare between New York and Houston is $276, but for $7 additional you can get a round-trip ticket. However, there's also an **All Aboard America** program, which is a round-trip ticket for $250 allowing three stops over a 45-day period. Once again, promotions come and go, so make inquiries when you call to be sure you're obtaining the cheapest fare. There are also special family fares, senior citizen fares, etc.

**GETTING ORIENTED:** A travel guide provides lots of information, but maps and brochures fill in the blanks. One of the best sources is the **State Department of Highways and Public Transportation,** Travel and Information Division, P.O. Box 5064, Austin, TX 78763 (tel. 512/465-7401). You can write or call them for the following free items: a series of ten *Texas Trail Maps* detailing scenic roads and out-of-the-way places; the *Official Highway Travel Map; Texas, the Friendship State,* a pictorial guide to Texas; the *Texas Travel Handbook,* a comprehensive 192-page guide to the state; a quarterly calendar of events; brochures like *Flags of Texas, Flowers of Texas, Texas Facts,* and *Texas Rocks and Fossils;* and *Texas Public Campgrounds,* a directory of several hundred facilities administered by federal, state, and local government authorities in Texas.

You can also call or write with your questions about any aspect of Texas travel. Or visit one of their many offices in the state where brochures are on display and knowledgeable staffers on hand to answer questions and help you plan travel routes. The **tourist bureaus** are located in: Amarillo, on I-40 East (tel. 806/335-1441); Anthony, on I-10 (tel. 915/886-3468); Austin, in the state Capitol (tel. 512/475-2028); Denison, on U.S. 75/69 North (tel. 214/465-5577); Gainesville, on I-35 North (tel. 817/665-2301); Langtry, on U.S. 90, Loop 25 (tel. 915/291-3340); Laredo, on I-35 North (tel. 512/722-8119); Orange, on I-10 East (tel. 409/883-9416); Texarkana, on I-30 East (tel. 214/794-2114); Valley, at the junction of U.S. 77 and U.S. 83, in Harlingen (tel. 512/428-4477); Waskom, on I-20 East (tel. 214/687-2547); and Wichita Falls, on U.S. 277/281/287 North (tel. 817/723-7931).

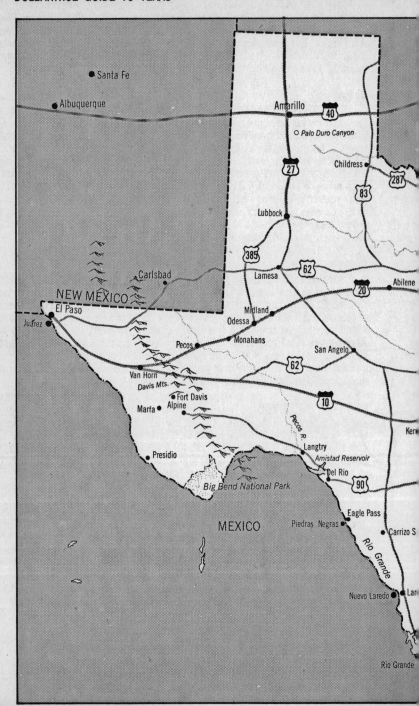

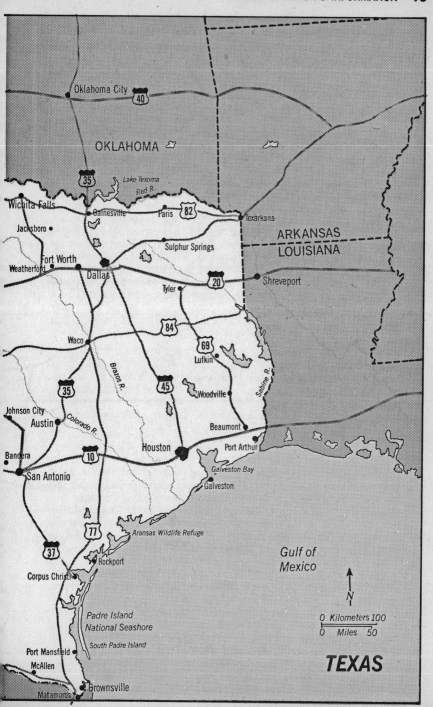

Other excellent sources are the **local chambers of commerce and convention and visitors' bureaus,** which are listed in the city chapters.

**GETTING AROUND TEXAS:** The size of the state is the biggest obstacle to seeing it. If you can, consider flying at least part of the time or most of your trip to Texas will be spent on the highway.

## By Air

The airline with the most flights around the state is **Southwest,** which recently added to its offerings when it acquired Muse Air, now renamed **TranStar.** Southwest serves Amarillo, Austin, Corpus Christi, Dallas, El Paso, Harlingen, Houston, Lubbock, Midland/Odessa, and San Antonio. TranStar adds Brownsville and McAllen to those destinations. You can also connect via Southwest to Albuquerque, Chicago, Denver, Kansas City, Las Vegas, Little Rock, San Diego, San Francisco, Los Angeles, New Orleans, Oklahoma City, Ontario (Calif.), Phoenix, Saint Louis, San Diego, San Francisco, and Tulsa. TranStar connects with several cities in Florida. Southwest calls its peak flights executive class, its off-peak flights pleasure class. Either way, they're quite inexpensive. At this writing, even the longest trip, Houston to El Paso (over 700 miles), is just $75 pleasure class, $95 executive. And shorter flights are much less; for example, Dallas to Austin costs $34 and $49 respectively. Children under 2 not occupying a seat fly free; accompanied children under 12, or those 12 to 21 flying alone, pay pleasure-class fares no matter when they fly, as do senior citizens. Inquire about special promotional fares when you reserve.

## By Bus and Train

Generally, you'll find bus service available between Texas cities, and occasionally there's train service as well. Both are listed in the individual city chapters of this book. If you come to Texas via bus or train, consider taking advantage of free stopovers included in round-trip fares (as described above).

## By Car

Air travel offers the advantage of conserving valuable vacation time. But if you have the time, traveling by car offers optimum flexibility. The terrain you drive through getting from here to there can be as interesting as the connecting destinations. The State Department of Highways and Public Transportation puts out a marvelous series of **Texas Trail Maps** for drivers covering various areas of the state (for instance, *Ride the Texas Hill Country Trail, Mountain Trail, Plains Trail,* etc.). They tell you about scenic roads and fascinating but out-of-the-way sights you'd probably miss if you stayed on the freeways. These free brochures are real trip enrichers. To get them, write or call the **State Department of Highways and Public Transportation,** Travel and Information Division, P.O. Box 5064, Austin, TX 78763 (tel. 512/465-7401).

Very few areas of Texas are easily seen without a car. A few car-rental companies are listed in each chapter of this book. One of the best-represented and most reasonably priced firms is **Budget Rent a Car** (tel. toll free 800/527-0700). They have many locations in Texas, including Abilene, Amarillo, Arlington, Austin, Bay City, Beaumont, Brownsville, Clear Lake, College Station, Copperas Cove, Corpus Christi, Dallas, El Paso, Fort Worth, Galveston, Harlingen, Houston, Killeen, Laredo, Longview, Lubbock, McAllen, Midland,

## MILEAGE BETWEEN TEXAS'S MAJOR CITIES
*Distance in Miles*

| | Amarillo | Austin | Big Bend | Brownsville | Corpus Christi | Dallas | El Paso | Fort Worth | Galveston | Houston | Laredo | Lubbock | McAllen | San Antonio |
|---|---|---|---|---|---|---|---|---|---|---|---|---|---|---|
| Amarillo | | 485 | 484 | 784 | 654 | 363 | 508 | 344 | 655 | 608 | 621 | 122 | 747 | 509 |
| Austin | | | 474 | 331 | 194 | 202 | 583 | 192 | 208 | 162 | 233 | 377 | 304 | 80 |
| Big Bend | | | | 636 | 524 | 559 | 329 | 584 | 651 | 603 | 434 | 360 | 578 | 406 |
| Brownsville | | | | | 160 | 526 | 806 | 518 | 384 | 357 | 202 | 672 | 58 | 275 |
| Corpus Christi | | | | | | 386 | 698 | 440 | 234 | 210 | 144 | 535 | 152 | 145 |
| Dallas | | | | | | | 647 | 33 | 292 | 241 | 435 | 327 | 504 | 282 |
| El Paso | | | | | | | | 614 | 791 | 743 | 607 | 382 | 751 | 571 |
| Fort Worth | | | | | | | | | 315 | 264 | 426 | 293 | 494 | 267 |
| Galveston | | | | | | | | | | 51 | 348 | 569 | 382 | 245 |
| Houston | | | | | | | | | | | 312 | 518 | 346 | 199 |
| Laredo | | | | | | | | | | | | 510 | 144 | 153 |
| Lubbock | | | | | | | | | | | | | 635 | 397 |
| McAllen | | | | | | | | | | | | | | 238 |
| San Antonio | | | | | | | | | | | | | | |

Richardson, San Angelo, San Antonio, San Marcos, Sugar Land, Texarkana, Tyler, Waco, and Wichita Falls.

The company's hotel/car-rental packages can be worth looking into. A current plan in Houston, for instance, gives you a 50% discount off weekend rates, 25% off weekday rates, at a Hilton hotel when you rent from Budget. Other promotions offer bonus miles in conjunction with airline frequent-flyer programs (for instance, United, Western, Air Canada, CP Air, Midway, USAir, and Pan Am). And a new company offering is the "Super Rez Club" for frequent renters. Your credit information is stored in a computer, so Budget can prepare the rental agreement in advance, saving you time at the counter. There's also a "Rapid Return" service. Promotions are subject to change, of course, but there are always special discounts and programs; be sure to ask about them when you reserve.

Other widely represented car-rental companies offering similar options and reachable via toll free telephone numbers are **National** (tel. 800/328-4567), **Hertz** (tel. 800/654-3131), and **Avis** (tel. 800/331-1212).

## 2. Traveling in Mexico

There are several border towns along the 1,800-mile stretch of the Rio Grande dividing Texas and Mexico. Both Texans and tourists make frequent excursions across the river for shopping, nightclubbing, and other south-of-the-border binges. Some border towns feature bullfights and thoroughbred or dog racing. And they all have *mercados* (markets) offering fabulous bargains to glib-tongued buyers and big tourist-oriented restaurants featuring (usually) less-than-fabulous food and mariachi bands. At the markets you can get everything from piñatas and paper flowers to large, sequined sombreros and serapes. Among the best buys are leather and suede items, pottery, handmade furniture, onyx chess and backgammon sets (and other items), goatskin rugs, perfumes, baskets, embroidered dresses, vanilla, and tequila. And there are wonderful things for children too.

Passports or visas are not required for U.S. citizens crossing into Mexico, unless you're going beyond the nearest border town or staying longer than 72 hours. Once every 30 days you're allowed to bring back—duty free—articles for personal or household use up to $400 in retail value, plus a gallon (only a quart for Texans) of liquor and 100 cigars. These are per-person limits, and those under 21 are not allowed to bring in liquor. Certain Mexican goods (mostly crafts items) can be brought back in unlimited quantities; U.S. Customs can tell you which ones.

Generally, people in the markets speak English, and you can always shop with American dollars so no currency conversions are necessary. And most shops also honor major credit cards.

**DRIVING IN MEXICO:** First of all, driving is not for the timid. Streets are narrow and crowded, sometimes one-way streets are unmarked, and Mexican driving is, to say the least, an anarchistic affair. You'll notice a disproportionate number of dented and dilapidated cars; they got that way "by accident." It is acceptable to honk your horn often. And when you park and a man materializes to guide you into the space, it is customary to tip him for this "service." Red-and-white signs that say ALTO, similar to stop signs, *are* stop signs.

If you do drive in Mexico—and I don't really recommend it—be sure to purchase insurance (your hotel can tell you where to get it) or to get a rider on your regular auto insurance before you leave home. Regular American auto insurance doesn't cover driving in Mexico.

It's so much easier and less expensive to park on the Texas side of the river (there's always a large lot) and walk across, I can't see too much reason to drive over. The markets are usually within walking distance, but if you want to ride, a taxi is cheaper than the extra insurance (bargain about the fare) and there are minibuses that ply the route from border to market.

The other hassle of driving is that you have to wait in a long line of cars going through Customs to cross back, an especially unpleasant affair in summer when your car becomes an oven and you have to turn off the air conditioning for fear of overheating. Walkers never have a wait.

One final caveat: Don't park in a Mexican no-parking zone; your license plate will be removed, and you'll have to pay a fine to reclaim it.

**¿QUÉ HORA ES?:** Mexico doesn't observe daylight saving time, so for the part of the year when the U.S. does, the two countries are out of sync timewise. Keep it in mind.

## 3. Texas Lodgings, Food, and Nightlife

**HOTELS:** Texas has built too many lodgings in most cities—a good situation for you, the prospective guest. That means that you can almost always get a room even at the last minute, and hotels are working harder to please. Of course, it's still a good idea to reserve in advance, thus assuring yourself the optimum choice and the best values. You'll find full mailing addresses for all hotels should you wish to write for reservations.

### Reduced Rates

Many Texas hotels offer weekend rates, some just on Friday and Saturday nights, others also on Sunday. When reserving, always ask for a special rate if your stay includes a weekend, specifying it once again when you register. At some hotels it isn't automatically given, and if you've not requested it when reserving, you won't get it when checking out. You can also request a weekly rate if you're staying five days or more at a hotel; often it will be granted. And though most people don't realize it, many properties—especially smaller ones—are willing to bargain on rates. For the most leverage, approach a small hotel or motel late in the afternoon; if their rooms aren't filled, chances are they might prefer to rent at a reduced rate than to keep a room empty and make no money on it. Of course you risk being snubbed, but if your temperament allows for it, you'll meet with occasional success.

### Children

It seems obvious, but since so many hotels have begged me to explain, I will. When listings say "children under 12" or "children under 18," or whatever, stay free, it means *in a room with their parents*. Your kids will not be given a gratis room of their own. If you are traveling with children, hotels that don't charge for them are obviously a good idea.

### Frills

Most hotels try very hard to pamper visitors. Generally, you can count on being able to call housekeeping for an iron and ironing board; in many cases, hair dryers and even curling irons are available as well. Expensive hotels almost always offer twice-daily maid service; while you're out for dinner a maid comes in, puts new towels in the bathroom, remakes your bed if necessary, and turns down the covers, usually leaving a little treat such as a Godiva chocolate. Some hotels that don't do this automatically will do so on request, either gratis or for a small extra per-night charge.

If you stay at a first-class hotel, you'll enjoy the services of a concierge who will arrange anything you desire, as long as it's legal. Need a suit pressed at 2 a.m., want restaurant reservations made in Paris (Texas or France), have a sudden craving for caviar, or feel you just won't be able to sleep without a down pillow? Just ring up and the concierge will do his or her best for you. Even lesser properties generally go out of their way to offer these special services, but most guests don't take advantage. You should! You're paying for it. And it's convenient to have someone making your airline and restaurant reservations while you're out sightseeing. Where there's no concierge, there's often a guest relations person; if not, just inquire at the desk.

## The Concierge Level

A fairly recent development that has been gaining in popularity during the 1980s is the concierge level or floor, a hotel-within-a-hotel concept. It's a special floor—usually an upper floor where rooms offer good views. Guests on this floor usually enjoy upgraded room decor and amenities (you may find fancy toiletries, a hair dryer, and a scale in the bath) and are pampered with nightly turndown and free daily newspaper delivery. Often registration and checkout are simplified (you do it on the floor, avoiding lines in the lobby), and a special concierge is on duty just to serve the floor.

There's always a plush lounge where a complimentary continental breakfast and Happy Hour hors d'oeuvres are served. In some cases (Marriott hotels are notably lavish) the hors d'oeuvre spreads are so abundant you can skip dinner. The lounge is always an extremely comfortable place, where you can meet and mingle with other guests. Business people are the largest clientele of concierge-level floors, but they offer a pretty good deal to anyone wanting to combine big hotel facilities with small hotel intimacy.

Rates are usually just about $15 or $20 more per night—not much when you consider all the extras.

## Hotel Chains

A few chains deserve special mention here. In the upper-bracket category, **Four Seasons** hotels really deliver the luxury you're paying for. Every detail of decor and service is *comme il faut*. Listings in various chapters will elucidate.

Down a price notch, **Marriott** properties are also notable for offering good value for your money. They additionally feature bonuses for frequent travelers (you can work toward free air fares, car rentals, rooms, etc.) similar to those offered by, and in some cases, interchangeable with, airline and car-rental bonuses. Marriott Corporation is working hard to make it worth your while to stay with them whenever you travel. Ask about these programs when you reserve.

Both Four Seasons and Marriott properties offer special low-fat, low-cholesterol menus in all of their restaurants—even the gourmet dining rooms.

For the budget traveler, the San Antonio–based **La Quinta Motor Inns** offer a uniformly high standard of excellence at a low cost. They all utilize Spanish-style exterior and interior decor. La Quinta Inns are housed in terracotta-roofed buildings, usually of cream-color stucco or Mexican brick. Inside, white stucco walls are hung with prints of southwestern desert scenes, the color scheme utilizes earth tones, dark Spanish-style furnishings include a table with three armchairs, and you also get color cable TV with movie and other special stations, a full tub/shower bath, and a phone on which local calls are free.

All La Quintas have swimming pools, serve free coffee in the lobby each morning, and are located next door to inexpensive 24-hour restaurants (such as Denny's). I've yet to see a La Quinta—and I've inspected at least a dozen of them—that was not a clean, well-run property. Some have on-premises lounges. All have some no-smoking rooms and are equipped for disabled guests. Parking is free. Prices are generally about $50 for two, and children under 18 stay free with their parents. Almost every city in Texas has at least one La Quinta property. You can call toll free 800/531-5900 and request a nationwide directory.

And for rock-bottom budget rates, there's **Motel 6,** offering clean and comfortable no-frills rooms with air conditioning and shower baths. Like La Quinta properties, they have swimming pools and are located adjacent to inexpensive restaurants. Motel 6 rates are pretty much standardized across the nation: give or take a few dollars at various locations, they're $19.95 for one person, $23.95 for two, $27.95 for up to four people, including a crib where necessary. A TV can be rented on a daily basis for 99¢ black-and-white, $1.49 color. For a directory of Motel 6 locations, write to Motel 6, Inc., 51 Hitchcock Way, Santa Barbara, CA 93105. These budget hostelries tend to get fully booked; reserve as far in advance as possible.

In Texas, you'll find Motel 6 properties in Amarillo, Arlington, Austin, Brownsville, Corpus Christi, Dallas, El Paso, Ft. Worth, Galveston, Grand Prairie, Houston, Laredo, Lubbock, McAllen, and San Antonio.

## CAMPING: For a free directory of hundreds of facilities administered by federal, state, and local government authorities called *Texas Public Campgrounds,* contact the **State Department of Highways and Public Transportation,** Travel and Information Division, P.O. Box 5064, Austin, TX 78763 (tel. 512/465-7401). Information about commercial campgrounds is available from the **Texas Association of Campground Owners,** 6900 Oak Leaf Dr., Orange, TX 77630. For information on **camping in state parks** there's an in-Texas toll-free number: 800/792-1112.

## RESTAURANTS AND FOOD: Get ready for some good eatin'! Though the big cities have their share of sophisticated haute-gastronomie restaurants—among them several that rival anything New York or Los Angeles has to offer—it's the intrinsically Lone Star cuisines that are going to knock your socks off.

### Mexican and Tex-Mex
Sometime on your trip, treat yourself to a Mexican breakfast—a tortilla filled with scrambled eggs, chorizo sausage, potatoes and/or cheese, served up with a steaming cup of coffee. Mexico is the only country in the world that ever invented a better breakfast than the U.S. of A. The big rage in Tex-Mex fare is fajitas—thin strips of char-broiled beef skirt steak, marinated in a special sauce and served sizzling on a cast-iron platter with pico de gallo (a relish made of diced tomatoes, green peppers, onions, and cilantro) and other accompaniments that might include guacamole, fried onions and peppers, and grated cheese. Everything gets wrapped in freshly made hot flour tortillas. Fajitas are addictive. Tacos al carbón—similar to fajitas but already wrapped in tortillas and topped with melted cheese—are a delicious variation. You'll also want to try queso flameado—melted Monterrey jack cheese mixed with shallots and chorizo sausage; top it with pico de gallo and roll it in flour tortillas. Yum! And then there are nachos made with fresh tortilla chips and topped not just with cheese but with pieces of fajita meat, jalapeño peppers, and guacamole. Nachos with a margarita are the best team since Gilbert and Sullivan.

## Texan

As for totally *Texan* food, you can never go wrong ordering steak. The beef is nearly always top-quality. In fact, even in ethnic restaurants you'll do well to order beef dishes. If you like your steak or burgers rare, though, don't just mention it—drive the point home. Look the waitress in the eye and say in a commanding voice, "I want the steak rare. Rare. I mean rare. I mean it. Rare! Tell the chef." With this method, you'll occasionally get a steak that is not well done.

At least once you must try chicken-fried steak, a dish that takes bad-for-you-beef and makes it badder. With batter. That's right. It's peppered steak thickly coated in batter, deep-fried, smothered in rich cream gravy, and served with mashed potatoes.

The official state food is chili, and if Washington lobbyists (many of them Texans) are successful, it will become the nation's official food. Chili is serious business in Texas. Aficionados band together in groups such as the Chili Appreciation Society, whose slogan is "The aroma of good chili should generate rapture akin to a lover's kiss." The best "bowls of red"—and some of the worst—are found at chili cookoffs where you can go around tasting the entries of participants. And Tolbert's, a restaurant in Dallas founded by chilihead Frank X. Tolbert, is almost a shrine to the faithful. The best Texas chili is without beans, cheese, sour cream, and other eastern desecrations.

The other major Texas specialty is barbecue, the best barbecue in the world. The best of this genre is always served in dives (many are listed in various chapters of this book), and, like chili, at barbecue cookoffs.

Finally, though Texans drink plenty of beer (especially Lone Star, Texas's "national beer"), the beverage of choice is iced tea—not the pallid powdered mixes you get in other parts of the country, but delicious fresh-brewed tea served in Texas-tall glasses with fresh mint and a wedge of lime. Unlimited refills are free. And speaking of Texas tall, you'll find big portions are the rule at restaurants here.

There's just one trouble with Texas food. There seem to be only three vegetables—guacamole, okra, and baked potatoes.

## Louisiana

One additional cuisine you'll experience here is Créole-Cajun. Louisiana is just next door, and Texans love gumbo, blackened redfish, poorboy sandwiches, and all the rest. Delicious fresh gulf seafood makes this one of your best—and healthiest—Texas dining options.

## Cookoffs

You don't know nothin' about Texas until you've been to a barbecue, chili, and/or fajita cookoff. Don your jeans and boots and wear a T-shirt that proudly displays your beer belly. Cookoffs are great fun. You can walk around sampling each chef's concoctions until the fear that your jeans will burst stays your spoon. Then retire your utensil and enjoy the festive atmosphere, which almost always includes live country music and dancing. It might also run to contests (anything from cow-chip-throwing to fiddling), an auction, pony rides and petting zoos for the kids, volleyball games, rodeo events, children's beauty contests, dunking booths, armadillo races, etc. Good, clean family fun. And some cookoffs are held in conjunction with rodeos and country headliner concerts. The granddaddy of them all is the World Championship Chili Cookoff held in the ghost town of Terlingua, Texas, every October. Some cookoffs charge admission, but often the food and entertainment are free. To find cookoffs, you can check local newspapers and inquire at tourist offices. But the most complete listings are in the *Goat Gap Gazette,* the very entertaining chilihead newsletter whose masthead proclaims: "It comes out about 11 months a year. Nothing serious is included in its columns." An annual subscription is $11; send your check to the Goat Gap Gazette, 5110 Bayard Lane No. 2, Houston, TX 77006. For a single issue write a month or two in advance with a cover letter specifying the dates of your trip so you receive relevant listings. Send $1 with your request.

### Happy Hour Food

Numerous discos and hotel lounges offer vast all-you-can-eat buffets on weekday afternoons for the price of a drink. If you just want the food, order a club soda and you can put away quite a meal for about a dollar. And even regular drinks are usually low priced during Happy Hour. Many of these buffets are mentioned in my nightlife and hotel listings. If you're traveling on a shoestring, this is the way to do it with style.

**TEXAS NIGHTLIFE:** Texans like to party, so even the smallest towns tend to have a disproportionate number of clubs. It's always been that way. Frontier towns often had a dozen bars before the first general store or church was built. Today's clubs range from down-home honky-tonks to flashy discos and include an ample number of lavish dance halls where "I can tell by his outfit that he is a cowboy" types (in real life, lawyers and other urban folk) dance the Texas two-step and the Cotton-eyed Joe. You know what I'm talking about. You saw John Travolta do it in the movie—at Gilley's, the granddaddy of the honky-tonks and the first of the urban cowboy bars. Gilley's, near Houston, and Billy Bob's in Fort Worth, are the two biggest, mind-bogglingest honky-tonks in the state. Numerous clubs are listed in the upcoming chapters of this book, but I will warn that they tend to come and go faster than a one-night stand. Call before you go.

Comedy clubs have also spread rapidly across Texas. If you've never been, they're forums for up-and-coming comics, the guys who perform on the Carson and Letterman shows. And they're much funnier when the restrictive TV codes are lifted. I've never had a less than entertaining evening at any comedy club in the state; I recommend them.

In big cities, you'll also find a full range of theater, classical concerts, ballet, etc., along with headliner performances. And you'll never have a better chance to see your favorite country stars.

*Chapter II*

# HOUSTON: SOUTHWEST SUPERCITY

1. Houston History
2. Getting There
3. Orientation
4. Hotels
5. Restaurants
6. Sights
7. Shopping
8. After Dark

THE YEAR 1986 marked the Sesquicentennial Celebration (150 years) not only of the state of Texas but also of the city of Houston, the fourth-largest and fastest-growing metropolis in the nation. It's not surprising that it grew to supercity status; after all, it was founded by New Yorkers.

## 1. Houston History

Named for Gen. Sam Houston, the first president of the Texas Republic and hero of San Jacinto, the city was the 1836 venture of two fortune-seeking New York brothers, land speculators Augustus C. and John K. Allen. They purchased 6,642 acres of land near the headwaters of the Buffalo Bayou from John Austin's widow for about $9,300, talked the new Texas Congress into moving its headquarters to the city, and lured numerous settlers by billing Houston as a future leading commercial center and world port. Though the Allens' claims were ultimately realized, Houston's beginnings were shaky. After three years Congress abandoned the sweltering mosquito-infested city for the Austin hill country. Epidemics of cholera and yellow fever decimated the population, and mud bogs made much of the city impassable when it rained.

Three factors saved Houston from ruin. The arrival of the railroad tied Houston to Galveston and all of the interior; it became "the city where 17 railroads meet the sea." With the discovery of oil in nearby Southeast Texas in the early 1900s, Houston was on its way to becoming one of the world's major petroleum industry and oil-field equipment centers; "black gold" made many Houstonians overnight millionaires. And the 1900 hurricane and tidal wave that devastated Galveston—one of the world's worst natural disasters—gave Houston the time and the opportunity to complete the widening and dredging of the Buffalo Bayou while her competitor, Galveston, was occupied in rebuilding. In 1914 President Woodrow Wilson fired a cannon that officially opened the Port of Houston—a port capable of accommodating every type of ocean-going vessel. Along with the burgeoning oil industry, it signaled Houston's transition from an agricultural backwater to a multifaceted megalopolis. Today thousands of ships dock at this port city each year, and major refineries, petrochemical factories, and other industrial plants stretch along the 50-mile man-made strip that brings the gulf right to Houston's door.

Over the years Houston has been called many things—"Queen City of the South," "Oil and Gas Capital of the World," "Southwest Supercity," and "Baghdad on the Bayou" (like any city worth its salt, it has a reputation for sin; as early as 1838 diarist John Hunter Herndon maligned it as "the greatest sink of dissipation and vice that modern times have known," and more recently evangelist Billy Graham predicted that "most Houstonians will spend an eternity in hell"). In 1962, when the National Aeronautics and Space Administration (NASA) located its flight-control and astronaut-training facility just southeast of the city, Houston became "Space City, U.S.A." The first words from the moon were "Houston . . . the *Eagle* has landed."

The Houston of the 1980s is, much like Los Angeles, an urban/suburban sprawl, its 565 square miles of real-estate developments, industry, and massive shopping centers connected by 222 smog-producing, meandering miles of freeway. It doesn't have the glamor of Los Angeles, but since it's a Texas city, its offerings tend to bigness. The famed Texas Medical Center, one of the world's largest medical facilities, is composed of 30 institutions, with world-famous staff associates including heart surgeons Drs. Michael deBakey and Denton Cooley. As for the Astrodome, creator of this super-arena Judge Roy Hofheinz once asked visiting Prince Rainier if he'd like to have the Astrodome in Monaco. "Marvelous," replied Rainier, "then we could be the world's only indoor country."

Houston is home to five universities and 56 foreign consulates. It's the international banking center of the Southwest and headquarters of 800 major companies, some of whose corporate dollars support her widely acclaimed ballet, symphony, opera, museums, and theaters. Downtown Houston is a showplace of modern architecture—a pristine cityscape of gleaming glass skyscrapers.

Houston is the most sophisticated urban center in Texas. But it's still Texas —home to the world's biggest, brawlingest honky-tonk, host of the annual Houston Livestock Show and Rodeo, and a town where cowboy boots and hats are seldom considered inappropriate attire, even in the most high-falutin' places. Scratch a Houston Yuppie and you may just find a beer-drinkin', football lovin', rugged individualist, wild western, urban cowboy.

## 2. Getting There

**BY AIR:** Houston is served by two major airports—**Houston Intercontinental Airport,** 16 miles north of downtown, and the smaller **William P. Hobby Airport,** 9 miles southeast of downtown. Among the airlines flying into Intercontinental are Aeroméxico, Air Canada, Air France, American, Aviatec, British Caledonian, Cayman Airways, Continental, Delta, Eastern, KLM, Pan American, Piedmont, South African Airways, Southwest, TACA, TWA, United, USAir, VIASA, Western, Metro Airlines, Royale, and Texas Airlines. Hobby is serviced by Air 1, American, Chapparel, Braniff, Delta, Eastern, Frontier, Ozark, PeopleExpress, Republic, Southwest, Texas Airlines, and Fort Worth Airlines. Since some airlines have flights into both airports, make sure you know which you'll be using.

**BY BUS AND TRAIN:** With a downtown station at 902 Washington Ave., corner of Bagby (tel. 713/224-1577, or toll free 800/872-7245), **Amtrak** connects Houston with most major cities. Houston is also served by **Trailways,** with its terminal at 2121 Main St., between Gray and Webster (tel. 713/759-6500, or your local office, and **Greyhound,** whose terminal is at 1410 Texas, at Austin (tel. 713/222-1161, or your local office).

# 3. Orientation

**GETTING YOUR BEARINGS:** Downtown is an easily navigated grid; the rest is a meandering mess developed without any system or planning. First order of business is to get yourself a map. Learn the freeways and you'll at least minimize the time spent lost in limbo. Maybe.

The central part of Houston is ringed by **Loop 610,** a continuous 44-mile artery. Addresses are given as East Loop, West Loop, South Loop, and North Loop, referring to its sides. Where it starts getting really confusing is when people talk about West Loop South and West Loop North, etc.; they're referring to the south and north sections of the west side of the Loop. If that explanation left you feeling loopy, study the map and you'll probably understand it. If not, forget it for a while and check out the other freeways; they're a little less confusing.

**I-10** (also called the **Katy Freeway** west of downtown and the **East Freeway** east of downtown) runs the entire east-west length of Houston (in fact it goes all the way from Beaumont to San Antonio). It's in the northern part of town.

**U.S. 59** (also called the **Eastex Freeway** north of downtown, but more often referred to as the **Southwest Freeway,** which is what it is south of downtown), cuts more or less diagonally through town rising from the southwest corner to the northeast; somewhere in the middle it has a horizontal stretch.

**I-45** (called the **Gulf Freeway** south of downtown and the **North Freeway** north of downtown) is a north-to-southeast artery that connects Houston to Galveston (that's why it's called the Gulf Freeway).

One thing almost all the freeways have in common is that they're usually jam-packed at rush hour, so allow extra time for traveling at peak periods.

Other important streets to know are **Westheimer Road,** which parallels I-10 about a mile south of it and, at Post Oak Road just outside the Loop, passes through the fashionable Galleria shopping area that is ringed by other posh stores and fancy hotels and restaurants. **Montrose Boulevard,** just above Hermann Park, is the arty district, the museum district, the gay district, and the hub of Houston's offbeat happenings. **Main Street** is downtown's, well, main street, and it continues south past the museum district, the Medical Center, and the Astrodome area, before heading out to the suburbs.

**INFORMATION SOURCES:** The **Greater Houston Convention and Visitors Council,** 3300 Main St., at Stuart, Houston, TX 77002 (tel. 713/523-5050, or toll free 800/392-7722 inside Texas, 800/231-7799 outside Texas), is a full-service organization geared to meeting the needs of tourists. Write or call before you go, and they'll send you an information kit containing *Houston Day & Night* (a two-month calendar of events), an attractive brochure called *Houston Discoveries* that gives an overall picture of local attractions, a map of Houston, an accommodations directory, and a few brochures on major sights. On request, they'll also include the very comprehensive *Houston Restaurant, Entertainment, & Shopping Directory*—so request.

On the phone or in person, the CVC will help you arrange accommodations at any price level. Their offices are open weekdays from 8:30 a.m. to 5 p.m., on Saturday from 9 a.m. to 3 p.m. If your time is limited, there's a drive-through window where you can pick up brochures and maps and get your questions answered in a hurry. Otherwise, there's free parking on the premises. The staff is multilingual, as is much of the available literature (French, German, Japanese, and Spanish). And the CVC is accessible to the disabled and offers them special tour advice and itineraries. It also maintains kiosks (racks of brochures only) at all three Intercontinental Airport terminals. When you visit, be sure to inquire about all special events going on during your stay.

**CLIMATE:** Summer temperatures, according to the charts, average 82°, but it always seems to me more like 95°. Houston is very steamy in summer. Winter temperatures, on the other hand, are a comfortable 53° to 61°, and spring and fall are delightful—the optimum times to visit, combining the best weather with the most happenings.

**GETTING AROUND:** I pity the person who doesn't have a car in Houston—unless your itinerary is very circumscribed, things will be difficult without one. There is a bus system, but the likelihood that one bus ride will take you from point A to point B in this megalopolis is small; you'll eventually get where you're going, but by the time you do, you might have forgotten why. Life is too short.

### Car Rentals

Most of the major car-rental companies are represented at both airports and elsewhere around town. **Budget** (tel. 449-0145 at Intercontinental, 643-2683 at Hobby) features very attractive hotel/car-rental packages in several price ranges and greatly reduced weekend rates. Also check out **Thrifty Rent-a-Car** (tel. 449-0126 at Intercontinental, 644-3351 at Hobby) and **National Car Rental** (tel. 443-8850 at Intercontinental, 641-0533 at Hobby).

### Buses

There are over 100 bus routes crisscrossing the Houston area, and close to 1,000 buses operating in the Metropolitan Transit Authority (METRO) network. If you plan to take them, your best option is to call 635-4000 6 a.m. to 8 p.m. weekdays, 8 a.m. to 5 p.m. weekends, for routing information (in English or Spanish). Just tell the person who answers the phone where you are and where you want to get to; you'll be given the best bus route, what time to catch the bus, and what the fare will be. Many downtown locations, Houston hotels, parks, and major sights are reachable by bus. You must have exact fare to board. Transfers are available if you have to change buses. Local service costs 60¢ and express fare is 85¢, with higher tariffs as you go farther afield.

There is weekday bus service to NASA (the 246-Bay Area Park and Ride Bus) for $2.05 each way, with departures from downtown Houston on the hour every hour between 8 a.m. and 3 p.m. You can catch the NASA bus on every other block of Milam between Preston and Jefferson. Buses from NASA back to downtown run every hour from 9:12 a.m. to 4:12 p.m.

## By Taxi

Except for short hops in the downtown area, taking taxis is an impractical way to traverse Houston's vast distances. The fare is $1.40 for the first fifth of a mile, 19¢ for each additional fifth. Firms offering citywide service include **Yellow Cab** (tel. 236-1111) and **United Cab** (tel. 699-8040).

## From the Airport

**Airport Express** (tel. 713/523-8888 or 523-5694) provides bus service from Intercontinental Airport to and from six central points in Houston—the Greyhound Bus Terminal at 1410 Texas Ave., the Downtown Hyatt on Polk Street between Louisiana and Smith, the Post Oak Terminal near the Galleria at 5000 Richmond, the Sharpstown Ramada at 6855 Southwest Freeway, the Greenway Plaza Terminal at 3769 Southwest Freeway, and the South Main Terminal near the Medical Center at 2201 Holcombe. Many hotels offer free pickup from the closest terminal. Buses operate from all three terminals (in conjunction with flight times) 24 hours a day in both directions. Cost is $6.50 each way, free for children under 12 accompanied by an adult. The company also provides frequent service between Intercontinental and Hobby Airports for $10 each way.

**Hobby Airport Limousine Service** (tel. 713/644-8359) operates buses between Hobby and four of the above points (not the Greyhound Terminal or the Ramada) for $4 each way (under 12, free). Departures are every 30 or 40 minutes in each direction between 5 a.m. and midnight.

**Taxi fare** from Hobby Airport to downtown is about $12 to $14, including a 75¢ airport departure tax. From Intercontinental you can pay flat rates to locations in five different zones or the amount on the meter, whichever is less. There's a zone map in the cab so you'll be able to figure out which zone you're going to. Fare from the airport to downtown is about $23, including a 50¢ airport departure tax.

Or make the trip by helicopter. A company called **Air Link** (tel. 713/975-8989, or toll free 800/231-4141) provides air-taxi shuttle service via helicopter between Intercontinental Airport and six Houston locations, with frequent departures throughout the day in both directions. Fare is $45 one way, $80 round trip, and many hotels offer free pickup from the nearest helistop drop-off point. Air Link has desks at all three airline terminals.

**ANNUAL EVENTS:** Major events are outlined here, but there's always a great deal more going on. Write in advance or call the **Greater Houston Convention and Visitors Council**, 3300 Main St., Houston, TX 77002 (tel. 713/523-5050, or toll free 800/392-7722 inside Texas, 800/231-7799 outside Texas), for a calendar of events taking place during the time you plan to visit. Also check the papers when you're in town.

## January

The year gets off to a running start with a world-class footrace, the **Houston-Tenneco Marathon.** Over 5,000 participants attempt to go the distance each year. This oil-company-sponsored run always begins at 8 a.m. near the

Tenneco Building, downtown at Milam and Clay. Phone 713/629-4489 for the date and further details.

## February

February is cowboy season. The exciting **Houston Livestock Show and Rodeo** opening day parade occurs mid-month; it begins downtown at Texas and Louisiana Streets with floats, marching bands, 6,000 horses, and a few hundred covered wagons from a dozen trail rides that originate in various parts of the state converging to join the procession. The same day, there are "Go-Texan Events" within the Astrodome complex including contests in barbecue cooking, fiddling, hay hauling, horseshoe pitching, and quilting. Admission, including parking, is about $5. The barbecue cookoff is judged the following day, and a $5 ticket (they usually have to be purchased in advance) allows participants unlimited samplings. The Livestock Show (admission $2, payable at the gate) is the world's largest, with exhibitors including both professional breeders and ranchers and young 4-H and FFA (Future Farmers of America) members. Some steers sell for as much as six figures! There are 16 scheduled rodeo performances in the two weeks following the parade, with saddle bronc riders, bareback riders, steer wrestlers, calf ropers, bull riders, and barrel racers competing for over $325,000 in prize money. And following each rodeo there's a concert by a major artist such as (in recent years) Ray Price, Waylon Jennings, Merle Haggard, the Gatlin Brothers, Crystal Gayle, and Willie Nelson. For information or advance tickets (reserved seats are about $10, including postage and handling; general admission, about $5), write or call the Houston Livestock Show and Rodeo, P.O. Box 20070, Houston, TX 77225 (tel. 713/791-9000). Ticket price includes the livestock show, rodeo, and concert—probably the best entertainment bargain left in the U.S. of A. Spring for the reserved seats; they're closer to the action. Sometimes tickets are available at the gate, but I suggest ordering in advance to avoid disappointment.

## March

In Texas, spring has arrived, and two weekends are set aside for the River Oaks Garden Club's **Azalea Trail** walks—a pilgrimage through selected gardens and homes of River Oaks, including the Bayou Bend gardens. Phone 523-2483 for details.

Later in the month, and occasionally beginning in early April, a major two-week extravaganza takes place all around town. During the **Houston Festival,** parks and plazas become outdoor stages for arts and crafts demonstrations and exhibits (both a juried and unjuried show, the latter called a "gypsy market"), international and Texas food booths, rock bands, C&W groups, jazz picnics, international music and dance (everything from Highlanders to Ukrainian folk), classical music performances, ballet, opera, special museum shows, theater, Latin groups, children's theater, mimes, comedy, and an outdoor art show extending for a mile along the Buffalo Bayou. That's not the half of it, and much of it is outdoors and free. There are several hundred events and exhibits each year. If you're in town in the spring, a full calendar is a must. To get it, write or call Houston Festival, 1964 W. Gray, Suite 227, Houston, TX 77019 (tel. 713/521-9329). They can also tell you which events require tickets and how to obtain them.

## April

More arts and craftiness. About 300 artists and craftspeople from all over the U.S. gather at the **Westheimer Colony Art Festival,** usually the third weekend of the month, to show and sell their wares. International food booths are part of the fun. It all takes place at the Liberty Bank parking lot, 1001 West-heimer at Montrose, from 9 a.m. to dusk. For further information, phone 521-0133.

And April is, in any case, an important month in Texas. On the weekend closest to April 21, the day the state won its independence from Mexico, there's the **San Jacinto Day Celebration** on the site of the decisive 1836 battle. Events include a parade, living history reenactments, musket salutes, and speeches by dignitaries. For further information, call 479-2421.

## May

Not to be missed for any reason, the famed **Fajita Meet** is held early in the month at the Cadillac Bar & Grill, 1802 Shepherd at I-10. For an admission of about $5 you can sample the fajitas proffered by about 25 Houston restaurants. Delicious! Bring an empty stomach. Call 862-2020 for details.

In Mid-May, KIKK Radio sponsors a **Cajun Festival** at the Miller Theatre with top Cajun performers like Frenchie Burke, Joe Douglas, and Rockin' Sidney. Admission is free. Bring a blanket and a basket of poorboy sandwiches. Call 772-4433 for information.

And at the end of the month, for a week beginning Memorial Day, the **Pin Oak Charity Horse Show** takes place at the Astroarena. This is a premier equestrian event, with ten performances. Champion riders from all over the country compete for the coveted silver trophies and blue ribbons, and a U.S. Grand Prix competition, featuring Olympic-quality show jumping, offers a $25,000 purse. Tickets are in the $5 to $12 range and can be ordered by phone via charge card (tel. 667-2494), or, subject to availability, purchased at the gate.

## June

The **Juneteenth Blues Festival** is a weeklong series of concerts at the outdoor Miller Theatre in Hermann Park. It's attended by over 100,000 people each year. Tickets are free, and you can get them at the box office between 11:30 a.m. and 1 p.m. on the day of performance. But don't worry if you don't get around to it; there's room for about 10,000 people on the lawn. The festival, featuring about 15 major blues artists, is sponsored by SumArts, a society that promotes contemporary performance and visual arts. Additional performances take place at Emancipation Park, but no tickets are needed. For information, call 528-6740.

In late June or early July, KIKK Radio sponsors a C&W concert called the **KIKK Radio Country Fair** featuring headliner entertainers like Charley McClain, John Conlee, Sylvia, and B. J. Thomas. A huge crafts fair, international food booths, and surrey and stagecoach rides are part of the fun. Proceeds go to cancer research. Tickets, available at the door, are about $5, and the event takes place at the Houston Farm and Ranch Club, off Hwy. 6, about two miles north of I-10. Call 772-4433 for information.

## July

As one would expect, there's much happening on the Fourth.

The old-fashioned **Foley's/Heritage Society Celebration** in Sam Houston Park, 1100 Bagby, includes patriotic music, early Texas crafts demonstrations, 19th-century games (like sack racing, egg-and-spoon racing, and haystack hunts for hidden treasures), mimes, clowns, face painting, oldtime dance demonstrations and lessons, square dancing, strolling costumed characters from our nation's past, historical reenactments, singers, bands, cloggers, and more—all of it culminating in a fireworks display. No admission charge. Call 651-6975 or 223-8367 for details.

**Major fireworks demonstrations** also take place at Sharpstown Center, 7500 Bellaire Blvd. (tel. 777-5391); AstroWorld (tel. 799-1234); in Clear Lake (tel. 488-7677); and at Gilley's, 4500 Spencer Hwy. (tel. 941-7990).

## August

The **Houston Jazz Festival,** the largest in the Southwest, once again sponsored by SumArts, is like the Juneteenth Blues Festival, a series of free concerts at Miller Theatre. The same information applies; details above.

## September

**Fiestas Patrias,** a two-week event beginning early in the month, originally celebrated Mexican Independence Day (September 16), but has evolved over the years into a general Hispanic festival. The schedule of events always includes a massive parade that draws 100,000 spectators to the downtown area, a major beauty pageant, another pageant to select a "Little Miss Fiestas Patrias," music, fashion shows, cultural programs, and a Grand Ball. There's much more. Call 926-2636 for further details.

## October

This is, for some reason, the most activity-filled month in town. The **Westheimer Colony Arts Festival** (see April) has another run, usually the third weekend of the month. Same information applies.

And **KIKK Radio** sponsors another concert, this time a freebie, at Miller Theatre. Major stars—like Eddie Rabbitt, George Strait, Ronnie Milsap, and Ricky Skaggs—perform. No tickets required—just show up early in the afternoon with a blanket and a picnic. Call 772-4433 for information.

The biggie is the **Texas Renaissance Festival,** beginning the first weekend in October and continuing for six weekends thereafter. It takes place in Plantersville, about 40 miles northwest of Houston (take I-45 north, make a left on Rte. 105, another left on Rte. 1774 and proceed six miles). While the festival is on, every Saturday and Sunday from 9 a.m. to dusk, Plantersville turns into 16th-century Europe with Shakespearean players, puppet shows, wandering minstrels, morality plays, jugglers, horse races, magicians, elephant rides, chariot races, jousters, a royal falconer, Renaissance games, crafts, and, of course, lots of hearty food. In addition to many booths offering everything from Scotch eggs to pizza, there's a full King's Gourmet Feast served up by beautiful wenches and enlivened by minstrels and other entertainers. Tickets, available at the gate, are $13 for adults, $6.50 for children 5 to 12 (under 5, free); sometimes discount coupons are available at Safeway's or Eckerd Drugs. The feast, at this writing, costs $50 if you reserve in advance, $60 at the gate. For information and tickets to the fair, contact Texas Renaissance Festival, Rte. 2, Box 650, Plantersville, TX 77363 (tel. 713/356-2178). For feast tickets, call or write Feast, Rte. 2, Box 655, Plantersville, TX 77363 (tel. 713/356-3002).

On a Thursday, Friday, and Saturday in early October, the Greek Orthodox cathedral sponsors the **Greek Festival** at 3511 Yoakum Blvd., between Harold and Kipling (tel. 713/526-5377). There's lots of Greek food (souvlaki, stuffed grape leaves, feta cheese puffs, and baklava) and Greek wine, as well as a dance program (Zorba, courtship dances, 1800s army dances, etc.), travel films, crafts and imported gift items, cathedral tours, and iconography displays. Admission is free during the day, $2 after 5 p.m. (there's more happening at night).

The **Martyn Farm Fall Festival,** usually the third weekend in October, takes place at the Armand Bayou Nature Center, 8600 Bay Area Blvd. Volunteers in turn-of-the-century costumes give guided farm tours, and there are demonstrations of instrument making, barrel making, blacksmithing, candlemaking, wool dyeing with plant materials, soapmaking, and rug hooking. Also bluegrass music, nature hikes, and hay rides. For details, call 474-2551.

## November

The **Annual Foley's Thanksgiving Day Parade** in downtown Houston is the major event of the month. Marching bands, floats, giant balloon characters, clowns, and celebrities—just like New York's Macy's parade. Call 651-6975 for information.

## December

On three evenings in mid-December, the Harris County Heritage Society sponsors free **Candlelight Christmas Tours** of the 19th-century homes and church in Sam Houston Park, 1100 Bagby. The buildings are candlelit with hurricane lamps and decorated in Victorian Christmas mode. Artisans give demonstrations of lacemaking, woodcarving, weaving, etc., and there's complimentary wassail for all. Choirs, musicians, and carolers entertain. Call 233-8367 for information.

# 4. Hotels

With 44 new hotels built since 1980, and still others under construction, it's not exactly difficult to find a room in this town. In fact, the city is overbuilt, which means: you can try bargaining for better rates, you're likely to get especially good weekend deals, and on the whole, you're going to get better value for your hotel dollar in Houston hotels than in other major cities. Nevertheless, I'd advise you to reserve in advance to give yourself optimum choice and procure the best rates. Houston hostelries range from old-world elegant to ultramodern, and there's even a motel that can claim "Elvis slept here."

Listings begin with the $100-and-up luxury-class categories, divided into deluxe and upper bracket; the latter are a bit less expensive than the former. The bulk of the selections fall in the moderately priced range—about $50 to $85 double; in several cases that price represents suite accommodations and even includes breakfast. A bed-and-breakfast and long-term-stay option are provided, and the section concludes with budget listings (under $40 for a double). I've selected hotels that offer the optimum in comfort, aesthetics, and service in their respective price ranges, as well as convenient locations in or near downtown, the Galleria, the Medical Center, Hermann Park, Memorial Park, or the Astrodome complex. There's something to suit every taste and budget.

**DELUXE CHOICES:** Victor Borge calls the **Lancaster,** 701 Texas Ave., at Louisiana, Houston, TX 77002 (tel. 713/228-9500, or toll free 800/231-0336), "one of the finest hotels in the world." Hermione Gingold, given a complimentary suite at another downtown luxury property when she starred in a production of *A Little Night Music,* checked out and paid for a room here. Offering a degree of service and a soothing ambience that harks back to the leisurely era when people traveled with steamer trunks, the Lancaster is indeed unique. Constructed in 1926 (in Texas that's ancient history) as the Auditorium Hotel, its advent marked the emergence of Houston as a great American city. Italian-born millionaire Michele DeGeorge hired distinguished architect Joseph Finger to design his 12-story brick hotel in neoclassic style with Italian Renaissance detailing and Florentine windows. Actors and actresses performing at neighboring theaters were regular guests at the Auditorium— including Gene Autry, who once rode his horse Champion down the stairs to a basement club and sang a few western ballads. In postwar years, as the neighborhood declined with Houston's

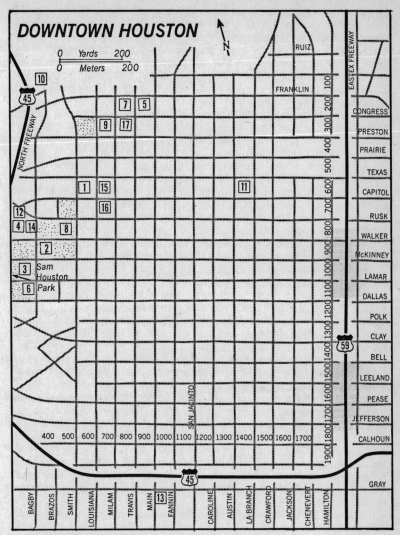

# DOWNTOWN HOUSTON

N

Yards 200
Meters 200

**KEY TO NUMBERED SIGHTS**

1. Alley Theater
2. City Hall
3. Sam Houston Park
4. Sam Houston Coliseum
5. Pillot House
6. The Long Row
7. Old Cotton Exchange
8. Tranquility Park
9. Convention and
   Visitors Center
10. Amtrak Station
11. Greyhound Terminal
12. Music Hall
13. Trailways Terminal
14. Albert Thomas Space
    Hall of Fame
15. Jones Hall for
    Performing Arts
16. Pennzoil Towers
17. Old Market Square Park

sprawl to the suburbs, the hotel began to deteriorate. But today downtown is once again a vital area, and in 1982 a multi-million-dollar renovation transformed the old Auditorium into the elegant European-style Lancaster. The brick exterior was repainted and highlighted by white terracotta cornices and trim. Large multipaned, burgundy-awninged showcase windows were enhanced by terracotta facing, colorful flags above, and flower boxes below. Brass-enclosed elevators were installed, and the marble staircase leading to the mezzanine level refurbished.

As a Lancaster guest, you're greeted at the beveled-glass doors by a smartly uniformed doorman who escorts you to the registration desk and announces you by name. The potpourri-scented lobby itself is a delight, with classical music playing and soft lighting from shaded lamps and sconces.

The guest rooms, pristinely decorated in four color schemes—forest green, claret, pale yellow, and white—feature two-poster, half-tester beds and lounge chairs with ottomans. Exquisite imported English floral-chintz fabrics create charming bedspreads, wallpapers, and draperies, and old English hunting-motif lithographs and Audubon prints adorn the walls. Bathrooms feature imported Italian statuary-vein marble vanities and floors, brass fixtures, and wrap-around mirrors, not to mention frills like Artesia water, a vase of fresh flowers, a thick terrycloth robe near a pile of bright white towels, an umbrella, a scale, and an assortment of designer soaps, colognes, aftershave lotions, body lotions, and shampoos. Ice is delivered to your room every afternoon, as are two newspapers each morning, and a selection of magazines is supplied. Your color TV, concealed in a handsome mahogany armoire, has a remote control device, while a bedside switch operates all the lights in the room. There are three phones—bedside, desk, and bath—and clock radios. Shoes are shined gratis if left outside your door at night.

Additional guest services include a full-time concierge who prides himself on never saying no, complimentary limo service within the business district on weekdays and to/from the Galleria on weekends, 24-hour room service, the availability of portable cellular phones with the hotel's number, in-room computers on request, messenger service, nightly bed turndown, picnic lunch baskets upon request, and access to downtown's most exclusive health facility, the Texas Club. The latter's offerings include a large indoor pool with adjoining sundeck, 12 racquetball courts, four squash courts, basketball, a one-third-mile indoor running track, a full spectrum of weights and Nautilus equipment, and an ongoing schedule of aerobics classes. And last but not least of the hotel's offerings is the charming Lancaster Grille, about which more in the restaurant section.

Rates at the Lancaster are $140 to $165 single, $165 to $190 double, from $275 for suites. A weekend rate (available Friday, Saturday, and Sunday—and Thursday in summer) of $105 includes parking (otherwise it's $9 per night), brandy at nightly turndown, and chocolates and wine on arrival. Inquire, too, about theater packages.

When celebrities are visiting town, you'll often find them at **The Remington on Post Oak Park,** 1919 Briar Oaks Lane, just off San Felipe Road, Houston, TX 77027 (tel. 713/840-7600, or toll free 800/231-9802). They appreciate all the luxuries offered at this $52-million property—the most expensively constructed hotel in the nation—which range from a chauffeured limo for guest use (no, it's not gratis, though service to/from the nearby Galleria is) to a concierge for whom no request is too difficult or too daffy. He managed, for instance, to procure two hairdressers for Boy George on short notice one Sunday afternoon—one to dye half his hair red, the other to bleach the rest. But don't think that the

Remington, though it caters to guests like Frank Sinatra and Brooke Shields, is all flash and glamor. Essentially, it's a small (248 rooms), elegant hostelry in the grand luxe tradition, designed to reflect the feel of visiting a Newport or Palm Beach mansion. The decor blends both modern and antique pieces, achieving a tasteful harmony. The stunning travertine marble floors in the hotel's foyers were hand-rubbed to impart an aged look. The entrance rotunda features a breathtaking floral centerpiece of exotic blooms in an antique jardinière, woodwork throughout the hotel is bleached oak, and two full-time brass polishers are employed keeping fixtures and railings lustrous. Off the lobby is the Living Room, a sublime setting for afternoon tea and cocktails. Its elegantly appointed black lacquer tables are set with Limoges china; an 18th-century lacquer screen with gilt and mother-of-pearl inlay that once belonged to the Emperor of China adorns one wall; peach silk pillows embellish plush couches; windows overlook a cascading fountain and tiers of potted flowering plants; and a harpist plays while you nibble at petit fours and buttered cucumber and cress sandwiches.

The Garden Room, the hotel's main dining facility, is decorated in delicate hues of peach, watermelon, and taupe. Walls are hung with mid-18th-century French pastoral prints; there are potted palms and exquisite flower arrangements; tables are, once again, set with Limoges china; and candles in large fluted glass holders add a romantic glow. Especially lovely is the conservatory area of this dining room; under a skylight, it's furnished in cushioned wicker pieces from China set amid huge pots of ficus and flowering foliage. During the day light streams in through multipaned arched windows; at night one dines under the stars. A dinner here might feature an appetizer of linguine salad with roast Chinese duck ($7.50), an entree of fresh Dover sole with brown butter and herbs ($27), and a raspberry soufflé ($6.50) for dessert.

Next to the Garden Room is The Bar, a handsome setting with dark oak beams, woodwork, and columns. Audubon bird prints and George Catlin Indian portraits adorn the walls, and you'll note a Frederic Remington bronze on the Florentine marble bar. Afternoons and early evenings there's live entertainment here—a pianist or combo, and sometimes a vocalist. A pubby lounge with leather furnishings and hunting prints on the walls adjoins. The Bar is a chic spot for Houston lunches and afternoon rendezvous.

There's also food service by the pool and sundeck. Additional hotel facilities include a posh French salon for men and women called Payot, offering massage, cellulite treatments, facials, leg waxing, all hairdressing services, tanning, manicures, and more. Guests can use the health club, plus tennis, racquetball, and squash courts over at the Houstonian (for details, see my recommendation of that hotel, below); free transportation is provided. On-premises shops include an exclusive leather boutique and a branch of Texas's foremost florist, Zen; they're responsible for all the magnificent arrangements in public areas.

On top of this, the rooms are all you'd expect—beds with beautifully carved mahogany headboards, gorgeous bedspreads, and down pillows; three phones (one bedside, one on your marble-topped desk, and one in the bath); a sitting area with a loveseat, armchair, and coffee table; a wicker basket of Gucci, Ralph Lauren, and Polo amenities—plus a terry robe—in the bath; an alarm clock AM/FM radio; and a color TV with HBO and other cable channels concealed in a handsome armoire. Color schemes combine muted beige with grays or forest green with rose hues. Of course, there's 24-hour room service, nightly bed turndown, complimentary shoeshine, and overnight pressing. And if you send your laundry out, it will come back to you wrapped in a box with cut flowers. No-smoking rooms and facilities for the disabled are available.

Rates are $155 to $220 for standard rooms (and a high standard it is), $195 to $240 for deluxe rooms (they're larger, on higher floors, and may have patios), $20 for each additional person, $105 per night (single or double) on weekends. Parking is $8.50 a night.

Opened in 1926, the **Warwick**, 5701 Main St., overlooking Hermann Park at the junction of Hermann and Montrose, Houston, TX 77251 (tel. 713/526-1991, or toll free 800/231-5701), is the oldest continuously operating hotel in Houston. The property has been owned since 1960 by oilman John W. Mecom, Sr., who refurbished it to the tune of $11 million and purchased $30-million worth of antiques to adorn its public areas and suites. The statues at the entrance are from an 18th-century Viennese palace. The lobby floors are Portuguese Rose Aurora marble; the paneling here and throughout the hotel comes from some of Europe's most famous 18th-century châteaux; and the spectacular chandelier has more than 5,000 pieces of crystal ornament. A priceless Aubusson tapestry adorns the rear wall. There's a plush lobby lounge (red-velvet cushioned Louis XV–style chairs amid potted palms and statuary), where weekday afternoons guests can enjoy piano-bar entertainment, and room-service fare is always available.

The LaFontaine Ballroom, with its graceful white Regency-period columns and doors, is the scene of the most lavish Sunday brunch in town ($25 per person). Breakfast and lunch are served daily in the charming Café Vienna, a small room paneled in oak from the Château La Motte au Bois in northern France and containing a magnificent 18th-century white faïence stove from Austria. The Hunt Room, a converted oak-paneled library from the Murat Palace, is an elegant setting for lunch or dinner. Sturdy oak tables are set with gleaming copper and lovely flower arrangements, black leather companion chairs contrast richly with the red Brussels carpeting, and a massive marble fireplace is (weather permitting) ablaze. A dinner here might consist of an appetizer of three pâtés with gherkins and brandied prunes ($5.50), followed by breast of chicken stuffed with mango, raisins, pinenuts, ginger, and honey ($14.50). And rounding out food and beverage facilities is the 12th-floor private Warwick Club; hotel guests become temporary members. Wrap-around windows offer panoramic views of Houston, and the view of the deluxe interior is just as pleasing. It's open for lunch, dinner, and nightly dancing to live music (big-band sound); a piano bar adjoins.

Guest rooms at the Warwick are decorated in the style of Louis XV, with caned furniture in painted and natural fruitwood finishes. The color scheme combines ivory, powder blue, and gold. More than half the rooms have a balcony. Amenities include phones in the bedroom and bath, cable color TV with movie channel and AM/FM clock radio. In addition to nightly turndown with Godiva mints, a fruit platter is delivered to your room about ten minutes after check-in, and a complimentary newspaper is left at your door each morning. Among the general hotel services and facilities are a lovely courtyard pool on a flagstone terrace surrounded by trees in planters; saunas for men and women; an on-premises travel agency, car-rental desk, hair stylist for men and women, florist, masseuse and masseur, and a Persian-rug shop; a full-service concierge; 24-hour room service; and complimentary limousine service to/from anywhere in the 610 Loop area. And, to my delight, only classical music (never the horror of "easy listening") is played in public areas—even the elevators. It's not surprising that this palatially elegant hotel is often headquarters for visiting royalty and heads of state; on my last visit a dinner was being set up for Crown Prince Philip of Belgium in the Presidential Suite.

Rates: $105 single, $125 double, $20 per extra person, free for children under 18. Inquire about reduced weekend rates when you reserve. Self-parking is $3 a night; valet parking, $7.50.

*Fortune* magazine once dubbed the **Four Seasons Inn on the Park,** Four Riverway, just off Woodway, Houston, TX 77056 (tel. 713/871-8181, or toll free 800/268-6282), "a parkside palace." It's a "palace" that has hosted royalty—Saudi Arabia's Prince Faisal and Crown Prince Harold of Norway, among others. As for "parkside," it's set on 28 forested acres, complete with lush thickets, sloping green meadows, and a reflecting pond that is home to numerous ducks and graceful Australian black swans. Near the pond are walls of cascading water, two immense swimming pools where you can do water ballet to underwater music, an expanse of lawn partly shaded by weeping willows, and a large sundeck area. And the tranquil park ambience is further reflected in the hotel's interior. Over $12,000 worth of fresh flowers are flown in from Amsterdam each month to adorn its public areas. The Italian green marble-floored lobby is hung with pastoral tapestries.

Café on the Green, a pool-view restaurant open daily from 6:30 a.m. to midnight, features gorgeous floral centerpieces, ficus trees, and latticework. And the tropically themed Palm Court—offering the same pond/pool/lawn view—has terraced fountains amid lush plantings, flower beds, and potted palms. Here, a pianist entertains every afternoon and evening, and a traditional tea with finger sandwiches, scones, and custardy fruit tarts, is served. Guests can also order vintage wines and champagnes by the glass or a light lunch at the Palm Court. Completing the hotel's food and facilities are La Reserve (a renowned gourmet dining room detailed in the restaurant section of this chapter) and the Black Swan Pub—very cozy with Persian rugs on bare oak floors, hunting prints on the walls, and dart boards (a bull's eye earns you a free lunch). It features 100 varieties of beer and lunch items ranging from prime rib to fajitas with English sherry trifle for dessert. And at night there's live music (top 40s) for dancing.

The Inn is an ideal choice for physical-fitness buffs. There are four tennis courts, bicycles are available for rides in the park, jogging trails abound in the area, and the lower level houses a fully equipped health club. It has exercise machines, a large-screen TV for aerobics videocassettes, a sauna for women, steamroom for men, whirlpool for both, and locker rooms stocked with razors, soaps, shampoo, body lotion, etc.

Guests also enjoy numerous luxuries—bedside remote control for one's cable color TV; a full-service concierge; twice-daily maid service and bed turndown; complimentary Artesia water; fresh flowers, a terry robe, and an extra phone in the bath; alarm-clock radios; free overnight shoeshine; 24-hour room service; complimentary transport via limo to and from a nearby airport, bus terminal and the Galleria.

The 383 rooms are fittingly exquisite, decorated in muted gray/green or taupe with charming floral-motif bedspreads and drapes, and framed prints of fruit and flowers on the walls. All rooms have a sitting area with a velvet loveseat and chair and a marble coffee table, and all offer stunning views of the Inn's park and reflecting pool or of nearby Memorial Park with the Houston skyline in the background. Deluxe rooms feature live plants and bath with hair dryer and bidet.

The tab for all this luxury living is $120 to $160 single, $145 to $185 double, with weekend rates reduced nearly 50%. There are also noteworthy weekend packages including frills like champagne upon arrival, buffet meals, and valet parking. Valet parking is otherwise $8 a night; self-parking, free. No-smoking rooms and special facilities for the disabled are available.

**THE UPPER BRACKET:** Linked to the Medical Center via a skywalk, and providing complimentary limousine service to any of its subdivisions, is the stunning new 26-story **Marriott Hotel** at 6580 Fannin St., Houston, TX 77030 (tel. 713/796-0080, or toll free 800/228-9290). Though Methodist Hospital allowed Marriott to build on its property in order to facilitate outpatient care (thus saving beds for people who really need them), don't think of this property as for the ailing only. Its location puts you within easy reach of the Hermann Park museums and zoo, downtown attractions and restaurants, and the Astrodome complex. In addition, this Marriott delivers an awful lot of luxury for the money. It has, in fact, hosted such notables as the Saudi Arabian royal family and the prime minister of Turkey.

Numerous plants, pink Italian marble, high-quality artwork, and Oriental antiques beautify the public areas, and the 398 guest rooms are charming. They feature moss-green carpets, pretty flower-and-peacock-motif bedspreads, brass lamps with pale-green shades, and gilt-framed floral prints on the walls. Some rooms have an armchair with hassock under a reading lamp as well as a desk. All offer full-length mirrors, cable color TV with Spectravision movies, and fancy bath amenities. Particularly luxurious and attractive are the concierge-level rooms where the extras include a phone, TV speaker, blow dryer, and scale in the bathroom; a small refrigerator; daily newspaper delivery; magazines in the room; an alarm clock; an AM/FM radio; a shoeshine apparatus; and nightly turndown with a Godiva chocolate. Concierge-level guests also enjoy fabulous views of Houston from their 25th-floor aeries and one of the most beautiful and best-equipped lounges of the genre, decorated with Oriental art and screens. Complimentary continental breakfast and afternoon hors d'oeuvres (both above the usual standard) are included in rates.

The hotel utilizes a health club connected with the Institute of Preventive Medicine at Methodist; hence, in addition to a full complement of weights and workout equipment, running track, volleyball, basketball and racquetball courts, whirlpool, and sauna, it offers classes in exercise, weight control, quitting smoking, and stress management. And for a fee you can measure the percentage of your weight that is body fat (not something I really want to know—I can guess). Further healthful activity is offered at a largish indoor pool with an adjoining Jacuzzi and sundeck.

There are, in addition to Chez Eddy at the health club (it serves healthful fare "high in imagination and low in cholesterol, sodium, and calories"), three dining options at the hotel. The most elegant is the Oriental-motif Choron's, with its rose marble floor, windows etched with lotus designs, Lalique-style lighting fixtures, flower arrangements in Oriental vases, and Indian sculptures on pedestals. Mesquite-grilled entrees and fresh seafood are featured at lunch and dinner. Deerfield's, less formal but equally appealing, offers marvelous buffets at breakfast, lunch, and dinner—all homemade fare, with fresh-baked breads and desserts, numerous salad-bar offerings, and delicious entrees. The $6.95 lunch is a great buy. One can also order à la carte. Another excellent buffet is the $4.75 lunch served weekdays at Fannin's, a plush eatery with a rose marble bar and burgundy ultrasuede walls cheerfully adorned with paintings of antebellum southern garden parties. The spread here includes homemade soup, cheeses, salads, an entree, and fresh-baked breads and desserts. At night Fannin's converts to a piano bar. All of the restaurants have no-smoking sections.

Further advantages accruing to Marriott guests are 24-hour room service; a lounge with sofas and game tables (puzzles, games, and cards are supplied); an adjoining shopping arcade in Scurlock Tower (reached via an interior passageway) that includes a chic multi-service salon for men and women, a stationery shop, pharmacy, and high-fashion boutiques; and a coin-op laundry.

Rates are $90 to $110 single, $100 to $120 double, the higher end representing concierge-level rooms. There are discounts for Medical Center patients and their families, and the weekend rate (Friday and Saturday nights) is just $65, single or double. Parking is $13.90 the first day, $9.40 each day thereafter, with a $3 surcharge for valet parking. No-smoking rooms and facilities for the disabled are also available.

No other Texas hostelry offers as many physical fitness facilities as the **Houstonian Hotel and Conference Center,** 111 N. Post Oak Lane, between Woodway and Memorial, Houston, TX 77024 (tel. 713/680-2626, or toll free 800/392-0784). It's set on 22 lushly forested acres, with a one-mile Astroturf jogging trail (lit at night) winding through the woods and a gravel walkway for more leisurely strolling.

On the premises, in a building adjoining the accommodations section, is the Fitness Center, its floor-to-ceiling windows overlooking verdant woods, beautifully manicured lawns, charming wooden bridges, flower beds, fountains, and gazebos. Its manifold offerings include eight lighted tennis courts, a full indoor gym for volleyball and basketball, eight racquetball courts, a large workout room with a full line of David equipment (considered by many to be the best there is) and other exercise machines, an ongoing schedule of aerobics classes, a one-ninth-mile indoor jogging track, steam room, sauna, whirlpool, flotation tank, sportswear boutique, pro shop, tanning bed, masseuse and masseur, and a full unisex salon for hair styling, manicures, pedicures, and facials. At the Preventive Medicine Center, a part of the Fitness Center, comprehensive medical evaluation is available. The Phoenix Spa, which is located in another building, is dedicated to rejuvenation through programs of diet, beauty, fashion, exercise, and personal growth. And there are two outdoor pools on the premises, one with a wooden deck where drinks and light fare are served and one Olympic-size with lanes for serious lap swimmers.

As for the hotel, its healthful tone is set in the sunny skylight lobby where arriving guests can help themselves from a basket of apples atop the registration desk. The lovely Atrium Café, just off the lobby, evokes the outdoors with umbrella tables and a waterfall. Salads and fruits are featured, and breakfast is served here daily. For more formal dining there's the Oak Room, its wall of windows overlooking lush greenery. The Oak Room's lunch and Sunday champagne brunch buffets are lavish displays highlighting fresh and healthful fare but also including sumptuously caloric entrees and desserts. An à la carte menu is also available.

The rooms—all with extraordinary forest views—are decorated in contemporary motif utilizing teal-blue or dusty-rose hues and color-coordinated striped or geometric-design cotton chintz bedspreads and drapes. A cable color TV, which has an in-house channel to orient guests to the Houstonian's numerous facilities, is concealed in a handsome oak or wicker armoire. Full-length mirrors, AM/FM clock radios, and a basket of complimentary Neutrogena toiletries in the bath complete the in-room amenities. Should you need anything additional, consult the hotel's very competent concierge.

For a slightly higher tariff, guests can stay on the concierge level, which offers a comfortable private lounge in which complimentary continental breakfast and afternoon hors d'oeuvres and champagne are served. A personal concierge is on hand to serve your needs, and room amenities are upgraded; for example, you get a terry robe in the bath. There are, of course, luxury frills for all at this in-town resort, nightly bed turndown with a Godiva chocolate and a complimentary *Wall Street Journal* each morning among them. And as the hotel is Vice-President George Bush's Houston residence, you can be sure security is taken seriously.

Rates are $98 to $118 single, $118 to $138 double, the higher end for units with sitting rooms with sofa and coffee table and concierge-level accommodations. An extra person pays $10 a night; children under 17 stay free. Weekend and holiday rates are reduced 50% or more. Overnight parking is $7, and valet parking is free during the day. Inquire about special packages, which run the gamut from mystery weekends (guests turn sleuth to solve a "murder" written, staged, and acted by professionals) to holiday celebrations, to get-in-shape-and-be-pampered spa programs. No-smoking rooms and facilities for the disabled are also offered.

The folks who bring you Lean Cuisine also operate the much-acclaimed **Stouffer Greenway Plaza Hotel,** 6 Greenway Plaza East, between Edloe and the Buffalo Speedway, Houston, TX 77046 (tel. 713/629-1200, or toll free 800/HOTELS-1). Located adjacent to the Summit, a 17,000-seat arena, the hotel is frequented by the performers and sports stars who play there—everyone from Willie Nelson, Kenny Rogers, and Barry Manilow to the Chicago Cubs and the Miami Dolphins. When the Ringling Bros. and Barnum & Bailey Circus plays the Summit, the hotel sponsors an elephant's dinner in the plaza with 40-foot troughs full of carrots, apples, and lettuce. But Stouffer's offers guests a richer diet than just glitz and glamor. It's opulent—from the plush marble-floored, crystal-chandeliered lobby to the large and luxurious rooms. Carpeted in pretty shades of mauve or teal, the latter have white walls adorned with Raoul Dufy watercolors and are furnished with white sofas and/or armchairs and hassocks. The look is low-key contemporary. Amenities include AM/FM radios, alarm clocks, color cable TVs with movie channel, special toiletries and extra phones in the bath, large walk-in closets, and full-length mirrors. And the hotel is so designed that all rooms overlook the pool and Greenway Plaza fountains.

The hotel's 17th and 18th floors comprise a concierge level, where a complimentary continental breakfast with fresh-squeezed orange juice is served in a private lounge each morning, and hors d'oeuvres are offered at cocktail hour. The lounge contains an honor bar, a TV, a backgammon table, phone (important calls can be taken here), and a stock of books and magazines. A concierge is on duty, and guests are further cosseted with frills like a hair dryer, nightly turndown with chocolate-covered strawberries, terry robes, and upgraded toiletries. All guests enjoy the luxury of complimentary morning coffee and a newspaper.

There's a large outdoor L-shaped pool (ample for laps) and an adjoining al fresco whirlpool set in a redwood deck. And in addition to an on-premises health club with Universal equipment and saunas, guests can patronize the deluxe Houston City Club, just next door, for a nominal fee. This sumptuous spa (regular membership is over $4,000 a year!) features ten air-conditioned indoor tennis courts, eight racquetball/handball courts, Nautilus equipment, saunas and steam rooms for men and women, massage, a pro shop, indoor and outdoor jogging tracks, and a club restaurant.

Of course, the hotel also has restaurants. The garden-themed, redwood-paneled Amelia's, serving breakfast, lunch, and dinner, wins points with me for playing classical background music. You can snack or dine (menus run the gamut from roast beef sandwiches to rack of lamb), but whatever you order it will be hard to pass up the six-inch-high, multitiered layer cakes, slathered with icing, that are temptingly displayed at the restaurant's entrance. Inexpensive lunches and Happy Hour cocktails (the latter enhanced by light rock and country tunes played by a live band) are offered at the pubby Justin's. There's also afternoon entertainment in the Lobby Bar, a relaxing setting for cocktails, tea and pastries, or premium wines by the glass. Marble tables, cotton chintz-upholstered wicker chairs, and moss-green sofas are set amid flowering plants, ivy, and potted palms. Contemporary jazz duos or a pianist perform. And perhaps best of all is the plush 21st-floor disco, City Lights, offering panoramic 360° views and dancing nightly to top-40s tunes and oldies. It's also used for lavish buffet lunches.

Rates at the Greenway Plaza are $110 to $140 single or double, $125 to $160 on the concierge level, $5 for an extra person, free for children under 9 (they also get coupons for free meals). Weekend and family rates are substantially reduced. Parking is $6 a night. Plus there are no-smoking rooms and facilities for the disabled.

**Marriott by the Galleria,** so named for its location four blocks from the shopping mecca at 1750 West Loop South (or the feeder road for 610), just north of San Felipe, Houston, TX, 77027 (tel. 713/960-0111, or toll free 800/228-9290), is a warmly inviting property—from the pretty, brick-floored lobby enhanced by stunning flower arrangements, to the basket of fresh apples at the front desk, to the 302 newly redecorated rooms. The latter are especially attractive, with rosy-mauve carpeting, pale-rose grasspaper walls hung with framed Oriental prints, turquoise ceramic lamps that harmonize nicely with the green-and-pink floral-print bedspreads, and handsome mahogany furnishings. Each has a table and chairs or a desk, one king-size or two double beds, cable color TV with Spectravision movies, and AM/FM alarm clock radio. A large indoor pool is the centerpiece of a lushly landscaped five-story glass atrium (they call it the "glass palace"), complete with a large outdoor sundeck, sauna, gazebo bar, and game room for kids. A health club is planned for the future, but until it is completed guests can use the luxurious President & First Lady Spa a block away (transportation is provided). The hotel's restaurant and bar/lounge are due for renovation at this time; however, the latter will probably continue to offer an elaborate complimentary Happy Hour buffet, serve premium wines by the glass, and feature live music for dancing and blackjack tables at night. The restaurant is moving from a western theme to a more contemporary look that harmonizes with hotel's new decor. Free transport is offered to/from the Galleria and an airport shuttle bus terminal.

Rates are $98 single, $115 double, with reductions offered for weekend stays. Children 18 and under stay free. Parking is free. No-smoking rooms are available.

If your taste is ultramodern, you'll love the **Lincoln Hotel Post Oak,** 2001 Post Oak Blvd., a block north of Westheimer, Houston, TX 77056 (tel. 713/961-9300, or toll free 800/231-9393), a creation of world-famous architect I. M. Pei. The dramatic 70-foot cascading glass vaults of the lobby enclose precast concrete walls and ficus trees ascending from Carnelian granite flooring to the skylight six balconied stories above. A lavish floral arrangement on a 19th-century Austrian Biedermeier table serves as a centerpiece, and two 18th-century Chinese Chippendale mahogany breakfronts (from the estate of J. P. Morgan) are displayed in the area.

Its chic Galleria location, luxury amenities, and impressive appearance combine to draw diplomatic, entertainment, and corporate elite to the Lincoln. George Bush gave a dinner here in honor of Rajiv Gandhi and his wife during the Indian prime minister's visit to the U.S., Placido Domingo has stayed here a number of times, and, to the delight of fellow guests, Al Jarreau once sat down and played piano in the lobby. Numerous amenities and services are offered: a multilingual concierge, complimentary shoeshine, nightly turndown with chocolate truffles, two phones in each room, a nice-sized pool and sundeck complete with poolside bar/snackbar, saunas for men and women, 24-hour room service, a unisex hairstyling salon, complimentary courtesy car to the Galleria and major business areas, car-rental desk, and the availability of a masseur and masseuse.

For a fee of $5 to $7.50 (depending on time of visit) guests can utilize facilities of a health club across the street—a swimming pool, racquetball courts, weight machines, an indoor jogging track, and aerobics classes among them.

The 386 rooms are attractively furnished and decorated in any of three color schemes: peach, beige, or soft teal blue. Your color TV, with AM/FM radio and movie channel, is concealed in an armoire. A digital clock is supplied, there are fine toiletries and full-length mirrors in the bath, and every room contains a sitting area with two armchairs and a small balcony.

The Lincoln has two restaurants. The Promenade, for casual, though elegant, dining, offers a sunny garden ambience with potted palms and trees amid peacock chairs and marble tables. The large geometrics of the carpeting, granite columns, and coved art deco ceiling add a pleasant contrast to the hotel's architecture. My favorite menu item is Le Grand Dessert, a sampler platter of all the restaurant's pies, cakes, and sweets!

The jewel-box-like Vendôme, paneled in honey-colored oak from a 19th-century château, is agleam with crystal chandeliers, 18th-century French bronze doré sconces, mirrored columns, and candlelight. A fireplace is set into the paneling, and 18th-century Flemish tapestries adorn the rotunda entrance foyer. French and regional haute-cuisine fare—lobster salad with truffles, loin of venison with black-currant purée sauce, and the like—is featured, with entrees in the $20 range. A sumptuous Sunday brunch ($22 per person) complete with ice sculptures, is served in the Promenade Lounge, also the setting for cocktail hour piano entertainment, nighttime jazz, and light fare. Another very pleasant precinct is the hotel's Brittany Bar, its rich cherrywood paneling set with beveled mirrors and a mural of southern French farm country. Comfortable chairs are upholstered in checkered green-and-white French country plaid, and the brass lamps on every table are reproductions of 19th-century French oil lamps.

Rates are $105 to $125 single, $125 to $145 double, $20 for an extra person. Children under 18 stay free in their parents' room. On weekends one or two people pay $80. Self-parking is free; valet parking, $7.50 a night. In addition, no-smoking rooms and facilities for the disabled are also offered.

**MODERATELY PRICED CHOICES:** All-suite hotels like the **Luxeford,** 1400 Old Spanish Trail, between Kirby and Fannin, Houston, TX 77054 (tel. 713/796-1000, or toll free 800/662-3232), have become increasingly popular accommodations choices in recent years, and with good reason. They deliver a lot of luxury and convenience at affordable prices. For openers, though the Luxeford's lobby is pleasant, it's not a splendiferous setting of fountains and ivied balconies under a skylit atrium. "We took some of the luxury out of the downstairs lobby and put it upstairs in the guest rooms," explained a hotel spokesperson. "That's where the guest spends the most time."

Saving money at the Luxeford begins at check-in; though bellmen are available, you can, without stigma, carry your own bags on luggage dollies supplied by the hotel. Similarly, though laundry service is offered, there's a washer/dryer for guest use on the third floor. And though there's a much-acclaimed art deco–motif, bistro-like restaurant, the Café Luxeford (delicious homemade gourmet fare is featured, along with fresh vegetables, fresh-baked herb breads and desserts, and premium wines by the glass), you can save money by cooking in your suite. It has a fully equipped kitchen with microwave oven, a small refrigerator/freezer, wet bar, and coffee maker. All the necessary cutlery, dishes, and cookware are available at the front desk, along with specially prepared gourmet microwave dinners.

Though the lobby's not posh, there is a pleasant lobby lounge for guests called the Club Room. With Oriental rugs on an oak parquet floor, a fireplace, well-stocked bookshelves, and comfortable furnishings, it's a fine place to relax over a drink at the end of a busy day. A complimentary continental breakfast (croissants, bagels and cream cheese, danish, granola, fresh fruit, juices, coffee and tea, even cappuccino and espresso) is set out on the Club Room sideboard each morning, and tea and coffee are available throughout the day. Houston newspapers are supplied gratis, while the *New York Times* and *Wall Street Journal* are available in the lobby. The Club Room also has an electric typewriter on a corner desk for guest use. And before you get to the Club Room, you'll receive a morning paper and orange juice at your door each morning.

The Luxeford's 191 accommodations are all one-bedroom suites with living room and kitchen. Each has a living room and bedroom phone, color TV with a choice of Spectravision movies, and radio, one of the latter with an alarm clock. Beds are king-size or double doubles. Decor is contemporary—pale-mauve carpeting, tan walls, brass lamps, quality oak furnishings, and mauve/silver/blue bedspreads and drapes. There's a mauve velvet sofa and armchair in the living room and a table with two chairs under a ceiling fan. You'll find full-length mirrors in closet doors.

Other facilities include a 24-hour fitness center with whirlpool, sauna, and Universal exercise equipment, and a small outdoor pool and sundeck. Gratis transportation is provided to and from the Texas Medical Center, an airport bus terminal, the zoo, nearby museums, Astroworld and the Astrodome (which is actually within walking distance, a factor that lures many sports figures and rock stars who play there to stay at the Luxeford). As for services, your shoes are shined overnight if you leave them at the door, and the front desk can handle concierge requests such as restaurant reservations and theater tickets.

The rates: $75 single, $85 double for a standard suite, $90 for a deluxe suite with a private whirlpool bath. An extra adult pays $10; children under 18 stay free. Parking and local calls are free. No-smoking rooms and facilities for the disabled are also available. The Luxeford probably offers more for your money than any other hotel in Texas.

Another hotel that features suite accommodations at regular room prices (145 of its 185 rooms are one-bedroom suites) is the **Wyndham Hotel Travis Centre**, 6633 Travis St., off University Boulevard, Houston, TX 77030 (tel. 713/524-6633, or toll free 800/822-4200). Located in the Medical Center area (patients get special rates), the Wyndham—rising 19 stories above a tree-lined boulevard—is an intimate hostelry where the leisure traveler can avoid the bustle and anonymity of convention activity. Off the lobby is a sedate 60-seat restaurant, the Garden Court, with marble-topped tables (candlelit at night) and rosy-hued furnishings amid potted palms. A pianist entertains at dinner, when the menu offers a choice of such nouvelle cuisine entrees as scaloppine of veal in lemon white wine sauce with spinach pasta ($14), along with lighter—and less expensive—fare including burgers, salads, and sandwiches. And though rich desserts (like the creamy white-chocolate mousse) are an option, the health-conscious diner can order from a full menu page of low-sodium, low-cholesterol, low-fat items. A delightful Sunday brunch here includes fresh-baked croissants, brioches, and breakfast rolls; fresh berries; fresh-squeezed orange juice; cheese and fruits; and assorted pastries and cakes for the price of your entree—perhaps poached Louisiana redfish with potato gnocchi and crayfish sauce ($12); it's worthy of consideration even if you stay elsewhere.

Wyndham suites are lovely and luxurious. Decorated in Fabergé colors of muted rose and pale green, each offers a full living room with sofa bed, armchairs, and coffee table; three phones (desk, bedside, and bath); an alarm clock radio; a color TV with cable stations and Spectravision movies concealed in a blond oak armoire; a wet bar and small refrigerator with ice maker; Water-Pik shower massage and upscale toiletries in the bath; and a king-size bed or double doubles in the bedroom. Since the first eight stories are parking levels, all accommodations are on higher floors and offer good views.

Additional guest amenities include an outdoor pool and jogging track, 24-hour room service, nightly turndown, a concierge, health club for men and women, sauna and whirlpool, gratis Perrier and Artesia water in every room, and complimentary transport to and from Hobby Airport, the Galleria, the Medical Center, Hermann Park museums, Astroworld, and the Astrodome. And though it's not an amenity, most guests will appreciate the very fine quality art (commissioned by Texas artists to harmonize with the hotel's interior) that adorns public areas.

Rates are $85 for up to four people in a king-size room (there are 40 of these) or one-bedroom suite, $150 for a two-bedroom suite. Weekend rates (Friday, Saturday, and Sunday nights) are $55 for any accommodation, and frill-filled packages are available as well. And a great boon, at this writing, is that rates include a full bacon-and-eggs American breakfast. That makes the Wyndham, already very competitively priced, one of the best hotel buys in town. And no-smoking rooms and facilities for the disabled are offered as well. Parking is $4 a night.

Just two blocks south of the Galleria is the **Galleria Oaks Corporate Inn,** 5151 Richmond Ave., between Sage and Post Oak Boulevard, Houston, TX 77056 (tel. 713/629-7120), a converted apartment complex offering 115 one- and two-bedroom suite accommodations. It's a friendly place offering a lot of personal service (in a pinch the director of sales once even sewed up a hole in a guest's pants). And there are occasional barbecues and fajita cookouts by the nice-sized kidney-shaped pool in the courtyard. Rates here include continental breakfast (fresh-baked croissants, danish, doughnuts, and tea or coffee) plus complimentary afternoon cocktails, both served in a comfortable lounge that also contains a TV, a large table, and soda, ice cream, and snack machines. Complimentary cocktails can also be enjoyed in the poolside gazebo. The suites —comprising one or two bedrooms, a comfortable living room, and a kitchen— are housed in a two-story building that encloses the courtyard. They're nicely furnished in a contemporary but homey fashion, with sturdy oak furnishings, tan or brown carpeting, forest-green bedspreads, sofas and chairs upholstered in wool plaids, and white stucco walls. Color schemes run to earth tones. Everything is neat as a pin and in excellent condition, and every suite includes a full kitchen with refrigerator, sink, dishwasher, stove (some have microwaves), wet bar, and dining table. Ample cutlery, dishes, and cookware are provided, as is coffee. All bedrooms have large walk-in closets and queen-size beds. And in-room amenities include a direct-dial phone and cable color TV with complimentary movie channel. There's an on-premises coin-op laundromat, and guests can utilize the posh President & First Lady Fitness Spa nearby; it features racquetball, handball, aerobics classes, a heated indoor pool, indoor jogging track, sauna, steamroom, whirlpool, and a full complement of workout equipment. Complimentary transport is offered to/from the Galleria and the Medical Center, and an airport shuttle bus terminal is half a block away. The hotel will also do your grocery shopping. Finally, the property is very nicely landscaped with several outdoor gazebos amid pink-blossoming crape myrtles and banana trees. And though there's no restaurant on the premises, there are plenty within easy walking distance.

Per-suite rates are $65 a day for a one-bedroom, $59 a day for stays of a week or more, $50 a day for stays of a month or more. For two-bedroom suites rates are $115, $100, and $75 respectively. Children under 12 stay free. Covered parking is free.

In today's harried, hurry-up world, owner/hosts Bob and Becky Harris of the **Allen Park Inn,** 2121 Allen Parkway, between Montrose and Taft, Houston, TX 77019 (tel. 713/521-9321, or toll free 800/231-6310), offer their guests a relaxing antidote—gracious southern atmosphere and country coziness. A series of white-shuttered brick buildings on five beautifully landscaped acres, with an entranceway fronted by white columns, the inn evokes the plantation era. And within its walls, the Tennessee-born Harrises make warm personal service their first order of business. The pleasant little lobby, with leather furnishings amid potted ficus trees and crystal chandeliers overhead, is decorated with Harris family antiques, as are other public areas. They include carved oak armoires, breakfronts, and grandfather clocks. Hallways are lit by shaded lamps. A large swimming pool and sundeck surrounded by palms grace the lovely central courtyard area, and there are wrought-iron umbrella tables on a garden patio for outdoor meals and cocktails; it's lovely to sit here sipping wine at sunset.

Though the 269 rooms are less quaint than their surroundings, they're nicely decorated and furnished with teal-blue carpeting and floral-print bedspreads and draperies. They're equipped with double doubles or king-size beds, cable color TVs with in-house movies, clocks, and radios, and some even have hair dryers. Most offer views of the landscaping—expanses of lawn, flower beds, neat rows of plants in clay pots, and flowering trees; others look out on the downtown skyline. About 20 rooms have full kitchens, and others have sinks and refrigerators. Additional on-premises amenities include a workout room with Universal equipment, whirlpool and sauna, a hair stylist, coin-op washer dryer, round-the-clock room service, a shoeshine operation, and a gift shop.

There's a charming restaurant, the Nashville Room, its walls lined with historic prints of Nashville and, when weather permits, a fire ablaze in its brick fireplace. Twenty-four hours a day, it dishes up moderately priced down-home specialties like chicken-fried steak in thick cream gravy, deep-fried oysters, and slabs of country ham with eggs and grits. A bar/lounge adjoins.

The inn has become a popular choice with entertainers, who, according to Becky, like the privacy and personal service. Much of the cast of *Terms of Endearment* stayed here during filming, and Debra Winger and pals partied in the bar. Other celebrity guests have included Dan Travanti and Jo Beth Williams (who were doing a TV movie nearby), Kris Kristofferson, Burt Lancaster, and the Pointer Sisters.

Rates are $42 to $62 single, $52 to $68 double, $125 to $175 for up to four in living room/bedroom suites equipped with wet bars, three phones, and two TVs. Children under 12 stay free, an extra person pays $6 a night, and weekend rates are reduced. Parking is free. Facilities for the disabled are also offered.

In the 1960s four hotels were built to comprise the Astroworld Hotel Complex. But over the years mergers were made, and there now remains the **Astro Village Hotel Complex,** 2350 South Loop West, (I-610) at Kirby, Houston, TX 77054 (tel. 713/748-3221, or toll free 800/231-2360), which includes at the same address and under the same ownership (a Florida company called Servico) a Holiday Inn (tel. 713/799-1050, or toll free 800/HOLIDAY). In toto, the complex offers 1,000 rooms, four swimming pools, four kiddie pools, two restaurant/lounges, and Houston's largest ballroom. Guests at either section can utilize facilities of both. The Astrodome attractions are right across the street.

The decor throughout is standardized, so wherever you stay your room will be decorated in one of three color schemes (teal blue, forest green/coral, or autumn tones) and contain two doubles or one king-size bed. Clean and attractive, they are equipped with all the expected amenities, plus seating areas, full-length mirrors, and balconies. There are lanai rooms with patios or balconies overlooking a swimming pool. And the pools provide a goodly choice of attractive settings (one is situated in a live oak-bordered courtyard), sizes (laps are an option), and sunning areas. At all of them you can order room-service fare poolside.

Astro Village has a large lobby, usually bustling with activity, and containing an Info Houston computer to acquaint guests with local dining, shopping, business, and sightseeing options. A large dining room, open daily from 6:30 a.m. to 10 p.m., serves international buffets (Mexican, Oriental, Italian, etc.) at lunch on weekdays ($6.50) and Sunday champagne brunches ($12.50), in addition to à la carte offerings and a children's menu. Complimentary hors d'oeuvres are served in a lobby lounge weekday afternoons. Additional amenities are a unisex hair salon, car-rental desk, dress shop, gift and sundry shop, and a florist. The Holiday Inn section also has a cheerful all-day eatery with seating in black leather booths and green-shaded lamps suspended over the tables. Its comfortable adjoining lounge offers a jukebox and backgammon tables.

Astro Village's rates are $59 to $85 single (the higher end represents better room location), $10 for each additional person, free for children 17 and under. In the Holiday Inn section singles pay $59 to $63; doubles, $66 to $72; an extra person, $7; children under 18, free November to April (the rest of the year they pay extra-person rates). Facilities for the disabled are available. Weekend rates are sometimes offered, as are packages including AstroWorld and WaterWorld tickets (inquire when you reserve), and senior citizens get a 10% discount year round. Parking is free at both hotels.

A good choice in the low-to-moderate price category are the three below-listed Rodeway Inns, beginning with the well-run nine-story, 300-room **Rodeway Inn Towers Hotel,** 2130 W. Holcombe Blvd., at Main Street, Houston, TX 77030 (tel. 713/666-1461, or toll free 800/228-2000). Here you'll enjoy rather attractive accommodations of the standard motel genre; they're carpeted in chocolate-brown with taupe or mauve bedspreads and drapes or in light blue with navy spreads and drapes. In addition to all the expected amenities, the cable color TV has a 24-hour movie station, there's a dressing area, and a basket of bath amenities includes shampoo, soap, and Scope. All beds are double or king-size. On the fourth floor is a good-sized swimming pool and sundeck, as well as gazebos hung with potted plants. There's a pretty little coffeeshop, with Breuer chairs at tan-clothed tables, navy carpeting, and a trellised planter of live chrysanthemums and silk purple flowers. Open from 7 a.m. to 10 p.m. daily (there's room service the same hours), it features reasonably priced sandwiches, omelets, salads, and heartier entrees. The second-floor lounge, Pebbles, is the scene of a weekly guest-appreciation party with free cocktails and hors d'oeuvres; ask about it when you check in. Finally, a coin-op laundry is provided, as is free transport to/from the Medical Center and the Astrodome complex.

Rates are $45 single, $51 double, $6 for an additional person (children under 18, free). There's a reduced rate for Medical Center patients, and summer rates also tend to be a little lower. Parking is free. No-smoking rooms and facilities for the disabled are also offered.

A pleasant, well-run little property, the **Rodeway Inn Downtown,** 1015 Texas Ave., between Main and Fannin, Houston, TX 77002 (tel. 713/224-4511, or toll free 800/228-2000), has 75 neat and newly renovated rooms in a seven-story building. They all have freshly painted tan walls hung with nicely chosen framed prints, tan carpeting, and color-coordinated drapes and bedspreads in one of four color schemes (teal blue, navy, rust, or brown). In-room amenities include a color TV with free movie channel, a table and two upholstered chairs, and a desk; in those units characterized as "executive choice," you'll also find king-size beds, gratis toiletries, AM/FM radios, and reclining chairs. In addition to the regular rooms, there are 70 rooms available for long-term stays. To attract a business clientele, the Rodeway offers secretarial services, a Federal Express mail drop in the lobby, and free transport to any location in the downtown area. You can also catch a bus from the door to the Galleria. Out back are a small pool and sundeck, and the abundantly colorful Carmen's (its walls are painted plum, orange, and turquoise) serves pretty good Mexican and American fare from 7 a.m. to 8 p.m daily. Room service is available the same hours, and free coffee is served in the lobby each morning.

Rates are $40 to $50 for one person, $50 to $60 for two, $60 to $70 for "executive choice" rooms, $10 for an extra adult, free for children under 17. The weekend rate (Friday, Saturday, and Sunday nights) is just $32 for any room in the house. Long-term stays are $150 a week for one, $200 a week for two, $375 a month for one, $475 a month for two.

Fronted by a Mediterranean-blue awning, the 110-room **Rodeway Inn,** 5820 Katy Freeway (I-10), at Washington Avenue, Houston, TX 77007 (tel. 713/869-9211, or toll free 800/228-2000), offers a lot in the low-priced category. Housed in a two-story brick building with white doors and shutters, the rooms are cheerfully decorated and in excellent condition. They feature patterned teal-blue bedspreads and drapes, attractive furnishings, and warm tan carpeting. Along with all the usual amenities, they offer cable color TV with HBO and other special channels, as well as extra-long double or king-size beds. Deluxe rooms, priced just a bit higher than the rest, feature remote control for the TV, full-length door mirrors, desks, and hair dryers and baskets of toiletries in the bath; some also have small refrigerators. There's a small pool and sundeck, and the proximity of Memorial Park, just across the street, puts guests close to many recreational facilities. A laundromat is just a block away, and a 24-hour Denny's adjoins. Local phone calls are free, which can be a boon if you're doing business (some hotels charge up to 75¢ per). And complimentary coffee and doughnuts are offered in the lobby each morning.

Rates are $38 to $50 for one person, $48 to $60 for two, $50 to $55 and $55 to $65, respectively, for deluxe rooms. Extra adults pay $6; children under 16 stay free. Reduced weekend rates are offered subject to availability. Parking is free, and no-smoking rooms are also offered.

The low-priced hotel chain, **La Quinta Motor Inns** (details in Chapter I), has nine properties in Houston, the most conveniently located of them at 401 Southwest Freeway (I-59) at the Weslayan exit, Houston, TX 77027 (tel. 713/623-4750, or toll free 800/531-5900). The Greenery restaurant on the premises serves a low-priced breakfast, lunch, and dinner, and the Cantina, a bar/lounge, adjoins. Rates are $46 single, $53 double, $5 for an extra person (children under 18, free). Weekend rates are further reduced, and facilities for the disabled are available.

**BUDGET BETS:** A very high recommendation goes to the **Grant Motor Inn,** 8200 S. Main St., between Braesmain and Kirby, Houston, TX 77025 (tel. 713/668-8000), a 64-room property opened by Gene and Lee Grant in 1940 and now run by their son, Harry. The Grants have always taken pride in their immaculate, affordable, family-operated enterprise, and Harry provides guests with personal attention and niceties like free coffee and doughnuts in the lobby each morning and, just outside the lobby, two Cinzano umbrella tables so you can enjoy this continental breakfast al fresco. Many of the rooms are in single-story white stucco, terracotta-roofed buildings that enclose a large expanse of lawn, in the center of which are a nice-sized swimming pool, a sundeck with umbrella tables, a children's pool, and playground equipment. The older section has rooms in brick buildings surrounding another courtyard. In the small, wood-paneled lobby, where clocks keep you abreast of the correct time in Tokyo, Los

Angeles, New York, London, and, incidentally, Houston, books and magazines are provided. On the premises is a coin-operated laundry, and irons and ironing boards available from housekeeping.

The rooms are neat as a pin and tastefully decorated; they have white stucco or exposed brick walls, sturdy Spanish-style dark oak furnishings, and attractive cotton bedspreads, and each is fitted out with cable color TV with a 24-hour movie channel (for $1 a day, you can rent a remote-control device at the desk), AM/FM radio, digital alarm clock, direct-dial Touchtone phone, a table and two chairs, full-length mirror, extra-long beds, and bath with tub and/or shower. Some have patios, and the "honeymoon" room has a canopied bed with a mirrored ceiling (it costs $45 a night). But it's not the only special room here. Before he was famous, Elvis Presley used to play frequent engagements at the now-defunct Starlight Ballroom down the street, and he always stayed in Room 123. "Even then he drove a Cadillac," notes Harry. Parking is free, and mostly covered—a real advantage in Houston's sultry summers when auto interiors can double as ovens.

Rates are $27 to $30 for one person in a room with a single bed, $31 to $34 for one or two in a room with a double bed, $35 to $38 for two in a double-double or king-size bed, $34 to $37 for two people in a room with a double and a single bed, $5 for each additional person, $2 for children under 12. No-smoking rooms and facilities for the disabled are also offered.

*Note:* Harry is toying with changing the name of the motel, so if someone answers the phone and says something other than "Grant Motor Inn," don't be surprised; everything else will remain the same.

Within walking distance of the Astrodome complex is the **White House Motor Hotel**, 9300 S. Main St., between Murworth and Westridge, Houston, TX 77025 (tel. 713/666-2261). Its colonnaded white façade does ever so slightly suggest 1600 Pennsylvania Avenue, and it also has a rather grandiose lobby with crystal chandeliers suspended from 20-foot ceilings, gold-flocked turquoise wallpaper, and a spiral staircase leading to the mezzanine. The 220 rooms are in neat two-story balconied white buildings with charcoal-gray doors and shutters. The buildings enclose a large courtyard of lawn and sundeck around the hotel's pièce de résistance—a gorgeous Olympic-size swimming pool. As a serious swimmer (you may have noticed I always indicate which pools are large enough for laps), I might consider staying here for the pool alone. Belying the prim white exterior, rooms are a tad on the gaudy side, utilizing, shall we say, overly bright blue, green, and gold color schemes. But at these rates you didn't expect *Architectural Digest* interiors, right? And they are clean and do offer air conditioning, double or king-size beds, tub/shower bath, color TV, and direct-dial phone. Many overlook the pool. Additional amenities are a small room with video games and pinball machines off the lobby; free transport by van to/from Hobby Airport, an Intercontinental Airport bus terminal, and the Medical Center; the White House Club, offering Happy Hour complimentary hors d'oeuvres and reduced-price drinks; and a full restaurant serving very reasonably priced meals.

Rates are $34 single, $38 double, $4 for each additional person (free for children under 14). Reduced rates are available to Medical Center patients, and facilities for the disabled are offered. Parking is free.

Just down the road apiece, and under the same ownership, is the **Chief Motel**, 9000 S. Main St., between McNee and Murworth, Houston, TX 77025 (tel. 713/666-4151). Its 126 rooms are in white balconied buildings with yellow and orange doors, and, once again, though clean and freshly painted, they are not "inspired." They do, however, contain the full complement of in-room amenities offered at the White House, and some have sofa beds in addition to a double bed. Walls are white concrete block. The pool here—nice-sized but not Olympic—and sundeck are in the parking lot, not a garden courtyard, and there's no restaurant or bar, though coffee is served in the lobby every morning. But if it offers less than the White House, the Chief also charges less: $26 single, $30 double, $4 for an additional person (under 14, free), and $24 for Medical Center patients. And there is free transport between the two properties, so guests here can avail themselves of all the additional facilities down the street. Both properties are well run.

For men 18 and over, there's the very conveniently located **Downtown YMCA**, 1600 Louisiana St., between Pease and Bell, Houston, TX 77002 (tel. 713/659-8501). It's not only the cheapest place in town to stay, it's clean and secure, and it houses one of the finest fitness centers in Texas, which guests can use for a small fee. Facilities include an Olympic-size indoor pool, sundeck, whirlpool, massage, steam and sauna rooms, exercise classes, 21 racquetball/handball courts, two squash courts, indoor and outdoor running tracks, Nautilus/Universal and CAM II air-resistance equipment, volleyball and basketball courts, a pro shop, tanning booths, and locker rooms. Gym clothing, towels, soap, and shampoo are available. Guests can also participate in social activities for residents ranging from chili cookoffs to ice cream and cookie parties, not to mention Sunday Bible-study classes over coffee and doughnuts. A nondenominational chapel is on the premises, by the way, and a chaplain is on call 24 hours a day. For secular get-togethers there's a tenth-floor lounge / game room / library. The front desk doubles as a tourism information center and sells theater tickets. And rounding out the facilities are wake-up service; weekday maid service; food vending machines; a low-priced restaurant specializing in healthful fare (granola / fresh fruit / yogurt / salads), but, not to worry, you can also get a cheeseburger or club sandwich; and a coin-op laundry.

The 138 air-conditioned rooms aren't fancy, but they're quite pleasantly decorated with colorful bedspreads and curtains and sturdy furnishings (a dresser, twin beds, desk, chair, and lamp); framed pictures on the walls add a homey touch. Each contains a large color TV and a switchboard phone (you can receive incoming calls around the clock, but outgoing calls must be made at a hall phone). Baths are in the hall. There's no curfew, but bringing nonresidents to your room—particularly distaff ones—is *verboten*.

The Y attracts an interestingly diverse international clientele, and the downtown location puts you within reach of bus transportation to any part of the city.

Rates are $15 a day, $60 for a full week. Reserve as far in advance as possible.

And finally there's a **Motel 6** (details in Chapter I), 9638 Plainfield Rd., at Bissonet (tel. 713/778-9606). It's a bit out of the way, but, barring traffic jams, you could scoot downtown on the Southwest Freeway in about 20 to 25 minutes.

**BED-AND-BREAKFAST:** The B&B concept has yet to catch on in a big way in Texas. Should you prefer this type of accommodation, however, there does exist Marguerite Swanson's **Bed&Breakfast Society of Houston**, 921 Heights Blvd., Houston, TX 77008 (tel. 718/868-4654), to help you. Her rosters contain only about 20 listings in Houston and its environs, so for the best selection at the best prices, contact her as far in advance as possible. All properties are carefully screened for cleanliness, comfort, and security, as are hosts for friendliness. And all the society's hosts are required to offer at least a hearty continental breakfast—fresh-baked breads, fresh fruit, and tea or coffee—though some cook up considerably more. The listed properties are quite varied. Some have swimming pools and/or hot tubs. There's an antique-furnished Victorian residence complete with a front porch swing, a home whose decor is influenced by American Indian art, and a hilltop farmhouse on 80 acres (not right in the city, obviously). There's no minimum stay or enrollment fee. Rates are in the $30 to $35 range for singles, $40 to $50 for doubles.

**LONG-TERM STAYS:** Real-estate entrepreneurs have been hard at work here in the last decade, and multiple-unit apartment developments have sprung up in vast numbers. Many of these units can be rented furnished on a long-term basis (minimum three months), and even if your stay is a bit shorter, you might find the price, usually including many on-premises facilities, acceptable. A management company with over 3,000 apartments for rent in locations all over Houston is **Fox & Carskadon,** 3131 Briar Park, Suite 100, Houston, TX 77042 (tel. 713/974-7377). Typical of its offerings is **Tennis World,** at Wilcrest and Westheimer (though others are more centrally located), where amenities include five swimming pools, a clubhouse, a fitness center with workout equipment, sauna and Jacuzzi, free cable TV, eight lighted tennis courts, and kitchens with dishwashers. Some apartments have wood-burning fireplaces. Furnished efficiencies are about $320; one-bedroom units, $415; two-bedrooms, $490; three-bedrooms, $600. You can call Tennis World (tel. 713/977-6081) or the main F&C office (they can book all Houston properties) collect to arrange rentals.

# 5. Restaurants

Houston is one of the best restaurant cities in the country, and I have ten pounds to prove it. It's not as diverse in its offerings as cities like New York and Los Angeles, but what it does, it does superbly. That includes all the Texas specialties—steak, Tex-Mex, Mexican, Créole, and barbecue—and, surprisingly, Italian cuisine. Houstonian restaurateurs do fabulous things with pasta, combining it with escargots, lobster, caviar—and even fajitas. Rapturous descriptions follow.

**LUXURY ESTABLISHMENTS:** If money is no object, plunk down your dollars at these elegant eateries and enjoy sumptuous cuisine in sublime surroundings. If not, use a credit card. Do note that some of these restaurants are much more affordable at lunch and/or have entrees that are moderately priced (for example, pastas) along with more expensive fare.

### American Gourmet / French / Continental

Houston's most glamorous restaurant, the haunt of the rich and royal, is **Tony's,** 1801 Post Oak Blvd., between Westheimer and San Felipe (tel. 622-6778). When King Hussein and Queen Noor come to town for Medical Center checkups, they have Tony's send over food to the hospital. And among those who've thrown parties in the renowned private wine room are John Travolta, Princess Margaret, Ladybird Johnson, and Luciano Pavarotti. *Esquire* magazine calls it "Houston's answer to New York's Le Cirque."

Cede your car to the valet outside (though diners have been known to arrive by helicopter) and pass through the heavy bronze doors into an elegantly appointed room fronted by a lavish food display table. Walls covered in raspberry velvet are hung with owner Tony Valone's collection of oil paintings, including a Françoise Gilot (her daughter, Paloma Picasso, always takes a seat facing it). Mahogany-framed chairs are upholstered in a charming floral fabric, there are planters of seasonal flowers and fresh-cut flowers on the white-linened tables, soft lighting emanates from shaded sconces, and mahogany columns and moldings add a note of substance. Tony is almost always on hand, greeting guests and keeping a sharp eye on operations (one reviewer described his activity as "stalking the room"). The "A" section tables are in the center of the main dining room—the best spot for seeing and being seen.

But even if you're seated in "Siberia," there's good reason to spend your shekels here. Tony's is more than a glitterati gathering place; it's one of the premier restaurants of Texas. You might begin your meal with an appetizer of rollatini de melanzane ($9)—eggplant stuffed with sun-dried tomatoes, prosciutto, parmesan, ricotta, and mascarpone cheeses, topped with béchamel sauce and a touch of marinara. It's exquisite. Some excellent entrees include poached gulf redfish with broccoli and Dijon mustard sauce ($18.50); grilled capon with a golden chutney of pears, peaches, raisins, yellow peppers, lemons, and oranges ($17); and a uniquely Texan haute-cuisine creation—lobster fajitas ($18.50). Actually, you can't go wrong whatever you order—the kitchen prepares everything superbly, from a simple sole meunière or veal chop to roast duck with wild rice and plum sauce. But do order at least an appetizer portion of one of Tony's pasta dishes—perhaps cappellini with lump crabmeat and lobster in white wine, cream, and butter sauce; or his spicy raviolis stuffed with veal and spinach in lemon / butter cream sauce. And do indulge in a selection from the fabulous four-tiered dessert cart. The tiramisu, a concoction of mascarpone cheese, cream, custard, and rum-soaked lady fingers ($6.50), is ambrosia for the immortals; ditto a white-chocolate vacherin with meringue, chantilly cream, and rich chocolate sauce ($6.50). Throughout the meal, many splendid items will arrive gratis at your table—pâté and toast with zucchini sticks, a bowl piled high with fresh seasonal fruits, and an after-dessert plate of liqueur-filled chocolates and amaretto cookies. Most luncheon entrees are in the $9.50 to $14 range. As for the wine list, Tony's has a vast cellar housing about 100,000 bottles of wine, some dating to the early 1800s.

Open weekdays for lunch from 11:30 a.m. to 2 p.m., for dinner Monday to Saturday from 6 to 11:15 p.m. Reservations essential.

*Note:* If Tony's is beyond your budget, you'll be glad to know that as we went to press owner Tony Valone opened a second, more moderately priced restaurant called **Anthony's,** 4611 Montrose, between Richmond and the Museum of Fine Arts (tel. 524-1922). It's casually elegant with a classic "nuovo" decor (whatever that might be; I'm quoting a press agent): 15-foot ceilings, pale-gray walls hung with whimsical Italian graphics, terracotta tile floors, arch-shaped windows, and lots of plants in terracotta urns. Many entrees are in the $9 to $12 range, and award-winning chef Mark Jay Cox has a very impressive résumé. Like Tony's, the new establishment offers a very comprehensive wine list. Dress can be anything from black tie to running clothes. Open for lunch weekdays from 11:30 a.m. to 2 p.m., for dinner Monday to Saturday from 5:30 p.m. to "late" (press agent again), on Sunday till 9:30 p.m. Reservations are essential; Anthony's is already mobbed at mealtimes and its goings-on reported in Houston's society columns.

A new restaurant that has already created quite a flap among reviewers is the cozy, gem-like **Georgia's,** 2171 Richmond Ave., at Greenbriar (tel. 523-6640). For one thing, there's no prettier place to dine. Georgia's glitters with Austrian crystal, Lalique chandeliers, and flickering candlelight. Its speakeasy-style front door, with a circular beveled-glass window, came from a New Orleans mansion. The chairs, at flower-bedecked, white-linened tables, are Queen Anne and Chippendale. White-trimmed burgundy walls are hung with handsome gilt- and mahogany-framed mirrors, and polished cotton white- swagged draperies and café curtains further enhance the intimate ambience. Attired in his trademark outfit—suspendered slacks and a crisp white cotton shirt—owner

Tom Lile (his wife's name is Georgia) is almost always on hand to extend a gracious personal welcome to diners. But more important, inspired German-born chef Kurt Sedlmeir is in his display kitchen turning out culinary masterpieces. His haute-cuisine creations are international in scope, highlighting fresh seafood. The menu changes daily, so I'll simply describe some of the more sublime items I've enjoyed here. If anything I've listed takes your fancy, just request it, whether or not it's on the menu; usually Kurt will prepare it. He does a spectacular appetizer of escargots swimming in garlicky butter with melted brie ($5.50), another of mesquite-smoked goose breast with lingonberries and tart crushed apples ($6.35). There are peerless pastas such as cold fettuccine with fajitas and guacamole; jalapeño fettuccine with blackened redfish in Créole sauce; pasta with escargots, capers, and green pepper in cream sauce; and, perhaps the ultimate, angelhair pasta with lobster and caviar in a rich cream sauce garnished with dill—all in the $10 to $11.50 range as entrees, $7 to $9 as appetizers. Equally memorable are a red snapper entree topped with crabmeat in cream sauce ($13.95), filet steak stuffed with foie gras and topped with morel/cognac sauce ($17.95), and a simple but excellent veal chop ($15.95). Kurt's desserts are decadently delicious, especially his white-chocolate mousse, rich with whipping cream and topped with a sauce of puréed raspberries ($5), his white-chocolate cheesecake ($3.75), and his German apple strudel in vanilla sauce ($2.95). Completing Georgia's catalog of virtues, service is excellent, and the wine list offers many good selections in the moderate-priced category.

Open for lunch weekdays from 11:30 a.m. to 2 p.m., for dinner Monday to Saturday from 6 to 10 p.m. Reservations essential. By the way, you may have a little difficulty locating the place; it's hidden within another Lile-owned restaurant called the **Bayou City Oyster Company** at the same address. Moderately priced and specializing in Créole fare, Bayou City is also well worth patronizing.

Some of Houston's finest restaurants are found in the city's premier hotels, and among the most acclaimed of these is **La Réserve**, at the luxurious Four Seasons Inn on the Park, 4 Riverway Ave. (tel. 871-8177). Here an innovative French cuisine (the menu changes daily) is served in a most gracious setting. A stunning floral arrangement on a centerpiece display table, beautifully appointed tables agleam with crystal and fine china, and beveled-glass french doors provide the sparkle; taupe velvet banquettes, shaded brass candle lamps, and mahogany paneling evoke the substantiality that bespeaks old-world luxury. The most intimate dining area, called Le Pavillon, has tables under a mirrored ceiling and crystal chandeliers.

Every other month La Réserve does a special promotion such as caviar and vodka, featuring a sample platter of caviars and a choice of vodkas, plus appetizers and entrees featuring the former. Other such promotions have highlighted various mushrooms, soufflés, and game meats like quail, partridge, wild hare, and Scottish elk. These haute-cuisine specialties are fun, and they provide a good opportunity to enhance one's culinary savoir faire. However, German executive chef Ludger Szmania's menus are never less than thrilling at any time. The salmon, smoked on the premises, is the best I've ever had—and I've had a lot. At dinner, you might opt for an appetizer of stuffed quail wrapped in a crêpe ($9.50) or a timbale of smoked goose breast with caviar ($9), and continue with an entree of chanterelle-stuffed tenderloin of beef with madeira sauce ($22) or baby Coho salmon and golden caviar wrapped in Savoy cabbage ($19.50). And don't pass up the heavenly desserts of pastry chef Otto Iselin, like his light-as-a-feather franchipan, a 1,000-layer pastry filled with crushed almonds and black cherries and served in a light vanilla sauce anglaise ($3.25).

Luncheon entrees are a bit less expensive (in the $15 range) and prix-fixe, calorie-fixe menus ($18 for a 500-calorie lunch; $28 for a 650-calorie dinner) are always offered. La Réserve is proud of its large selection of eaus de vie cognacs, brandies, and liqueurs, and its extensive, well-chosen wine list. It's open for lunch weekdays from 11:30 a.m. to 2 p.m., for dinner Monday to Saturday from 6:30 to 10:30 p.m. Reservations are essential.

And while I'm on the subject of Inn on the Park, you might also consider these posh precincts for an elaborate Sunday brunch—crêpes, pasta dishes, terrines of pâtés, carved meats, salads, eggs Benedict, scrumptious pastries, and much more for $20.50 per person. There's also a marvelous southwestern/Créole buffet ($17.95) at the hotel's Café on the Green every Friday night, a Viennese dessert table in the Palm Court on Friday and Saturday nights from 10 p.m. to 1 a.m., and a Bagel Nosh in the Café every Saturday from 10 p.m. to midnight—cream cheese, lox, smoked whitefish, smoked trout, kosher salami, corned beef, and a complimentary Sunday paper for $11 per person. The two latter buffets are excellent after-theater dining choices, as is Le Bar (adjoining La Réserve) for after-theater drinks.

Another notable in this category is **Le Restaurant de France** at the Hotel Meridien, 400 Dallas St., at Bagby (tel. 759-0202), an establishment where both decor and cuisine are characterized by elegant simplicity. You won't find crystal chandeliers and swagged draperies in this less-is-more interior. Instead, this rose-carpeted room has sheer white curtains, fresh flowers and tall white taper candles in silver holders atop white-linened tables, and handsome cherry and walnut burl paneling. At the entrance is a display of beautiful faïence china. Taped classical music is played at lunch, while at dinner a harpist sets the tone. In addition, there's a charming wine cellar dining area, the perfect spot for small dinner parties of two to seven people; it must, of course, be reserved in advance.

Alsace-born nouvelle cuisine chef Bernard François Hermann has served as head chef at such New York bastions of haute cuisine as La Réserve and Le Cygne, and he is a member of the select Academie Culinaire de France. His exquisite presentations are decidedly in the nouvelle mode ("you eat first with your eyes," says Hermann), but the portions, I'm happy to report, are uncharacteristically plentiful for the genre. The menu changes seasonally. On recent visits I've enjoyed as appetizers a marvelous mixed salad of avocado, grapefruit and orange sections, haricots verts, diced tomato, julienned mushrooms, artichokes, and thinly sliced white turnips in walnut oil dressing lightly touched with beurre blanc ($4.50), and a creamy, lightly saffroned cold crab soup ($5.50). Exceptional entrees include a pink, juicy roast loin of lamb in garlic cream sauce ($18.50) and medallions of venison with seasoned apples and lingonberries in a lightly creamed reduction sauce sweetened with currant jelly ($25.50). Also memorable: An entree of boneless quail stuffed with a rosemary- and thyme-flavored quail mousse; it is braised in port wine with pears and served in natural juices spiked with a touch of brandy ($15.95). For dessert try the apple tart, its paper-thin sliced apples resting on a delicate feuilleté pastry and topped with crème fraîche ($5). Prix-fixe luncheon menus are available in the $25 range (in addition to à la carte listings), and a full Sunday brunch is just $21 per person. It changes weekly, but typically includes a glass of champagne; selections from the hors d'oeuvre table (smoked salmon, poached turbot, salads, pâtés, etc.); an entree, perhaps grilled red snapper with purée of leeks, beef Wellington, or fresh linguine in vegetable cream sauce; cheeses such as English Stilton and Normandy brie; and a buffet of pâtisseries.

Le Restaurant de France is open for lunch weekdays from 11:30 a.m. to 2 p.m., for dinner nightly from 6 to 10 p.m. Reservations essential.

The most popular place in town for pre- or post-theater dinners is the warmly cozy **Lancaster Grille** at the Lancaster Hotel, 701 Texas Ave., at Louisiana (tel. 228-9502). In decor it's reminiscent of Washington's posh Jockey Club, with red-and-white-checkered tablecloths, gilt-framed 19th-century oil paintings of English hunt scenes adorning forest-green walls, brass sconces shaped like hunting horns, polished oak floors, and shuttered windows. A red rose in a silver vase graces every table, and as in all the Lancaster's public areas, classical music is played in the background. It's a small restaurant, seating just 58.

And it's not just for theater dining. I can't think of a more tranquil way to start the day than over breakfast at the Grille—perhaps with "the Texan," which includes fresh-squeezed orange juice, eggs, a six-ounce prime strip steak grilled to order, a selection of fresh-baked rolls and muffins with English preserves and honey, and café au lait ($9.50—I said it was tranquil, not cheap). Of course, one can enjoy the same ambience over a croissant and coffee ($3.25). At lunch or dinner try the cream of onion soup spiked with apple brandy and served in a hollow boule (a large scooped-out round French bread) that has been touted by *Gourmet* ($4). Dinner here might also begin with a warm salad of poached duck served over bibb lettuce in a Grand Marnier vinaigrette and garnished with fresh fruit ($6.25), or fresh lump crabmeat tossed in a piquant mustard dressing served over julienne spinach ($7.25). Chef Michael Malet's innovative entrees include gulf red snapper baked in parchment with apples, bananas, almonds, and white wine ($16.95), and grilled boneless duck breast served with a sauce made of hibiscus tea and green peppercorns ($15.95). Desserts can run the gamut from fresh raspberries or blackberries with cream to a rich white-chocolate mousse. Most luncheon entrees are in the $8.95 to $11 range.

The Lancaster Grille is open weekdays from 6:30 a.m. to midnight, on Saturday from 7:30 a.m. to midnight, and on Sunday from 7:30 a.m. to 10 p.m. Reservations essential at lunch and dinner.

Country elegance is the keynote at owner / chef Joe Mannke's delightfully cozy **Rotisserie for Beef & Bird,** 2200 Wilcrest Dr., at Olympia Drive (tel. 977-9524). The entrance is lined with photos of notables who have dined here—Gerald Ford, Cesar Romero, Alistair Cooke, and Tom Jones among them. Within, the white-hatted Mannke tends an open brick hearth hung with copper pots; an antique cast-iron stove serves as the dessert display table, and cream-colored walls are hung with prints of ducks and quail. There are shelves of knickknacks and open wine racks, a sideboard display of decorative china, and curtained windows. Planters are used to create intimate dining areas. Warmer ambiences just don't exist. Diners are seated in comfortable leather-upholstered spindleback armchairs at tables set with Villeroy & Boch china and oversize European silverware. A plate of rye bread wedges and smoked salmon pâté is brought to your table with the menu.

As a chef, Mannke has impressive credentials. He started his apprenticeship at the age of 14 at the famed Hotel Beyerischer Hof in Munich and went on to become executive chef at New York's Stork Club. In Boston, he opened Anthony's Pier Four, the largest seafood restaurant in the U.S., with 65 chefs under his supervision! A position as executive chef at the Hyatt Regency brought him to Houston in the mid-1970s, and in 1978 he opened his own restaurant specializing in Texas game birds and fresh seafood.

Among the appetizers at Beef & Bird, I'm partial to the traditional French onion soup au gratin topped with a large dollop of gruyère cheese ($3.25); deliciously juicy and tender baked oysters, their flavor enhanced by creamed spinach, buttered breadcrumbs, and bits of bacon ($5.50); and Texas game pâté with raspberry ginger sauce ($5.50). Spit-roasted birds—such as roast young goose with apple brown Betty and red cabbage ($14.95), and roast pheasant served with grapes, pinenuts, and a delicate wild mushroom sauce ($15.95)—are a specialty. Other noted entrees feature the choicest cuts of beef char-broiled on the open hearth; try the thick, juicy filet mignon ($17.95). In season, Mannke offers specialties like fresh filet of sea bass sautéed in brown butter and topped with fresh crayfish ($15.95). All entrees are accompanied by fresh vegetables, a delicious garden salad tossed with garlicky dressing, and crusty hot yeast rolls dusted with flour (it's hard to eat just one). For dessert there's bread pudding with hot whiskey sauce ($2.95), fresh-baked cobbler with ice cream ($3.50), and praline ice cream pie with chocolate hazelnut sauce ($3.50). The wine list—a vast selection of over 400 varieties—has won awards, and a few premium wines are offered each night by the glass, along with ports and sauternes. Especially in winter, consider a move to the adjoining lounge for dessert and liqueurs (or port) before a blazing fire.

Open for lunch weekdays from 11:30 a.m. to 2 p.m. (entrees are in the $7.50 to $10 range), for dinner Monday to Saturday from 6 to 10 p.m. Reservations essential.

## Créole

As we all know, Créole cuisine is the rage of the age, and Texas, just next door to Cajun country, can blacken a redfish with the best of them. Lafayette, Louisiana's famed Don's Seafood, owned by brothers Don, Willie, and Ashby Landry, was cloned in Houston in 1976. Within two years it became one of the 25 busiest restaurants in America, so the Landrys opened Willie G's (1981), and its success spawned yet a third venture in 1983, the Magnolia Bar & Grill.

Owned by five native Cajuns, among them Willie Landry's sons Bill and Floyd, the **Magnolia Bar & Grill**, 6000 Richmond Ave., at Fountainview (tel. 781-6207), bristles with the excitement of culinary creativity as well as chic sparkle. Its elegant decor is reminiscent of New Orleans, with slowly whirring fans and authentic Tiffany lamps suspended from lofty gray wood ceilings, plantation shutters on oversize windows, an impressive marble-topped, turn-of-the-century mahogany bar, and large planters of philodendrons and ficus. The cocoa-colored walls are hung with large black-and-white photographs by Elmore Morgan, Sr., who documented Louisiana life in the 1940s for *National Geographic* magazine. There's also a charming semicircular skylight room in back. And over the buzz of conversation there's soft Dixieland music.

The Cajun owners also operate a wholesale food distribution company called Louisiana Foods. They go down to the boats in Louisiana twice a week to select the freshest and best-quality seafood, and purchase fresh peppers and spices from New Orleans and sweet potatoes grown in the sandy soil north of Opelousas. The quality of these and other carefully culled fresh ingredients is one of the reasons a Magnolia meal is such a special experience. The other is the talent in the kitchen.

For starter's, request an appetizer (it's not on the menu) of embrouchets—char-grilled shrimp and oysters wrapped in bacon. Lightly battered deep-fried softshell crabs ($6.25) are another excellent appetizer selection, ditto the fried crab fingers ($6.50) and the rich seafood gumbo ($3.95 for a bowl, $2.75 for a cup). Succulently satisfying entrees—all served with garlic bread—include a filet of redfish stuffed with fresh lump crabmeat ($12.95); baked eggplant stuffed with shrimp and crabmeat ($11.95); and Opelousas duck, slow baked, basted with cooking juices, seasoned with cayenne, paprika, and orange sauce, and served with Louisiana rice dressing and yams ($12.95). But a meal at the Magnolia needn't be expensive. You can always come in for a dozen raw oysters ($5.25) or to wrap your mouth around an incredible shrimp, roast beef, or oyster poorboy sandwich ($5.25 to $5.95). Or for the pig heaven of an all-you-can-eat Sunday brunch buffet ($14.95) where a 40-foot table is laden with Cajun specialties, including desserts like Louisiana bread pudding and blackbottom cheesecake. A well-selected wine list highlights California wines.

Open Monday to Thursday from 11 a.m. to 11 p.m., on Friday and Saturday till midnight, on Sunday from 10:30 a.m. to 11 p.m., with brunch served till 2:30 p.m. No reservations are taken, so arrive early or late to avoid the crowds. The same applies for the two below-listed establishments.

Though I like the ambience best at the Magnolia, Don's and Willie G's also merit your patronage. If you have time, try all three.

**Don's,** within walking distance of the Galleria at 3009 S. Post Oak Blvd., between Richmond and Westheimer (tel. 629-5380), has a more casual atmosphere and attracts a less glitzy family crowd. At the entrance are blown-up photographs of Willie Landry and his wife and of the original Don's in Lafayette, with the hungry masses mobbed outside awaiting the privilege of entrance (it looks like opening night of a new Spielberg film). The week after Don's opened in Houston, without any advertising, there was a similar crowd at the door here. Don's has a nautical feel, partly because circular "windows" in slatted-wood dividers create a porthole effect. During crayfish season (October through June), opt for one of Don's preparations of this delicious lobster-like delicacy— perhaps quick-fried crayfish in a light batter seasoned with cayenne ($12.95) or a creamy, garlicky crayfish bisque yielding a potpourri of spicy sensations ($9.50 for an entree-size bowl). Also highly recommended is the Landry special—a cup of okraless seafood gumbo (one food critic called it the most authentic in Texas) followed by a casserole of crabmeat au gratin and small portions of stuffed shrimp, deviled eggplant, shrimp Créole, and salad ($12.95).

Don's is open Sunday to Thursday from 11 a.m. to 10 p.m., on Friday and Saturday till 11 p.m.

Finally, there's **Willie G's,** 1605 Post Oak Blvd., between San Felipe and Loop 610 (tel. 840-7190), a bustling and boisterous haunt of Houston oilmen and lawyers. A lot of deals have been made at Willie's bar and glossy butcher-block tables. But moneyed clientele aside, the ambience is casual. Come in jeans if you like. Wood-paneled walls are hung with Louisiana-themed posters, plants abound, and there's a stainless-steel-topped oyster bar (try the Louisiana bluepoints; they're great!). Aproned waiters and waitresses wade through the crowds bearing platters laden with fried catfish and stuffed shrimp. Green-checkered curtains add a homey warmth. Once again, fresh seafood is prepared in traditional Cajun style—there's no freezer or microwave in this kitchen.

Willie G's is open Monday to Friday from 11 a.m. to 11 p.m., on Saturday from 5 to 11 p.m., and on Sunday from 5 to 10 p.m.

## Italian

Houston has some of the best Italian restaurants in the country, and one of the reasons is the presence of the gastronomically gifted Mandola family, who in one way or another seem to have involvements in about half the restaurants in town. Grace Mandola (a.k.a. "Mom") taught all three of her charming Italian sons to cook. Tony, the oldest, was the first to do so professionally, in the early '70s at the famed Ninfa's (he later married Ninfa's daughter). Then Damian Mandola, in partnership with Nash D'Amico and others, opened the superb and still-extant D'Amico (details below) in 1977. The same year, Tony and his other brother, Vincent, opened Nino's (named for their dad), now run by Vincent alone. Tony opened his fabulous Blue Oyster Bar in 1983, and Damian left D'Amico to start Damian's in 1984. Grace Mandola works at Tony's on the Gulf Freeway (a pin on her dress identifies her as "Mama"), where she has a small cult following. I gladly join the crowd of admirers, having enjoyed some of the best meals of my life at Mandola-owned and -influenced restaurants. "Mom's" banana / key lime pie (at Tony's) makes me feel like I'm floating on a pink cloud of bliss.

I'll start with **Nino's,** 2817 W. Dallas St., at La Rue (tel. 522-5120), a restaurant dubbed by *Esquire* as one of the nation's 125 greats for "business, romance, late nights, and old friends," and that's just one of numerous accolades from the fraternity of restaurant critics. A devoted following thinks nothing of waiting an hour (reservations are taken Monday to Thursday nights only) for the privilege of digging into Vincent's Italian specialties. Housed in a converted 1939 grocery store, Nino's offers a cozy, homelike setting with white lace curtains in the windows, lots of plants, and gilt-framed oil paintings on the walls. There's also a framed photograph of the Mandola paterfamilias, Nino, taken on his wedding day (Mrs. Mandola says it was the only time she ever managed to get him dressed up, so she took a picture). There's another, more intimate dining room upstairs, its wood-paneled walls hung with travel posters. And the candlelit lounge up front is always crowded with waiting diners who might stay the pangs of hunger by ordering some appetizers—perhaps the fried mozzarella cheese topped with marinara sauce ($3.85); a half pound of crab claws sautéed in lemon, butter, garlic, and spices ($11.50); or, in season, fried peewee softshell crabs, dredged in seasoned breadcrumbs and served with lump crabmeat topping ($5.25). For the main course, try the fettuccine scampi—shrimps, fresh mushrooms, and chives, sautéed in butter sauce and tossed with fettuccine ($11.50)—or the equally recommendable Vincent's chicken Angelina—rolled breast of chicken stuffed with spinach, prosciutto, and fontina cheese in marsala sauce with sautéed mushrooms ($13.50). A selection from the mostly Italian wine list is essential to the true enjoyment of all this spectacular fare. And the almond-crusted raspberry pie is a not-to-be-missed dessert. The above items are among Vincent's pricier menu listings, but it should be noted that one can also select homemade pasta dishes in the $7 to $8.50 range, and that very good pizza is an option. Furthermore, at lunch a number of items are much reduced in price.

Open Monday to Friday for lunch from 11:30 a.m. to 2:30 p.m., for dinner Monday to Thursday from 5:30 to 10 p.m., on Friday and Saturday till 11 p.m.

**Damian's Cucina Italiana,** 3011 Smith St., at Rosalie (tel. 522-0439), is by far the most elegant of the Mandola restaurants. Walls are painted in Pompeii terracotta wash and decorated with a grapevine-motif frieze and a pastoral mural; rosy lighting emanates from small, shaded wall sconces; arched room dividers create intimate dining areas; white-linened tables display vases of country flowers. A potted palm here and there completes the picture. Among the unforgettables at Damian's are appetizers of gnocchi verdi, the most delicate of dumplings made with spinach, ricotta, and parmesan, and served in tomato cream sauce ($4.95) and peppers and anchovies ($4.50)—sweet red peppers roasted and peeled, marinated in virgin olive oil with garlic and finely chopped anchovies, and served with buffalo mozzarella cheese and capers. Those, by the way, are in addition to a delicious eggplant and pinenut relish with garlic toast, which appears on your table gratis. Among the most exquisite entrees are shrimp Damian, fresh gulf shrimp sautéed in white wine, lemon, butter, and virgin olive oil with Italian parsley and shallots, served with fettuccine Alfredo ($15.50); tortellini alla panna, a pasta stuffed with pork, chicken, mortadella, ricotta, and parmesan in Alfredo sauce ($8.25); and spaghetti carbonara, in an eggy cream sauce with Italian bacon, whipping cream, fresh-grated parmesan, and sautéed scallions and garlic ($8.25—at least an appetizer portion is a must). All the above are to die for. Ditto an off-the-menu dessert (just ask) of zabaglione with fresh raspberries and Chambord liqueur. Italian wines are featured.

Open for lunch weekdays from 11 a.m. to 2:30 p.m. (same menu), for dinner Monday to Thursday from 6 to 10:30 p.m., on Friday and Saturday till 11:30 p.m. Reservations essential.

*Note:* The above-mentioned Tony's is listed farther along in this chapter.

The charming interior at **D'Amico**, 2407 Westheimer Rd., a block east of Kirby (tel. 524-5551), has been described as an Italian grandmother's parlor, and the fare within these lace-curtained precincts as "so good, it's amazing you can ever get a table." Both accounts are true. D'Amico does look like grandma's parlor—assuming grandma had excellent taste. Decorated in warm shades of rose and mauve with burgundy carpeting, it's pinkly lit by fringed, silk-shaded Victorian lamps suspended over the tables. Windows all around are curtained in white lace, there are hanging wicker baskets of plants, and vases of fresh flowers grace every table. Framed photographs of Italy adorn the walls. And as for the classic Italian fare, it inspired one reviewer to kiss the chef and *Gentleman's Quarterly* to rate the establishment as one of America's ten best Italian restaurants.

Owner / chef Tony Rao, ably assisted in the kitchen by his cousin, David Bua, recently returned from a food and wine trip to Italy. He gained 15 pounds and added many exciting new dishes to his menu like the superb capelli d'Angelo—angelhair pasta tossed with lump crabmeat in a creamy tomato sauce with fresh basil ($8.50). It's a terrific choice for your appetizer—here called *primi piatti* (first plates)—as is a dish of roast sweet red peppers and anchovies served with capers in virgin olive oil ($6). In addition to the *primi piatti* you order, a gratis platter of crispy breaded fried mozzarella arrives at your table soon after you're seated, and a silver tray of fresh-baked crusty Italian bread with plenty of butter accompanies each course.

Under the menu category of *secondi piatti* is an Italian saying that translates "Let 100 hands partake in the feast with God's blessing—but not from my plate!" And in fact the only thing that might keep one's gluttony from getting out of hand is the occasional view of a sumptuous multi-tiered dessert cart at nearby tables; room must be left. But first there are entrees like a mixed grill of veal chop (exquisite), ribeye steak, chicken breast, and rack of lamb ($20.50). The meats are crisp and brown outside, juicy and tender inside, their flavors enhanced by a salmoriglio sauce of olive oil, garlic, bay leaves, and red wine vinegar. It's all perfection, as are the accompanying vegetables, perhaps asparagus spears cooked al dente and lightly buttered. Another specialty is the trota al toto, filet of trout topped with fresh lump crabmeat in a white wine / lemon / butter sauce spiked with parsley and pinenuts ($19). Many diners, of course, simply summon Tony to their table, discuss food preferences, and leave the ordering in his hands, including the choice of appropriate wines (usually Italian) to best complement the dishes. For dessert, fresh raspberries in zabaglione sauce ($6.50) or an almond-crusted raspberry tart ($4.50) are both heavenly, and the chocolate cheesecake ($4.50) is not without its devotees. Service, provided by waiters in black tie and long white aprons, is deft and friendly.

Open for lunch weekdays from 11:30 a.m. to 2 p.m. (most entrees are in the $8 to $11 range), for dinner Monday to Saturday from 6 to 11 p.m., on Sunday from 5:30 to 10:30 p.m. Reservations essential.

## Moroccan

Step into the exotic world of **Casablanca**, 14025 Memorial Dr., at Kirkwood (tel. 531-9060), a series of sumptuous tented rooms in which a belly dancer in sequins and chiffon swirls to the strains of Andalusian music, and soft, romantic lighting filters through cut-brass lamps. Vibrantly colored Berber carpets cover the floors; goatskin poufs and straw bread baskets from Fez are strewn about. Seat yourself on a low, cushioned velvet banquette at a table inlaid with intricate arabesque design. A waiter will wash your hands in the *mghasselle,* an ornate antique silver urn; as is the custom in Morocco, dinner will be eaten sans utensils. Thus begins the leisurely affair that is a Casablanca dinner. Do order a bottle of wine; it's de rigueur with this multicourse prix-fixe ($17 to $20.50) feast. You'll begin with a piquant vegetable soup in lamb broth, followed by a salad of spicy eggplant purée and pickled vegetables that is scooped into crusty hunks of fresh-baked bread. Next comes b'stilla, a heavenly delicacy consisting of shredded chicken, eggs, and spices wrapped in tender flaky pastry and dusted with powdered sugar and cinnamon. Your entree will depend on which dinner you've ordered. Not to be missed is the lamb mrouzia with honey sauce and almonds; it's spiced with onion, nutmeg, coriander, and saffron. Additional choices might include a fragrant chicken tajine with pickled lemons and olives or browned beef in a tangy sauce garnished with prunes and sprinkled with roasted sesame seeds. Meats are always cooked to falling-off-the-bone tenderness, making them easy to eat with the fingers (the proper method is to use only the first three fingers of the right hand). A platter of couscous and steamed vegetables—perhaps squash, carrots, turnips, onions, and chick peas —accompanies all entrees. After the main courses, the waiter once again washes your hands, this time in hot towels perfumed with rosewater. Dessert is fresh fruit and cookies and a refreshing spearmint tea that, according to owner Ben Hadj, aids digestion and sweetens the breath. Tea is a veritable ceremony: the waiter pours it with panache from a height of several feet. By this time you're practically lying on the floor like a sated sheik; give in to total hedonism, order an after-dinner drink, and watch the dancing girls.

Open for dinner nightly from 6 to 11 p.m., and for lunch (smaller in scope) weekdays from 11 a.m. to 2 p.m. Reservations suggested.

## Steak and Lobster

Oil-rich millionaires, real-estate magnates, athletes, and men who don't eat quiche dine at **Ruth's Chris Steak House,** 6213 Richmond Ave., at Greenridge (tel. 789-BEEF). The decor couldn't be more fitting. Its five color TVs that soundlessly air all sporting events, row of functional-looking round clocks that tell the time in nine major cities, exposed brick and carpeted walls plastered with oil company logos (all provided by patrons) and photographs of offshore drilling operations, New York and American Stock Exchange electronic ticker-tape boards, and famous sign over the entrance reading "Through these portals pass the finest oil field trash in the world," all contribute to the men's-club ambience. Seating is in tufted burgundy leather chairs and there's track lighting overhead. Though owner Bob Ruby (a colorful ex-radio talk show host) claims his patronage has changed over the years ("It's a 'rulier' crowd today," he laments. "The good ol' boy who used to come in and drink a fifth of Crown Royal has been replaced by the guy who orders Pouilly-Fuissé"), don't think Ruth's Chris has gone effete or Yuppie. It's still a reasonably rugged lair of macho Houston.

You have to be a bit macho to manage Ruby's hefty platters of steak, all of it prime-grade Chicago beef aged 21 days, cut on the premises, broiled to your specifications, and sent to your table swimming in clarified butter. A filet of tenderloin is $22; a petite filet (eight ounces), $17; the classic T-bone, $27. With your entree comes a delicious loaf of fresh-from-the-oven bread on a silver tray and a fabulous house salad (try the tangy remoulade dressing made with Créole mustard). Lots of diners share a steak (there's a $2 surcharge for splitting) and go to town on side dishes—creamy lyonnaise potatoes ($3.75); the biggest, thickest, breadiest onion rings you've ever had ($4); fresh asparagus au gratin ($5.75); and/or perhaps cauliflower au gratin ($5). All the fresh veggies come from a fancy produce shop called Jamail's.

The shrimp cocktail in rémoulade sauce is also worthy of consideration. The wine list is extensive, and, there are, by the way, entrees other than steak, including grilled shrimp, live Maine lobster, chicken amandine, pork chops, and veal chop. Whatever you've selected, your diet's doomed, so go ahead and order Ruby's super-creamy cheesecake with crushed pecan crust ($4) for dessert.

Open weekdays from 11:30 a.m. to 11 p.m., on Saturday from 5 to 11 p.m. A reduced menu is offered at lunch. No reservations; arrive at off-hours to avoid the crowds.

**MODERATELY PRICED CHOICES:** The following selections are in the price range most people choose when dining out, yet some, like Dong Ting, offer a very luxurious ambience.

## American

In summer Houstonians wisely avoid non-air-conditioned environments and in winter it's usually just a bit too cold for al fresco dining. But now and again a balmy day comes along. That's the time to combine an expedition to Rice Village, a charming shopping area, with lunch at **Allegro,** 2407 Rice, between Kelvin and Morningside (tel. 528-2409), a delightful outdoor café serving fresh, homemade fare. It's a good choice for continental breakfast: fresh-baked butter croissants, brioches, and apricot or cheese danish are offered with your morning caffè latte. Rest up from shopping over such luncheon fare as a three-cheese lasagne salad ($6.50), a croissant sandwich of avocado and brie with basil / garlic mayonnaise ($4.75), or lemon-mint chicken salad in cantaloupe ($5.75). Or stop in for afternoon tea (if not afternoon cappuccino or espresso) and luscious desserts like whiskey-flavored chocolate zabaglione cake ($3.50); Bavarian fruit torte (layers of frangipan, vanilla sponge cake, and Mandarin orange-flavored cream, topped with fresh seasonal fruits; $3.75); or chocolate velvet cake (layers of hazelnut meringue and chocolate mousse flavored with crème de cacão and kirsch; $3.50). The menus change daily, but the above items are typical. Wine and beer are available.

Open Monday to Thursday from 7 a.m. to 10 p.m., on Friday and Saturday to midnight, and on Sunday for brunch from 9 a.m. to 4 p.m.

## Chinese

**Dong Ting,** 611 Stuart St., between Louisiana and Smith (tel. 527-0005), is a restaurant very much stamped by the personalities of its urbane owners. San and Jo Hwang are Hunanese (their families have been friends for several generations), and they offer Houstonians the regional gourmet dishes they grew up on. Jo is the very charming hostess, graciously welcoming diners to the Hwang's lovely restaurant. San sees to the rest. Though he comes from a family that numbered several prominent chefs and his mother was a superb cook, San first studied Chinese history at a California university and went on to become a journalist in San Francisco. But early instincts eventually came to the fore, as did sound business sense. Houston, where two of his brothers were already settled, certainly had no superfluity of fine Chinese restaurants in 1978, the year San opened the original Dong Ting. For that matter, it still doesn't.

The Hwangs recently moved from their original location to this plush downtown setting. Formerly a French restaurant, under the new regime it retains beautiful oak beams and paneling from a 19th-century New Orleans hotel, a large crystal chandelier from the same source, and ornate mirrored columns—all of which harmonizes exquisitely with the Huangs' added Orientalia. This includes a 16th-century Ming Dynasty Buddha, delicate hand-painted murals of

17th-century Chinese derivation, calligraphy scrolls done by San's great-grandfather, and display cases of his collection of ancient Chinese ceramics and sculptures (including 2,000-year-old tomb figurines, an 8th-century Tang Dynasty horse, and Sung Dynasty Celadon). If you're interested in Chinese art, ask San to show you around; he's extremely knowledgeable. The Chinese-style black lacquer chairs upholstered in rose fabric were made especially for the restaurant. An elegant back room is predominantly French in feeling with latticed cherrywood walls and ceiling, crystal chandeliers and candelabra sconces, and Louis XVI–style chairs. There's also a delightful awninged garden with a goldfish and water lily pond, plus white wrought-iron furnishings amid banana palms; it's used for cocktails and after-dinner drinks. And the pièce de résistance is an exquisite wood-paneled wine cellar dining room where $300 dinners are offered for up to 12 people at a stunning round rosewood table.

A good beginning at Dong Ting is an order of lamb dumplings ($4.75) served on a bed of shredded cabbage with hot sauce and vinegar; feathery light and spiced with minced ginger root, they won't spoil your appetite for forthcoming courses. The same can be said about a piquant salad of minced chicken and shredded cucumber ($3.60) in a sesame / lemon / rice vinegar dressing with a touch of yellow mustard. For entree selections, consider the tender smoked Long Island duckling, marinated in salt, anise, and peppercorn, then steamed and roasted ($12); steamed fresh baby red snapper with black bean and ginger ($9.95); crispy snow peas sautéed with roasted pumpkin seeds and sliced garlic ($7.95); and stir-fry onion-pepper beef in a brown sauce ($9). A side order of crabmeat fried rice ($7.75) is also heartily recommended. All the dishes I've enjoyed here are characterized by a melange of subtle flavors that make for exciting new taste discoveries with every forkful (or chopstickful).

You might adjourn to the comfortable bar / lounge or the garden for dessert and liqueur or jasmine tea. Try the delicious Peking Dust ($3.50), a whipped cream and chestnut creation that was a favorite dish of the empress dowager; San learned its preparation from the chef at the famed Jin Jiang Hotel in Shanghai.

Open Monday to Thursday from 11:30 a.m. to 11 p.m., on Friday to 11:30 p.m., on Saturday from 5:30 to 11:30 p.m. Reservations essential. At dinner, a pianist plays Chinese music.

## Indian

There are two Indian restaurants attempting to curry favor with Houstonians, and both are noteworthy.

At the **Taj Mahal,** 8328 Gulf Freeway, at the Bellfort / Howard exit (tel. 649-2818), chef Madan Lal, trained at India's prestigious Oberoi hotels, mans the kitchen—part of it is glassed in so you can watch the culinary action at his tandoori ovens. Ambience is achieved by Indian paintings, brass trays, and rugs, and Indian ragas played as background music. Tables are covered in white linen. If you're not familiar with Indian fare, come by at lunch when a $6.50 buffet will give you an opportunity to sample a wide selection of dishes. On my last visit they included vegetable pakoras (batter-dipped, sautéed vegetables); black lentils cooked in onions, nuts, cream, and fine herbs; tandoori chicken; lamb with creamed spinach; rice with peas; salad; raita (whipped yogurt with cucumbers, onions, potatoes, and herbs); naan (tandoori-roasted bread); and an Indian dessert called gulab jamun (a sweet flour-and-milk confection in rosewater-and-honey sauce). You can also order à la carte, perhaps beginning with crisp vegetable samosas stuffed with delicately spiced potatoes, peas, and herbs ($2), and continuing with one of the tandoori specialties such as chicken tikka masala in a sauce of onions, tomatoes, butter, and cream. Combination dinners that allow you to enjoy a variety of dishes are also offered, and there's a full bar.

Open for lunch Tuesday to Friday from 11 a.m. to 2 p.m. and weekends from noon to 2 p.m.; for dinner Tuesday to Thursday and Sunday from 6 to 10 p.m., on Friday and Saturday till 11 p.m. Reservations suggested on weekends.

**India's**, 5704 Richmond Ave., between Chimney Rock and Fountain View (tel. 266-0131), also features lavish, all-you-can-eat luncheon buffets—here priced at $7.50. It offers a pleasantly exotic setting with many large plants, latticework partitions, Casablanca fans overhead, and, once again, Indian background music. Not to make too many comparisons, but India's, too, has a display kitchen allowing full view of the tandoori chef at his clay ovens. (I await the day when Texans institute the tandoori cookoff.) Only the buffet is offered at lunch.

At dinner you might consider sharing an entree with your companion and sampling a number of such side dishes as samosas stuffed with spiced ground lamb, peas, and herbs ($3.25); deep-fried battered prawns ($6.75); raita ($1.75); and fresh-from-the-tandoori oven buttered naan stuffed with almonds, pistachios, and cashews ($2.25). For your entree selection, keep in mind that tandoori specialties are featured. You might try a mixed grill for $11.50 that includes chicken, lamb, prawns, and fish, all served with rice and salad. I'm also partial to India's lamb biriyani, a fragrantly flavored blend of rice, dried fruits, nuts, and spices ($9.50); if you like hot food, ask for a bowl of hot sauce on the side. Dessert choices include mango ice cream ($2.50) and creamy rice pudding with honey, nuts, and raisins ($2.25).

Open daily for lunch from 11 a.m. to 2 p.m. and for dinner from 5:30 to 10:30 p.m. All bar drinks are offered. Reservations suggested on weekends.

## Iranian

Whatever Houston is, it's not exotic. That's why a Persian restaurant romantically named **Khayyam**, albeit prosaically placed in a shopping center at 2727 Fondren Rd., just north of Westheimer (tel. 974-6977), falls under the category of rare and refreshing fruit. Inside it looks a bit like a gypsy tea parlor, though much larger, with gold-tasseled red velvet drapes, walls hung with framed photos of Persian mosques and colorful oil paintings illustrating the poetry of Omar Khayyám, and bright-red carpeting and tablecloths. Taped Persian music helps set the Middle Eastern tone, and everything looks better at night when candles glow in red glass holders. For ambience, the best time to come is Friday or Saturday night when a belly dancer entertains from 10 p.m. on. For good food that is also authentic (many Iranians eat here), come anytime. Entrees are served with rice, a basket of warm pita bread, and a plate of radishes, scallions, feta cheese, fresh sweet basil and mint leaves; the cool leaves provide a superb counterpoint to the salty feta. Start off with deep-fried pastries filled with ground beef, chickpeas, and parsley ($3.25), or a rich, spicy soup made with chickpeas, ground beef, tomato sauce, and homemade yogurt ($1.75). For your entree the combination of kebab murgh (chicken) and shish kebab ($7 at lunch, $9.25 at dinner) is unbeatable, delicately but very flavorfully spiced and char-grilled to juicy perfection. Only the baklava was less than exceptional; consider saving your feta cheese and pita for dessert. There's a full bar. Service is a bit slow (some of the staff speaks limited English) but friendly.

Open for lunch Monday to Saturday from 11:30 a.m. to 3 p.m., for dinner Monday to Thursday from 6:30 to 11 p.m., on Friday and Saturday till 2 a.m., on Sunday from 2 to 10 p.m.

## Seafood

**Tony Mandola's Blue Oyster Bar,** 8105 Gulf Freeway (I-45), between Bellfort and Broadway (tel. 640-1117), is the third of the above-mentioned Mandola brothers' enterprises. It's a tiny place with just a half dozen or so tables and additional seating on chrome barstools at an art deco glass-brick counter lit from behind by blue neon. Snag one of these tables or stools and sit yourself down to a meal you'll long remember. "Everything," says Tony, "is homemade, except the ketchup." Fresh gulf fish and seafood are featured, and the blackboard menu offers a diversity of items that include Tex-Mex, Créole, and Italian fare.

Start out with an order of oysters Rockefeller ($5.85 for eight); Tony sautés spinach in butter with scallions and garlic, adds Créole mustard, anchovy paste, Pernod, and "secret spices," packs this divine mixture atop fresh-shucked oysters, and bakes them topped with hollandaise. Or consider other appetizers like his scrumptious, hearty seafood gumbo, his grandmother's old Louisiana recipe ($4 a bowl); excellent ceviche served with fresh-made avocado; and shrimp cocktail Vincente containing fresh cilantro and chiles, tomatoes, and chopped onion, served with pico de gallo and garnished with avocado wedge and lime ($6.25). Fish and seafood entrees, usually fried in a light batter, include oysters ($6.25 a dozen), red snapper ($9.25), catfish ($7.75), shrimp ($7.50), and (my favorite) softshell crabs ($8.95)—all served with homemade fries, "coon ass" coleslaw (it's studded with bits of shrimp), and Tony's own rich and creamy tartar sauce. A big bowl of lemon wedges is on every table, and homemade tortilla chips with salsa are served gratis when you order. On Tuesday and Thursday there's a special of homemade spaghetti with shrimp and crabmeat sauce. Crayfish dishes are also heartily recommended in season. And absolutely not to be passed up for any reason is Mama Grace Mandola's incredible banana key lime pie ($2.75 per heavenly slice).

Tony's isn't fancy; come as you are. It has New York bar-style white tile flooring, neon beer signs over the bar, and sky-blue ceramic tile walls. There's a full bar, but I'd opt for the iced tea served with fresh mint.

Open Monday to Thursday from 11 a.m. to 10 p.m., on Friday and Saturday till 11 p.m., on Sunday from noon to 9 p.m. You can't make reservations, so arrive at off times to avoid long lines. There's another location at 1608 Shepherd Dr., between Memorial Drive and I-10 (tel. 864-0915).

## Steak

**Texas Tumbleweed,** 1007 Gessner Rd., just north of I-10 (tel. 464-9507), is more than just a place to dig into a juicy, sizzling, mesquite-grilled steak. Part of a Houston-based chain that spoofs itself by advertising "tough steaks, watered-down drinks, and high prices" (of course offering just the opposite), it's an only-in-Texas phenomenon. Owner Jack Ray is a former world-champion duck and goose caller who has appeared on the "Merv Griffin Show" and in a "do-you-know-me" American Express commercial. Like all Texas Tumbleweeds, the Gessner location is a big rustic barn of a place with six-foot-long, red-and-white-checkered oilcloth-covered picnic tables enclosing a dance floor. Wednesday through Saturday nights there's live country music from 7:30 p.m. till closing. Diners frequently take to the floor and (when not upstaged by the occasional western gunfight) execute a proficient Texas two-step worthy of John Travolta. The pine-paneled walls and columns are decorated with murals of the West, neon beer signs, Texas flags, and wood-plank signs made up from guests' business cards or bearing mottoes like "God Bless John Wayne," "Free Beer Tomorrow," and "Don't Throw Bones at the Band." Low lighting comes from enamel lamps overhead, candles in red glass holders, and the glow of the mesquite fire. Waiters and waitresses, mostly college students wearing faded jeans, bandanas, and cowboy hats, introduce themselves as Cactus Flower, Sundance, and the like. And kids are given a Texas Tumbleweed sheriff's badge. It's a great place for family dining.

Go at dinner on a music night to catch the show. Though these gargantuan steak meals are plenty without appetizers, you're probably going to hang around a long time to enjoy the music, so what the heck? Start out with a round of nachos ($3.50) or golden nuggets (jalapeños stuffed with cheddar cheese, breaded, and deep-fried; $3.50). Moving on to entrees, the "cowboy," a massive 24-ounce porterhouse, is just $14.95, but for my bird-like appetite the $10.95 "wagon wheel," an eight-ounce bacon-wrapped filet, is amply filling. All entrees are served with salad, blazin' saddle beans, and hot homemade bread and butter. A baked "tater" on the side will add $1.25 to your tab; homemade hot peach cobbler topped with vanilla ice cream, $2.50. There's a full bar, and "for the little deputies" the Tumbleweed offers a mesquite-grilled trailburger with fries for just $3.25. Mesquite-grilled chicken and chicken-fried steak are additional options.

Open weekdays for lunch from 11 a.m. to 2 p.m. (prices are about $1 lower per item), from 5 to 10 p.m. Sunday to Tuesday, till 10:30 p.m. on Wednesday and Thursday, till 11:30 p.m. on Friday and Saturday.

## Tex-Mex

**Primo's,** 519 Rosalie, at Smith (tel. 528-9158), gets my vote for the best fajitas in Houston (maybe in Texas)—which in itself is ample recommendation. In fact, all the food here is incredibly *delicioso*. It's a festive-looking place with a beachy Mexican resort decor, complete with painted palm trees. Walls are hung with photographs of Zapata and Pancho Villa, there are lots of plants, and the oilcloth-covered tables are adorned with fresh flowers. There's always music on the jukebox—Mexican, rock, or country—and enhancing the south-of-the-border setting, at the entrance a Mexican woman pounds out tortillas. Primo's has provided fare for many Houston festivals and catered parties for Ray Charles, Kris Kristofferson, B. B. King, and other headliners who play Rockefeller's, the nearby club; *Texas Monthly* magazine calls Primo's "*segundo* to none."

All food here is freshly prepared from the finest ingredients. Cognoscenti often opt for an off-the-menu item called *revolución*—a mixed-grill platter piled high with fajitas and char-broiled chicken breast and shrimp, served with Mexican rice, refried beans, excellent tangy guacamole, tortillas, and pico de gallo ($13.95). Of course, all its elements can also be ordered separately for considerably less. Back on the menu, consider the carne guisada, tender cuts of beef simmered with fresh tomatoes and onions ($8.95). For appetizers there are choices like cold shrimp in spicy red sauce ($9.95), queso fundido, which is melted Monterrey jack cheese flavored with sausage and shallots ($6.25), and fabulous nachos topped with melted cheese, jalapeños, fajitas, and guacamole ($7.95 for an immense order). Meals conclude with delicious homemade desserts, including a marvelous creamy flan and rich praline cheesecake ($3.25 for either). Primo's serves Mexican breakfasts too: $3.25 for chorizo sausage and scrambled eggs wrapped in two tacos with a cup of hot coffee. And at Happy Hour, weekdays from 3 to 6 p.m., free hors d'oeuvres accompany dynamite margaritas ($1.75).

Hours are 7 a.m. to 10 p.m. Monday to Saturday, on Sunday to 9 p.m. There's a second location at 77 Harvard, at the corner of Washington Avenue (tel. 880-2470).

**Ninfa's,** 2704 Navigation Blvd., between Nagle and Delano (tel. 228-1175), is more than just another Tex-Mex eatery; it's a revered Houston institution whose history is as well known locally as the Alamo's. It all began when Mexican-born Ninfa and her Italian husband, Domenic "Tommy" Laurenzo, combined heritages, creating a company to sell wholesale pizza dough and tortillas. After Tommy died in 1969, Ninfa, with five children to support, decided to augment her income by turning a small portion of the factory into a ten-table Mexican restaurant. She opened her doors in 1973 with just $16 in the cash register and only her kids as help. But her menu pioneered dishes culled from every region of Mexico, at that time unheard of in Texas, along with her still-famous avocado-based green sauce and the use of fresh cilantro. Word spread of Ninfa's tacos al carbón, and soon carloads of hungry Houstonians began crossing the tracks to the Mexican barrio to try them. After a year she added another 24 tables; after two years she doubled the size of the restaurant to 3,800 square feet with 175 chairs. Today there are nine Houston locations plus one in Dallas—all flourishing, and all keeping to the high standard of the original. And Ninfa herself has achieved national renown; she's been featured in *Newsweek,* the *New York Times, Forbes,* and *Business Week;* has been voted "Woman Restaurateur of the Year" by the Texas Restaurant Association; and has appeared on the "Today Show."

The original Navigation location, next door to the house where Ninfa raised her family, is a festive setting with pink-bordered cream-colored walls, painted with floral designs; stained-glass lighting fixtures; and seating in colorfully painted wicker chairs with variegated cushions. At the entrance, a sturdy-looking Mexican woman rolls out and grills the fresh tortillas in front of an open kitchen. The place is always mobbed. In-the-know-diners, which includes just about everyone except out-of-towners, ask for the "off" menu of chef's specialties and peruse it while munching tortilla chips dipped in the famous green (it's made with avocado, sour cream, green tomatoes, and fresadilla tomatoes, among other things) and red (tomato- and chili-based) sauces. Curtido (carrots marinated in oil, vinegar, and very hot chiles) also comes gratis; it's so good you can't stop eating it, but it's so hot you wish you could. There's an excellent ceviche appetizer: bay shrimps and scallops marinated in lime juice with onions, tomatoes, cilantro, and avocado chunks ($4.75). Entree specialties include chicken flautas (chicken sautéed in butter, wine, and tomato sauce, rolled in corn tortillas, deep-fried, and served with guacamole and sour cream; $6.50 for two) and parillada mixta, a mixed grill of your choice, possibly including shrimp, fajitas, pheasant, quail, chicken, and / or ribs cooked over mesquite and served with fresh onion, bell peppers, tomatoes, and stuffed green peppers. The latter item isn't on either menu; just ask for it. Everything you order is fresh and prepared in small batches. Praline cheesecake with fresh whipped cream is the perfect ending to this high-calorie feast.

Ninfa's is open from 11 a.m. to 10 p.m. Monday to Thursday, to 11 p.m. on Friday, from noon to 11 p.m. on Saturday, and from noon to 10 p.m. on Sunday. Reservations essential.

One final note: Though Houstonians swear the Navigation location is the best, I think it's just sentiment; I've never had a less than superb meal at any Ninfa's. Check the phonebook for the nearest location.

Business people mob the place after work every day, by dinnertime there's often an hour or longer wait for tables, and it's not unusual to see celebrities. The **Cadillac Bar,** 1802 Shepherd Dr., a block south of I-10 (tel. 862-2020), is a scene everybody makes eventually. It's rowdy, it's funky, and it's fun. There's likely to be someone standing on a table and writing on the walls. In fact, every inch of the cream-colored walls is covered with graffiti, a custom spontaneously started years ago, which the owners, at first reluctantly, accepted; they now repaint every year and start from scratch. The ambience is a blend of Mexican music, animated conversation (fairly often interupted by the delivery of singing telegrams), lots of pickup action at the bar, and the bustle of waiters carrying sizzling platters of fajitas through the crowds. In the bar area, adorned with neon signs, sombreros serve as lampshades. The dining room has high-backed wicker chairs at white linen-clothed tables and a large Mexican flag draped on one wall.

If there's a wait for a table, order up the house special, a Mexican flag ($3), at the bar; a layered flaming drink of liqueurs the colors of the Mexican flag, it's made with white crème de menthe, grenadine, and chartreuse. Of course, a margarita ($2.75) would taste better, but either will get you in the proper let-loose spirit. For openers, you can't go wrong with the Cadillac's queso flameado con chorizo, a spicy melted cheese and sausage dish ($3.85) to be scooped up with chips. The guacamole's another good choice. Chef Rufino Delgado makes some great fajitas ($11.95), and his other specialties—like cabrito, tender milk-fed goat ($11.95); softshell crab ($10.95); and mesquite-roasted quail ($11.95) —are also noteworthy. Or order *everything*—at an all-you-can-eat buffet ($11.95) any Saturday or Sunday from noon to 3 p.m. It consists of about seven main courses, fresh fruit, omelets, coffee, and unlimited champagne.

Open Monday to Thursday from 11 a.m. to 10:30 p.m., on Friday to midnight, on Saturday from noon to midnight, and on Sunday from noon to 10 p.m. Reservations essential at lunch and dinner, though none can be made Saturday nights after 7 p.m.

### Thai

**Renu's,** 1230 Westheimer Rd., at Commonwealth (tel. 528-6998), is a much-acclaimed Thai eatery that *Esquire* called one of the 100 best new restaurants in the U.S. in 1981. I'm happy to say that owner/chef Don Parnarom (Renu is his wife) has maintained the quality that evoked such early praise. *Houston City* magazine recently rated Renu's as one of the 20 best restaurants in Houston! Though Don has a degree in stage design from an Italian university, here he highlights the skills gleaned from an older sister who is director of a culinary school in Bangkok. His dishes are not only delectable, they're totally authentic and prepared from fresh ingredients: the Parnaroms grow lemon grass, anise leaves, and other exotic herbs in their home garden.

An appetizer of beef sate ($5.40) is highly recommended so that you can taste Don's heavenly peanut sauce. I'm also very partial to mee krob, a pungently spiced, crispy noodle dish ($4.50), and pad thai, imported noodles tossed with shrimp, bean curd, preserved radish, ground peanuts, and bean sprouts ($4.95). Among the entrees, you can't go wrong with sautéed chicken with cashew nuts, bamboo shoots, and dried pepper ($5.95); shrimp clay pot (shrimp, vegetables, ham, glass noodles, and bean curd steamed in a clay pot; $7); a steamed seafood curry served in a rabbit fashioned out of tin foil ($7.95); or a dish called tiger cries—medium-rare steak with a chili/garlic dip ($6.25). Be forewarned that the latter is so named because it's so hot it could make a tiger cry. There's a full bar, and in addition to menu items, specials are always listed on the blackboard. Prices are a tad reduced (about 50¢ per item) at lunch. Thai food tends to be pretty torrid, but the refreshing desserts will restore your palate to a temperate zone. I'm partial to the sticky sweet rice that is steamed in coconut milk and served, in season, with fresh mango (at other times, topped with Thai custard). Renu's is a casual but quite comfortable place with pine walls and paneling, Formica tables, linoleum tile floors, and orange vinyl booths along one wall. Subdued lighting adds a bit of atmosphere.

Open Tuesday to Friday from 11 a.m. to 2:30 p.m. and 5 to 10:30 p.m., on

Saturday and Sunday from 3 to 10:30 p.m. Reservations suggested on weekends.

## Vietnamese

**Vietnam Kitchen,** 2929-C Milam, at the corner of Anita (tel. 520-7106), is, quite simply, the best Vietnamese restaurant I've ever encountered. It's an unpretentious little place in a so-so section of downtown (don't worry—it's a seedy, but perfectly safe area), with a plain-but-pleasant interior: linoleum-covered floors, silver foil wallpaper, red vinyl chairs and tablecloths. A large number of the diners are Vietnamese, always an indication of authenticity.

Begin your meal with an appetizer of the Kitchen's crispy chao gai, Vietnamese eggrolls (six for $3.75). They're served with a basket of fresh mint leaves, parsley, lettuce and cucumber slices; the proper, and very rewarding, procedure is to wrap the leaves, cucumber, and an eggroll in a lettuce leaf and dip the whole thing in fish sauce. Lemon-grilled beef ($8.50), an equally extraordinary culinary creation, is eaten in similar fashion. You wrap it in thin rice pancakes along with shredded carrots, bean sprouts, pickled onions, sliced cucumber, mint, and parsley. The two above items are musts; they're just incredibly good. But if you're ordering additional dishes, consider the barbecued shrimp wrapped around sugarcane ($12.25), the "special soup" made with squid, shrimp, chicken, pork, and vegetables ($5 for four people), and the stir-fry shrimp with assorted vegetables, snow peas, carrots, Chinese cabbage and straw mushrooms ($7). Wine and beer are available. Portions are very hefty.

Open 9 a.m. to midnight Sunday to Thursday, till 3 a.m. on Friday and Saturday.

**BUDGET:** Included here are some of the best burgers and barbecue in Texas.

## Barbecue and Burgers

Dining at a barbecue restaurant in Kansas City, Vice-President George Bush once risked future Missouri votes by exclaiming, "This place is okay, but you should go to Houston and try Otto's." **Otto's,** 5502 Memorial Dr., at the corner of Reinicke (tel. 864-2573), has been eliciting rave reviews since Annie and Otto Sofka got into grilling in 1955. Today, son Marcus oversees the hickory pits. George and Barbara Bush come in regularly when they're in town (he likes ribs, she orders links).

The food at this joint—and a joint it is, with imitation wood paneling, linoleum tile floors, and rustic pine booths and tables—is fabulous. The ribs, cooked with the fat on for extra juiciness and trimmed before serving, are falling-off-the-bone tender and authentically smoky in flavor. Otto's barbecue sauce achieves a pungently spicy perfection. The coleslaw is crisp, the potato salad even better than your mom's, the baked beans better than Boston's. Everything's so good, I'd opt for sharing an all-meat platter of sausage links, beef, ribs, and ham ($7.25) and ordering individual portions of potato salad, beans, and slaw (85¢ each). Fresh-baked bread accompanies all orders. Draft beer is $1.05; a slice of homemade pecan or pumpkin pie, $1.25. And sometimes barbecued chicken is on the menu.

Otto's has a second section serving burgers made from meat ground on the premises, its "dining area" even funkier than the other. If the weather is good, the outdoor tables are your best bet. Inside, Otto's is decorated with pictures of chimpanzees, kitschy art, and plaques with mottoes.

Otto's is open for barbecue Monday to Saturday from 11 a.m. to 9 p.m.; for burgers weekdays from 9 a.m. to midnight, on Saturday to 6 p.m. No credit cards.

## Chili and Burgers

There are about 50 branches of **Chili's** in Texas, and the one at 5930 Richmond Ave., at Fountain View (tel. 781-1654), is the first in Houston and the second in the chain. Its chili was recommended to me by no less a connoisseur than Jo Ann Horton, editor of the chilihead newspaper, *Goat Gap Gazette*. All the Chili's eateries look pretty much alike. They have white stucco and wood-paneled walls, the latter painted a pleasant shade of green and the totality plastered with framed color photographs of chili cookoffs. Seating is in upholstered wood booths at ceramic-tile tables (candlelit at night) under hanging lamps made of old chili pots. Floors are brick. There are lots and lots of plants, and there's usually a lively bar area. The setting is rustic and casual, but very comfortable. It's a great choice for family dining.

The "bowl of red" for which the restaurant's named is $3.25 with or without beans and cheese. Equally popular here are the fabulous half-pound burgers with mustard, lettuce, tomato, onion, pickle, and mayonnaise ($3.50); numerous toppings (cheese, chili, sautéed onions, hickory sauce, guacamole, etc.) are available. Other big items are fajitas served with guacamole, cheese, and sour cream ($6.95); a barbecued half chicken served in a basket with sauce, barbecued beans, and a crispy tortilla shell filled with salad ($6.50); and a barbecued chicken sandwich with bacon, tomato, swiss, and dressing on a sourdough bun ($4.50). The fresh-cut home-style fries ($1.50) are a must, but if you like them without salt be sure to specify. There are no desserts, but your beverage choices run the gamut from wine to strawberry margaritas to chocolate milkshakes.

Open Monday to Thursday from 11 a.m. to 11 p.m., on Friday and Saturday to 1 a.m., and on Sunday from 11:30 a.m. to 11 p.m.

## Mainly Burgers

The **Fuddruckers**, at 3100 Chimney Rock Rd., a block north of Richmond (tel. 780-7080), is one link in a widespread Texas chain that features a build-your-own-burger format. They all have spacious warehouse-like interiors in which products used in food preparation form part of the decor: sacks of potatoes and flour, boxes of cheese sauce and ketchup, sides of beef, and jars of pickles are stacked here and there in large quantities. There are also old saloon-like elements such as fan lamps suspended from pressed-tin ceilings, sturdy oak furnishings, handsome oak bars, neon beer signs, and checkered tablecloths. The total effect is quite pleasant, and the burgers are great.

Upon entering a Fuddruckers, you first get on a cafeteria line to order. Choices include a half-pound burger on a buttery fresh-baked bun ($4.25), a steak sandwich ($5.25), and a chicken breast sandwich ($3.85), with such inexpensive side-order options as fries, beans, chili, and sautéed onions. A children's three-ounce burger or hot dog platter with fries, a cookie, and a 16-ounce soft drink is $2.25; wine or beer for the adults is $1.95. Having procured the basics, the diner now proceeds to the frills—a buffet table of jalapeños, salsa, chopped and sliced onions, lettuce, chopped and sliced tomatoes, big crocks of melted cheddar and jalapeño cheeses, pickles and relish, barbecue sauce, sauerkraut, Hellman's mayonnaise, and Heinz ketchup—everything required to create the burger of your dreams. All that's left to do is sit down and eat till your eyes bubble. There are fresh-baked brownies and chocolate-chip cookies for dessert, à la mode with Blue Bell ice cream if you wish, over at the bakery counter. While you're lingering over coffee the kids can play video games—

Fuddruckers is an A-1 choice for family dining. The quality hamburger meat is fresh ground on the premises, and everything else is made from scratch.

Fuddruckers is open Monday to Saturday from 11 a.m. to 11 p.m., from noon to 10 p.m. on Sunday. Check the phonebook for additional locations.

## Mexican

Mexican friends tell me the food at **Doneraki,** 2836 Fulton St., at Halpern (tel. 224-2509), tastes just like *madre* used to make. It's owned by three Mexican brothers—César, Victor, and Jorge Rodriguez—who, starting out with $500 and household kitchen equipment in 1973, have created an extremely popular and successful restaurant. Though the menu lists a few Tex-Mex items, I'd suggest passing them up and trying some authentic dishes you may not have come across before: for example, the caldo de rez, a rich and chunky cilantro- and cumin-spiced beef soup containing cabbage, corn (on the ear), carrots, onions, peppers, squash, tomatoes, and celery. Fresh cilantro and onions and large bowls of three delicious sauces—a guacamole-, sour cream-, and cilantro-based green, chili con queso, and a spicy red—are served gratis with your tortilla chips. The rice accompanying entrees is special too; it's boiled in a broth with Mexican spices, potatoes, red peppers, onions, cumin, garlic, and carrots. And the refried beans are slow-cooked with pork drippings. A specialty is the tacos al carbón del trampo ($4.25)—a kind of Mexican beef souvlaki—served with flour or corn tortillas and pinto bean soup made with beer and bacon. If you're really adventurous, tell Victor you're looking for new taste sensations and ask him to order for you. Don't pass up the excellent sugar- and cinnamon-flavored Mexican coffee at the end of your meal, perhaps with creamy cold rice pudding.

Doneraki, by the way, is an attractive eatery, a festive south-of-the-border setting with a Mexican fountain centerpiece, terracotta-tile floors, lacy white wrought-iron chairs with blue cushions, fans overhead, and lots of hanging plants thriving in the light streaming in from all-around windows. There's a glass-enclosed café area up front.

Open Monday to Thursday from 11 a.m. to midnight, Friday through Sunday from 8 a.m. (come by for a Mexican breakfast) to 3 a.m. At night mariachi bands entertain. Reservations suggested.

## Trendy American

Just a block from the Fine Arts and Contemporary Arts Museums, **Butera's,** 5019 Montrose Blvd., at Bartlett (tel. 523-0722), not surprisingly, attracts an arty clientele. It's a good choice for a casual meal when you're sightseeing in the area. The somewhat haphazard interior evokes New York's East Village; both the plants and the works of local artists displayed on white and forest-green walls seem almost arbitrarily placed. Interior seating is at butcher-block tables, but, if weather permits, I always head for the sidewalk café with garden furnishings under a striped awning.

Service is cafeteria style, and everything is made from scratch on the premises. Sandwiches are made to order with fillings like turkey, roast beef, creamed herring, cream cheese and lox, chicken salad, cheeses, Genoa salami, and corned beef available between slices of whole wheat, rye, white, French bread, pumpernickel, onion or Kaiser roll. An equally wide selection of dressings is offered. Prices are about $3 to $5, depending on how Dagwoody you get. There's also a large choice of salads, everything from deviled eggs ($2.65) to broccoli and new potato ($1.85) to prosaic macaroni ($1.50). A cheese, fresh fruit, and pâté platter served with French bread is $11.50 (serves two). And those with hearty appetites can opt for an Italian sausage hero ($4). Something here for everyone, surely. Beverage options include a large wine selection and

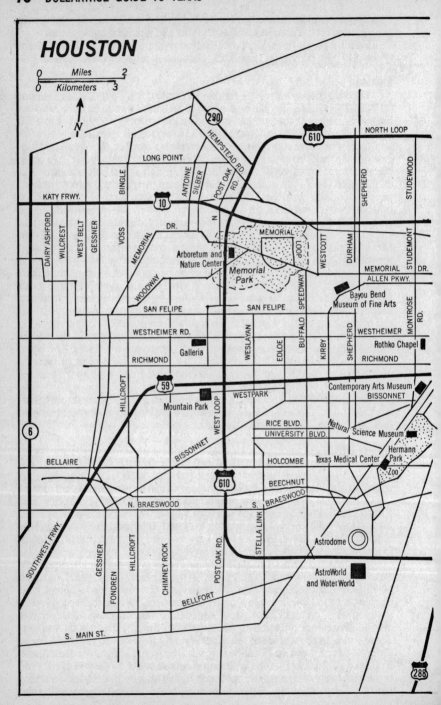

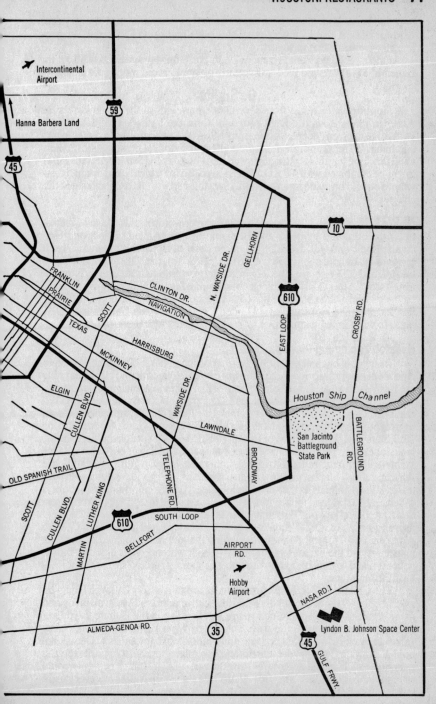

over 100 beers from all over the world, as well as fresh-squeezed orange juice. And for dessert there's a very good chocolate mousse ($1.95), plus Häagen-Dazs ice cream or frozen yogurt.

Open weekdays from 11 a.m. to 8 p.m., on Saturday and Sunday till 6 p.m. Lunchtime is always mobbed; arrive early or late to avoid waiting for a table.

# 6. Sights

Houston sights range from several fine museums to the headquarters for America's manned space-flight program, from the battlefield of San Jacinto (where Texas won independence from Mexico) to child-pleaser theme parks and hands-on museums, from nature centers to historical preservations. Allow a full day for Clear Lake attractions and most of a day for San Jacinto; the latter might be combined with a Port of Houston cruise for which, please note, reservations should be made far in advance. Spectator sports are also included in this chapter.

**HERMANN PARK:** A little over a mile from downtown, this 545-acre recreation area bordered by Main and Hermann Streets, Almeda Road, and Holcombe Boulevard (tel. 520-7056), is in the heart of Houston's museum area. It contains an 18-hole public golf course (tel. 529-9788), the Miller Outdoor Theatre (tel. 520-3290) offering the largest program of free cultural events in the nation (see "After Dark"), picnic areas, excellent children's playgrounds, ballfields, and a large bronze equestrian statue of Sam Houston pointing toward San Jacinto. The Houston Civic Garden Center and Rose Garden is a lovely place to walk amid beautiful plantings and statuary. Also in the park are:

## Houston Zoological Gardens

Its humble beginnings in 1905 were a collection of rabbits, raccoons, capuchin monkeys, prairie dogs, and Mexican eagles, along with one black bear, one great horned owl, and an alligator pond—all in Sam Houston Park. But the animal population began to grow and by 1925 a tract of land was set aside in Hermann Park to house over 400 animals. Today there are about 2,500, representing 588 species, and the Houston Zoological Gardens, entrance on 1513 Outer Belt Dr., just east of Fannin (tel. 523-5888), occupies 50 acres lushly landscaped with palms and shade trees, fountains, and flower beds. Attendance at this delightful zoo ranks fifth among U.S. menageries. Natural habitats house African zebras, hippos, giraffes, rhinos, cheetahs, and gorillas, along with such lesser-known animals as the serval (a long-legged cat), colorful-faced monkeys called DeBrazzas, and fennec foxes (the smallest of all foxes). From Australasia there are fierce-looking Tasmanian Devils, blue-and-green striped Fijian iguanas, and wallabies. Other equally interesting residents hail from Eurasia, North America, and Tropical America (including the luxuriantly maned golden lion marmoset and the hideous vampire bat—yes, it will suck your blood). And an aquarium and several bird areas are home to some of the zoo's most awesomely beautiful creatures.

The Children's Zoo here is excellent. It contains a Zoo-Lab with hands-on exhibits, the Texas Wild Building housing native animals (like armadillos and flying squirrels) and Aquatunnel where fish that live in the Buffalo Bayou are represented, petting areas (donkeys, sheep, goats, etc.), a hatchery where fuzzy yellow baby chicks can often be seen, and a nursery of baby animals. Occasional puppet shows and animal demonstrations take place here. Just opposite the zoo is another child-popular feature—a train ride that travels a two-mile route around the park. Tickets are 80¢ (infants free), and departures are every eight minutes from 10 a.m. to about 5:30 p.m.

The Houston Zoo (also known as the Hermann Park Zoo) is open from 9:30 a.m. to 8 p.m. May 1 to September 30, till 6 p.m. the rest of the year. Strollers and wheelchairs are available at the front gate, as are maps of the zoo. Inquire at the information booth about special films and other programs, as well as feeding times for the alligators, vampire bats, and sea lions. Admission free.

## Houston Museum of Natural Science

Established in 1909, this fine natural science museum at 1 Hermann Circle Dr. (tel. 526-4273) began with a small collection of insects, butterflies, and stuffed animals and birds kept in the City Auditorium. The present building, opened in 1969, houses what has grown into one of the largest natural science museums in the Southwest.

On the lower level, exhibits deal with the development of energy from human brawn and fire to nuclear and solar power; communications (printing, telegraph, telephone, radio, motion pictures, video, satellites, etc.); space science (a piece of lunar rock, space mission artifacts, and a replica of the astronauts on the moon are displayed); chemistry; and gems and minerals. A ten-minute nature program is shown in a darkened room, and another room invites the visitor to guess how fast various animals can run and how high they can leap (did you know a tortoise plods along at .16 miles per hour, while a peregrine falcon whizzes by at 180 mph, or that a kangaroo can leap 42 feet?). Geared to kids is a table with tactile items like coral, petrified wood, and deer horns, to pick up and touch.

The main floor is dominated by a 70-foot *Diplodocus* dinosaur skeleton, one of several prehistoric residents of the Central Hall. Fossils include an 80-million-year-old dinosaur egg. In the Hall of the American Indian, in addition to feather headdresses, rugs, pottery, basketry, and silver and turquoise jewelry, there are sculptures by artist Frederic Remington. You can also explore the *Beaver Mark IV,* a deep-diving submersible, and learn about drilling for oil, the refinery process, and products made from petroleum (would you believe Tide, Sweet 'N Low, flashbulbs, and styrofoam cups?) in the Hall of Petroleum Science and Technology.

Tableaus of African animal life and displays of African art and artifacts are on the second floor, as are the Hall of Texas History (exhibits on the Alamo, branding a maverick, guns that won the West, etc.) and the Hall of Texas Wildlife.

In addition to the regular collection the museum mounts many special exhibits such as "4,000 Years of Chinese Jade" and "Peru's Golden Treasures." And do ask at the desk about films, field trips, lectures, and demonstrations (some of them geared to children), of which there is a full annual program.

On the premises of the museum is the **Burke Baker Planetarium,** open for daily afternoon shows, weekends year round at 2, 3, and 4 p.m., and during the week at 2 and 3 p.m. Monday to Friday May 31 through the end of August, 4 p.m. only Wednesday to Friday the rest of the year. Shows range from a *Galaxy Grand Tour* to *All Systems Go,* the latter commemorating 25 years of America in space.

Museum hours are 9 a.m. to 5 p.m. Tuesday to Saturday, noon to 5 p.m. on Sunday and Monday. Admission is free, but donations are appreciated. Planetarium shows cost $2 for adults, $1 for children under 12.

**SAM HOUSTON PARK:** Nestled in the shadow of downtown skyscrapers, Sam Houston Park, 1100 Bagby St. (tel. 223-8367), is a 19th-century time capsule, a segment of Houston's past preserved under the auspices of the Harris County

Heritage Society. Here six historic 1800s houses and a small country church have been restored and refurnished in period styles to create an outdoor museum set among rolling lawns and Victorian gardens. Also on the premises is a reconstructed "Long Row" of mid-19th-century shops. One-hour guided tours of the buildings (focusing on architecture, interior decor, and lifestyles of the period) depart from the Long Row on the hour and half hour, Monday to Saturday from 10 a.m. to 3 p.m. and on Sunday between 1 and 4 p.m.

Before you begin your tour, visit the new **Gallery of Texas History** next to the Long Row; it houses a comprehensive exhibit on Texas and Houston history from 1519 to the present. The gallery offers visitors a foretaste of the future Texas Museum of History and Technology that will be built on this site by 1990. There's also a ten-minute film on Texas history shown continuously in the Long Row Building that you can watch before or after your tour. Because of time limitations, the tours take in only four—but not always the same four— buildings; if you want to see the others, ask your docent how it might be arranged. A little background on each follows.

**Kellum-Noble House:** Built in 1847–1848, this is Houston's oldest residential structure on its original site. Nathaniel Kelly Kellum was one of the major building contractors in Houston in the 1840s, and his home was visited by many Texas notables, including Sam Houston. The Noble family bought the house in 1851, and their granddaughter, Eloise Witt, lived here until the city acquired the property as its first public park in 1899. The plantation-style home, with its broad porches and wide doors and windows, has elements of Greek revival architecture, which was very popular in the first half of the 19th century. In the formal parlor are a side chair and table that belonged to Sam Houston, as did the walnut sideboard in the dining room.

**Nichols-Rice-Cherry House:** One of the last surviving examples of the antebellum urban elite residences on the Texas upper Gulf Coast, this Greek revival structure was the home of two prominent Houston entrepreneurs and a leader of the art community. It was built by Ebenezer B. Nichols between 1845 and 1850, and in 1856 Nichols sold the house to his business partner, William Marsh Rice, whose vast fortune funded Rice University. Nichols and Rice were major importers with heavy investments in shipping and early railroads. The final owner, Mrs. Emma Richardson Cherry, was a leader in the creation of the Houston Art League, a forerunner of the Museum of Fine Arts. The Cherrys lived in the house until her death in 1954. The house is furnished with many fine American Empire, early rococo revival, and Gothic revival pieces. There's an exquisite Duncan Phyfe piano in the parlor, and the master bedroom, with its massive Gothic pieces, is quite grand: pillars on the canopied bed are over eight feet high! It contrasts dramatically with poor nanny's bed in the nursery, designedly narrow and stiff so she'd sleep lightly and wake quickly to the children's call.

**Pillot House:** A Queen Anne–style residence, Pillot House was built in 1868 by French-born timber merchant Eugene Pillot. He constructed the first attached kitchen in Houston at the back of the house, and was one of the first in the area to install gas lighting and build a home with running water. Pillot was a major theatrical entrepreneur in Houston and Galveston. Leading performers like Maurice Barrymore, Lillie Langtry, Otis Skinner, and Edwin Booth played his Opera House. His grandson, also named Eugene, lived here until the 1960s. When the house was moved to Sam Houston Park in 1965, along with it came a pair of cast-metal dogs that flanked the entrance, the original iron fence, the walk, and many plants—sago palm, pink and white oleander, crape myrtle, fig trees, and a deep-purple climbing rose. The Society has refurbished the parlors in the rococo revival and Eastlake styles popular in the 1860s and 1870s, respectively. The imitation bamboo furnishings of one of the bedrooms reflects 1880s aesthetics influenced by the Japanese pavilion at the 1876 World's Fair. There are many indications of ostentation, including closets, which in the 19th century were taxed as additional rooms. The beautiful doll at the foot of the bed in the French bedroom belonged to the family doctor; women pointed to parts of its anatomy to tell where it hurt without betraying Victorian modesty.

**San Felipe Cottage:** The lifestyle of a German middle-class family, the Ruppersburgs, is reflected in this unpretentious dwelling built in the late 1860s and remodeled in the 1870s and 1880s. A sewing machine, an apparatus an immigrant family would have been proud to own, is prominently displayed in the parlor, along with the elaborate trunk such a family might have brought from Europe and possessions such as a collection of Clabber glass. The cuckoo clock in the dining room would also have been a reminder of home.

**The Old Place:** Climbing farther down the social ladder, the Old Place is a rudimentary frontier cypress cabin built, it is believed, in 1824. Here an entire family would live in one small dirt-floored room, sleeping on mattresses filled with Spanish moss. Since uninvited animals (like raccoons) often wandered in, foods were kept on high-hung shelves. Believed to be the oldest standing structure in Harris County, the house was occupied briefly (in 1843) by Christian Duer, whose diary provides a bleak insight into frontier life in the Houston area. "Now, alas," wrote Duer, "when after years of struggles with good and bad fortune my brightest hopes have faded and fallen like the sear and yellow leaves of autumn—when perhaps no being on earth save one cares for my weal or woe except through interest—now alas my soul is cold—my feelings are blunted and earth has no pleasures for the heart chilled and satiated by a knowledge of the world and an intercourse with mankind." Pretty grim, but keep in mind that Duer wrote it when alone on Christmas Day; it could be an early case of the holiday blues one reads so much about today. Later more affluent owners used the original structure as the framework for a pleasant Victorian cottage, but the Heritage Society was able to remove these modifications and get down to the hand-hewn cedar studs and beams.

**Staiti House:** This 1905 residence of prominent Houston oilman Henry Staiti is currently being remodeled. The interior will not be open to the public until 1990.

**St. John's Church:** Built in 1891 to serve the Swiss and German immigrant farmers who made up its Lutheran congregation, St. John's originally cost just $860. Its arched windows and shutters are in 19th-century Gothic style, but the basic form of the church is classical revival. The church was—and is here—placed in an east-west direction for religious reasons (facing the rising sun and Jerusalem). The floors, which had been preserved by linoleum over the years, are original, as are the cypress plank pews, the pulpit, organ, and hymn board. St. John's is typical of the small countryside churches that played such a large part in the lives of early Texas settlers.

**The Long Row:** In the early days of Houston (the 1830s), founder John Kirby Allen ordered the construction of a row of connected buildings on Main Street to house the government until the capitol building was completed. It became known as the Long Row, and with the completion of the Capitol, it soon evolved into Houston's first shopping center. The actual Long Row was destroyed by fire in 1860, but the Heritage Society reconstructed it in Sam Houston Park in 1967. It contains the charming Yesteryear Shop where you can buy all kinds of country-store items (patchwork quilts, dried flower wreaths, wicker picnic baskets, etc.) and, in so doing, help support the Heritage Society. And there's also a delightful plank-floored tea room serving homemade fare—sandwiches on fresh-baked bread, soups, salads, and desserts—at tables adorned with baskets of flowers. It's open for lunch weekdays from 11 a.m. to 1:30 p.m.

*Note:* The Heritage Society Parking lot is a bit hard to find. It's on the south side of Allen Parkway.

**MEMORIAL PARK:** The Hogg family that gave the city the stunning Bayou Bend Collection also contributed 1,000 nearby pine-forested acres to this beautiful and very necessary recreation area. Later, another 503 acres were purchased, further enlarging the park. It is so named because it was dedicated in 1925 to the memory of Houstonians who died in World War I.

Memorial Park, four miles from downtown Houston at I-10 and Loop 610 (tel. 641-4111), offers a wealth of leisure activities. Among its facilities are an 18-hole golf course (tel. 862-4033), picnic areas with barbecue grills, 22 tennis courts (four lit for night play; tel. 861-3765), baseball and soccer fields, polo grounds, an archery range, a swimming pool, playgrounds, and jogging/biking/hiking trails.

## Houston Arboretum and Nature Center

This 155-acre wilderness is right in the heart of Houston at 4501 Woodway Dr. (tel. 681-8433). For nature lovers, it is a veritable oasis in the asphalt desert where native vegetation has been preserved in a rapidly expanding city. There are five miles of hiking trails, including a crushed-granite, three-quarter-mile, self-guided loop tour winding through upland, lowland, and ravine habitats—from groves of loblolly pine festooned with trumpet creeper to wetland area where wading birds, frogs, and turtles can be observed amid the rushes. The trail is posted with interpretive signs along the way, and a booklet further elucidating its natural attractions is available at the Visitor Center. Don boots, jeans, and insect repellent when you visit (there are snakes, poison ivy, and mosquitoes). Free guided walks on Sunday afternoons and other nature programs are well worth attending; call to find out what's on during your stay. But equally worthwhile is a solitary few hours on the trails (you have to start early in the morning to avoid crowds) watching for birds (there are 158 species), catching glimpses of forest animals, and listening to the wind rustling in the trees. A gift shop and children's discovery room are located at the Visitor Center.

Grounds are open from 9 a.m. to 6 p.m. November to April, till 8 p.m. the rest of the year. Visitor Center hours are 9 a.m. to 5:30 p.m. Monday to Saturday, 1 to 5:30 p.m. on Sunday.

**THE MUSEUM OF FINE ARTS:** The original neoclassical-style wing of the Museum of Fine Arts, 1001 Bissonet St., at Main Street (tel. 526-1361), opened its doors in 1924, and subsequent years have seen half a dozen architectural additions. But as important as the architecturally notable buildings are their contents—a collection of 14,000 works spanning some 4,000 years of art history. In the recently redesigned Upper Brown Pavilion Galleries of European Art, 23,000 square feet of gallery space houses a chronological display of approximately 400 highlights from the museum's permanent collection, including paintings, sculptures, and decorative art objects. This portion of the museum, designed by Mies van der Rohe in 1974, is flooded with light from 244 windows and centers on the Grand Hall. Following a sequence of ten intimate, carpeted galleries, the viewer moves through art time from "Antiquity: The Emergence of a Western Tradition," to "The Late 19th Century and Emergence of the Modern Era." Following the sequence is a suite of rooms showcasing late 19th- and 20th-century works from the John A. and Audrey Jones Beck Collection, including such artists as Bonnard, Derain, Matisse, and Signac.

Another 1986 addition was the Lillie and Hugh Roy Cullen Sculpture Garden, designed by Isamu Noguchi. A one-acre landscaped plaza with walking paths of carnelian granite interspersed with islands of grass and trees, the garden has free-standing concrete walls of different heights and shapes designed to form backdrops for the sculpture. Vine-covered walls enclose the area, shielding the garden from traffic noise. And Noguchi has designed outdoor furniture that offers comfortable seating while complementing the overall design. Among the 19th- and 20th-century works displayed in the garden are sculptures by Maillol, Matisse, David Smith, Rodin, di Suvero, and Bourdelle.

Highlights of the museum's lower level include galleries of ancient Mexican, Oceanic, Oriental, and African art, as well as an excellent photography collection and Frederic Remington's vivid paintings of the turn-of-the-century West. And, of course, there's an ongoing schedule of changing exhibitions, of which some recent examples are "Dutch and Flemish Masters"; "Kandinsky in Paris: 1934–1944"; "Leonardo da Vinci Drawings of Horses from the Royal Library at Windsor Castle"; and "Akbar's India: Art from the Mughal City of Victory."

This is a vital and exciting art museum, of which any city might be proud. It's also a good place to catch classic films—everything from Disney to Buñuel—on weekends (for film information, call the above-listed number and ask for extension 105). Other events here include frequent lectures, gallery tours, jazz concerts, poetry readings, theatrical performances, symposia, and chamber music recitals.

Plan to have lunch or afternoon tea when you visit. The lovely marble-floored Museum Café, its pale-gray walls hung with art posters, serves homemade soups, sandwiches, salads, fresh-baked desserts (like key lime cheesecake), a wide choice of teas, wines, and blackboard-menu specials like poached breast of chicken with tarragon-lime mayonnaise and beef carbonnade with apricots. A wall of windows overlooks the garden terrace, and if the weather is fine you can dine al fresco. The café is open Tuesday to Saturday from 10 a.m. to 4:30 p.m., on Thursday till 7:30 p.m., on Sunday from 1 to 4:30 p.m.

The museum is open Tuesday to Saturday from 10 a.m. to 5 p.m., on Thursday till 9 p.m., on Sunday from 1 to 6 p.m. Admission is free, but a $2 donation is suggested.

## CONTEMPORARY ARTS MUSEUM: Contemporary is certainly *le mot juste* to describe this award-winning ultramodern-looking structure at 5216 Montrose Blvd., at Bissonet (tel. 526-3129). A stainless-steel parallelogram, its interior space was "intended to serve as an artist's medium, stimulating imaginative works rather than merely functioning as a space in which to exhibit them." The floors are raw pine, and the warehouse-like exposed-steel ceilings are 20 feet high. Frankly, it makes me long for less contemporary times (but then, much of the 20th century does). The current building dates to 1972 but the museum itself was founded in 1949, and since that time it has been keeping Houstonians abreast of the art world's latest movements and manifestations. The first exhibit, *This Is Contemporary Art,* included a Waring blender, Eames furniture, and a model of Frank Lloyd Wright's house, Falling Water, in Pennsylvania. Subsequent shows have highlighted works of Lyonel Feininger, Dove, Calder, Miró, Modigliani, Picasso, Rothko, de Kooning, Rauschenberg, Vasarely, Resnick, and numerous others, and themed exhibitions have run a wide gamut from "Beaux Arts Drawings" to "Mexican Movie Posters" to "Audio Works by Artists." There are always two concurrent exhibits, one upstairs, one down.

Admission is free. Docent tours (also free) are conducted every Sunday at 2 and 4 p.m. Inquire about lectures, concerts, films, and other special events at the information desk. Museum hours are Tuesday to Saturday from 10 a.m. to 5 p.m., on Sunday from noon to 6 p.m.

**THE BAYOU BEND COLLECTION:** Under the auspices of the Museum of Fine Arts, this excellent decorative arts collection at 1 Wescott St., just west of Kirby off Memorial Drive (tel. 529-8773), is housed in the historic former 28-room mansion of Miss Ima Hogg. The only daughter of the late governor, James S. Hogg, she conceived, with her brother, James, the idea of forming a collection of early American furniture for eventual display in a Texas museum. She began collecting in 1920 with the purchase of a country Queen Anne armchair, the house was built in 1928, and in 1957 she turned the entire property—building, contents, and 14 surrounding acres of woodland and formal gardens—over to the Museum of Fine Arts. It is open to the public for 1½-hour tours by reservation only; admission is $4, $3 for senior citizens, and there's a minimum age requirement of 14. Women are requested not to wear high heels to protect the floors, (if you forget, slippers are provided). It's worth making a reservation to see the whole of this incredible collection. You can, however, view the first floor's contents during open house from 1 to 5 p.m. the second Sunday of every month. The house is closed to the public entirely during the month of August. Garden tours must be arranged far in advance. Ima Hogg continued adding to the collection until her death in 1975 at the age of 93. A portrait of her in 1948 graces the entry.

A tour of the house is like an American decorative arts course from 1660 to 1860, the colonial through Victorian eras. Each room houses the best art and furnishings of its period. There are pieces by noted 18th- and 19th-century cabinetmakers Duncan Phyfe and John Henry Belter, and works of art by major artists of the period including John Singleton Copley, Charles Willson Peale, James Peale, Rembrandt Peale, Thomas Sully, and Gilbert Stuart. Also notable are collections of American and English ceramics, metalware (silver, pewter, and brass), works of art on paper, textiles, carpets (Persian and Turkish rugs as well as Aubussons), and folk art. One room is designed to reflect the architecture of Shirley, the Carter mansion in Virginia. The Pine Room, a 1720 interior, is furnished in the American version of the William and Mary style. The third quarter of the 18th century is illustrated in the Massachusetts Room, furnished in Chippendale rococo pieces. Elegant simplicity and excellent craftsmanship characterize the Newport Room, copied from a prosperous Rhode Island merchant's home. Several rooms display federalist interiors. The Maple Bedroom, which was occupied by Miss Hogg's companion/lady's maid, has a folk art decor and rural furnishings from 1730 to 1840. And as a Lone Star native, Miss Hogg had to have a Texas Room with lithographs on the Gothic pine-paneled walls and china in the cupboard commemorating the war between the United States and Mexico.

The gardens contain copies of Carrara marble statues of Clio and Euterpe that Miss Hogg saw at the Vatican, and another of the goddess Diana, each in her own formal setting. Clio, the muse of history, presides over a formal garden of parterre design popular in 17th-century England. Diana, goddess of the hunt, is framed by arcs of water from a fountain pool as she stands amid majestic trees, evergreens, and azaleas. And Euterpe, the muse of poetry and music, is by a tranquil woodland walk. There are fountains, reflecting pools, topiary displays, waterfalls, woods, ravines, gazebos, and a bird sanctuary, and bronze deer graze in a pristinely beautiful garden where all the blossoms are white.

**THE ROTHKO CHAPEL:** Perhaps the most unexpected attraction in Houston is the Rothko Chapel, 3900 Yupon St., a block south of Alabama (tel. 524-9839), created by artist Mark Rothko as a "religious environment and sacred place" at the suggestion of patrons John and Dominique de Menil. Rothko proposed the octagonal design, worked closely with the architects, and made 14 extremely minimalist, almost all-black paintings to be hung within it. In 1971 the chapel was formally consecrated to ecumenical "worship and meditation, spiritual events and encounters." Situated in a reflecting pool opposite the entrance is a 26-foot-high steel sculpture by Barnett Newman, *Broken Obelisk,* dedicated to Martin Luther King, Jr. The chapel is the scene of frequent concerts, religious celebrations and ceremonies, and lectures by religious leaders ranging from Jain priests to the Dalai Lama. Martin Luther King's birthday (January 15) and the December 10 anniversary of the United Nations Declaration of Human Rights are observed every year.

But most of all this is a place to which many individuals come for prayer and meditation. There are hand-hewn wooden benches and cushions on mats on the floor where one can sit in silent contemplation. The total silence—something we seldom experience in modern life—is perhaps the most appealing feature of this unusual sanctuary. The guest book shows that people's reactions are widely varying. They range from "awe inspiring" and "the chapel has an energy which stirs the soul" to "the emperor's new clothes" and "please shut this place down before all of Houston is brainwashed." By now I'm sure your curiosity is piqued.

The chapel is open daily from 10 a.m. to 6 p.m. There's no admission charge.

**THE MENIL COLLECTION:** Shortly after press time the collection of art patrons John and Dominique de Menil (the people behind the Rothko Chapel) will go on display in a new Houston museum. The Menil Collection will occupy the 1500 block of Sul Ross Street, between Mulberry and Mandell (tel. 524-9028), a 2.9-acre site adjacent to the Rothko Chapel. The building, designed by architect Renzo Piano (he also designed the Centre Georges Pompidou in Paris), will be on an intimate human scale and constructed of materials that harmonize with surrounding buildings. It will be long and low-roofed with gray painted wood siding and a cast ferroconcrete roof with louver-like elements to admit natural light. The interior will be divided into 20- by 40-foot modules.

The collection itself numbers some 10,000 items ranging from Paleolithic to contemporary art. Among its strengths are Mediterranean antiquities, Eurasian and European artifacts, and a large body of African art. Surrealists Max Ernst and René Magritte are particularly well represented, as are American and European painting and sculpture of the last four decades.

Though the museum won't be completed when we go to press, it should be open by the time you read this. Call for hours and further information.

**SAN JACINTO BATTLEGROUND STATE PARK:** Just 21 miles from downtown Houston off state Hwy. 225 (from the southeast corner of Loop 610, take Hwy. 225 east about 15 miles to Hwy. 134 and follow the signs) is a 327-acre state park (tel. 479-2421) on the site of the Battle of San Jacinto, the 18-minute skirmish that led to the independence of Texas from Mexico. Texas declared its independence on March 2, 1836. Following the debacle of the Alamo (March 6, 1836), the main body of the Texas army began to retreat eastward, pursued by Santa Anna. Less than a month later a Texas force under Colonel Fannin was forced to surrender near Goliad and was slaughtered by order of Santa Anna. Both armies arrived at the battle site on April 20, the Texans camping on the shore of the Buffalo Bayou near the present site of the battleship *Texas,* the Mexicans at the east end of the plains. On April 21, 1836, Sam Houston and his ragged band of 927 Texans stormed Santa Anna's fort in a surprise afternoon attack, when many of the Mexican officers were in their tents taking a siesta. To quote a cherished line from my high school history text, "'Remember the Alamo, remember Goliad' was the cry of the revolting Texans." The Mexicans, 1,200 in number, were quickly routed (630 killed, 208 wounded, and the remainder taken prisoner), while Texas casualties numbered only 9 dead and 30 wounded, among them Houston, whose ankle was shattered by a rifle bullet. Santa Anna seized a horse and fled; however, the next day he was spotted by cavalry patrols and, though he claimed to be merely a soldier, his fine underwear gave him away. (No, I don't know how the Texans happened to see his underwear.) The cavalrymen knew he was someone important but didn't guess his true identity until they brought him into camp and some Mexican prisoners shouted out "El Presidente!" The war was over and Sam Houston was president of the new Republic of Texas, ten years later to become part of the United States.

## San Jacinto Monument

In 1842 an anonymous poet wrote an "Ode to San Jacinto" in which he expressed the hope that "In future time, then may the pilgrim's eye see here an obelisk point to the sky. . . ." As with most memorials, however, it was a long while from conception to creation. Efforts to create a fitting monument were initiated by the Texas Veterans Association in 1856. And in the 1890s the Texas legislature allocated funds for the state to purchase the battlefield from its private owners. But it wasn't until 1936, with patriotic fervor enhanced by Texas Centennial celebrations, that adequate funding was amassed actually to begin building. The world's tallest masonry memorial (at 570 feet high, it's 15 feet taller than the Washington Monument), completed in 1939, is constructed of Texas Cordova shell limestone noted for its creamy color and million-year-old embedded fossils. It's made up of 500-pound blocks with an allegorical frieze at the base of the shaft depicting eight important episodes in the history of the Republic of Texas and a 35-foot-tall Texas Lone Star at the top. Like the Washington Monument, it is fronted by a reflecting pond and offers beautiful panoramic views from its observation tower.

## San Jacinto Museum of History

The splendid spire and star monument, visible for miles around, does more than just commemorate the 927 men who fought for and won Texas's independence from Mexico. It commemorates Texas history from the period prior to the discovery of America through the end of the 19th century in a museum inside the monument's base. Exhibits are divided into historical segments, beginning with "The Pre-Conquest Native," which contains Mayan, Toltec, and Aztec artifacts. Later periods—documented with weaponry, books, paintings, photographs, coins, costumes, letters, official seals, personal artifacts, battle artifacts, flags, and maps—include the conquests and exploration of the Spanish conquistadors and the French under La Salle, the mission era, Spanish colonial life, the Mexican revolution against Spain, and Texas history from the revolution through early statehood.

Admission to the monument and museum are free; the elevator to the observation deck (489 feet up) costs $2 for adults, 50¢ for children under 12. Hours are 10 a.m. to 6 p.m. daily.

## The Battleship *Texas*

The 27,000-ton U.S.S. *Texas*, moored at the battleground since San Jacinto Day 1948, is the oldest surviving battleship of its kind (the large-gun or dreadnought class) in the world, and also the only surviving battleship that fought in both World Wars. Launched in 1912, the *Texas* saw action in 1918 as a member of the Sixth Battle Squadron of the Grand Fleet. During World War II she was involved in battle aiding General Patton in seizing Casablanca as a base for military and naval operations, and later in the invasion of Normandy and at Iwo Jimo and Okinawa. The Texas Parks and Wildlife Department took over the ship in 1983, and they're currently in the midst of a ten-year restoration project to return the ship to its 1944 condition. As part of this work, the ship may be drydocked in Galveston for repairs during part of 1987. An admission fee of $2 for adults, $1 for children 6 to 12 (under 6, free), includes a map and brochure for a self-guided tour of the *Texas*; just follow the arrows. The ship houses the world's largest collection of naval documents, photographs, and ship's plans of the dreadnought era (the British ship H.M.S. *Dreadnought* was the prototype for this style of vessel, hence the name).

Exhibits include a memorial to the cruiser *Houston,* which was sunk in the Pacific during World War II; among its displays is the ship's actual bell and a machine gun, both recovered by the Indonesian government after 31 years in the water. Another exhibit documents the exploits of the *Texas* at Normandy, with maps, charts, photos, actual naval communiqués, and the 240-pound German shell that pierced the ship. An audio-visual orientation provides background on the ship's history.

Below decks (it's not air-conditioned, to duplicate actual conditions) you'll see the cramped sleeping quarters (note the many hammock hooks all over the ceiling; there weren't enough beds, so many crew members slept in hammocks). You'll also see evaporators that desalinated water for all uses other than drinking, Texas navy correspondence, the barbershop, operating room, sick bay, tailor shop, soda fountain (the *Texas* was famous in World War II for its banana splits made with homemade ice cream), post office (all mail coming in or going out was censored), dentist's office, laundry (just before the war the crew once steamed lobsters in the sheet steamer, and sheets smelled like fish for months afterward), and the room in which high-level officers dined.

On the main deck you can examine antiaircraft guns that downed kamikazes and the 54-foot-long guns mounted in rotating turrets and designed to shoot 1,500-pound shells to distant targets. How distant? "From here," a park ranger explained, "we could take out downtown Houston with these guns." Also on the tour are the living area for the crew members (it's not the Hyatt), a machine shop (everything mechanical the crew needed was made right on board), three stories of engine rooms, and the horrendous brig composed of hot and airless solitary cells four by six feet in length and width and about four feet in height.

The ship is open to visitors from 10 a.m. to 6 p.m. May 1 through the end of August, till 5 p.m. the rest of the year. Call 479-2411 for further information.

## San Jacinto Inn

Though it's not officially part and parcel of the monument, the San Jacinto Inn (tel. 479-2828) is adjacent to it and the ideal place to dine when you're sightseeing in the park. Originally built in 1917 and rebuilt in 1927, it is itself a bit of Texas history. However, the building now housing the restaurant is not the 1927 structure (it was slowly sinking into the channel, so the owners built an exact replica on safer land). On a wall lined with volumes of guest books from 1927 on (you'll sign one when you come in) is a photograph of the new building juxtaposed next to the sinking one.

The restaurant itself is reminiscent of an old-fashioned resort dining room with high peaked ceiling, dark wood beams and posts, wide-plank pine floors, and pale-green shiplap walls covered with photographs of Texas scenes like the famous XIT Ranch and a fire at Spindletop (the first big oilfield in Texas); also depicted are Russian astronauts who dined here in the early 1970s (the inn had a menu in Russian printed up for the occasion). The restaurant still has its original bentwood chairs at the white-linened tables, many of which offer views of the Houston Ship Channel. A rustic pine-paneled bar called Santa Anna's Retreat adjoins. Over the bar is a painting of Santa Anna surrendering to Sam Houston, the original of which hangs in the Capitol building in Austin. Order the house specialty drink, the Yellow Rose of Texas, a rum punch similar to a mai tai.

Dinner is an all-you-can-eat affair served family style. It changes seasonally, but a typical menu might include a shrimp cocktail, oysters on the half shell, fried oysters, fried fish, fried chicken, homemade french fries, hot biscuits, and dessert of sherbet. Cost is $19.50 per person, $10 for children 8 to 11, $6 for ages 4 to 7. All the food is fresh and homemade.

Dinner is served from 6 to 10 p.m. weekdays, from 5:30 to 10 p.m. on Saturday, and from 1 to 9 p.m. on Sunday. Reservations are suggested.

**THE PORT OF HOUSTON:** Though most people don't think of it that way, Houston is one of the world's busiest seaports—the third largest in the United States in total tonnage and a leader in foreign trade. More than 5,000 ships call here each year, and in addition over 3,500 barges are handled annually in the Turning Basin. On a free 1½-hour narrated sightseeing tour aboard the M/V *Sam Houston,* the Port Authority's air-conditioned, 100-foot inspection boat, you can see the workings of the port—grain elevators, transit sheds, cargo wharves, refineries, and large vessels turning—and also pass the exact spot where Santa Anna surrendered. Coffee and soft drinks are provided to passengers gratis. There's only one catch: you have to reserve six to eight weeks in advance for weekdays (further ahead for weekends) by writing or calling Michael Scorcio, Port of Houston Authority, P.O. Box 2562, Houston, TX 77252 (tel. 713/225-4044). There are trips at 10 a.m. and 2:30 p.m. Tuesday, Wednesday, Friday, and Saturday; at 2:30 p.m. only on Thursday and Sunday (no departures on Monday or during the month of September). The boat sails from Gate 8 of the Sam Houston Dock, six miles from downtown. Take I-10 east to North Wayside; go south and exit to the left at Clinton Drive (the second overpass), which will take you directly to Gate 8.

**CLEAR LAKE:** NASA headquarters and the Armand Bayou Nature Center are both in Clear Lake, 25 miles southeast of Houston via I-45. As it's on a lake, boating and water sports are popular here. If you'd like to explore Clear Lake's recreational aspects, visit or write to the **Clear Lake Area Chamber of Commerce,** 1201 NASA Rd. 1, Houston, TX 77058 (tel. 713/488-7676); the office is open weekdays only from 8:30 a.m. to 5 p.m.

As you'll likely be spending the better part of a day visiting the two sights described below, I'll recommend a place to dine. **Jimmy Walker's,** 201 Kipp (tel. 334-2513), is situated right between Clear Lake and Galveston Bay, and all-around windows provide great views of the passing parade of sailboats, sleek yachts, fishing craft, and tugboats, and the gulls atop weathered dockposts. There are graduated seating levels, so all tables offer water views. The restaurant is attractive inside too, with white-linened tables (lit by oil lamps at night) and oak-wainscoted gray walls hung with nautically themed art. Fresh seafood is featured—items like char-broiled shrimp kebab brushed with butter ($13.95) and deviled crab cakes ($10.95). At lunch weekdays there are specials in the $5.50 to $8 range.

Open Sunday to Thursday from 11 a.m. to 10 p.m., on Friday and Saturday till 11 p.m. Reservations essential at dinner. It's a little tricky finding the place. Take Hwy. 146 south just over the bridge and double back on Texas Avenue to make a right on 2nd Street, which becomes Kipp.

## Lyndon B. Johnson Space Center

The focal point for America's manned spaceflight programs, the LBJ Space Center, NASA Rd. 1 (tel. 483-4321), is where our spacecraft are designed, developed, and tested. Here astronauts are selected and trained, and manned space missions are planned and controlled. The center, located three miles east of I-45, is open to visitors, admission free, from 9 a.m. to 4 p.m. seven days a week. Take NASA Road to the Visitor's Entrance Gate and start your self-guided tour (allow three to four hours) at the Visitors Center in Building 2. At the information desk, pick up a map of the complex and free tickets for a visit to Mission Control. Adjoining the desk is the Teague Auditorium where films about NASA flights are shown every half hour.

Among the exhibits in **Building 2** are a replica of the Apollo 11 lunar module *Eagle* that took Armstrong and Aldrin to the moon in 1969, three-dimensional photos of the moon's surface (glasses provided), a display of astronaut "fashions," the actual *Apollo 17* command module that orbited the moon in 1972, photographs of the earth's surface taken from space, displays of space, displays of space paraphernalia (you can try on a space helmet or photograph yourself in a cardboard astronaut cutout), exhibits on the numerous side benefits of the space program (like intercontinental TV and location of mineral resources), astronaut foods (freeze-dried chewing gum, pot roast, bacon, and other none-too-appetizing-looking dishes), actual capsules from *Mercury* and *Gemini* spacecraft, exhibits on the history of rockets and the use of animals in space, logs kept by Lovell and Borman on the *Gemini* mission, and of course, moon rocks. Films and video displays are used throughout the exhibit area.

In **Building 3** you'll find a pretty good cafeteria and a gift shop (both accept cash only), the latter offering some great stuff for kids, including astronaut suits, space models, books, and videotapes.

**Building 5** highlights *Skylab,* including a full-size model, a film about *Skylab* missions, the actual command module, exhibits on sleep monitoring and off-duty equipment (a Velcro dart board, novels, exercise gear), and a walk-through model of the interior of *Skylab* that was used by astronauts to practice tasks in preparation for missions.

**Building 30** houses the Mission Control Center (you've seen it on TV). Here space operations are supported by teams of engineers and technicians utilizing sophisticated communication, computer, and data-display equipment. If you've procured a ticket at the information desk you can (unless MCC is closed to visitors, as it is during shuttle missions) get a 30-minute briefing here on the history and future of space exploration.

**Building 9A** (sometimes closed to visitors if astronaut training is going on) contains a full-size replica of the space shuttle *Orbiter.* Here astronauts train to develop the skills and techniques necessary to operate the system in space, like manipulating payloads with the shuttle arm. The shuttle can carry up to 65,000 pounds into space—about the same amount as 1½ Greyhound buses. You can also explore a full-size replica of the crew compartment of the spacecraft.

**Building 31A,** the lunar sample building, contains most of the 800 pounds of lunar material astronauts have brought back to the earth. It is being tested by scientists here.

The Space Center complex is spread over 1,620 beautifully landscaped acres; it's pleasant walking, but it's a lot of walking, so wear comfortable shoes. The exhibits are very well planned to appeal to both the space-knowledgeable and space cadets in the crowd. About 1.4 million people visit NASA every year, making it the number two tourist attraction in Texas after the Alamo.

## Armand Bayou Nature Center

Close to NASA's Johnson Space Center, but another world altogether, is the 1,800-acre Armand Bayou Nature Center, 8600 Bay Area Blvd. (tel. 474-2251), a wildlife refuge where three ecosystems—tall grass prairie, hardwood forest, and Galveston Bay marsh—converge. White-tailed deer, rabbits, and raccoons are frequently seen, and coyotes, foxes, great blue herons, alligators, armadillos, and vultures are sometimes spotted. The Nature Center is also one of the best birding areas in the United States.

There are three loop trails to explore, each of them 1½ miles long, and to enjoy them you must be properly dressed—wear long pants and comfortable boots, and douse yourself with mosquito repellent. Remember that this is wilderness, not a wilderness theme park—there are snakes and poison ivy. Start out at the center's information building, where you can view an exhibit area, inspect the gift shop wares, and find out about interesting programs here on a wide range of subjects such as herb gardening, hunting fall mushrooms, dye plants, and insect study. There are also marvelous naturalist-led activities like canoeing on Armand Bayou, candlelight dinners at the farm, and nature and birdwatching walks. The area around the information building is landscaped with native plants, many of them flowering.

In addition to the trails, the center includes the Jimmy Martyn Farm with an 1890s farmhouse furnished in period pieces and a timber frame barn full of hay and animals. At the farm visitor center there are exhibits and a slide show about the history of the area, early cattle ranching and farming, and Jimmy Martyn, who farmed here until his death in 1964 but never modernized. He did not have electricity, running water, a telephone, or a TV, even in the years when astronauts were training for space flights practically next door. The farmhouse kitchen, complete with wood-burning stove, is used for domestic arts demonstrations. Kids can pet the animals—rabbits, sheep, goats, mules, and chickens—see a cow being milked, help gather eggs, hear a rooster crow, and learn about antique farm equipment and its uses. There are farm tours at 10 a.m. and 1 p.m. on Saturday, at 1 p.m. only on Sunday. Usually on weekends there are also demonstrations of butter churning, corn grinding, quilting, and other farm activities. And during the fall, when the sugarcane crop is harvested, you'll see cane being converted to syrup.

You can reach Bay Area Boulevard from I-45. If you're coming from NASA, go west on NASA Road, north on El Camino Real Boulevard, and east on Bay Area Boulevard.

**ASTROWORLD AND WATERWORLD:** Part of the vast Astrodomain complex —one of the top tourist attractions in the country—are two adjoining theme parks under the auspices of the nation's largest network of amusement parks, Six Flags.

**AstroWorld,** opened in 1968, is a 75-acre park at Loop 610 and Kirby Drive (tel. 799-1234), offering over 100 rides, shows, and attractions. It's divided into 12 theme areas representing America's past (like "Western Junction" and turn-of-the-century "Americana Square") and international cultures (like "Oriental Corner" and "Plaza de Fiesta"), also including a "little people's paradise" called the "Enchanted Kingdom." It's all beautifully landscaped, with over 600 varieties of plants, flowers, shrubs, and hanging baskets. The "wacky wabbit" hangs out at the Enchanted Kingdom, and his Looney Tune friends roam about elsewhere. Foot-weary visitors can take a peaceful cable-car ride between far-apart sections of the park and get a bird's eye view of its layout from 100 feet up. For thrill seekers there's the famed Texas Cyclone (highly rated by roller-coaster aficionados); the Skyscreamer, a free-fall drop from a 128-foot tower that evokes the sensation of jumping from a ten-story building; the thrill of shooting the rapids at Thunder River, a ten-acre whitewater river with whirl-pools, rapids, and waterfalls; a roller coaster with an 80-foot-high loop called Greezed Lightnin' (you go through forward, then backward); and a water-flume ride called Bamboo Shoot. Less dizzying are a riverboat ride through an authentic coastal wetlands environment and a Victorian carousel. A net crawl, trampoline, and a journey through a maze are a few of the treats for the younger set.

It's exhausting traipsing around the park, but you can rest up intermittently at one of the many shows that run continuously throughout the day: a dolphin revue, costumed character show, a Sens-O-Sphere film (the action comes right at you), a snake show, waterski exhibit, a variety of music shows including a major revue, a Don Rickles–like buzzard (a bit milder of course), and incredible Chinese acrobats. The shows change a bit from year to year, but that's a typical format. There are 44 food stands and four restaurants, so you won't go hungry. And topping off the day's excitement in summer is a spectacular fireworks display. There's much more, as you'll discover when you visit.

A one-day ticket for unlimited admission to all rides, shows, and attrac-tions is $15.50 (free for children under 2). It also includes admission to a headlin-er concert at the Southern Star Amphitheatre, though sometimes there's a supplement of up to $5 if a really big star is performing; see "After Dark" for details. You can also purchase a two-day ticket or a combination ticket for a day at AstroWorld and a day at WaterWorld for $20.95. The park is open daily from June through the end of August and on weekends mid-March to June and Sep-tember through late November. Call for hours.

The newer **WaterWorld** (same address and phone; a tram takes you to "WaterWorld Junction") opened in 1983 with 15 acres of water recreation activ-ities. You can float lazily on inner tubes along the 900-foot Hokey Pokey River, jump waves in the 30,000-square-foot Breaker Beach pool, race down water slides at speeds of up to 40 mph into a body of water, go tubing on a Run-A-Way River, and spiral your way down corkscrew body slides with names like Hurri-cane, Typhoon, and Tidal Wave. For little kids there's Squirt's Splash, a safe water play area. And, yes, there's a large pool where you can swim and dive. Bring your bathing suit. Men's and women's dressing rooms are provided, and lockers and rafts can be rented. Life jackets are offered free of charge, and all activities are supervised by certified lifeguards. There's a restaurant surrounded by 25-foot waterfalls.

The park is open weekends from early May to June and then daily through the end of August. Call for hours. Tickets are $11.95 (free for children under 2).

**HANNA BARBERA LAND:** About 22 miles north of downtown Houston, on the east side of I-45, Hanna Barbera Land, 1401 Hanna Barbera Dr. (tel. 350-0914), is a 30-acre theme park in which kids meet up with Saturday-morning pals like Yogi Bear, Scooby Doo, Huckleberry Hound, Fred Flintstone, and the Smurfs. There are 200-foot water slides (wear cotton pants or shorts, not jeans which take forever to dry—or better yet, bring the kids' bathing suits) a Ghoster Coaster with a 360° loop, an old-fashioned carousel, pedal boats, and a minia-ture train. You can rest up between rides at a musical revue in the 1,000-seat Showplace Amphitheatre, at a costumed-character outdoor rock 'n roll show, or a lively puppet show. Kids can climb the Tinker Toy–like three-story construction (complete with nets) in Silly Stix, "swim" in a pool of brightly colored balls, or pet the cows and pigs at McScrappy's Farm. At Papa Smurf's Forest Restaurant, the blue folks entertain diners with song and dance; the menu features inexpensive deli sandwiches, pizza, nachos and burritos, and foot-long hot dogs. And the Funsonian houses participatory computer games. There are plenty of shaded areas, including picnic grounds, in the park—essential in the hot Houston summer. Attractions are geared to children 13 and under.

The park is open June, July, and August plus spring and fall weekends. Days and hours change annually, so call before you go. The admission price of $8.95 for adults (children under 2, free) gives you unlimited access to all rides, shows, and attractions.

**THE CHILDREN'S MUSEUM:** Opened in 1985, the Children's Museum, 3201 Allen Pkwy., at Rosine (tel. 52-AMUSE for a recording of events, 522-1138 for other information), is a hands-on paradise for the under-12 set. Via an exhibit called Choice of Many Hats (a row of child-size hatted figures—a fireman, police officer, chef, Indian chief, cowboy, etc.—with mirror faces) children can assume visual career identities. In the Pocketa, Pocketa: Things Kids Collect room (so named because kids' collections originate in pockets), they can draw with Magic Markers on a washable wall and examine collections of stamps, coins, rocks, shells, etc. The Culture and History Room houses temporary exhibits, at this writing a simulated Mexican Village in which kids can dress in Mexican clothes, grind corn and make tortillas, try their hands at Mexican embroidery, make paper flowers, and play customer or salesperson in a Mexican store. At the Recycle Center children learn to creatively reuse cast-off materials by making rockets out of Minute Maid juice cans and otherwise utilizing pieces of styrofoam, wallpaper samples, cartons, and fabric scraps. The Magic Space Time Machine is like being inside a kaleidoscope. Kids play consumer or supermarket employee at a Safeway Mini-Market, complete with carts, a cash register, and shelves abundantly stocked with real products. And of course there are computers in a section called Kidtechnics, where hi-tech attractions include a talking computer; opportunities to correspond with a computer "penpal," make a dot-matrix self-portrait, and create computer art; a shadow sculpture room where brightly hued rainbow silhouettes can be created; musical stairs (you compose as you walk up and down); and a video studio where future Donahues can interview one another and then see the tapes.

An excellent gift shop specializes in creative and affordable items, and there are frequent demonstrations on subjects like nutrition, mask making, and science in a classroom on the premises (sometimes it's also used for performing arts).

The museum is open Tuesday, Wednesday, Thursday, and Sunday from 1 to 5 p.m., on Saturday from 10 a.m. to 5 p.m., and on Friday morning from 10 a.m. to noon. Admission is $1 for children under 12 and senior citizens, $2 for adults. Take the Waugh Drive exit from Allen Parkway.

**MOUNTAIN PARK:** This seven-acre adventure playground for tots at Southwest Freeway (U.S. 59) and Loop 610 (tel. 668-4300) could be the highlight of your child's vacation. It has a Legoland with over 300,000 pieces to utilize in construction, Granny's Attic of dress-up clothes, a ball crawl, a sensorium maze (kids use touch and hearing to find their way through), a climbing network of ropes and nets, a water slide with adjacent baby pools, a science room with hands-on exhibits, and an arts and crafts workshop where activities can range from woodwork to face painting. The kids can make videotapes of themselves and play them back in the TV studio, and instruct each other to "open wide" at the dentist's office. A large sandbox, table tennis, basketball, and volleyball are also provided.

Mountain Park is open daily April to September, Thursday to Sunday only the rest of the year. Call for hours. Admission is $3.50 for children (under 2, free), $1 for adults. The water slide is an additional $3 for children, $5 for adults.

**SPECTATOR SPORTS:** There are three major facilities for sports events in Houston. Most notable, of course, is the **Astrodome,** Kirby Drive and South Loop 610 (tel. 799-9500 for information, 799-9555 to charge tickets), billing itself as "the world's foremost sports, entertainment, and convention center" and "the Taj Mahal of Stadia." This vast, air-conditioned, multipurpose domed sports stadium is the home of the Houston Oilers (NFL), the Houston Astros (baseball), and the University of Houston Cougars (college football). Other events of note here include the Houston Livestock Show and Rodeo (see annual events), tennis (this is where the famous Billy Jean King/Bobby Riggs match took place), truck and tractor pulls (2,000-horsepower trucks and tractors race while pulling weights of up to 60,000 pounds), motorcycle races, polo matches, track and field events, and auto thrill shows. Sports events at the Astrodome are enhanced by a state-of-the-art video instant-replay board, upholstered seating, and excellent sound and lighting systems.

If you'd like to tour the facility, you can do so daily (unless tours are pre-empted by afternoon events) at 11 a.m., 1 p.m., and 3 p.m. In summer there's an additional tour at 5 p.m. Cost is $2.75 (children under 7, free). Call 799-9544 for tour information.

The **Summit,** six miles south of downtown Houston at U.S. 59 and Timmons Lane (tel. 627-9470), is the 17,000-seat home of the Houston Rockets (NBA). Championship tennis, horse shows, hockey, indoor soccer, ice shows, boxing, wrestling, and the Harlem Globetrotters have also been featured here.

Finally, there's the 8,000-seat **Sam Houston Coliseum,** part of the Civic Center, 810 Bagby, at Walker (tel. 222-3267), where major tennis matches take place and there's wrestling every other Friday night.

# 7. Shopping

Shopping centers comprise about 90% of the scenery in Houston. Just drive along any major artery and you'll see dozens of them, usually centered around vast Wal-Mart, K-Mart, and Target stores that sell everything from electronics and major appliances to toilet paper, from clothing for the whole family to office supplies—all at substantial discounts. They're so easy to find I'm not going to detail them below. Major malls, including the famed Galleria, are listed, however, along with other stores and shopping areas that are unique, pricewise or merchandisewise. One surprise is that Houston, the most 20th century of cities, is great for antiquing. And since the listings below are alphabetical, that's where I'll begin.

**ANTIQUES AND FLEA MARKETS:** The **Trade Mart,** 2121 W. Belt Dr. North, at Hammerly Boulevard (tel. 467-2506), contains over 100 shops in one immense air-conditioned free-span building 1½ times the size of a football field. Even the aisles are ten feet wide. The goods aren't flea-markety; this is all quality merchandise, in great condition and beautifully displayed. About 90% of the "shops" sell antiques, collectibles, and decoratives. The rest deal in a variety of merchandise that includes Korean brass and eelskin, wicker, wallpapers, Mexican embroidered dresses, and plants. Whatever you're looking for, be it French country furniture, depression glass, Victoriana, 18th-century porcelain, or art nouveau jewelry—you'll find it. Merchandise is competitively priced, and prices are often negotiable. There are snackbars, rest rooms, and five acres of parking.

A very different cup of tea is the carnival-like **Common Market,** 6116 Southwest Freeway (U.S. 59) on the north access road off the Westpark exit (tel. 782-0391). Billing itself as "the largest flea market in the Southwest," it occupies 14½ acres, 9 of which are parking space. Most of it is outdoors under the shade of corrugated roofing on stilts or nylon tenting, and the merchandise —old and new—includes everything in the world; for example: western wear, shoes, breadboxes, bird cages, appliances, incense, vacuum cleaners, fruits and vegetables, coins, knives, Mexicana, watches, baby strollers, plants, cosmetics, used jeans, bicycles, clothing, furniture, toys, fake ID cards, jewelry, tires, feathers, books, marble flooring, hardware, and luggage. That's just a small percentage. This flea market addict's paradise has been going for over two decades. Great bargains can be found by the canny shopper, be it a package of ginseng tea for $1.50 or a rare coin for $4,000. There are seven snackbars and wine and beer to keep you going.

Another biggie, **Antique World,** West Loop 610 at Beechnut, in the Meyerland Plaza Shopping Center (tel. 666-2344), has 100 dealer spaces in a 30,000-square-foot, air-conditioned building. It's a mixed bag, but there's ample wheat among the chaff to make for fun browsing and buying. There are toys, dolls, lamps, furniture, glassware, brass beds, stained-glass hangings, antique clothing, jewelry, patchwork quilts, and vintage Mickey Mouse items.

One of the biggest and the best is **Trading Fair II,** 5515 South Loop 610, at Crestmont (tel. 731-1111), with 400 dealers and 160,000 square feet of air-conditioned shopping space on two floors. It's been going for about a dozen years. Each dealer mans a clean, neat little shop, generally selling good-quality merchandise. A sampling of wares—new, old, and antique—includes golf clubs, records, needlework supplies, dolls, art, comic books, Indian crafts, Hawaiian wear, dollhouse and real furniture, Depression glass, Christmas decorations, brassware, luggage, gaslamps, toys, baskets, and 14-karat-gold fingernails. It's a pleasant place to shop.

A Mini Mall, a Maxi Mall, and a Metal Mall (the latter describes the building, not its wares) comprise **The Market Place,** 10910 Old Katy Rd., between West Belt and Wilcrest on the north side of I-10 (tel. 464-8023), with 125,000 square feet of merchandise under its combined roof. Best buys are in the Mini Mall, where mostly new, but some used and antique, items are sold at 25% to 50% below retail. It contains about 80 shops offering a mix of shlock, kitsch, and quality—from beautiful Kashmiri papier-mâché boxes to collections of old baseball cards, from dollhouse mansions to dashikis, from Oriental rugs to a place called Porcelain Palace that will paint your portrait on a china plate from a photograph. A snackbar called Rainbov s End has good homemade chili, barbecued brisket, and fresh-baked brownies, peach cobbler, and banana nut bread. Antiques and collectibles are competitively priced in the Maxi and Metal Malls —about 300 shops offering a mix of junk and quality similar to the Mini's. There are additional eating places and rest rooms.

A smaller grouping of select shops (20 dealers under one roof) makes up the **Antique Center of Houston,** 2500 Sage Rd., at Westheimer (tel. 961-4123). For the most part, everything sold here is top-quality, and the surroundings are plush. Dealer's wares run the gamut from African tribal arts to Louis XV armoires, from Georgian highboys to china, crystal, and art glass. There's a nice restaurant on the premises.

**BOOKS:** Happy to say, **Crown Books** has come to Houston, with 11 stores, perhaps the most conveniently located of which is at 6100 Westheimer Rd., between Hillcroft and Fountainview (tel. 266-0501). Crown is the Washington, D.C.–based discount bookstore chain that offers discounts of 10% to 49% on all its books (including bestsellers), magazines, calendars, and audio and video cassettes. A hefty 40% off *New York Times* hardback bestsellers makes this a great place to shop for gifts. Check the phonebook for the closest location.

**DRUGS:** A major Texas chain with 110 Houston-area stores, 11 of them open 24 hours a day, **Eckerd Drugs,** retails many low-cost generic products under its own label. Check the Consumer Directory under "Pharmacies" for a convenient location.

**DRY CLEANERS:** A few clever young entrepreneurs have revolutionized the dry-cleaning industry in Houston, and I only hope their innovation spreads around the country like wildfire. By streamlining operations to achieve optimum efficiency, they've managed to offer the remarkable price of $1.25 for cleaning any garment (that includes silks and satins that usually run sky high), and furthermore they do the job in one day. The result has been a general lowering of dry-cleaning prices and couponing all over town, but nobody can match these innovators. They do an excellent cleaning job, by the way, and offer friendly service in the bargain. They are: **Biarritz Cleaners,** in the Lakeside Plaza Shopping Center at 1100 Wilcrest (tel. 782-3838); **Regal,** 2631 Revere St., at Westheimer (tel. 526-8207); and **Eldorado,** 11175 Fondren Rd., near Bellfort (tel. 995-5310). You pay when you bring your clothes in.

**MALLS AND SHOPPING CENTERS:** Located in a ritzy part of town amid other posh Post Oak shops like Guy Laroche, Polo, and Courrèges, **The Galleria,** on Westheimer between Sage and South Post Oak (tel. 621/7251), was the prototype that inspired the malling of America. In addition to over 300 shops, it contains under its 12-story atrium skylight roof, a 400-room Westin hotel, an Olympic-size ice-skating rink, art galleries, four movie theaters, a full health club, a jogging track, and a choice of more than 20 restaurants. Among its most prestigious stores are Neiman-Marcus, Gump's, Tiffany & Co., Mark Cross, Lord & Taylor, Cartier, Gucci, Charles Jourdan, Laura Ashley, and Louis Vuitton. The most recent additions (in 1986) were a Macy's department store and a 4,000-square-foot garden. And, besides stores selling everything from maternity clothing to musical scores, this ultimate one-stop shopping mecca offers an American Express office, a travel agency, doctors, opticians, photo processing, a stockbroker, hairdressers, bank, and Christian Science Reading Room.

Predating the Galleria by a decade is the **Sharpstown Center,** 7500 Bellaire Blvd., at Southwest Freeway (tel. 777-5391). Opened in 1961, this landmark mall has undergone several facelifts and is therefore attractively contemporary in appearance. Sharpstown puts on a fabulous fireworks display every July Fourth. Its 230 stores include three department stores—Foley's, Montgomery Ward, and J. C. Penney—and though you might buy a diamond ring or a Rolex watch on the premises, the accent is on more practical purchasing. Where Galleria has Caswell-Massey and Ted Lapidus, Sharpstown has Walgreen's and Lerner Shops. And replacing posh restaurants is a big food court on the upper level where barbecued beef sandwiches, corn dogs on a stick, and Orange Juliuses are sold. There's also a Wyatt's cafeteria. Numerous services are offered: a bank, travel agency, auto leasing, post office, Ticketmaster outlet, apartment location services, opticians, hairdressers, an amusement center (video games for the kids)—even a U.S. Armed Forces recruitment office.

**Town & Country Center,** 800 West Belt North, at I-10 (tel. 468-1171), adds to the fun of shopping at its 155 stores an ongoing series of promotions that include fashion shows, food festivals, home shows, contests for the best Halloween costume (one for merchants, one for local kids), car shows, Fourth of July fireworks, aerobics competitions, and celebrity appearances (like Susan Howard, who plays Donna on "Dallas"). The mall is anchored by four department stores—Neiman-Marcus, J. C. Penney, Joske's, and Marshall Field's—and its other shops offer anything you might be looking for, from western wear to waterbeds.

Not a mall at all, but a quaint and, well, village-like shopping center, **The Village** is a 15-block area bounded by Sunset and University Boulevards north and south, Greenbrier and Kirby east and west. There are over 500 restaurants, services, and shops along its tree-lined streets, and these streets are ever in a process of further greening and enhancement via the addition of flower boxes, benches, fountains, bike racks, and canvas awnings. Though some of the stores are pragmatic (there's even an H & R Block), more typical are places like the Village Weaver (where the owner shares premises with her dog, Meg, and an angora rabbit, Anna), La Taste (for gourmet foods, potpourri, dried flowers, and French wines), the Houston Potter's Guild (handmade works of ten local potters), House of Coffee Beans, a shop selling Guatemalan arts and crafts, Bountiful Baskets, and the Aquarian Age Bookstore. Needless to say, there are quite a few antique shops and art galleries. Occasional art exhibits, concerts, and wine tastings enliven the shopping experience, and there are a number of good restaurants in which to recover from its rigors. The Village has been evolving since the 1930s.

Still quainter are the picturesque **Gardens of Bammel Lane,** bounded east and west by Sackett Avenue and Bammel Lane, north and south by Earl Street (a block below Westheimer) and Phil Fall (tel. 523-8580). Here, 14 shops and one restaurant are housed in 15 beautiful restored Victorian homes, connected by brick walkways, wrought-iron fencing, and a charming garden courtyard complete with greenhouse, fountain, gazebo, and ornamental benches. In front of each house is a bronze plaque detailing its history. The merchandise sold here is all of the highest quality. Ragazzi features darling European clothing for children (your search for Dior undies for little Suzy is over). Lots of antique lace and linen, along with other Victoriana, can be found at the Gypsy Savage. Karalia is a boutique featuring exclusive, exquisite, and extremely expensive lines of women's clothing. J. Newton Lloyd Antiques specializes in 17th- and 18th-century English furniture. And so on.

Just two blocks away on Ferndale are two wonderful stores you should visit while in the area. Country French Cottons has the most beautiful fabrics I've ever seen. And next door, Carol Leverett Antiques sells English country collectibles. It all makes wonderful browsing.

Do plan your Bammel Lane shopping excursion around lunch at **Hadley House,** one of the prettiest little restaurants in Texas. The wainscotted walls in its various rooms are painted in different colors—rose, robin's-egg blue, and cream —and adorned with framed prints of ducks, fruit, and flowers. There are fresh roses on every beautifully appointed table, the doors are beveled glass, the floors are bare pine, and windows are curtained in white lace. A brick-floored patio, its windows lined with flower boxes, overlooks the garden courtyard. Even the entrance foyer is charmingly furnished in wicker pieces with floral chintz cushions. All the food at Hadley House is homemade and delicious. You might lunch on fettuccine Alfredo ($5.25), a Cobb salad ($6.25), or a more serious entree like veal Oscar ($10.25). There are luscious desserts too. At night Hadley House is even lovelier by candlelight, and it offers gourmet entrees like filet mignon au poivre and veal Cordon Bleu in the $15 to $18 range. It's open for lunch weekdays from 11:30 a.m. to 2:30 p.m., on Saturday to 3 p.m.; and for dinner Monday to Saturday from 6:30 to 10:30 p.m.

**MEXICANA:** Billing itself as "the largest Latin market in the U.S.," **El Mercado del Sol,** at Navigation and Jensen (tel. 227-7555), has five floors brimming with Mexican merchandise—embroidered dresses, rugs, big paper flowers, piñatas, pottery, etc.—along with an on-premises Mexican restaurant and a number of concessions selling fast fajitas and the like. It's fun, but I do wish the quality of merchandise offered maintained a higher overall standard. As it is, it's a mix—some jewels, some junk. If your trip includes Mexican border towns or San Antonio, you'll do better at their markets; if not, check out El Mercado. It can conveniently be combined with a visit to Ninfa's, just a few blocks away (see restaurant recommendations).

**WESTERN WEAR:** Everything in western wear and then some can be found at **Stelzig's,** 3123 Post Oak Blvd., at Richmond (tel. 629-7779), which has been around almost as long as Texas (since 1870). It smells of freshly tanned leather, not surprising since they specialize in custom-designed leather items ranging from rifle scabbards to bolo ties. The store includes a complete tack shop department (branding irons, horseshoes, saddles, saddlebags, chaps, mane and tail whitener, you name it); a full line of western clothing for men, women, and children; a western art gallery; and an English riding wear department. It's still run by the Stelzig family who founded it.

## 8. After Dark

Whether you're looking for culture or country, rock or Rachmaninoff, you'll find it in Houston. There are discos by the dozen, comedy clubs, and jazz clubs. The city has nationally prominent opera and ballet companies, notable theater, a major symphony orchestra, and several facilities that feature headliner entertainers. Pick up the current issue of *Texas Monthly* or the Friday weekend sections of the *Houston Post* or the *Houston Chronicle* to find out what's on during your stay.

*Note:* Though this section is called "After Dark," there are daytime children's theater and concert options listed below.

**TICKETS:** The following outlets are convenient places to pick up tickets for whatever you'd like to see, and many of them are good information sources for area entertainment as well.

### Showtix

Under the auspices of a nonprofit organization called Arts for Everyone, SHOWTIX sells half-price tickets for all Ticketron events—sports, theater, headliner clubs, concerts, rodeo, etc.—at a booth in Tranquility Park at the corner of Walker and Smith (tel. 227-9292 for an up-to-the-minute, 24-hour recording of all available half-price tickets). You can purchase half-price tickets on the day of performance only (Sunday tickets are sold on Saturday) or advance-sale tickets at full price, the latter not just for the Houston area but for events nationwide (like Broadway shows). The booth is open on Monday from 11 a.m. to 2 p.m. and Tuesday to Saturday to 7 p.m. Cash and traveler's checks are the only accepted forms of payment. There's free 20-minute parking. While you're here, pick up a free copy of Arts for Everyone's bimonthly calendar of cultural events throughout the Greater Houston area; you can also get it by writing or calling Arts for Everyone, 1950 West Gray, #19, Houston, TX 77019 (tel. 713/522-

3744). Also check out the *Houston Post* on the last Sunday of every month when SHOWTIX runs an ad with coupons for half-price tickets available in advance.

## And Others

There are **Ticketron** outlets at all Joske stores and elsewhere around town. Call 526-1709 to find out the most convenient location or to charge tickets with your VISA or MasterCard.

A similar operation, **Ticketmaster,** has about 15 Houston locations; call 799-9555 to find out the most convenient office or to charge tickets. It handles only Houston events.

Finally, there's the **Downtown Ticket Center,** 1100 Milam, at Dallas (tel. 222-SHOW), which, like Ticketron, has tickets to just about everything in Houston and nationwide.

**MIXED BAGS:** Like most cities, Houston has many performance facilities that offer a wide range of entertainment, hence defying easy categorization. Most notable of these is:

## Civic Center Complex

Houston's answer to New York's Lincoln Center and Washington's Kennedy Center, the Civic Center Complex (tel. 222-3561), which in addition to vast convention facilities includes the 3,000-seat **Jesse H. Jones Hall for the Performing Arts,** 615 Louisiana, at Capitol, and the 3,023-seat **Music Hall,** 810 Bagby St., at Walker. In addition, the **Gus W. Wortham Theater Center,** which will occupy a square block bounded by Texas, Smith, Preston, and Buffalo Bayou, is scheduled for completion by mid-1987. At that time the Houston Grand Opera and the Houston Ballet will move their performances to the Wortham, which will actually consist of two separate facilities, a 2,300-seat auditorium and a 1,100-seat theater. Its advent will make it possible for Houston to host a greater number of cultural attractions, major musicals, and Broadway shows. Civic Center productions are detailed below under various headings.

## Tower Theater

A converted 1930s movie house, the 955-seat Tower Theatre, 1201 Westheimer Rd., at Yoakum (tel. 529-5966 or 621-8600), hosts three resident companies.

The **Delia Stewart Jazz Dance Company** (tel. 522-6375) does three productions here each year. The company's exciting and innovative work was described by one reviewer as "a repertoire of musical theater jazz that's joyful, soulful, sometimes mellow, and above all, fun." The Tower productions take place in August, November, and April each year. Tickets are $11 to $16, and they go quickly.

**Texas Opera Theater** (tel. 546-0290), the nation's largest touring company, under the auspices of the Houston Grand Opera, also performs here several times each year. They have a great logo—a cowboy hat with Valkyrie-like horns. TOT performers are young (average age is under 30) and talented, and their repertoire puts the emphasis on classic operas like *La Traviata, Die Fledermaus,* and *Carmen* (all sung in English), with occasional forays into more contemporary and/or avant-garde material such as *Sweeney Todd* and *Starbird,* a Space Age children's fable. The company has won widespread acclaim (CBS "Morning" host Charles Kuralt called it "one of the most ambitious and respected opera companies in the nation"), and if they're in town when you are, I urge you to catch one of their energetic productions. Tickets are $8 to $16.

The Society for the Performing Arts (tel. 227-1111), a nonprofit organization that brings quality classical and modern dance, recital artists, and theater to the Houston area, presents a series of small modern dance concerts here each year (more about this organization just below).

In addition, the Tower hosts occasional Broadway shows such as *Best Little Whorehouse in Texas* and *Pump Boys and Dinettes* (both with the original New York casts) and *Agnes of God* starring Elizabeth Ashley. Headliner concerts, like Judy Collins, Leon Russell, Jay Leno, Laurie Anderson, and Joan Armatrading, round out their offerings.

## Society for the Performing Arts

A nonprofit corporation formed in 1966 simultaneously with the opening of the Jesse H. Jones Hall for the Performing Arts, the Society for the Performing Arts (tel. 227-1111) is dedicated to bringing to Houston internationally acclaimed artists and attractions from the entire spectrum of the performing arts. And they do an excellent job of it. During a recent annual September-to-May season, they presented (primarily at Jones Hall) the Paul Taylor Dance Company, the Saint Louis Symphony Orchestra, the Joyce Trisler Danscompany, the San Francisco Ballet, the Canadian Brass, pianist Andre Watts, the Pilobolus Dance Theatre, the Philip Glass Ensemble, Balletap U.S.A. (a company formed by Maurice Hines and Mercedes Ellington), famed chamber music ensemble Academy of St. Martin in the Fields, Peter Schickele ("P.D.Q. Bach"), guitarist John Williams, Ballet Théâtre Français, Itzhak Perlman, and the Los Angeles Philharmonic conducted by André Previn. Quite a season! For a current year's calendar, call the above number or write to the Society of the Performing Arts, 615 Louisiana St., Houston, TX 77002.

## Miller Outdoor Theatre

Established in Hermann Park in 1923 and rebuilt in 1968, Miller Outdoor Theatre, 100 Concert Dr. (tel. 520-3291), offers a great diversity of programming every April to October that typically includes performances by the Houston Symphony, the Houston Grand Opera, and the Houston Ballet; a Broadway musical; a Shakespearean production; a bluegrass show; a jazz festival; a KIKK radio country music festival; and more. The audience sits under a canopy covering 1,667 seats or under the stars on a grassy hill, and it's a tradition to bring a picnic hamper. Best of all, everything is free. You can pick up tickets the day of the performance at the box office between 11:30 a.m. and 1 p.m.; otherwise just bring your blanket and sit on the grass.

**THEATER:** The **Alley Theatre**, 615 Texas St., at Louisiana (tel. 228-8421 for information or to charge tickets), is one of the largest and oldest (established 1947) regional resident theaters in the country. It supports a company of professional actors and playwright residencies, the latter at one time including Paul Zindel whose Alley première of *The Effect of Gamma Rays on Man-in-the-Moon Marigolds* went on to win a Pulitzer Prize. The Alley's current home, opened in 1968, contains the 798-seat Large Stage used for major productions of classical and contemporary works (like *Execution of Justice,* Cole Porter's *Kiss Me Kate,* Shakespearean plays, *Quartermaine's Terms,* and Beth Henley's *The Miss Firecracker Contest*), and the 296-seat Arena Stage for more intimate theater (such as David Mamet's *Glengarry Glen Ross,* the much-acclaimed revue *A . . . My Name Is Alice,* and Tina Howe's *Painting Churches*). The Alley has a year-round season at both stages, except for occasional dark Septembers. There's always a Christmas-themed show at the Arena (like Truman Capote's *A Christmas Memory*) from Thanksgiving through New Year's.

Tickets are in the $10 to $27 range. And buffet meals at the on-premises

Alley Brasserie (served two hours before the show) are $7 to $11. The Arena also puts on lunch-hour children's shows Monday to Saturday; tickets are about $5.

Major hit shows are presented in the annual **Broadway Star Series** (tel. 622-4153), mostly at the Music Hall and Jesse H. Jones Hall. A recent year's program included Liza Minnelli in *Liza,* Susan Anton and Elizabeth Ashley in *A Coupla White Chicks . . . , Dream Girls,* Noël Harrison in *Noises Off,* and *The Tap Dance Kid.* For a season calendar, write to Pace Theatrical Group, 4543 Post Oak Dr., Suite 200, Houston, TX 77027.

Since 1968 **Theatre Under the Stars** (tel. 622-TUTS for performance information, 526-1709 to charge tickets) has been offering Houston superb musical comedy entertainment under the artistic direction of its founder, Frank M. Young. Productions have brought nationally known performers to the TUTS stage—Hermione Gingold and Juliet Prowse in *A Little Night Music,* Robert Goulet in *On a Clear Day You Can See Forever,* John Schneider in *Oklahoma!,* Jane Powell in *South Pacific,* and Donna McKechnie in *A Chorus Line,* among them. The theater presents one free production each summer at Miller Outdoor Theatre. Tickets are available at the box office on the day of performance only, and people start lining up at 8 a.m. for an 11:30 a.m. box office opening. Don't worry if you don't have time for that kind of thing; you can always sit on the hill. Between October and May, TUTS presents five musicals at the Civic Center Music Hall, 810 Bagby, at Walker. A recent year's program included productions of Lerner and Loewe's *Paint Your Wagon, Annie, Sugar* (based on the screenplay *Some Like It Hot), Cabin in the Sky,* and Anthony Newley as *Chaplin.* Ticket prices are in the $10 to $30 range. The same year, the Miller Theatre production was a double bill of *The Boyfriend* and *Divorce Me, Darling!*

There are also occasional children's theater productions under the auspices of **Humphrey's School of Musical Theatre,** the exclusive source of juvenile talent cast in TUTS's major musical productions. These take place at 4235 San Felipe, at Midlane, and ticket prices are $5 or less. Call 622-1626 for information about children's shows.

The **Main Street Theater,** 2540 Times Blvd., just off Kirby in the Village Shopping Center (tel. 524-6706), offers a year-round season (with occasional dark periods) that always includes at least one comedy, one musical, one heavy drama, and one classical production. For example, a recent season's roster included *Golddiggers of 1633* (an original musical), *The Member of the Wedding, Twelfth Night, Marat/Sade,* Edward Albee's *Everything in the Garden,* and the Broadway hit *Baby.* In addition, three works of new playwrights are produced every summer. Casts are composed of actors from the Houston area. Tickets are in the $7 to $11 range.

MST also operates the **Theater for Young People**—high-quality children's shows geared to youngsters through early teens. There are performances most Saturdays and Sundays at 2 p.m. Tickets are about $5.

A resident company of about 25, often supplemented by local talent, run **Stages,** 3201 Allen Pkwy., at Rosine (tel. 52-STAGE). Their facility, behind the Children's Museum, houses two theaters: a 200-seat thrust stage with seating on three sides, and a 250-seat theater-in-the-round. The company puts on 10 to 12 productions each year, often utilizing both stages simultaneously. A typical calendar of productions includes such diverse offerings as *Pacific Overtures,* Molière's *Learned Ladies, The Fantasticks, The Madwoman of Chaillot, A Day in the Death of Joe Egg,* Christopher Durang's *Marriage of Bette and Boo, As Is,* and *Doonesbury.* Tickets are in the $10 to $13 range.

Under the same auspices is **Early Stages,** also using both theaters for daytime performances (Tuesday to Friday at 10:30 a.m., on Saturday at 10:30 a.m. and 1:30 p.m., and on Sunday at 1:30 p.m.) for children. Typical productions: *Snoopy, Charlotte's Web, Joseph and the Amazing Technicolor Dreamcoat,* and David Mamet's *Revenge of the Space Pandas.* Tickets are about $5.

**Theatre on Wheels,** based at the Carillon Arts Center, 10001 Westheimer, at Briar Park in the Carillon Mall (tel. 953-1666) is Houston's only full-time children's theater. A company of professional adult actors—sometimes supported by students in children's roles—TOW offers a year-round season of plays for young people, both here and throughout the state; as the name indicates, it's a traveling company. Their repertoire includes well-known works like *Punch and Judy, The Emperor's New Clothes,* and *Hansel and Gretel,* as well as original plays, some of them Texas-themed. Tickets are in the $4 to $8 range. There's a Chili's restaurant in the mall, a good place for pre- or post-theater meals with the kids.

The Fine Arts and Speech Department of Houston Community College offers diverse productions in the **Irwin Heinen Theatre,** 3517 Austin St., at Holman (tel. 630-1113), a converted synagogue that was built in the 1920s and is listed on the Texas and national registers of historic buildings. The school's performance season is September to May (and a full and varied season it is), plus one musical production in summer. An evening's entertainment here might be two one-act comic operas (*The Impresario* by Mozart and *The Telephone* by Menotti), a wind quintet recital, *A Midsummer Night's Dream,* an evening with Broadway songwriters Betty Comden and Adolph Green (songs and anecdotes), chamber music, a jazz concert, a performance by Chrysalis (a well-known local modern dance company), a concert given by Houston Symphony musicians, or *Jacques Brel Is Alive and Well and Living in Paris.* Tickets are usually under $10, with discounts available for students and seniors.

## OPERA, BALLET, AND SYMPHONY: The **Houston Grand Opera** (tel. 546-0200 for information, 227-ARTS to charge tickets), under the general direction of David Gockley, has grown since its founding in 1955 from a small company doing two productions a year to one of the nation's leading opera companies. They have an October-to-May season at the Jesse H. Jones Hall for the Performing Arts, 615 Louisiana, at Capitol, with four performances each of six major operas, sometimes featuring guest artists like Placido Domingo, Beverly Sills, Luciano Pavarotti, and Dame Joan Sutherland. They range from the classic to the avant-garde, from Puccini to Philip Glass. Guest artists are also featured in the Great Artist Series of recitals and concerts. Every spring there are free performances at Miller Outdoor Theatre.

In conjunction with the University of Houston, the **Houston Opera Studio** (a training program) presents a full opera, recitals, and evenings of operatic scenes featuring famous arias.

Tickets for major productions are $10 to $75. Houston Opera Studio productions, which take place at the Lyndall Finley Wortham Theater at the university, are usually under $10, and some are free.

*Note:* When the Gus. W. Wortham Theatre Center is completed (sometime in 1987, if plans proceed according to schedule) HGO productions will move there.

The **City Ballet of Houston** (tel. 468-3670) has been a going concern since 1958, dedicated to "providing audiences with both classical and original ballets of the highest artistic quality." Renowned professionals are often invited to work with the 26-member company, among them such notables as Robert Joffrey and Alexander Minz. The company performs October through May at various spaces around town, and since each facility has its own ticket sources, you have to call the above number to find out where the company is playing and how tickets can be obtained. There's an annual production of *The Nutcracker* with performances mid-November through December, and every year the Spring Repertory Performance at the Tower Theatre highlights several short works by the company's own and other established choreographers.

Formed in 1955 for the purpose of "conserving and advancing the art of dance," the **Houston Ballet** (tel. 227-ARTS) today performs about 50 times a year in a mid-September-to-late-May season at the Jesse J. Jones Hall for the Performing Arts (when the Wortham Theater Center is completed sometime in 1987, it will become the company's new home). Artistic director Ben Stevenson was formerly a principal dancer and balletmaster with the London Festival Ballet and a director of the National Ballet of Washington. Under his guidance, the company has gleaned rave reviews (the *San Francisco Chronicle* said: "For purity and classical precision, their only match in this country is the New York City Ballet"). A recent season featured works new to the company by George Balanchine and Jerome Robbins, along with a dramatic *Peer Gynt* and classics like *The Nutcracker* and *Giselle.* They also performed at the free Miller Outdoor Theatre. Tickets are in the $8 to $50 range.

The **Houston Symphony Orchestra,** one of America's oldest performing arts organizations (established 1912), performs over 150 concerts a year (year round except August), most of them at the Jesse H. Jones Hall for the Performing Arts, 615 Louisiana St., Houston, TX 77002 (tel. 224-4240 for information, 227-ARTS to charge tickets). Among the world-class conductors who have preceded current music director Sergiu Comissiona are André Previn and Leopold Stokowski. HSO has premiered music composed by Khachaturian, Villa-Lobos, Rachmaninoff, and Aaron Copland, and composers like Leonard Bernstein, Morton Gould, and Igor Stravinsky have been invited to conduct their own works. The orchestra regularly tours the country, and its concerts are carried on radio and TV stations, including the BBC. The Winter Series is HSO's largest program—some 60 concerts, often with guest artists—committed to the full range of classical music from concert favorites to challenging 20th-century works. The September-through-April Exxon Pop Series offers lighter material like Broadway music, folk, and jazz; these very popular concerts usually take place at the Music Hall. Each summer HSO presents a series of free concerts at Miller Outdoor Theatre in Hermann Park, including a traditional July Fourth celebration complete with fireworks. The Summer Festival at Jones Hall presents symphonic music during three weeks in July. Special holiday concerts celebrate Christmas and New Year's, the former always including performances of Handel's *Messiah.* In early summer HSO presents Cabaret Pops, featuring light symphonic fare. And in addition there are chamber music concerts and Saturday-morning programs for children. Write to the orchestra at the above address for the current season's concert calendar.

**HEADLINERS:** Any given week at least four or five major stars are playing Houston. They're likely to be at the following auditoriums:

The 1,668-seat **Cullen Auditorium** at the University of Houston, 4800 Calhoun St. (tel. 749-2607 or 749-1435), offers a full schedule of entertainment. The student program board books acts like the Eurhythmics, DEVO, jazz violinist Jean Luc Ponty, Miles Davis, Randy Newman, and Stevie Ray Vaughan. In addition, the Houston Baptist University Opera performs here every spring, and the Chinese Student Goodwill Mission, a touring group from Taiwan that does acrobatics, plays, Chinese opera, and kung-fu exhibitions, performs here each fall. Christian music groups also play this facility.

AstroWorld's **Southern Star Amphitheatre,** Loop 610 and Kirby Drive (tel.

799-1466), is a massive nine-acre, open-air entertainment facility with a seating capacity of 20,000 (3,000 reserved seats and 17,000 on the lawn). A hand impression in cement is made of each entertainer along a "Walk of Stars." Among those who have performed here are John Denver, Amy Grant, Kenny Loggins, Air Supply, Al Jarreau, the Beach Boys, Neil Young, WHAM!, Jimmy Buffet, Bob Dylan, and the Grateful Dead. Admission is included—sometimes with a supplement of up to $5—with your entrance ticket to the AstroWorld park (see "Sights"). Otherwise, most tickets—available at Ticketron and other major ticket agencies, or at the park on the day of performance only—are in the $12 to $25 range. Conversely, concert tickets allow you free admission to the park on the day of the event.

The 8,800-seat **Sam Houston Coliseum,** 810 Bagby St., at Walker (tel. 222-3267), a part of the vast Civic Center Complex, offers a number of headliner concerts each year. Among those who have appeared here are Kiss, Black Sabbath, José José, The Pretenders, and Ted Nugent. The facility is also used twice a year for a big country music jamboree with major stars, and for Christian and gospel concerts. For some shows you can charge tickets at the above box office number; other promoters work exclusively through Ticketron and/or Ticketmaster.

The **Summit,** six miles south of downtown at Hwy. 59 and Timmons Lane, is a 17,000-seat arena that hosts some of the biggest names in about 65 major rock and country events each year. Willie Nelson does an annual New Year's Eve concert here. Other stars who've played the Summit include Bruce Springsteen, Prince, Julio Iglesias, Kenny Rogers, Luciano Pavarotti, Neil Diamond, David Bowie, Diana Ross, and Eddie Murphy. Concert tickets can be charged through the box office (tel. 627-9452) three days after the first day of sale, but for the biggest names, go through Ticketron or Ticketmaster; 17,000 seats can fill up fast. For show information, call 961-9003.

A star too big for the Summit will play the **Astrodome,** Kirby Drive and South Loop 610 (tel. 799-9500 for ticket information, 799-9555 to charge tickets). Among those who've filled this arena's 66,000 seats are the Rolling Stones, the Who, and the Jacksons' Victory Tour.

**Rockefeller's,** 3620 Washington Ave., at Heights Boulevard (tel. 861-9365), is a very attractive nightclub with a dance floor in front of the stage and cocktail-table seating on the main floor and balcony above. Generally there's headliner entertainment Wednesday through Sunday (except when the club is taken over for private parties). Ray Charles, B. B. King, Betty Carter, Roy Orbison, David Allan Coe, Chick Corea, Mel Tillis, Randy Newman, Ella Fitzgerald, Kris Kristofferson, and Bonnie Raitt are among those who have performed here. Tickets are $5 to $35, depending on the performer (not all the names are as big as those listed above). You can charge them at the above phone number or purchase them from Ticketron.

**COUNTRY:** Everyone knows about **Gilley's,** 4500 Spencer Hwy. in Pasadena, just 20 minutes from downtown Houston (tel. 946-9842), the cavernous bar that *Urban Cowboy* made famous—or vice versa. Even before the movie, Gilley's was the honky-tonk to end all honky-tonks. Its size is awesome: the entire complex occupies over four acres, which, according to the *Guinness Book of World Records,* makes it the largest nightclub in the world. It encompasses a full western-wear boutique (along with the traditional stuff, you can buy Mickey Gilley jeans, jackets, calendars, signed color photographs, even underwear) and a long counter (above which the movie *Urban Cowboy* plays continuously) selling many of the same items. Then there are dozens of video games, pinball machines, pool tables, a punching bag, test-your-strength machines, arm-wrestling machines, and of course, El Toro, the famed mechanical bull (a ride costs $2 if you dare, and if not, you can have your picture taken on it and say you did). Hundreds of tables flank the dance floor. There's also a restaurant on the premises serving barbecue, steaks, pizza, nachos, and (from midnight to 2 a.m.) breakfast fare. In 1982 Gilley's added a 60,000-square-foot rodeo arena with seating for 10,000 and began offering a Wild West Rodeo every Saturday night at 8:30 p.m. Admission is $5.50.

During the week, Johnny Williams and the Bayou City Beats perform at Gilley's, while big names—like Willie Nelson, Waylon Jennings, George Jones, Hank Williams, Jr., Loretta Lynn, Conway Twitty, Johnny Paycheck, and David Allan Coe—usually play on Friday and Saturday nights. Mickey Gilley performs about ten times a year, and Johnny Lee ("Lookin' for Love") also puts in quite a few appearances.

The club is open nightly until 2 a.m. Admission is $2 to $20, depending on the performer. No credit cards. Don't miss Gilley's, an only-in-Texas phenomenon. You can bring the kids, by the way; many people do.

**Kat Bullews,** 2707 Wilson Rd., between Old Atascocita Road and Will Clayton Parkway (tel. 446-0879), has live country music every Friday and Saturday night—both big stars (like Mel Tillis, George Jones, Sylvia, Charly McClain, and Eddy Raven) and talented locals. There's a 4,000-square-foot hardwood dance floor. A restaurant is on the premises, ditto the requisite video games and pool tables. Admission is $3 to $20, depending on the performer.

Decorated with mounted steer, deer, elk, moose, and other hunting trophies—along with Mexican movie posters and neon beer signs—**San Antone Rose,** 1641 S. Voss Rd., at San Felipe (tel. 977-7116), is the archetypical urban cowboy club, "the home of the $4 hat and the $40 hatband." Like Fizz and Boccaccio (see below), it's a Mike Steinmann–owned club. There are many promotions: radio station parties with well-known DJs, Halloween costume parties, trivia contests, all-you-can-drink-for-$2 parties, battles of the bands, and suchlike.

With the cowboy craze on the wane, the club now offers a mix of DJ music —25% top-40s rock, 75% country. And blackjack tables, pool tables, a punching-bag machine, skeet shooting, and video games provide additional entertainment options. Open till 2 a.m. Tuesday to Sunday. Admission is $1.50 Tuesday to Thursday and Sunday, $2.50 on Friday and Saturday.

**DANCING:** The 21st-floor disco at the Stouffer Greenway Plaza Hotel, 6 Greenway Plaza East, between Edloe and the Buffalo Speedway (tel. 629-1200), **City Lights** is a romantic setting with windows all around providing panoramic city skyline views. Inside, there are plush furnishings amid plantings of ivy and ficus. A DJ plays top-40s and oldies seven nights a week. No cover charge.

The most chi-chi club in town is **Boccaccio,** 1800 Post Oak Blvd., between Westheimer and San Felipe (tel. 626-7141), a cardholder club that nonmembers can visit for $10. Very plush, with midnight-blue velvet banquettes and art deco lighting fixtures, Boccaccio, like Club A in New York, belongs to the elite international Club of Clubs (membership payable in 1,000 Swiss francs). It has hosted parties for everyone from Princess Christina of Sweden to Paloma Picasso to Joan Collins. A bottle of Dom Perignon here is served with fresh strawberries and lady fingers, and you might snack on beluga caviar or smoked salmon while you watch the action on the dance floor. Or sit down for a full dinner at SRO, the adjoining restaurant, where pizzas and pasta dishes (all in the $10 range) are available, along with mesquite-grilled entrees like redfish with orange hazelnut butter ($13). Boccaccio is open Tuesday to Saturday from 10 p.m.

to 2 a.m., and dinner is served at SRO from 6:30 p.m. on. Jackets and ties are de rigueur for men.

Under the same ownership (Houston nightlife guru Mike Steinmann) is **Fizz**, 6400 Richmond Ave., at Hillcrest (tel. 789-1197), specializing in sensory overload with a state-of-the-art sound system playing loud high-energy music, 18 video monitors (including three ten-foot-square screens that descend over the dance floor at given intervals), and a matrix board with 84 light levels. Slick dancers can jump up on a stage and strut their stuff, while nondancers can meet and mingle at the roulette and blackjack tables. There are even seating areas, including an outdoor wooden deck with umbrella tables, where conversation is possible. The music starts out relatively mellow early in the evening and increases in intensity as the night wears on. Fizz does lots of promotions: for example, for Monday-night football the club is decorated in team colors, and you pick a team when you come in; whenever they score a touchdown, you get a free drink. Julian Lennon, WHAM!, Mary Lou Retton, and Duran Duran have all thrown parties in Fizz's VIP room. There's an immense free buffet daily from 4 to 9 p.m., lockers are provided (you can't dance holding your purse), and women can have hair and makeup done outside the ladies room. Fizz is open nightly, till 2 a.m. Sunday to Thursday (admission $1), till 4 a.m. on Friday and Saturday (admission $1 before 8 p.m., $4 thereafter).

The suit-and-tie crowd at **Rialto**, 5351 W. Alabama St., at Rice Avenue (tel. 840-9720), is so Yuppie you could transport the whole scene to Washington, D.C., no questions asked. In line with the "rialto" theme, the walls are hung with framed theater posters. The DJ plays mostly top-40s hits at non-deafening decibel levels, a state-of-the-art sound / light system centers on the dance floor making audible conversation possible elsewhere, and you can sit on comfortable sofas and upholstered chairs and watch the action. There are blackjack tables on the upper level. Promotions include shows from high-fashion boutiques (this isn't the kind of place that has a Rambo night). Come between 5 and 9 p.m. Tuesday to Friday night and you can enjoy a 35-foot buffet of pâtés, oyster brochette, fresh veggies, pizza, seafood and pasta salads, chocolate-dipped fruit, and more for $2. Later arrivals can order champagne, cognacs, liqueurs, and snacks like caviar pie and oysters bourguignon. The Rialto is open Tuesday to Saturday nights till 2 a.m. After 9 p.m. on Sunday and Tuesday to Thursday there's a $2 admission charge, $5 on Friday and Saturday after 7 p.m.

**LIVE MUSIC:** Though **Fool's Gold**, 12845 Westheimer, a block west of Dairy Ashford (tel. 497-2501), is often thought of as a C&W club, it actually offers a considerable variety of live entertainment. Some of the better-known acts that have been booked here are Elvis imitator Johnny Harrah, Bachman-Turner Overdrive, the Bellamy Brothers, Johnny Rodriguez, and Earl Thomas Conley. There's always live music on Friday and Saturday nights, and sometimes during the week as well; otherwise a DJ plays rock and country hits enhanced by videos aired on two 20-foot screens. It's a big club—22,000 square feet with a 3,200-square-foot dance floor and a sizeable stage. Fool's Gold does frequent promotions like the Houston Pretty Lady Contest and a festival of Cajun music and food. In the country mode, there are five pool tables on the premises. There's also a recording booth at the entrance where (for $10) you can cut a record singing over instrumental tapes. Open nightly until 2 a.m. Admission is $5 to $10 when live performers appear, no cover other nights.

One of the most romantic settings in town is **Cody's Restaurant & Club**, 3400 Montrose Blvd., at Hawthorne (tel. 522-9747), a candlelit, tenth-story setting, which in this part of Houston is high enough to provide panoramic views. You can cozy up on a couch, sit at one of the cocktail tables, dine in the restaurant areas, or enjoy the downtown cityscape from one of two open-air roof patios. Live bands play mostly contemporary / progressive jazz from 9 p.m. Monday to Thursday, 9:30 p.m. on Friday and Saturday. Very simpático! The menu is reasonably priced; dinner here might begin with an appetizer of fried stuffed jalapeños ($4) or baked brie ($5) and continue with barbecued shrimp ($7.25) or veal marsala ($8.50), both entrees including salad, vegetable, potatoes, and bread and butter. No cover. The average drink is $3.50.

At **Remington's Bar & Grill,** 4608 Westheimer, a block east of the Galleria (tel. 850-0451), part owner/jazz singer Scott Gertner and his combo play what he calls "listenable and danceable intellectual bop." Whatever it is, it's great. Gertner sings and plays guitar, and his group consists of a drummer, bassist, keyboard player, lead guitar, and saxaphonist. They play Tuesday to Saturday nights to a large Texas following. On Sunday and Monday there's varied live entertainment, mostly jazz and rhythm 'n blues. Remington's is a cozy, comfy, and casual club with low log ceilings, prints of Frederic Remington western paintings on the walls, and a candlelit wooden deck. You can order drinks, a wide selection of imported beers, and finger foods like fried cheese, buffalo wings, and burgers. There's a small dance floor. Come early for the large free buffet weekdays between 4 and 8 p.m.—ribs, fajitas, shrimp, and more—and you'll not only get a good meal but a seat for the show. Entertainment begins at 9:30 p.m. and goes till about 1 a.m. Admission is $4 Thursday through Saturday, and the cover varies on Sunday and Monday.

The Bayou City Oyster Company, a popular Cajun restaurant at 2171 Richmond Ave., at Greenbriar (tel. 523-6640), recently opened the adjoining **Rhythm Kitchen,** a beautiful open-air eatery/bar where owner Tom Lile plans to host live bands and improv groups. All this was in the works at press time, so you'd best call before you go to see how things have proceeded. Seen on a hardhat tour, the Rhythm Kitchen was shaping up to something spectacular. Enclosed by a tall black wrought-iron fence, it has an octagonal center bar with piano keyboard tile design, fans overhead, and silhouettes of Dixieland musicians on plum-colored walls. A small menu will feature the most popular items in Houston—fajitas, ribs, chicken-fried steak, and a few Cajun specialties. Lile also owns Georgia's, which is part of this complex (see my restaurant recommendations). I'm sure this new enterprise will be well worth checking out.

**Fitzgerald's,** a rustic candlelit club housed in an 80-year-old Polish dance hall at 2706 White Oak, at Studemont (tel. 862-3838), presents a mix of blues, rock, and reggae, with an occasional comedy night thrown in. There's live entertainment seven nights a week, and over the years the club has hosted some big names—James Brown, Tina Turner, Stevie Ray Vaughan, Bo Diddley, B. B. King, Arlo Guthrie, and Jerry Jeff Walker. There are three levels. Downstairs in the back room are a pool table, a few video games, a dart board, and a blackjack table. There's a porch upstairs where you can catch a breath of fresh air and see if your hearing is still unimpaired. And the musicians play on the balcony level. Wear jeans. Fitzgerald's is funky, young, loose, and loud. Cover ranges from $3 to $25, depending on the performer; the above-mentioned big names are occasional, but the entertainment young owner Sara Fitzgerald books is usually good.

**COMEDY:** The **Comedy Workshop & Annex,** 2105 San Felipe, at Shepherd (tel. 524-7333), consists of two rooms—the Annex and the Cabaret. The Annex offers a Comedy Store set-up, featuring working professionals who live in the Houston area (some have been on "David Letterman" or the "Tonight Show"), and occasionally visiting stars like Robin Williams, Rodney Dangerfield, and Steve Wright. Sunday to Thursday nights there are 6 to 12 comics in each show, performing continuously from 8:30 p.m. to midnight; on Friday and Saturday the club presents three comics only, doing longer schticks, plus an MC. Friday shows are at 8:30 and 10:45 p.m., Saturday shows at 7:30 and 9:45 p.m., and midnight. Admission is $4 Sunday to Thursday, $6 on weekends. There's a full bar but no drink minimum. In the adjoining Cabaret, a resident professional company of six performs Second City–style revues Tuesday through Thursday at 8:30 p.m., on Friday and Saturday at 8:30 and 11 p.m. Admission is $5 during the week, $7 on weekends.

There's also a **Laff Stop** in town, at 1952A West Gray, between Shepherd and Driscoll (tel. 524-2333), featuring nationally known comedians (three per show). Once again, these are the guys you've seen on Carson and Letterman. Tuesday to Thursday and Sunday showtime is 8:30 p.m., Friday shows are at 8 and 10:30 p.m., and Saturday shows at 7:30 and 10 p.m., and midnight. Admission is $6.50 weekdays, $9 on Friday and Saturday, sometimes more if a big name (like Gabe Kaplan, Wayland Flowers & Madame, Professor Irwin Corey) is performing. There's a full-service bar, and light fare is available. On weekends there's a two-drink minimum (average drink is $3.50).

# Chapter III

# GALVESTON: A TREASURE ISLE

### 1. Getting to Know Galveston
### 2. Where to Stay
### 3. Restaurants
### 4. Sights and Other Attractions
### 5. Galveston Nights

A 32-MILE STRETCH of palm-fringed white sandy beach is just one of Galveston's lures. You'll also enjoy delving into this lazy resort town's less-than-peaceful past.

## 1. Getting to Know Galveston

**HISTORY:** Galveston has a wild and romantic history. During its early years it was a fishing place and burial grounds for the Karankawa Indians and a haven for pirate crews operating in the Gulf of Mexico, its tranquillity scarcely disturbed by the occasional brief arrival and departure of French and Spanish explorers. It wasn't an inviting place: rattlesnakes abounded and the Karankawas were cannibals. For many centuries the only white men to make a longish stay were Cabeza de Vaca and his crew who, having washed up on the island in 1528 after being lost at sea, spent six years as captive slaves of the Indians; they named it "The Isle of Misfortune."

In 1785 José Evia surveyed the Texas coast for Count Bernardo de Galvez, Spanish governor of Louisiana, and named the bay in his honor. Though the island was eventually named for him, Galvez probably never visited or gave much thought to the place.

The first Europeans to settle here were pirates, most notably the infamous and dashing Lafitte, who made Galveston his base of operations in 1817 and began exploring its potential as a port and trading point. Unfortunately, much of the "trading" he did involved robbing Spanish merchants of slaves, ships, and cargo. In 1821 he expanded his activities to include seizure of an American ship, and the United States Navy called a halt to his operations. Lafitte sailed off to ports unknown, leaving behind legends of buried treasure that exist to this day.

In 1836, with the victory of San Jacinto assuring the viability of Texas, Michael B. Menard, a leader of the new republic, bought the site of the present city and a few miles of coast for $50,000. The new city got a big boost in 1845 when Texas became part of the United States, an event that attracted investors and opened up communications and trade with European ports. The second part of the 19th century, especially the last quarter after Reconstruction, was "Galveston's Gilded Age." The city became the world's leading cotton port and the second-richest city in the U.S. based on per capita income. The town's merchant princes built Victorian mansions, many of them still extant, and the Strand, modeled after London's, became a financial hub known as the "Wall Street of the Southwest." Galveston was the most important city in Texas.

But all that was to change on September 8, 1900, when a hurricane of devastating proportions, followed by a tidal wave that tore across the island at 120 miles per hour, undid in one night the work of generations. More than 6,000 people were killed, thousands more were left homeless, and two-thirds of Galveston's buildings were washed away. It remains the worst natural disaster the United States has ever known. The grief-torn city rallied valiantly, building a 17-foot seawall and elevating the entire city about eight feet to protect the harbor from future storms. But during the recovery years Houston completed its ship channel, thus usurping Galveston's role as Texas's major port city for all time. In rebuilding, Galveston took the opportunity to beautify its streets, parks, and beaches, and a spirit of optimism was reflected in the luxurious new hotels going up along the gulf. Galveston was getting ready to concentrate on its resort attractions—and on Las Vegas–style vice.

Even before the storm, Galveston had a large red-light district of bawdy houses. And with Prohibition in 1918, it became a center of bootlegging. Big-time gambling started in the 1920s, most of it under the auspices of Sicilian immigrant brothers Sam and Rose Maceo. They operated the famed Hollywood Club, offering lavish dinners, headliner entertainment—Guy Lombardo, Frank Sinatra, Duke Ellington, Spike Jones, and Sophie Tucker, among others—and a full complement of craps, blackjack, and roulette tables in the back room. Much the same went on at their South Seas resort-style Balinese Room, and slot machines were common in restaurants, drugstores, and other public places throughout the island. Nobody minded much except an occasional Texas Ranger. The Maceo's contributed heavily to Galveston churches and charities and were consequently very popular. It wasn't until 1957 that state Attorney-General Will Wilson surprised everyone by keeping his campaign promise to enforce the law of the land in Galveston. Slot machines and gaming tables were smashed in the presence of news cameras, and the era of gambling in Galveston drew to a close.

The city slumped in the '60s and early '70s and was beginning to recede into somewhat seedy insignificance. But Galveston's feisty spirit soon came to the fore once again, sparked by a nationwide interest in historic preservation. In 1973 the Galveston Historical Foundation set up funding to purchase old buildings along the Strand and resell them to investors who would restore their former grandeur. They have been actively spearheading preservation efforts ever since, especially in the downtown area. One of the city's great 1980s benefactors is Galveston-born oilman and real-estate developer George Mitchell, who with his wife, Cynthia, has restored ten structures on the Strand and is responsible for some of the island's finest new hotels and restaurants. Another major philanthropist is the Moody Foundation, established in 1942 by the late Mr. and Mrs. William Lewis Moody, Jr., and still run by family members. The Moodys have committed millions to historical restoration, most notably the Center for Transportation and Commerce (details below).

Today Galveston is more than just a playground for Houstonians. The Strand is once again a thriving commercial center, lined with shops, galleries, and restaurants. In the East End and Silk Stocking Historical Districts there are so many preserved Victorian homes that architecturally one might consider Galveston the 19th-century equivalent of Colonial Williamsburg. Visitors can ride about in style aboard an authentic horse-drawn carriage or explore the island in an old-fashioned trolley car. There's much to see—from tours of historic homes to a restored square-rigged 1877 merchant ship and a marine park with performing dolphins and sea lions. And of course not the least of Galveston's offerings is that above-mentioned beach and such attendant attractions as boating, fishing, surfing, diving, and waterskiing.

**GETTING THERE:** Galveston is just 50 miles south of Houston. The Gulf Freeway (I-45) leads right into Broadway, the city's inviting central street, its wide esplanade planted with tall palms, live oaks, and oleanders.

You can fly in to either of Houston's airports and board a ten-passenger **Galveston Limousine Service** van at any terminal to any Galveston location. There are frequent departures in both directions seven days a week. The price from Hobby Airport is $15 per person to any Galveston hotel, $3 additional for other island locations. From Intercontinental you pay $18 and $21, respectively. For details, call 409/765-5288, or in Houston, 713/223-2256.

A company called **Excursion Trains Incorporated** (tel. 713/522-0574) has been negotiating with Amtrak and plans in the near future to run luxury-class art deco–style passenger trains between the Amtrak depot in downtown Houston and the old Santa Fe railroad terminal in Galveston at the Strand and 25th Street. If all goes according to plan, they should be offering one or two trips daily in each direction by the time you read this. Call for details.

Finally, **Greyhound** connects Galveston with all U.S. cities. The terminal here is at 4913 Broadway (tel. 409/765-7731).

**ORIENTATION:** Make your first stop the **Galveston Convention & Visitors Bureau,** 2106 Seawall Blvd. (tel. 409/763-4311, or toll free 800/351-4237), in the Moody Convention Center. Open weekdays from 8:30 a.m. to 5 p.m., weekends from 9 a.m. to 5 p.m., they can provide maps, brochures, and information. You can also purchase Treasure Isles Tour Train tickets here; in summer a ticket booth just outside sells tickets for the Galveston Flyer and other attractions.

Another excellent, and very conveniently located, place to find out what's happening in town is the **Strand Visitors Center,** 2016 The Strand (tel. 409/765-7834). Headquarters of the Galveston Historical Foundation, the center can provide detailed information about local attractions along with maps, brochures, and a self-guided walking tour. They also sell tickets to most major attractions (discount ticket packages are available), rent out audio cassette tours of the Strand ($2 or $3 per couple), operate a gift shop on the ground floor, and rent out bicycles. A 20-minute film on the *Elissa* is shown here throughout the day. Summer hours are Sunday to Thursday from 9:30 a.m. to 6 p.m., on Friday and Saturday till 8 p.m.; the rest of the year the center is open from 10 a.m. to 5 p.m. weekdays, 9:30 a.m. to 6 p.m. weekends.

### Island Tours

The **Treasure Isle Tour Train** (tel. 765-9564), a colorful open-air tram that makes a circuitous 1½-hour loop tour around the island, departs from 21st Street and Seawall Boulevard. Taped commentary describes attractions along the 17-mile route—Fort Crockett, historic homes, the Seawall, downtown, the shrimp fleet, and the yacht basin. During May there are four departures daily, in summer five, and September to December and March 1 to May 1 there are two, weather permitting. And every once in a while the train goes out during the December-to-February period. Adults pay $3.50; children 3 to 12, $1.75; under 3, free. Call for exact departure times.

The **H. R. H. Carriage Company** (tel. 763-7084) offers horse-drawn carriage rides through the Strand and other historical districts of Galveston. Hire your carriage from the Strand and 21st Street, just across from the Visitors Center, or from the Galvez Hotel west parking lot at Seawall and 21st. Or call for reservations. The company will be happy to customize a tour to suit your interests and/or provide narration. Cost is $25 per hour, $15 per half hour.

The **Galveston Flyer** (tel. 763-0884) is a quaint replica of a 1920s trolley, and it functions both as a tour vehicle and a means of getting around town when sightseeing. Your ticket is valid throughout the day, and you can board at any stop and stay on for the entire route—a one-hour narrated tour of historic Galveston—or get on and off as many times as you like. There are departures on the hour between 9 a.m. and 5 p.m. daily from 21st Street and Seawall Boulevard. Some of the stops along the way include Ashton Villa (24th and Broadway), the Tremont House (23rd and Ship's Mechanic), the Railroad Museum (25th and the Strand), Pier 19 (20th and Water), the Strand Visitors Center (21st and the Strand), and Bishop's Palace (14th and Broadway). It also stops at a few hotels. Adults pay $4; seniors, $3.50; children under 12 pay $3.

**GETTING AROUND:** Galveston, an island, is about 30 miles long and 3 miles across. Being so small, it's one of the few places in Texas where you can do a lot of walking.

Also consider renting a **bicycle;** they're available at shops all along the beachfront (for example, at 25th and Seawall, 3114 Seawall, and 1102 Seawall). These shops also rent roller skates, surrey-type three-wheelers, tandems, and surfboards.

You can **rent a car** at **Budget,** 2028 Broadway (tel. 409/744-0000). Also represented here is **Thrifty,** 602 Broadway (tel. 409/762-3506).

Galveston has a pretty comprehensive **bus** system under the auspices of **Island Transit** (tel. 762-2903); you can call that number for routing information weekdays between 8 a.m. and 5 p.m. Generally, if you're on any main street you can find a bus that will at least take you close to where you're going.

**Taxis** cost $1 for the first one-fifth mile and 20¢ for every fifth of a mile thereafter. Call Yellow Cab at 765-5557 or 763-3333.

**WHEN TO COME:** Galveston is a year-round destination. As I'm writing this, it's January, and while other cities are snowbound, here it's 70° (the average annual temperature) and the trees still have their leaves. Though beachcombing and bike riding are year-round pastimes, the best water weather is from about May to September; hurricane season is June to November, but mostly in the late summer and early fall. Since you can't predict when they'll come, don't stay away for fear of hurricanes, but do pay attention to August and September weather reports.

**ANNUAL EVENTS:** In an effort to make Galveston a year-round destination, the town sponsors an ongoing series of special events. Those listed below are the biggies, but check at the Convention & Visitors Bureau (tel. 409/763-4311) or the Strand Visitors Center (tel. 409/765-7834) to find out what else is happening during your stay.

The first major event of the year is **Mardi Gras,** with about ten days of events peaking the weekend before Ash Wednesday. A recent year's celebration included mask-making parties for children and adults, special theatrical performances, a Chinese New Year fête, art shows, masked balls, costume contests, concerts, a Créole cooking demonstration, a children's parade, and of course, a dazzling nighttime parade with floats and marching bands. Many of the historic homes offer special happenings as well, like a Dixieland brunch at

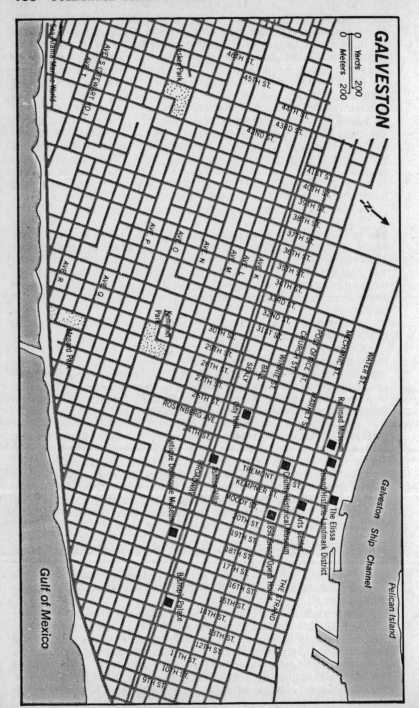

GALVESTON

Yards 200
Meters 200

Ashton Villa. Contact the Convention & Visitors Bureau or Strand Visitors Center for details. Some events require tickets.

There's an **Easter Egg Hunt,** generally the Saturday before Easter Sunday at Ashton Villa (tel. 762-3933). And the first or second Sunday following Easter the **Blessing of the Shrimp Fleet** takes place. Elaborately decorated shrimp trawlers compete for pageant honors and receive clergy blessings for a safe and productive harvest.

The first two weekends in May Galveston's Historical Foundation invites visitors to tour eight of the island's historic homes not usually open to the public, with special events, exhibits, and celebrations. Related **Historical Homes Tour** events might include a candlelight cocktail buffet, a Victorian "genteel junk sale," colorful Cinco de Mayo (a Mexican holiday) celebrations, lectures, and more. Advance tickets are required; call 765-7834.

**July Fourth** is celebrated with a family picnic and ice cream crank-off at Ashton Villa. At night there are usually fireworks at Stewart Beach.

Galveston's best-known celebration is **Dickens on the Strand,** a fun-filled weekend early in December. For two days the Strand and its neighboring blocks become 19th-century London streets and most of the local populace dresses in period costume. Special happenings include a parade of costumed characters from Dickens books, numerous street performers (jugglers, fire eaters, mimes, dancers, singers, musicians, and comics), 19th-century fare (wassail, mulled wine, and roasted chestnuts), a special performance of *A Christmas Carol,* Victorian games, crafts booths, illuminations of Broadway and beachfront hotels, candlelight tours and morning teas at historic homes, port cruises, special feasts at local restaurants, and a parade of Clydesdale horses. There's much more. Stop by the Strand Visitors Center for a full calendar of events.

## 2. Where to Stay

Galveston offers the most diverse accommodations options of any city in Texas. They include charming bed-and-breakfast lodgings (some of them in converted Victorian edifices), a gracious early 1900s resort, plush modern waterfront hotels, and budget motels.

**BED-AND-BREAKFAST:** A grand old Galveston lady, the 1879 Renaissance revival Leon & H. Blum Building in the Strand National Historic Landmark District has been converted by developers George and Cynthia Mitchell into a lavishly elegant 120-room hotel. The **Tremont House,** 2300 Ship's Mechanic Row, Galveston, TX 77550 (tel. 409/763-0300, or toll free 800/874-2300), is a gem—one of the most stunning hostelries in Texas. A four-story block-long arcaded building with a mansard roof, dormer windows, and an enormous ornamental cornice as a crowning centerpiece, Tremont House is styled to re-create the atmosphere of a legendary 19th-century Galveston hotel of the same name. The original hosted six presidents, Sioux chiefs Spotted Horse and White Eagle, Buffalo Bill, Clara Barton, and the Vanderbilts; from its door, Sam Houston made his last public speech, denouncing Texas's secession from the Union.

Guests ascend an ebony marble staircase to the pristinely white, wicker-furnished atrium lobby, where classical music sets an elegant tone, and tall Alexandria palms grow toward sunlight streaming in through skylights four stories overhead. The lobby houses the lovely Toujouse Bar, its intricately carved 1888 rosewood bar flanked by trompe l'oeil marble pillars and its walls adorned with beautiful gilt-framed oil paintings and antique marine-theme prints. Afternoon tea, featuring an assortment of English and herbal brews, tea sandwiches, and sumptuous pastries, is served here daily. Following tea, there's a champagne hour during which premium vintages are offered by the glass along with fruit and cheese platters, and Tuesday through Sunday nights there's piano bar entertainment. Just off the lobby, also an airy atrium under a four-story skylight, is the Merchant Prince, perhaps Galveston's most exquisite dining room. White-linened tables are centered around a putti fountain and planters of azaleas, walls are exposed brick, bentwood chairs and banquettes are upholstered in forest green, and classical music (often of the baroque period) is always played. It looks like the courtyard of a Mediterrean villa. The fare is nouvelle American, light and delicious. I heartily recommend the smoothly creamy lobster consommé ($4.50) as an appetizer or the escargots sautéed with pasta in a delicate cream and brandy sauce ($6.95). For your entree, perhaps the filet of red snapper with mussels in saffron cream sauce ($13.25) or sautéed gulf shrimp with a fondue of tomato flavored with fresh basil ($12.75). Seafood is always superbly prepared here; at lunch I adore the Merchant Prince salad of shrimp, crabmeat, mussels, and lobster on a bed of greens ($8.75). At Sunday brunch there's a special menu offering elegant prix-fixe meals for $14.95.

Off the Tremont House lobby you'll discover high-fashion clothing boutiques for men and women and an exclusive antique shop. A canopied crosswalk connects to the Wentletrap restaurant, also Mitchell owned, about which more below.

The hotel's gracious ambience of course extends to its guest rooms, many of which open, via glazed french doors, onto bottle-green ironwork balconies overlooking the central atrium. Decorated in restrained Victorian motif, with glossy-black / crisp-white color schemes, they have hardwood oak floors topped with hand-woven Irish rugs, French Bussac fabric curtains (a charming fruit-and-flower print), and white enamel and brass beds (all king- or queen-size) with ruffled white eyelet cotton spreads and pillow shams. Victorian-reproduction furnishings include massive oak armoires that conceal your cable color TV and contain desks topped with black leather embossed folders and gray felt blotters. Fans are suspended from the 14-foot ceilings. Even the bathrooms are stunningly appointed with black travertine marble vanities, hand-painted Italian tile walls, thick white Fieldcrest towels hung on heated racks, and big baskets of Crabtree & Evelyn toiletries. Tremont House cossets guests with remote control for your TV, a bedside switch that operates room lights, AM/FM radio, Artesia water in rooms, nightly turndown with gourmet chocolates, a concierge on hand around the clock to do your bidding, 24-hour room service, and complimentary overnight shoeshine.

Rates for one person are $70 to $110 January through the end of March, $100 to $150 April 1 through mid-September, $90 to $120 the rest of the year. An additional person pays $10, and children under 12 stay free. Both valet and self-parking are free. Special facilities for the disabled are also available.

The **Virginia Point Inn**, 2327 Avenue K, Galveston, TX 77550 (tel. 409/763-2450), is the flawlessly run and extraordinarily charming B&B operation of Tom and Eleanor Catlow. They called it Virginia Point because that was where Tom's great-grandfather, Texas Sen. Robert S. Guy, was stationed during the Civil War, and from whence he wrote a letter home extolling the beauty of near-by Galveston. The letter is on display in the parlor, and many of the 19th-century senator's furnishings and objets d'art grace the inn.

The house itself, a 1907 neo-Mediterranean mansion, is surrounded by spacious gardens landscaped with fruit trees, live oaks, palms, roses, and a stretch of verdant lawn, the latter ideal for badminton and croquet. The very hospitable Catlows offer a great deal to their guests. Their bedrooms and public areas are impeccably tasteful, and they serve a hearty breakfast each morning, including cold ham, cheeses, fresh fruit salad, fresh-squeezed juice, dry cereals, hot-from-the-oven croissants or muffins, and coffee. Every afternoon a cheese tray is set out with wine, tea, fruit, and biscuits. And there's always a crystal decanter of sherry on the dining room table. They also keep a small microwave oven and refrigerator for guest use, offer gratis bicycles, and provide fresh flowers, baskets of soap and potpourri, and bathrobes in every room.

Floors throughout the house are edge-grained pine, which the Catlows have stripped and refinished and keep waxed to a high polish. In the cozy parlor, where these floors are adorned with a Persian rug, there's a burgundy velvet Empire sofa before the working fireplace, and bookcases are stocked with reading materials. An English grandfather's clock chimes the hours, one of 12 antique clocks to do so on the premises. There are always large and lovely floral arrangements gracing the parlor and other rooms. Evenings, guests sometimes gather around the piano in the music room. And the dining room, its lace-curtained windows embellished with floral chintz cornices, centers on a large English mahogany table set with silver serving trays and Royal Worcester china. Breakfast and afternoon tea can be enjoyed here or al fresco on an adjoining porch.

The five bedrooms are delightfully furnished in quality antiques, not the usual B&B flea-markety finds. Yours might have a hand-turned walnut spool bed with an early American patchwork quilt, a creamy white porcelain pitcher atop a Victorian dresser, an Oriental rug, Queen Anne desk, big humpback trunk, or copper plate and bronze wood-bladed Emerson fan. Most rooms share baths, and all but one have screened-in porches with hanging plants and wicker rocking chairs. They're painted in pretty colors—pale blue, buff, apricot, or pastel yellow—with neat white window trim and moldings, and the walls are hung with framed Audubon prints, antique English hunting prints, and the like. All accommodations contain large closets and full-length beveled mirrors, and the master bedroom offers a working fireplace and private bath.

Parking is free. The house is air-conditioned and heated. Rates are $85 single, $95 to $135 for doubles and twins. Virginia Point Inn is a treasure.

The **Matalí,** 1727 Sealy, at 18th Street, Galveston, TX 77550 (tel. 409/763-4526), was built in 1886 by Isabel Offenbach, the composer's sister who was married to a Galveston ship's chandler. Amadeo Matalí, a later owner for whom the house is named, was an Italian tile maker and cement layer who built many of Galveston's sidewalks. He lived here from 1928 to 1981, after which Dan Dyer, Matalí's charming host, bought the Victorian mansion and turned it into a successful B&B accommodation. He's furnished it in cozy / cluttery period style, purchasing Oriental rugs for the Texas pine floors and turn-of-the-century antiques. The parlor is a comfortable sitting room with a velvet-upholstered loveseat facing a cherrywood fireplace, potted palms, and cabinets filled with objets d'art. The sofa in front of the game and music room fireplace, from a Louisiana plantation, is upholstered in striped satin burgundy grosgrain fabric and flanked by Victorian plantstands from a French Quarter home. There's an oak game table (games are provided), and guests can also play the piano or listen to Dan's sizable collection of 78s on the 1917 Victrola (it works perfectly!) Another fireplace warms the dining room, its table set with fine china and Waterford crystal. Twelve-foot ceilings add grandeur to all Matalí rooms, and cypress and pine woodwork enhance the decor throughout. Each of the three bedrooms has a private balcony, and as there are two baths, one resident gets private facilities and the other two share. You'll find magazines and brochures about local attractions, AM/FM clock radios, bowls of potpourri, fresh flowers, and Crabtree & Evelyn soaps in all the rooms. They're named for previous owners. The Fisher Room has striped floral wallpaper, a cherrywood bed, upholstered wicker armchairs, lavender wall-to-wall carpeting, and a ficus tree in a large basket. The lovely Offenbach Room, painted pale apricot, has a rose carpet on a stenciled floor; it's furnished with white wicker pieces and a large marquetry-adorned armoire with beveled oval mirror. And the Maas Room, also featuring a dusty-rose / apricot color scheme, has a beautifully tiled walnut fireplace and a walk-through bay window leading to a plant-filled balcony with a hammock. Evenings, it's lovely to sit out on the front porch or on the bench in the front yard which is shaded by elm and magnolia trees.

Rates include a big breakfast of fruit, quiche, fresh-baked muffins, fresh-squeezed orange juice, and coffee, plus an evening cheese tray. September through March, one or two people pay $75, $95 the rest of the year, with reduced rates for longer stays.

The **J. F. Smith Inn,** 2217 Broadway, Galveston, TX 77550 (tel. 409/765-5121), built in 1885 by a prosperous hardware merchant, is another of Galveston's converted Victorian mansions. It's owned by a group of investors, but hostess Donna Harbaugh is always on the premises providing warm, personal care and southern hospitality. The entrance hall has its original stained-glass panels and Venetian-glass chandelier, and all of the windows in the house—some with antique-glass panes—retain their original shutters. Also intact are numerous old cherrywood fireplaces, gold-leaf moldings, and the beautiful Eastlake-design walnut and mahogany staircase and banister with its ornate Grecian-style newel post lamp. Public areas are delicately scented with incense. Walk-through windows lead to a lovely wooden porch overlooking a flower garden shaded by a magnolia tree and lit by a gaslight streetlamp at night. There's also a flower-bordered brick courtyard with garden furnishings under a cherry laurel, pecan trees, and Texas palms.

In the Victorian double parlor, with two working fireplaces, the original gaslight chandeliers are suspended from an exquisite 14-foot white pressed-tin ceiling (it looks like ornate plasterwork). Cream-colored walls are hung with gilt-framed 19th-century oil paintings, dark varnished Texas pine floors are enhanced by a Chinese rug, and Chinese pottery is displayed on various tables. The massive mahogany dining room table is under another stunning Venetian-glass chandelier with ornate carved medallion.

All six guest rooms are equipped with private bath, AM/FM radio, and direct-dial phone (local calls are free). They're charmingly furnished in antiques, but, as all the pieces are for sale, decor changes from time to time. You might draw a canopied half-tester bed or a four-poster with eyelet spread and ruffled pillow shams, a satin armchair with tufted hassock, an art nouveau chandelier, or a turn-of-the-century marble-topped walnut sideboard. One accommodation has its own front porch. Guests are cosseted with terry robes, fresh flowers, books and magazines in the bedrooms; Crabtree & Evelyn soaps in the bath; and nightly turndown with a chocolate on the pillow. Sherry, tea, coffee, and homemade cake are available in the dining room throughout the day, and the continental breakfast served here includes fresh fruit, fresh-squeezed orange juice, homemade breads and cakes, and coffee. Full American breakfast is also an option, and wine and cheese is served every evening. The house is air-conditioned and heated. There's an ice machine for guest use, and off-street parking is free.

Rates are $85 to $100, single or double. No children under 12 accepted.

**ON THE WATERFRONT:** The most lavish of the beachfront hotels is the 15-story **San Luis,** 5222 Seawall Blvd., Galveston, TX 77550 (tel. 409/765-8888, or toll free in Texas only 800/392-5937), an elegant resort property fronted by an imposing entranceway lined with palms and tropical plantings. High above the Seawall, it commands a superb view of the gulf. Like many an exciting Galveston development, the San Luis is a creation of George and Cynthia Mitchell, who opened their new hotel in 1984 with a bang—a fabulous fireworks display hosted by celebrity-of-all-trades George Plimpton. The relaxed resort atmosphere that characterizes every facet of the San Luis is experienced as soon as you step into the spacious marble-floored lobby, furnished with oversize cushioned wicker chairs and art deco sofas. At the registration desk the hotel's mascot, a talkative macaw named Phidias (George Mitchell's middle name) welcomes guests with a raucous "Hello!" or "Shut up!" It depends on his mood. In front of the hotel, screened by lush greenery, is a stunning and sizable free-form heated swimming pool surrounded by tropical gardens, swaying palms, a cascading waterfall, and rockscapes. It features a Caribbean-style swim-up bar and a thatched-hut concession serving food and exotic drinks. From the vast sundeck area guests can while away a lazy hour watching the surf roll in on the beach across the street. Or walk down to that beach where umbrellas, chaise lounges, cabañas, and paddle trikes can be rented. Guests also have gratis use of six tennis courts across the street and of the facilities of the Galveston Country Club (a ten-minute drive from the hotel), including an 18-hole golf course, pro shop, four tennis courts, and an Olympic-size pool.

The 244 balconied rooms all offer panoramic water vistas and front doors opening to al fresco corridors overlooking the city and Houston beyond. They're attractively decorated in South Seas shades of blue and green, furnished with handsome oak pieces and fitted out with all the modern amenities including color TVs with a wide choice of cable stations. Closets have full-length mirror doors, and bath amenities include a basket of Crabtree & Evelyn toiletries.

The Spoonbill Restaurant, serving all meals, overlooks palms and hibiscus through a wall of floor-to-ceiling windows. It's furnished with bamboo chairs and plushly upholstered floral-motif booths amid a garden of indoor plants. Lavish buffets are served at Sunday brunch off-season, and during the summer smaller buffets are offered at breakfast. A la carte menus feature selections for both snacking and serious dining; at dinner you might order a full meal of pan-fried redfish in lemon butter with vegetables and potatoes du jour ($11.95) or a triple-decker deli sandwich with potato salad and coleslaw ($6). The adjoining Waterspout Lounge, sporting the same view and a similar decor, offers live music for dancing nightly except Monday (seven nights in summer) and complimentary hors d'oeuvres during Happy Hour. And for continental dining in an intimate setting there's Maximilian's, named for the Habsburg prince who ruled Mexico in the 1860s under Napoléon III; when French rule collapsed, his wife, Carlotta, fled to Galveston en route to France. You can read the rest of the story on the menu. Maximilian's is richly decorated in shades of tan and moss green, with lotus-motif etched-glass panels and room dividers. Candles in crystal holders and shell-shaped wall lamps cast a soft, romantic glow over the room. Open for dinner nightly, Maximilian's features continental haute cuisine. Scrumptious appetizers include a terrine of duck with sauce tangerine ($5.25) and oysters wrapped in bacon, delicately battered, and deep-fried ($6.50). For the main course, you might select roast breast of chicken with figs and herbs in wild plum sauce ($14.95) or veal chops with cream and chives ($16). And the dessert cart offers sumptuous treats like the pecan jewel—a graham-cracker-crust pastry topped with coconut, rich dark chocolate, and pecans, the entirety dipped in white chocolate ($3.25).

Both self- and valet parking are free. Rates are seasonal: from mid-November through mid-March singles pay $79 to $115; mid-March through mid-May and early September through mid November, $84 to $132; and mid-May through early September, $92 to $156. An extra person pays $10; children under 14 stay free, and, subject to availability, special reduced rates are offered Sunday to Thursday. The upper range of the above-quoted rates are for higher floors and corner rooms with two-sided views and oversize oval tubs in the bath. Facilities for the disabled are available.

*Note:* The San Luis also has luxurious condominiums available for longer stays; call 409/740-0219 for details.

Originally dubbed "the Queen of the Gulf," the gleaming-white **Hotel Galvez,** at 21st Street and Seawall Boulevard, Galveston, TX 77550 (tel. 409/765-7721, or toll free 800/228-9290), established in 1911, was reopened as a Marriott property to elaborate fanfare in 1980. A cannon boomed, thousands of colorful balloons were released into the air, and marchers attired as 18th-century Spanish grenadiers paraded to the chime of bells signaling the rebirth of a grande dame. The premier hotel of Galveston's heyday, the Galvez hosted dozens of notables from Franklin D. Roosevelt to Frank Sinatra. Bandleader Phil Harris married pinup girl Alice Faye in a seventh-floor suite, and in the hotel's lavish ballroom countless debs made their entry into Galveston society. Marriott's $13-million renovation involved a study of the original architect's plans to accurately re-create public areas, while upper floors were gutted to construct the kind of modern rooms today's traveler expects.

Entered via a grand porte cochère on Bernardo de Galvez Avenue, the stunning lobby has been totally restored to reveal its dark oak-beamed ceiling and ornate column capitals. The floor has been redone in terrazzo covered by patterned Axminster carpets, a reproduction of the original front desk has been installed, exquisite chandeliers have been repaired and rehung, and an imposing portrait of Count Bernardo de Galvez once again graces a lobby wall. Outside, the stucco finish of the Spanish-style architecture has been repainted, terracotta roof tiles have been repaired, and the palm-fringed grounds have been relandscaped to resemble an English garden. The arcaded Promenade, with its large arched windows overlooking the gulf, has resumed its Victorian loggia appearance with cushioned antique wicker sofas and armchairs amid potted palms and slowly whirring fans overhead. Its walls are decorated with Galvez family crests.

In the central area of the lobby set off by café-curtained partitions, is the Spanish Renaissance–style Galvez Dining Room, once again painted the cream and gold of yesteryear, its intricate moldings and gilt-topped columns restored, and its brass candelabra chandeliers suspended on heavy chains from lofty coffered ceilings. It's open for breakfast, lunch, and dinner, the latter meal featuring entrees ranging from grilled shrimp, glazed with a thick barbecue sauce over Créole rice ($12.50) to blackened redfish ($13.50); fresh seafood, Cajun style, is a specialty. For dessert there's fresh-baked peach cobbler topped with real whipped cream and/or Häagen-Dazs ice cream. At Sunday's spectacular champagne brunch ($15.95), a pianist entertains. The Galvez Lounge, centered around a rectangular bar with stained-glass panels, has exquisite high ceilings, arched multipaned doorways, antique fans with art nouveau fixtures, and matching wall sconces. High-energy bands play top-40s tunes here for dancing nightly except Sunday until 2 a.m.; it's a very popular spot. You can get away from the music and enjoy a quiet drink and conversation in the adjoining Peacock Alley, its decor much like the above-described Promenade. Also adjoining is the delightful plant-filled bamboo- and wicker-furnished Veranda, where you can watch the sun go down over the gulf while enjoying late-afternoon cocktails.

The 228 rooms, all offering gulf or city views, have grasspaper-covered walls hung with sepia photographs of Galveston in the 1930s. Most are cheerfully decorated in art deco colors—dusty rose, sand, and turquoise. Parlor rooms have king-size Murphy beds and sofas so they can double as hospitality suites. All rooms are equipped with cable color TV offering a choice of Spectravision and HBO movies and alarm clock radios.

There's no charge for self-parking. Rates are seasonal: $64 to $104, single or double, May 1 to September 3; $55 to $75 the rest of the year. An extra person pays $10; children under 18 stay free. Higher-rated rooms are for gulf views, and facilities for the disabled are available. The Galvez offers many terrific midweek packages (subject to availability), and also sponsors mystery weekends (guests become detectives and solve a staged crime), Mardi Gras weekends, Dickens weekends, and more; inquire when you reserve.

For budget travelers, there's a very well-located **Econo Lodge,** 2825 Butterowe (61st Street), Galveston, TX 77551 (tel. 409/763-6262, or toll free 800/446-6900), just a block from the beach and a pier purveying the "three Bs" necessary to fishing—bait, bucket, and beer. A large shopping center also adjoins. The Econo offers clean and well-equipped motel rooms, each with two doubles or one queen-size bed, a tub / shower bath, a direct-dial phone, oak furnishings, and color TV. They're carpeted in brown, tan grasspaper wall coverings are adorned with photographs of the Galveston beach, and bedspreads and curtains are floral prints. There's a small pool and sundeck, and complimentary coffee is served in the lobby throughout the day.

Rates are $34.95 for one person (one bed), $39.95 for two people (one bed), $44.95 for two people (two beds), $5 for an extra person, no charge for children under 12. Off-season and midweek rates are often reduced if the hotel is not fully booked.

## 3. Restaurants

When you're surrounded by water, you can't go wrong ordering seafood. Most restaurants here specialize in it, but you'll also find a few excellent Mexican eateries and a bit of continental and Cajun flair. In addition to the listings below, keep the hotel dining rooms in mind, most notably the Merchant Prince at Tremont House, Maximilian's at the San Luis, and the Galvez dining room, all detailed elsewhere in this chapter.

George and Cynthia Mitchell have restored the 1871 League Building to create a stunning restaurant named for a rare Texas spiral seashell. The **Wentletrap,** 2301 The Strand, at Tremont (tel. 765-5545), designed in Renaissance revival style, is a massive three-story brick building with a cast-iron façade and New Orleans cornice. It's entered via an exquisite three-story atrium lounge under a lofty skylight. On the star-patterned black-and-white tile floor, wicker sofas and bentwood chairs are set amid potted palms, and an imposing turn-of-the-century carved oak bar occupies the far wall. In the restaurant itself—separated by exposed brick archways from the lounge area—trellised planters of greenery and beautifully appointed flower-bedecked tables create an elegant garden ambience. During the day, light filters in through a wall of windows draped in sheer white linen; at night candles glow in crystal holders.

Continental haute cuisine is featured. At dinner start out with crabmeat bisque liberally laced with sherry ($4.75) and so ambrosial one would like to order it by the tureenful. Other good appetizer choices are oysters Rockefeller (broiled with parmesan, spinach, and hollandaise topping) and oysters diablo (broiled in a pungent garlicky tomato sauce with fresh chopped herbs and topped with bubbling mozzarella), $6.50 each. Specialties among the entrees include red snapper piled high with fresh sautéed mushrooms meunière ($15); lump crabmeat (in season) sautéed in butter, garlic, cayenne pepper, and lemon, quickly flamed in cognac, and served with asparagus tips ($16.95); egg-coated veal sautéed with lemon, capers, and artichoke hearts ($15); and roast sliced capon topped with cherries flamed in brandy ($15.50). There are fresh-baked desserts like lemon / orange torte with fresh whipped cream ($3.95), and an extensive wine list highlights French and California selections. Luncheon fare offers a choice of lighter entrees—avocado stuffed with crabmeat ($10.50) and a classic quiche Lorraine ($7.50)—along with heartier dishes, most of them priced in the $8 to $11 range. And a special Sunday brunch menu includes an appetizer (perhaps chilled strawberry cream soup) and dessert (cherries Jubilee or chocolate mousse) with the price of entrees like eggs Hussarde—poached eggs on grilled Canadian bacon and crisp bread in wine sauce and hollandaise ($10.50). Every other Sunday a jazz trio plays New Orleans Dixieland music at brunch.

The Wentletrap is open Monday to Saturday from 11:30 a.m. to 2:30 p.m. and 6 to 10 p.m. (to 11 p.m. in summer), on Sunday from noon to 3 p.m. There's free parking across the street at lunch and valet parking at night. Reservations suggested on weekends. Jackets required for men evenings; at lunch you can wear anything but your bathing suit.

The Hill family has been running seafood restaurants in Galveston since the early 1940s, almost as long as they've been in the fish business. **Hill's Pier 19,** at 20th and Wharf (tel. 763-7087), is right on the waterfront overlooking the shrimp fleet and fishing boats—one of the most picturesque settings in Galveston. The place abounds in rustic charm. Downstairs, the tables are set amid chianti-bottle-festooned, weathered pier posts driven into pilings below; the restaurant is actually right over the water. But the best views of port activity are from the upstairs knotty-pine-paneled dining room and the two-level outdoor deck with barrel-pedestaled tables. Any window seat provides great waterfront views of fishing boats and scavenging shore birds (pelicans, herons, and seagulls); from the higher levels you can also see the *Elissa* and cargo ships.

All the fish and seafood served here is fresh, much of it bought right off the boats docked outside. Service is cafeteria style. All dinners include fries, coleslaw, bread, and homemade red and tartar sauces. A platter of deep-fried jumbo gulf shrimp, Galveston Bay oysters, or scallops is $9.25; softshell crabs are $10.25; shrimp stuffed with blue-shell crabmeat dressing, $12.50. For a less expensive meal you might order a bowl of shrimp gumbo ($3.25) and an oyster or shrimp poorboy sandwich ($3). There are also low-priced listings for children, and homemade desserts like carrot cake ($1.25). Beer and wine are available. Don't miss Hill's; it's part of the Galveston experience.

The restaurant is open daily from 10:30 a.m. to 8 p.m., till 9 p.m. in summer. In season, particularly, it's mobbed at mealtimes, and any time of year you'll enjoy the best views if you come at off-hours. If there's no room in front of the restaurant, you can park free in the lot on 20th Street, off the Strand.

Founded in 1911 by Italian immigrant S. J. Gaido, and still an all-in-the-family operation, **Gaido's,** 39th Street and Seawall (tel. 762-0115), is Galveston's most renowned seafood restaurant. Nothing frozen or processed is served here. Gaido's is still shucking oysters, peeling shrimp, and fileting fresh fish the way they've been doing it for 75 years, and all sauces and salad dressings are prepared from old family recipes. It's a classic American seafood restaurant, with rough-hewn beams and wooden columns, a wall of windows overlooking the gulf, ship lanterns and fans overhead, and large white-linen-clothed tables. At night, especially in season, people often wait an hour or more for one of those tables, sustained in the bar by a continuing parade of cocktail waitresses bearing plates of complimentary fried fish, crab balls, cold shrimp, and other hors d'oeuvres. Or if you're afraid of ruining your appetite (I never am), you might browse in the adjoining gift shop or peruse display cases of Mrs. Gaido's collection of crystal.

Portions at Gaido's—served up by old retainer–type waiters, many of whom have been with the restaurant for decades—are extremely hefty and include a choice of vegetables or baked potato (topped with butter, melted cheddar, and a big dollop of sour cream) and hot, fresh-baked rolls with butter and apple jelly. The best deals are full dinners, the most complete of which includes, for $5.95 plus entree price, a salad, appetizer (perhaps a crabmeat or shrimp cocktail in rémoulade sauce), vegetable, beverage, and dessert (like chocolate brownie cake). For an entree, you might select a close-to-foot-long brochette of plump shrimp and scallops interspersed with crispy bacon ($12.25), a platter of 17 juicy oysters prepared five different ways ($16.25), or (in season) deep-fried softshell crabs ($15.25). Of course, you can also order à la carte. Special low-priced dinners are offered for children under 12 ($6) and senior citizens ($12 for the equivalent of the above-described dinners). And a wide selection of wines, many of them available by the glass, is also available, along with imported and draft beers and all bar drinks.

From September through the end of February Gaido's is open Tuesday to Thursday from 11:30 a.m. to 2 p.m. and 5 to 9 p.m., on Friday and Saturday from noon to 10 p.m., and on Sunday from noon to 9 p.m. The rest of the year hours are 11:30 a.m. to 10 p.m. daily. No reservations.

One of the most delightful restaurants in Galveston, conveniently located right on the Strand (at no. 2021), is Larry and Carolyn McDowell's **Le Paysan** (tel. 765-7792). Housed in an 1894 building (a one-time ship's chandlery) it has a wall of high arched windows overlooking the action on the street. Wood-bladed fans are suspended from a high beamed ceiling, walls are painted a delicate gray, and tables are covered with pretty floral-print cotton topped with burgundy linen runners and adorned with small bouquets of fresh flowers. Potted azaleas and other plants, plus the fact that the McDowell's play only classical music and light jazz, further enhance the ambience. At night tables are more elegantly appointed and lit by candles in brandy snifters.

The first thing you'll notice upon entering is the large bakery / pastry counter up front filled with toothsome treats. These fresh-baked offerings make Le Paysan a great choice for croissant and café au lait breakfasts or leisurely afternoon teas. The menu features French country fare—everything homemade and fresh, with many entrees utilizing locally caught fish and seafood. At lunch you might order a crock of traditional onion soup topped with a chewy sufficiency of melted Gruyère ($3.25) and a cheeseburger pommes frites ($5.75) or buttered croissant sandwich stuffed with sliced turkey breast and topped with a white wine/Gruyère sauce ($5.50). Save room for Le Paysan's creamy cheesecake ($2.75). At dinner a recommendable beginning is an order of escargots in puff pastry topped with a buttery / garlicky crème fraîche, perhaps followed by an entree of breast of duck rôti with lingonberry purée and Chambord liqueur served with a bouquetière of vegetables and wild rice ($14.95). All dinner entrees include fresh-baked bread and butter and a house salad with Dijon vinaigrette dressing; a homemade sorbet is served between salad and entree. In addition to dessert cart offerings there are specialties like soufflé Grand Marnier ($4) and Paysan flambé—a chocolate *sac* filled with fresh berries, smothered in vanilla sauce, and flamed to melting in Grand Marnier and brandy ($20 for four). A carefully chosen and reasonably priced wine list features French and California vintages, all of them available by the glass. Finally, Le Paysan has a special Sunday brunch menu listing items like eggs Benedict ($6) and shrimp in white wine sauce en croûte ($7.75), along with selections from a waffle bar with toppings like fresh berries, chocolate sauce, pecans, fresh whipped cream, honey, and maple syrup ($6.50).

Le Paysan is open weekdays from 7:30 a.m. to 10 p.m., on Saturday from 8:30 a.m. to 10 p.m., and on Sunday from 10 a.m. (brunch served 11 a.m. to 3 p.m.) to 10 p.m. Closed Monday during winter. Reservations suggested at dinner.

A cheerful restaurant that serves up excellent home-style Mexican fare is

**Poco Loco,** 5302 Broadway (tel. 744-8828). Owners Joe and Crystal Gandara claim they opened the place because they got tired of driving up to Houston every time they wanted Mexican food. They decorated their establishment in festive Mexican flag colors: grass-green floors and window trim, white stucco walls (hung with Mexican rugs), and red oilcloth-covered tables adorned with fresh flowers. Light streams in through large windows; there are *Casablanca* fan chandeliers overhead; and wicker-seated wooden chairs, painted with colorful flowers, further enliven the setting, a large converted Coca-Cola plant.

Everything here is fresh and homemade—even the tortilla chips and tangy/tomatoey salsa—and purposely nongreasy. High-quality beef and Joe's secret marinade make Poco Loco's fajitas ($8.25)—served with grilled onions, Spanish rice, deliciously spiced frijoles a la charra, and hand-rolled flour tortillas—some of the best anywhere. A similar dish, served with more or less the same accompaniments is tacos al carbón, the steak already rolled in tortillas and topped with aged cheddar cheese sauce ($7). Also excellent are pechugas de pollo, tender deboned chicken breasts gently sautéed in a savory sauce of wine and garlic butter and garnished with fresh bell pepper, tomatoes, and grilled onions ($7.25, same accompaniments). If you want to try several dishes, there's a goodly choice of combination platters. And for dessert the very good flan ($2.95) is light and satisfying, but you can also opt for a more substantial sopapilla, a cinnamon-powdered pastry puff, topped with ice cream for $1.95. During the week there are luncheon specials priced under $5.

Poco Loco's margaritas are powerful, and the best way to enjoy them is in the bar where sporting events are aired on a 45-inch TV; order up a dish of guacamole ($4.25; it's first-rate) and chips, a platter of nachos topped with ground round, refried beans, aged cheddar, guacamole, and jalapeños ($5.25), and/or a spicy queso con chorizo (baked cheese topped with sausage; $5.25), and you're set for the afternoon. Poco Loco also serves great Mexican breakfasts, like huevos sincronisado—eggs over easy with bits of fajitas, chicken, and salsa, smothered in melted cheese and served between two corn tortillas with refried beans and pico de gallo ($4.75). Joe claims it will cure a hangover. There's a Happy Hour buffet with complimentary hors d'oeuvres from 4 to 7 p.m. Monday to Thursday, and on Friday and Saturday nights live bands play Mexican music and bossa nova. Future plans call for an upstairs jazz club.

Poco Loco is open Monday to Thursday from 7 a.m. to 10 p.m., on Friday to 11 p.m., on Saturday from 9 a.m. to 11 p.m., and on Sunday from 9 a.m. to 9 p.m.

A recent development on the local culinary scene was the opening of a branch of Houston's **Primo's,** 7711 Broadway (take the 71st Street exit off I-45; tel. 744-1617). Like its Houston counterpart, this Primo's has a playa resort decor. It's painted in shades of shell pink, aqua, and turquoise, festooned with colorful paper decorations, and enhanced by many green plants. There are fans overhead, and tables are covered in variously patterned oilcloths. Mariachi bands entertain on weekends. Especially nice is the glassed-in patio area where tables are candlelit.

The menu features the mixed grill that is so popular at the original restaurant: char-broiled fajitas and chicken breast served with rice, beans à la charra, guacamole, pico de gallo, and broiled peppers and onions ($11.50). Other specialties are char-broiled shrimp with more or less the same accompaniments ($11.95) and red snapper filet sautéed in butter, garlic, and lemon juice, served with Mexican rice and refried beans ($8.25). A large order of nachos topped with cheese, fajitas, and guacamole is $7.95; there are also many combination platters in the $6 to $8 range. Try the praline cheesecake for dessert ($3.25).

Primo's is open Monday to Thursday from 11 a.m. to 10 p.m., on Friday and Saturday to 11 p.m., and on Sunday from noon to 9 p.m.

The **Little Shrimpboat Restaurant,** 2227 Seawall Blvd. (tel. 762-8590), is named for the owner of the land, not its size. In fact it's fairly large, and it has one of the best locations on the island—right over the water. In winter it's a popular local hangout, and in summer, when diners can sit out on the wooden deck and watch the sailboats, cavorting dolphins, and scavenging seagulls in the gulf, it's mobbed with tourists. I love it anytime of year; it's one of the coziest and friendliest places in town.

Inside, the cedar-paneled walls are hung with photos of Galveston in the 1920s, large pieces of coral are displayed on shelves, and there are aquariums and many hanging plants. Seating is in Mediterranean-blue deck chairs, all tables have water views, and there's always good country music playing. In summer there's live jazz or C&W out on the deck, and if you happen to hit the right day you might even hear Willie Nelson do a tune or two (he's a friend of the owner's). My favorite meal here is the fried crabcake platter ($7.50), which like all dinner entrees comes with a salad and baked potato topped with chives, cheddar, and sour cream. Other dinner choices are a fried oyster platter ($7.50), fried shrimp and oysters ($9), chicken-fried steak ($5.50), and a 16-ounce T-bone steak ($10.50). You can also order a shrimp or oyster poorboy ($4), a roast beef sandwich ($4.25), or a platter of nachos ($2.50). The key lime pie ($1.50) is a satisfying dessert choice. Wine and beer are available.

Hours are 11 a.m. to 10 p.m. daily, later (often till 2:30 a.m.) in summer. While you're in the neighborhood, you can check out two adjoining souvenir shops that are fun to explore.

"Everyone from the mayor of Galveston to Joe the garbageman eats here," says Camella Chessir, who, with her husband, Sam, owns **The Warehouse,** a cozy barbecue joint at 101 14th St., at the corner of Water Street (tel. 765-9995). And why not? The Chessirs' open-pit specialties, prepared over an oak and pecan wood fire, are smokily and succulently delicious. My recommendations are the barbecued smoked sausage plate or the smoked chicken, either priced at $5.95 and served with homemade potato salad or coleslaw, baked beans, and a big slab of buttered homemade bread. You can also order hefty sandwiches on homemade bread, like smoked sausage, chili, and cheese ($4.50), sliced barbecued beef ($3.60), or a one-pound cheeseburger ($5.25). Most barbecue places offer scanty pickings in the way of dessert, but Camella comes through with a marvelous fresh-baked hot peach cobbler ($1.50) that shouldn't be ignored. The Warehouse is unpretentious in decor: Formica tables, linoleum floors, orange vinyl chairs, Tudor-beamed stucco and dark wood-paneled walls hung with mirrored and neon beer signs, and poolhall-type beer-logo chandeliers overhead. The jukebox is always on, and the ambience is definitely simpático.

Open Monday to Saturday from 10 a.m. to 8 p.m., on Sunday (summer only) from 11 a.m. to 6 p.m.

**Sonny's,** 19th Street and Avenue L (tel. 763-9602), is a funky local hangout, totally off the usual tourist-beaten track. Authenticity and some great menu items are its lures. Lawrence Puccetti opened Sonny's (named for one of his sons) in 1944, and the restaurant is now run by his other son, Larry, and Larry's son, also Larry. The "decor" consists of imitation wood-paneled walls hung with photos of old Galveston, red linoleum carpeting, and red leather booths and chairs at Formica tables. A 22-foot shuffleboard table takes up about a quarter of the restaurant, and a bit more space is used for video games and pinball machines. The TV over the bar is always on, especially if sporting events are being aired, and the jukebox is usually going as well. Sonny's was held up in 1971, and a plaque over a bullet hole on the bar counter commemorates "the now famous gunfight between Jr. Puccetti and three armed robbers . . . evidence of the brutal confrontation." It all sounds pretty wild and noisy, but Sonny's is usually pretty low key. Medical students, bankers, DAs from the nearby county courthouse, and local families are all regular patrons.

Come by for lunch or dinner on Friday; that's the day Larry cooks up his delicious and hearty shrimp gumbo ($3.75 for a good-size bowl, $4.25 for a larger one). Other times, opt for one of Larry's terrific barbecued beef sandwiches ($2.50, $2.75 with cheese), a large bowl of chili ($3), an all-beef burger ($1.80), half a dozen fresh oysters ($3), or a fried shrimp sandwich that's not listed but is available ($4). Wine and beer are available, but Sonny's, uniquely in my experience, does not serve coffee.

Open Monday to Wednesday from 11 a.m. to midnight, on Thursday and Friday to 2 a.m.

## 4. Sights and Other Attractions

You'll be amazed how much there is to see and do on this tiny island. In summer especially, you could easily spend a couple of weeks getting acquainted with Galveston's rich history and architectural treasures and enjoying her numerous recreational facilities. I'll begin with the former.

**THE STRAND:** This quaint historic district extends from 20th to 25th Streets at the northern end of the island, a block north of Water Street. Close to the docks where merchandise was brought in from exotic ports, its ornate Victorian buildings housed 19th-century traders, merchants, bankers, and shippers who made their fortunes from waterfront-related activities. Galveston was "Queen City of the Gulf," and the Strand was known as the "Wall Street of the Southwest." Wholesalers headquartered here supplied goods of every description to neighboring states. Before the Civil War slave auctions were held on the sidewalks, and interspersed with stores selling everything from saddles to French perfumes there were quite a few fine saloons for gentlemen. The Strand was the scene of frequent parades and pageantry, including elaborate Mardi Gras celebrations and an annual Parade of the Butchers, featuring the local meat men dressed in grotesque costumes. There was also a daily parade of patent medicine vendors, mule-drawn carts loaded with bales of cotton, performers of every persuasion (one man made a good income eating glass), and tourists, including many famous visitors. Not all were enchanted; Union Gen. Phil Sheridan commented while visiting the city, "If I owned Texas and hell, I'd rent out Texas and live in hell." Years later he recanted the statement, but may have come to feel that way again when he was caught here during the 1900 hurricane. Even a foppishly dressed Oscar Wilde once visited the Strand to give a lecture on decorative art.

Today the Strand is once again a thriving commercial center, its 19th-century cast-iron commercial buildings beautifully restored and its sidewalks lit at night by gas streetlights. It is lined with browsable boutiques and simpático restaurants, souvenir shops and art galleries, including full mall-like buildings of them on the order of San Francisco's Ghirardelli Square, though less commercial in feel. The Railroad Museum is at the 25th Street end, and the square-rigged *Elissa* is berthed at Pier 22 close by. An audio cassette tour of the Strand can be rented at the Strand Visitors Center, 2016 The Strand (tel. 765-7834).

### Shopping the Strand

There are probably over 100 shops in this five-block stretch. Beginning at 25th Street and working your way down, some of the highlights include the following:

**Candles N' More,** 2410 The Strand, housed in a small warren of shops, sells a wide variety of scented and unscented hand-dipped candles in shapes ranging from unicorns to cowboy boots. The **Country Peddler,** at the corner of 24th Street and the Strand, carries handcrafted cottage industry items only—folk art cookie jars, hand-woven rugs from Appalachia, Christmas tree ornaments, and much, much more. Beautiful imported clothing for women from Greece, India, Peru, Guatemala, and other countries is featured at **Morgan's,** also at 24th and the Strand, along with great jewelry. Stop in for a hot-fudge sundae or some homemade fudge at **La King's Confectionary** (no. 2323), a delightful old-fashioned ice cream parlor that also houses a display of antique candy-making equipment; all ice cream and candy sold here is homemade. The delightful aroma at **Crabtree & Evelyn** (no. 2311) is a heady mix of potpourri, fine soaps, and other exquisite toiletries produced in the countryside of England. **Whampoa Import Merchant** (no. 2301) specializes in antiques and traditional crafts from China, Japan, Hong Kong, the Philippines, Indonesia, Thailand, and India.

Just south of the Strand at 213 Tremont, stop into **Breads, Spreads, and More** for glorious picnic baskets filled with pâtés, cheeses, French breads and croissants, dried fruits, and fresh-baked southern pecan pie.

The newest and most spectacular development on the Strand is **Old Galveston Square,** occupying an entire block between 22nd and 23rd Streets. It houses 32 shops and restaurants, plus a branch of a sophisticated Houston nightclub called Cody's (see Chapter II) in a converted Civil War–era building that was once a Wells Fargo office. A 14-ton sculpture from the New Orleans World's Fair called *The Jazz Trumpet* graces the atrium lobby, and there are Tiffany stained-glass windows in the building. This is the only Strand structure of sufficient magnitude to require escalators. Old Galveston Square opened with a gala sesquicentennial celebration in May 1986 hosted by Johnny Cash.

For certain, don't pass up **Col. Bubbie's,** 2202 The Strand, with an incredible assortment of authentic government surplus—over 10,000 items from over 100 countries including everything from hand grenades to French World War II helmets, from military boots to K-rations. Bubbie's is patronized by soldiers of fortune and has actually supplied emerging nations with military uniforms!

The **Shell Vendor** (no. 2114) is one of many shell shops in Galveston. It carries big decorator shells, shells culled from all over the world, shell lamps, and lovely shell jewelry. You can buy a gorgeous selection—a nice gift for a child—for just a few dollars.

The **Old Peanut Butter Warehouse,** 100 20th St., just north of the Strand, sells estate antiques, a vast selection of Depression glass, and American and European antique furniture. And since it's housed in a turn-of-the-century peanut butter factory, and the name of the establishment gets everyone's mouth watering, they also sell homemade peanut butter cookies, fresh-ground peanut butter, and other culinary concoctions. Background music is provided by a player piano.

**BISHOP'S PALACE:** The most magnificent of Galveston's historic preservations is the grandiose Bishop's Palace, 1402 Broadway (tel. 762-2475), designated one of the nation's 100 most outstanding buildings by the American Institute of Architects. Erected in the 1880s at a cost of $250,000, it was the home of Col. Walter Gresham, a wealthy Virginia planter and lawyer who fought in the Civil War. However, the family fortune was lost during the war, and Gresham moved to Texas in 1866 with $5 in his pocket. He soon opened a law practice in Galveston and went on to become involved in the railroad business and the cotton industry, and to assume political office. Obviously, he prospered, and in 1887 commissioned the state's most notable architect, Nicholas

Joseph Clayton, to design a mansion for him.

Six years in the building, and representing the epitome of late 19th-century taste and culture, the four-story home was a Renaissance revival structure, with an ornate exterior composed of native Texas limestone, red sandstone, and pink and blue granite. Gresham collected magnificent fireplaces, and planned rooms around them; there's even a false fireplace worked into the stairwell under the magnificent 55-foot central rotunda. Fronted by elaborate lacy wrought-iron verandas and porches atop cast-iron columns, the house has a high pitch roof covered with Belgian terracotta tile, its turrets topped with winged horses of Assyria. Both the horses and the gargoyles flanking the outside steps were hand-carved on the premises by master craftsmen. Intricate carving and detail also characterize the grand curved oak staircase to the second floor and woodwork throughout the house; some of the doors utilize different wood veneers (antique oak and burled walnut) to match room interiors on either side. Each room is finished with a different wood, though all the floors are inlaid oak, each square separately attached with wooden pegs.

Gresham and his family lived here until his death at age 79 in 1920. In 1923 the building was purchased by the Catholic Diocese of Galveston, hence the name Bishop's Palace. Bishop Christopher E. Byrne referred to his residence as "my palace in the sky." Though the building is now open to the public for tours, it is still the residence of the current bishop when he visits the city. One of the few Galveston homes to survive the 1900 storm, during which it sheltered hundreds of refugees, the Bishop's Palace is totally preserved in its original state. Many of the Greshams' furnishings and fixtures remain, including a 350-pound Baccarat crystal chandelier with 14-karat-gold plating and a fabulous oak sideboard in the formal dining room. Cherubs' faces on the dining room ceiling and atop second-floor column arches are said to be likenesses of the Greshams' sons. The chapel, created by Bishop Byrne, has elaborately hand-stenciled walls and stained-glass windows from Munich.

Conducted 45-minute tours are given Monday to Saturday from 10 a.m. to 5 p.m. and on Sunday from noon to 4 p.m. between Memorial Day and Labor Day (noon to 4 p.m. daily the rest of the year); closed Tuesday year round. Admission is $3 for adults, $1.50 for ages 12 to 18, 75¢ for children 12 and under.

**ASHTON VILLA:** The lifestyle of the urban elite during Galveston's Gilded Age is gloriously reflected in the opulent brick mansion of James Moreau Brown. An adventurous New Yorker, Brown went west to seek fame and fortune, settling in Galveston in 1843 where he formed a prosperous hardware business and went on to become a wealthy entrepreneur and civic leader. By 1859 his merchant prince status and growing family warranted the building of Ashton Villa, an imposing three-story residence on the corner of Broadway and 24th Street (tel. 762-3933). He named his new home for his wife's Revolutionary War forebear, Lt. Isaac Ashton, and designed it in the prevailing classical style, embellished with newly fashionable Italianate elements. His workforce consisted of his own slaves.

Distinguishing architectural features included long windows topped by cast-iron lintels and ornate verandas with Gothic revival detail. The main house connected to the kitchen and slave quarters via a breezeway, and a brick arcade led to the stable and carriage house. Brown installed the city's first indoor plumbing and gas lighting system, adding the novelty of electricity in the 1880s. A later addition was a massive vaulted family room. Brown's daughter, Rebecca Ashton Brown ("Miss Bettie"), who inherited the house, built a subsequent addition in 1898 for her divorced sister, Mathilda, and her three children. (Later occupants, the Shriners, demolished the slave quarters and kitchen outbuilding and constructed a large ballroom in the 1920s—but I'm getting ahead of the story.) Miss Bettie, a renowned belle and hostess, studied art in New York and Düsseldorf and traveled extensively. Her paintings can today be seen throughout the house, and off the formal reception area is a room containing some of her acquisitions from abroad—in her day a mini-Smithsonian collection of mummies' heads, turquoise from the Holy Land, baskets, etc. (she used to travel with 18 mahogany trunks).

Over the years much history took place here. After the Civil War the Emancipation Proclamation was read to Galvestonians from an Ashton Villa balcony, and some accounts claim that the city's treaty of surrender was drafted at a table in the house. And during the 1900 storm water rose to the top of the 11-foot doors. However, the house survived both war and flooding, if not in peak condition. In 1973 it was scheduled for demolition, but, fortunately, the Galveston Historical Foundation intervened. Detailed archeological studies and excavations have uncovered a vast store of information about the house, its occupants, and 19th-century lifestyle and customs. The house has been restored as far as possible to its late 1800s' appearance, and about a quarter of the original furnishings have been reinstalled. Photographs in every room show the house as it actually was.

On 30-minute tours conducted on a continuous basis from 10 a.m. to 4 p.m. weekdays, from noon to 5 p.m. weekends, visitors can see an audio-visual program on the hurricane that devastated Galveston in 1900. The tour includes the formal dining room, the formal parlor/music room (it's said that a piano floated out its window during the great storm and saved the life of a man, who used it as a raft), the formal reception room with its 22-karat gold-leaf medallion chandeliers, Miss Bettie's beautiful bedroom and adjoining sitting room, Mathilda's bedroom, and the master bedroom in which Mr. Brown died of cancer in 1895, leaving an estate of $4 million. There was a special staircase for children in order to keep carpets and art objects intact.

Tours cost $3 for adults, $2.50 for students ages 12 to 18 and seniors, $1.50 for children 6 to 12; under 6 and over 80, free.

**THE ELISSA:** Christened in 1877 in Aberdeen, Scotland, the *Elissa* (tel. 765-7834), an iron barque (a three-masted, square-rigged sailing vessel) with a towering 103-foot mast, is now restored to her former grandeur and moored at Pier 21 adjacent to the Strand, recalling the days when Galveston was a leading world port. In the late 19th century, 15 or 20 such ships would anchor in Galveston harbor on any given day, loading and unloading cargo and setting sail for foreign ports. The Galveston Historical Foundation found her headed for demolition in a Greek scrapyard in 1974, renewed portions of her hull, and towed her to America for total $4.2-million reconditioning to a museum ship that could sail on a limited basis. Rigging (26,000 feet of it) and ship's gear was re-created with the aid of photographs, blacksmiths made new fittings, carpenters laid new decks and repaired topside structures, and the hull was painted. By dedication day in July 1982 the *Elissa* was her old self again.

The *Elissa* was built to the order of Henry F. Watt, a Liverpool sea captain. Her first sail in December 1877 was to Brazil with a cargo of Welsh coal, and during a 90-year career in seaborne trade she traveled the east coast of South America and visited U.S. and Canadian ports, as well as India, Burma, Australia, and Chile. In 1897 Watt retired and sold her to a Norwegian owner, who for the next 14 years kept her in full rig and glory. But from then on, subsequent owners cut her down, installed an engine, removed her proud sails, and made progressive modifications. By 1969 she was renamed the *Achaeos* and reduced to smuggling bonded American cigarettes from Greece into Italy.

It was here that marine archeologist Peter Throckmorton found and purchased her for $11,000. He intended to sell the ship to San Francisco's Maritime Museum, but negotiations floundered, leaving him with an expensive white elephant on his hands. Galveston, a port the ship had visited twice in its heyday, then entered the picture, purchasing and restoring the ship as part of a growing effort toward preservation of buildings and other artifacts from the city's glorious past.

You can board the *Elissa* for a self-guided tour weekdays from 10 a.m. to 5 p.m., weekends to 8 p.m., with extended hours in summer. It costs $3.50 for adults, $3 for students and senior citizens, $2.50 for ages 6 to 12 (under 6, free), with a maximum family admission of $10. There are a lot of informative signs, and exhibits probe the *Elissa*'s life at sea and restoration. You can also see a 20-minute film on the restoration in the cargo hold or at the nearby Strand Visitors Center, 2016 The Strand. Near the ship are a nautical gift shop and a boat workshop, where, at this writing, dinghy lifeboats and a cutter are being made. The *Sea Child*, a playground boat that kids can climb around on and steer, is on the dock. If you can't find street parking, there's a garage at 25th and Water Streets where you can park for $2 all day.

**THE CENTER FOR TRANSPORTATION AND COMMERCE:** This fascinating five-acre museum of rail memorabilia at the Strand and 25th Street (tel. 765-5700) centers around Galveston's Victorian train depot, the Santa Fe Union Station building designed in 1897 by noted architect Nicholas J. Clayton. Galveston greeted her first train in 1861 and had her own railroad, the Gulf, Colorado, & Santa Fe, by 1873. Steam locomotives moved in and out of the Southwest's major port city carrying cargo and passengers to Texas and connecting with rail networks throughout the nation. The railroad flourished for close to a century in Galveston, but by the early 1970s the old station was scheduled for demolition. It was rescued by the Moody Foundation, restored to its original art deco splendor, and renamed Shearn Moody Plaza. The museum opened to the public in 1982.

The entry plaza, housing the ticket office/gift shop (the latter featuring many items of interest to both child and adult train buffs) also contains the 1929 Baldwin Prairie 2-6-2 steam locomotive on a simulated turntable, formerly Engine No. 1 of the Waco, Beaumont, Trinity & Sabine Railroad (called the Wobbly, Bobbly, Turnover, & Stop because it derailed so often). Four audio-visual presentations in the plaza area detail Galveston history from 1528 to the present. The elegant art deco waiting room of the depot is today populated by 39 cast-from-life plaster figures on whose programmed audio conversations visitors can eavesdrop. The depot is complete with pot-bellied stove, stationmaster's office, and telegraph operator. You can observe the indentations in the marble floor where, over the years, people waited on ticket lines. And in addition to conversational effects, train arrivals and departures are announced, and whistles and steam engines can be heard in the background. The Gallery of Commerce highlights the cargoes—coffee, tea, cotton, grain, etc.—that have been shipped through the Port of Galveston. Adjoining is a working HO-gauge model railroad traveling around the port, complete with miniature steamships, wharves, and warehouses.

Behind the depot, on four tracks, are 43 late 19th- and early 20th-century railroad cars open for exploration. Some of these are also peopled by plaster figures, such as a porter making up a berth and a child climbing into bed. Others contain collections of railroad memorabilia, and one operates as a theater showing railroad-theme movies. Among the cars on view are steam locomotive boxcars, baggage cars, a mail car, parlor and Pullman cars, a logging engine, and cabooses. The opulent 1929 *Anacapa,* described by the *New York Times* as "the most elegant private car on the rails today," carried its wealthy passengers in cosseted comfort. It was used through the 1950s for campaign excursions by Eisenhower and Stevenson. Visitors can sometimes board a 1922 steam locomotive, the ex-Magna Arizona Railroad Engine No. 555, for an "iron horse" excursion along the wharves (fare is a $1 supplement to museum admission; call for departure schedule). The 555 has appeared in many Hollywood and TV movies, and in a commercial testing whether American Tourister luggage could withstand being run over by a train. The Garden of Steam, an outdoor exhibit, details the development of steam-driven devices. Throughout the year there are frequent special events and exhibits (like antique, classic, and custom motorcycles). The museum provides more than a history of railroads; it's a very good orientation to all of Galveston's past.

Hours are 10 a.m. to 5 p.m. daily. Admission is $4 for adults, $3 for senior citizens, $2 for children under 12 (under 4, free), $10 maximum for families. Parking is free on the premises. Allow about 1 to 1½ hours for your tour.

**THE 1839 SAMUEL MAY WILLIAMS HOME:** One of the founding fathers of Galveston, and a relatively unknown father of the state, Samuel May Williams was a statesman, shipper, land speculator, banker, and early Texas entrepreneur. He arrived in Texas from Rhode Island via a circuitous route through Central America, with a Spanish mistress in tow, in 1822. Despite a dubious past involving the use of an alias to escape debtors, Williams soon resumed his rightful name, sent the mistress packing, and became assistant in colonial affairs to Stephen F. Austin. His pre-Texas life remains shrouded in mystery to this day. By 1831 he had amassed a fortune and acquired 48,000 acres of land in return for services to the Mexican government. Later, when Texas went to war for independence, Williams helped finance its army and navy; it is said he bore a tenth of the cost of the revolution against Santa Anna. Once independence was gained he spent much of his time up north raising money for the new republic, though all the while operating Texas's leading mercantile establishment in Galveston.

Williams and his family lived in the house at 3601 Avenue P (tel. 765-1839), a Greek revival version of a Louisiana bayou-style residence, until his death in 1859 when the house was sold to his business partner, Philip C. Tucker. The Tucker family lived here until 1954. In 1984 the house was opened for self-guided tours by the Galveston Historical Foundation, which presents an audio-visual program on the premises, a history of both Williams and his home that provides quite a bit of Texas history background as well. One of the oldest homes in the city, it has been completely restored to its 1854 appearance. A cupola atop the house (much like New England's widow's walks) allowed Williams to watch over the doings at the port. It's not a surprising feature, since the home was an early version of a prefab, constructed in Maine and shipped to Galveston. In the parlor are the family's original piano and horsehair-covered sofa, and the other rooms are furnished in authentic period pieces. Oil portraits of Williams and his wife, Sarah, hang in the parlor. The kitchen, where a slave once tried to poison the family by putting ground glass in the food, was originally separate from the house for fear of fire, though today it's attached. Trunks and trunks of William's letters and documents are still extant, some of them, along with photographs, on display here. The draperies and cornices in the master bedroom were fabricated from descriptions found among Williams's receipts.

The house is open for tours Monday to Saturday from 9:30 a.m. to 4:30 p.m., on Sunday from 11 a.m. to 4:30 p.m. (closed the last two weeks in January). Eight rooms are open to view. Admission is $2.50 for adults, $2 for students and seniors, $1.50 for children 6 to 12 (under 6, free); maximum for families, $7.

**EAST END HISTORICAL DISTRICT:** Many of the Greek revival, Queen Anne–style, and Victorian homes that flourished in Galveston's Gilded Age occupy a National Historic Landmark District, more or less bounded by Market Street and Broadway north and south, and 11th and 19th Streets east and west. A walking (or riding) tour map of the exact area is available at the Strand Visitors Center (details above), pinpointing 100 noteworthy structures in the area and telling a little about each. Ranging from cottages to mansions, the listings include several creations of Galveston's most famous architect, Nicholas J. Clayton. It's a fascinating tour, especially for those interested in period architecture.

**THE SILK STOCKING HISTORIC PRECINCT:** A small, elegant neighborhood of restored historic homes, the Silk Stocking District occupies 24th and 25th Streets (the latter also called Rosenberg Avenue) between Avenues N and L. A pocket of Victorian architecture, it is, like the East End District, fun to explore, though no brochure is currently provided. If you want details about architectural highlights, the Strand Visitors Center can fill you in.

A block outside the area is the **Texas Heroes Monument,** Broadway and 25th Street, a 72-foot tribute to the heroes of the Texas Revolution. A bronze statue of *Victory* points a laurel wreath in the direction of San Jacinto, and scenes of important Texas battles are set in panels at the base.

**GALVESTON COUNTY HISTORICAL MUSEUM:** Operated by the Galveston Historical Foundation and located in the 1919 City National Bank Building at 2219 Market St. (tel. 766-2340), this small county museum features permanent and visiting exhibits relating to the history of Galveston County and the state of Texas. The building itself is one of the county's architectural treasures, a masterpiece in marble and granite with a dramatic arched ceiling and ornate interior plasterwork. It was donated in 1972 by a member of the Moody family, Galveston benefactor Mary Moody Northen. The collection includes fossils and artifacts from architectural digs in the area, a large photographic collection documenting Galveston history (many fascinating hurricane pictures), costumes from Mardi Gras and various balls, turn-of-the-century clothing, drawings and plans of famed local architect Nicholas Clayton, Karankawa arrowheads and pottery shards, the beacon from the 1893 South Jetty Lighthouse, old letters and documents, Civil War cannonballs, and more. Special exhibits have highlighted areas like Victoriana, Mexican toys, and antique radios.

Admission is free. The museum is open weekdays from 9 a.m. to 4 p.m., on Saturday from 11 a.m. to 4 p.m., and on Sunday (summer only) from 11 a.m. to 4 p.m.

**SEA-ARAMA MARINE WORLD:** Located on West Beach at Seawall Boulevard and 91st Street (tel. 744-4501), Sea-arama Marine World is the Gulf Coast's premier sea-life park, a 31-acre educational/entertainment facility with a large and diverse population of marine mammals, fish, reptiles, and birds. The park has a national reputation for its excellent research programs, its work with injured sea animals and birds, and its efforts to preserve endangered species like the ridley sea turtle and the brown pelican. They've been operating for over two decades, but a recent landscaping added new palms and plantings.

A one-price ticket costing $10.95 for adults, $7 for children 4 to 12 (under 4, free), provides admission to all shows and exhibits. The former include a dolphin revue, a sea lion show, an exotic bird show starring macaws and cockatoos, shark feeding, seal and sea lion feeding, marine animal-training workshop, and a waterski show. Over 20 killer sharks are among the denizens of the 200,000-gallon oceanarium, and other exhibits display alligators, black swans, river otters, and giant land turtles.

Open daily from 10 a.m. to 5 p.m. A snackbar and picnic area are on the premises.

**THE MOSQUITO FLEET:** That's a rather unappealing name for the picturesque shrimp fleet docked along the Pier 19 wharves, just below 20th Street. It's not so called because there are a lot of mosquitoes hanging around, but because the boats have a kind of mosquito-like appearance. There's lots of activity here throughout the day. In addition to shrimp boats, visitors can observe bustling port activity nearby: big banana ships from Central America and cargoes of plywood, sugar, and grain arriving and being unloaded; huge metal cranes in operation, and railroad engines moving cargo around the wharves. The port is still a vital commercial center, and along with tourism and oil, a major source of income to the city. The best vantage place for viewing the Mosquito Fleet and port ships is Hill's Pier 19, a rustic waterfront seafood restaurant described above.

**THE ANTIQUE DOLL MUSEUM:** Collectors, little girls, big sisters, and moms will all enjoy the Antique Doll Museum, 1721 Broadway (tel. 762-7289), housed in a restored pre–Civil War cottage with additions by architect Nicholas J. Clayton, who also designed the Santa Fe Union Station building and Bishop's Palace. It was moved to its present location by mule team in 1886. The dolls on display here, the personal collection of Mr. and Mrs. Lee Trentham, date from 300 years ago to the present. There are "bye-lo" baby dolls with bisque heads, one of the most popular dolls ever made; wonderful Old South black character dolls from the '50s made by Maggie Head Kane; original Kewpies; a 17th-century wooden-headed Queen Anne; French dolls from the 1800s and early 1900s; limited-edition dolls; early rag dolls; a pregnant doll; Hawaiian clay dolls; and many famous figures like Ike and Mamie, George and Martha, Queen Victoria, Prince Rainier and Princess Grace (with little Caroline), and Frederick Douglass. One room houses a complete doll circus, another a model of the Galveston depot peopled by dolls, and a third a nursery of baby dolls. And of course there's a gift shop stocked with wonderful dolls.

Admission is $3 for adults, $2 for children 6 to 12 (under 6, free). The museum is open Tuesday to Saturday from 10 a.m. to 5 p.m., on Sunday from 1 to 5 p.m. Closed in January.

**THE AUTOMOBILE MUSEUM:** Oil millionaire Don Childress displays his incredible collection of antique cars in a 20,000-square-foot showroom at 1301 Tremont St., at Avenue M (tel. 765-5801). On exhibit are some 100 automobiles, give or take a few loaned out for Hollywood movies at any given time (like *The Godfather* and *The Sting*). The collection includes the 1937 Rolls-Royce given to Eva Braun by Adolph Hitler, a 1929 Packard once owned by a prince of New Zealand, a 1933 Buick Phaeton (one of three left in the world), one of Elvis Presley's white Cadillacs (1955), a 1929 paddy wagon, a 16-cylinder Cadillac, a 1925 Gardener (the only one of its kind in the U.S.), and Childress's very first car, a 1914 Dodge.

Open daily from 10 a.m. to 5 p.m. Admission is $4 for adults, $2.50 for seniors and children 6 to 12 (under 6, free); maximum for families, $10.

**BAY CRUISES:** You haven't seen a port city until you get out on the water. A variety of cruises are offered aboard the **Colonel** (tel. 763-4666), a 152-foot, 800-passenger, diesel-powered paddlewheeler. A Moody Foundation project named for Civil War Col. William Lewis Moody, this 19th-century-style vessel is gaily Victorian in its appointments and furnishings, including an open-air promenade deck with lacy white wrought-iron tables and chairs. Two-hour cruises depart from the 22nd Street Wharf next to the *Elissa,* and the boat is boarded half an hour before departure time.

Daily Bay Cruises, with historical narration by the captain, are scheduled once or twice daily year round. Passengers learn about Galveston's past while viewing its present port activities. Adults pay $8 and children 4 to 12 pay $4 (under 4, free).

Evenings there are **Dinner/Jazz Cruises,** also year round, featuring Créole or seafood all-you-can-eat buffets and a Dixieland band. Adults pay $24; children under 12 pay $15.

And for adults only, in summer only, there are romantic **Moonlight Cruises on the Bay** every Saturday night at 10 p.m. You can dance to a live band and whisper sweet nothings under a sky full of stars. Cocktails are available. Price is $8.

Departures are, of course, weather permitting. Reservations are required for the dinner cruise.

**PARKS AND BEACHES:** Galveston is a resort city with abundant recreational facilities. Its oldest and principal beach area is **Stewart Park,** Seawall Boulevard and Broadway (tel. 765-7424), where you'll find all beach services, bath houses, restaurants, concessions, gift shops, a children's amusement park, and rental operations offering water paraphernalia. Parking costs $2.

A little farther afield, along a six-mile stretch of FM Road 3005 between 7½ Mile Road and 11 Mile Road (tel. 744-6750 for Park 1, 737-1544 for Park 2, and 737-1206 for Park 3) are the three lovely **West Beach Parks** offering most of the above facilities, plus a waterskiing cable operation. Parking costs $3. There's horseback riding nearby at Sandy Hoof Stables (tel. 740-3481).

Both Stewart and the West Beach Parks are popular family beaches, but out on the west part of the island there are miles of secluded beach where parking is free and you can avoid the crowds if you're willing to eschew concessions.

Teens and young 20s party at **R.A. Appfel,** on the far eastern end of the island.

**Galveston Island State Park,** a 2,000-acre facility off FM 3005 at 14528 Stewart and 13 Mile Road (tel. 737-1222), offers over 1½ miles of gulf beachfront, several miles of nature trails with bird-viewing blinds and boardwalks over the bayous, a bike trail, picnic areas, camping facilities with electricity and showers, and freshwater lakes (including six ponds stocked with bass and bream), and surf fishing. There's a $2 entrance fee to the park.

**Seawolf Park,** across the Galveston Ship Channel (take 51st Street north, which becomes Seawolf Parkway; tel. 744-5738), has a 380-foot fishing pier over Galveston Bay, picnic areas, imaginative children's playgrounds, and a World War II submarine and destroyer escort to explore. It's a lovely place to sit under tall palms and watch the parade of passing ships. Parking is $1.

**AND OTHER RECREATION:** A wide choice of sports activities is accessible to visitors in this outdoor-minded city.

## Fishing

Seemingly infinite numbers of boat operators offer fishing excursions, and choices range from deep-sea to freshwater fishing.

A reasonably priced and well-run operation is **Buccaneer** (tel. 763-5423), with at least two four-hour fishing trips departing from Pier 19 daily throughout the year. Bay fishing trips cost $9 for adults, $6 for children under 12, $2 extra for tackle, rod, reel, and bait. Deep-sea trips cost $37 to $43 weekdays (it depends which boat you use), $48 to $53 weekends. Deep-sea fisherpeople might snag red snapper, grouper, king mackerel, and ling; from the bay, sand trout, croaker, redfish, and drum are common. Also recommended is Jack Elliott's **Pelican Boat Rental** (tel. 762-2400). You'll find the brochures of dozens of additional anglers for your business at your hotel or either of the visitors centers.

Of course, you can also fish off the piers. The **Gulf Coast Fishing Pier** at 90th Street and Seawall (tel. 744-2273) or the **61st Street Fishing Pier** (tel. 744-5681) both provide the four "Bs" (bait, beer, benches, and bathrooms), along with food concessions, running water, and fish-cleaning tables. The Gulf Coast Pier even has a walk-in cooler where you can leave your catch until you're ready to go home. Both piers charge $2.

If you're over 17 and under 65, you need a license to fish off the piers. You can get it, along with all fishing gear, at **Sportsman's Paradise,** 2001 61st St., at Heards Lane (tel. 744-0171). Out-of-state residents pay $15 for a license good for one year, $8 for a five-day license. State residents pay $5 for a 14-day license.

## Tennis

The **Galveston Racquet Club,** 8300 Airport Blvd. (tel. 744-3651), has nine private courts open daily from 7 a.m. to 9:30 p.m. by reservation. Lessons are available, and there's a pro shop on the premises. They charge a $5 guest fee, and $2.50 per hour before 5 p.m., $3.50 after 5 p.m.

**Free public courts,** with no reservations required (they're first-come, first-served, so to speak), include four courts in Schreiber Park at 81st Street and Beluche, five Menard Park courts at Seawall Boulevard and 27th Street, and six courts, surrounded by palm trees, at Lasker Park, 43rd Street and Avenue Q. All of these are lit for night play. Call 766-2138 for information.

## Golf

The **Pirates Golf Course,** 1700 Syndor Lane, west of Stewart Road (tel. 744-2366), is a challenging 18-hole course complicated by water hazards and coastal breezes. It offers full clubhouse services. Fees are $5 weekdays, $6 weekends.

## Riding

Horses can be rented from **Sandy Hoof Stables,** 11118 West Beach, between 7 and 8 Mile Roads (tel. 740-3481). Guided or unguided rides along the beach cost $9 per hour.

## Scuba

**Aquasphere,** 112 23rd St., just off the Strand (tel. 765-7001), offers scuba trips both out on the gulf and farther afield (like Cozumel). Equipment can be purchased or rented, and instruction is available. They also rent and sell snorkeling equipment, and can tell you the best spots.

## Biking

See "Getting Around," above, for rental sources. Galveston is ideal for bike riding; you can pedal along the traffic-free Seawall for miles, and the entire island is pancake flat. Many bike-rental outlets along Seawall also rent roller skates.

## Jogging

Once again, you can't beat the Seawall. Serious runners will consider moving here.

## 5. Galveston Nights

There was a time, just a few decades ago, when Galveston was one of the hottest nighttime towns in the nation. Not so anymore, but there are a few pleasant ways to pass an evening here.

**THE STRAND STREET THEATRE:** A professional repertory company presents a year-round theater season at the Strand Street Theatre, 2317 Ship's Mechanic Row (tel. 763-4591). Productions include both new and well-known plays, among the latter, in recent seasons, *The Gin Game, Gemini, El Grande de Coca-Cola, Gypsy,* and Agatha Christie's *The Mousetrap.* Performances are generally on Thursday, Friday, and Saturday nights at 8 p.m., and Sunday matinees. All tickets are under $10, with special prices for students and seniors.

**THE 1894 GRAND OPERA HOUSE:** Totally restored within to its turn-of-the-century appearance, this grand brick edifice at 2020 Postoffice St. (tel. 765-1894) has hosted some of the most famous actors of the 20th century—Otis Skinner, George M. Cohan, and Lillian Russell, among them. Work is now under way to restore the building's exterior, and soon the majestic cupola will once again grace the top of the old Grand.

The year-round season here includes very diverse offerings. A recent season featured the Houston Symphony Orchestra with Marvin Hamlisch conducting, Texas Opera Theater performances of *Carmen* and *Die Fledermaus,* a modern dance company, Hal Holbrook in *Mark Twain Tonight,* chamber concerts, and headliners Rita Moreno and the Four Freshmen. Annual productions always include a musical version of Dickens's *A Christmas Carol* in conjunction with "Dickens on the Strand" festivities, *The Nutcracker* each December, and five concerts by the Galveston Symphony Orchestra. Prices vary with the attraction; you can almost always get tickets at the box office.

**MARY MOODY NORTHEN AMPHITHEATRE:** This 1,800-seat outdoor amphitheater in Galveston Island State Park at 14528 Stewart Rd. (tel. 737-3440) boasts state-of-the-art sound, light, and staging equipment. Throughout the summer season (early June through Labor Day) it offers alternating performances Tuesday through Sunday nights of *Hello Dolly* starring Marilyn Maye and *The Lone Star,* a lively musical about the history of Texas with spectacular battle scenes, frontier songs, and rousing dance numbers. Though the Mary Moody has been presenting it for a decade, *The Lone Star* was the official play of the 1986 Texas Sesquicentennial. Tickets are in the $7 to $9 range, about half price for children 12 and under.

A Texas-style barbecue ($5.50) is offered before the show at the Theatre Restaurant from 6 to 8 p.m., but since the facility is in a lovely park, many people opt for picnic dinners (there are tables) instead. Tickets are available via Ticketron and at the box office.

**NIGHTTIME MISCELLANY:** An art deco–motif nightclub at the Key Largo Hotel, 5400 Seawall (tel. 744-5000), **Hemingway's,** offers live entertainment nightly from 9 p.m. to 1:30 a.m. It's both posh and cozy, with comfortably upholstered armchairs and sofas, lots of plants, and a handsome bar with an ornate stained-glass backbar. The combos here are really good; they play top-40s tunes and mellow rock, and there's a small dance floor.

**Hennessy's,** 45th Street and Seawall, in the Fort Crockett Shopping Center (tel. 763-9191), is an immense disco that offers a mix of top-40s tunes, hard rock, country, and soul music. The lighting is disco, and the pool tables in the back are country. It's open Tuesday to Sunday till 2 a.m., but the action doesn't really pick up till after 11 p.m. on weekdays, earlier on weekends.

One of the nicest nightspots in town is the **Wentletrap Lounge** (see restaurant recommendations for a description) at 2301 The Strand (tel. 765-5545), where a very talented pianist plays show tunes and jazz classics on weekend nights, usually with a more extensive schedule in summer. It makes for an elegant evening.

In a similar vein, there's piano-bar entertainment Tuesday through Sunday nights at the Tremont House **Toujouse Bar,** 2300 Ship's Mechanic Row (tel. 763-2300). See the hotel recommendations for a full description.

Behind Le Paysan (again, see my restaurant recommendations) is **Le Bistro,** 2021 The Strand (tel. 765-7792), a bar lounge featuring live jazz artists on Friday and Saturday nights (extended schedule in summer). Classy light fare like smoked salmon, pâté and cheese plates, and crudités is available.

Finally, you can dance to high-energy bands at the gorgeous **Galvez Lounge,** 21st Street and Seawall Boulevard (tel. 765-7721). It's open Tuesday to Sunday nights till 2 a.m.

*Chapter IV*

# CORPUS CHRISTI: THE TEXAS RIVIERA

## 1. Bay City Basics
## 2. Hotels
## 3. Restaurants
## 4. Attractions
## 5. Nightlife
## 6. Padre Island National Seashore

THE "BEAUTIFUL BAY" was discovered in 1519 on the Catholic feast day of Corpus Christi by Spanish sea captain Alonso Alvarez de Piñeda who was mapping the coast of Texas. Believed to be the first white man to view the site, de Piñeda named it, charted it, and left it. Like Galveston, Corpus Christi then remained through the early 1800s a smuggler's rest (legends of buried treasure persist to this day), inhabited only by coastal Indian tribes and transitory traders.

## 1. Bay City Basics

In 1840, Col. Henry L. Kinney, a young Pennsylvania-born Irishman who went west to recover from a broken romance with Daniel Webster's daughter—and to escape from heavy debts—purchased 44,280 acres of land for about $4,000 from a Mexican captain. He set up Kinney's Ranch and Trading Post on what would evolve into the city of Corpus Christi. Kinney's quarters were fort-like, since Mexicans had a tendency to arrive with troops and try to convince him to leave. But he held on, and in 1845, when Gen. Zachary Taylor brought thousands of men to Corpus to back up Texan territorial claims, his little settlement flourished. Grog shops alone increased in number from 2 to 200. It was a pretty wild and lawless little town. One newcomer described it as "the most murderous, thieving, gambling, God-forsaken hole in the Lone Star State or out of it," and Taylor himself noted there were "no ladies . . . and very few women."

When the fighting with Mexico ended, Taylor and his troops departed, leaving Kinney with something of a ghost town on his hands. With admirable foresight, he quickly rallied, proclaiming Corpus Christi "the Naples of the Gulf" and advertised for settlers in European and American newspapers. He began deepening the ship channel at the bay's entrance in 1848 to enhance port activity, and when 1849 brought the Gold Rush, he lured prospectors by promoting Corpus Christi as "the best way to California"! By 1852 Corpus Christi was incorporated as a city, was a government-recognized port, and had held the first Texas State Fair. It went on to survive Civil War bombardment, yellow fever epidemics, vicious raids by armed Mexican bandits, Indian attacks, hurricanes (like Galveston, the city is now protected by a seawall), and oilfield fires.

Today Corpus Christi is the nation's ninth-busiest port. Its air and water, despite the fact that 1,300 producing oil and gas wells ring the city, are among the purest in the country. And its second-largest industry is tourism, with holiday weekenders often numbering over 100,000.

Many visitors approach Corpus Christi via the majestic Harbor Bridge spanning the ship channel (234 feet at its apex), which offers breathtaking daytime vistas of the sun-dappled, 152-square-mile bay and port activity, and, after dark, a glittering light show. Dubbed "the Sparkling City by the Sea" and "Crown Jewel of the Texas Coast," Corpus Christi has a classic Riviera waterfront (Shoreline/Ocean Drive). Its wide grand-boulevard esplanade is studded with tall palms and pink- and fuchsia-blossomed oleander. On one side are miles of white sand beach and yacht-filled marinas; the other is lined with luxury highrise hotels, condos, and the palatial villas of oil tycoons and political power brokers.

Directly across the gulf from Tampa, Florida, the city is a migration point for hundreds of species of birds flying south for the winter—a pattern followed by many American midwesterners and Canadians. They come for some of the best beaches in Texas, and all the attendant resort activities—golf, tennis, swimming, surfing, birdwatching, hunting, fishing, boating, and beachcombing. Padre Island, a hauntingly beautiful wilderness area also described in this chapter, begins just a half-hour drive from downtown.

**WHEN TO COME:** Barrier islands protect Corpus Christi from the magnitude of storm devastation that plagues other gulf cities, and sea breezes off the gulf make for cool summer evenings. The average annual temperature is 71.2°, there are 255 days of sunshine each year, and January, averaging 56.9°, is the coldest month. Summer is the biggest tourist season; in April (spring break time for Texas college kids) you might as well be in Fort Lauderdale; October is bliss— hot enough to swim but not to swelter.

**GETTING THERE:** Both **Trailways** and **Greyhound** have bus service into Corpus Christi; terminals are at 702 N. Chapparal (tel. 512/882-2516) and 819 N. Broadway (tel. 512/884-9474), respectively.

**Corpus Christi International Airport** is served by six airlines, none of them international carriers, however. To or from the airport you can take a **Texas Riviera Transportation** (tel. 512/289-0191) van to (or from) any point in Corpus Christi; price is $6 per person. A **taxi** from the airport to bayfront hotels is about $11.

There's train service between Corpus Christi and Laredo via the **Texas-Mexican Railway Company** (tel. 512/289-1818 from Corpus, 512/722-6411 from Laredo). Fare is $39.95 for adults, $20 for children under 12.

By **car** it's a few hours' drive from anywhere you're likely to be. From San Antonio, 150 miles to the northwest, Corpus Christi is about a 2½-hour drive via I-37, which takes you right into Shoreline Drive. From Brownsville, McAllen, and Laredo, it's a three-hour drive via U.S. 77 and Hwy. 44, U.S. 281 and Hwy. 44, and U.S. 59 and Hwy. 44, respectively. Houston is 200 miles away via U.S. 59 and I-37.

**GETTING ORIENTED:** Make your first stop in town the **Corpus Christi Convention & Tourist Bureau,** 1201 N. Shoreline Dr., Corpus Christi, TX 78403 (tel. 512/882-5603). Their staff is bilingual (Spanish and English), and they have brochures in those languages plus French, German, and Japanese. The CTB can provide information about all Corpus Christi attractions, events that will be on during your stay, and resort activities. Write to them in advance for an annual vacation guide called *Texas Tropical Coast,* accommodations and restaurant guides, a sports guide, visitor map, and answers to any questions you have about the area. The bureau is open Monday to Friday from 8:30 a.m. to 5 p.m. and on Saturday to noon. On Saturday afternoon and Sunday you can obtain tourist information at the Corpus Christi Museum.

**GETTING AROUND:** It's certainly helpful to have a car in Corpus Christi. **Budget** has locations at the airport (tel. 512/289-0434) and at 3737 South Padre Island Dr. (tel. 512/855-8400). Also represented both at the airport and downtown is **National** (tel. 512/289-0515). **Hertz** (512/289-0777) maintains convenient rental desks at the Marriott and Hershey hotels. Toll-free numbers for all rental-car operations are given in the introductory chapter.

There are **city buses** you can take around town. Call 882-1722 for routing information.

A **taxi** costs $1.25 at meter drop, $1 per mile after that. Call Yellow Checker Cab at 884-3211.

**ANNUAL EVENTS:** Several major events take place in Corpus Christi each year, along with any number of one-time affairs ranging from gun shows to quarter horse expositions. Check with the Convention & Tourist Bureau (tel. 512/882-5603) to find out what will be on during your stay. Also call the bureau for ticket information if no other number is provided below.

**Buccaneer Days,** an 11-day festival in late April/early May, commemorates the landing of Alonso Alvarez de Piñeda, the Spanish explorer who discovered Corpus Christi Bay in 1519. It officially begins when "pirate queens" (Buc Days beauty contest entrants) capture the mayor and force him literally to "walk the plank." Other than mayor dunking, activities include an ongoing carnival with rides and attractions, sports competitions, regattas, a Junior Parade, an illuminated night parade, tractor pulls, concerts, bayfront fireworks, the crowning of a King Alonso, his queen, and princess, and a coronation ball. Tickets are required for some events. Call 512/882-3242 for details.

The **Deep-Sea Roundup** takes place in July, 25 miles east in Port Aransas. Originally called the Tarpon Rodeo, it's the oldest fishing tournament on the gulf (since 1932), attracting serious anglers from all over the world. It's fun to see the weighing-in at the dock of hundreds of pounds of kingfish, sailfish, marlin, redfish, and shark, and proud fisherfolk posing with their trophies for the traditional photo. For information, call 512/749-5919.

The three-day **Texas Jazz Festival** in mid-July features famous musicians from all over the country. It includes a jazz cruise aboard a three-decked paddlewheeler, a jazz mass, and numerous concerts—almost all of them free. Among those who've taken part in past years are Cal Tjader, the George Shearing Quintet, Dick Hyman, Stan Kenton, Al Hirt, and Zoot Sims.

**Bayfest** is a late-September family fall festival with three days of events along five waterfront blocks, beginning at the Bayfront Plaza Convention Center. Water-related events (a boat parade, jetski and sailboard demonstrations, dolphin gymnastics, aquarium exhibits, junior fishing contests, a sailboat regatta, and an anything-but-a-boat-that-will-float race) are featured, along with a street parade, continuous musical entertainment (jazz, country, mariachis, you name it), over 75 food booths purveying everything from tacos to turkey legs, arts and crafts booths, and fireworks. For details, call 512/887-0868.

The first week in December, the mayor flips a switch lighting most of the sailboat masts in the marina, the official Christmas tree on Shoreline Drive, and bayfront office building façades. It's called **Harbor Lights.** Mr. and Mrs. Santa arrive by boat and pass out candy to all the children, elves collect children's letters to Santa, and there's caroling, dancing, and family entertainment. Christmas is also celebrated with a **Christmas Tree Forest** at the Art Museum of South Texas, an exhibition of spectacularly decorated trees. Over the years they've included trees embellished with everything from seashells to handcrafted dolls. The event always has a theme (like Victorian Christmas, Winter Wonderland, or Fairytales of Christmas) and tableaux and wreathes are exhibited along with the trees. Call 512/884-3844 for further details. Annual productions of Handel's *Messiah* and *The Nutcracker* are also part of Corpus Christi's Christmas season.

## 2. Hotels

Ideally, you'll want to stay right on the waterfront in Corpus, enjoying the scenic views and proximity to the palm-fringed beach. In summer, on weekends (especially holiday weekends), and during college spring break, you'd best reserve far in advance.

The block-long **Corpus Christi Marriott,** 707 N. Shoreline Dr., between Starr and Taylor, Corpus Christi, TX 78401 (tel. 512/882-1700, or toll free 800/228-9290), enjoys a beautiful beachfront location within walking distance of museums, restaurants, and the tourist bureau. Its completion in 1984 signaled the start of a transition for Corpus from sleepy beach town to a Texas Riviera resort. The first beachfront hotel built since 1973, this Marriott property has a casual and airy resort feel, its public areas decorated with beautiful paintings and tapestries and abundantly abloom with greenery and flowers in wicker, clay, and brass pots. Even in the lobby, which contains a bay-view cocktail area, the registration desk is festooned in English ivy.

The 350 rooms are delightfully decorated in seashell colors like pale peach and cream, with frosted raspberry accents. Beds (all king-size or doubles) are bamboo-framed and covered in pretty floral-print spreads. Other furnishings include a big oak dresser/desk and a table with two bamboo chairs. All rooms have balconies and offer bay views. They're also equipped with AM/FM radios, alarm clocks, color TVs with HBO and other cable channels, and full-length mirrors.

Capers is the hotel's all-purpose dining room, and a very pretty one it is. Comfortable upholstered bamboo and wicker chairs are set amid ficus trees in big wicker baskets, and most tables offer excellent bay views. A lavish $13.95 Sunday champagne brunch is served here. It includes a large selection of salads, bagels with lox and cream cheese, antipasto, cheeses, an omelet and waffle bar, blintzes, roast beef au jus with creamed horseradish, a choice of entrees (such as blackened redfish, beef sirloin tips, and chicken teriyaki), potatoes, a choice of fresh vegetables, fresh-baked breads and rolls, a large dessert display, and complimentary champagne. It does change a bit from week to week, but those are the general outlines. Even if you're staying elsewhere, consider popping over on Sunday for this fabulous feast.

The Marriott's fine dining facility is Monty's, plushly decorated in shades of mauve and apricot, with velvet couches and bamboo furnishings. Its stucco walls are hung with attractive tapestries and watercolors of the Southwest. You can cozy up on one of those sofas for cocktails, or sit down at a candle lamp-lit table for a full dinner—perhaps an appetizer of seafood-stuffed artichoke hearts topped with melted cheese and flavored with vermouth ($4.95), followed by filet mignon with mushroom cap and sauce béarnaise ($14.95). Entrees include soup or salad, fresh-baked bread, and rice pilaf or a baked potato with all the trimmings. Monty's also serves up lobster, roast beef, lamb, and veal entrees. It's open for dinner only. Bentley's is the Marriott's popular nightspot for high-energy music (more about this in nightlife listings, below).

The third floor is the pool area, centered on two attached hexagonal pools —one indoors, one outdoors, with a swim-through glass partition. You can bask in the sun on a weathered-pine deck overlooking the bay, relax in the indoor whirlpool or sauna, have a drink at the bar, or work out in the exercise room; there's even a game room for the kids.

A courtesy van provides free transport to/from the airport. Nightly turn-down with Godiva chocolates is available on request. A car-rental desk is on the premises. And there's free indoor parking. Rates are $75 to $100, single or double, the higher end of the scale representing executive king-size accommodations with sofas or better bay views. An extra person pays $10; children under 18 stay free. There's a weekend rate from Friday to Sunday of just $60 per night, and attractively priced packages are available.

No sooner did Marriott open its doors, than **The Hershey**, 900 N. Shoreline Dr., between Twigg and Mann, Corpus Christi, TX 78401 (tel. 512/887-1600, or toll free 800/533-3131), usurped its position as new kid on the bay with a Valentine's Day opening and free Kisses for all. Owned by a corporation established by Milton Hershey of chocolate bar fame (you get one when you check in), this new property is Corpus Christi's most luxurious hostelry. Even in its first year it attracted such prestigious guests as ex-President Ford, Farrah Fawcett, and Gene Hackman.

The hotel's facilities include a large indoor-outdoor pool and whirlpool with an adjoining children's pool, whirlpool, a lovely redwood sundeck, game room for kids, and the Lanai Lounge for drinks and light fare; you can also order from room service poolside. On the second floor is a sizable workout room with Keiser pneumatic-resistance equipment, saunas, locker rooms, and showers. Rock music is piped in for aerobics, and the spa area has its own sun-deck where you can bask in peace since there are no kids romping about. Speaking of kids, the hotel offers packages (among others), which include organized activities for them. Two racquetball courts round out the sportive facilities. They have a viewing area where drinks and food are available, and the attend-ant on duty can find partners for you or arrange lessons. There are several shops and services off the lobby, including a large gift shop that also carries resort wear, a high-fashion women's clothing boutique, a unisex hair salon, a car-rental desk, American Airlines desk, and a shoeshine stand. Complimentary transport to/from the airport is provided.

For dining, there's the lushly planted Glass Pavilion, with a wall of windows overlooking the bay and trees growing toward a glass greenhouse ceiling. Fresh flowers on every table further enhance the garden ambience. The dinner menu offers choices ranging from salads and burgers to full meals—something for every mood and budget. You get a Hershey's Kiss with your bill. A bay-view lounge, the Topsider, adjoins. The Glass Pavilion is very pretty, but the Her-shey's other restaurant, the 20th-floor, multi-tiered Reflections, is almost awe-inspiring. Decorated in subtle gray/blue tones, it has 18-foot windows offering panoramic bay views from every seat. White-linened tables are exquisitely ap-pointed with fine silver, crystal, and china, and the setting is saved from austeri-ty by many trees and plants. It's open for lunch weekdays (one of the best times to enjoy the view) with entrees ranging from sausage of veal and Boursin cheese ($7.95) to a sandwich of smoked salmon, cucumber, and cream cheese on black bread ($5.25). A typical Reflections dinner might include an appetizer of escargots and artichoke hearts ($5.50) or lobster bisque ($5), followed by an entree of mesquite-grilled strip steak in three-mustard sauce ($15) and a dessert of fresh fruit Grand Marnier ($3.25). At night Reflections is a romantic spot. Another food and beverage facility is the High Tide Lounge (about which, more in night-life listings).

Rooms at the Hershey are done in resort colors like sea green, coral, and mauve. They all have balconies overlooking the bay (your bed also faces the bay view), full-length mirrors, two phones (bedside and desk), cable color TVs with HBO and Cinemax stations, and AM/FM alarm clock radios. Guests are pampered with baskets of fine toiletries in the bath and nightly turndown with—guess what? The 18th-floor of the hotel is a concierge level called the Main Line Club. Rooms here have king-size beds and sofas, small refrigerators, and digital scales. In the bath is a seashell filled with Gilchrist & Soames bath products (cologne, fine talc, bath cube, soap, and potpourri) and in the closet a plush terry-cloth robe. Main Line Club guests enjoy a beautiful private lounge with a reading room area, card table, a selection of newspapers and magazines, a color TV, and a stereo. In addition to the hotel concierge, there's a special concierge stationed in the lounge to give personal attention to Main Line guests, and room rates include complimentary continental breakfast and a cocktail hour buffet.

Rates are $85 to $95 single, $95 to $105 double, $10 for an extra person, no charge for children under 18. Concierge-level rooms are $125 per night, single or double occupancy. Parking—both self- and valet—is free. And facilities for the disabled are provided as well.

The **Friendship Sea Shell Inn,** 202 Kleberg (just over the Harbor Bridge), Corpus Christi, TX 78402 (tel. 512/888-5391, or toll free 800/453-4511), is a two-story, 26-unit motel right on the beach that is very popular with families. The rooms, all of which overlook the bay, are large and homey—not as slick as a chain motel's but clean and pleasant. Over half have fully equipped kitchenettes (stove, oven, sink, refrigerator, cookware, and dinnerware), most beds are king- or queen-size, all accommodations have full dining tables, and some contain sofas. They're heated in winter, air-conditioned in summer, and equipped with direct-dial phones, full tub/shower baths, and cable color TVs with Cine-max movies and other special stations. Just outside your door are a nice-size swimming pool and sundeck, a kiddie playground, a shuffleboard court, and gas barbecue grills for preparing picnics on the beach. Roam down to the next beach and you can rent umbrellas and such from the concessions of the more expensive Sandy Shores hotel and also utilize their restaurants and bars. There's a washer/dryer for guest use, local phone calls cost only 25¢ (low for hotels), and shaded parking (which means your car does not convert to an oven in the hot sun) is free.

Rates are seasonal: November through February, singles or doubles pay $35; March to mid-May and September/October, they pay $50; mid-May through Labor Day, $61. Rooms with kitchenettes are $5 to $6 higher across the board. There's no charge for children under 12. Sunday through Tuesday rates are sometimes lower, subject to availability; there's a 10% reduction for stays of a week or longer in summer; the rest of the year, if you stay six days the seventh is free, and monthly rates are even further reduced.

The **Sea Ranch,** 4401 Ocean Dr., between Airline and Robert, Corpus Christi, TX 78412 (tel. 512/853-7366), is an attractively rustic-looking motel with a weathered pine façade and barn-red exterior room doors. It's a family operation run by Josef and Marta Gluck, whose kids, Michael and Marta, help out in summer when they're not away at college. Petra, Michael's pet donkey, lives here year round (she's a favorite with visiting children), and there's also a small and friendly dog named Spunky heading up the security department.

There are 34 units (6 with kitchenettes) furnished in a hodgepodge of homey pieces; Mrs. G. haunts flea markets and garage sales. Most have nice wallpapers and pine paneling or wainscoting, and all are equipped with direct-dial phones, tub/shower baths, and color TVs. Some have refrigerators, and kitchenette rooms include stoves and sinks as well (guests supply their own dishes and cookware). There's a comfortable pine-paneled, lodge-like lounge off the lobby with a working fireplace, couches, and cowhide rugs on the brick floor. A breakfast of coffee, sweet roll, and orange juice is available here for $1.60, and magazines and decks of cards are provided. Outside is a courtyard area with picnic tables, a nice-size pool and sundeck, a whirlpool, swings, shuffleboard, and a tennis court. Chairs are provided on the second-level balconies.

Rates mid-May to Labor Day are $43.50 single, $57.50 for two or three people in a room. The rest of the year singles pay $39.50; two or three, $52.50.

# 3. Restaurants

Corpus Christi restaurants capitalize on the city's waterfront location, offering great seafood, sometimes with a Cajun accent. In addition to the listings below, consider Monty's at the Marriott and Reflections at the Hershey, both very elegant choices that are fully described in the hotel listings above.

Some of the best Cajun food in Texas can be found at the **Water Street Oyster Bar,** 309 N. Water St., between Lawrence and Williams (tel. 881-9448), a simpático seafood eatery housed in a converted auto-transmission shop. Owner Brad Lomax has used the auto shop interior to create a hi-tech decor with exposed pipes and high black batt-insulated, steel-beamed, skylight ceilings. One brick wall is decorated with a large mural of Botticelli's (*Birth of Venus* on the halfshell) with the Corpus Christi Harbor Bridge in the background. On another, diners can sign their names, and among those who've availed themselves of the opportunity are actors Matt Dillon and Hal Holbrook, one of the Pointer Sisters, former Dallas Cowboy Walt Garrison, and the Jefferson Starship. Large potted leafy plants enhance the decor. It's nice to sit up on the balcony level and watch the doings below, or in good weather, on the outdoor patio. Downstairs, you can observe food preparation in the glassed-in kitchen, a popular feature of Cajun restaurants.

WSOB's bay oysters are so fresh they flinch when you squeeze a lemon on them. Start out with an order of half a dozen ($3.25) or a dozen ($6). Another marvelous appetizer (also available as an entree) is the picayune shrimp broiled in a 20-ingredient Cajun sauce (it contains everything from brown sugar to clarified butter to vermouth) served with freshly baked bread for dunking and extra napkins ($6.25 as an appetizer, $10.50 as an entree). The blackened redfish—Paul Prudhomme's three-pepper recipe, laced with spicy Cajun butter and seared to a turn on a white-hot griddle ($10.50)—is also extremely meritorious. Ditto the embrochette platter of eight gulf oysters, each wrapped in shrimp and bacon and fried ($10). All entrees are served with fresh-baked bread (the kind you can't stop eating), rice pilaf, and a large portion of fresh vegetables du jour cooked to al dente perfection. For dessert try the New Orleans bread pudding with bourbon sauce ($1.75).

The restaurant is open Sunday through Thursday from 11 a.m. to 11 p.m., on Friday and Saturday till midnight. They don't take reservations, so come during off-hours if you want to avoid a 45-minute-or-longer wait.

In a waterfront city there has to be a restaurant out on the water. In Corpus Christi, it's the **Wayward Lady,** 22 Cooper's Alley L-Head (tel. 887-9716), a barge built as a paddlewheeler. She broke her moorings during a storm while she was being constructed, hence her risqué name. The interior rooms are all lavishly Victorian. On the first level is the Oyster Bar, entered via saloon doors, with a burgundy rose-patterned carpet on white tile flooring, pressed-copper ceiling, and ornate wall sconces and chandeliers. Even if you don't dine on the *Lady,* come by in the late afternoon sometime, order a platter of cold shrimp or raw oysters and a glass of wine, and watch the sun set over the bay and the passing parade of boats. The dining room on this level is called the Captain's Lady. The most casual and least expensive of the four on board, it's nevertheless very attractive; the decor is similar to the Oyster Bar, but seating is in plush white leather booths at marble-topped tables. Lunch or dinner, you can enjoy a blackened redfish sandwich on croissant ($5.25), a crab Louis salad ($6.25), a fajita platter ($7.25), or a full meal beginning with half a dozen oysters on the halfshell ($4.25), followed by spicy broiled shrimp ($10.25), and pecan pie with ice cream ($3) for dessert.

On the second-level Texas Deck are the lovely Yellowstone and the Hiawatha Rooms, named for a paddlewheeler and a steamboat, respectively. Both have gray velvet-upholstered booths and chairs at tables set with sea-green linen cloths and coral napkins. Walls are shell pink, and windows are framed by pale-rose curtains. Menus in these two rooms are identical. A typical meal here might include an appetizer of shrimp cocktail in rémoulade sauce ($5.85) or a bowl of zesty Cajun-style seafood gumbo ($3.75); an entree of blackened redfish with hollandaise sauce, fresh-baked bread and butter, vegetable of the day, and rice pilaf ($12.25), and bread pudding with bourbon sauce for dessert ($2.95).

Both the Captain's Lady and Texas Deck restaurants have a low-priced children's menu for "little mates" 12 and under, with full meals in the $4 to $6.50 range.

The plushest and most pricey is the Victorian Room on the third deck, with burgundy velvet chairs at elegantly appointed tables lit by hurricane lamps, teak-paneled walls, crystal chandeliers suspended from a beamed oak ceiling, and swagged draperies. If you like, you can begin with drinks on the outdoor deck before settling into these posh precincts. A rose is given to each lady diner. The menu here is being revamped at press time, so I can't quote exact entrees. Gourmet continental cuisine will probably be featured, with most entrees in the $15 to $20 range.

Finally, up top there's a deck with umbrella tables. You can't order up here, but you can bring a drink from the restaurant or bar. It's a great spot for watching Wednesday regattas. And for romantic meals à deux and intimate dinner parties, there's the pine-paneled Wheel House, four stories up and offering 360° views of the bay and marina. It seats two to nine people in tufted-velvet comfort. There's a $50 charge for using this private dining facility, plus, of course, the cost of your meal from the Victorian Room menu.

The Captain's Lady is open daily from 11 a.m. to 11 p.m., the Hiawatha and Yellowstone Rooms serve lunch daily from 11 a.m. to 2 p.m. and dinner from 5:30 to 10 p.m., and the Victorian Room serves dinner only Tuesday to Saturday from 6 to 10 p.m. Reservations suggested. Whichever room you choose, it's worth dining early to get a window table. Off-season hours are reduced, so if you're here other than in summer, call ahead.

**Snoopy's Pier,** 10875 S. Padre Island Dr., on the Laguna Madre (tel. 949-8815), is not a place you'll happen upon accidentally. In fact this laid-back boating and fisherman's hangout is hard to happen upon purposefully. Take South Padre Island Drive all the way out to the John F. Kennedy Causeway and make the first turnoff to the right after you get off the bridge; then, if floundering, ask someone or just follow the crowds. On summer weekends Snoopy's serves 600 to 800 people, though many of them arrive by boat (not car) and tie up at the marina. It's one of those special places that is totally original and totally authentic—a real find. The first owner named the place (then a private club-house operation) by asking his little daughter what to call it. In 1978 Ernie Butt-ler, a commercial fisherman, and his wife, Corky, bought Snoopy's and turned it into a restaurant open to the public.

Snoopy's is housed in a rustic pine A-frame, its walls decorated with hang-ing fish net, hats left by customers, photos of area boating and fishing activities, and Snoopy and Woodstock fishing from a boat called the *Miss Lucy*. A big cast-iron fireplace made from a ship's boiler occupies the center of the room; in winter it provides heat and is used for mesquite grilling, and in summer it's filled with plants and driftwood. There are oilcloth-covered tables and wood benches interspersed among weathered pier posts. Additional seating is on a shaded out-door wooden deck and a screened-in porch, both providing wonderful views of the marina and a variety of shore birds on the Laguna. Service is cafeteria style, and all the fish and seafood is fresh-caught. A fried-shrimp plate with tossed salad and fries is $7.35; a combination plate of fried fish, shrimp, and oysters with fries costs $9; a shrimp sandwich runs $3; an oyster sandwich is $2.50, and the broiled catch of the day with rice and salad, $6.75. There's a full bar. Open daily from 11 a.m. to 10 p.m.

People often say the best, and most authentic, Mexican food is served in dives. That's not necessarily the case, but **Old Mexico Restaurant,** 3329 Leopard St., at Nueces Bay Boulevard (tel. 883-6461), is the kind of place they have in mind. A family-run operation for over three decades, Old Mexico is a second home to owners Joe and Josephine Lopez and their grown sons, Zeke and Jerry. Though it's patronized by local families and teens, a lot of the regulars look like something out of *Let Us Now Praise Famous Men* (on my last visit I dined across from an old geezer in undershirt and suspenders). As for the decor, artificial brick walls are hung with paintings on velvet of Mexicans and Indians, tables are Formica, floors linoleum tile, ceilings styrofoam.

"The Lopez family has always lived to eat," says portly owner Joe. They cook everything from scratch, including corn that is stone-ground on the prem-ises to be made into tortillas and tacos. Beans are cooked overnight; rice is deli-ciously spiced with chicken broth, fresh garlic, tomatoes, onions, and bell peppers; even the chili gravy is prepared from an old family recipe. It's hard to beat the Old Mexico dinner—guacamole salad, chile con queso, a meat-filled taco, an enchilada, a tamale with chili gravy, beans, rice, and homemade praline candy for dessert ($6.50). And if you order a smaller combination meal or à la carte, you can dine heartily for $5. Both Mexican and American children's plates are $2.50, and wine and beer are available.

Old Mexico is open daily from 11 a.m. to 9:30 p.m., and it's always mobbed at dinner; come early to avoid the crowds.

You can always do with a good hamburger, and **Rusty's Burgerfactory, Bakery & Bar,** 4256 S. Alameda, at Everhart, in the Town & Country Shop-ping Center (tel. 993-7307), is where you'll find one. The buns are hand-rolled and fresh baked on the premises (you can see this happening through a display window), and the meat is freshly ground on the premises daily from select cuts of the choicest chuck. Everything else that goes into or onto your burger is also fresh and high quality; Rusty's claims to offer "an honest hamburger." The place itself is casual and attractive, with white trellised partitions, oilcloth-covered tables, fans overhead, and white walls decorated with neon beer signs and murals depicting the bay. There's even an enclosed tableau of a beach scene complete with a surfboard and flamingoes. Rock music played at comfortable decibel levels completes the picture. The tropical-motif stainless-steel bar is stocked with all the major Virgin Island runs; a Goombay Smash—pineapple, rum, apricot brandy, and secret ingredients ($3.25)—is the restaurant's specialty.

A half-pound "honest hamburger" with melted cheddar is $4, $4.25 with guacamole and melted Swiss, $4.50 with cheddar and chili or cheddar and bacon. Do order thick skin-on ranch fries on the side ($1.25) and crisp, lightly battered onion rings ($1.75). Other options include a chicken salad sandwich on a fresh bun, made with fresh-cooked diced chicken tossed with fruit, walnuts, and dressing ($5.25); fajitas with all the trimmings ($6.25); and a bowl of home-made chili ($3.25). Unlike most Texas hamburger restaurants, Rusty's has desserts too, baked on the premises. A brownie topped with vanilla ice cream and hot fudge is $2.

Rusty's is open daily from 11 a.m. to 10 p.m., till 11 p.m. in summer. There's another location at 1645 Airline at Williams, where the service is cafeteria style and a duo plays folk/country/rock nightly till 1 a.m.

## 4. Attractions

Essentially, Corpus Christi is a resort town—a place to kick back and relax on the beach and work on your backhand. In addition to fun in the sun, the city does offer a few museums and an important Naval Air Station that is open for tours.

**RECREATIONAL ACTIVITIES:** Corpus Christi's waterfront location and balmy climate make outdoor pursuits year-round activities.

### Fishing

Fishing calendars are easy to come by in Corpus Christi; you can find them at the tourist bureau, and very likely, even at your hotel. The bureau's *Corpus Christi Sports Guide* brochure provides very detailed information. Year round, you can fish for red snapper, scamp, grouper, amberjack, redfish, speckled trout, sand trout, and more, and other species swim through area waters on a seasonal basis.

You can go out on a four-hour **bay fishing** excursion aboard the *Capt. Clark,* a 65-foot boat with a spacious lounge, snackbar, and sundeck (tel. 884-4369 or 643-7128). There are three trips daily departing from Peoples Street T-Head at 7:30 a.m., 2 p.m., and 8 p.m. Bait is included. Tackle rod and reel can be rented for $4.50. Excursions cost $13 for adults, $7 for children under 12, $1 additional for the 8 p.m. sailing. Departures are daily except Tuesday from October 1 to March 1. Other excursion boats also depart from Peoples Street T-Head.

**Deep-sea fishing** expeditions and party boats can be found in nearby Port Aransas, a 30-minute drive from Corpus. Call Fisherman's Wharf (tel. 888-8093) or Deep Sea Headquarters (tel. 749-5597). Or contact the Port Aransas Chamber of Commerce (tel. 749-5919).

If you have your own gear, some of the best trout and redfish waters are along the **Intracoastal Canal,** which runs the length of the Laguna Madre out near the John F. Kennedy Causeway. You can wade in or sit on a pier along the causeway; try the Waterworks Marina, 13245 S. Padre Island Dr.

Other convenient **fishing piers** are at the T-Heads, and at several locations along Ocean Drive. Most charge a small admission.

For other than party-boat fishing, you need a license if you're over 17 and under 65. Nonresidents pay $15 a year, $8 for a five-day license. Texas residents

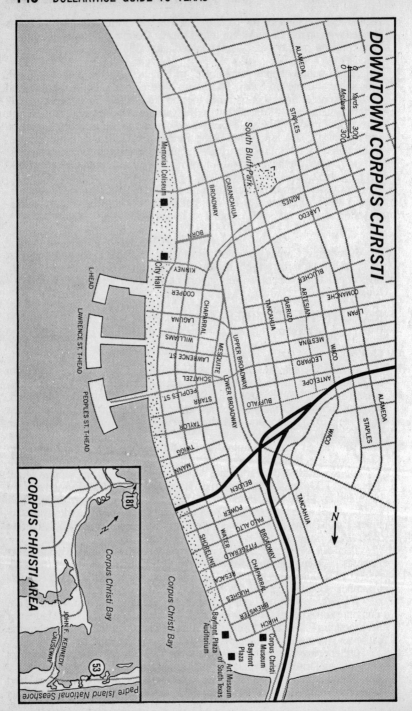

DOWNTOWN CORPUS CHRISTI

CORPUS CHRISTI AREA

can get a 14-day license for $5. They're available at local convenience stores and fishing-gear shops such as the Full Stringer, 2342 Rodd Field Rd. (tel. 992-4660).

## Beaches

Most central is **McGee Beach,** a small beach right on Shoreline in front of the Memorial Coliseum at Park Street. There's a food concession, and the breakwater is lit for night fishing.

A better choice is the **Corpus Christi Beach** at the northeastern tip of the city, just over the Harbor Bridge. A two-mile stretch of white sand beach, it offers shaded picnic tables with charcoal grills, rest rooms, showers, and children's play areas. In season you can rent aqua trikes, Sunfish, and catamarans at the U-Haul Rental Center on the beach near the Sandy Shores Resort or farther down at the Villa del Sol.

The third notable beach is on Padre Island, about which more later.

## Sightseeing Cruises

A fully narrated one-hour tour aboard the *Flagship,* a 400-passenger paddlewheeler, takes you into the bay and provides a view of port activity. The boat has an air-conditioned main deck, a snack concession, and a full bar; it's also used for moonlight cruises, some with dancing to live bands. Departures are from the Peoples Street T-Head. One-hour day trips cost $5.50 for adults, $3.50 for children under 12. Regular night tours (1½ hours) cost $6 for adults, $4 for children. A 1½-hour night cruise with live music is $7 for adults and $4 for children. And a summer-only late-night music cruise (9:30 to 11:30 p.m. Friday and Saturday) is $9.50 for adults, $5.50 for children. Other cruises depart daily except Tuesday between October 1 and March 1. For departure schedules and further information, call 884-1693 or 643-7128.

## Aquarentals

Along the seawall, in front of the Marriott, or behind City Hall, is **Corpus Christi Surreys by the Sea** (tel. 643-8715), renting pedal-powered surreys with a fringe on top. They seat two adults and have a kiddie basket up front. At the **Peoples Street T-Head** you can rent sailboards for windsurfing, aqua trikes, jetskis, paddleboats, Sunfish sailboats, and small catamarans. Sailboats—captained or bareboat charters—and houseboats can be rented at **L-Head** (tel. 881-8503); you can also inquire there about sailing courses. **Scuba and snorkeling** are, like deep-sea fishing, best in Port Aransas (tel. 749-5919).

## Golf

There are two 18-hole public golf courses, the **Corpus Christi Golf Center,** 4401 Old Brownsville Rd. (tel. 883-3696), and the **Oso Beach Golf Course,** 5600 S. Alameda (tel. 991-5351). Both offer pro shops and cart rentals, and are open daily. The Corpus Christi charges $2 weekdays, $2.75 weekends; Oso Beach charges $4.75 weekdays, $5.75 weekends.

## Tennis

The municipally run **H.E.B. Tennis Center,** 1520 Shely (tel. 888-5681), has 24 Laykold courts open weekdays from 9 a.m. to 10 p.m., till dark on Saturday, 1 p.m. till dark on Sunday. There's a $2 charge for 1½ hours of daytime use, $2.50 for nighttime use. NCAA championships are often held here.

Another municipal facility is the **South Bluff Center,** 502 King St. (tel. 883-6942), open Tuesday to Sunday from 8:30 a.m. to 10 p.m. Daytime 1½-hour play costs $1.75, $2.25 at night. They offer seven Laykold courts.

**THE ART MUSEUM OF SOUTH TEXAS:** Right on the bay at 1902 N. Shoreline Dr. (tel. 884-3844), this attractive art museum was designed by noted architect Philip Johnson in 1972. Gleaming white in the Corpus Christi sun, it's made of reinforced poured concrete, with vast expanses of bronze-tinted glass providing natural light and beautiful bay views as a backdrop to the art. The first floor is a sweep of unimpeded white space, with areas sized to present both large and small works at optimum effectiveness. The second floor has an upper gallery under a peaked skylight ceiling and a spectacular 60-foot walkway.

As the only fine arts museum in about a hundred-mile radius, AMST tries to offer an eclectic view of art media, historical periods, and works of all nations, though primarily featuring American and regional artists. Past exhibits have included "Johns, Stella, Warhol: Works in Series," "George Catlin American Indian Paintings," a photographic essay on the Big Thicket wilderness area, "Currier & Ives Prints," "Haitian Painting: The Naïve Tradition," "Greek and Roman Sculpture from the Boston Museum of Fine Arts," "Louise Nevelson Graphics," "Navajo Pictorial Weaving," "Etchings by Rembrandt and His Followers," "Winslow Homer Watercolors," and "Edward Hopper: Development of an American Artist." That's about as diverse and fascinating a group of shows as I've ever encountered at any museum, and it represents only a meager sampling of what AMST has presented over the years. In conjunction with shows, there's an ongoing schedule of classic films, lectures, dance performances, concerts, and other programs. Do find out what will be on during your stay.

Hours are Tuesday, Wednesday, and Friday from 10 a.m. to 5 p.m., on Thursday from noon to 8 p.m., weekends from noon to 5 p.m. There's no admission charge, but donations are appreciated.

**THE CORPUS CHRISTI MUSEUM:** Located in the Bayfront Plaza area at 1900 N. Chaparral St. (tel. 883-2862), this general museum is, like the art museum, the only one of its kind in the vast surrounding South Texas area. And like the art museum, it attempts a wide-ranging educative purpose. Because of its very diverse holdings, it's known as the "city's attic."

The North Building, for the most part, houses exhibits on area history and artifacts: antique kitchen implements including a raisin slicer and grape seeder; old school primers and spelling books; 200 photographs of early Corpus Christi; replicas of an early Corpus Christi house made of shellcrete bricks, a general store, and a trading post; war relics; the gun of a man who was hanged; and great grandpa's pipes and shaving equipment. Also in this section: an international doll collection; animal tableaux of wolves, bears, jaguars, mountain lions, etc.; Eskimo and Indian artifacts; a tableau of Béranger's discovery of the Aransas Pass in 1720; and the mummy of a pre-Inca girl.

The South Building displays include additional animal tableaux, exhibits on archeology (including a replica of the Rosetta Stone) and communications, weapons and implements from settler days, and a mummy's hand! In the Hall of Man you can peruse items from Persia, Japan, Indonesia, India, the Philippines, Egypt, Korea, Africa, and Australia. And the Hall of Marine Science contains shells, whale skeletons, ship models, ships in bottles, and exhibits on ship carpentry and shrimping, an important Texas industry. There are also changing shows highlighting the works of local artists, hands-on exhibits (fossils, petrified wood, an armadillo, etc., can be fondled), a Rock and Mineral Hall, and a series of aquariums.

Most exciting is a new $2.3-million wing under way at this writing that will add over 25,000 square feet of space to the museum and house a "Naval Aviation in South Texas" exhibit and artifacts from an ongoing excavation of the oldest recovered shipwreck in the western hemisphere. The latter involves three silver-laden Spanish ships that ran aground at Padre Island in 1554. It includes cannons, an anchor, part of a keel, coins and gold, pewterware, shipboard tools, and much more. The exhibit tells the story of the original voyage and the archeological efforts to recover the artifacts. Until the new wing opens, probably in 1988, these will be housed in the North Building.

The museum offers a full program of lectures, movies (they range from comedy classics like *Abbott & Costello Meet the Mummy* to more educational subjects like *Caves: The Dark Wilderness*), concerts, jazz, ballet folklorico, clowns, clog dancers, belly dancers, magicians, piano recitals—even treasure hunts for children. It's well worth investigating what will be on during your stay.

Admission is free. Museum hours are Tuesday to Saturday from 10 a.m. to 5 p.m., on Sunday from 2 to 5 p.m.

## HERITAGE PARK: A four-acre historic preservation project on the 1600 block
of North Chaparral Street adjoining the Bayfront Arts & Science Park, Heritage Park contains seven restored homes built between 1851 and 1908. The park itself is landscaped in period fashion, with globe street lamps and a gazebo in the courtyard.

Only one home is open for tours, but you can explore the others from the outside and read their historical markers. An example of High Victorian architecture, **Sidbury House,** built in 1893, doubles as headquarters for the local Junior League. Volunteers from that organization offer free 45-minute docent tours Tuesday to Thursday from 9:30 a.m. to 12:30 p.m. All of the furnishings in the house are authentic period pieces, many of them in the Eastlake style. They include a Seth Thomas clock, a Tiffany mantel clock with matching candlesticks, an 1893 Steinway piano, Louis XVI–style chairs, and an 1850 Jenny Lind table. Items like a bamboo hall rack reflect the Oriental influence prevalent at the time. For details, call 883-9352.

## U.S. NAVAL AIR STATION: Once the largest naval air station in the world, this
Corpus Christi facility is still the place pilots of all multi-engine propeller-driven planes receive advanced training. It's all the way out east at the end of Ocean Drive, so even if you're dragged here unwillingly by a navy buff spouse, you'll enjoy the beautiful scenery en route. Established in 1941, the station was one of the American coastline navy bases constructed as Nazi Germany began waging war on Europe. By the war's end over 35,000 aviators had earned their wings here.

Free 45-minute tours are given on Thursday at 1 p.m. only. No reservation is required. Tell the guard at the gate you want to take the tour and he'll direct you to a parking lot. The actual tour is via a 37-passenger bus (not surprisingly, an important navy base doesn't like people just wandering about unsupervised). In the way of day-to-day living operations, you'll see the base housing area, chapel, hospitals, theater, store, gymnasium, bowling alley, dining facility, and fire department. The tour also visits the flightline (where you'll see the types of aircraft pilots learn to fly here), the synthetic trainer building (where pilots use computer technology to simulate actual flights), a helicopter repair hangar, the supply building, and the public works building. For further details, call 939-2568.

## THE MUSEUM OF ORIENTAL CULTURES: This rather unexpected museum
at 426 S. Staples, at Marguerite (tel. 883-1303), is basically the collection of Corpus Christi native Mrs. Billie Trimble Chandler, who went to Japan after World War II to teach children of Americans in the occupation forces and collected a

vast store of Oriental art and artifacts during her 17-year stay. In 1973 she donated her treasures to the people of Corpus Christi, and other benefactors have since contributed additional pieces. Like many a private collection, it's a mixed bag of valuable art, reproductions, and items of greater personal appeal than museum quality, but that all combines to make for interesting perusal. A highlight is a collection of 1,000 clay Hakata dolls displayed in dioramas representing various aspects of Japanese life—Emperor Hirohito and his empress in the Imperial Palace, fishermen, farmers, laborers, worshippers at the Horuji Temple, etc. Also well represented are red clay *haniwa* figures, reproductions of Japanese grave art from A.D. 300 to 700. Then there are samurai artifacts, Indian jewelry and brassware, Tang Dynasty masks, Noh masks, handmade silk kimonos, geisha fans, Hindu and Buddhist art, porcelains and cloisonné and a 1766 Japanese Buddha—all displayed in rooms with Chinese red walls and floors. There are special exhibits from time to time focusing on specific countries, like "Korea: Land of the Morning Calm" and "Decorative Arts of India," or exhibiting the works of well-known Asian artists. A library of books on Orientalia on the premises is open to the public, and the museum sponsors occasional events ranging from martial arts demonstrations to Japanese dance programs.

The museum is open Tuesday to Saturday from 10 a.m. to 4 p.m. Admission is $1 for adults, 50¢ for students, and 75¢ for senior citizens.

## 5. Nightlife

For a small town, there's quite a bit to do, including some pretty plush places to dance. Ballet, symphony, theater, and headliner concerts are featured on a fairly regular basis. In addition to the listings below, check out the Art Museum of South Texas (tel. 884-3844) and the Corpus Christi Museum (tel. 883-2862), both of which offer an exciting schedule of cultural events. Also consider moonlight cruises aboard the *Flagship* (tel. 884-1693).

The **Bayfront Plaza Convention Center,** 1901 N. Shoreline Dr. (tel. 883-8543), is sometimes used for headliner concerts. Among those who've played this facility are Tom Jones, Engelbert Humperdinck, Donny and Marie, George Carlin, George Strait, KISS, Wayne Newton, and John Conlee. You might also catch a Broadway road company show like *Annie* or *A Chorus Line* at the Convention Center, and it's the home of the Corpus Christi Symphony Orchestra and the Corpus Christi Ballet Society. Call to find out what's on during your stay.

Just next door, the **Harbor Playhouse,** 1 Bayfront Park (tel. 882-3356), offers a year-round theater season ranging from comedies to classics. The performers are members of a community theater group that has been in existence since 1925. The current facility dates to 1975. Productions in recent seasons have included *Joseph and the Amazing Technicolor Dreamcoat, A Streetcar Named Desire,* Shaw's *St. Joan, Carousel,* and *Bullshot Crummond.* Tickets are under $10.

One of the liveliest spots in town is the **High Tide Lounge** at the Hershey, 900 N. Shoreline Dr. (tel. 887-1600). Decorated in shades of gray and silver, it has a contemporary look and lighting that pulsates to the beat of the music. Come during weekday Happy Hour to enjoy a complimentary buffet with afternoon cocktails and stay on to dance to music provided by the high-quality Las Vegas–style lounge acts that perform here Monday to Saturday nights.

Also at the Hershey is the stunning 19th- and 20th- floor **Reflections,** an elegant restaurant with an adjoining lounge that offers piano-bar music from 7 to 10 p.m. Monday to Thursday nights and a combo for dancing on Friday and Saturday. Great views, and very romantic.

Another very happening hotel nightspot is **Bentley's** at the Marriott, 707 N.

Shoreline (tel. 882-1700), which also gets the evening going with a lavish Happy Hour buffet—shrimp, rib roast, crab, taco bar—and rocks all night to high-energy music played by a DJ. It's plush and attractive, with comfortable sofas and armchairs lit by shaded table lamps and lots of greenery endlessly reflected in mirrored walls and columns. There's music nightly. On Friday and Saturday a $2 cover is charged.

A large but comfortable club of the urban cowboy genre, **Dallas,** 24 Parkdale Plaza, between Everhart and South Staples (tel. 852-8088), is decorated with palm trees, maps of Texas, and neon beer signs. The music is mostly C&W, with a little top-40s rock thrown in now and again. Most patrons, be they rodeo riders or office workers, are attired in tight jeans, boots, and cowboy hats. There are pool tables and a shoeshine stand, both de rigueur for a cowboy bar, and the action centers around an octagonal bar. Dallas is always mobbed. There are frequent promotions, such as pajama night, toga night, beach party, modeling contests, dance contests, and flakiest of all, "foolish night." Most nights, it's just a great place to dance and hang out. Open nightly. Minimum age is 21. Cover charge is $3. Ladies are admitted free on Monday and Wednesday nights.

**Kramer's,** 6057 Weber Rd., between Caravelle and O'Day Parkway in the Las Palmas Shopping Center (tel. 857-5411), is a Los Angeles–slick, hi-tech-decor oldies club with an adjoining chi-chi diner. It attracts a Yuppie crowd, and attracts them in droves; if you haven't taken assertiveness training, you'll never get to sit down. Thursday through Saturday nights, come a little early (for the Happy Hour buffet) and avoid long lines outside. It's a let-loose atmosphere within, people dancing on the bars and tables to music from the '50s, '60s, and early '70s—a lot of Motown/*Big Chill* sounds. A bright red '55 Thunderbird convertible nestles against a 3-D wall mural of a palm-studded beach, but you won't see much of the decor through the wall-to-wall people. In the diner, you and your honey can romance over burgers and milkshakes. The club stays open till 2 a.m., the restaurant till 4 a.m. Minimum age 23. No cover.

Finally, there's **Mingles,** 4244 S. Padre Island Dr., between Everhart and Weber (tel. 851-8315), an every-night, high-energy scene where cowboys mingle with Yuppies, and the DJ plays a mix of oldies, C&W, and top-40s tunes. Big and ski-lodgey in feel, with pine-paneled walls, a two-tiered balcony, and a stuffed Kodiak bear at the entrance, Mingles has antique merry-go-round horses suspended over the dance floor from a 30-foot ceiling. There are pool tables, video games, and big plush couches away from the action where conversation is plausible. Rebel yells increase in number as the evening wears on, and people are more likely to jump up on the bar and strut their stuff. The action gets under way about 10 p.m. and continues till 2 a.m. On Sunday night there's free barbecue on a wooden deck out front. Minimum age is 21. No cover.

## 6. Padre Island National Seashore

A party of Spanish surveyors wrote about Padre Island in 1766, "Her treasure is the gold of her sun, the silver of her moonlight, and the sapphire of her pearl-crested waves."

Though the island was more verdant and forested in those days, the description still evokes the magic of Padre, the largest barrier island in the United States, extending 113 miles along the Gulf Coast from Corpus Christi to Mexico. Three miles at its widest point, and in some places just a few hundred yards wide, it is one of America's most unspoiled wilderness areas. Only the north and south ends (especially the latter) are developed; the central 63½ miles was declared a national park by President John F. Kennedy in 1962 and is under federal protection.

Whether you merely visit the beach at the northern extremity, or penetrate the wilder interior in a four-wheel-drive, you'll experience some of Padre's subtle mystique. Like much of the Texas Gulf Coast, Padre was originally a hunting and fishing area for the legendary Karankawa Indians—a tall (over six feet) and handsome tribe who practiced cannibalism. Some accounts claim they merely ate parts of enemies to ingest their strength; other, more lurid writings have them tying victims to a stake and slicing off pieces of flesh to eat before their very eyes. Whichever was the case, the Karankawa were extremely hostile to white folks who happened upon their land, and they let it be known.

Alonso Alvarez de Piñeda charted the island along with Corpus Christi in 1519, naming it Las Islas Blancas (the White Islands), but it was later renamed for Father (Padre) Nicholás Ballí, a Spanish missionary who received the island as a land grant in the early 1800s. Ballí's descendants still make occasional claims on the island, which they consider rightfully theirs. In the 1970s they once blocked the Queen Isabella Causeway (entrance to South Padre) to dramatize their position. Ballí tried, without success, to bring Christianity to the Indians. He did, however, initiate the first extensive cattle-ranching operation here—an enterprise that would eventually change the island's topography to a desert-like landscape as grazing animals destroyed vegetation that had built up over centuries. Treasure-laden Spanish galleons voyaged past the island for hundreds of years, often running aground in gulf storms, especially at a treacherous ship's graveyard called Devil's Elbow. Pirate attacks were also not uncommon. In 1554 a fleet of Spanish ships ran into trouble here, and 300 survivors were marooned on the island. It wasn't much of a sanctuary: only two survived attacks by the Karankawa and the hardships of a 350-mile trek in oppressive heat to Mexico, where they hoped to meet up again with civilization. A fortune in gold and jewels, from these and other wrecks, is still buried in the island's shifting, wind-formed dunes. There's also the treasure left here by cattle rancher John Singer (brother of the sewing machine Singer), who buried $80,000 and his wife's emeralds in a jar under an oak tree when fleeing north at the outbreak of the Civil War. When he returned at the war's end, his ranch, the tree, and the jar, had been blown away by hurricanes. Of course, much of the island's ostensible buried treasure has probably blown out to sea; during a hurricane it is said that pirate Jean Lafitte once sailed right across Padre just to show that it could be done.

Indian history, pirate lore, and buried treasure make for a romantic backdrop, but the essence of the Padre Island experience is a communion with nature, primitive and unruly. Since cattle were rounded up and removed from the island in 1971, a great deal of the natural vegetation has returned. In spring, especially, the beaches are blanketed with wildflowers—brilliant emerald-leaf railroad vine with big purple blossoms, masses of pink seaside phlox, white-stemmed wild indigo, red and orange Indian blanket, morning glories, flame flowers, gentian, and evening primrose—all in dramatic contrast to the stark-white sand. Dolphins, and less frequently, whales, frolic in the water, and pelicans, herons, sandpipers, and gulls scavenge for fish. Over 350 species of birds are year-round or seasonal visitors, the latter including thousands of winter ducks and geese. Because Padre is separated from the mainland by the Laguna Madre, a body of salt water that varies in width from three to ten miles, the fauna found on the island differs from that of the mainland. At least one species, the kangaroo rat, has evolved in a way unique to the island.

**HOW TO VISIT PADRE ISLAND:** From Ocean Drive hotels in Corpus Christi it's about a 30-mile drive to the northern tip of Padre Island. Go east on South Padre Island Drive (Texas Hwy. 358), cross the John F. Kennedy Causeway over Laguna Madre, and turn south on Park Road 22. From that turnoff, you can only take a conventional car for 14 miles. The first 8½ miles are on hard-surfaced road, at the end of which you'll come to the **Malaquite Visitor Center** (tel. 512/949-8068), which is staffed by park rangers. Offering extended programs and information, this is a *must* starting point for down-island travel beyond the 14-mile limit. The Visitor Center is on a pleasant white sand beach, offering showers, rest rooms, an observation deck, sheltered picnic tables, and, in summer, a concession selling beach necessaries like suntan lotion and sunglasses, and a snackbar. The center itself—open 9 a.m. to 4 p.m. daily, till 6 p.m. in summer—features exhibits on Padre and, in summer, a wide range of naturalist slide shows, beach walks, and campfire programs. Participation in these programs, along with beachcombing, camping (there are sites on the premises available for $4 a night), swimming, sunning, fishing, and bird-watching in the Malaquite Beach area, is, for the most part, the extent to which you can explore Padre Island without a four-wheel-drive vehicle. You can drive a regular car out on hard sand for another 5½ miles, an area where free camping is also permitted. And you can take the kids to swim in the calm, shallow waters of **Bird Island Basin,** part of the Laguna Madre off Park Road 22, also a popular area for windsurfing and catamarans. Come early in the morning to watch the shorebirds.

**DOWN-ISLAND TRAVEL:** To go beyond 14 miles south of the northern entrance, you must have a state-licensed four-wheel-drive vehicle or all-terrain cycle. They can be rented in Corpus Christi, but the companies that rent them seem to come and go every year, and in summer they usually have to be reserved in advance. Before you leave home, call National Park Headquarters at 512/937-2621 or the Visitor Center for up-to-date information on rentals. They can also tell you about guided trips. The cost of a four-wheel-drive is about $75 per day, plus gas. A recorded message giving information on tides, weather, shelling, beach conditions, and fishing is provided from 8 a.m. to 4 p.m. daily; call 512/949-8175.

Remember, when you get out into the unspoiled wilderness, you're on your own. You may encounter no one else for miles. Be sure you're properly equipped with a shovel, wooden boards, and a car jack (sand-engulfed vehicles are a common problem), sturdy high boots (there are rattlesnakes in the grasses), rubber boots for wading into the water, mosquito repellent, suntan lotion, extra gasoline, a CB radio, a first-aid kit, and adequate water and food supplies. For pleasure, bring binoculars for bird-watching, a camera, fishing gear (there are an estimated 600 to 800 varieties of saltwater fish along the seashore), and shell-collecting buckets.

The first area you'll encounter at the four-wheel-drive cutoff is **Little Shell Beach,** much of its surface made up of coquina clam shells. Ten miles farther along is **Big Shell Beach.** Shelling is particularly good during the winter months, as is birdwatching.

Tales of lost treasure notwithstanding, metal detectors are *verboten;* the Archeological Resources Act makes scavenging a felony, so if you come upon a trunkful of doubloons you're legally required to turn them in. Riding on the dunes is also illegal, because their fragile vegetation is easily destroyed.

It's also possible, of course, to hike down-island, once again taking many precautions. The fact that you have to carry all the water you need will probably impose limitations, unless you can arrange with a driver to meet you along the way. Whatever your hiking or driving plans, be sure to notify a ranger before departing.

All these warnings are not to scare you off, but to help you have an adventure rather than a misadventure. Exploring Padre Island isn't for everyone. Its

# Chapter V

# THE RIO GRANDE VALLEY: THE BEACH AND THE BORDER

### 1. Brownsville/Matamoros
### 2. South Padre Island
### 3. McAllen/Reynosa

THE FERTILE RIO GRANDE VALLEY, a 140-mile strip of southernmost Texas, is the Lone Star State's top agricultural-producing region and a popular annual vacation spot for some 200,000 "winter Texans." When their hometowns are snowed in and a 10° day is considered a heat spell, these American midwestern and Canadian snowbirds wing their way down to the valley for months of fun and sun in a semitropical clime where orange blossoms and roses bloom at Christmastime. The average winter temperature in the region is over 70°. South Padre Island offers not only an idyllic climate but also some of the most beautiful beaches in the state, terrific fishing, and water sports. Brownsville and McAllen are most notable (from the tourist's point of view) for their proximity to Mexico. A day or two in either of these cities will probably give you ample time to explore the immediate south-of-the-border attractions. And since Brownsville/Matamoros is just a 25-minute drive from Padre, McAllen about 1½ hours, you might consider setting up headquarters for a week or so at the beach and making side trips to other area cities.

## 1. Brownsville/Matamoros

Brownsville is the largest city (pop. 100,000) of the Rio Grande Valley, and it's not only a stone's throw from Mexico, it practically is Mexico. Over 70% of the population is Hispanic.

The city's early history is a typical tale of the wild and woolly West. Though the Spanish had missions and villages along the Rio Grande by 1749 (including a flourishing trade center that would become Matamoros in 1826), it wasn't until 1850 that a young adventurer from Connecticut, Charles Stillman, organized a government to the north and got Brownsville officially incorporated. In 1846, during the Mexican War, Zachary Taylor fought to reinforce America's claims

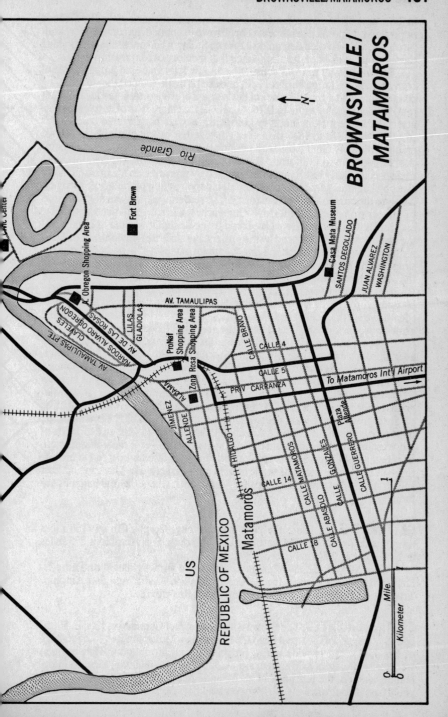

BROWNSVILLE/
MATAMOROS

—N—

Rio Grande

Fort Brown

Casa Mata Museum

SANTOS DEGOLLADO

JUAN ALVAREZ

WASHINGTON

J. Obregon Shopping Area

AV. TAMAULIPAS

LILAS

GLADIOLAS

AV. DE LAS ROSAS

VARDOS ALVARO OBREGON

CLAVELES

AV. TAMAULIPAS PTE.

ProNaf
Shopping Area

Zona Rosa Shopping Area

CALLE BRAVO

CALLE 4

CALLE 5

PRIV CARRANZA

To Matamoros Int'l Airport

JIMENEZ

ALLENDE

ALDAMA

HIDALGO

Plaza
Allende

CALLE GUERRERO

CALLE GONZALES

CALLE MATAMOROS

CALLE ABASOLO

CALLE 14

CALLE 18

Matamoros

US

REPUBLIC OF MEXICO

Mile

Kilometer

0

in the area, building a fort for this purpose on the north bank of the Rio Grande opposite Matamoros. He named it Fort Brown in honor of its commander, Maj. Jacob Brown, who died defending it. When Stillman laid out a village adjoining the fort four years later, he also named it in memory of Major Brown.

In those days the town consisted of a few huts scattered among fields of corn and cotton. Large herds of wild horses and cattle roamed the surrounding countryside, and a general tenor of lawlessness prevailed. A noted local inhabitant, William Neale, wrote in 1876, "I believe that more men of desperate character, desperate fortunes, and evil propensities were congregated here on this frontier from 1846 to 1848 than ever got together in any other place." Neale credited the 1849 Gold Rush with purging the area of the worst of the desperados, luring them to California. But even with the most lawless factions gone, Brownsville's early history was long marked by warfare with Mexico and incursions by banditos so vicious as to threaten depopulation of the whole area and paralyze the burgeoning cattle industry. The settlers were also plagued for years by attacks from bands of Indians—Comanches, Cherokees, Apaches, Creeks, and Kickapoos. (Of course a case could be made that it was the Mexicans and the Indians who were plagued by the settlers, but since this is a book about Texas we'll consider matters from the Lone Star point of view). The worst of the incursions was by Mexican leader Juan Cortina, who organized frequent raids with the aim of redeeming the north country. On September 28, 1860, he invaded Brownsville with a force of about 200 men who woke the town before daylight by riding through the streets with guns ablaze shouting "Meuran los Gringos!" (death to the Americans) and "Viva México!" Cortina broke down the jail and armed prisoners to join him. He held the area until the end of December when Gen. Robert E. Lee, with the help of the Texas Rangers, drove him out. However, border warfare continued for another decade with both townfolk and outlying ranches occasionally falling victim to Mexican assault, arson, and robbery.

Today, except for typical bordertown driving, it's all quiet on this western front. Brownsville is a tranquil town laced with freshwater *resacas* (shallow lagoons formed where the Gulf of Mexico merges with the Rio Grande) and miles of citrus groves and cotton fields—all under the beautiful blue Texas sky. The most scenic street is a 2½-mile stretch of Palm Boulevard with an esplanade of tall Washingtonian palms. And in the downtown area—especially Washington, Elizabeth, and Levee Streets between 8th and 14th Streets—it's fun to browse through block after block of exotic merchandise displayed in Mexican and East Indian stores. But save your pesos for Matamoros, where the real bargains are found.

**GETTING THERE:** From the closest major city, Corpus Christi (160 miles away), take Texas Hwy. 44 west and U.S. 77 south. San Antonio is 275 miles away; Houston, 357; and Laredo, 208.

**Muse Air** (tel. 512/544-2828) has flights into Brownsville/South Padre Island International Airport from Houston, Dallas, Austin, and San Antonio. **Trailways** provides bus service into downtown Brownsville.

**GETTING ORIENTED:** The **Brownsville Chamber of Commerce,** 1600 E. Elizabeth St., just down the street from the Fort Brown Motor Inn (tel. 512/546-3721 or 542-4341), can provide maps, brochures, and information. They're open weekdays only, from 8:30 a.m. to 5 p.m., and they also maintain a tourist information center at the junction of U.S. 77 and FM 802 (tel. 512/541-8455), which you'll pass if you're driving in. It's open weekdays from 8:30 a.m. to 5 p.m. and on Saturday from 9 a.m. to 1 p.m. For advance information, write to the chamber at P.O. Box 752, Brownsville, TX 78522.

**GETTING AROUND:** Unless you plan only to post yourself at the Fort Brown Motor Inn and make on-foot or taxi excursions into Matamoros, you'll probably want a car. Both **Budget** (tel. 512/542-5684) and **Avis** (tel. 512/542-7756) have airport locations, as do a number of other companies. Brownsville has a pretty good **bus** system (call 541-8359 or 541-5514 for routing information). Though major hotels offer free transport to/from the airport, public buses also ply the route.

There are always **taxis** lined up outside the Fort Brown, and, this being a few blocks from Mexico, rates are negotiable. Don't pay more than $10.

**ANNUAL EVENTS:** Since 1938 Brownsville has been celebrating **Charro Days,** a week-long fiesta in late February. The holiday celebrates the Mexican cowboy. It begins with a *grito* (the Mexican answer to a rebel yell) and continues with days of events on both sides of the border—street dances, grand balls, costumed parades, Mexican rodeos, bullfights, strolling mariachi bands, a children's parade, fajita cookoffs, and jalapeño-eating contests. For details (some events require tickets) call 512/542-4245.

Contact the Chamber of Commerce to find out about other events in the area during your stay. A lot goes on in winter when the population almost doubles with sun-seekers.

**WHERE TO STAY:** The accommodation of choice in Brownsville is the **Fort Brown Motor Inn,** 1900 E. Elizabeth St., just off International Boulevard, Brownsville, TX 78520 (tel. 512/546-2201, or toll free 800/541-3333), a beautiful 17-acre property set on a lagoon and landscaped with bougainvillea, hibiscus, palm groves, splashing waterfalls, and gazebos. You can easily walk to Mexico from the Fort Brown; the bridge is just two blocks away. The hotel offers many resort facilities, among them two tennis courts lit for night play, a shuffleboard court, and a large palm-shaded swimming pool with an adjoining sundeck and baby wading pool. You can phone up and order from room service at poolside, and best of all you can watch the sun go down while enjoying a before-dinner margarita in an outdoor whirlpool set into a latticework gazebo. There's another pool with a waterfall and additional Jacuzzi overlooking the resaca.

Also overlooking the resaca, through big windows, is the hotel's very pretty coffeeshop, with stone, brick, and latticework walls and many indoor plants. The facility also has shaded outdoor seating. Its menu features Mexican and American breakfasts, low-priced luncheon buffets, and dinner choices ranging from chicken-fried steak to carne asada. There's fancier dining at the Resaca Club, a snazzy-looking nightspot with red velvet curtains, Spanish furnishings, and white-linened tables lit by candles in red glass holders. A large bar under a stained-glass ceiling nestles in one corner. The bar is open from 11 a.m.; however, the best time to come is from 4 to 8 p.m. when a two-drink minimum (and a scotch and soda is just $1.50) entitles you to an extraordinary all-you-can-eat buffet of fresh mushroom salad, nachos, chile con queso, tomatoes, cucumber salad, carrot salad, finger sandwiches, carne guisada (beef tips in gravy), guacamole, and sliced beef served from a carving station. There's also a full à la carte menu, which you might consider for late-night dining while you watch the nightclub acts—Las Vegas lounge-style entertainment, with two shows a night (Monday to Saturday at 10 p.m. and midnight) and dancing in between. There's no cover or minimum for the shows. A typical dinner at the Resaca Club might begin with an order of cheese/bean/guacamole/jalapeño nachos ($4.25), followed by an entree of prime rib with Yorkshire pudding ($14.25), breast of chicken with mango sauce ($13.95), or shrimp stuffed with crabmeat ($14.50). For dessert, there's baked Alaska ($6.95 for two). Outside the Resaca Club is the Hawaiian Lanai, a terracotta patio under an awning with Polynesian furnishings amid potted evergreens and hanging plants. You can enjoy dinner or drinks out here, and the music can be heard via speakers.

Rooms at the Fort Brown have king-size or double beds, covered with navy or beige cotton print spreads; carpeting is tan, rust, or beige, and the wallpaper is off-white. In-room amenities include cable color TV with movie channel, an AM/FM radio, and a Bible left open to the 23rd Psalm. Many rooms offer pool or resaca views, and some have patios. Poolside suites are especially nice; they have terracotta tile floors, white stucco walls, lots of plants, and private Jacuzzis. One even has a waterbed.

On the premises are a gift/resortwear shop, beauty parlor, and car-rental desk, and there's a small shopping center, including a car insurance outlet, just across the street. Complimentary transport to/from the airport is available.

Rates at the Fort Brown are $42 to $48 single, $49 to $59 double, $75 single or double for a corner suite with a couch, $135 single or double for a poolside suite with private Jacuzzi, $165 for an ultraluxurious penthouse suite. An extra person pays $7, and children under 12 stay free. Parking is free.

There's also a **La Quinta Inn** in town at 55 Sam Perl Blvd. and Fronton Street, Brownsville, TX 78520 (tel. 512/546-0381, or toll free 800/531-5900). It's a very nice, well-run property, with a medium-size swimming pool and sundeck, a 24-hour Denny's just next door, and a lounge called the Conquistador decorated with suits of armor and Mexican antiques, the latter featuring extensive Mexican buffets at Happy Hour. The property is conveniently located between the old and new bridges.

Rates are $38 single, $43 double, $48 for three or four people; children under 18, free. No-smoking rooms and facilities for the disabled are available. See Chapter I for further details on La Quinta.

**WHERE TO EAT:** One of the best choices in Brownsville is **Antonio's**, 2403 Boca Chica Blvd., between North Street and Los Ebanos Boulevard (tel. 542-6504), a cheerful little restaurant where great meals are prepared from scratch. There are two dining rooms. The front room has stucco and adobe walls hung with sombreros, Mexican crafts, and paintings on velvet of matadors. Along with terracotta floors, tables covered in variegated checkered oilcloths, a latticework partition, and wrought-iron amber lamps, it all combines to create a festive south-of-the-border setting. The second room is sunny and filled with plants.

Antonio's has really superb food, and the best time to experience it is at Wednesday's buffet dinner, an all-you-can-eat affair that lets you experience many house specialties. Come early—lines begin forming by 5:30 p.m. When you sit down at Antonio's, you'll get a big bowl of homemade tortilla chips with guacamole-based green sauce and pico de gallo made with big chunks of tomato. An appetizer of queso con chorizo—spicy sausage in melted cheese ($3.75)—is also a good way to make use of your chips. Do save some room, though, for entrees like deep-fried, breaded chile relleños stuffed with meat and spices, covered with Spanish sauce, and served with rice and beans ($4); fajitas served with rice, beans a la charra, and flour or corn tortillas guacamole, ($5.50); and Antonio's Monterrey special—grilled steak topped with ranchero sauce, a beef taco, a cheese enchilada, guacamole, rice, and beans ($6.75). For dessert, the rich and creamy flan ($1.25) is heaven. Also consider Antonio's for

Mexican breakfasts—two eggs over easy with ranchero sauce, fried potatoes, refried beans, chorizo sausage, beef tips with gravy, and flour tortillas ($4.25).

Hours are Monday to Thursday from 8 a.m. to 10 p.m., on Friday and Saturday till 11 p.m.

The **Oyster Bar Too,** 153 Paredes Line Rd., between Boca Chica Boulevard and Las Casa Street (tel. 542-9511), offers a simple fresh-seafood menu in an unpretentious setting. It looks like a coffeeshop, with red vinyl booths and chairs at Formica tables and fluorescent lighting overhead. I like it best during the day when sunlight streams in through the large windows. A large oyster or shrimp cocktail here costs $4, $2.50 for a smaller serving; a large bowl of rich seafood soup is $5.95, $3.25 for a cup. That's almost all there is in the way of appetizers, except for raw oysters on the halfshell ($3.50 per half dozen) or boiled regular shrimp ($3.95) or jumbo shrimp ($4.50). For an entree, you might select the delicious stuffed shrimp ($8.45), a whole fresh baby snapper broiled or fried ($11.95), fried shrimp or oysters ($7.45), or perhaps the super seafood platter of three raw oysters, three cocktail shrimp, three fried oysters, three fried shrimp, and a fried filet of fresh fish ($11.95). All of the above are served with homemade french fries or baked potato, salad, and very tasty hot rolls with butter. There's a full bar, but no desserts are offered.

Open daily from 11:30 a.m. to 2:30 p.m. and 5 to 9 p.m. There's another location, **Oyster Bar I** (the original, opened in 1950), at 1057 E. Levee St. (tel. 542-9786).

**BROWNSVILLE SIGHTS:** The **Gladys Porter Zoo,** 500 Ringgold St., between 6th Street and Palm Boulevard (tel. 546-7187), houses 1,800 animals on 31 beautifully landscaped acres lush with bougainvillea, palms, bamboo groves, cactus gardens, orchids, poinciana, and hibiscus. The population includes over 450 species of wildlife—mammals, birds, reptiles, amphibians, invertebrates, and fish—including some species found in no other zoo in the world. It has been called one of the ten best zoos in the country by professionals for its natural animal habitats and its programs in research, conservation, and breeding. The zoo is built around a meandering resaca system, which is populated by numerous waterfowl—cranes, storks, black swans and baby cygnets (they're not ugly, they're cute), geese, scarlet ibis, roseate spoonbills, and lovely pink- and coral-hued flamingoes—along with seasonal freeloaders like raucous grackles, cormorants, gulls, black-bellied tree ducks, and egrets. At the children's zoo, youngsters can pet or rub noses with goats, sheep, and baby llamas. The area also houses a nursery of baby animals including gorillas and orangutans whose antics are a delight to watch.

In major areas, animals from tropical America, Indo-Australia, Asia, and Africa roam freely in large cave- and rock-like enclosures built of blown concrete, their free-form appearance adding a sculpture-garden aspect to the zoo's landscaping. There are fleet African antelopes, ostriches, striking red- and white-faced (and bummed) mandrills, white rhinos, cute fluffy lemurs from Madagascar, spectacular Indian peacocks, brilliantly plumed Ceylon junglefowl (the progenitor of our modern domestic chicken), Australian wallabies, and brightly colored birds from America's tropical jungles.

Of course, that's not the half of it. The herpetarium and aquarium displays are fascinating—not to mention indoors and air-conditioned, and there are picnic tables, tree-shaded benches, food concessions, a gift shop, a playground, and a large swimming pool on the grounds. Though the chief way to see the zoo is on foot (there's an easy-to-follow route), on Sunday only from 1:30 to 3:30 p.m. you can take a 20-minute train ride for 50¢.

The zoo is open daily from 9 a.m. to an hour before dusk. Adults pay $3.50

and children 2 to 14 pay $1.50. Get a map at the ticket booth and ask about any special programs (films, speakers, concerts, etc.) that may be taking place during your stay.

Charles Stillman was the founder of Brownsville, purchasing a large tract of land adjoining Fort Brown in 1849. The Stillman name is today reflected in street names—St. Charles (for himself), Elizabeth (for his wife), and St. Francis (for his father). Stillman's 1850 southern colonial-style home, the **Charles Stillman House** at 1305 Washington St. (tel. 542-3929), built of handmade brick with New England slate shingles, has been restored by the Brownsville Historical Association with assistance from the founder's descendants. Stillman lived here through 1867 when, following a stroke that left him paralyzed, he joined his family in Cornwall, New York. Prior to that he had a marital arrangement of the kind we think of as very jet-age 20th century. During an 1853 yellow fever epidemic Stillman sent his wife and six children to Cornwall, and they stayed on there while he made frequent trips back and forth. When Stillman left, he sold the house to the Mexican consul in Brownsville, whose family lived here through 1956. Stillman's great-grandson bought the property in 1957 and restored it, furnishing it with period pieces gleaned from various family members.

The front door to the house is a "Christian" door, with the shape of a cross in the center and six square partitions; the upper four represent the gospels, and the lower two symbolize an open bible. The door opens into a spacious central hall, furnished with Stillman family pieces like a 1770 grandfather clock in a carved cherry case that belonged to Elizabeth Stillman's Yankee grandparents, an iron sea chest (1830) that was a gift to Stillman from one of his sea captains, a replica of a framed sampler done by Elizabeth's mother, a Benjamin West engraving, and an original Maxfield Parrish painting. The parlor, its floors covered with Aubusson needlepoint carpets, is furnished with pieces from the 1850s that came from the Stillman family home in Cornwall. One of Elizabeth's dresses is displayed on a mannequin, there are three steel engravings by Thomas Cole, and the black-and-white chandelier—used with candles—was made in England by Josiah Wedgwood. The master bedroom has a Victorian hand-carved maple four-poster with a long-handled bed warmer from Elizabeth Stillman's grandparents' home; on the wall is a framed engraving by Benjamin West. The "dining room" you see today was also a bedroom originally, but its appointments well exemplify the period.

Another room on the premises (added in 1900) houses a small museum of historical Brownsville relics, such as the first spike driven into the Southern Pacific Railway, old photos, arrowheads, the city charter, and Confederate weapons. The museum leads into the 1850 kitchen, with its original tile floor, brick hearth, and spinning wheel. Antique kitchen utensils are displayed over the fireplace. A kitchen door opens on the courtyard where the old cistern is located and you can see what remains of the original garden and the carriage house. In the latter, one of the Stillman's buggies is on display.

The house is open weekdays only, from 10 a.m. to noon and 2 to 5 p.m. Admission is $1 for adults, 15¢ for students. Park at the municipal lot on 14th and Adams.

The **Port of Brownsville** is a thriving operation, surrounded by about 200 companies including a huge manufacturing facility for offshore drilling platforms called Marathon LeTourneau. In addition to cargo-handling facilities, the port boasts one of the finest fishing harbors on the gulf, with approximately 500 shrimp boats permanently based here and over 1,000 others loading or unloading at the docks each year. It connects to the Gulf of Mexico via a 17-mile channel and is a terminus of the U.S. Inland Waterway System. The port's not set up to accommodate tourists, but if you'd like to drive over and see the action—railroad cars transporting cargo, grain elevators, big ships, transit sheds, etc.—take Hwy. 48 east to Rte. 511, make a right and then a left at the first stop sign. To see the shrimp boats, just take Hwy. 48 as far as Marathon LeTourneau and look for the gate on the right-hand side. If shrimp is being loaded or unloaded, you'll have to ask the guard for permission to come inside; it's usually granted.

**SPORTS:** Golf, tennis, hunting, and fishing excursions are all popular activities in Brownsville. Details are available at your hotel desk or from the chamber of commerce (tel. 546-3721 or 542-4341).

**NIGHTLIFE:** The **Resaca Club** at the Fort Brown Motor Inn, 1900 E. Elizabeth St. (tel. 546-2201), is the hub of nighttime entertainment in Brownsville. There's no cover or minimum to enjoy the Vegas-lounge-style entertainment here. Details above.

**MATAMOROS:** Though it's listed last here, Matamoros is the primary reason tourists other than winter Texans visit Brownsville. Named for patriot, priest, and general Mariano Matamoros, one of the leaders of Mexico's War of Independence, it is the largest of the Rio Grande Valley cities. Some of Matamoros's architecture dates to the 18th century, and the market streets are lively and colorful. I've seen some terrific street performers in the market and once encountered a man trying to sell an eagle!

Though shops begin just across the bridge on Calle Alvaro Obregon, make your way on foot or by taxi to the main market area about half a mile farther along. Bounded by Calles 8 and 10 east and west, Calles Bravo and Abasolo north and south, this four-block area contains the old and new markets, a warren of hundreds of shops selling every variety of Mexican wares—sombreros, piñatas, embroidered dresses, pottery, onyx, leather goods, striped serapes, guitars, baskets, rugs, hammocks, dolls, brassware, and much, much more. Low-priced liquor is also a lure. Be sure to bargain everywhere; if you're good at it, you can radically reduce prices. The market shops are open seven days a week from about 9 a.m. to 6 p.m.

If you walk to the market, carry a map, since no Mexican you meet along the way is likely to be able to provide directions, even though it's only a few blocks from the border and they probably have lived here all their lives. I don't know why this is, but it is. I've occasionally had Mexicans point skyward in response to queries as to the whereabouts of the local *mercado*.

If you drive across, be sure you're insured. I don't recommend it, because driving in Mexican bordertowns is a hair-raising experience, and once you're in, you'll have a long wait in a hot car getting through Customs on the way out. Cars pay a 60¢ toll each way; pedestrians, 16¢. Car insurance is available at **Sanborn's,** 1922 E. Elizabeth (tel. 542-7222). You can park Stateside across the street from the Chamber of Commerce, or in the International Friendship Garden lot, both right across from the Gateway Bridge. Once you've crossed the bridge, you can get a taxi to the market for $5 or less (negotiations are a must) or hop a 25¢ taxi van; it's packed, and it's not air-conditioned, but you'll only be aboard for a few minutes.

If you're a very cautious type, you might want to take a **Gray Line tour** into Matamoros. They run daily except Sunday and include a little sightseeing along with shopping stops. A 3½-hour excursion costs $11 for adults, $5.50 for children under 18. Call 542-8962 or inquire at your hotel desk for departure times.

Personally, I think it's much more fun to do it on your own, and a really passionate shopper will want to spend additional hours sifting through the merchandise.

Take a margarita break from shopping at **Las Dos Republicas,** Calle 9a across from the New Market, a comfortable adobe-walled, terracotta-floored lounge where you can sink into a big tufted-leather armchair and rest your market-weary feet. It's quite an attractive place, with wrought-iron candelabra chandeliers suspended from a 30-foot beamed ceiling, and entertainment that ranges from mariachi and marimba bands to an organist playing "Secret Love." You can order a plate of guacamole or nachos here too, and a specialty is a drink called piña de la casa that is sipped from a fresh-cut whole pineapple.

## A Meal in Matamoros

**Garcia's,** 82 Alvaro Obregon, just a block from the bridge on your left (tel. 31566), is the archetypical Mexican bordertown restaurant that caters to the stream of American tourists crossing over from stateside. It is—as they all are—ostentatiously elegant, in this case with a teak beamed ceiling that evokes an ocean liner dining room and seating in striped velvet chairs at white-linened tables. Light streams in from sheer-white-curtained windows all around, and there's always entertainment—an organist playing music that ranges from Mexican to merry-go-round. As for the food, you'll notice the only Mexicans in the place are the ones who work here, which should clue you in. Why, then, am I recommending Garcia's? Because there's no place more authentic in Matamoros where you can be sure not to pick up a case of *turista,* and because restaurants like Garcia's are a not-to-be-missed part of the border scene.

Prices are certainly reasonable. A Mexican plate consisting of a taco, enchilada, chile relleño, tamale, Mexican-style rice, and refried beans is $4; stuffed jumbo shrimp is $8.25; and if you want to get exotic you can order quail au vin ($4.95), baked cabrito (baby goat; $7.95), or broiled frog's legs ($5). For dessert a flan is just 55¢, but you can also opt for crêpes Suzette or baked Alaska flamed tableside ($2.95). There are extra-low-priced luncheon specials each day; for example, for $4.65, a full meal of soup du jour, fajitas, a taco, an enchilada, refried beans, jumbo french fries, onion rings, tortillas, and dessert. Light fare is also served in the adjoining bar/lounge where a band plays from 8 p.m. to midnight daily. It's furnished with tufted gold leather chairs.

Garcia's is open Sunday to Thursday from 11 a.m. to 10:45 p.m., till 11:45 p.m. on Friday and Saturday nights. Reservations suggested at dinner.

The restaurant is on the second floor. Downstairs is a large, air-conditioned market under the same ownership selling the full range of Mexican goods you'll find elsewhere in town. Browse around before or after you dine.

# 2. South Padre Island

Padre Island history and topography are described in some detail in Chapter IV. The southern end of this 113-mile barrier island, however, is another world. Unlike the wild and barren landscape of shifting dunes to the north, South Padre has been civilized and tamed. High-rise hotels and condominiums line the beachfront, and visitors enjoy an idyllic resort where the average annual temperature is a pleasant 74° and aquasports are year-round activities. There's fishing (the Laguna Madre has the heaviest fish population of any bay along the Gulf or Atlantic Coast), boating, shelling, swimming, snorkeling, sailing, scuba-diving, and parasailing—not to mention land sports like golf and tennis.

To reach South Padre Island, you drive along the majestic 2.6-mile Queen

Isabella Causeway, Texas's longest bridge, gracefully arching over the Laguna Madre to connect the island with the Rio Grande Valley mainland. A statue of Padre Ballí, for whom the island was named, faces oncoming traffic with arms outstretched in welcome. It was erected in response to pressure from his descendants, a group that is still peeved because they feel the island is rightfully theirs. The first impression is an enchanting one of shimmering turquoise and sapphire waters under the clear Texas sky.

Padre has an inviting expanse of pristine white sand beachfront, and its main street, Padre Boulevard (Hwy. 100) is flanked by beach on one side, marina-lined bay on the other. Cross streets are colorfully named for fish (Pike, Dolphin, Red Snapper), plants (Hibiscus, Oleander, Gardenia), and planets (Venus, Jupiter, Saturn). On either end of the city is a park, Andy Bowie to the north and La Blanca to the south, the latter offering a protected area where youngsters can swim in calm, shallow waters.

How long should you plan to spend on South Padre? As long as you can!

**GETTING THERE:** From Brownsville, 25 miles away, take U.S. 77/83 south and Texas Hwy. 100 east, which becomes the Queen Isabella Causeway after Port Isabel. To get to Brownsville from other parts of Texas, see Section 1 of this chapter.

**GETTING ORIENTED:** Stop in at the **South Padre Island Tourist Bureau,** 600 Padre Blvd., right next door to the Hilton (tel. 512/943-6433, or toll free 800/ 527-1121; when an operator answers ask for Express no. 2927). They can provide maps, brochures, and information on accommodations, restaurants, and all sporting activities. You can write to the bureau in advance at P.O. Box 2095, South Padre Island, TX 78597. Hours are Monday to Friday from 9 a.m. to 4:30 p.m., on Saturday and Sunday from 10 a.m. to 3 p.m.

**GETTING AROUND:** Tiny South Padre Island, the city part of it just four miles long and a few blocks wide, is easily traveled via **bicycle.** You can rent one at **Jeeper's,** 5308 Padre Blvd. (tel. 943-6314); they also rent Jeeps and mopeds.

However, to get across the causeway you'll need a car. You can rent one at **Car Port Rentals,** 3200 Padre Blvd. (tel. 943-3789), or from **Avis,** 101 W. Dolphin (tel. 943-1392). Both offer free pickup and return to/from your hotel.

**Gray Line** (tel. 512/943-2144) offers shuttle service between island hotels and airports in Brownsville and Harlingen in conjunction with arriving and departing flights. Cost is $12 to Harlingen, $30 to Brownsville, the latter by prior arrangement only.

In summer, a little red choo-choo train, the **Coast Line,** runs up and down the island daily from 10 a.m. to dark, taking 55 minutes for a round trip. There's no fare (it's the town's way of saying "We're glad you're here"), and there are about ten stops along the way where you can board or debark.

Taxi rides in town cost $3, $5 to Port Isabel, $30 to Brownsville. If you need one, call Shrimp Boat Taxi at 943-5681.

**ANNUAL EVENTS:** Not so much an annual event as a yearly invasion, **spring break** is when Padre becomes a Texan Fort Lauderdale. Unless you like an *Animal House* atmosphere, it's best to stay at one of the upscale hotels while the college kids are on the loose.

Many fishing tournaments take place during July and August, most notably the **Texas International Fishing Tournament** and the **South Padre Island Invitational Billfish Tournament.** The latter begins with about 125 yachts lining up and starting out at the same time (quite a show) and ends with the winner pocketing over $300,000! Fishing tournaments often include other events like barbecue cookoffs and family activities. If you'd like to enter one, contact the tourist bureau for details; otherwise, it's always fun to watch the weighing-in and hear about the ones that got away.

Every October there's a **seven-kilometer run** in celebration of the beautiful Queen Isabella Causeway, followed by a progressive ball in the evening. Participants begin at one location for cocktails, proceed to another for dinner, a third for dancing, etc. Tickets (about $30 per person) are available through the tourist bureau.

The first weekend in December is a great time to be here. That's when 50 or more boats compete in a marine **Parade of Lights,** festooning their craft with multicolored lighting displays and other decorations. It's quite beautiful to see.

**WHERE TO STAY:** It's a good idea to book ahead in this popular resort town. Sometimes hotels are packed during big fishing tournaments, and during spring break the place is overrun with college kids.

Occupying 14 beachfront acres (and don't I know it, having toured the property in 95° weather) is the luxurious **Bahia Mar Resort Village,** 6300 Padre Blvd., South Padre Island, TX 78578 (tel. 512/943-1343, or toll free 800/531-7404), with its own on-premises lagoon and a wide range of vacation facilities. Opened in 1973, the Bahia Mar was the first plush, Miami Beach–like property on Padre. It consists of a 200-room, 12-story hotel (the top two floors are suites only) and 147 condominium units in weathered-wood buildings. At this writing a total renovation and upgrading is in the works, so some description will be a little sketchy. Off the terracotta-tiled lobby are a piano-bar lounge and a gift shop that carries an extensive line of resortwear for men and women. La Paloma dining room, which also offers live piano entertainment, overlooks the pool and has a patio for outdoor dining. Steak and seafood dinners are featured, with such offerings as a 12-ounce filet mignon with mustard béarnaise sauce for $16 and a shrimp and scallop casserole in butter/white wine sauce topped with seasoned breadcrumbs ($11.75). Both come with fresh vegetable and potato. The Club at Bahia Mar, a 350-seat facility, offers live entertainment Monday through Saturday nights—sometimes fairly big names like the Platters, the Supremes, and the Impressions. Paneled in raw oak and decorated in teal blue and sea green, the club is open till 2 a.m.; between sets a DJ plays music for dancing.

Other on-premises facilities include two tennis courts lit for night play, shuffleboard, a club-shaped pool with adjoining outdoor whirlpool, a second large pool in the condominium section with adjoining kiddie pool, a beach bar (summer only) for drinks and snacks, volleyball nets, and a private white sand beach where umbrellas, chairs, and other beach amenities can be rented. Guests can use a nearby health club offering weight rooms, racquetball, exercise classes, massage, steam, Jacuzzi, and tennis for a small fee, and they're also welcome to play golf at the Brownsville Country Club's 18-hole course. Off the Bahia Mar's beach, sailboats can be rented and a 32-foot party barge departs for luncheon and sunset cruises. An activities director organizes fun and games for guests of all ages, and, of more pragmatic interest, there's a washer/dryer for guest use and complimentary transport is available to/from Brownsville and Harlingen airports by prior arrangement.

Of the 200 rooms, 64 are standard doubles, while the rest have kitchenettes or are full suites. Since they're set for redecoration at this writing, I won't describe them except to note that they're equipped with all the modern amenities. Some of the condominium accommodations—rentable for stays of three days or longer only—have been redone beautifully in pastels and resort colors with lovely turquoise or forest-green carpeting. They're very elegantly appointed. A couple of pluses at the Bahia Mar include a landscaped river walk that meanders through the property and water views from just about every room.

Rates for a standard room are $85 to $92 single, $92 to $100 double, with suites from $105. An extra person pays $10 per night (children under 12, free). Parking is free. One-bedroom condominium units with fully equipped kitchens begin at about $575 per week.

Just a few minutes' drive from Padre beaches is the quaint and lovely **Yacht Club Hotel,** 700 Yturria St., two blocks north of Hwy. 100, in Port Isabel, TX 78578 (tel. 512/943-1301). Built in 1926 as an ultra-exclusive private yacht club for the Rio Grande Valley elite, it housed such notable guests as Charles Lindbergh, war journalist Ernie Pyle, and Dale Carnegie. During the Depression, when the elite dwindled, yacht club member John Shary bought the property and turned it into a hotel. Since 1979 the hotel has been under the auspices of local developers Ron and Lynn Speier, who have completely refurbished and redecorated rooms and public areas and added a dining room and pool, all the while maintaining the Yacht Club's inherent 1920s charm. The white stucco building is in the Spanish style, with terracotta roofing and a white wooden balcony. It's fronted by palms and lush foliage and a terracotta patio overlooking a boatyard across the street—a very simpático setting for the complimentary continental breakfast enjoyed by guests here each morning.

Within, there's a small lobby with wood-bladed fans suspended from a beamed stucco ceiling and an adjoining gift/sundries/resortwear shop. Over the lobby fireplace hangs the immense hotel crest made in Madrid. The front desk offers personalized service; they'll make tour arrangements and restaurant reservations, arrange fishing and boating excursions, watersports, etc.

Whether or not you stay here, do come by for a meal in the dining room, specializing in locally caught snapper, oysters, and shrimp. Under a high ceiling with dark wood beams, it offers seating amid potted palms in comfortable red leather armchairs at candlelit, white-linened tables set with pewterware. The white stucco walls are hung with sepia photos of the area in the '20s and '30s, and burgundy velvet-curtained windows look out on tropical foliage. A dinner here might begin with jalapeños stuffed with blue crab ($4.95) or a ceviche salad ($5.95). For an entree, the broiled red snapper filet ($14.50) and shrimp and scallop seafood brochette ($13.95) are both very recommendable, and non-seafood fanciers can opt for prime rib ($16.95). There's an extensive wine list, and lime pie ($2.50) is the featured dessert. Evenings, a Spanish guitarist entertains in the adjoining lounge. The restaurant is open for dinner nightly except Wednesday, and reservations are essential.

The 24 rooms are small but pleasant, not in the least bit plush or fancy. They have imitation wood-paneled-walls hung with beach-themed art, dark-green bedspreads and curtains, and bamboo/rattan furnishings. Amenities include cable color TV and air conditioning, but no phones (the front desk can take incoming messages). Upper floors have a pleasant shaded balcony overlooking the Port Isabel Channel. Out back are a small pool and sundeck nicely landscaped with banana palms and hibiscus.

Rates are $40 a night, single or double, for a room with one double bed, $50 for a suite with bedroom plus living room (the latter has a studio couch/bed), $5 for an extra person. Parking is free. The Yacht Club offers a tranquil and inexpensive alternative to Padre's luxury beachfront hotels.

**WHERE TO EAT:** In addition to the restaurants below, try the **Yacht Club Hotel dining room,** detailed above. You can't go wrong ordering shrimp anywhere in this fleet-filled town.

A good choice for dinner, **Louie's Back Yard,** 2305 Laguna Blvd., at Ling (tel. 943-6406), is a restaurant right on the bay that offers spectacular views of the passing boat parade. It's particularly nice to sit out under the palms on the brick patio in ornate black wrought-iron chairs with big Mediterranean-blue cushions. Come early so you can enjoy the sunset. Inside the chairs are ornate white wrought iron, tables are lit by candle lamps, and a wall of windows overlooks the bay.

Dinner is a $15.95 buffet (half price for children under 10). It's quite a lavish spread, at last count including six salads, fresh broccoli in cheese sauce, zucchini, mashed potatoes, Swedish meatballs, prime rib, fried shrimp and scallops, flounder, a seafood casserole au gratin, pasta with shrimp and clam sauce, and cantaloupe. Hot rolls and butter are brought to your table, and there's cheesecake or ice cream parfait for dessert, but it's extra. A guitar duo entertains at dinner. Later on there's a DJ playing top-40s tunes, and you can dance on an outdoor platform right on the bay—very romantic.

Louie's is open for cocktails (also nice at sunset) from 4:30 p.m. to 2 a.m. Tuesday to Sunday, for dinner Tuesday to Thursday and Sunday from 5:30 to 10 p.m., till 11 p.m. on Friday and Saturday nights. Reservations are essential.

Stunning water views and good food combine to make **Bermudas,** 205 W. Palm, just off Laguna Boulevard (tel. 943-4308), a terrific choice. It's one of the best places in town to watch the sun set over the bay and, later, the glittering lights of the causeway come on. Stay on a little longer and you can dance to live combos and disco music under a starlit sky. There's seating both inside and out. The upstairs room, paneled in rough-hewn pine, has cushioned bamboo furnishings amid potted palms and hanging plants. Picture windows all around provide every table with a bay view. Outdoors, seating is in comfortable cushioned green-and-white-striped garden chairs.

Fresh seafood is featured, and even at dinner you can choose light fare like a basket of fried oysters with fries and hushpuppies ($6.25) or three tacos ($4)—or have a full dinner of stuffed crab with salad, rolls, and baked potato ($9.25). Among the dessert choices are chocolate-covered strawberries ($3.25), strawberry shortcake ($3.25), and ice cream drinks ($4.50). Low-priced lunch specials are featured on weekdays.

Open daily from 11 a.m. to 11 p.m., with entertainment until 2 a.m. on Friday and Saturday, till midnight Monday to Thursday. Reservations essential at dinner. Bermudas closes in winter.

**Cappuccino's,** in Port Isabel on Tarnava Street just off Hwy. 100 on the right (tel. 943-4201), is an Italian restaurant housed in a turn-of-the-century stockyard building that later served as a city jail. The outside, as is still evident, was a railroad station. In keeping with the period, Cappuccino's has Victorian lamps and wall sconces with fringed silk shades and wood-bladed fans suspended from a rustic beamed ceiling. Tables are adorned with fresh flower arrangements. Less Victorian in derivation are ochre brick walls hung with gilt-framed oil paintings and decorated with a brightly hued mural of parrots and toucans. Most *intime* is a seating area off the pine-paneled bar. And there's a comfy upstairs lounge under a sloped ceiling where the original brick is exposed. The entire effect here is rather charming, especially at night when tables are lit by oil lamps and the background music is Italian opera.

The menu was devised by a chef in Rome, and everything on it, including pasta and sauces, is homemade. All luncheon entrees come with a salad; dinner entrees with salad, soup, and homemade breads. A side order of garlic bread is recommended at either meal. At lunch, pasta dishes like lasagne ($4.85) and stuffed shells ($4.50) are featured. At dinner, appetizers include fried zucchini with lemon wedge ($4) or fettuccine Alfredo ($4.50), from whence you can proceed to fresh seafood entrees (such as fresh gulf catch in butter and almond sauce for $12.25, or green and white fettuccine with sautéed shrimp and scallops in a dilled white cream sauce for $13). Veal dishes such as saltimbocca—veal topped with prosciutto and mozzarella, sautéed in wine and butter ($13)—are also featured, and pasta dishes are in the $9 to $11 range. If you can't decide what to order, have the *cominazione* plate of lasagne, veal parmigiana, manicotti, fettuccine Alfredo, and fresh vegetables ($12.45). Creamy zabaglione ($3) is the not-to-be-missed dessert here.

Cappuccino's is open for lunch weekdays from 11 a.m. to 2 p.m., for dinner Monday to Saturday from 6 to 11 p.m. Reservations suggested for dinner. Friday and Saturday nights there's entertainment—usually a vocalist or guitar player—in the upstairs lounge.

**THE SIGHTS:** Just about everyone who visits Padre Island goes to see the "Turtle Lady," Ila Fox Loetscher, founder of a group called Sea Turtles, Inc. (STI), that is dedicated to the preservation and protection of Kemp's ridley sea turtles, an endangered species. The group also concerns itself with conservation of all marine turtles. At her home at 5805 Gulf Blvd., between Palmetto and Parade Drives (tel. 943-2544), Ms Loetscher cares for sick and injured turtles, maintains breeding tanks, and gives "Meet the Turtles" programs to increase awareness about ridleys and other endangered species. She explains that sea turtles always return to the place they were hatched to do their nesting, and there's only one rookery in the world for ridleys—a beach 50 miles north of Tampico, Mexico. However, for years, Mexican poachers have been selling ridleys' oil for cosmetics, their skins for boots and purses, and their eggs for aphrodisiacs. By 1974 the species was reduced to just 500 members. Ms Loetscher, along with other concerned parties, has attempted to establish a new and protected rookery, originally on the shores of South Padre Island. From their first batch of 2,000 eggs, 1,100 hatched, but only seven returned to nest (it takes seven to nine years, by the way, till the new turtles are old enough to nest). In 1978 they moved the rookery to the northern end of Padre near Corpus Christi, a more protected area. Since, in nature, only an estimated 1% of the eggs from each nest survive their first year, STI has incubation programs to up the odds. Newly hatched ridleys are kept in a protected tank for a year before being returned to the sea too big and strong to fall prey to seagulls and fish. An arrangement with Mexico gives STI 2,000 eggs a year, and they are also helping to build up the Mexican rookery.

At her hour-long outdoor turtle shows, given Tuesday and Saturday mornings in summer at 10 and 11 a.m., and Tuesday and Thursday afternoons at 1 and 2 p.m. November through April, Ms Loetscher gives a delightful and informative talk with enough humor and whimsy to keep the kids in the audience interested (she dresses the turtles in costumes) while very effectively getting her conservationist message across to all ages. A donation of $1 is requested, and T-shirts are sold to help finance the operation. Since this is Ms Loetscher's home (she's given the entire downstairs floor to the turtles, and she lives upstairs), and Ms Loetscher is over 80, call before you go; sometimes something comes up and she has to cancel.

The **Port Isabel Lighthouse**, 100 Queen Isabella Blvd., at Tarnava (tel. 943-1172), has long been a dominant feature of the southern tip of the Texas Gulf

Coast. A navigational light became a necessity in the mid-1800s to guide increasing maritime commerce through Brazos Santiago Pass to Port Isabel. The brick tower was completed in 1853, topped by a stationary light that could be seen for 16 miles. During the Civil War both Union and Confederate troops used the lighthouse as an observation post, but after shipping declined at the end of the century, it was abandoned. In 1950 it was designated a historic site and remodeled by the State Parks Board. It is now once again marked on sea charts as an aid to navigation, and its mercury-vapor beacon is seen by ships in the gulf.

The site is open to visitors (kids love the circular climb) from 10 to 11:30 a.m. and 1 to 5 p.m. daily. From the top (60 feet) you can enjoy a panoramic view of Port Isabel and Padre. Future plans call for guided tours that will further elucidate the role played by the lighthouse in local history and an adjacent visitor center with exhibits on early lighthouse technology and operation. Adults pay $1 for admission, and children 6 to 12 pay 25¢.

Also on Port Isabel, at Maxan and Yturria, is the **Lady Bea,** a restored shrimp boat typical of those traversing Gulf of Mexico waters in search of seafood. The Rio Grande Valley shrimp fleet is the largest in the nation. The ship is open for exploration 24 hours a day, and like the lighthouse, it is the first phase of a larger plan—a maritime museum and park. Admission is free.

**Ocean Safari Marineland** is a 9½-acre attraction located in Isla Blanca Park (tel. 943-3271 or 943-4502), featuring bird, fish, and animal performers and exhibits. There are sea lion stunts, dolphin acrobatics, a petting zoo, a circus show starring six species of jungle cats, bicycle-riding and card-playing macaws, and a snake handler who kisses a deadly Indian cobra! All that and baboons, too. Admission is $7.50 for adults, $6.50 for senior citizens, $5.50 for children 4 to 12 (3 and under, free). Summer hours are 11 a.m. to 7 p.m. daily; the rest of the year the schedule varies, so call ahead.

More family fun is offered at **Jeremiah's Landing,** 100 S. Padre Blvd. at the southern end of the island in front of the Holiday Inn (tel. 943-2131), an amusement center with a 240-foot, three-flume water slide, an 18-hole miniature golf course, electronic game room, outdoor entertainment on summer nights, a snackbar, and a piña colada/mimosa bar. Hours vary seasonally. Admission is $7 per hour. It's open March to October only.

The **Isabella Queen,** a paddle wheeler constructed to travel the shallow waters of the Laguna Madre Bay, offers 2½-hour narrated Sunday champagne brunches, sightseeing cruises, dinner cruises with live music, and sunset cruises. All departures are from behind Louie's Back Yard. For a schedule and prices, call 943-7891.

The **Pan American University Coastal Studies Laboratory** in Cameron County Park (tel. 943-2644) is a research facility that maintains an exhibit area open to the public with displays of local plants and animals, a small aquarium, and a goodly collection of shells. Hours are 1:30 to 4:30 p.m. daily except Saturday and holidays.

Take the kids, or the kid in yourself, over to **Sunnies Candyland,** 1604 Padre Blvd. (tel. 943-5062), a huge store selling homemade candy, including about 20 flavors of fudge varying from rocky road to vanilla pecan. They serve it in tiny ice cream cones. Sunnies also carries souvenirs and gift items.

**BEACHES AND PARKS:** The city part of South Padre extends just four miles south to north, but Padre Boulevard continues for three miles farther among the dunes. Any part of the seven-mile stretch of beach is clean and open to use. Of course, the beaches in front of major hotels offer the most concessions and facilities. Take the kids to **Cameron County Park** where the water is calm and shallow. **Islas Blancas Park,** however, has picnic areas and barbecue grills. Above the seven-mile road limit, Padre Island reassumes its wilder nature and a state-licensed four-wheel-drive is required for trips farther north.

**AQUASPORTS:** There are many options for both bay and deep-sea **fishing,** including party boats, individual charters, and pier fishing. **Jim's Pier** (tel. 943-2865) has a bay party boat, the *Danny B.*, departing every morning at 8 a.m. and every afternoon at 2 p.m. for a four-hour fishing trip; cost is $10 per person, $12 with tackle, bait supplied in either case. They also offer deep-sea trolling and fishing excursions and private charters. Call for details. Most fishing services—including supplies, tackle, and licenses—are available from **Fishermans Wharf,** 211 W. Swordfish (tel. 943-7818). The 5,840-foot-long, state-owned **Queen Isabella Fishing Pier,** located on the old causeway, offers 24-hour fishing, with 2,800 feet lit for night use. Tackle, bait, and human food are available. Cost is $1 for adults, 50¢ for children 13 to 17 (12 and under, free).

Serious anglers should contact the tourist bureau; they have extensive information about all aspects of Padre Island fishing.

Waterskiing rides and lessons are available from the **South Padre Island Ski School** under the auspices of Captain Bill (tel. 943-6386).

You can rent sailboats and water trikes from the beach in front of the Hilton, just next door to the tourist bureau. Sailboat rides, rentals, and lessons are available through **Island Sailboats,** 212 W. Dolphin St. (tel. 943-5061).

Windsurfing rentals and lessons are offered at **Southcoast Windsurfing** in Cameron County Park (tel. 943-8840).

Ever been parasailing? Attached to a motorboat like a waterskier, you float along in an open parachute about 100 feet up in the air. You can do it at **South Padre Para-Sailing,** just across from the Bahia Mar at 6201 Padre Blvd. (no phone). A 45-minute ride costs about $25.

Or perhaps you'd prefer just to sit on the beach. **Etc. Rentals,** 101 Morningside, near the Bahia Mar (tel. 943-9535), rents umbrellas, chairs, barbecue grills, tents, etc.—also mopeds.

**LAND SPORTS:** There's an 18-hole public **golf** course in Port Isabel at the Outdoor Resort on Garcia Street (tel. 943-5921); fee is $6. And the four Hilton **tennis courts,** lit for night play, are open to the public. Call 943-6511 (ext. 437) for information.

**CAMPING:** Full hookups, cabins furnished with bunk beds and mattresses, and tenting areas are available through the **Cameron County Parks System,** P.O. Box 2106, South Padre Island, TX 78597 (tel. 512/943-5493). Call for details.

**NIGHTLIFE:** There's plenty to do after dark on South Padre. In addition to shows mentioned above at the **Bahia Mar** (headliners), **Louie's Back Yard** (disco), **Cappuccino's** (vocalist or guitarist in the upstairs lounge), **Bermudas** (live combos playing dance music), the **Yacht Club** (a Spanish guitarist), and **Jeremiah's Landing** (usually bands for dancing), the Hilton and the Holiday Inn usually have lounge shows. A free local newspaper called the *Island Times,* available at the tourist bureau or your hotel, provides full listings.

**TRIPS TO MEXICO:** Best bet is to drive up to Brownsville, park on the Texas side (see details above in Brownsville/Matamoros section of this chapter), and spend a day shopping, browsing, and drinking margaritas.

**Gray Line** offers three-hour tours from Padre to Matamoros Monday to Saturday at 9 a.m. and 3 p.m., on Sunday at noon. Cost is $14 per person. Call 943-2124 or 943-2144 for details.

### 3. McAllen/Reynosa

In 1986 McAllen was just 75 years old, half as old as the sesquicentennial-celebrating state of Texas. It all began when rancher John McAllen set up a village called West McAllen in 1905 shortly after the Missouri Pacific Railroad completed their line into the area. The "village" consisted of a depot and bank. Later John Closner, a country sheriff, and William Briggs, a Louisiana promoter, set up East McAllen on a townsite two miles east of the village. Eventually east and west merged, and in 1911 the city was officially incorporated. McAllen's early years were marked by border raids from Mexican bandits, most notably the soldiers of Pancho Villa. After well-organized plans for an uprising against the U.S. were found on a revolutionary soldier arrested in McAllen in 1915, a National Guard regiment, the 69th New York Infantry, was dispatched to the area to settle the matter once and for all. The town grew to accommodate the influx of soldiers and kept growing after they left. By 1920 the city had 5,000 residents and the finest hotel in the Rio Grande Valley. Gone were the days when the only available entertainment was shooting rattlesnakes in the front yard.

Today McAllen, dubbed the City of Palms for its swaying tropical trees, is a tranquil and pleasant little community of 88,600, its ranks swelled by an influx of 50,000 winter Texans each year between December and April. The *U.S. News and World Report* named it one of the ten best places in the nation to retire. The hub of the Texas citrus belt in a county that has the highest agricultural production of any in the state, McAllen is surrounded by orange and grapefruit groves and fields of vegetables and cotton. Though it is a prettier city than Brownsville, it is also farther from the border, and Reynosa doesn't offer as much in the way of shopping or local color as Matamoros. If you have time to visit only one Rio Grande Valley border town, choose the latter. A better reason to visit McAllen is its proximity to the Santa Ana National Wildlife Refuge, which should not be missed.

**GETTING THERE:** Two carriers, Muse Air and Continental Airlines, fly in and out of **Miller International Airport,** conveniently located on the southern end of town. **Trailways** (512/682-5513) has bus service into town, its terminal right on North Broadway. By **car** Brownsville is 58 miles away via U.S. 83, and South Padre Island is 25 miles farther along. Other not-too-distant cities are Laredo (144 miles), Corpus Christi (152 miles), and Monterrey, Mexico (150 miles).

**GETTING ORIENTED:** Visit the **McAllen Chamber of Commerce,** 10 N. Broadway, at Ash Street (tel. 512/682-2871), for maps, brochures, and information on all the city's offerings. You can write to the Chamber in advance at P.O. Box 790, McAllen, TX 78502. Office hours are Monday to Friday from 8:30 a.m. to 5 p.m.

**GETTING AROUND:** At Miller International Airport, you'll find several major car-rental companies, among them **Budget** (tel. 512/686-0323), **National** (tel. 512/686-5124), and **Dollar** (tel. 512/687-7297).

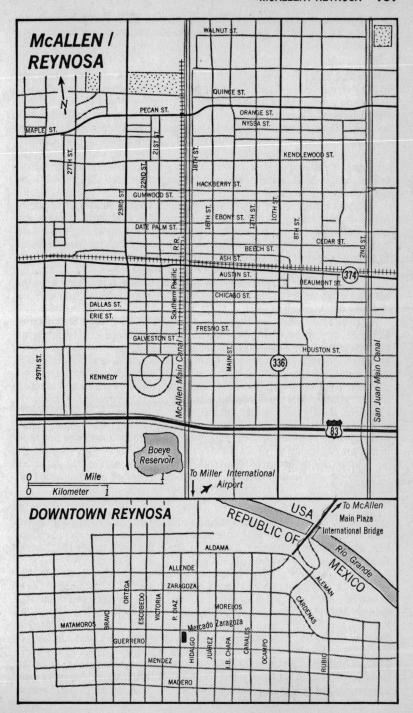

# McALLEN / REYNOSA

N

WALNUT ST.
QUINCE ST.
PECAN ST.
ORANGE ST.
NYSSA ST.
MAPLE ST.
27TH ST.
21ST ST.
18TH ST.
KENDLEWOOD ST.
22ND ST.
HACKBERRY ST.
23RD ST.
GUMWOOD ST.
16TH ST.
EBONY ST.
12TH ST.
10TH ST.
DATE PALM ST.
R.R.
8TH ST.
CEDAR ST.
2ND ST.
BEECH ST.
ASH ST.
AUSTIN ST.
BEAUMONT ST.
374
CHICAGO ST.
DALLAS ST.
ERIE ST.
FRESNO ST.
Southern Pacific
GALVESTON ST.
McAllen Main Canal
29TH ST.
MAIN ST.
HOUSTON ST.
San Juan Main Canal
KENNEDY
336
83

Boeye
Reservoir

0 Mile 1
0 Kilometer 1

To Miller International
Airport

# DOWNTOWN REYNOSA

ALDAMA
ALLENDE
ZARAGOZA
ORTEGA
ESCOBEDO
VICTORIA
P. DIAZ
MORELOS
MATAMOROS
BRAVO
GUERRERO
Mercado Zaragoza
HIDALGO
JUAREZ
B. CHAPA
CANALES
OCAMPO
MENDEZ
MADERO
REPUBLIC OF
USA
To McAllen
Main Plaza
International Bridge
Rio Grande
MEXICO
ALEMAN
CARDENAS
RUBIO

If you need a taxi, call **T.V. Taxicab** (tel. 682-9772). A taxi between the airport and downtown hotels costs about $6, but most hotels offer free transport.

**ANNUAL EVENTS:** German Night, a small version of Oktoberfest, takes place in late February/early March. There are food booths selling sausages and funnel cakes, and you can dance to oompah music. Tickets are about $5, obtainable at the Chamber of Commerce. About the same time of year, the **Rio Grande Valley International Spring Music Festival** is a week of special concerts at the Civic Center. Tickets are available from the Civic Center box office (tel. 686-3382).

Early May brings **Springfest,** a three-day celebration with a parade, the crowning of a Miss Springfest, live entertainment, arts and crafts displays, food booths, games, and contests. Some events require tickets. Call 682-6221 for details.

McAllen pulls out all stops for **July Fourth.** On the Sunday immediately before or after Independence Day there's a fajita cookoff with live bands and other festivities. On the Fourth itself there's a parade on Main Street, food booths and arts and crafts displays are set up in Archer Park (at Broadway and Beech), an aquafest takes place at the Municipal Pool, and there are concerts followed by fireworks. Call 682-5563 or 682-9873 for specifics.

The **International Balloon Festival** in mid-November brings 50 or so colorful hot-air balloonists to the area for a race. Other highlights of this event are clog dancing, Mexican folkloric dancing, bands, games, and food booths.

**Candlelight Posada,** usually the second Friday in December, is a beautiful Christmas celebration that attracts about 20,000 visitors each year. Blending the cultures of the U.S. and Mexico, it includes the lighting of thousands of twinkling lights in the area surrounding Archer Park, dozens of food booths (everything from Christmas pies to tamales), music and dance on outdoor stages, and caroling. The climax is the candlelit Posada procession, a traditional Mexican pageant in which Mary and Joseph's search for an inn is reenacted, with choirs, musicians, shepherds, wise men, and angels in tow. Hundreds of local residents join the march, carrying song sheets and candles. The singing of "Silent Night" in the park by all assembled, the ringing of bells, and the reading of Scripture herald the procession's arrival at the Nativity.

For details about any of the events described here, and to find out about other happenings during your stay, contact the Chamber of Commerce (tel. 682-2871).

**WHERE TO STAY:** No problem getting a room in McAllen except during two busy times of year—white-wing dove season, the first two weekends in September, when hunters converge from all over the U.S., and October 10–12 when there's a big air show in nearby Harlingen.

A beautiful Mexican-style hotel that has a twin in Laredo is **La Posada,** 100 N. Main St., between Ash and Beech, McAllen, TX 78502 (tel. 512/686-5411, or toll free 800/531-7156). The first hotel not only in McAllen but in the Rio Grande Valley, La Posada (originally called Casa de Palmas, or House of Palms) was built in 1918, an awe-inspiring structure in a town that consisted at the time of two old frame hotels, a small bank, a feed store, and a saloon. It immediately became the hub of all fashionable society gatherings. In 1939, $100,000 was spent on expanding the property, making it even more noteworthy. In 1951 Twentieth Century–Fox housed Marlon Brando and the entire crew of *Viva Zapata!* here during filming. And Bob Hope, Anthony Quinn, Lyndon

B. Johnson, and even Howard Hughes are among those who have signed the guest register over the years.

La Posada is still a bit awe-inspiring today, or if not that, at least a very pleasant surprise to the arriving traveler. The property occupies an entire city block. Guests pass through a gleaming-white stucco archway into a beautiful balconied central courtyard enclosed by an arcade and centered on a Mexican fountain and inviting swimming pool. A terracotta sundeck is lushly planted with palms and tropical foliage. It feels like a tropical resort in some exotic country, and force of habit will probably have you out on the deck in a bathing suit sipping a rum drink two minutes after check-in.

On the premises is an attractive restaurant with arched multipaned windows, Saltillo tile floors, a beamed ceiling, and wrought-iron chandeliers overhead. Seating is in Spanish leather chairs at white-linened tables, candlelit at night. Lunch and dinner, the menu caters to a variety of dining moods; you can order a chef's salad ($6.25), a burger with fries ($5), a Mexican platter like cheese enchiladas topped with chili con carne with rice, refried beans, and guacamole ($6.25), or a full gourmet dinner beginning with smoked salmon and cream cheese ($5.65), followed by an entree of sautéed flounder with lemon butter and caper sauce ($8.25), and concluding with a selection from the dessert tray. Prices are extremely reasonable, and there are kiddie plates that can be ordered by anyone under 95. Adjoining is a cozy lobby bar overlooking the pool and courtyard, the scene of piano-bar entertainment Thursday through Sunday nights. And a new second-floor restaurant, specializing in rôtisserie, is in the works at this writing.

The 170 rooms are decorated in bold color schemes—orange and black, red and black, or green and black, with gold or bright red carpeting. They have beamed ceilings and white stucco or exposed yellow Mexican brick walls, in some cases hung with prints by Spanish artists like Goya and Velázquez. All double-doubles (there are 47) face the courtyard pool, and some have balconies. A washer/dryer is provided for guest use, and free transport is offered to/from the airport. The hotel van also makes frequent trips to and from the International Bridge at no charge, providing guests with easy access to Reynosa.

Rates are $57 single, $66 to $77 double, $5 for an extra person (children 12 and under, free), $45 single or double on weekends (Friday, Saturday, and Sunday nights). Parlor suites, with living room areas and wet bars, are $80 single, $90 double. Covered parking is free. No-smoking rooms and facilities for the disabled are available as well.

Though La Posada would be my first choice, it's no longer the only luxury property in town. Nearing completion at press time is **Embassy Suites**, 1800 S. 2nd St., near U.S. 83, McAllen, TX 78503 (tel. 512/686-3000, or toll free 800/ EMBASSY), with 168 all-suite accommodations housed in a very attractive terracotta-roofed, Spanish-style building, its exterior walls faced with stone brought in from Mexico. Entered via a stunning nine-story atrium lobby under a skylight ceiling, it offers a wide range of facilities—a medium-size indoor pool and whirlpool with adjoining outdoor sundeck, an exercise room with Universal equipment (aerobics classes are given in the afternoons), steam and sauna, and a kiddie pool. Remington's, the hotel's dining room (not completed when I visited), will specialize in mesquite-grilled steak and seafood and feature a 32-item salad bar/buffet of hot and cold items and a dessert bar. In an adjoining lounge, piano-bar entertainment is planned.

Rooms, decorated in apricot or burgundy/gray color schemes are furnished in contemporary oak pieces. Each has a living room sofa that converts to a double bed, a dining area with a table for four, a kitchen/wet bar with a mini-refrigerator and small microwave oven, plus two phones and two cable color TVs (living room and bedroom). There's a concierge in the lobby, and rates include a full American breakfast served in the atrium courtyard.

Singles pay $65; doubles, $75; children under 18, free; an extra person, $10. Inquire about reduced weekend rates and rates for longer stays. Facilities for the disabled are also offered.

More budget-minded options include a 122-room **La Quinta** at 1100 S. 10th St., one block north of U.S. 83, McAllen, TX 78501 (tel. 512/687-1101, or toll free 800/531-5900). Courtesy pickup from the airport is offered. The rate for one person is $44 to $48; for two people, $48 to $53; $5 for an additional person (18 and under free).

There's also a **Motel 6** at 700 U.S. 83, corner of 8th Street, McAllen, TX 78501 (tel. 512/682-1071), with 93 units and a swimming pool.

Motel 6 rates and details about both of these budget chains are in Chapter I.

**WHERE TO EAT:** The Della Croce family has been operating the **Executive Steak House**, 1500 N. 23rd St., between Pecan and Orange (tel. 686-5541), for over two decades, and they have a large local following. The name notwithstanding, it's a casual kind of place (you can wear jeans if you like), with forest-green carpeting, gold leather chairs on caster wheels at oak tables set with green napkins, a few plants here and there, and walls adorned with limited-edition prints by western artist G. Harvey (these deserve a second glance). Somewhat harsh lighting makes for an ambience that is less than romantic, but Gary Della Croce promises candlelight dinners in the future, and I hope he delivers—it would make a world of difference.

But ambience or no, you can't go wrong here. At lunch a Mexican buffet of eight or nine dishes is just $5, and you can also order à la carte items like a six-ounce filet mignon wrapped in a strip of bacon with salad and potato for $9.50, or a less-expensive sandwich or salad. All dinner entrees include salad bar selections, a cup of homemade soup with homemade croutons, a basket of delicious hot rolls with butter, a baked potato (they're cooked in small batches, so they're always freshly prepared), and corn on the cob or the vegetable of the day. Steaks are all USDA choice. A filet mignon is priced the same as at lunch, a 12-ounce T-bone is $12.50, and a 12-ounce sirloin strip, $13.50. Other choices include prime rib ($12.50), chicken-fried steak ($6.50), and fresh-from-the-gulf fried oysters ($8.50), jumbo shrimp ($10.50), and trout ($10.50). The conclusion to this very satisfying meal is fresh-baked apple or banana pie topped with real whipped cream ($1.75). Beer and wine are available.

Open for lunch weekdays from 11:30 a.m. to 2 p.m., for dinner Monday to Saturday from 5 to 10 p.m.

A totally authentic little family-run barbecue joint—with a Mexican accent —is Juan and Maricelda Villarreal's **The Red Barn**, 4701 N. McColl Rd., at Minnesota (tel. 631-8332). A local magazine poll voted their barbecue the best in the Rio Grande Valley by a wide margin. The interior is pure Texas kitsch: two rooms with white stucco walls, ruffled red-and-white floral-print curtains framing the windows, and tables covered with red cloths protected by clear-plastic sheeting and adorned with vases of red cloth flowers. In the front room a color TV is always on, but if you don't want to watch it you can sit in the back. Food is eaten off styrofoam plates with plastic utensils.

The Villarreals' homemade potato salad is the kind you remember from childhood family picnics; their beans are Mexican style, flavored with cilantro, tomato, and bacon; the barbecue sauce is smoky, spicy, and delicious; and

Maricelda's homemade cakes—carrot with cream cheese icing and thickly iced chocolate—are just like mom's. Plates include rice, beans, potato salad, tortillas, and pico de gallo or jalapeño. With ribs (they're great) a plate is $4.25, same for brisket, chicken, or sausage; $4.50 for a combination of the above or fajitas. You can also get any of the above in a sandwich. Out back you'll see the huge pile of mesquite wood that flavors this praiseworthy barbecue. There are also picnic tables under shade trees outside where strolling mariachi bands occasionally entertain diners.

Open Monday to Thursday from 10 a.m. to 8 p.m., on Friday and Saturday to 9 p.m., on Sunday from 11 a.m. to 8 p.m. No credit cards.

**WHAT TO SEE:** To preserve the area's rapidly vanishing wildlife, the U.S. Fish and Wildlife Service has set aside 2,080 acres as the **Santa Ana National Wildlife Refuge** (tel. 787-3079). From McAllen it's just a 20-minute drive (take U.S. 83 east, go south on FM 907—a scenic country road—and take a left on U.S. 281), well worth a day's visit if you like exploring an undisturbed and lush natural environment. A unique habitat, the refuge combines tropical and temperate influences in the same area, so there are some very rare birds and plantlife here. Over 371 species of birds make their home at the refuge at different times of the year, and early morning is the best time to view them. If you're not an incorrigible night person, it's well worth rising at the crack of dawn to see the sun coming up over the lake and shore birds wading in the morning quiet. Very early arrival also lets you enjoy the trails in solitude.

Woodland areas are forested with evergreen shrubs, cedar elms, Jerusalem thorn trees, Texas persimmon, sugar hackberry, Mexican leadtree, honey mesquite, Texas ebony, and sandpaper trees, many of them festooned in Spanish moss. And over 450 species of native plants include pretty red Turks cap (a favorite food of the hummingbird), many cactus, purple sage, red mint, and asterlike blue eupatorium.

There are three lakes, and 15 miles of hiking trails wind through the property, much of it posted with interpretive signs. You can drive a 6.7-mile tour loop, but you really won't see much if you don't get out and walk. Trails off the loop lead you further into the wilderness.

In winter (early December through mid-April), the Audubon Society operates a narrated train ride through the refuge; it costs $2 for adults, $1 for children under 12, and runs four times a day (call for exact hours). The rest of the year, you're usually on your own, though tours sometimes leave from the information center. You can also see nature films here on request; call before you come.

All trails, one of which is handicapped accessible, begin and culminate near the information center, where there are exhibits to see and you can purchase books on wildflowers, birds, and other natural subjects. To enjoy your walk, wear boots, douse yourself with mosquito repellent, bring binoculars, and if you're planning on a long hike, carry a canteen; there are no rest rooms or other facilities out on the trail. Though the beauty of nature is thrilling enough at anytime, you never know when you'll see something as magnificent as thousands of broadwing hawks overhead en route to South America or spot an ocelot or jaguarundi peering through the bushes. In spring, and whenever it rains, the wildflowers are a delight.

The center is open weekdays from 8 a.m. to 4:30 p.m., weekends and holidays from 9 a.m. to 4:30 p.m., the walking trails from sunrise to sunset daily, and the tour loop road from 9 a.m. to 4:30 p.m. daily, except when the Audubon train is running.

The **McAllen International Museum,** 1900 Nolana Loop, at Bicentennial Drive (tel. 682-1564), opened in 1976, is the major cultural bastion of the Rio Grande Valley. An accredited arts and sciences museum, it is much stronger in the former category. Its South Gallery, opening onto an enclosed hacienda courtyard reflective of McAllen's Mexican influence, usually houses traveling exhibits; the crescent-shaped North Gallery is designed to present paintings, sculpture, and photography; and the Hall of Exhibits covers scientific, anthropological, and historical subjects.

The museum's permanent collection is strong in Mexican folk art. It also contains a large number of Picasso lithographs and works by 17th- and 18th-century European artists. There are about 25 temporary exhibits each year, such as "John Sloan, A Printmaker," "Works by Women" (Helen Frankenthaler and Georgia O'Keeffe, among others), "Mexican Masks," "The Rowdy London of Hogarth," and "Currier & Ives." Not all are art-related, like "Creatures of Darwin's Galápagos" and "Exploring Microspace." And in fact the museum's science section is scheduled for considerable growth in the near future. It now contains ancient Texas fossils, minerals, and exhibits on paleontology, astronomy, meteorology, and oceanography. In addition to exhibits the museum offers an ongoing program of workshops, films, recitals, lectures, dance performances, and concerts—even meet-the-artist wine and cheese parties. Children's art and science programs take place Saturday mornings at 10 a.m. Find out what will be happening during your stay when you visit.

Admission is free, though donations are appreciated. Hours are Tuesday to Saturday from 9 a.m. to 5 p.m. and on Sunday from 1 to 5 p.m. The entire month of December each year, the museum is filled with Christmas trees decorated by children.

The modernistic **Virgin de San Juan del Valle Shrine** (take U.S. 83 east to Raul Longoria Road in San Juan, make a left on Nebraska; tel. 787-0033) was built just a few years ago, but its history goes back to 17th-century Mexico. In 1623 a young girl believed dead was brought back to life in front of a small statue of the Immaculate Conception that had been placed by Spanish missionaries in a church in Jalisco called San Juan de los Lagos. In their migration to Texas, Mexicans retained their devotion to this manifestation of the Virgin, and in 1954, with 60,000 pilgrims present, a shrine was dedicated here to house the sacred image (a reproduction, actually). In 1970 a pilot flew a plane directly into that shrine, destroying it completely except for the tower, which still stands, and the statue itself. The present shrine was completed in 1980.

Visible from U.S. 83, it is fronted by three immense brass doors adorned with theological symbols, representing faith, hope, and charity. The stained-glass windows depict religious events, and the 15 mysteries of the rosary are illustrated in a faceted-glass window at the entrance. The central figure in the spacious interior is, of course, the statue, flanked by life-size ceramic figures representing the sick, the elderly, farm workers, and migrant workers. There are also figures of a priest, a nun, and a bishop. To one side of this area is a room where visitors may light candles, to the other side is a room for leaving *promesas* (small tokens of appreciation) such as a lock of child's hair, notes, and pictures. After the Vietnam War some people brought in uniforms or medals in thanks for the safe return of loved ones. The shrine is visited by 10,000 people a year, many of them Mexican-Americans. There are three masses a day, five on Sunday. A gift shop on the premises sells religious articles. And on weekends a 30-minute video (in Spanish) about the shrine is shown several times a day.

Open daily from 6 a.m. to 8 p.m., it's about a 20-minute drive from McAllen.

The **McAllen Hudson Museum,** N. 10th St., at Freddy Gonzalez Drive (tel. 383-5763), is one of those privately owned, eclectic, curator's-nightmare collections with displays ranging from antique cars to Egyptian scarabs. George Gillespie and Tex Ray, retired importers of Mexican giftware, began collecting and restoring old Hudson cars in the 1940s. George also amassed an extensive collection of coins and antiques during his military travels, and continued adding to it over the years. Eventually, storage became a problem for both men, so in 1980 they opened the museum as a solution. There are 21 cars on display, the oldest being a 1931 Essex and the latest a 1957, the last year Hudson produced an automobile. Other exhibits include Civil War bullets, a working 1902 player piano, Mexican funerary art, antique guns and swords, Greek and Roman artifacts, fossils, ancient coins, and letters to Jack Ray (Tex's father) from Robert F. Kennedy and John F. Kennedy commending him for help in keeping the peace during integration of the first black students at the University of Mississippi (Jack Ray was a federal marshall at the time). Almost as interesting as the museum displays is the gift shop, which carries a full line of Mexican wares, along with Chinese teapots, chairs made from horns of African cattle, skin-care products, and inlaid boxes from Agra.

Hours are Monday to Saturday from 9:30 a.m. to 5:30 p.m., on Sunday from 1 to 5:30 p.m. Closed Monday in summer. Admission is free.

## SPORTS: Both **hunting** and **fishing** are very popular in McAllen and surrounding Rio Grande Valley areas. There are outsize white-tail bucks, bob-white quail, wild turkeys, numerous waterfowl, white-wing doves, and other wildlife, and varieties of fish too numerous to list. Many organizations based in McAllen offer hunting and fishing expeditions both in the area and Mexico. One such is **Club Exclusive & Big Bass Tours,** 2600 S. Main (tel. 512/687-8513, or toll free 800/531-7509). The **McAllen Chamber of Commerce** (tel. 512/682-2871) is also well versed in these areas.

The 27-hole, par 35-36-36 **Palm View Golf Course,** South Ware Road, just west of the airport (tel. 687-9591), is open to the public. As for **tennis,** there are 16 courts lit for night play at McAllen High School, 23rd and La Vista, which you can use free of charge from 6:30 to 11:30 p.m. And for a fee, you can play days at the private **Racquet Club,** North 10th at 7 Mile Rd. (tel. 383-6268). There are nine courts open from 8 a.m. to 11 p.m.

## NIGHTLIFE: From October to the end of April touring Broadway shows play the **McAllen Civic Center** at U.S. 83 and 10th Street, including in recent years *42nd Street, Sophisticated Ladies,* and *Noises Off.* Tickets are in the $10 to $40 range. There are also occasional headliners like Rich Little and Ben Vereen, ballet performances, and concerts. The Chamber of Commerce handles tickets and can tell you what will be on during your stay. Call 512/682-2871 for details.

A disco called the **Big Apple** in McAllen? That's right. Located at 2322 N. 10th and La Vista (tel. 687-2672), it's decorated with framed posters and photographs of New York City. The music is top-40s, both DJ and live rock groups. It's a nice-sized, comfortable club, with upholstered chairs at tables around the sunken dance floor, a game room (pool tables and video games), 15-foot video monitors, and a concession that sells T-shirts with the logo "The Big Apple, McAllen, Texas." Many promotions take place here—Rambo nights, modeling contests, singing contests, girls-in-miniskirts-get-in-free nights, Madonna-lookalike nights, etc.

Open nightly from 8 p.m. to 2 a.m. There's no cover Sunday to Friday before 9:30 p.m.; otherwise, Wednesday cover is $1, Thursday is $2, and on Friday and Saturday, $3.50.

**Southern Nights,** 500 E. Hackberry, at McColl Road (tel. 682-4133), has been voted the best dance hall in the valley. There are live C&W bands nightly —all top local groups—and the adjoining restaurant serves up a good chicken-fried steak. Big and rustic, its rough-hewn pine walls adorned with the requisite neon beer signs, Southern Nights has a ten-foot monitor for airing C&W videos, football games, and the occasional old western movie. You can pick up an iced longneck at the beer wagon. Monday to Wednesday nights raw oysters or boiled shrimp are $1, ladies are admitted free on Monday till 11 p.m., and Thursday night's the two-step contest. Stick around till the wee hours, especially on weekends, and things tend to get nice and wild.

Open from 9:30 p.m. to 2 a.m. nightly. Cover charge is $2 on Thursday, $3 on Friday and Saturday, $1 on Sunday, free other nights.

A little more chi-chi than the two above-listed is **Players in the Night,** 1101 Chicago, at 10th Street (tel. 630-0440), where seven nights a week a DJ spins top-40s tunes and takes requests ranging from C&W to jazz. The crowd runs to professionals in their 30s, and the ambience is fairly elegant—marble-topped tables, art prints on the walls, beveled-glass doors, lots of mirrors, and an etched-glass mural. A pool table and video game room are upstairs.

Open nightly till 2:30 a.m. No cover.

**REYNOSA:** About eight miles south of McAllen via Hwy. 336, Reynosa is a bustling city of 350,000 with a cluster of tourist-oriented shops and restaurants just over the bridge called the **Zona Rosa** (Pink Zone) and, a little farther on, a large market called **Mercado Zaragoza.** The latter is the best shopping area in town, a warren of dozens of stores off a traffic-free pedestrian mall that is entered at the corner of Hidalgo and Matamoros Streets. Though not as good a market in terms of variety and quality of goods as you'll find in Matamoros or Nuevo Laredo, it is colorful, particularly along Colon Street where there are donkey carts and fruit and vegetable stands. And the plaza, centered on an old church, is rather picturesque.

Once again I advise parking on the Texas side to avoid driving in chaotic Mexican traffic and long lines on return. It's really not a very long walk from the bridge to Zaragoza—about ten short, fairly interesting blocks—but you can get a taxi for about $6 (bargain) or hop a crowded, non-air-conditioned van for 25¢. There's McAllen parking behind the Goodyear sign for $2 per day. If you stay at La Posada, complimentary transport to and from the International Bridge is provided. There's a 50¢ fee if you cross the bridge by car, 10¢ for pedestrians, 5¢ for each sheep, goat, or hog you have in tow (just quoting the sign). If you do decide to drive across, insurance can be purchased at **Sanborn's,** 2011 S. 10th St. (tel. 682-3401).

The most popular place to eat in Reynosa is **Sam's,** corner of Allende and Ocampo (tel. 20034), just a block from the bridge in the Zona Rosa. A large room with red carpeting, white-linened tables, and gold leather chairs, it is lit by fluorescent lighting and looks like the kind of room used for wedding receptions by fraternal organizations (most Mexican border restaurants do). However, $7.50 will get you a very hearty meal here with a choice of two different meats— filet mignon, baked cabrito (that's baby goat), fried chicken, turkey with dressing, roast pork, quail, or frogs' legs—served with avocado salad, french fries, fried onions, fresh tomatoes, pickles, Mexican rice, rolls and butter, jalapeño peppers, beans, and toasted tortillas. Or you might just relax from the rigors of shopping with a piña colada and a bowl of chile con queso. Along similar lines are **La Cucaracha** on Aldama Street (tel. 20174) and the smaller **Meson de Colorado** on Aleman Street (tel. 27979).

There's off-track betting at the **Reynosa Turf Club,** just around the corner from Sam's on Aldama Street; simulcasts of races throughout the U.S. are shown on video monitors here.

# LAREDO: GATEWAY TO MEXICO

THE RIO GRANDE officially divides Laredo in Texas from Nuevo Laredo in Mexico, but since the former city has a 90% Hispanic population, it's sometimes hard to tell the difference. Originally it was all part of one Spanish colony called Nuevo Santander. In 1755 Capt. Don Tomas Sanchez de Barrera y Gallardo, a veteran Spanish officer, established a settlement called Villa de San Agustín de Laredo, centered on the site of the present Plaza San Agustin and named for the hometown of his superior officer. The settlement consisted of three families who shared 66,000 acres of grazing land. Land was distributed in lots in 1767. Untypically, Laredo was neither a military nor a mission town; its rancher residents lived by trading mules, wool, and hides to itinerant merchants. By 1789 there were 700 residents (not counting Indians), a stone church, and 85 dwellings—four of stone, two of adobe, and the rest merely *jacales* (rude huts).

The community was not a peaceful one; it suffered frequent Comanche and Apache raids and saw action in various wars for its first 150 years. The Comanche especially were a dominant force on the frontier through the late 1800s. During the years of border struggles between Mexico and Texas, Laredo was a "no-man's land" caught in the middle. It was here that Santa Anna planned his famous attack on the Alamo, and much fighting occurred in the town's environs. Neglect by both governments led residents of the river communities to form a government of their own in 1840, the Republic of the Rio Grande. Its capital was Laredo, and its capitol building, today a museum, was on the site of the present La Posada Hotel. Though it lasted only 284 days before the area was reclaimed by Mexico, the Rio Grande Republic added a seventh flag over Texas. Following the defeat of Mexico in 1848 the Rio Grande became the official border. Those north of it were Americans; those who wished to become Mexican citizens moved across the river and founded Nuevo Laredo.

Laredo saw heavy action during the Civil War but bravely overcame federal assaults and held the area for the Confederacy. However, it was then plagued by the rigors of Reconstruction, a misery added to continuing depradations by Mexican gangs and the Indian menace. In spite of these difficulties, Laredo flourished as an important transportation center connecting San Antonio, Corpus Christi, and Monterrey. In 1881 two rail lines were built to the town, and by the end of the century the population had increased to 6,000 (including many Anglo-Americans) and a bridge connected *los dos Laredos*. Almost overnight Laredo went from a sleepy "gateway-to-Mexico" adobe village to an important Lone Star State town with a booming economy. And the economy experienced another boom after World War I when natural gas and oil were discovered here.

## 1. Laredo Basics

Today Laredo is a very pleasant little Texas town centered around the picturesque San Agustin Plaza with its beautiful cathedral, 1930s bandstand, and gas-mantle lamps amid palms, orange trees, and rose bushes. The historic downtown area is very Spanish in feel, with many buildings of considerable architectural interest. The town radiating from this quaint center is made up of narrow, tree-lined streets extending outward to a tranquil suburbia of ranch houses fronted by well-tended lawns.

Visitors can explore not only the famed "streets of Laredo," but also the colorful Mexican streets of Nuevo Laredo, an easy walk from the plaza area. Nuevo Laredo is the best market town of the Texas border, and it offers the additional attractions of greyhound and horse racing. If you have time to visit only one Texas border town, Nuevo Laredo is a good choice.

**GETTING THERE:** From McAllen, Laredo is a few hours' drive (144 miles) via U.S. 83, a not-very-scenic ride through brush country. As you approach, you'll notice that most of the radio stations you get are in Spanish. From Corpus Christi, also 144 miles away, take Hwy. 44 west to U.S. 59. And San Antonio is just 153 miles to the north via Interstate 35.

Two airlines—American Eagle and Royale—have flights into **Laredo International Airport** (tel. 512/722-4933), conveniently located in the northeast section of town.

**Trailways** (tel. 512/723-3629) and **Greyhound** (tel. 512/723-4324) have terminals in the downtown area.

And the new **Texas-Mexican Railway Company** (tel. 512/722-6411 in Laredo, 512/289-1818 in Corpus Christi) connects Laredo with Corpus Christi. Fare is $39.95 for adults, $20 for children under 12.

**WHEN TO COME:** The sun shines on Laredo 322 days a year, and the average annual temperature is 74.3°. Since the main reason you'll visit is to traipse through Mexican markets in Nuevo Laredo, the trip is more enjoyable spring through fall; summer temperatures, especially in August, often hover at 100°. But if summer's the only time you can come, don't worry too much; you can easily cool off after a marketing morning by spending an afternoon in the hotel pool.

**GETTING ORIENTED:** Stop in at the **Laredo Chamber of Commerce,** 2310 San Bernardo (tel. 512/722-9895), for maps, brochures, help with accommodations, and the answers to your questions about local facilities and attractions. When you visit, be sure to find out about any special events going on during your stay. The chamber of commerce is open weekdays only, from 8:30 a.m. to noon and 1 to 5 p.m. You can also write in advance for information to P.O. Box 790, Laredo, TX 78042.

**GETTING AROUND:** Most likely you'll want to rent a car if you haven't driven here. **Budget Rent a Car,** at the airport (tel. 512/726-3681), has a large selection of Ford and Lincoln Mercury cars, vans, mini-vans, and pickup trucks. Another option is **Sears Rent a Car** at the airport (tel. 512/726-3682) or 1 Auto Rd. West (tel. 512/723-6391).

There's a **city bus system** called El Metro; phone 722-0951 for routing information.

A **taxi** between most hotels and the airport should cost about $6 to $8. The charge is $1.75 at meter drop when you get in and 20¢ per mile after that. Some drivers will bargain in advance about the fare. If you need a taxi, call Yellow Cab (tel. 723-8285) or Red Top (tel. 723-3711).

**ANNUAL EVENTS:** Laredo has a busy calendar, with most events seeming to involve the crowning of a festival queen. Perhaps every Laredo lass gets her moment in the spotlight. Contact the **Laredo Chamber of Commerce** (tel. 512/722-9895) for additional happenings during your visit and details on events described below if no other phone number is provided.

Laredo is a big hunting area, and the last week in January the sport is celebrated at **Fiesta Caceria,** a hunt feast in which food booths fill the Civic Center grounds offering hunted game prepared in various gourmet styles. This is your chance to sample rabbit mole, rattlesnake meat, grilled venison sausage, barbecued wild pig, and other dishes made from anything that can be shot and cooked. There are also hunt-related crafts booths (like tanning) and an art auction of works by Texas and New Mexico artists. Fiesta Caceria coincides with the **Stockman's Ball** attended by ranchers from far-flung areas. A Border Olympics Queen is chosen, and there's always a contest for the best-dressed couple, another for the best dancers—both western style. Tickets to the ball are about $20. Call 512/722-0589 for details.

For nearly a century Laredo has been making a big whoop-de-do over **George Washington's Birthday,** with celebrations around the week of February 22 centering on a big fiesta and military parade of Mexican troops with tanks marching through the streets. A parade queen (Pocahontas) is crowned, as is a jalapeño queen (she kisses the winner of a jalapeño-eating contest), and there's a debutante ball—a re-creation of an actual ball Washington attended, with all guests in colonial garb and assuming the identity of prominent 18th-century personages. All this and fireworks too! Tickets to the ball cost about $20, and some other events also require tickets. Call 512/722-0589 for further information.

**Border Olympics**—high school and college athletic competitions—take place the first week in March at the Shirley Field Stadium. Tickets are $5 or less; inquire at the Chamber of Commerce.

In mid-March the **Laredo International Fair & Exposition** is a fair, rodeo, and stock show with lots of western excitement. Call 512/722-5662 for details.

If you like beauty contests, you can see **Miss Laredo** chosen at a pageant in early March.

**Frontier Days** is a fun event late in May, with booths on the Civic Center grounds selling early Texas crafts and foods, gunslinger shows, rattlesnake shows, and other settler-related activities. Tickets are about $3, available at the gate.

The last Saturday in June, the **Chamber of Commerce Dance** is attended by over 600 people each year. A farewell is said to the past president, and a new chamber president is welcomed. The event is always themed (recently, for example, a Mexican cabaret), and a dinner is served. Tickets are about $20.

People from all over Texas come to Laredo's **Fourth of July Fiesta/**

**Borderfest** celebration, a history-oriented affair with demonstrations of early Texas skills (like roof thatching), a parade, the crowning of a Borderfest Queen, arts and crafts booths, local bands, and mariachi contests. There's also a Seven Flags over Laredo dance pageant. Call 512/722-9898 for details.

September 16 is **Mexican Independence Day** (El Dieciseis de Septiembre), and every hotel in town puts up a table in San Agustin Plaza offering tourists wine and cheese, margaritas, and ojo rojo (red eye)—a punch made with Southern Comfort, rum, orange juice, pineapple juice, and grenadine. Other activities the week of the 16th include athletic contests, skeet shooting, a beauty pageant, balls, bullfights, rodeo events, lots of music, fashion shows, and much more. It's a pretty big deal. Details at the chamber of commerce.

Early in October there's another **Stockman's Ball,** pretty much like the January event.

## 2. Where to Stay

It always amuses me that bordertown hotels charge extra for rooms with views of the Rio Grande. A Customs officer might be willing to pay extra for a window onto this not-very-scenic river, but I don't know why anyone else would. As in McAllen, the lovely stucco, terracotta-roofed La Posada is *numero uno*. If you're coming to town for the George Washington's Birthday celebrations, be sure to reserve in advance.

**La Posada,** 1000 Zaragoza, Laredo, TX 78042 (tel. 512/722-1701, or toll free 800/531-7156), is an excellent choice for a number of reasons. Its colonial Spanish architecture and palm-fringed courtyards are so lovely it's almost worth coming to Laredo just to stay here. All resort amenities are offered, and the location, on picturesque San Agustin Plaza, just two blocks from the bridge to Mexico, couldn't be better. A hotel since 1961, the structure itself dates to the mid-1800s and incorporates the capitol building of the short-lived Republic of the Rio Grande, now a museum. En route to your room you'll pass through the arcaded white stucco courtyard where Posada guests laze about the pool, order drinks from the Mexican-tile bar, and enjoy the music of a marimba band. It's beautifully landscaped with bougainvillea and other tropical plantings. There's a second pool in a courtyard in the newer wing, this one with a swim-up bar and an adjacent fountain and goldfish pond.

Off the lobby is the main dining room, decorated in classic Mexican style. Both Mexican and American breakfasts are served here—everything from a bagel with cream cheese to huevos rancheros. Lunch and dinner selections are equally eclectic, ranging from a chef's salad ($6.25) or a burger with steak fries ($5) to Mexican combination plates ($8) and full continental dinners. Prices are very reasonable. Outside the dining room is a nicely landscaped terracotta terrace with a waterfall fountain and wrought-iron garden furnishings—the setting for Mexican buffet brunches ($8.25) on weekends.

For more elegant dining, try the upstairs Tack Room, a delightfully cozy, brick-floored restaurant with a Victorian horse-racing motif. Pale-gray walls are hung with beautiful equestrian prints, wood-bladed fans are suspended from a wood-plank ceiling, copper pots gleam in the open kitchen, and cheerful 1890s music emanates from an old oak player piano (some nights a pianist entertains instead). Seating is in plush green booths at candlelit oak tables set with pewterware. And over the copper-topped bar are stained-glass depictions of the races at Ascot. Open for dinner only, the Tack specializes in char-broiled steaks and seafood. A typical meal might include an appetizer of baked crabmeat with cheese, wine, and herbs ($6.25), followed by a five-ounce bacon-wrapped filet mignon and a four-ounce lobster tail with drawn butter ($20), and a dessert of lemon mousse cake ($3).

After dinner, guests might enjoy a liqueur out on the balcony overlooking the plaza. Or head over to the subterranean Import Lot, a sophisticated nightclub where Las Vegas–like lounge acts are featured Monday to Saturday nights. Once a convent, the Lot has original stone walls and arched windows overlooking the Rio Grande. It also overlooks the U.S. Customs import lot where trucks going into Mexico are inspected, hence the name; you can see, and sometimes smell, the furnaces where contraband marijuana is burned. Light fare, such as chili-filled baked potatoes and beer-battered fried shrimp, is available.

Yet a fourth La Posada dining room is the Tesoro Club, *muy elegante* with pink linen-clothed tables lit by hurricane lamps, dusty-rose velvet booths, red velvet wall coverings, and satin-curtained windows. A big bouquet of roses serves as a centerpiece at this most romantic of the Posada's—and of Laredo's—restaurants. French haute cuisine is featured. You might begin with shrimps sautéed in a creamy garlic sauce ($6.25) or a Caesar salad prepared tableside ($8 for two). Among the entree choices are a superb entrecôte au poivre, a 12-ounce steak in brandy/red wine/cream sauce prepared tableside ($17); poached fresh salmon with lobster sauce ($14.50); and crabmeat-stuffed jumbo shrimp with champagne sauce ($17.50). Entrees include a salad, stuffed baked potato, and homemade rolls and butter. Flambé desserts are a specialty, and there's a good wine selection. After dinner or between courses you can dance to music provided by a marimba band.

The hotel's 272 rooms are Spanish in style. They have white stucco and Mexican brick walls hung with works of Spanish masters, beamed ceilings, heavy wood furnishings, and gold carpeting, draperies, and bedspreads. Most overlook the courtyard pool or the Rio Grande, and all are equipped with phones and cable color TVs with Spectravision movies. The new building has a concierge level with an intimate fireplace lounge; guests here get complimentary continental breakfast and afternoon cocktails, enjoy the services of a private concierge, and are pampered with nightly turndown, terrycloth robes, deluxe bath amenities, clock radios, and daily newspaper delivery. General hotel services include complimentary transport to and from the airport, free valet parking, and use of the nearby Laredo Country Club's 18-hole golf course, tennis and racquetball courts, sauna, swimming pool, and restaurant.

Rates are $56 to $62 single, $67 to $80 double, $5 for an extra person (under 12, free). The higher end of the scale is for rooms with pool or river views. Concierge-floor rooms are $150 a night, single or double occupancy. Inquire about weekend rates, offered subject to availability.

Another property offering proximity to the border is the 207-room **Laredo Hilton**, 1 S. Main Ave., adjacent to the River Drive Mall, Laredo, TX 78040 (tel. 512/722-2411, or toll free 800/445-8667). There's free van transport to and from Bridge No. 1, seven blocks away. And the mall is a convenient shopping center with about 60 stores. Kirk Douglas lived at this Hilton during the filming of *Eddie Macon's Run*. Entered via a south-of-the-border-style lobby with Saltillo tile floors and exposed Mexican brick walls, the Hilton is a 15-story circular tower. Hence each of the large and sunny guest rooms has a curved wall. They also have full picture windows overlooking the city or the river, attractive modern furnishings, cable color TVs with HBO movies, and brown/tan color schemes. Executive rooms additionally offer sofas and desks at no extra cost. There's a medium-size swimming pool with surrounding Astroturf sundeck and a restaurant, the Coffee House, that overlooks it. Open daily from 7 a.m. to 7 p.m. it offers reasonably priced coffeeshop fare—both Mexican and American —and adjoins a bar/lounge also facing the pool.

A more elegant setting is the semicircular, 15th-floor Windows on the Rio, with Spanish-style leather chairs and banquettes at tables clothed in dusty rose.

Windows provide panoramic vistas from all seats, and a mirrored wall further enhances the effect. The menu is mostly continental with a few Mexican and Créole entrees. Begin with a salad Sarah Bernhardt—artichokes, hearts of palm, and fresh greens in Dijon mustard dressing ($3.25). Main-course choices include blackened red snapper ($8.25), prime rib with burgundy sauce ($12.25), and sautéed golden-brown Monterrey hen garnished with guacamole, jack cheese, and mole sauce ($9.75). All entrees include soup or salad, fresh vegetable du jour, and saffron rice or potato. From the adjoining bar/lounge, Reflections, you can see miles out into Mexico. It's a romantic spot for dancing at night; a DJ plays mostly mellow rock tunes, and light fare is available.

The Hilton offers free transport to and from the airport, parking is free, and guests enjoy in-room coffee makers and nightly turndown with gourmet chocolates. Rates are $47 to $64 single, $52 to $69 double, $5 for an extra person (free for children of any age—even if you're 50 and traveling with your aged parents). Higher rates are for rooms with river views. Inquire about packages offering savings and such special features as facilities for the disabled.

**Family Gardens Inn,** 5830 San Bernardo Ave., at Mann Road, Laredo, TX 78041 (tel. 512/723-5300), is, as the name hints, a family-oriented hotel with gardens. Couples should head for the romantic La Posada, but if you've got the kids in tow this is the place. A brand-new property, it's centered on a large courtyard with a swimming pool, kiddie pool, outdoor Jacuzzi, sundeck (umbrella tables and chaise longues), and a marvelous playground with bridges, things to climb on, long twisting slides, and a big sand lot. While the kids are at play, adults can sip frozen margaritas at a white-tiled poolside cabaña bar under a green roof. All rooms have pretty latticework balconies or patios overlooking the courtyard, with green wrought-iron garden furnishings. And the entire outdoor area is beautifully landscaped with jasmine and honeysuckle vines climbing decorative trellises, banana palms, and other tropical foliage. At night, it's lit by old-fashioned globe lamps.

The 94 rooms are in neat white stucco buildings with green peaked roofs and door moldings. They're large and pretty, with weathered barn-plank walls hung with framed Oriental prints, handmade oak furnishings and mirror frames, sienna floral-print bedspreads and draperies, and slate-gray carpeting. All have baths (24 have shower only, no tub), direct-dial phones, satellite TVs with movie channels and other pay-cable stations, wet bars, small microwave ovens, and small refrigerators. There's a bedside switch for the TV.

At a 24-hour convenience/food store off the lobby, you can buy dinners and snack fare, plus all other necessities from motor oil to Pampers. The laundry room has washing machines, dryers, video games, and a folding table; irons and ironing boards are available on request. Free transport is offered to/from the airport and the bridge, complimentary coffee is served in the lobby each morning, and qualified babysitters are available. A lot of thought and care have gone into this immaculate and well-run property; there's even a free kennel for dogs on the premises.

Parking is free, and as hospitable manageress Barbara Brunson points out, "you can't beat the prices with a stick." One person pays $38 to $41; two people, $41 to $44; children under 18, free; $5 for an extra person. No-smoking rooms are also available.

# 3. Where to Eat

Laredo's 90% Hispanic population and border proximity make Mexican food a good bet. And because Mexican border towns tend to cater to tourists, you'll often find better, less Americanized restaurants on the Texas side. Such is the case in Laredo, home to the superb **El Asador Suizo,** 4120 San Bernardo (tel.

724-9646), a charming, plant-filled little place where Mexican rugs and pottery, copper pots, and utensils adorn white stucco walls, and decorative baskets are hung from the ceiling. All the furnishings are from Mexico, including the pretty tiled fountain that is the room's central focus.

Grilled specialties are featured, as you can see in the glassed-in kitchen. Queso flameado dishes ($5.35)—melted cheese with various toppings (bacon, Mexican sausage, jalapeños, etc.)—are especially good here; order one as an appetizer to be scooped up with hot homemade tortillas. Other excellent beginnings include a fabulous guacamole ($2.75 small, $4 large) and tortilla soup with onions, avocado, cheese, lemon, hot sauce, and chips in a chicken-broth base ($3 small, $4 large). A worthy entree selection is beef enchiladas suizas topped with cheese, hot sauce, and sour cream, and served with roasted sweet green peppers, cilantro-flavored beans, and guacamole ($5.50). If you're with a group, however, go for the anafre, a sampler platter of queso flameado, guacamole, beans, Polish sausage, short ribs, rib steak, loin-tip steak, shish kebab, chicken, and fajitas, served with tortillas and fresh cilantro, dill, and scallions—it's $35 for four, $50 for six. Another, less expensive way to try everything is at weekday buffet brunches ($6). There's a full bar, featuring a selection of Mexican beers, and homemade desserts include incredible flans in a variety of flavors—pecan, chocolate, vanilla, butterscotch, or coconut ($2).

El Asador Suizo is one of the best Mexican restaurants in the Lone Star State. Open daily from noon to 11 p.m.

Scrumptious and totally authentic Mexican barbecue specialties are what the Sanchez family have been offering for over 15 years at **Catulla-Style Pit Bar-B-Que,** 4502 McPherson, at Taylor (tel. 724-5747). It's a large and funky eatery, seating 200 in a room with linoleum-tile floors, red vinyl chairs at Formica tables, hanging plastic plants, wagon wheel chandeliers, and walls hung with hunting trophies, animal skins, and oil paintings of Mexico. The immense barbecue pit is out back. And large as it is, Catulla is often mobbed, so there's a waiting area up front with rustic hand-carved mesquite furniture and an old cast-iron pit like the cowboys used in the old days.

Everything is fresh and homemade. Try the smoky and tender barbacoa de cabeza (steamed shredded beef; $3.79), a tampiceña plate (char-grilled thin steak with rice, beans, and guacamole; $4.25), or the incredibly delicious gisado, a steak cooked in special seasonings, topped with gravy, and served with rice, beans, and tortillas ($4.10). Catulla is a great place for Mexican mariachi breakfasts—corn or flour tortillas stuffed with beans, eggs, sliced beef, potatoes, etc.—with a good cup of steaming hot coffee. A crew of four spends dawn to dusk in the kitchen turning out fresh tortillas—over 3,000 every day. The Sanchez family (Manuel, wife Ricarda, and sons Manuel, Ramon, and Jorge) are from Catulla, Mexico, and their food is indigenous to that region. Beer is available.

Open Tuesday to Sunday from 8 a.m. to 6 p.m.

A Laredo institution for over four decades, **Golding's,** 1702 Santa Maria Ave., at Callaghan Street (tel. 723-9733), has an old-fashioned elegance reminiscent of a resort-hotel dining room. Carpeted in burgundy, it has forest-green chairs and white-linened tables set with pewter plates and vases of fresh flowers. Owner Freddy Longoria is an African hunter, so mounted trophies (rhinoceros, deer, elk, and water buffalo, among others), paintings of animals, African carvings, and spears line the cream-colored walls. Old mirrors framed in white woodwork are further adornments, and there are candelabra chandeliers overhead. At night, tables are lit by candles in amber glass holders.

Golding's is known for steaks, but the menu also features Mexican and seafood dinners. All entrees include selections from a very nice salad bar, garlic toast, fried onion rings, and a baked potato or vegetable of the day. Appetizers run the gamut from escargots bourguignons ($6.75) to nachos ($4); entrees, from chicken-fried steak with mushroom gravy ($8.50) to an eight-ounce filet mignon ($13.50), to fried jumbo shrimp ($13.50), to cheese enchiladas topped with meat chile sauce and served with Spanish rice, refried beans, and guacamole ($5.75). In addition to the regular menu there are daily lunch and dinner specials. There's an eclectic wine list featuring wines of many nations at prices ranging from $10 to $100 a bottle. For dessert, the homemade flan ($1.75) is a good bet.

Open Monday to Saturday from 11 a.m. to 11 p.m., on Sunday to 9 p.m.

Got the munchies, but don't feel up to a full meal? Head over to **La Reynera Restaurant & Bakery,** 1819 San Bernardo, at Sanchez (tel. 722-6641), an old-fashioned Mexican bakery that's been run by the Gonzalez family since 1928. Marvelous aromas greet you upon entering. There are a few counter stools and booths if you want to eat here, but you can also take out the empanadas filled with pumpkin and sweet potato, gingerbread pigs, sweet rolls, chocolate-filled cinnamon sticks, and other goodies from the glass showcase. La Reynera has great coffee too.

## 4. What to See and Do

Included here are museums, a walking tour, a little shopping, sports and recreation, and nightlife.

**THE NUEVO SANTANDER MUSEUM COMPLEX:** At the west end of Washington Street, on the Laredo Junior College campus, there's a mini-Smithsonian-like museum complex that opened in 1977, on the town's 222nd anniversary. When you get to the end of Washington Street, make a left and go one block to the Old Fort Chapel. The museum consists of several restored mid-1800s buildings that were once part of Fort McIntosh, the citadel from which Laredo settlers battled marauding Mexicans, Indians, and Union soldiers.

The **Old Fort Chapel,** built at the turn of the century, is now a museum of regional history. Free guided tours of the complex depart from the chapel on a continuous basis throughout the day. The building itself is used to house traveling exhibits, usually of regional interest such as Navaho blankets, Texas political cartoons, and a display on underwater archeology off the Gulf Coast. Occasionally, however, the exhibits are not Texas related (a recent example: working models of Michelangelo's drawings).

The **Museum of Military History,** housed in an 1880 U.S. Army Guardhouse (you can still see the old prison cells), contains exhibits on military history, weaponry, clothing, army posters, etc.

At the **Museum of Science and Technology,** once the Commissary Warehouse, you can view a 15-minute slide show on early Laredo ranchers, see a typical 19th-century Laredo dwelling (a thatched-roof shack, its size limited by the scarcity of timber in these parts), and view a tableau of a vaquero (Spanish cowboy) and an American cowboy around the fire with a chuckwagon in the background. There are also farming exhibits and two fancy horse-drawn carriages—one from the U.S., one from Mexico. Don't ask me why it's called a science and technology museum.

More understandable in concept is the adobe- and sandstone-walled **Museum of Art,** housed in the U-shaped Commissary, the oldest building in the complex. Changing shows of regional and nonregional artists are featured.

There's also a small **children's museum** with hands-on, science-related exhibits.

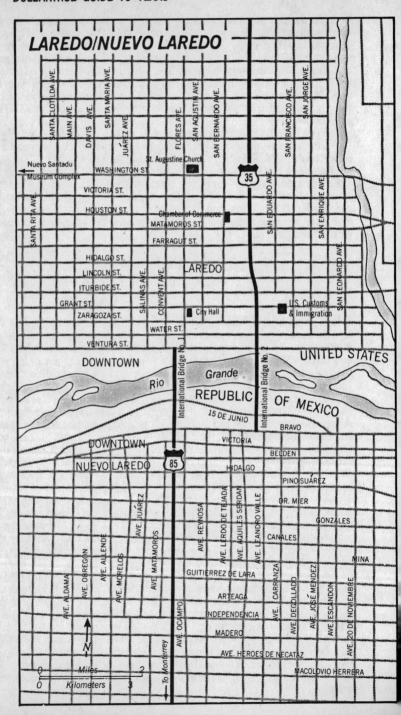

The complex is open Monday to Friday from 9 a.m. to 4 p.m., on Sunday from 1 to 5 p.m. Admission is free. For further details, call 722-0521, ext. 321.

## Museum of the Republic of the Rio Grande

Officially part of the Nuevo Santander Complex, this museum is located apart from the rest, adjacent to the La Posada Hotel, 1005 Zaragoza St. (tel. 727-3480). The over-150-year-old thatch-roofed building was the capitol of the short-lived republic. It still has the original adobe walls, mesquite ceilings, and window sashes. Three rooms show a typical 1830s bedroom with rope-mattress bed, a living room, and a kitchen with limestone water filter for making potable the water of the Rio Grande. In a front room (added in 1860) there are frontier exhibits including an Indian costume worn to the first Washington's Birthday parade in 1899, old furnishings, period clothing, arrowheads, cannonballs, photographs, a 19th-century Bible, and other such historical artifacts.

Hours are Tuesday to Sunday from 10 a.m. to 5 p.m. Admission is free.

**A WALKING TOUR OF LAREDO:** At the Chamber of Commerce you can pick up a walking-tour brochure and map of the "streets of Laredo," focusing on 35 architectural and historical highlights in the downtown area. It begins at the Gothic revival **St. Augustine Church,** on the east side of San Augustin Plaza—the starting point not only of your tour but of Laredo's history. The third church to be erected on this site, it dates to 1872 and is believed to be the burial site of city founder Tomas Sanchez. The church spire is a local landmark, and the stained-glass windows within are notable.

Other sites include many 19th-century homes; the **capitol building** of the 1840 Republic of the Rio Grande (now a museum); **La Posada** Hotel (formerly Laredo's high school from 1916 to 1935); the **home of Col. Santo Benavides,** a local hero who led Confederate forces in Laredo during the Civil War and successfully repulsed the Union Army; the art moderne **Plaza Theater;** the **Laredo National Bank,** which probably has the most beautifully designed and furnished interior of any bank you've ever seen; the old **County Courthouse** (1906), designed by noted Texas architect Alfred Giles; several old hotels and churches; and **City Hall.**

**City Hall Square,** bounded by Hidalgo and Lincoln north and south, San Agustin and Flores east and west, was built in the 1880s as a public market. It is currently being transformed into a mini-Ghirardelli complex of shops, food outlets, and cafés—a shopping/festival center that will be enlivened by street performers and arts and crafts displays. It will become the center for many local fêtes and activities. Surrounding streets have been repaved with interlocking bricks, and storefronts have been restored to their original appearance.

The tour is most interesting. Note that many of Laredo's downtown streets are named for Mexican and American heroes—Zaragoza, Lincoln, Hidalgo, Washington, etc.

**SPORTS AND RECREATION:** Hunting is extremely popular in Laredo—for dove, quail, ducks, geese, javelina, coyote, bobcat, boar, and whitetail deer, among other prey. Several outfitters offer hunting excursions on both sides of the border. One of the best is **Quality Whitetail International,** 110 Century Dr. North (tel. 512/727-6938 or 722/6242). Their fully guided, six-day, first-class hunt includes transportation, accommodations, meals (with wine and other alcoholic beverages), a professional guide, and skinning; taxidermy is available at an extra charge. Cost is $3,000. That's the deluxe way to hunt; the company has many lower-priced packages as well. For additional information and outfitters, contact the Laredo Chamber of Commerce (tel. 512/722-9895).

**Casa Blanca Park,** in the northeast section of town out on U.S. 59, offers a number of recreational facilities. Its 1,600-acre man-made lake is excellent for waterskiing and bass fishing, there's an 18-hole municipal golf course and pro shop on the premises (tel. 727-9218), rowboats can be rented on the lake, there are playgrounds for kids, and shingle-roofed picnic tables with adjacent barbecue pits overlook the water.

Serious swimmers will want to do their daily laps at the Olympic-size **Civic Center Swimming Pool,** 2200 San Bernardo (tel. 722-0478). Mid-May through the end of September, it's open to the public daily from 1 to 8 p.m. for a minimal charge.

The **Laredo Country Club,** on McPherson Road (tel. 727-3569), welcomes visitors to use its facilities on a fee basis. These include an 18-hole golf course, tennis and racquetball courts, a swimming pool, and a sauna.

Try your skill at **skeet and trap shooting** out at the 1,300-acre **La Bota Ranch** on FM 1472 (Old Mines Road) 3½ miles west of I-35 (tel. 723-1994 or 723-6328). Gun rental is $3 per round, including 25 clay pigeons. The price of a round is $5, and ammo is $6 a box. Lessons, given on Monday, Tuesday, and Friday, are $25, all inclusive. There's an air-conditioned clubhouse on the premises where trap- and skeet-related gear and snack fare are available. Hours of operation are 6 p.m. to midnight on Wednesday and Thursday, 3 p.m. to midnight on Saturday and Sunday. A water park is planned on the premises in the future.

## SOME SHOPPING NOTES:
You'll probably get in all the shopping you want in Nuevo Laredo, but you can also find a goodly selection of Mexican wares in Laredo proper. Mexican curio shops line San Bernardo Avenue between Calton Road and Garden Street, about a mile-long stretch. Most notable of these establishments is **Vega's,** 4002 San Bernardo, at Ugarte (tel. 724-8251), its premises chockablock with piñatas, hand-blown glass figures, belts, papier-mâché animals, Indian dolls, onyx, pottery, furniture, etc.

It's also worth mentioning that **Laredo's Mall del Norte,** on I-35 between Hillside and Mann Roads (tel. 724-8191), is the largest shopping mall in South Texas. Laredo's answer to the Galleria, it includes a Sears and Montgomery Ward among its 130 stores, not to mention the only Catholic church in a United States mall.

## NIGHTLIFE:
Keep in mind the above-mentioned **Import Lot** at La Posada, featuring Las Vegas–like lounge acts Monday to Saturday nights, and **Reflections,** the 15th-floor disco (in Laredo that's a skyscraper) at the Hilton. Other choices include the following:

**Rox-z,** 4610 San Bernardo Ave., just south of Calton Road (tel. 723-0517), is a big, slick disco with a state-of-the-art sound system and fog machine, a 12- by 9-foot video monitor, a sizeable dance floor, a game room with three pool tables and video games, and two blackjack tables. The walls are decorated with Dayglo murals of South Texas and New York City. The music is top-40s with some European tunes thrown in for sophisticated measure. And there are frequent special events featuring *Playboy* playmates, rodeo stars, live rock acts, soap opera stars, etc.

Open Tuesday to Sunday till 2 a.m. There's a $3 cover on Thursday nights, $4 on Friday, $5 on Saturday.

At **Golding's,** 1702 Santa Maria Ave., at Callaghan Street (tel. 723-9733), there's entertainment Tuesday to Friday in the lounge from 7 p.m. to midnight. If Raul Puente, a well-known classical Mexican guitarist, is playing during your stay, be sure to come by. Otherwise, the entertainment will probably be a combo for dancing. For further details, see my restaurant recommendations.

Finally, there's **Whistle Stop,** in the Mall del Norte, I-35 between Hillside and Mann Roads (tel. 722-4893), the only place in Laredo you can hear live rock music. And you'll really hear it—this music is outrageously loud. The bands play C&W Monday and Tuesday nights, top-40s music Wednesday to Sunday; the latter nights there's a $3 cover.

Open 8 p.m. till 2 a.m.

# 5. Nuevo Laredo

About 30 million people cross the two bridges connecting Laredo and Nuevo Laredo each year—more than at any other crossing. It's the most picturesque of the Tex-Mex border towns, and it has the largest market areas offering the best selections of quality goods. Unlike other border towns, most of its residents even speak English. Most people cross over on International Bridge No. 1 at the bottom of Convent Avenue. Car toll is 75¢; pedestrian toll, 15¢. My advice is to park on the Texas side at the River Drive Mall, Zaragoza and Water Streets (there's no charge), and walk across. The market area begins about two blocks from the bridge. The main drag, Guerrero Street, is lined with shops for several miles, with additional boutiques on the side streets. Beginning right across the bridge, some of the best shops are:

**La Casona,** across from the famed Cadillac Bar at 2712 Belden, has beautiful pottery, furniture, rugs, and glassware.

**Mercado Las Arcos,** entrance on Belden and Ocampo, is a clean, pleasant, air-conditioned mall with many shops.

**Vega's,** Guerrero and Victoria Avenues, sells a full line of Mexicana—pottery, onyx, papier-mâché, clothing, baskets, etc. It's been here since the early 1930s.

**Marti's,** at the corner of Victoria and Guerrero, has two levels of first-quality merchandise—designer Mexican clothing, exquisite jewelry, wedding dresses, leather and suede coats, fine crystal from Monterrey, and much more, in elegant surroundings. A harpist plays Mexican music while you shop.

**Nuevo Mercado Maclovio Herrera,** at Belden and Guerrero, is a new, air-conditioned indoor market with lots of shops.

**Mona Variety,** just across the street at 401 Guerrero, is a very good dress shop that also carries a nice line of jewelry and brassware.

At **Maria Christina,** another mall at 631 Guerrero, you can find the pottery of Heron Martinez, a noted Mexican craftsman from the state of Pueblo.

And much farther along—about a $5 taxi ride from the rest of the market—**Rafael de México,** Guerrero at Anahuac, is a huge store chock-full of the beautiful furnishings created by Rafael Costilla, along with hammered brass and copper mirror frames, pottery, folk art sculpture, rugs, and many wonderful crafts items.

Those are highlights, but there are hundreds of other establishments to explore as well. Passionate shoppers should allow a full day. In addition to merchandise, you'll enjoy Nuevo Laredo's street musicians, some of them groups of children who sing and play Mexican instruments.

Of course, you have to take a break at some point. The in place for refreshments since 1926 has been the **Cadillac Bar,** right near the bridge at Belden and Ocampo (tel. 20015), its wainscotted cream walls hung with photos of Laredo in the '20s and '30s and mounted hunting trophies. Sit down at a white-linened table and order up one of the Cadillac's potent margaritas, very heavy on the tequila and made with Cointreau instead of the less expensive Triple Sec. The restaurant's Ramoz gin fizz is also renowned. Menu options run the gamut from snack fare like nachos ($3) to a full dinner such as a Créole-style shrimp cocktail, salad, broiled fresh-caught red snapper, homemade french fries, refried beans, homemade rolls with butter, and coffee—all for $10.95. Every imaginable drink —from a Colorado Bull Dog to a Cuba Libre—is available, along with a wide choice of wines, beers, and liqueurs. A pianist is usually on hand, playing all kinds of music—Mexican, country, and corny.

The Cadillac Bar is open daily from 10 a.m. to 11 p.m.

**NUEVO LAREDO DOWNS:** One of the fun things to do in Nuevo Laredo is spend a day at the races. Nuevo Laredo Downs, six miles south of the bridge on Monterrey Highway (tel. 512/726-0549), is a full-fledged thoroughbred track racing horses on Saturday afternoons at 2 p.m. and greyhounds Wednesday to Sunday nights at 8 p.m. On Sunday at 2 p.m. horses race during June and July, greyhounds the rest of the year. To get there by car, go south on Guerrero and just follow the signs. But you don't have to drive; an air-conditioned bus goes to/from any major hotel or the River Drive Mall for just $5 round trip.

Laredo Downs is a beautiful track, with state-of-the-art betting equipment, shops (including a Ralph Lauren Polo boutique), and dining facilities. I enjoy the races most when comfortably ensconced at a table at the exclusive **Turf Club** restaurant, which has a full window wall overlooking the track. There's a $10 minimum if you dine here, and that amount will get you a very full meal. The food is not gourmet quality, but the setting is so pleasant you won't really care. Best bet is to spend your $10 minimum on a drink or two and a botana plate of mixed appetizers. The Turf Club also does a pretty good tortilla soup, and there are fancy desserts flamed tableside in cognac, like bananas Foster. So popular is the Turf Club restaurant that you have to reserve a seat at least a day in advance; call the above number or, if you're elsewhere in Texas but wish to phone ahead for reservations, call toll free 800/292-5659. The restaurant is open Wednesday to Friday from 6 to 10:30 p.m., on Saturday and Sunday from noon to 10:30 p.m.

There's a more plebian restaurant, **La Canasta,** on the track level. It's not as elegant as the Turf Club, but it is air-conditioned, has no minimum or reservations-only policy, and offers a good view of the track. There are also several bars and snackbars.

General seating for greyhound races is 25¢ (non-air-conditioned) to $1, 50¢ (non-air-conditioned) to $2 for horse races.

At the track there are race books, so you can bet on races all over the United States while you're here. If you'd like to do so while watching simulcasts, head for the downtown **Turf Club** at Bravo and Ocampo (tel. 23800).

# Chapter VII

# SAN ANTONIO: THE ALAMO CITY

### 1. San Antonio Basics
### 2. Hotels
### 3. Restaurants
### 4. Sights and Attractions
### 5. Alamo City Nights

SAN ANTONIO IS ONE OF THE OLDEST cities in the West, and wonderfully, vast portions of its past are preserved and restored. The Alamo, a mission turned fort that dates to 1718, is just one of five still-extant missions from the days of Spanish rule. From a later era is La Villita, a restored 200-year-old riverside community in the heart of downtown. Market Square and Main and Military Plazas are also remnants of early San Antonio. They were headquarters in the 1800s of the famed "chili queens" who spiced the San Antonio air purveying "bowls of red" from steaming kettles.

But San Antonio is a tourist mecca not just for its historical attractions. Its natural and man-made beauty reach an apogee on the River Walk in the heart of downtown—three of the loveliest miles in America. San Antonio, past and present, will enchant you.

## 1. San Antonio Basics

**HISTORY:** The city's picturesque history, filled with bloody Indian warfare and the roar of cannons, begins at the river. When an expedition of Spanish soldiers and priests first discovered the lushly forested headwaters of the San Antonio River in 1691—an area corresponding to today's downtown—it was a wilderness whose only residents were the Coahuiltecan Indians. The explorers admired its "broad plains, the most beautiful in New Spain," named the site San Antonio de Padua in honor of the saint whose feast day it was, and went on their way. The Indians, no doubt, went on calling it Yanaguana (Peaceful Waters) as they always had.

It wasn't until 1718, when French encroachments forced Spain to look after its claims in the area, that the first settlement arrived. The Spanish governor of Texas, Martín de Alarcón, and Franciscan Father Antonio Olivares established a town called Villa de Béjar, a presidio or fort called San Antonio de Béjar, and a mission, San Antonio de Valero (better known for its later incarnation as the Alamo).

The mission/presidio setup was an archetype of Spanish colonization in the New World. At the missions the Indians were to be converted to Catholicism and trained in farming and the rudiments of European culture. The presidio was there to see that they went along with the scheme. From the Indian point of view it wasn't such a hot proposition; they were expected to form a class of peasants to work for the European elite who would arrive to populate the area. Nor was the system the smoothly oiled colonization machine Spain intended. Not only did many Indians heartily resist, but Spanish military, civil, and religious sectors, despite a common allegiance to the Crown, were in constant conflict. Even Alarcón and Olivares arrived separately, refusing to travel together because of mutual dislike. The clannish settlers were a snobbish bunch of elitists. They looked down on the soldiers as lowlife mercenaries—which indeed they were. And the Franciscans had no use for either group.

In 1731 when 56 settlers arrived from the Canary Islands there were five missions in San Antonio. And there wasn't much else. The immigrants had been promised land, but found the best land already appropriated by the missions—as was the Indian labor force they had expected to serve them. Instead they were assigned a site for a town, which they were expected to build with their own hands on a hostile frontier where vicious Apache and Comanche attacks were a constant threat. Angry and resentful, but unable to hop an Iberia jet back home, they set about building their town on the site of what is now Main Plaza. Thus was added yet another squalling faction to the divisive local scene.

In spite of it all, San Antonio continued to grow. The presidial captain's house (later the Spanish Governor's Palace) was built in 1749, a time that represented the height—such as it was—of the mission era. Though thousands of Indians had been brought into the missions, they died there in great numbers, victims of European diseases for which they had no immunities. Perhaps the Indians' mental state as a subjugated people had something to do with their poor health as well; their birth rate also declined sharply. And even those who survived never really assimilated. Unwilling workers with inadequate tools, they were viewed in an un-Christian light by the friars as "vile, cowardly, treacherous, and lazy." At the end of the century the missions, now housing only a handful of Indians, were secularized and used to quarter Spanish troops. San Antonio de Valero, renamed the Alamo for a previous post of that name occupied by the same cavalry group, came into being. As the new century dawned, a new country, the United States, was moving westward toward the Spanish frontier. And Mexico was chafing under royal rule. Bloody battles in which thousands were slaughtered took place in San Antonio between the Spanish and Americans, and drought, cholera, and flood added to the city's many tribulations.

The years 1821 to 1836 brought a wave of Anglo-American immigration under the colonial program of Stephen F. Austin. It was at the start of this period that Mexico won independence from Spain, and at its end that Texas broke free of Mexico. The events leading up to the rebellion against Mexico and the final debacle at the Alamo—followed shortly thereafter by Texas's independence—will be covered in depth a little farther along in this chapter.

San Antonio was incorporated as a city of the Republic of Texas in 1837. It didn't mean the end of warfare with Mexico, which continued on a sporadic basis along with the ongoing Indian reign of terror. Indeed, the Comanches boasted that San Antonio was really their town and they only let the settlers stay to raise horses for them. Things changed for the better when Texas became the 28th state of the Union in 1846 and gained America's military backing. The population also began to shift. Visiting Easterner Frederick Law Olmsted noted in the early 1850s that "the sauntering Mexicans prevail . . . but the bearded Germans and the sallow Yankees furnish their proportion." There were French, Scottish, and Italian immigrants too. No longer was San Antonio a totally Hispanic culture.

The Civil War accelerated San Antonio's role as a military and commercial center. And after the war it grew rich in the cattle trade as adventurous residents rounded up herds from the millions of free-roaming longhorns and drove them north. Successful trail drivers returned and spent their money in town. By 1870 San Antonio (pop. 12,256) was the largest city in Texas. It was a boisterous place, peopled by rowdy cowboys, wealthy merchants, sheep ranchers, and speculators. Bars, bawdy houses, and casinos were everywhere to be found, and shoot-outs were common. The railroad chugged into town in 1877, electric lights went on a decade later, and by 1886 there was even a fancy French restaurant.

San Antonio entered the 20th century as a civilized modern city. And it continued developing as such, happily with a concurrent awareness of its heritage that inspired a widespread preservation effort. Mayor Maury Maverick made brilliant use of President Roosevelt's WPA program to revitalize the downtown area, creating the spectacular River Walk and restoring La Villita. The San Antonio World's Fair, HemisFair '68, celebrated the city's 250th anniversary, an event providing a new sports arena, convention hall, theater, museum, and tower.

San Antonio today is one of the most interesting and delightful cities in the state, perhaps offering the visitor more than any other Texas town. If the Alamo forefathers could see it, I think they'd feel they didn't die in vain.

**GETTING THERE:** By car, San Antonio is just 80 miles south of Austin via I-35, 199 miles west of Houston on I-10, 153 miles north of Laredo on I-35, and 145 miles north of Corpus Christi via I-37.

**San Antonio International Airport,** above Loop 410 in the northern sector of town, is served by over a dozen major carriers, including Southwest, American, Continental, TWA, United, Delta, Eastern, Pan Am, and USAir.

Both **Trailways** (tel. 512/226-6136) and **Greyhound** (tel. 512/277-8351) have bus terminals downtown, the former at 301 Broadway, the latter at 500 N. St. Mary's. Frequent bus service in and out of town is available.

And **Amtrak** (tel. 512/223-3226, or toll free 800/872-7245) has service to and from several major cities. The Amtrak station is at 1174 E. Commerce St.

**GETTING ORIENTED:** Stop in at the **Visitor Information Center,** 317 Alamo Plaza, directly in front of the Alamo (tel. 512/299-8155, or toll free 800/531-5700), for comprehensive information about all San Antonio sights, accommodations, restaurants, events, etc., and to pick up maps and brochures. It's open daily from 9 a.m. to 5:30 p.m. If you'd like to write in advance, the address is P.O. Box 2277, San Antonio, TX 78298.

**GETTING AROUND:** There are numerous options for getting around town. So many attractions are centered in the downtown area (where parking, by the way, is a problem second only to traffic jams) that you actually can manage without a car.

There's an excellent bus system, **VIA Metropolitan Transit,** that can get you just about anywhere in town at 50¢ a hop; call 227-2020 for routing information or check with the Visitor Information Center. VIA even has service between the airport and major hotels, with departures in both directions about every 45 minutes between 6 a.m. and 8 p.m.; fare is just $1.

**A taxi** between the airport and downtown hotels will cost you about $11;

taxi fares are $1.45 when the meter drops, $1 per mile after that, plus a 50¢ airport departure charge. If you need one, call **Checker Cab** (tel. 222-2151) or **Yellow Cab** (tel. 226-4242).

In addition to buses, VIA operates **old-fashioned trolley cars** à la San Francisco—authentic reproductions of rail streetcars that actually traveled the streets of San Antonio over 50 years ago. They make stops at most downtown hotels, at several restaurants, and at La Villita, Southwest Craft Center, and other attractions. And a ride only costs a dime. Call 227-2020 for routing information.

That's not the only streetcar. The **Old 300,** a restored bright-yellow-and-green electric streetcar that was in service here from 1913 to 1933, is back on the track. It makes a round trip from the San Antonio Museum of Art to the Pearl Brewery, past the Hays Street overpass to St. Paul Square. You can board at the Museum of Art, 200 W. Jones Ave., Tuesday to Friday at 11 a.m. or 2:30 p.m., on Saturday and Sunday at 10:30 and 11:30 a.m., and 1, 2, 3, or 4 p.m. Admission is by presenting a same-day ticket from the Museum of Art, the Witte Museum, or the Museum of Transportation (all detailed later in this chapter).

Yet a third trolley ride is a 35-minute narrated tour on the **Yellow Trolley** departing from the Alamo hourly between 10:30 and 5:30 p.m., weather permitting. On it you'll see, and hear the history of, the Alamo, the King William area (Victorian homes), San Fernando Cathedral, the Mexican Market, La Villita, the Spanish Governor's Palace, HemisFair, and more. The ride ends back at the Alamo. Fare is $4.25 for adults, $1.75 for children 6 to 14 (under 6, free). For details, call 533-3992.

One of the most delightful ways to see the town is from a **horse-drawn carriage.** They depart from in front of the Alamo and charge $20 per couple for a half-hour tour of the downtown area (children under 12 ride free). There's some talk about moving these buggies, so if you don't see them in front of the Alamo, stop in at the Visitor Information Center and ask where they've gone. Or call the operators—Alamo Carriage (tel. 534-1051), Yellow Rose (tel. 225-6490), or Lone Star (tel. 656-7527).

And now that I've told you all the ways to get around without a car, you'd probably still rather have one. So would I. Most major **car-rental companies** are represented at the airport. **Budget** has locations not only at the airport but at 410 E. Commerce St. downtown, and at 338 N.E. Loop 410 in the northern part of the city; phone for all Budget locations is 512/349-4441. Call **National,** at the airport only, at 512/824-1841.

**ANNUAL EVENTS:** Festive San Antonio celebrates all year long. There's always something special going on you'll want to get in on. For further details about the events listed below—and additional happenings during your stay—contact the **Visitor Information Center,** 317 Alamo Plaza (tel. 512/299-8155).

The Christmas spirit lingers into early January in San Antonio, with **Los Pastores,** a centuries-old miracle play at the San José Mission. It depicts the devil trying to keep the shepherds and other pilgrims from finding the Christ child. There's no admission charge. Call 922-0543 for details.

Later in the month, usually the second or third week, is the **Great Country River Festival** with continuous country-western entertainment by major recording artists (George Strait, Johnny Rodriguez, and Gary Morris) on river barges, at the Arneson River Theater, and on open river patios. There's no admission charge. Call 227-4262 for details.

A biggie is the mid-February **Livestock Show and Rodeo,** ten action-packed days of rodeo events on the official National Rodeo Circuit, with C&W star performances included in your ticket price. You can also check out prize-winning steers, pigs, chickens and other livestock exhibits. It's held at the Freeman Coliseum, 3201 E. Houston (tel. 224-1374). Tickets are available at the door and through major ticket outlets.

For **St. Patrick's Day,** the San Antonio River is dyed green and renamed the "River Shannon." During two weekends in March, the one closest to the 17th and the one prior, there's Irish music, dancing, and singing on the River Walk, and riverside cafés sell green beer. On the second weekend there's a big parade down Houston Street to Alamo Plaza with bands, drill teams, floats, clowns, dance groups, military units, etc. After the parade, an annual wreath-laying ceremony in front of the Alamo commemorates the 12 Irish-born men who died defending it.

The major event of the year is one that's been celebrated for nearly a century here—**Fiesta San Antonio,** the third week in April, with ten days of events including sports competitions (everything from rugby to Mexican horsemanship), dozens of concerts ranging from Sousa to salsa, costumed dancers, a gigantic carnival with rides and midway attractions, art shows around the city, balls, coronations of festival queens and kings, military displays, food booths vending every extant variety of ethnic fare, oyster bakes, balloon races, gown exhibits, house tours, fireworks, special theater and concert performances, and eight parades—the Hispanic Parade of the Ugly King (Rey Feo), a solemn march to the Alamo, a river parade with about 40 decorated barges, the Battle of Flowers Parade with lavish flower-bedecked floats, and the torch-lit Fiesta Night Parade, among others. The festivities include **Night in Old San Antonio—** actually a four-night extravaganza in which early San Antonio fiestas, many of them ethnic, are reenacted; everyone gets stuffed with barbecue, meat-filled pastries, bowls of chili (the Chili Queens are resurrected), paella, and other treats; there's flamenco, bluegrass, dancing, and the breaking of *cascarones* (confetti-filled eggshells) over unsuspecting heads. Some four million people attend Fiesta events each year; it's one of the biggest celebrations in Texas. Some events require tickets; call 512/227-5191 for details.

San Antonio's large Hispanic population celebrates **Cinco de Mayo,** Mexico's independence from France, with a parade the first weekend in May, and music, food, and folkloric dancing in Market Square. Call 299-8600 for details.

**Fiesta Noche del Rio** begins in June and goes on all summer long. It's a colorful three-hour musical festival of song and dance performed under the stars at the Arneson River Theater. The audience sits on grass-tiered seats and enjoys lavishly costumed Las Vegas–style production numbers with a Latin beat. Performances are on Tuesday, Friday, and Saturday nights at 8:30 p.m. Cost is $6.50 for adults, $2.50 for children 6 to 12 (under 6, free). Tickets are available at the box office 1½ hours prior to the show, or through Rainbow Ticketmaster in HemisFair Plaza (tel. 224-3000). For additional information, call 512/226-4651.

Also in June, the three-week **San Antonio Festival** features opera, symphony, ballet, recitals, and jazz concerts, many of the productions by international companies. A recent year's program included productions of *Aïda,* a Benjamin Britten miracle play called *Noye's Fludde,* a Buenos Aires group's *Tango Argentino,* a showcase of song and dance from Madrid, Prokofiev's *Romeo and Juliet,* Beethoven's Ninth Symphony, a Dixieland jazz mass, works by Bach and Mendelssohn, the U.S. Air Force Band and the Singing Sergeants, a country and western jamboree, and much more. For details and ticket information, call 512/226-1573. Or write in advance for a calendar and ticket order form to San Antonio Festival, 306 N. Presa, Suite 7, San Antonio, TX 78205.

**July Fourth** celebrations include a flag-waving patriotic parade with military bands, cavalry units, tanks, and floats; lots of food booths; free entertainment; and fireworks. The Visitor Information Center can provide a schedule of the day's events.

The **Texas Folklife Festival,** held the first week in August, takes place at the Institute of Texan Cultures in HemisFair Plaza. Participants experience a multitude of cultures—those of the 30 ethnic groups that developed the state of Texas. Every kind of dish is represented (Cornish pastie, chicken teriyaki, Greek baklava, Alsatian sausage, etc.); dancers in traditional costumes perform Polish mazurkas and Scandinavian polkas; there are mariachi bands, German oom-pah bands, and Irish fiddlers; and at crafts demonstrations you'll learn to make candles, wagon wheels, saddles, horseshoes, boots, lye soap, and other products the settlers had to produce for themselves. Storytellers spin yarns about life in the frontier days, and you can participate in frontier games like watermelon-seed-spitting and corn-shuckin' contests. Tickets are $6.50 for adults, $2.50 for children 6 to 12 (under 6, free). Call 226-7651 for details.

**Diez y Seis de Septiembre,** during the week of September 16, celebrates Mexican independence (this time from Spain), with many activities, mostly at La Villita on the River Walk. There's entertainment and food, arts and crafts booths, etc.—all of it Mexican themed. Market Square also has Diez y Seis festivities. Call 229-8600 for details.

The first weekend in October, hundreds of artists from all over the state display their works on the River Walk at the **River Art Show.** Call 226-8752 for details.

Two ethnic celebrations occur every October, the two-night **Greek Funstival** at La Villita, with stuffed grape leaves, moussaka, baklava, and dancing à la Anthony Quinn. The retsina flows freely. It's usually toward the end of the month.

There's also an **Oktoberfest** (substitute sauerkraut and sausage for grape leaves and moussaka, strüdel for baklava, beer for retsina, oom-pah for Anthony). It takes place at Beethoven Hall, 422 Pereida, near South Alamo. Call 222-1521 for details and ticket information.

The **Holiday River Parade,** the day after Thanksgiving, officially kicks off the Christmas season with the lighting of Christmas lights along the River Walk and a parade of gaily decorated barges.

**Christmas** is abundantly celebrated in San Antonio. First there's the **River Walk Lighting**—thousands of lights sparkling in trees along the river, and carolers aboard riverboats singing Christmas songs. It goes on all month.

The first two weekends of December, hundreds of candles line the River Walk for the **Fiesta de las Luminarias.** It represents the lighting of the Holy Family's way to Bethlehem. It's quite beautiful.

The second Sunday in December is **Los Posadas,** a reenactment of Mary's and Joseph's search for an inn. A procession winds along the River Walk as the participants sing traditional songs and hymns until it reaches La Villita where a clay figure of the infant Jesus is placed in a crèche. Piñata parties for children follow in the plazas of La Villita, and hot chocolate and cookies are served to all. Call 224-6163 for further information.

Another celebration is **Fiesta Navideñas,** a three-day Christmas festival in Market Square with mariachi and conjunto bands, Mexican folk dancing, piñata parties, traditional holiday food, and a blessing of pets by the bishop of the Archdiocese of San Antonio (dozens of children arrive carrying dogs, cats, goats, geese, and hamsters, many of the animals sporting big Christmas bows). The kids also receive goodies from "Pancho Claus."

There's much more, varying each year but usually including performances of *The Nutcracker,* exhibitions of Christmas madonnas, tours of decorated homes, special church services, and events at the Alamo.

## 2. Hotels

There are exquisite hotels overlooking the river and exquisite hotels not overlooking the river. One property directly across the street from the Alamo, the **Emily Morgan,** is so sophisticated in concept it would be considered avant-garde in New York or Los Angeles. I especially recommend it for honeymooners and those with the honeymoon spirit. It's romantic.

It's usually not hard getting a room in San Antonio, but be sure to book ahead in April during Fiesta and between March and June, a heavy convention period.

The **Emily Morgan Hotel,** 705 E. Houston St., just across the street from the Alamo, San Antonio, TX 78205 (tel. 512/225-8486, or toll free 800/824-6674), is named—despite some controversy—for "The Yellow Rose of Texas." Emily Morgan, the girl who inspired the song, was a beautiful mulatto who was a member of the household staff (really a slave) of Col. James Morgan, a commander of rebel forces in the struggle against Santa Anna. The Mexican leader, a notorious ladies man, was smitten with her, and she became one of the spoils of his campaign. But Emily remained a loyal Texan. She collaborated with Sam Houston by sending him word via slave boys of Mexican troop movements and kept Santa Anna dallying in his tent at San Jacinto while the rebels charged the camp. Some Texans consider her a heroine; others, including some of the Daughters of the Republic of Texas (descendants of settlers who arrived in Texas before 1846), view the hotel's name with disdain. "She was a prostitute," claims one San Antonio woman. "Naming a hotel right across the street from the Alamo after her is like throwing mud on the Alamo." However, owners are betting that tourists, like Santa Anna, will succumb to Emily Morgan's charms, and I daresay they will. It's one of the most stunning hostelries in Texas.

Constructed in 1926, this 13-story building (designed by noted architect Ralph H. Cameron) originally housed a medical center and office space. Its neo-Gothic exterior belies an Italian art deco interior of such exquisite and sophisticated perfection that even those with the most highly developed aesthetic discernment will be nowhere jarred. The gleaming marble-floored lobby is adorned with abundant arrangements of fresh flowers and large potted ferns; opaque multipaned glass partitions give the area an Oriental feel. Here, from early morning to late at night, a concierge is on duty to serve you.

Off the lobby is Sarducci's, a highly stylized northern Italian restaurant with bare oak floors, a wall of beveled mirrors, beautiful art deco lighting fixtures, and Wedgwood blue–clothed tables appointed with fine china, crystal, and silver. Lots of light streams in during the day from a wall of café-curtained windows. The less-is-more interior is strikingly effective, the fare exquisitely prepared and presented. At dinner, you might order antipasti of roasted peppers and grilled zucchini ($4.50) or lightly breaded artichoke hearts, deep-fried and delicately sautéed in Italian herbs ($5.25). There's a choice of four pastas— thin spaghetti, gnocchi verdi (green potato dumplings), tortellini (meat-filled pasta twists), and green fettuccine—which can be topped with any of five sauces: marinara, bolognese, Alfredo, primavera, and pescatora (fish and tomato). Half portions range from $4.50 to $5.50, and full portions run $7.95 to $8.95. Other entrees include grilled swordfish marinated in Italian herbs and cooked with garlic and butter ($14.25), sautéed veal and prosciutto with chanterelles and fontina cheese ($14.50), and boned quails stuffed with chicken livers, bacon, and mushrooms flamed in cognac ($15). At lunch most entrees are in the $6 to $11 range. Either meal, order the tartufo ($3.50) for dessert—an immense chocolate bonbon made of chocolate ice cream, coated with sinfully rich dark chocolate fondant, and topped with fresh whipped cream and strawberries. All fare is fresh and homemade, and an extensive selection of wines is available. Sarducci's is open for lunch and dinner daily.

Another facility on this level is the plant-filled, art deco Lobby Bar, where a classical guitarist or harpist entertains Tuesday to Saturday from 5 to 10 p.m. Afternoon tea (gourmet teas, pastries, and finger sandwiches) is served weekdays from 3 to 6 p.m., and complimentary hors d'oeuvres and wine are offered daily from 5 to 7 p.m.

The 177 rooms are luxuriously decorated in shades of rose ash and cloud blue on alternating floors. Custom pecan-burl armoires opposite the beds conceal cable color TVs (you have a remote control for bedside operation) and serve as bureaus. Horizontal maple blinds grace cathedral windows, and full mirrored walls along the entry expand the feeling of spaciousness while allowing guests a full view of their appearance. A hundred of the rooms have deep Jacuzzi tubs and small refrigerators, and in most of these you can swivel the TV to an angle that lets you watch it in the tub. (Plaza rooms have large windows next to the tub so you can enjoy a view of the Alamo while bathing.) Other bath amenities include fancy toiletries (soaps, shampoo, conditioner, rinse, and hand lotion), a hair dryer, shoeshine pads, sewing kit, scale, and a miniature yellow rose in a vase. In the bedroom you'll find satin clothes hangers in the closet, an AM/FM clock radio, and beautiful art, the latter among hundreds of pieces of museum-quality works throughout the hotel. Guests are pampered with gourmet chocolates at nightly turndown and complimentary breakfast in bed (pastries, fruit, soft boiled egg, fresh-squeezed orange juice, and coffee, served on a tray with a yellow rose). The daily paper is also delivered, of course.

Additional facilities include a small pool, whirlpool, sundeck with umbrella tables, saunas for men and women, and an exercise room, plus no-smoking accommodations and facilities for the disabled.

Rates are $75 for one or two people in a room with one double bed, $85 with one queen-size, $90 with two doubles, $100 with a king-size, $105 to $120 with a king-size bed and Jacuzzi tub. An extra person pays $10; children under 12 stay free. Inquire about low-priced weekend packages.

As I've stated elsewhere in this book, you'll never go wrong at a **Four Seasons** hotel, and the San Antonio representative of this plush chain, at 555 S. Alamo St., between Nueva Street and Durango Boulevard, San Antonio, TX 78205 (tel. 512/229-1000, or toll free 800/268-6282), is no exception. It delivers luxury on a grand scale. There's a complimentary limo for guest use between 7:30 and 9:30 a.m. weekdays to deliver business people to appointments in high style. And even the elevators have Persian rugs! In-room amenities include terry robes, full-length mirrors, remote-control cable color TVs, hair dryers, lots of skirt hangers in the closet, and alarm clock radios. Every night the maid turns down your bed and refreshes your ice bucket, leaving a chocolate and a poem on your pillow and a bottle of Artesia water on your night table. Place your shoes outside the door at night and you'll find them shined in the morning next to your complimentary newspaper. Fresh flowers are left in your room each day, you can order up from room service round the clock, and a concierge will procure anything else (if it's legal) you desire.

Four full-time gardeners are employed keeping the 6½-acre grounds green and gorgeous. The landscaping, complete with waterfalls, makes for such a resort feel that you'll forget you're in the heart of the city. Saltillo tile and brick pathways meander through the property's flower beds and manicured lawns (there's a small putting green on the latter), and past the largest anaqua tree in the United States (the chef makes jelly from its berries). Chinese pheasants roam the grounds; in spring you'll see chicks. A couple of 19th-century buildings on the property are used for receptions; they're not of interest to the transient guest, except that they add an historic air to the gardens. A large swimming pool, whirlpool, sundeck, and baby pool nestle amid hibiscus, palms, banana trees, and pampas grass. There's a poolside margarita bar with shaded tables under an arbor, and room service can be ordered by phone.

The Four Seasons' spa is the only health club I've ever seen that has two working fireplaces; it also contains a full complement of Universal workout equipment, separate saunas for men and women, and a fully supplied locker room (towels, hair dryers, toiletries, etc.). Additional health-oriented features are two Laykold tennis courts lit for night play and complimentary bicycles (you can even get a tandem and have the concierge order a picnic basket for two); jogging maps are available from the same source.

Off the lobby, itself enhanced by Persian rugs and stunning flower arrangements, is the Palm Terrace. Sink into a plush sofa amid the potted palms for classical music or jazz and afternoon tea complete with homemade scones and Devonshire cream. This delightful facility is also the setting for piano-bar entertainment Thursday to Sunday from late afternoon till about 10 p.m.

The hotel's gourmet restaurant, Anaqua (after the tree), is an elegant dining room with forest-green carpeting, sienna velvet-upholstered armchairs, cream linen-clothed tables set with beautiful Shenango china and fresh flowers, and picture windows looking out on a rose garden, three fountains, and a Seward Johnson sculpture of a man seated under an oak tree. Classical or jazz music and much greenery enhance the setting. Wild game, veal, and seafood are featured, meats are smoked on the premises, and the sous chef maintains an herb and vegetable garden on the grounds. The menu changes daily. Dinner might begin with house-cured breast of goose with nectarines ($5.95), a fragrant crayfish bisque ($4.25), or a warm salad of lobster with vegetables vinaigrette ($8.25). On my last visit entrees included filet of rainbow trout in pecan butter sauce ($14.95), roast duckling with currants and Pinot Noir sauce ($19.50), and sautéed Coho salmon with chives and cream ($17.95). Delectable desserts and a comprehensive wine list are, of course, available. And as at all Four Seasons restaurants you can order from the "Alternative Cuisine" menu of gourmet low-fat, low-calorie fare. Luncheon entrees are in the $8 to $10 range.

Last but not least, the rooms. They're large and lovely, with hand-stenciled walls and hand-painted bedboards. Color schemes are rich browns and forest greens, and walls are hung with matted photographs of the San Antonio River and other original art. Especially nice are the top-floor rooms with 15-foot cathedral ceilings.

Though not on the River Walk, the Four Seasons is just a short stroll away, and the Alamo and HemisFair Plaza are also close by.

Rates are $100 to $130 single, $120 to $150 double, $15 per extra person (free for children under 18). Inquire about low weekend rates. Self-parking costs $1.50; valet parking, $4. And no-smoking rooms and facilities for the disabled are also offered.

One of the loveliest hotels gracing the River Walk is the white-limestone, Spanish colonial-style **La Mansión del Río**, 112 College St., between St. Mary's and Navarro Streets, San Antonio, TX 78205 (tel. 512/225-2581, or toll free 800/531-7208). Its 1850s building was originally a religious school started by four French brothers, later headquarters for the San Antonio Bar Association law school where many of the state's most distinguished lawyers earned their degrees. An official historic landmark, it became a hotel in the late 1960s. Fronted by a graceful arched bridge over the river, its lushly landscaped façade is one of arcades and balconies. Terracotta-tile roofing, rough-hewn ceiling beams, wrought-iron-railed spiral staircases, and a central courtyard are additional aspects of the hotel's Spanish heritage. The hotel is entered via a beautiful Saltillo-tile lobby strewn with area rugs.

The 335 rooms are charmingly decorated in pale-peach, mauve, jade-green, and coral-shell hues. All have one Mexican brick wall and weathered beamed ceilings. Belgian tapestry chairs flank an oak table, the cable color TV (with remote device) is concealed in a handsome oak armoire, there's a marble-topped bar (stocked), and a clock radio. In the bath you'll find a terry robe, fancy toiletries, a makeup mirror and full-length mirror. Some of the large rooms have seating areas, and many accommodations offer balconies facing the river or courtyard. Speaking of the courtyard, it contains a small pool and sun-deck amid abundant tropical foliage and a ceramic-tiled Mexican fountain. Food and drink are available.

Soft gray carpeting, pale-peach stucco walls, and flower-bedecked peach-clothed tables make the hotel's El Capistrano Restaurant a delight. Arched windows overlook the pool, and in one dining nook a ficus tree grows toward a skylight overhead. It's open for all meals. Breakfast choices run the gamut from huevos rancheros ($6) to birchermuesli (oatmeal with mixed nuts and fresh fruit; $5) to a Belgian waffle smothered with strawberries and whipped cream ($4.95) or a toasted bagel with cream cheese ($1.50). Hotel breakfasts always tend to be pricey, but lunch and dinner here are very reasonable. The menu lists such Mexican fare as fajitas with guacamole and pico de gallo ($8.25), as well as smoked pork, chicken, or ribs with steak fries ($6.50), and a sirloin steak with baked potato ($10.50). And to backtrack a minute, there are marvelous Mexican appetizers like queso flameado with chorizo sausage and flour tortillas ($3.25) and a paella salad ($5.25). For dessert, it's hard to beat chocolate flan with Kahlúa sauce ($2.25).

After dinner, adjourn to El Coleijo, a stunning bar/lounge. Sink into a plush muted-jade velvet sofa in front of the adobe fireplace, sip a cognac, enjoy the piano-bar entertainment, and know total contentment. Las Canarias, the hotel's gourmet restaurant, is undergoing a total renovation at this writing, though it will probably be completed by the time you visit. It will have a wine bar and feature a flamenco show.

Guests at La Mansión are pampered with full concierge service and nightly turndown with Godiva chocolates.

Rates are $95 to $140 single, $115 to $160 double, $12 for an extra person (under 17, free). Higher tariffs are for larger rooms with water views. Parking is $6 a night, and facilities for the disabled are available.

The **San Antonio Marriott River Walk,** 711 E. River Walk, between East Commerce and Market Streets, San Antonio, TX 78205 (tel. 512/224-4555, or toll free 800/228-9290), has 502 rooms, half of them with a view of the River Walk. President Reagan stayed here in 1984 when he addressed the State Bar of Texas. It's a beautiful resort property. The window-walled fifth-floor recreation area, under a soaring 60-foot opaque-glass atrium skylight, has a large indoor/outdoor swimming pool, a Jacuzzi nestled amid large potted palms and ficus trees, a sundeck, and a game room for kids. You can order drinks and food from room service on the deck, and (in summer) there's an indoor bar at this level.

Rooms have creamy stucco walls hung with Oriental prints, dusty-rose carpeting, and very pretty floral bedspreads and drapes in colors complementing the rose/mauve/sea-green scheme. All are equipped with cable color TVs and clock radios, attractive furnishings, and baths with full-length mirror doors that turn inward to give you the full three-dimensional treatment. Riverside rooms have balconies.

There's a plush lobby bar with bamboo furnishings and macramé wall hangings, where guests enjoy piano-bar music with afternoon cocktails on weekdays. It has outdoor river-view patio seating as well. Another waterside patio facility is Gambits, right on the River Walk level. Come by during weekday Happy Hour and partake of a buffet including complimentary baked potatoes stuffed with butter, cheddar cheese, and crumbled bacon topped with sour cream and chili con queso. Tortillas stuffed with fajitas and guacamole are just 50¢; an order of shrimp, 25¢. Pile your plate high, order a drink, and sit out on the brick terrace watching the sun go down. Monday to Saturday nights a DJ plays top-40s tunes for dancing at Gambits, and some weekends there are country bands out on the patio.

The fancified coffeeshop at the Marriott, the Cactus Flower Café, serves breakfast, lunch, and dinner buffets ($5.95, $7.50, and $8.50, respectively) under a striped awning. The decor is very pleasant. White stucco walls are adorned with colorful painted wood trays and other Mexican craft items. There are bamboo furnishings and booths, a wood-beamed ceiling, and enough plants to create an indoor garden ambience. À la carte menus are also offered at every meal. You could begin a Cactus Flower dinner with an order of potato skins topped with bacon, cheddar, and sour cream with chives ($3.95), and go on to an entree of roast prime rib with creamy horseradish sauce ($13.95) or veal sautéed with bay shrimp, garnished with avocado and tomatoes, and topped with melted jack cheese ($13.95). Or simply order a Cobb salad ($6.50). There are all-American desserts like deep-dish apple pie topped with ice cream ($3.10) and a hot-fudge sundae ($3.25). A kids' menu is offered at lunch and dinner, and if you're watching calorie and fat intake, you can order from a special "Good for You" menu.

On the premises are a car-rental desk, American Airlines desk, a concierge, shoeshine stand, and a gift/resortwear shop. The VIA airport limo stops at the door.

Rates are $109 single, $130 double, $15 for an extra person (under 12, free). Parking is $4.50 a night. Reduced weekend and family rates are based on space available. No-smoking accommodations and facilities for the disabled are available as well.

If you'd like to stay in the northern section of town, close to the airport, across the street from two major malls, and near restaurants and nightlife, there's **Marriott North,** 611 NW Loop 410, just west of San Pedro Avenue, San Antonio, TX 78216 (tel. 512/340-6060, or toll free 800/228-9290). Rates are 15% to 20% lower than you'd pay for similar luxury downtown, and you're only a 15-minute drive from the River Walk here. Free parking is another advantage. Marriott North has 389 rooms, all with king-size or double-double beds, color TVs with Spectravision movies and special cable channels, and alarm clock radios. Decor is in shades of brown and tan with handsome oak furnishings.

Right off the lobby is B. J. Bentley's, a plush all-purpose hotel eatery where wine racks and planters serve as room dividers. Lavish buffet meals, complete with ice sculptures, are served daily at breakfast, lunch, and dinner, they're especially sumptuous on Friday and Saturday nights (when seafood and prime rib are featured, respectively) and on Sunday at brunch. You can also order à la carte fare at all meals. Dinner entrees run the gamut from stir-fried chicken and cashews with rice pilaf and fresh vegetables ($11.50) to fajitas with all the trimmings ($12.25), and there's Häagen-Dazs ice cream for dessert with chocolate brandy sauce ($2.85). The adjoining lounge features live music for dancing Tuesday to Sunday nights, and airs football games on a large-screen TV on

Monday. During Happy Hour this lounge is the scene of a large complimentary buffet, usually Mexican; you can indulge from 4 to 8 p.m. any weekday.

An indoor/outdoor pool, open year round, adjoins a pleasant sundeck, an indoor whirlpool, video game room, and separate men's and women's saunas. Guests have health-club privileges at a spa across the street with workout equipment and racquetball courts. A large gift shop offers a full line of resortwear in addition to the usual sundries. And free transport is provided to and from the airport and the malls across the street. All in all, this is a very nice hostelry, its public areas adorned with much well-chosen art.

Rates are $89 single, $99 double, no charge for an extra person of any age. A honeymoon package includes suite accommodations, breakfast, dinner, and a bottle of champagne for just $109.95 a night—a steal! If you have no significant other, fall in love with yourself and book it alone. No-smoking rooms and facilities for the disabled are also offered.

The original section of the historic **Menger Hotel,** 204 Alamo Plaza, San Antonio, TX 78295 (tel. 512/223-4361, or toll free 800/241-3848), dates to 1859, with later additions from the modern era (1950 and 1968). According to management, the core structure is the oldest hotel in the United States standing in its original form. In its heyday it was one of the finest hotels west of the Mississippi. Owner William A. Menger, a German brewer, stored hops and malt in the basement, but mint juleps were served on the patio. Teddy Roosevelt recruited his Rough Riders in the Menger's bar, stockmen made important deals over ale during the cattle drives, and Presidents Taft, McKinley, Roosevelt (he returned in 1905, this time as president, and was honored at a lavish banquet), Eisenhower, and Nixon have signed the register, as have stars like Lily Pons, Joan Crawford, John Wayne, James Stewart, Robert Mitchum, Sarah Bernhardt, and Beverly Sills. During the Civil War the Menger sheltered both Grant and Lee (at different times, of course). Writers Oscar Wilde and O. Henry made it their San Antonio headquarters. And Roslyn Carter campaigned for her husband in the Colonial Room in 1976.

You'll get a feel for the old grandeur in the stunning, balconied Victorian lobby with ornate marble columns rising 40 feet to a stained-glass skylight ceiling. Lobby walls are hung with gilt-framed mirrors and large oil paintings, and an immense Oriental rug adorns the white tile floor. Rooms in this section have 12-foot ceilings, and many are furnished in Victorian antiques and reproductions—massive carved mahogany beds, marble-topped dressers and tables, and the like. Also lovely is the hotel's courtyard centered on a large swimming pool and sundeck amid vine-covered trellises, palms, tropical shrubbery, and hibiscus.

Rooms in the newer sections are spacious and attractive, also high-ceilinged (ten feet), decorated in contemporary styles utilizing brown and pale-green color schemes. Some have french doors leading onto balconies. Whichever section you stay in, you'll have modern amenities including full tub/shower bath and cable color TV with free in-room movies. Some rooms in the old section have twin beds.

The Patio Dining Room, the hotel's fine dining facility, is being renovated at this writing; it will have a Spanish-style decor and feature classic continental cuisine. There's also a Spanish-motif coffeeshop on the premises, a dress shop, and a drugstore. And you can quaff ale in the same bar where Teddy Roosevelt recruited the Rough Riders. It's an exact replica of the bar in London's House of Lords, except for the photographs of old San Antonio on the wall (I'm assuming here; I've never been to a bar in the House of Lords).

Don't come expecting a Williamsburg-quality restoration. Some of the older public areas reflect the hotel's former grandeur, but for the most part the Menger is just a moderately priced, very well-located hotel (across the street from the Alamo and a block from the River Walk) with a lot of history.

Parking (valet only) is $4 a night with in-and-out privileges. Rates in the old section are $55 single, $68 double or twin, $90 to $110 for a parlor suite with one bedroom. In the newer section singles pay $65; doubles, $77; and a parlor suite is $149. An extra person pays $5; no charge for children under 12. Inquire about weekend rates and packages.

An organization called **Bed and Breakfast Hosts of San Antonio,** 166 Rockhill, San Antonio, TX 78209 (tel. 512/824-8036), has about 25 B&B homes on its rosters, some of them right near the River Walk. All have been carefully screened by the service's owner, Lavern Campbell, and all offer breakfasts that range from continental to full American. At one restored Victorian home the hostess offers to prepare authentic Mexican dinners for her guests. Another is close to a canoeing concession on the river. And the hostess of a third keeps her kitchen stocked with Mexican pastries. Rates range from $27.50 to $85 a night, single or double, with a considerable range in between.

For budget travelers, a good bet is **La Quinta Market Square,** 900 Dolorosa St., at San Saba, San Antonio, TX 78207 (tel. 512/271-0001, or toll-free 800/531-5900). It has 121 rooms, a medium-sized courtyard pool beneath the palms, and the usual Mexican architecture/interior decor. Local phone calls are free. The location is great—right across the street from Market Square and a few blocks from La Fiesta, in other words within close walking distance of about a dozen restaurants and numerous shops. Rates are $46 to $52 single, $52 to $57 double, $5 for an extra person (under 18, free). No-smoking rooms and facilities for the disabled are also available. You'll find details about the La Quinta chain in Chapter I.

## 3. Restaurants

San Antonio not only has some fabulous restaurants, but they're in some of the most beautiful situations as well. It's part of the San Antonio experience to have at least one meal at a **River Walk** restaurant—if weather permits, one with outdoor seating. Also lovely are the colorful **Market Square cafés** (see "Sights") where mariachi bands entertain while you dine. **Los Patios,** a group of three delightful restaurants, nestles in rustic woodlands on the banks of the Salado Creek. And the most romantic dining option is a banquet on the river aboard a **floating barge,** available through any River Walk hotel or restaurant. The charge is $30 an hour plus the cost of your meal; you can order up anything from cocktails and hors d'oeuvres to a full dinner.

Finally, consider fine dining rooms at posh hotels like **Anaqua** at the Four Seasons and **Sarducci's** at the Emily Morgan; both are superb. The first two listings are on the River Walk.

**P.J.'s,** 1 Riverwalk Pl., at St. Mary's and Convent Streets (tel. 225-8400), is the second San Antonio enterprise of award-garnering gourmet gurus Beajan, Ali, and Arjon Tabatabai (see also Arthur's, below). Iranian natives, longtime Texans, and naturalized Americans, these brothers three create culinary magic in all quarters. At P.J.'s it takes the form of French nouvelle cuisine with an Italian accent. Hors d'oeuvres chauds include the very popular shrimp P.J.'s, sautéed in Pernod- and lobster-flavored beurre blanc with julienne of snow peas, carrots, and fresh beets ($7.50). Also notable in this category are gâteaux de crabe (more familiarly known as crabcakes), delicately tinged with cayenne and green onion and sautéed in beurre blanc ($7.95). Go on to order an entree of filet of sole stuffed with lump crabmeat and fresh asparagus sauced with sherry ($15.50) or perhaps milk-fed veal chops sautéed with shrimp in lobster sauce and garnished with mushrooms ($18.50). To top off your dinner, there's a heavenly mille-feuilles—puff pastry layered with whipped cream and fresh tropical fruit with a burnt-sugar glaze topping ($5.50). P.J.'s use of the highest-quality and freshest local and imported produce, meats, and fish (they don't even own a freezer); of garden-fresh herbs for seasoning; fresh-baked breads and pastries; and homemade pastas and sauces (they even make their own ricotta) combines to make dining here a memorable experience . . . as does the beautiful setting.

Overlooking the River Walk, the restaurant is decorated in Fabergé colors —coral and jade wall-to-wall carpeting, jade-green lattice-and-fan-design archways framing the windows, paintings and sculptures of flamingos, exposed wine racks, and caned chairs at pink-clothed tables. At lunch (when most entrees are in the $7.50 to $10 range) there are sometimes fashion shows from ultra-chic San Antonio boutiques. At night the restaurant is romantically candlelit, and there's a band for dancing in the plush adjoining lounge. Validated parking is available at One Riverwalk Parking (700 N. St. Mary's St.) at lunch and dinner; valet parking as well at dinner. You can park your car here and take the house limo to and from performances at the Majestic. And P.J.'s caters barge dinners for $35 and up per person, plus boat rental.

Open for lunch weekdays from 11:30 a.m. to 2:30 p.m., for dinner Monday to Saturday from 6 to 11 p.m. Reservations essential.

Also try the Tabatabais' latest venture, **Ruffino's,** 9802 Colonnade (tel. 641-6100), a less formal—and less expensive—northern Italian restaurant. It opened after I left San Antonio, but I hear glowing reports from local pals. Most entrees at Ruffino's are under $10.

The **Little Rhein Steak House,** 231 S. Alamo, next to the Hilton (tel. 225-1212), offers a choice of cozy indoor seating or patio tables on the River Walk. The building dates to 1847, and its interior dining room has a pine-plank ceiling and stone walls hung with painted beer trays and beer-themed posters and artwork, a decor more bräuhaus than Bauhaus. Seating is in green leather-upholstered captain's chairs at candlelit, white-linened tables, and soft lighting emanates from large amber-glass fixtures, ceiling fan lights, and globe wall sconces. Sheer white curtains framing the windows add a homey touch. There are two additional stone-walled dining rooms downstairs, the low-ceilinged, terracotta-floored Crockett and Bowie Rooms, both with white wood furnishings. A porch dining area overlooks the river, and outdoor patio seating is graduated so that just about all tables have good water views. Some even have good views of the Arneson River Theatre, enough to be almost considered "gratis" admission to performances there.

The Little Rhein specializes in simple, traditional fare, perfectly prepared. All entrees include a large salad in a tasty garlic dressing, a dish of black-eyed peas, a baked potato, and a loaf of brown bread with honey and parsley butter. Order up a USDA prime beef steak—perhaps an 8-ounce filet mignon ($19.95) or a 16-ounce Texas T-bone ($19.95)—and you can't go wrong. Other good choices are shrimp scampi sautéed in white wine and garlic ($19.75), Alaskan king crab with drawn butter and a petit filet ($25.50), and a 12-ounce cut of prime rib ($17.75). A bottle of wine from the reasonably priced list is de rigueur with meals like this. And leave a little room for that traditional American dessert—a hot slab of apple pie with buttery, flaky crust topped with vanilla ice cream ($3.25).

Open for dinner nightly from 5 to 11 p.m. Reservations suggested. The Little Rhein offers barge dinners on the river by prior arrangement.

**Paesano's,** 1715 McCullough Ave., at Locust Street (tel. 226-9541), is the domain of the ebullient Joe Cosniac and his half-brother, Nicola Pacelli. Traditionally trained in the culinary arts in Italy from tender years, they came to the United States in the late 1950s and exhibited their fare at three World's Fairs before settling into this super-successful San Antonio establishment in 1969. Now they're famous enough to have done a "do-you-know-me?" American Express commercial and to attract long lines every lunch and dinner, always including the city's most prominent political power brokers and socialites. Their restaurant is a cozy warren of intimate, red-carpeted dining areas with red-clothed tables lit by candles in red glass holders. Wood-paneled walls are hung with gilt-framed oil paintings. It all combines to create a very warm ambience. For parties of 5 to 16, private wine room seating is available (reserve in advance).

All the food is fresh and homemade, and all entrees include salad, a side order of spaghetti, and a big basket of garlic toast. The salad isn't the usual limp iceberg lettuce affair usually included in restaurant dinners; it's a delicious melange of hearts of palm, artichoke hearts, avocado, tomato, and lettuce in a piquant vinaigrette. Start out with an appetizer of eggplant parmigiana ($4.25) and follow up with an entree of Nicola's signature dish, shrimp Paesano—fresh, tender shrimp browned crisp in a light batter and smothered in velvety-smooth, lemony, butter/garlic sauce ($13.95); the latter is also offered as an appetizer for $5.25. Another excellent choice is veal saltimbocca—tender, milk-fed veal sautéed in a white wine sauce flavored with sage, butter, and garlic and topped with prosciutto and spinach ($14.95). You can't go wrong with pasta dishes here either, even a simple manicotti or lasagne ($9.25). And for dessert there's cappuccino ice cream pie with bitter-chocolate crust and chocolate sauce ($2.50) or New York cheesecake ($2.50). You'll find a wine list on the menu, but that merely scratches the surface of what's available. If you want something better, ask for the upscale list; they'll be happy to break out a $200 bottle of Château Lafite-Rothschild for you. No hard liquor is available—only wine and beer. In addition to the regular menu there are daily lunch specials priced at $5.95 to $7.95.

Paesano's is open Tuesday to Friday from 11 a.m. to 2 p.m. and 5 to 11 p.m., on Saturday from 5 to 11:30 p.m. and on Sunday from 5 to 10 p.m. The restaurant doesn't take reservations, so arrive early to avoid a long wait.

Like P.J.'s, **Arthur's,** 4001 Broadway, at Hildebrand Avenue (tel. 826-3200), is owned by the very charming Tabatabai brothers. Lady Bird Johnson has had luncheons here, and the Nooners, a group of federal judges and millionaires who throw lavish dinners at carefully chosen restaurants, have honored the restaurant with their custom. One reviewer describes Arthur's clientele as "local power brokers . . . old money, new money . . . and out-of-town money." It does take a bit of money (old, new, or otherwise) to dine here, but it's well worth it.

Arthur's exotic interior is stunning. Jade-green walls are hung with hand-carved sandalwood mirrors, tables are covered in sea-green cloths and lit by hurricane lamps, and intricate sandalwood screens serve as room dividers. An exquisite hand-carved Indian brass chandelier graces the center of the room, and antique Indian sculptures further beautify the setting. (The room's designer, Rosemary Augustine, did the late Mrs. Indira Gandhi's home.)

The fare is classic continental/American cuisine, complemented by a very extensive selection of California wines. Listed geographically, the wine menu encompasses a spectrum of 75 noted wineries between Monterey and Mendocino. Begin your dinner with an appetizer of large mushroom caps stuffed with butter-sautéed gulf backfin crabmeat, shallots, and a touch of Dijon mustard, the stuffed caps broiled and topped with creamed hollandaise ($6.95), or perhaps cold spaghetti tossed in vinaigrette with small, al dente chunks of broccoli, cauliflower, asparagus, and tomato, and tender crabmeat, shrimp, and scallops ($6.95). For an entree I suggest mignons of beef Stanley sauced with madeira, garnished with bacon, and topped with horseradish ($17.95) or a mixed seafood grill of salmon, swordfish, red snapper, scallops, and shrimps served with grilled tomato, bacon, and béarnaise ($18.95). A refreshing salad of seasonal greens, fresh vegetables, and fresh-baked French rolls and butter accompany all entrees. The irresistible dessert is a soufflé made with praline liqueur and pastry cream topped with vanilla custard sauce ($5.50). Complete the evening with an after-dinner drink in the adjoining piano bar where the popular Noboko Trio plays contemporary jazz until 2 a.m. nightly.

Arthur's is open for dinner nightly from 6 to 11 p.m. Reservations essential.

**Los Patios,** 2015 N.E. Loop 410 at the Starcrest exit, is actually a group of three delightful restaurants, six shops, and a garden center—all nestling on the verdant, lushly forested banks of the Salado Creek. The plant-filled **Gazebo** (tel. 655-6190), with big windows overlooking the greenery and outdoor patio seating under shade trees, is a light and airy garden restaurant. Seating is in leather-upholstered wrought-iron chairs, and pots of flowers prettify every table. In winter there's a cozy blaze in the large fireplace. The menu specializes in light, ladies' luncheon–type entrees like finger sandwiches with soup or salad ($6.95), quiche Lorraine with vegetables and fruit salad ($6.95), crêpes filled with chicken and mushrooms and served with fruit salad ($6.95), and even chicken à la king served with vegetable and salad ($6.50). This is the kind of place you'd take your mom for lunch when she's in town; there are even fashion shows. For dessert there's lemon cream cheese pie ($2.50)—so much for the diet everyone's on.

**Hacienda** (tel. 655-6225) is a charming cantina centered on a stone fountain, with numerous indoor plants and windows overlooking the woods. It has a lofty cathedral ceiling with a skylight, terracotta-tile floors, and walls adorned with Mexican art. Start off here with an order of six cheese-filled jalapeños ($2.95) or cheese and bean nachos ($3.45). Entree selections range from a combination plate of one cheese enchilada, one chicken enchilada, and one beef taco with pinto beans and guacamole ($7.50), to green chile quiche with guacamole salad and pinto beans ($6.95). For dessert, try a sugary buttermilk praline (75¢).

Most sublimely sylvan of the three is the **Brazier** (tel. 655-9270), a rustic, lodge-like setting with a stone floor, beamed ceiling, and rough-hewn paneled walls. Windows all around overlook a waterfall and goldfish pond on one side, ducks in the creek on the other. And there's actually a tree growing through the ceiling. All three eateries have outdoor patios, but the Brazier deck, in the woodsiest setting, is the nicest. Mesquite-grilled specialties are featured, such as a whole chicken breast with green chile sauce ($7.50) or fresh fish in lemon butter sauce ($8.50). Both entrees include rice pilaf, selections from the salad bar, and hot jalapeño and butter biscuits. Fresh strawberry pie ($2.50) is a refreshing dessert.

All Los Patios facilities serve wine, beer, and cocktails. After your meal, take a stroll around the 33 landscaped acres and browse in the boutiques and galleries. Shops are open from 10 a.m. to 5 p.m. daily. Restaurants are open for lunch only, weekdays from 11:30 a.m. to 2 p.m., on weekends and holidays to 2:30 p.m.

Proximity to several attractions—Brackenridge Park, the McNay Art Institute, the Quadrangle, and the Witte Museum—makes **Cappy's,** 5011 Broadway, at Mary D Avenue (tel. 828-9669), the perfect spot to break for lunch or wind down for dinner after a day's sightseeing. During the day it's light and sunny; at night, romantically candlelit. The main dining room has exposed brick and weathered barnwood walls hung with a changing art exhibit, terracotta-tile floors, and a rough-hewn beamed ceiling. A glass-enclosed patio with pine-plank floors adjoins, and upstairs is another very pleasant dining area—a cozy loft under a peaked, beamed pine ceiling. Dozens of green plants enhance the setting throughout.

The fare is fresh and all-American. Among other things, Cappy's does a fabulous mesquite-broiled cheddarburger ($4.25), and it's a good place to try traditional Texas chicken-fried steak smothered in peppery country white cream gravy ($6.50). The wilted spinach salad ($2.75 small, $4.25 large) with fresh mushrooms and tangy warm bacon dressing is a signature item. Other possibilities include mesquite-grilled sausage and spicy marinara over homemade pasta ($6), redfish sautéed in browned butter/wine sauce topped with almonds ($9.50), and half a pound of sizzling fajitas served with grilled onions, guacamole, black beans, pico de gallo, and flour tortillas ($7.50). Nachos ($4.25) here, by the way, are *muy bueno,* and iced tea comes with fresh mint. For dessert there's a double chocolate cake iced with fudge, covered with pecans, and topped with a scoop of vanilla ice cream ($2.50), or hot apple pie topped with cinnamon, brown sugar, and vanilla ice cream ($3).

Cappy's is open Monday to Thursday from 11 a.m. to 11 p.m., on Friday and Saturday to midnight, and on Sunday from 10 a.m. to 10 p.m. Reservations suggested at all meals. The restaurant offers a park-and-ride service (park here, eat, and they'll provide round-trip bus service for $2.50) to and from the Majestic theater. There's another Cappy's at 123 N.W. Loop 410 (tel. 366-1700); same menu, same hours.

Another good choice in the Brackenridge Park/museum area is **Viet-Nam Restaurant,** 3244 Broadway, at Natalen Avenue (tel. 822-7461), a cheerful little eatery with four brown-carpeted dining areas. Its cream-colored walls are decorated with Oriental paintings and mirrors, Vietnamese screens serve as room dividers, there are crystal chandeliers overhead, and two pretty, arched stained-glass windows depict fruit and flowers.

The food here is authentic and very reasonably priced. At lunch a full meal —eggrolls, shish kebab, and fried rice—is just $5.95. Order a side dish of lettuce mixed with fresh mint and cilantro, and use it to wrap the eggrolls; then dip the whole concoction in tangy fish sauce. These eggrolls, by the way, are deliciously crisp and spicy. In fact, all of owner Snow Eisenhauer's fare is scrumptious. At dinner you might order crab/asparagus soup ($1.95) followed by spicy chicken with peanuts, green onions, and peppers ($7), or crab suprême—crabmeat with onions, ground pork, and glass noodles ($8.50). Either meal, don't pass up those eggrolls or the egg custard (95¢) for dessert; it's much like a French flan. Wine and beer are available, but you might want to go the nonalcoholic route with fresh-squeezed lemonade or jasmin iced tea.

Viet-Nam is open daily from 11 a.m. to 10 p.m. There are always big crowds at lunch and dinner, so arrive off-hours if you want to avoid a wait.

Traditional Texas barbecue is served in rough-and-tumble joints on styrofoam plates with plastic utensils, and if there's any fancifying it might be a dispirited little arrangement of plastic flowers on your Formica table. **The County Line,** 606 Afton Oaks Blvd. (tel. 496-0011), is part of a super-successful chain that has cleaned up the barbecue act and made it possible to dig into your ribs in a more rarefied atmosphere. The interior is an art deco 1930s roadhouse setting with cream-colored pressed-tin ceilings and dark-stained pine walls plastered with collages of old sheet music (Judy Garland, Fred Waring, and Kate Smith), glamor photos of Jean Harlow and Marlene Dietrich, and posters advertising Old Gold cigarettes and Studebaker cars. Wurlitzer jukeboxes and appropriate-to-the-era background music bolster the theme, while forest-green carpeting and curtains make for coziness. And lest you imagine that all this ambience has ruined the ribs, let me assure you that at least 300 people a night don't think so. In fact, unless you arrive very early, you can count on a wait for seats of at least a half an hour. However, that's passed pleasantly enough with a drink on the tree-shaded wooden deck or in the attractive bar/lounge.

The menu is simple, and portions are enormous. Platters served with homemade coleslaw, potato salad ("The recipe is mom's," says Rib King owner Randy Goss), and pinto beans include a choice of ribs ($10.50), barbecued beef ($9.50), sausage ($8.50), a mixture of all three ($9.50), or chicken ($8.50). A child's plate is $5.50. For just $12.50 ($5 for children under 12) you can order country style; that means you get a big platter of meats (ribs, brisket, and sausage) with generous bowls of potato salad, slaw, and beans, plus a loaf of home-made bread (à la carte it costs $3)—and seconds on everything at no extra cost! Hard to beat that, but you probably couldn't manage seconds even on the regular meals, especially if you leave a little room for some delicious homemade ice cream ($1.75). Beer, wine, champagne, and mixed drinks are available, as are immense mugs of iced tea with fresh mint and lime. Doggy bags are gladly given (except with country-style dinners).

To get here, take Hwy. 281 north, go west on North Loop 1604 and drive about 1½ miles until you see Afton Oaks on your left. Hours are Sunday to Thursday from 5 to 10 p.m., on Friday and Saturday to 10:30 p.m.

What could be lovelier than a picnic in beautiful Brackenridge Park? First-rate fixings are available from a gourmet shop called **Le Fromage,** 4001 Broadway, at Hildebrand Avenue (tel. 828-4744). You can stop in and purchase marvelous sandwiches and salads on the spur of the moment, or provide 24 hours notice and have owners Erika and Walter Barth create a fancy basket for two, including plates and utensils. There are six standard picnics for two ranging in price from $10.95 to $28.95. The last includes iced caviar, pâté, imported brie or camembert, French mini-toasts, thinly sliced Bavarian ham, herbed cheese, pasta salads, Dijon mustard, and a dessert of almond pound cake and Australian glazed apricots. Wines, beers, and champagnes are available.

The shop is open weekdays from 10 a.m. to 5:30 p.m., on Saturday to 4 p.m. You can also eat at tables on the premises.

Two chain restaurants that are great choices for inexpensive family meals have branches in San Antonio. Their identical counterparts have already been described in Chapter II (Houston), so I'll merely give the particulars here and ask you to turn back to those pages for full descriptions. They're **Texas Tumbleweed,** 13311 San Pedro Ave. (U.S. 281), at Bitters Road, on the southwest corner (tel. 496-1122), open Sunday to Thursday from 5 to 10 p.m., on Friday and Saturday till midnight; and **Fuddrucker's,** 115 Alamo Plaza, at Commerce (tel. 223-9944), open Monday to Thursday from 11 a.m. to 10 p.m., on Friday and Saturday to midnight, and on Sunday from noon to 10 p.m. The latter, housed in a restored 19th-century building that occupies a square block, is very convenient to the Alamo.

## 4. Sights and Attractions

I haven't counted up the sightseeing highlights in each chapter, but it seems to me that San Antonio has the most. There's so much to do, I'd advise reading

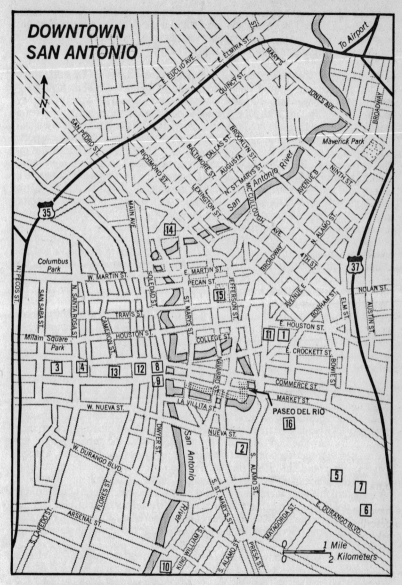

## DOWNTOWN SAN ANTONIO

### KEY TO NUMBERED SIGHTS

1. The Alamo
2. La Villita
3. Market Square
4. Fiesta Plaza
5. Tower of the Americas
6. The Institute of Texan Cultures
7. San Antonio Museum of Transportation
8. Main Plaza
9. Military Plaza
10. King William Historical Area
11. The Heart of Texas
12. San Fernando Cathedral
13. Spanish Governor's Palace
14. Southwest Craft Center
15. Travis Park
16. Convention and Visitors Bureau

through this section and planning your days with geographic proximity in mind; it will save time and footweariness. You'll find it refreshing to alternate serious sightseeing (like touring the Alamo and the Missions) with a stroll in the zoo or Botanical Gardens or a splashdown at Water Park USA.

**THE ALAMO:** This is San Antonio's major attraction, visited by some three million people each year. Every Texan—and probably every American (certainly those who were around in the Davy Crockett fad years)—knows the story of its 13-day siege in 1836. But Alamo history predates that battle by over a century. Built in 1718 as the Mission San Antonio de Valero, the first in a chain of missions built along the San Antonio River, it always had a fort-like aspect. The mission's ostensible purpose was to spread Christianity and educate the Indians, but not all Indians welcomed these "advantages." So even though an actual fort (or presidio) was less than a mile away, the mission itself had to be a stronghold against raids. In its most productive period San Antonio de Valero was home to over 300 Indians of seven tribes who, under the Franciscan friars' direction, operated a farm, a ranch, and subsidiary ventures like carpentry and blacksmith shops. The church you see today was built in 1744.

By 1793 the Indian population was so decimated that the Catholic church closed the mission. In the early 1800s the Spanish cavalry moved in and renamed the structure Pueblo del Alamo (Alamo means cottonwood tree); it was used as a hospital treating both soldiers and civilians. Mexican troops replaced the Spaniards in 1821. Now began the events leading up to one of the most famous battles in history.

Mexico had just won its independence from Spain in 1821 after 300 years of colonialism. Inexperienced in self-government, it wasn't a stable country; 13 presidents came to power and were overthrown during the next 15 years. The seeds for Mexican friction with Texas were quickly sown. In order for pioneers to settle in Mexican Texas, they were expected to embrace Roman Catholicism, and to be legal, their marriages had to be blessed by a priest. Since most of the pioneers were Protestants, accustomed to the right of religious freedom taken for granted in the United States, this was a source of considerable contention. In 1827 Mexico prohibited slavery. Though the Texans got around this injunction by tricky legislation that freed their slaves under contracts binding them to their masters for life, the ban also caused resentment. And the former Americans were used to more freedom than they now enjoyed. As Mexican Gen. Manuel Mier y Teran noted in 1828, "they carried their constitutions in their pockets." In 1830 the Mexican government put a stop to further American immigration to Austin's colony. As Austin feared would happen, this edict merely deterred the better-quality southern gentleman-type settlers he had hoped to attract; frontier riffraff, unconcerned with the niceties of laws, poured in, doubling the population in four years. Soon the Texans were asking for independent statehood in Mexico and for other reforms.

In 1833 Austin met with Santa Anna, who agreed to most of the reforms but not to statehood—at least to Austin's face. He could just as well have agreed to everything, since he then had Austin seized on his way back to Texas and thrown in jail. Santa Anna's government, at first supported by the Texans, had become increasingly repressive. On October 2, 1835, the Mexicans, who had begun worrying about a Texas rebellion, tried to retrieve a six-pound cannon they had given the colonists to fight Indians. The Texans refused to surrender it in a brief skirmish, and the first shots of the revolution were fired. At a gathering at Washington-on-the-Brazos later that month, a provisional government was set up with Henry Smith as governor and Austin as commander-in-chief of the army. Soon battles began erupting between the Texans and the Mexicans. On

December 9, 1835, at the siege of Bexar, the rebels captured San Antonio. But their victory was short-lived. On February 23, 1836, Santa Anna, heading an army of about 4,000 men, marched into San Antonio to retake the city. The Texans, under Lt.-Col. William B. Travis and Col. James Bowie, retreated to the Alamo with 157 men to await reinforcements. Answering Santa Anna's demand for surrender with cannon fire, Travis sent the following message via courier "to the people of Texas and all the Americans in the world" on February 24:

> *Fellow citizens and compatriots — I am besieged, by a thousand or more of the Mexicans under Santa Anna — I have sustained a continual bombardment & cannonade for 24 hours & have not lost a man — The enemy has demanded a surrender at discretion, otherwise, the garrison are to be put to the sword, if the fort is taken — I have answered the demand with a cannon shot, & our flag still waves proudly from the walls — I shall never surrender or retreat. Then, I call on you in the name of liberty, of patriotism & everything dear to the American character, to come to our aid with all dispatch — The enemy is receiving reinforcements daily & will no doubt increase to three or four thousand in four or five days. If this call is neglected, I am determined to sustain myself as long as possible & die like a soldier who never forgets what is due to his own honor & that of his country — Victory or Death.*

But save for 32 men and boys from Gonzales who slipped through Santa Anna's lines in answer to Travis's call, reinforcements never came. For 12 days the Texans and Mexicans engaged in an artillery duel, and though the Texans were far outnumbered, they were better armed and better marksmen. Still, as the days passed they exhausted ammunition and supplies. By March 5 the situation inside the Alamo had become so desperate that Travis called his battle-weary men together, drew a line on the ground with his sword, and in an emotional speech described the hopelessness of their position. Then he said, "Those prepared to give their lives in freedom's cause, come over to me." All but one man crossed the line; Louis Rose, a veteran of Napoleon's retreat from Moscow, risked the contempt of his peers and chose to escape. Jim Bowie, stricken with typhoid and pneumonia, was unable to walk across but asked that his cot be carried over. Thus 188 men and boys sealed their doom.

On March 6, with bugles sounding the dreaded "Deguello" (a Spanish march signaling merciless death to the defenders), Santa Anna advanced against the Alamo. Three hours later it was all over. Bowie died on his cot with his pistols empty of ammunition and his knife bloodied. Colonel Travis, only 26 years old, fell across his cannon shot through the forehead. Davy Crockett, a frontier Tennessee legislator and three-time U.S. congressman, perished in fierce hand-to-hand combat with knife and rifle butt, taking many Mexicans down with him. They are the most immortalized heroes of the Alamo, but to Texans this small band that killed or wounded a third of Santa Anna's men as they fought to the death are all great heroes. Just a little over a month later, on April 21, Sam Houston avenged the Alamo at San Jacinto, winning Texas independence for all time.

## Visiting the Alamo

The Alamo is located right in the heart of the downtown area at Alamo Plaza between East Crockett and East Houston Streets (tel. 225-1391). It's reachable from an exit off the River Walk. The state purchased its historic buildings and grounds in the early 1900s and turned the property over to the Daughters of the Republic of Texas "to operate and maintain as long as it does not cost the state any money." This they gladly do. When you walk up from the River Walk, though the familiar building is across the street, you're already in the Alamo. You'll see part of the original walls, indicating the outline of rooms (Indian quarters) that were once here. The complex originally extended to the gazebo on the south. Today the chapel and the Long Barrack are the only two original buildings left. There are no guided tours of the Alamo, but a 15-minute history talk is given in the chapel on the hour from 10 a.m. to 4 p.m., except at noon. A Texas Daughter at the desk will be happy to answer any questions not covered in the talk. And a ten-minute film, a reenactment of the battle, runs continuously in the Long Barrack. It's a good orientation; see it before you tour the rest of the premises.

The chapel is about 95% as it was originally, barring a few changes made by the army in the 1840s. As you enter, you'll see a scale model of the Alamo of 1836. To the right is the Baptistry, where 16 women and children (families of the defenders) hid during the battle and survived. To the left is the Confessional, its stained-glass windows dating to 1904. Here you'll see the original Alamo chime. Part of the chapel is the Sacristy, where religious services were held. Today it's the Flag Room, used for a display of flags of the 20 states and six foreign countries whose representatives died here. There are a number of exhibits in the chapel, such as an original Bowie knife, artifacts and weaponry from the battle, a ring that belonged to Travis, paintings of the battle, etc. A special group of displays highlights the four commanders of the Alamo: Travis, Crockett, Bowie, and Lt. James Bonham. Bonham, a lawyer and military aide to the governor of South Carolina, gave up his practice to join the Texans' cause. He left the Alamo twice during the siege in futile attempts to secure help and returned through a hail of enemy fire to aid the defense, though he knew the situation was hopeless. Like Travis, he died at his cannon.

In the gift shop area, where you can purchase Texas centennial china and Davy Crockett caps for the kids, there are additional displays of weaponry and artifacts.

The well in the Convent courtyard, under a massive live oak, dates to the 18th-century mission period. Also outdoors are stone tables and benches under the trees where visitors are welcome to picnic. There are two monuments, one dedicated to the 32 men from Gonzales who rallied to the cause, the other a 1914 gift from Japan.

The Long Barrack, scene of the final showdown (over 130 Texans were killed in this building) is now a museum. Exhibits here document the mission period, not just of this mission but of the others in San Antonio. There are displays on early Spanish and Indian residents, on the lives of the men who fought here, on early Texas settlers, and on other battles with Mexico. You'll also see Republic of Texas treasury notes and Santa Anna's ceremonial robe.

Admission is free, but though the Alamo is state owned, it is not state funded, so donations are appreciated. Closest public parking is at the Allright lot on Crockett and Houston, but most of you will be able to walk over from your hotels.

**THE PASEO DEL RIO (RIVER WALK):** Other than Paris, I can't think of any city that makes better use of its river. A three-mile meandering stretch of the San Antonio River comprises the utterly delightful River Walk—a horseshoe-shaped bend in the heart of downtown sequestered from the daily hubbub 20 feet below street level. Flanked by high ivy-covered stone walls, it is a subtropical terrain of tall shade-providing cypress trees, palms, flower beds, and lush foliage. Thousands of birds twitter in the branches overhead, and the cobblestone pathway is punctuated by fountains, waterfalls, graceful arched stone bridges, statuary, interesting shops, and waterside cafés and restaurants. Picturesque barges float along at a leisurely pace carrying sightseers and, at night, people dining in the open air by candlelight. Dozens of festivals, pageants, art shows, and other events take place here, so the River Walk is almost always in the midst of a celebration. And even when nothing special is going on, you're likely to encounter street musicians and vendors selling wares from impromptu carts.

There are many exits leading up to the street, which means that you can use the scenic River Walk to get from here to there as San Antonians do on a daily basis. It's very pleasant on foot, but don't worry about wandering too far from your hotel; you can always hop a river taxi for $1.50 back to your starting point. There's also a 30-minute narrated tour barge that departs from just across the street from the Hilton at the Market Street Bridge; it also costs $1.50, but unlike the taxis, it makes no stops. Or go out under your own steam in a paddleboat built for two ($5 deposit, $1.50 for a half-hour rental); they're available near the Hilton from 9 a.m. to 10:30 p.m. Ramps (at Crockett and St. Mary's Streets, off Market just west of Losoya, and on the south bend of the river at Presa) make the River Walk accessible to the handicapped. Dinner barges are available from all River Walk hotels and restaurants for $30 an hour plus the price of food, which can range from a simple picnic to a gourmet meal. It depends on the source.

## La Villita

Right on the River Walk at 418 Villita St. (tel. 229-8614) is a little 200-year-old town, an early community around which a major metropolis grew. Originally settled by squatters who built rude shelters of stone, mud, or wood in the shadow of the Mission San Antonio de Valero (the Alamo), La Villita remained a makeshift affair until an 1819 flood destroyed much of the west bank of the San Antonio River. La Villita, with its higher east-bank elevation, survived the flood and began to prosper as San Antonio residents realized that high land was good land. In 1836 the surrender of Mexican troops was signed in the "Cos House" here. And by the time Texas became a state in 1846, opulent Victorian mansions built of limestone had replaced many of the huts.

La Villita flourished through the turn of the century, but soon after the area fell on hard times as commercial and industrial ventures encroached. Proximity to factories and auto repair shops caused wealthier citizens to flee to the suburbs, turning their once-proud homes into rooming houses for the not-so-well-heeled. By 1939 the San Antonio police commissioner described the area as "one of the worst slum districts in San Antonio . . . a hangout for winos, all sorts of vice, and a terrible-looking, dirty neighborhood." Mayor Maury Maverick decided to take the matter in hand. He arranged a $100,000 revitalization grant from the National Youth Administration and began a WPA project removing debris and eyesore architecture and restoring the beautiful older homes. As La Villita became more attractive, other money flowed in and the old town soon became a center for community events. In 1969 the La Villita Historic District of San Antonio was created, and it was extended in 1975. La Villita is also a National Register Historic District.

Today its 25 restored buildings, spanning a century of architecture, provide working space for artists and craftspeople, house quaint boutiques and restaurants, and are a major sightseeing attraction along the River Walk. The Arneson River Theatre is here as well.

It's great fun to browse among the shops. Their wares include Texas and

Mexican spices, fajita seasonings and jalapeño jellies, Mexican imports, hand-made cowboy boots, clothing, antiques, jewelry, and souvenirs. There's a German bakery, a charming country store for quilts and calico, and many an art gallery, including the headquarters for the River Art Group, an organization of 600 artists who have rotating shows of their work in the 1855 Florian House (Building 14). While wandering in and out of the buildings, you'll come across many studios where working artists demonstrate their skills and sell finished works—stained glass, glassblowing, candlemaking, photography, pottery, leatherwork, and painting, among them. The setting is often enlivened by weddings, parties, and festivals going on in La Villita's three outdoor plazas.

You can attend nondenominational services in the 1879 German Methodist Episcopal Church, now called the Little Church of La Villita. Have your cards or palm read by the Blue Lady in Palisado House (Building 25), former home of an 1800s psychic. Dine in one of the restaurants. Or pose for portrait artist Jesse Sanchez. In summer, be sure to attend a production at the Arneson River Theatre (details in my nightlife listings, below).

La Villita shops are open from 10 a.m. to 6 p.m., most of them seven days, though some close on Sunday.

**MARKET SQUARE:** One of the many charming areas of San Antonio is the lively Mexican-themed pedestrian mall bounded by San Saba, Santa Rosa, Dolorosa, and Commerce Streets. Restaurants spill out onto the street in awninged cafés with umbrella tables—the best vantage point to watch the bustling crowds, street acts, caricaturists, and frequent festivities. Traders, beggars, craftsmen, and strolling musicians walked these colorful streets when the area was an open-air market in the 1800s. It was the home of San Antonio's famed "Chili Queens"—first purveyors, some say, of the state's national dish. People came from near and far to sample the smouldering brews the queens stirred all day in large pots on charcoal fires, and the pungent aroma of chili filled the air.

Today's re-created Market Square is centered around a vast *mercado* selling everything you could purchase south of the border—curios, candles, pottery, jewelry, papier-mâché animals, piñatas, handcrafted dolls, embroidered cotton dresses, straw products, leather goods, onyx, paper flowers, you name it. In summer there are frequent Mexican folkloric ballet performances on a stage by the fountain. And a number of restaurants vie for your patronage.

I like **La Margarita,** 120 Produce Row (tel. 227-7140), a delightfully airy, plant-filled restaurant with exposed brick walls, overhead fans suspended from a high, cream-colored pressed-tin ceiling, and large multipaned windows overlooking the street. If it's not too hot or too cool, eat outside at an umbrella table. At lunch a pianist entertains. Famous for frozen margaritas, this eatery is also a good place for a lunch of queso flameado (melted Monterrey cheese with bits of chorizo sausage scooped up with tostaditas; $4.25 for two) and a sizzling platter of fajitas (a full pound of char-grilled meat, served with grilled onions, guacamole, pico de gallo, and a basket of tortillas wrapped in a green cloth napkin; $11.50, also serving two people). An order of charra beans simmered in a pot liquor with cilantro, chiles, pork, garlic, and spices is $1.25.

Hours are 11 a.m. to 10 p.m. Sunday to Thursday, to midnight on Friday and Saturday. Evenings, mariachi bands stroll Market Square wandering in and out of the restaurants.

If you arrive early in the morning, have a Mexican breakfast at **Mi Tierra** (it means "my land"), 218 Produce Row (tel. 225-1262), a San Antonio institution under the auspices of the Cortez family for over four decades. The family also owns the above-mentioned La Margarita, next door. At the entrance is a tempting glass display case filled with pan dulce—Mexican pastries, breads, and sweets. Mi Tierra is open 24 hours a day and decorated for Christmas year round. Huevos rancheros with bacon, ham, or pork chop is $4.35; with a cup of coffee (75¢) that's a totally satisfying breakfast, but you can also improvise breakfast tacos to your liking. And a full Mexican menu is served at all times, as are piña coladas, frozen daiquiris, and pitchers of margaritas.

Market Square shops are open daily from 10 a.m. to 6 p.m., till 8 p.m. in summer. Across San Saba Street is the colorful **Farmer's Market,** where produce comes in for distribution throughout the city. It's always fun to walk around market stalls piled high with fruits and vegetables, and five times a year the facility is used for senior citizens' arts and crafts shows with displays (all for sale, of course) of handcrafted wooden toys, crocheted animals and other items, hand-tooled belts, and such.

**FIESTA PLAZA:** You can continue the browsing begun at Market Square at this second colorful market a block farther along. Fiesta Plaza occupies four square blocks bounded by Matamoros, Frio, South Pecos, and Buena Vista Streets (tel. 271-0408). Inside a large terracotta-roofed, candy-pink stucco building, complete with Mexican fountains and Saltillo-tile floors, are 58 shops and restaurants and an entertainment stage. The latter, in an immense indoor courtyard under a 30-foot skylit ceiling hung with colorful banners, has lacy white wrought-iron tables and chairs where shoppers can eat or drink while enjoying the free shows—mariachi bands, flamenco dancers, clowns, acrobats, and occasionally even big-name performers like Eddie Raven and José Greco. It's a good idea to call before you go and find out what's on and when, so you can time your visit accordingly.

The shops are very varied. They include an international art gallery, a Chinese grocery, Vega's (a renowned Mexican import shop), the House of Onyx, clothing boutiques, western wear, toys, pottery, jewelry, candles, and much more. There are also vending carts to check out. As for the available cuisine, it's international in scope, providing a choice of Indian, Filipino, Italian, Mexican, Japanese, Chinese, and American fare. And if none of it appeals to you, you can always shop here and dine back at Market Square. Hours are 10 a.m. to 10 p.m. seven days a week.

**BRACKENRIDGE PARK:** As if San Antonio didn't have enough scenic outdoor attractions, it also has one of the prettiest urban parks in the state. Bounded by Broadway, McAllister Freeway (Hwy. 281), and Hildebrand Avenue, it's a 343-acre greenbelt, with ducks and paddleboats cruising the river that winds through its forested grounds.

Brackenridge has all the facilities one looks for in a park. There are **riding stables** at 840 E. Mulberry (tel. 732-8881), where you can rent horses for use on the park's bridle paths at $10 an hour. Numerous joggers do their daily run on park paths shaded by groves of live oaks. At 2315 Avenue B is an 18-hole **municipal golf course** (tel. 226-5612); fee is $5 weekdays ($4.50 after 3:30 p.m.) and $5.50 weekends ($5 after 3:30 p.m.). Other recreational options include bike rental, a baseball diamond, playgrounds, and picnic groves with barbecue grills —everything for a perfect day in the park.

**The Brackenridge Eagle,** 3918 N. St. Mary's St. (tel. 735-8641), is a miniature train ride that leaves from near the zoo and makes stops at various points around the park on its 3½-mile route. There are two trains on the line, one with a small-scale replica of an 1835 steam locomotive, the other with a scale model of a modern diesel. Hours are 9 a.m. to 5 p.m. weekdays, 9:30 a.m. to 6:30 p.m. weekends. Adults pay $1.25; children under 12, 85¢. Another marvelous way to traverse the park is via the **Skyride**, 3883 St. Mary's St. (tel. 732-8481), which goes back and forth between the zoo and the Japanese Tea Gardens, providing incredible park and skyline views en route. In summer it's also a little cooler up here. The Skyride runs from 9:30 a.m. to 5 p.m. Monday to Friday, till 8 p.m. weekends May through August, till 6 p.m. weekends the rest of the year. Adults pay $1.75, and children under 3 ride free.

In addition to the above-mentioned facilities, park attractions include the following:

## The Japanese Tea Gardens

These beautiful gardens, entered through a graceful stone archway flanked by flower beds, is on the site of an old rock quarry that provided the limestone used to build the state Capitol and many homes in San Antonio. Ray Lambert, San Antonio's first park commissioner, envisioned the transformation from rock quarry to rock garden, and with funding from local businessmen and labor from the city prison, the project was completed in 1918. A Mexican Village—a group of four houses in which Mexican families lived and made pottery and baskets to sell to tourists—was part of the original plan. The structures are still here, but no longer occupied. The landscaping is charming, with pebble pathways winding through colorful flower beds, ponds of shimmering goldfish and lotus, quaint arched bridges, and an immense stone pagoda. In summer there are outdoor performances here—concerts, ballet folklorico, etc. During World War II anti-Japanese sentiment forced a name change to the Chinese Tea Gardens, but recently the city of San Antonio hosted the Japanese ambassador to the United States and as a long-overdue gesture of goodwill, changed it back. Be sure to see these spectacular gardens.

## The San Antonio Zoological Gardens and Aquarium

Limestone rock quarries and the San Antonio River form the backdrop for this beautifully landscaped 50-acre menagerie at 3903 N. St. Mary's St. (tel. 734-7183). Established in 1910 and moved to its present location in 1914, the zoo houses over 3,000 animals representing more than 700 species. It is known for its African antelope collection, one of the world's largest, and its outstanding bird population. The animals live in natural, moated habitats, and many breed in captivity. You'll see a lot of baby animals. The African Safari Trail links several exhibits of birds and animals to simulate an East African setting. In the walk-through aviary dioramas display birds in miniature natural habitats. Artificial rocks, streams, and waterfalls enhance a gorilla exhibit. And there's a noteworthy aquarium on the premises. A highlight is the excellent children's zoo, where a rustic boardwalk overlooks grasslands and a waterfowl pond, and infant animals are on display in a nursery complex. A boat ride follows a meandering canal past an Asian Island (pelicans and cormorants are the inhabitants), a South American Island (a jungleful of monkeys), a Galápagos Island, and an Australian Barrier Reef with an underwater aquarium tunnel for viewing giant sharks nose to nose. An imaginative playground area and animal-petting zoo are also part of this facility. Pick up a map at the entrance and find out about special programs and activities—elephant shows and rides, sea lion demonstrations, and lectures. This is the largest zoo in the Southwest and one of the top zoos in the country. Don't miss it.

Hours are 9:30 a.m. to 6:30 p.m. daily April to October, to 5 p.m. the rest of the year. Admission is $4 for adults, $2 for children 3 to 11 and senior citizens (under 3, free).

## The Witte Museum

In existence since 1923, the Witte, 3801 Broadway (tel. 226-5544), houses an extensive collection of southwestern artifacts, from dinosaur bones to the advent of radio—much of it enhanced by narrative slide and video shows. This is a great museum for kids. The curatorial staff has done a remarkable job of making its exhibits accessible and fascinating to all age groups. In the dinosaur section, visitors can handle real dinosaur bones and view skeletal reconstructions of the *Triceratops* and the 2,000-toothed *Anatosaurus,* fossils from the Cretaceous period when Texas was a sea, and actual casts of dinosaur footprints found in the state. A video display debunks dinosaur myths from old movies. Farther along, an intriguing Animal Senses exhibit enables visitors to experience what birds, animals, fish, and bugs see, smell, and hear. Sounds of South Texas spotlights birds in a tableau as they trill their individual calls. In South Texas Ecology, you'll walk through a simulated riverbed. And two additional downstairs galleries highlight the Alamo and the lifestyles of people of the Lower Pecos area (now Val Verde County) from 7000 B.C. to A.D. 1500.

Upstairs are costumes from the current year's Fiesta (see "Annual Events"), a glassed-in curator's room where you can watch staff members working on museum artifacts, and an exhibit demonstrating the highly developed culture and arts of the Indians titled "They Call Us Savages." On the grounds in Brackenridge Park two log cabins and three historic homes are on view.

Open Tuesday to Saturday from 10 a.m. to 5 p.m., with extended hours on Thursday till 9 p.m., and on Sunday from noon to 5 p.m. June through August it stays open until 6 p.m. Admission is $3 for adults, $1.50 for students, military, and senior citizens, $1 for children 6 to 12 (under 6, free). There's free admission for all on Thursday between 3 and 9 p.m. The *Old 300* streetcar stops at the door.

While you're here, pick up a calendar of events, which will also fill you in on happenings at the art and transportation museums, under the same auspices. Activities include singles nights, workshops (like costume making), field trips (for example, canoeing on the San Antonio River or hiking Padre Island with a naturalist), and lectures.

## The Texas Rangers Museum

Right next door to the Witte Museum at 3805 Broadway (tel. 822-9011), you can learn about the legendary Texas Rangers, the force first formed in 1823 by Stephen F. Austin to protect his colony of 300 settlers from Mexican hostilities and marauding Comanche, Apache, and Karankawa Indians. These brave and dedicated enforcers of frontier law have been described as "men who could ride straight up to death." There were originally ten men who "ranged" over wide areas scouting movements of the Indians, hence the name. This activity required good horsemen, so the rangers were for many years a mounted force. In 1845, when Texas joined the Union, American forces came to the aid of the Rangers in the bitter battles with Mexico, and the Rangers became temporarily a unit in the U.S. Army.

During the Civil War, Rangers activity was in abeyance, but the group resurfaced to help deal with the chaos left after Reconstruction. At that time they expanded their activities (though still dealing with Mexican and Indian raids) to include mob control and the capture of murderers, train robbers, cattle thieves, and brigands. Under Capt. Leander H. McNelley the Rangers recaptured a large herd from the notorious bandito Cortina, a success that greatly enhanced their can-do reputation. (McNelley displayed the bodies of Mexicans killed in this conflict in a public square at Brownsville to discourage future cattle theft.) By the 1880s the presence of the Rangers was widely felt throughout Texas, and lawless frontier days were coming to an end.

The Rangers are still in operation today, one of the world's strongest forces of law. Their informal motto is, "No man in the wrong can stand up against a man in the right who keeps on a-comin'."

At the museum you'll see numerous Ranger mementoes and memorabilia —guns, spurs, branding irons, saddles, correspondence, mounted heads of longhorn cattle, trail maps, photographs, news clippings, and documents. The walls of the Trail Driver's Room are lined with 295 photographs of some of the 40,000 pioneers who drove over ten million head of cattle to northern markets in the years 1870 to 1890. The museum has collected the photographs from descendants of these men. A large oil painting in this room by noted western artist H. W. Caylor depicts a trail ride of 96 miles with no water. Photographs of past presidents of the Trail Driver's Association line the President's Room. And 1800s furnishings from frontier homes are displayed in the Pioneer's Parlor.

The museum is open daily from 10 a.m. to 5 p.m. Adults pay $1 admission, and children 6 to 12 pay 25¢ (under 6, free).

**THE SAN ANTONIO BOTANICAL GARDENS:** Beautifully landscaped areas abound in San Antonio, but one that should not be missed is this tranquil 33-acre garden at 555 Funston Pl. and North New Braunfels Avenue (tel. 821-5115). Even the visitor center here, with its cypress doors and beveled-glass windows and panels, is something to see. Start off by picking up a map of the gardens. Just outside is a fountain plaza with wrought-iron benches and a wisteria arbor; the exquisite fountain, hand-carved from Mexican volcanic stone, is similar in design to the Generaliffe fountain in Spain. In the nearby Garden for the Blind, scented plantings like lavender and sage are featured and elucidated upon in Braille plaques. Golden-hued koi carp swim among water lilies in the delightful Aquatic Garden.

A large section is devoted to native Texas plants of three areas: Southwest Texas, East Texas, and the Hill Country, the latter resplendent in springtime with fields of buttercups, bluebonnet, orange and red sumac, and other wildflowers. That's also the best time to see the flowering dogwoods in the East Texas area and the white-blossomed yucca of the Southwest. Though one thinks of Texas as relatively unforested, these native habitats have dozens of different trees—sugar maples, river birch, gum trees, black walnut, honey locust, ash, elm, beech, magnolia, sycamore, wild black cherry, and large, spreading chestnuts, among others. Also in this area are several early Texas log and adobe buildings from various parts of the state that have been dismantled and reconstructed on the premises. Elsewhere, a Biblical Garden is planted with flora mentioned in the Bible—crown of thorn, fig trees, myrtle, and bulrushes. Formal gardens include beds of annuals and perennials (marigolds, asters, snapdragons, and other typical backyard blooms), an herb garden, and a fragrant rose garden of hybrid teas, climbers, floribundas, and antique roses. From an elevated observation point—a hilltop gazebo capped with an antique weathervane—all the gardens are visible.

In the works at this writing, and probably extant as you read this, is the new $6.5-million Lucile Halsell Conservatory, a 90,000-square-foot complex designed to display tropical palms, rain forest ferns, an orangerie, and desert cacti.

Visitors will follow a tunnel into a subterranean world of varied ecosystems within a series of tent-like pavilions. Only the lines of the glass roofs will be visible from above ground.

The gardens are open Tuesday to Sunday from 9 a.m. to 6 p.m. Admission is $2 for adults, $1 for children 13 and under.

**THE SAN ANTONIO MUSEUM OF ART:** Opened in 1981, this very fine San Antonio museum at 200 W. Jones Ave., between Broadway and Dallas Street (tel. 226-5544), occupies a turn-of-the-century romanesque building that once housed the Lone Star Brewery. Its architecture is quite striking, encompassing a skywalk adorned with neon tube art that is visible from the freeway below. The skywalk connects twin four-story towers and itself offers panoramic views of the city skyline on one side and the San Antonio River on the other.

Exhibits cover a wide spectrum. A gallery of Texas paintings and decorative arts includes furniture used by early settlers, chairs made of horns, quilts, Texas Campaign dinnerware, and works by Texas painters. Other galleries focus on Pre-Columbian sculpture and pottery, contemporary American art (George Segal, Hans Hofmann, Stella, etc.), 18th-century Americans (Gilbert Stuart, John Singleton Copley, Benjamin West), 19th-century Americans (John Singer Sargent, Marsden Hartley, Arthur B. Davies), Oriental art, and Mexican folk art from the collections of Robert K. Winn and Nelson Rockefeller. A highlight is a superb photography gallery displaying works of Ansel Adams, Diane Arbus, Edward Steichen, Walker Evans, Dorothea Lange, and others.

Additionally, there's a 2½-acre sculpture garden with oak-shaded paths and rest areas. And on the top floor, reached via sleek glass elevators, is the lovely Terrace Café, where 20-foot windowed walls provide sky and skyline views. It also has outdoor seating on a large wooden deck. Light fare—cheeses, sandwiches, homemade soups, fresh-baked banana bread, fresh fruits, and fancy teas—is offered at very reasonable prices. It's open from noon to 4 p.m. Tuesday to Sunday.

Regular exhibits are supplemented by temporary shows such as "Chinese Export Silver" and "Paintings from the École des Beaux-Arts: 1797–1863." There's also an ongoing schedule of events including concerts, lectures, workshops (spend an afternoon learning Chinese brush painting), and classic films. Pick up a calendar when you visit. It will also fill you in on happenings at the Witte Museum and the Museum of Transportation, which are under the same auspices.

The museum is open Tuesday to Saturday from 10 a.m. to 5 p.m. with extended hours till 9 p.m. on Thursday, and on Sunday from noon to 5 p.m. June through August it stays open until 6 p.m. Admission is $3 for adults, $1 for children 6 to 12 (under 5, free), $1.50 for military, senior citizens, and students. There's free admission for all on Thursday from 3 to 9 p.m. You can get here, by the way, via the *Old 300* streetcar.

**THE MARION KOOGLER MCNAY MUSEUM:** One of the finest art museums in Texas, the McNay is located at 6000 N. New Braunfels Ave., at U.S. 81 (tel. 824-5368). Upon her death in 1950, oil heiress and art patron Marion Koogler McNay bequeathed her exquisite Mediterranean-style mansion, many of its original furnishings, 23 acres, and her vast collection of paintings, sculpture, and drawings as an endowment to establish and support a museum of modern art. The mansion, built in 1927 for McNay and her third husband, Dr. Donald T. Atkinson (she married five times), was then and is now one of the largest and most elaborate in San Antonio. The acres surrounding it, some left in their native state, others beautifully landscaped with fountains, ponds, and flower beds, today are an outdoor setting for the museum's fine sculpture collection. The museum would be worth visiting to see the house and grounds alone, and the collection inside, focusing on the post-impressionists but touching on many other periods, is one any city would be proud to claim.

Highlights include works by Gauguin, Picasso, Henry Moore, Lautrec, Van Gogh, Pisarro, Bonnard, Klee, Maillol, Rodin, Arp, and Matisse. In the entrance hall is a bust of McNay and the first important painting she purchased, Diego Rivera's *Delfina Flora*. Two special galleries and their adjoining loggias are devoted to the permanent installation of Gothic and medieval art presented to the museum in 1955 by Dr. and Mrs. Frederic G. Oppenheimer. Another later donation, the Lang Collection (housed in its own galleries), is rich in modern sculpture and American art, with paintings by Homer, Marin, O'Keeffe, Picasso, Mondrian, Hopper, Dubuffet, and Léger. The Southwest Gallery houses Mrs. McNay's notable collection of New Mexico Indian art, and one of her own works, a painting called *Navajo Women Weaving*. A stairway lined with stained-glass panels leads to the upper-floor galleries where panel paintings, stained-glass art, textiles, tapestries, and stone sculpture of the 16th century are exhibited. And the Great Gallery in the Emily Wells Brown Wing is used to display large canvases, including four important works by Albert Gleizes. A comprehensive art reference library, focusing on 19th- and 20th-century art, is open to the public Tuesday to Friday from 9 a.m. to 5 p.m.

The museum itself is open Tuesday to Saturday from 9 a.m. to 5 p.m. and on Sunday from 2 to 5 p.m. Admission is free, but donations are gratefully accepted. Inquire at the desk about gallery talks and special events.

**HEMISFAIR PLAZA:** World's Fairs never really end; they always leave a few attractions behind, landmarks of glory days. In San Antonio this 92-acre plaza at South Alamo and Market Streets is the leftover from HemisFair '68, an exposition that marked the city's 250th anniversary. Two HemisFair Plaza attractions are the Institute of Texan cultures and the San Antonio Museum of Transportation. But the most obvious remnant is one that has altered the city's skyline.

### Tower of the Americas

As early as 1964, architect O'Neil Ford began working on the design for a tower to crown San Antonio's 250th birthday party exposition. However, financing for the project lagged, and it wasn't until February 1967 that construction actually began. Then it proceeded at a frenzied seven-days-a-week pace in order to complete the building by the fair's opening in April 1968. It was done just in time, at a cost of $5½ million.

At 750 feet, the tower is the second highest in the western hemisphere. It is named in honor of all the countries and peoples of the Americas and their bond of friendship. Six Venetian glass mosaics depicting the great American cultures of the past ornament the base, and reflecting pools circling the tower sparkle in the sun by day and glitter with lights after dark.

Three high-speed elevators offer a vertical panorama as they whisk visitors to the 550-foot level in 43 seconds. That's the revolving **restaurant** (tel. 223-3101), where diners enjoy a 360° view every hour of the Alamo City and beyond. Seating is in plush burgundy velvet banquettes at pink-clothed tables, every one of them offering the full view. Dining here needn't be expensive. At lunch you can opt for a chef's salad ($5.75) or soup and sandwich ($4.50), though options also include full meals: an appetizer of stuffed mushrooms

($3.50), followed by prime rib with baked potato, vegetables, and hot bread and butter. At dinner, when tables are romantically lit by shaded brass candle lamps, it is a bit pricier. Only serious entrees are offered, like red snapper in Pontchartrain sauce ($11.95) and filet mignon ($13.75), both with the same accompaniments as above. Either meal, there's a low-priced children's menu for under-12s with entrees under $5. There are also some great desserts like a scoop of ice cream rolled in pecans and topped with hot fudge ($2.25). Restaurant patrons pay half price for the elevator ride, park free (it's $1.25 otherwise), and can visit the observation level after the meal at no extra charge. You've probably eaten in these rotating rooms with a view before. Even when the food's not quite Cordon Bleu, you always enjoy it. The Tower of the Americas restaurant is open for lunch daily from 11:30 a.m. to 2:30 p.m., for dinner Sunday to Thursday from 5:30 to 10 p.m., on Friday and Saturday till 10:30 p.m. Reservations essential at dinner.

The **observation deck** (tel. 299-8615) is 605 feet high and the elevator ride to it costs $1.25 for adults, 75¢ for children under 12. Open daily from 10 a.m. to 11 p.m., it offers a gorgeous 360° view, expandable if you spring for another 10¢ for a telescope. It's especially nice to walk around outside. There's a gift shop on this level (and for some ill-conceived reason, video games, tempting junior to ignore the experience in favor of killing off electronic aliens).

Yet a third way to enjoy the tower is from the **Cloud Room,** a cocktail lounge ten feet above the restaurant but not revolving. Semicircular in shape, it offers only a 180° view, still terrific (though who had the idea of multi-paned windows I'd like to know). It's open for drinking and dancing in the sky seven nights a week, admission free, till midnight Sunday to Thursday, till 2 a.m. on Friday and Saturday.

## The Institute of Texan Cultures

The Texas experience, past, present, and future, is explored here in exhibits depicting the lives and contributions of 25 ethnic and cultural groups. But there's nothing dry and scholarly about it. Like other San Antonio curators, the institute's staff has been extremely innovative in presenting its material in a fashion that fascinates. At the chuck wagon, visitors chat with "Cookie" about life on the great Texas cattle drives. They join in corn grinding and tortilla making in the Mexican area, learn spinning and weaving from a Norwegian immigrant, soak up Indian lore while sitting around a tepee, mail a letter in a 1914 post office from Geronimo, Texas (it's one place you can buy stamps on Sunday), and listen to stories about black families in the early 1900s in an actual East Texas sharecropper's cabin. All the "characters" in interpretive areas are in period costumes. In the Czech section there's a video display of native folk dancing, in Spain a video about late 1800s folk healer Don Pedrito. A lively multimedia show called *Faces and Places of Texas* is shown daily at 10:15 a.m., noon, and 2 p.m. in a domed theater, and there are Texas-theme puppet shows and folk music performances throughout the day.

Other exhibits highlight oil, farming, and other state industries, and every ethnic section has a "histowall" documenting its people's contributions to the development of Texas. On weekends, fall through spring, there are "mystery history" games for children of all ages. In fact, weekends are the best time to come; that's when the most is happening here. In addition to permanent displays there are changing exhibits in the lower-level gallery, such as "Reach for the Sky," exploring aviation history in Texas, and "Scholars, Scoundrels, and Schoolteachers," an overview of the state's educational system. The gift shop carries many locally made craft items and interesting publications.

The institute is located at 801 S. Bowie (tel. 226-7651). It's open Tuesday to Sunday from 9 a.m. to 5 p.m. No admission charge, but donations are appreciated.

## The San Antonio Museum of Transportation

Dozens of vehicles from the days when cars were called "roadsters" are on view at this fascinating transportation museum, along with antique bicycles, motorcycles, horse-drawn vehicles, a stagecoach, a fire engine steam pumper (once used by the city, it was drawn by three horses), an 1878 hearse, a hunting carriage, an 1890 surrey with a fringe on top, a 20-passenger mule-drawn trolley, even a Chinese rickshaw. The facility houses several 1920s Rolls-Royce cars; a 1915 Model T Ford; the 1917 Pierce Arrow used by President Woodrow Wilson during World War I; the 1940 Ford "deluxe woodie," one of the first modern station wagons and one of the earliest wood-paneled models; a 1948 MG TC (considered one of the best-looking postwar cars, it started the two-seater sports car craze); the much-maligned 1959 Edsel; President Lyndon B. Johnson's 1964 white Lincoln convertible; a 1906 Pungs-Finch, the only one of its kind still in existence; and an 1899 Locomobile—starting it took over 45 minutes and involved 20 separate steps! All the cars are in operable condition.

Museum admission ($3 for adults, $1.50 for students and senior citizens, $1 for children 6 to 12; under 5, free) entitles you to a two-mile round-trip excursion aboard *Old 300*, a 1913 electric streetcar. Open Tuesday to Saturday from 10 a.m. to 5 p.m., on Thursday to 9 p.m. (admission free 3 to 9 p.m.), and on Sunday from noon to 5 p.m. For further information, call 226-5544.

**THE LONE STAR BREWERY AND BUCKHORN HALL OF HORNS:** This complex of only-in-Texas museums at 600 Lone Star Blvd., between Probandt Street and Roosevelt Avenue (tel. 226-8301, 226-8303 on weekends and holidays), deals in longhorns and longnecks. The whole shebang is on the grounds of the Lone Star Brewery, a facility capable of turning out 1½ million barrels of beer per year.

The **Buckhorn Saloon,** established on Dolorosa Street in 1881, moved here in 1956 and now serves as the hospitality room where visitors are entitled to two free beers or one free root beer. The original Buckhorn was a favorite gathering place for trappers, traders, cowboys, and cattlemen. Owner (and passionate hunter) Albert Friedrich decorated his establishment with a collection of longhorn cattle horns, antlers, and rattlesnake rattlers, and over the years his assortment burgeoned as customers would bring in horns of their own in exchange for drinks. Not that drinks cost that much in the 1880s—for a nickel at the Buckhorn you could get a beer and help yourself to unlimited quantities of sausage, hard-boiled eggs, cheeses, meats, and bread. Nonetheless, over the years the Friedrichs collected over 32,000 sets of horns and antlers and 23,000 rattlers. Friedrich's wife helped with the interior decor, designing pictures, patterns, frames, and lettered signs from rattlesnake rattlers and skins. And his father made furniture for the place from cattle and buffalo horns, including a special chair for honored visitor Teddy Roosevelt.

This unique saloon is re-created at the Brewery, complete with the original marble-pillared cherrywood back bar and brass foot rail and the world's record 78-point whitetail deer. The cash register is from 1913, and the turn-of-the-century globe chandelier with crystal prisms was converted from gas to electricity. The collection of horns, and more than horns, has grown so vast over the years that it doesn't all fit in the bar area. Hence the Hall of Horns, where you'll see the overflow plus stuffed animals and mounted heads including lions, rhinos, zebras, giraffes, a gorilla killed by Teddy Roosevelt, wolverine, moose, boar, polar and Kodiak bears, and the lynx that was in the Lincoln Mercury commercials. The trophies are displayed in five geographical areas—Asia, Africa, Europe, North America, and Texas—along with tableaux and murals of nature scenes ranging from Tanganyika to Texas hill country, displays of guns, and saloon memorabilia. One particularly grisly exhibit are two deer-head trophies with locked horns (sometimes, our guide explained, deer enter into combat, their horns lock, and coyotes, attracted by the noise, come to feast on the defenseless but still living animals). Other oddities on display here are dressed fleas, two-headed calves, a doe with deer horns, Siamese lambs, albino animals, drawings made with bullets, the Lone Star shovel (reputedly the world's largest shovel), and a church fashioned from 50,000 matchsticks. In the adjacent Hall of Fins are exhibits of mounted fish ranging from a 1,056-pound black marlin to a palm-sized piranha, not to mention a convincingly Satanic-looking devilfish. Then there's the Hall of Feathers wherein hundreds of colorful stuffed birds are displayed in their natural habitats, including a few pairs of the now-extinct passenger pigeon. But that's not all, folks.

On the premises is the **Hall of Texas History Wax Museum,** with wax tableaux of Jean Lafitte plundering Spanish treasure from Gulf Coast ships, De Vaca meeting the Indians on Galveston Island, La Salle planting the flag of France on Texas soil, scenes from the Alamo, Sam Houston, Texas Rangers, and all the rest. The exhibits are enhanced by sound effects (barking dogs, folk tunes, mission bells, gulls and surf) and explanatory narratives.

And next door to the museum is the **O. Henry House,** an 1855 adobe house once the residence of O. Henry on South Presa Street. It was moved here in 1960, an apt choice since the writer was a frequent visitor to the Buckhorn Saloon. It was while in this house that O. Henry published his famous *Rolling Stone* newspaper. A wax figure of O. Henry sits doodling at his desk (he was also a political cartoonist), and the furnishings include some pieces that date from his 1895–1896 tenancy. His books and writings are displayed.

All this excitement (and I haven't even mentioned the trick mirrors) costs just $2.25 for adults, $1 for children 6 to 12 (under 6, free). The museum is open daily from 9:30 a.m. to 5 p.m. Half-hour tours of the Hall of Horns depart from the saloon every 30 minutes; allow another 45 or so minutes to see the rest.

**SAN ANTONIO MISSIONS NATIONAL PARK:** In the era when Spain owned half the world, conquistadores came to Texas to see what one of the last outposts in the New World would yield in the way of wealth and treasures. With them came the Franciscan friars to establish a chain of 38 Texas missions, five of them along a 12-mile stretch of the San Antonio River. As religious representatives of the royal government, they served the dual task of subduing natives and utilizing those natives as a source of free labor. Indians worked the mission farms and ranches in exchange for food, shelter, and education in Christianity and the ways of the West. From mission settlements grew many of today's Texas towns, San Antonio among them, and nowhere else in the state is mission culture so well preserved in the modern age. In addition to the famed mission-turned-fort, the Alamo, the city has four still-extant restored missions, all with active parishes, the five structures together comprising a unique national park that winds its way south from the Alamo along the banks of the San Antonio River.

Of course you'll visit the Alamo, but the others are also of interest, both architecturally and in terms of recapturing the spirit of Spanish-ruled Texas. A mission tour brochure is available from the Visitor Information Center across the street from the Alamo, and you can also inquire there (tel. 299-8155) about bus tours of the trail departing from the Alamo. I prefer to drive, perhaps stopping for a picnic lunch on mission grounds. By car, go south on Alamo Street and look for the blue-and-white signs. Wear comfortable walking shoes; you'll be putting in a lot of footwork. All the missions are open daily from 9 a.m. to 6 p.m., and charge no admission.

**Mission San José y San Miguel de Aguayo,** in the 3200 block of Roosevelt Avenue, at Mission Road (tel. 922-0543), is the most grandiose of the four. A classic example of Spanish colonial architecture, it was founded in 1720, shortly after the Alamo. There's no guided tour, but you can view an informative slide show about all San Antonio missions at the visitor center and pick up a self-guided tour map that will be enhanced by informative signs, mechanical narrations, and displays of mission artifacts.

One of the largest and most beautiful missions in the state, it was built within a fort-like compound with stone walls, ramparts, and bastions to protect itself from Indian attack. You'll see the old well, the granary where thousands of bushels of corn were stored, the water-powered mill, pottery kilns, the *acequia* (irrigation ditch) that channeled water to mission fields, the Indian quarters (two rooms with a fireplace and a buffalo-hide-covered cot), and priest's quarters. The limestone church has a square bell tower and ornate façade with beautifully ornamented stone carvings of cherubs, scrolls, and statues of St. Joseph (San José) framing the wooden doors. There's an exquisite window known as Rosa's Window on the south side of the church, also surrounded by ornate stonework. The interior is less elaborate, with high vaulted ceilings and wooden pews on rock floors.

The best time to visit is on a Sunday when there's a noon mariachi mass; arrive early to get a seat. If your schedule allows time to visit only one of the four missions, this is the best choice.

It is not, however, the first mission south of the Alamo. That's **Mission Nuestra Señora de la Purisima Concepción de Acuna,** 807 Mission Rd., at Felisa (tel. 532-3158), its church built in 1755, and built so well that no restoration was necessary. It is America's oldest unrestored stone church. The mission itself began in San Antonio in 1731, predating the church you see today. Original frescoes, completely faded away on the other mission churches, can be seen at this symmetrical twin-towered church. A self-guided tour (once again, pick up a map in the office when you come in) takes you to the textile workshop where the Indians wove fabrics for blankets and clothing, and an old well, not yet run dry, remains. The church altar is under a Moorish dome. You can also visit the sacristy and the convento (missionary living quarters).

Next on the trail is **Mission San Juan Capistrano,** 9101 Graf Rd. (tel. 532-5840), a less grandiose mission with a stark church having only one bell tower. The square's trees and foliage are a charmingly rustic setting for the church, convento, and ruins of a guest room and Indian quarters. Pick up a tour brochure at the entrance and follow the plaques around the square. An interesting feature here is a small museum with exhibits about on-site archeological digs and the Coahuiltecan Indians (arrowheads, pottery shards, coins, etc.). Like Concepción, the San Juan Mission moved to San Antonio in 1731 (both originated earlier in East Texas). It began with only crude grass huts, but by mid-century had a church whose remains can be seen today along with those of a larger church begun in the 1760s and never finished. The present church, originally a granary, dates to sometime after 1800. Its interior is modest, with a simple raftered ceiling, white walls, and wooden pews.

The southernmost compound in the park is **Mission San Francisco de la Espada,** 10040 Espada Rd. (tel. 627-2021), still in a pastoral setting of surrounding farmland as it was centuries ago. Like the two above missions, it moved from East Texas to San Antonio in 1731. Many of its buildings are in ruins, but its *acequia* system (irrigation ditch) is still intact and carrying water to the mission fields. Only the chapel and information center are open to the public, but you can also examine a corner bastion with holes in the rock for cannons and muskets. Most isolated of the missions, Espada was most vulnerable to Apache attack. Its inhabitants risked death when they wandered outside its walls. The stone chapel, with its three-bell tower and Moorish arch-framed doors, dates to 1756. Follow the trails to the San Antonio River and you'll find some nice spots for picnicking.

**THE HERTZBERG CIRCUS COLLECTION:** This unusual museum of big-top memorabilia, at South Presa and West Market Streets (tel. 299-7810), is actually part of the San Antonio Public Library system. Aficionado Harry Hertzberg collected thousands of circus mementoes during his lifetime, including a library of books on subjects circusy like *Memoirs of a Midget* and *Lions, Tigers, and Me.* He left it all to the library in 1940. An extensive collection of Tom Thumb's tiny things include his 1843 carriage (seemingly big enough for a two-year old), vest, and violin; Mrs. Thumb's miniature piano and itsy-bitsy boots; and a piece of their wee wedding cake. There are exhibits of clown shoes, circus costumes, knife-throwers' knives, animal trainers' whips, a trapeze, claws from Clyde Beatty's lion (Simba), circus posters from all over the world, and photographs of big-top stars, Buffalo Bill's Wild West Show, Annie Oakley, and others. Visitors also get to see an old ticket wagon from the Gentry Bros. Circus, a freak case of famous sideshow personalities, P. T. Barnum's collection of letters and photographs, and Toto, a mechanical clown in garish costume and grotesque makeup who was a model of a 19th-century Viennese clown. Two additional highlights are a complete miniature three-ring circus with bareback riders, menagerie, performers, music, horse stables, cowboys, etc., and the Tom Scaperlanda Collection of circus lore, a gift from Hertzberg's friend and fellow fan.

Open May to October only, Monday to Saturday from 9 a.m. to 5:30 p.m., on Sunday from 1 to 5 p.m. Admission is free.

**MAIN AND MILITARY PLAZAS:** Since the early 18th century Main and Military Plazas, also known, respectively, as Plaza de las Islas and Plaza de Armas, have been a focal point of government, civil, and social activities. Both have seen much history. The first civil settlement in Texas was founded on Main Plaza by Canary Islanders (hence the name "las Islas") in 1731, the first permanent military quarters on Military Plaza in 1722. The Governor's Palace on Military Plaza was the setting for the approval of Moses Austin's petition to bring the first Anglo settlers to Texas. And on Main Plaza, at the start of the Civil War, Gen. David Twiggs surrendered all U.S. arms and equipment to the Texas secessionists. Like nearby Market Square, the plazas were a venue for the famed "chili queens," they were the scene of processions to mourn the death of a king of Spain and honor the coronation of a new king, and they were the site from which wagon trains departed for Mexico and on El Camino Real. They also contained San Antonio's first courthouse, school, jail, hanging tree, gambling houses, and hotel.

The two adjoining plazas are bounded north and south by Commerce and Dolorosa Streets, east and west by Soledad and Santa Rosa. On a walking tour beginning at Main Plaza you'll see the **San Fernando Cathedral** (tel. 227-1297), San Antonio's first parish church built in 1738 and Texas's first place of worship. Remains of Alamo heroes are entombed in the chapel at the left-hand side of the entrance. From its tower, Col. Francis Johnson raised the flag of victory on December 12, 1835, marking the rebels' short-lived defeat of Mexico. The church still has a very active parish. The **Bexar County Courthouse** dates to the turn of the century. And the **Main Plaza Building** (once the Frost Bank) was built in 1922 on the site of the Frost family's wool business, an enterprise established in 1848.

In Military Plaza you'll find the **Spanish Governor's Palace** (tel. 224-0601), early residence of the presidio or military captain who represented King Philip V of Spain. It was built in 1749. When San Antonio was made the capital of Spanish Texas in 1770, it came to be called the Governor's Palace. After the fall of Spain in 1821, the building served as a secondhand clothing shop, a tailor's, a bar, restaurant, and school. It was restored to its original appearance in 1931 and furnished with authentic period pieces. You can take a self-guided tour of the house and its delightful garden (the latter with a fountain and wishing well), Monday to Saturday from 9 a.m. to 5 p.m., and on Sunday from 10 a.m. to 5 p.m. Admission is 50¢ for adults, 25¢ for children 7 to 14 (under 7, free).

Other Military Plaza highlights are the Victorian **Plaza de Armas Buildings; City Hall,** built in 1899; the **Artes Graficas Building,** constructed in 1910 as the palace livery stable; and the old **Continental Hotel,** originally the Clede Hotel when it went up in 1898. The **Navarro State Historic Site,** 228 S. Laredo (tel. 226-4801), was the home of Texas's foremost Hispanic statesman, José Antonio Navarro, who lived under five of the six flags of Texas. Navarro participated in the convention that ratified annexation of Texas to the Union. Guided tours are given Tuesday to Saturday from 10 a.m. to 4 p.m. Adults pay $1; children 6 to 12, 25¢.

**THE KING WILLIAM SECTION:** In the late 1800s this 25-block, tree-lined area near downtown on the south bank of the San Antonio River was the poshest residential district of the city. Originally settled by wealthy German merchants, it is now a zoned historic district and once again a very fashionable place to live. Victorian mansions that deteriorated in the 20th century are being restored and the area is of such architectural note that it has become a tourist attraction. The district to explore is loosely bounded north and south by King William and Alamo Streets, east and west by St. Mary's and Gunther Streets. A walking tour map is available from the **San Antonio Conservation Society,** 107 King William St. (named for King Wilhelm I of Prussia). You can drive through, but of course you'll see it much better on foot. One mansion, **Steves Homestead,** 509 King William St. (tel. 225-5924), is open to the public for tours daily from 10 a.m. to noon and 1 to 5 p.m. Admission is $2 for adults, $1 for children under 12.

**WATER PARK USA:** The kids have been good sports traipsing around to museums and sightseeing attractions (or maybe they haven't). Either way, you all need a refreshing break, and Water Park USA, I-35 between Coliseum and Binz-Engleman Roads (tel. 227-1100), is a place where everyone can cool off and relax. A 15½-acre water-attractions complex, it offers a variety of ways to get wet. On the Double Dipper, two 230-foot daredevil speed slides, you can whiz into the water at a speed of 25 to 30 mph. Other slides with names like Roaring Thunder, the Twister, and Texas Tornado are 350-foot serpentine streams of water. There's an 18,000-square-foot wave pool, ten feet at its deepest point, with mild-to-wild wave patterns; a 1,025-foot river for floating, rafting, tubing, or swimming; an 8,000-square-foot pool for serious laps; and Pollywiggle Pond and the Waterwalk for little splashers. Sandy beaches, sunbathing areas, a snackbar, buffet restaurant, gift shop, dressing room, video game arcade, and lockers complete the facilities.

The park is open May 1 to October 1, and, weather permitting, early spring and late fall. Hours are 10 a.m. to 10 p.m. daily. Admission is $9.95 for ages 8 to adult, $6.95 for ages 3 to 7 (under 3, free), $6.45 for senior citizens or entry after 5 p.m.

**FORT SAM HOUSTON:** This 1876 fort, site of the first ever military flight (in 1910), is today the Fifth Army headquarters and home of Brooke Army Medical Center. Located at Grayson Street and New Braunfels Avenue (tel. 221-1211), its attractions are as much idyllic as military. Its quadrangle looks like a scene from a Disney movie, with ducks, geese, chickens, guinea hens, peacocks, rabbits, and deer—all extremely tame and unafraid of humans—wandering on the lawn amid ancient shade trees. Kids love it, and you couldn't find a nicer spot for a picnic on the grass.

In 1886 Geronimo, his son, Chappa, Chief Natchez (son of Cochise), and about 30 other Apaches were confined in the Quadrangle and watched from the tower. That tower is still standing, and its Seth Thomas clock, with faces on all four sides, still counts the hours. The clock chimes every half hour when a hammer hits the old 600-pound bell. A stone tablet beneath its south face expresses the grim sentiment, "AD 1876. In Peace, Prepare for War." In 1898 the Quadrangle depot outfitted and supplied the famed Rough Riders on their way to Cuba in the Spanish-American War.

A walking tour map is available; it highlights the house where General Pershing lived in 1917, a small museum about the history of the post (tel. 221-6117; open from 10 a.m. to 4 p.m. Wednesday to Sunday, admission free), the gravesite of Pat the artillery horse who served the post for 26 years, Dwight D. Eisenhower's 1916 and 1941 homes, the First Flight Memorial, the chapel dedicated in 1909 by President Taft, the U.S. Army Medical Museum (tel. 221-2358; open weekdays from 8 to 11:30 a.m. and 12:30 to 4 p.m., admission free) detailing army medical history from 1775, and an old blacksmith's shop.

The Quadrangle is open daily from 8 a.m. to 4 p.m. There's no admission charge.

**THE HEART OF TEXAS:** Just across the street from the Alamo (at 307 Alamo Plaza, to be exact), is a 26,000-square-foot "entertainment center" featuring an hourly 45-minute multimedia show about everything Texan. It utilizes 32 film and slide projectors and 16 sound speakers throughout the auditorium to totally engulf the audience in the action. The narrator plays straight man to the main character, a scruffy frontier-days' itinerant tinker. The tinker's wares are old pots, pans, and dreams; he has a loom for weaving rainbows and a drill for drilling wishing wells. There's lots of rousing western music and beautiful photography focusing on rodeos, a buffalo-chip-throwing contest, armadillo races, the famed Terlingua chili cookoff, Judge Roy Bean, the advent of oil, and Texas outlaws, immigrants, sports, music, and Rangers. You'll see vistas of prairies, canyons, deserts, pine forests, and mountains. It's lots of fun, and there are even a few good Texas jokes, but I won't spoil it for you by telling them here. Or give away the dramatic special effects.

Take the kids. Admission is $3.25 for adults, $1.50 for children 5 to 11 (under 5, free). There are continuous showings from 11 a.m. to 5 p.m. daily. Call 222-2400 for further details.

On the premises are a candle shop, a souvenir shop, the Yellow Rose Saloon, an ice cream parlor, and an arcade with old-fashioned nickelodeons (they cost a quarter).

**THE SOUTHWEST CRAFT CENTER:** Housed in a converted 1840s French Catholic Ursuline Order convent, this artist's complex at 300 Augusta St. (tel. 224-1848), is today used for classes, workshops, exhibitions, special events, and a charming restaurant. On the premises are ongoing classes and resident artists' studios where weaving, spinning, pottery, sculpture, painting, papermaking, jewelry, life drawing, and calligraphy are practiced. Visitors are welcome to wander about the studios and classrooms, though sensitivity to the situation is requested. In other words, watch an artist at work or observe a class in session, but don't interrupt what's going on.

While you're here, take a stroll around the beautifully landscaped old convent gardens, explore the interior of the Ursuline chapel, see the changing show in the Emily Edwards Gallery, and peruse the beautiful works (all for sale) of resident artists and students. There's a terrific bookstore/gift shop on the premises, and occasional art fairs take place on the grounds. On weekdays you can have lunch in the Copper Kitchen, a monastery-like stone-walled dining room with wood-plank floors, a beamed ceiling, and seating at long wooden tables. The fare is all home-cooked. There are sandwiches, salads, one hot entree each day (usually Mexican) and fresh-baked desserts. Wine and beer are available. Five or six dollars will buy a nice meal in these quaintly pleasant surroundings.

The galleries are open weekdays from 10 a.m. to 4 p.m., on Saturday to 3 p.m. The grounds and gardens are open from 8 a.m. to 10 p.m. daily. Admission is free. Pick up a map and events schedule at the front desk.

**ARTISANS' ALLEY:** Started in 1975, Artisans' Alley, 555 Bitters Rd. (tel. 494-3226), is a nostalgic and rustic turn-of-the-century shopping center constructed with old wood and architectural salvage. Its 24 shops sell mostly crafts items; there's a woodsmith, a stained-glass artist, a candlemaker, and a southwestern art shop. At other Alley stores you might purchase monogrammed gifts, antiques, crocheted items, crystal jewelry, silk flower arrangements, ceramic birdhouses and birdbaths, out-of-print history books, Mexican imports, and all the ingredients needed to make wine and beer. Have lunch or a snack in the Tea Room, and ask the psychic over at Cosmic Connection what your future will bring.

Open Tuesday to Saturday from 10 a.m. to 5:30 p.m., on Sunday from 1 to 5 p.m.

**SPORTS:** In the spectator category, the **NBA Spurs** play at the Convention Center Arena, South Alamo and Market Streets, during the October-to-April basketball season. Call 224-9578 or 299-8566 for ticket information.

If you're in town in February, don't miss the **Livestock Show and Rodeo** (details in "Annual Events").

That's what to watch. Participant sports are even better represented. See the discussion of **Brackenridge Park** (above) for riding, golf, paddleboating, jogging, biking, and baseball.

You can play tennis in San Pedro Park at the **McFarlin Tennis Courts,** 1503 San Pedro Ave., at Ashby Place (tel. 732-1223); fees at these 22 lighted outdoor municipal courts are $3.50 per court for 1½ hours of play. After the game, cool off in the park's large swimming pool.

Then there's the **Racquetball Club,** 7700 Torino (tel. 344-8596) and the **Racquetball and Handball Club,** 121 N.W. Loop 410 (tel. 349-2733).

And the above-mentioned pool at San Pedro Park is just one of 21 **city swimming pools;** see the blue pages of the phonebook for a complete listing under "Recreation Facilities."

**A GUIDED TOUR:** There's so much ground to cover in San Antonio that if your time is limited, a guided tour may be the answer. **St. Anthony Tours** (tel. 512/828-3096) offers tours of major sights, mission tours, and customized tours to your exact specifications—all in air-conditioned cars, vans, and buses. It even has trips to Johnson City to see the LBJ Ranch and boyhood home, to the Mexican border town of Del Rio, to Brackettville (where the movie *The Alamo*, starring John Wayne, was shot), to Laredo, and other points. Call for details.

## 5. Alamo City Nights

San Antonio offers big-city culture—symphony, theater, ballet—along with a dab of disco, a frisson of folklorico, and a soupçon of C&W. In other, less-alliterative words, something for everyone. In addition to the below-listed options, keep in mind the **Cloud Room** at the Tower of the Americas, a nightclub in the sky for cocktails and dancing; the piano bars at the **Four Seasons** and **La Mansión del Río** hotels, and best of all, the jazz bar at **Arthur's.**

**THE SAN ANTONIO PERFORMING ARTS ASSOCIATION:** This marvelous nonprofit organization brings big-name talent to town during its fall through spring season, with performances at various theaters and facilities. A typical season's lineup might include the San Francisco Ballet performing *A Midsummer Night's Dream,* Philip Glass, the Erick Hawkins Dance Company, Les Grands Ballets Canadiens, Kathy Rose (a multimedia evening of dance and animated film), the Houston Ballet doing a Christmas performance of *The Nutcracker,* Itzhak Perlman, *Mummenschanz* (Switzerland's sensational mimemask theater), the Academy of St. Martin in the Fields (a renowned chamber music ensemble), Ballet West (from Salt Lake City) performing Tchaikovsky's *Sleeping Beauty,* pianist Murray Perahia, operatic baritone Sherrill Milnes, and the avant-garde Bill T. Jones / Arnie Zane & Company dancers. That's a cultural season any city could be proud of.

For a current performance schedule and ticket information, write or call the San Antonio Performing Arts Association, 110 Broadway, Suite 230, San Antonio, TX 78205 (tel. 512/224-8187). To charge tickets, call 226-2626 or 224-3000.

**THE MAJESTIC PERFORMING ARTS CENTER:** Broadway road shows and other important productions play the Majestic, 212 E. Houston St. (tel. 226-9535), a lavish 1929 movie palace that has been restored to its original grandeur. Its interior, which has been alternately described as Moorish and Texas baroque, was perhaps best summed up by a Corpus Christi reporter who said, "Imagine the inside of a Fabergé egg and you're almost there." Designed to resemble an open courtyard with floating clouds and twinkling stars, it has cedar trees, stuffed pigeons, reproductions of classical statuary, and ornate buildings with arched windows, Spanish balconies, and parapets. When it was completed, the Majestic was the second-largest motion picture theater in the U.S., with seating for 3,743 patrons. Today it has 2,486 seats, and the foyer has been enlarged to accommodate a 70-foot bar.

The theater was restored by Pace Management Corp., one of the nation's premier presenters and producers of live entertainment; they reopened it in 1981 with a smash hit, *The Best Little Whorehouse in Texas.* Subsequent productions have included *Annie, A Chorus Line, Hello Dolly!* starring Carol Channing, *The King and I* with Yul Brynner, *Sugar Babies* with Mickey Rooney and Carol Lawrence, *Man of La Mancha* with John Raitt, Richard Harris in *Camelot*, Barbara Eden in *Woman of the Year*, Martin Landau in *Dracula*, and *Jerry's Girl's* starring Carol Channing, Leslie Uggams, and Andrea McArdle.

In addition to Broadway shows, the theater also books headliners like Debbie Reynolds, Englebert Humperdinck, Robin Williams, Liberace, José Feliciano, the B-52s, George Carlin, Rich Little, Paul Anka, James Taylor, David Copperfield, Joan Rivers, Lionel Hampton, Tom Jones, and B. B. King. They've also hosted performances by the Dallas Symphony Orchestra, the Dance Theatre of Harlem, the Preservation Hall Jazz Band, the Chicago Symphony Orchestra, and "P.D.Q. Bach." For a current program (their season is year round), contact the theater at the above address or phone number. To charge tickets, call 226-2626.

Some restaurants have dine-and-ride packages which obviate the parking problem. Call the theater for details.

**THE SAN ANTONIO SYMPHONY:** Founded in 1939, the San Antonio Symphony is one of America's major symphony orchestras under the gifted direction of Maestro James Sedares. Performing over 165 concerts each fall-through-spring season, the orchestra has featured such notable guest artists as pianist Lorin Hollander, conductor Maxim Shostakovich, flutist Jean-Pierre Rampal, and violinist Itzhak Perlman, along with popular stars like Sammy Davis, Jr., Toni Tennille, Judy Collins, Shirley Jones, and even Phyllis Diller. In addition to its classical and pops series, the symphony performs family concerts, free concerts, and children's concerts, one of the latter of which was narrated by the city's mayor, Henry Cisneros; the program was called *The Mayor Meets Babar.*

Performances take place at various spaces around town, including the Lila Cockrell Theatre, Laurie Auditorium, and the Majestic. For a performance calendar, write or call the San Antonio Symphony, 109 Lexington Ave., Suite 207, San Antonio, TX 78205 (tel. 512/225-6161). To charge or reserve tickets, call 223-5591. Ticket prices range from $8 to $18.

**THE ARNESON RIVER THEATRE:** Part of the restored village of La Villita, the Arneson (tel. 299-8614 for performance times and ticket information) is a delightful open-air theater with a stage right on the river. If there are performances during your visit, it's a must—an integral part of the San Antonio experience. In summer there are events Tuesday through Sunday nights. Every Tuesday, Friday, and Saturday its *Noche del Río*—a three-hour Latin-themed musical with spectacular Las Vegas–style costumes and lavish production numbers. On Wednesday nights you might catch anything from modern jazz to country. Every Thursday night the theater features *Fandango,* a program of Mexican dance, Spanish guitar, and flamenco. And every Sunday night the Ballet Folklorico de San Antonio takes the stage. Tickets, usually under $10 for any performance, are sold at the door. The Arneson stage is also used for productions in conjunction with River Walk festivities throughout the year.

**THE HARLEQUIN DINNER THEATRE:** Dinner theatre is always a delightful way to spend an evening, especially if the dinner is presentable and the play well presented. Such is the case at the Harlequin, 2652 Harney Rd., in Fort Sam Houston (tel. 222-9694). A cast of competent local actors mount about eight productions a year in a year-round season. Past shows have included Agatha

Christie's *The Mousetrap, Enter Laughing,* the Rodgers and Hart musical *Babes in Arms,* Neil Simon's *I Ought to Be in Pictures, Deathtrap, H.M.S. Pinafore, You Can't Take It With You,* and *The Sound of Music*—mostly mysteries and musicals, but they've also attempted more serious drama, like *Member of the Wedding.*

It's not Broadway, but neither are the prices—$14.50 on Wednesday and Thursday nights, $15.50 on Friday and Saturday nights. Admission includes an all-you-can-eat buffet dinner with fried chicken in gravy, stuffed roast pork, fried shrimps and scallops, crab rolls, roast beef, vegetables, baked and mashed potatoes, an extensive salad bar, fresh-baked loaves of bread and butter, and tea or coffee with a homemade dessert such as lemon chess tart. Alcoholic beverages are extra. A bar/lounge adjoins the theater.

Call the above number for information and/or to reserve tickets.

**DISCOS:** San Antonio's "rock-till-you-drop" club is **Zig-Zag,** 2803 N.E. Loop 410, at Perrin-Beitel Road on the southeast corner (tel. 654-8737), a big, snazzy place with hundreds of twinkle lights and neon stars aglow against a black ceiling creating an indoor starlit night. Wear your whites and you'll glow iridescently as does the limelight tubing decoration that depicts the Eiffel tower, the New York skyline, the canals of Venice, and other international scenes on black walls. There are four bars, and the action is enhanced by ten-foot-square video monitors. Weekdays there's a Happy Hour buffet from 6 to 8 p.m., Monday-night football games are aired on the monitors, and there's usually some zany promotion in progress—a wheelbarrow race, best legs contest, Roman orgy chariot race, or beach party (everyone comes in a bathing suit)—with prizes for contest winners. The music is top-40s rock, and the action really gets under way after 11 p.m.

The club is open Sunday to Thursday nights till 2 a.m., on Friday and Saturday till 4 a.m. Admission is $2 for men, $1 for women Sunday to Thursday, $3 for all genders on Friday and Saturday.

Another very happening place is **Fizz,** 9631 San Pedro Ave., at McCarty Road (tel. 342-7081), a glittery setting where music is enhanced by 25 TV monitors (including one on the dance floor that combines 12 screens), a state-of-the-art light show, and special effects. Like Zig-Zag, Fizz features frequent promotions: beach parties complete with sand, a swimming pool, and hot tub set up in the parking lot; Rambo contests; everyone-in-pajamas slumber parties; beauty contests; Gong shows; and the like. A lavish complimentary buffet is served weekdays from 4 to 8 p.m. There are blackjack tables ($10 buys $2,000 worth of chips, but there's a $100 minimum bet), video games, and pool tables. Monday to Saturday a DJ plays high-energy music, and on Sunday nights there are usually live reggae groups. You can buy specialty drinks like the "Café au Hait"—Kahlúa, chocolate ice cream, and dark crème de cacao—at the ice cream bar.

Fizz is open Sunday to Thursday till 2 a.m., on Friday and Saturday till 3 a.m. Admission is $1 Monday to Thursday, $3 on Friday and Saturday, free on Sunday.

**COUNTRY:** Big names from Nashville alternate with talented local acts at the **Blue Bonnet Palace,** I-35 at Selma (tel. 651-6702), a mini-Gilley's offering a great night's entertainment. The setup is classic C&W joint, with an immense dance floor flanked by long rows of tables on either side. A big draw here is a 40,000-square-foot rodeo arena where two half-hour bull-riding shows, complete with rodeo clown, are offered nightly at 10 and 11:30 p.m. And urban cowboys can try their hand at calf-roping on a spring-loaded calf. Some of the big names who've played the Bluebonnet are Charley MacClain, Ronnie McDowell, Steve Warner, and Mel MacDaniel.

The club is open Friday and Saturday nights only, from 7:30 p.m. to 2 a.m., and usually about 2,000 people show up. Admission is $4 to $6, depending on the act.

# Chapter VIII

# COWBOY COUNTRY

### 1. Bandera
### 2. Kerrville

PROBABLY MORE THAN ANY OTHER part of the state, these two Hill Country towns are archetypically Texan. This is ranch country and dude ranch country. Pack your jeans, boots, and Stetson hat, and you're ready to go. Here's your chance to get on a horse, chow down around the campfire with the cowboys, attend a local rodeo, go on a hayride, and join in a hoe-down. The best time to visit is during peak season, May 1 to September 30 and on holidays throughout the year, when the dude ranches are full and the most comprehensive activities schedules are offered. On the other hand, the rest of the year it can be a more contemplative and personal experience. You'll get to enjoy the spectacular Hill Country scenery in tranquil solitude and meet locals when you're not just one of a mass of summer people.

You won't have really seen Texas until you've spent a few days on a Hill Country ranch, and a good case could be made for spending your whole vacation there. After a day or two of the outdoor life, most people wish they could stay forever.

## 1. Bandera

The self-proclaimed "Cowboy Capital of the World," this picturesque mountain region of farms and ranches on the banks of the cypress-lined Medina River is as Wild West as the state gets. Forested with cedar, live oak, cottonwood, elm, cypress, mesquite, hackberry, and pecan, and criss-crossed with clear, spring-fed streams, it's a place where nature achieves a wild and rugged grandeur. It's easy to imagine a row of Indians ranged along the hilltops, about to descend with war whoops and arrows flying to attack the cowboys riding the range below. Bandera is the cowboy movie landscape etched in the minds of millions throughout the world—what we all expect, and hope, Texas will be.

It's not so long ago that Bandera was a rugged frontier town in Comanche country, much like those depicted in cowboy movies—except that the Indians sometimes won. By the time the first settler arrived Texas was already part of the Union. Amasa Clark made his way west from New York in 1852 and remained until his death in 1927 at age 102; he fathered 19 children. In 1853 Charles de Montel and John James mapped out the townsite, with wide streets off the public square, today still the center of town and site of the county courthouse, jail, and library. De Montel was a German immigrant who came to the U.S. in 1835, changed his name from Scheidemontel, joined the Texas army, and became friendly with Sam Houston. He helped guard Santa Anna at San Jacinto. John James, a young Englishman whose imagination was fired by accounts of the Alamo, arrived in Texas in 1837 at the age of 18. They established James, Montel & Co. Mills, a horse-powered sawmill to produce lumber and shingles to build the town.

Early residents describe Bandera as "a land of wild men and wild beasts." A group of 250 Mormons who came fleeing persecution in 1854 were so discouraged by Indian raids and other vicissitudes of frontier life that they pressed on to Utah in 1858. But other, hardier immigrants replaced them, and the town began to grow. Bandera history is filled with Indian massacres, hangings, bank robberies, posses, gunfights, jailbreaks, and sheriff shootings, along with the usual pioneer hardships of cholera, drought, famine, and flood. Life was hard and amenities were few. And indeed there were "wild beasts": panthers, Mexican lions, and bears were numerous in the region.

In 1856 a colorful element was added when a military post, Camp Verde, was established and garrisoned with a few cavalry companies to help protect the settlers from hostile Indians. A caravansary of 73 camels, complete with 12 Armenian drivers and their families, was brought in to transport supplies between Bandera and other remote frontier outposts. During the Civil War, Confederate forces took charge of camp and camels. The federal government sold them after the war and abandoned the post in 1869. But some of the camels had wandered off, and they were occasionally seen in the wild for many years afterward. A pillow Amasa Clark made from the hair of Camp Verde camels (he worked herding them for a while) is on display at the Frontier Times Museum.

There are dozens of colorful stories about Bandera. Legend has it that William J. Ryan, a local schoolteacher in the 1880s, was actually Lincoln assassin John Wilkes Booth. Booth ostensibly perished in a Virginia fire, but his body was never positively identified, and some sources say he made good his escape. Ryan did leave Bandera under a cloud when it was noised about town that he was a fugitive from justice, wanted for a crime committed in another state. From photographs, he does look exactly like Booth.

Many of today's Bandera residents are descendants of the rugged pioneers who built the town. They're a special breed with firm handshakes and unshakable opinions, not necessarily the same ones. There's still a lot of wildlife here; thousands of sportsmen arrive every year to hunt the abundant whitetail deer, turkey, Russian boar, javelina, dove, and quail. There's still quite a bit of wild life, too, as you'll discover over at Arkey Blue's Silver Dollar Saloon. Bandera folks have an anything-goes, anything-can-happen-here kind of attitude that keeps things hopping. Just 50 miles from San Antonio, it's another world.

**GETTING THERE:** Chances are you'll be coming from San Antonio, just 46 miles southeast of Bandera via Hwy. 16. You can drive or catch a **Kerrville Bus** (tel. 512/257-7454) between the two cities.

**GETTING ORIENTED:** For information on all local attractions and events, visit the **Bandera Chamber of Commerce,** 503 Main St., between Hackberry and Pecan (tel. 512/796-4312). It's open weekdays only, between 9 a.m. and 5 p.m. (except when Judy goes out to lunch). You can also write to them in advance for information at P.O. Box 171, Bandera, TX 78003.

**GETTING AROUND:** You can arrange with the ranch you're staying at to pick you up at the bus station. After that, you really won't need a car, and you won't have one unless you've brought it with you. There are no car-rental outlets in Bandera.

**ANNUAL EVENTS:** Winters are pretty quiet in Bandera, but things start to perk up as the summer tourist season approaches. For details on any of the events listed below, call the chamber of commerce at 512/796-4312.

Starting in April and through Labor Day there's **Bo's Rodeo** (tel. 512/796-3139 or 796-4535) every Saturday night at 8 p.m. at an arena 4½ miles south of town on Chipman Lane. Cowboys and cowgirls compete in bronc riding, calf roping, team roping, barrel racing, steer wrestling, and bull riding. Following the rodeo events, there's country-and-western dancing to live bands. And concessions on the rodeo grounds offer Texas barbecue and soft drinks. Make a night of it. Admission is $3 at the gate. Bo also has Youth Rodeos on Friday nights, admission free. Anyone in town can give you driving directions to the arena.

Another all-summer-long event: **dances** at the Mayan Ranch every Tuesday and Thursday night.

**Funtier Days** is a Memorial Day Weekend celebration with a big parade of cowboys on horseback and floats, an outdoor dance with local C&W groups, dozens of arts and crafts booths, a rodeo, softball tournaments, and country contests—tobacco spitting, ice cream eating, arm wrestling, fiddling, etc. Anyone can enter. Tickets are required for the rodeo and dances; they're all under $5 and available at the door. Check with the chamber of commerce for a full schedule of Funtier activities.

Late in June, the **Night in Old Bandera** celebration occupies a full weekend with dog and pony shows, livestock displays, staged shootouts, buggy rides, horse races, street dancing, food booths, crafts demonstrations, and continuous entertainment. Members of pioneer families are singled out for recognition during special ceremonies. Details from the chamber of commerce.

Labor Day Weekend, people come from miles around to the **Cowboy Capital Pro Rodeo Cowboy Association (P.R.C.A.) Rodeo** in Mansfield Park. Top national performers compete in this event, and there's usually pre-show entertainment. For advance tickets, write to C.C.P.R.C.A., P.O. Box 1801, Bandera, TX 78003. It's about $5 if you buy them in advance, $7 at the gate. Children under 12 are admitted free.

The **Bandera County Fair** takes place early in October. It's the archetypical event with judgings of quilts, arts and crafts, cakes, breads, canned goods, etc. There's also an auction and pageants to select Miss Bandera, Mr. Bandera, Baby Bandera, Junior Miss Bandera, etc.

The Friday in November prior to the start of hunting season is celebrated with a **Hunter's Barbecue** at Mansfield Park, followed by a dance and auction.

Early December, usually the first Friday, is **Holiday Shopper's Jubilee.** All the shopowners decorate their storefronts and have big sales. There's a contest for the best decorations with prizes in the categories of traditional, western, and old-fashioned. There's also a parade with floats decorated in those three categories and judged. The Christmas tree at the courthouse is lit, sometimes there are special dances, and everyone joins in singing Christmas carols.

**WHERE TO STAY:** The two ranches described below are both excellent—the best I found in Bandera. Both include meals and a host of activities. Reserve as far in advance as possible; these ranches offer such a fabulous—and a low-priced—vacation that they get booked up quickly. And don't forget to pack your boots and jeans.

## The Flying L Ranch

The Flying L, a mile south of town on Hwy. 173, at Wharton Dock Road (mailing address is HCR 1, Box 32, Bandera, TX 78003; tel. 512/796-3001), has been dubbed the "country club ranch" by locals. Framed by the panoramic beauty of the Texas Hill Country, it occupies 542 forested acres of live oak, cedar, and mesquite. Go for a walk or ride in the morning stillness and you'll see many deer and jackrabbits, maybe even an armadillo or two.

The "country club" handle isn't because the Flying L is less western and rustic than its counterparts. It derives from the ranch's paved and lighted runway for private planes, its luxurious condos and Frank Lloyd Wright villas, and its manifold recreational facilities. These include two night-lit tennis courts, a challenging 18-hole golf course with pro shop and clubhouse restaurant, a large and beautiful outdoor pool with adjoining sundeck and cabaña hot-tub spa, an exercise room, and of course, a fine string of horses for daily guided trail rides. Lawn games include shuffleboard, volleyball, horseshoe and washer pitching, and table tennis. And an indoor rec room offers video games and bumper pool.

You can pack a picnic lunch and hike for miles through pristine woodlands. There's perch fishing and tubing on a creek that winds through the property. And especially in season, there are numerous daily activities—creekside sing-alongs, riding lessons, games, hoe-downs, breakfast and sunset rides with campfire meals, barbecues, square dancing, hayrides, live entertainment, and branding parties (they brand the Flying L right on your jeans—with paint). Summer also brings a full schedule of children's activities, and if a tour bus pulls in during your stay you can watch ranch hand "bandits" hold it up.

There are two basic accommodations categories. Most luxurious are the 16 attractively furnished and spacious condos, with large windows overlooking the verdant ranchlands or the golf green and fairway. Most have oversize Jacuzzi tubs (big enough for two) with mirrors on three sides, and two of the beautiful living rooms contain working fireplaces. They all have at least a kitchenette, and the two with fireplaces have huge fully equipped kitchens. Condo guests also enjoy patios with garden furnishings, some with barbecue grills. Like all Flying L accommodations, the rooms are air-conditioned and equipped with color TVs, clocks, king-size or double beds, and full tub/shower baths.

The Frank Lloyd Wright villas have full living rooms, some with fireplaces; they're furnished in homey country style. They don't have kitchens, but you do get a refrigerator. There are no phones in any rooms at the ranch, but public pay phones are available, and the desk will take messages for you.

Light breakfasts and lunches are served at the clubhouse restaurant, either indoors or at umbrella tables just outside. The ranch dining room is very attractive with picture windows overlooking the grounds, a big stone fireplace, and large wrought-iron chandeliers suspended from a beamed ceiling. A glassed-in sunroom adjoins. A big Texas breakfast here might include pancakes, scrambled eggs, tortillas, breakfast tacos, sausage, bacon, grits, juices, homemade biscuits with gravy, fresh fruit, pastries, hash browns, and coffee. Dinners usually feature barbecue, steak, or Mexican fare. Very popular is the three-meat barbecue—chicken, brisket, and sausage—grilled over mesquite wood with potato salad, corn on the cob, pinto beans, hot bread and butter, and piping hot cobbler with your coffee. Friday-night dinners and Sunday champagne brunches are open to the public.

Adjoining the dining room is the Branding Iron Saloon, its cypress-paneled walls and ceiling hung with myriad brands of local ranches. Scene of many nighttime happenings, the Saloon has a dance floor, a massive stone fireplace, a large-screen TV used for airing sporting events and movies, and a stone bar topped by a slab of cypress. At night the room is candlelit. A covered pavilion nearby is used for dances and barbecues; it adjoins the pool, so you can swim to the music or leave the kids in the pool while you dance. One last facility is a laundromat for guests.

Rates are $55 to $80 per person per night, the range depending on the type of accommodation, the time of week (weekends are higher) and time of year. They include daily breakfast and dinner and all recreational activities on the ranch. You can also rent on a room-only basis and pay separately for recreational activities. A 12% service charge is added to your bill, precluding the need for constant tipping. Parking is free. There are no facilities for the disabled, but the terrain is easily negotiable, most rooms are ground-floor level, and the staff will go out of their way to accommodate guests with special needs. Numerous package deals are offered, particularly in conjunction with holidays. Inquire when you reserve.

## The Mayan Dude Ranch

The Mayan Dude Ranch, two miles from the center of town (from the courthouse on Main Street, turn left on Pecan and follow the signs; mailing address is Box 577, Bandera, TX 78003; tel. 512/796-3312), dates from the early 1900s. The Hicks family—Don, Judy, their 13 kids, the kids' spouses, the kids' kids, and Don's mother, Gracie (otherwise known as the Hicks gang)—bought the place in 1951 and have been running it as a dude ranch ever since. The Mayan's magic begins when you drive up the entrance road under a canopy of tall trees, cross the Medina River that meanders through the property, and enter upon a panoramic mountain vista that stretches for miles into the distance. In the foreground horses graze at pasture, and if it's spring the fields will be covered with wildflowers. The ranch raises all its own horses, along with cattle and hay.

Guests are never lacking for something to do at the Mayan. There are riverside barbecues, country-western bands for dancing, karate and aerobics classes in the fully equipped fitness center, cowboy campfire breakfasts, river fishing and tubing, Mexican/Irish/Texas/Italian nights with the appropriate food and music, twice-daily trail rides, margarita-making contests, chili cookoffs, and wagon train rides. The Mayan takes its guests into town on a haywagon or stagecoach, tying up the horses at the still-extant hitching posts on Main Street. You can swim a few laps in the Olympic-size pool (complete with water slide), play Ping-Pong or tennis (there are two courts), join in lawn games (volleyball, shuffleboard, basketball, horseshoe pitching), arrange for guitar lessons, or take a hike in the woods. There are 320 acres to explore, and you'll likely see deer, wild turkeys, rabbits, and some of the 100 or so resident peacocks along the way. Or opt for the easy life and curl up under a shade tree with a good book. The daily schedule of activities arrives at your cabin each morning with coffee, juice, and a sweet roll. That's just to hold you over till breakfast—in the dining room or out in the woods after an early-morning trail ride. While a cowboy sings and strums guitar, you can work off an exercise-induced appetite with scrambled eggs, bacon, biscuits, sausage, hash browns, grits, cowboy gravy, barbecued meats, onions, mushrooms, and grated cheese (some items are meant to be rolled into tortillas), coffee, and juice.

Back at the ranch, accommodations are in log cabins and stone houses. The interiors are attractively rustic with cedar-paneled walls, rust or brown wall-to-wall carpeting, and rough-hewn wood furnishings. All have air conditioning, full tub/shower bath, one king-size bed or two double beds, and color TV—but no phone (the desk will take messages). There are porches where you can sit and enjoy the vista. All rooms offer beautiful rural views, some have sleeping lofts, and one has a cedar log treehouse the kids can play and sleep in.

In the main house there's a comfortable lodge-like, stone-walled lobby with a wagon-wheel chandelier suspended from a beamed ceiling. Off the lobby are the Peacock Bar, the dining room, a gift shop (western wear, etc.), and a game room/library with an immense stone fireplace. The Hickses keep a good supply of board games on hand. The cozy Peacock Bar, furnished in hand-hewn wood pieces, also has a comfortable leather sofa made of horns in front of the fireplace. A big picture window lets you enjoy the spectacular view. Lore, the bartender, has been at the Peacock for years; he's also a successful country song writer whose tunes have been recorded by Waylon Jennings, among others, and made the charts. A wood deck adjoins the Peacock for dancing under the stars, and there's another bar and dance floor on the premises as well. The dining room decor is similar to the bar's—rough-hewn wood beams, paneling, and furnishings, and big picture windows overlooking a beautiful piece of country (diners often see peacocks strutting around outside). A big flower arrangement adorns every table, and candle-shaped sconces on wooden posts create very nice lighting. It's a lovely room.

The Mayan's facilities include a guest laundry. And perhaps the best of the ranch's offerings is the Hicks family itself—a fun-loving and friendly crew who extend a warm welcome to guests.

Rates are $75 a day for adults, $40 for children 12 to 18, $35 for kids under 12. Weekly rates are $10 a day less for adults, $5 a day less for children. Three hearty meals a day and all activities are included in rates, and a 10% service charge is added in lieu of tipping. No ranch is really totally equipped for handicapped people, but Don and Judy will do their best to accommodate guests who need special help.

The Hicks family also owns the nearby Whispering Winds ranch, where they have ten one- to four-bedroom houses with full kitchens. Guests at Whispering Winds can participate in all Mayan activities. Rates are the same as above.

**WHERE TO EAT:** Most Bandera visitors stay at a ranch and eat all meals there —or out on the trail at a campfire cookout. But if you want to check out the local scene, try the places listed below. I do hope you get to have at least one breakfast or lunch at the Old Spanish Trail.

To Bandera folks the **Old Spanish Trail,** 305 Main St. (tel. 796-3836), is just the local hangout; they always refer to it as the OST. But if you come from anywhere but Texas you'll probably think it's plumb exotic. It doesn't quite date from Old Spanish Trail days, but the restaurant has been around for over 65 years. The regulars here are ranchers, rodeo performers, locals, and motorcycle riders from San Antonio. They don't look like a crowd you'd see in a Woody Allen movie.

In the front room, tables are covered with bandana-patterned red oilcloth, the wood-paneled walls are hung with old paintings of local ranches, and there are wagon-wheel chandeliers overhead. A sign on the cash register reads "Cows may come and cows may go, but the bull in this place goes on forever." Then there's the John Wayne Room in the back, with rough-hewn cypress tables and an oxen yoke on the wall that was used in the building of the San Antonio–Bandera highway. And of course there are paintings and photos of John Wayne.

The bar is festooned with pictures of old Bandera and the traditional elk head, the jukebox provides a background of country music, and there are video games in a back room. There have been some good ol' western brawls at the OST, and owner Harvey Raab enjoys telling of the time a girl threw a sugar container at her boyfriend, missed, and hit the deputy sheriff. It knocked him to his knees, a position from which he quickly rose to say, "Lady, you're under arrest."

So much for local atmosphere. You can get a good meal at the OST. Come by in the morning for breakfast tacos ($2.25 for two corn tortillas filled with scrambled eggs and a choice of sausage, bacon, ham, chorizo, potato, or refried beans). Of course, you can add ingredients for a price. Or order eggs and chili ($3.25) with hash browns or refried beans and hot biscuits or thick slabs of Texas toast. At lunch there are $3.25 specials like big platters of chicken-fried steak or macaroni and cheese. Other day or night options are a grilled-cheese sandwich with potato chips ($1.35), steak fingers with cream gravy served with french fries and Texas toast ($4), and Mexican meals like two chicken enchiladas—corn tortillas stuffed with chicken and Monterrey jack cheese, topped with sour cream, chili gravy, and green onions ($3.60). A side order of guacamole salad with cheddar and chips is $3.25. For dessert there are Gwen Raab's homemade pies—lemon, coconut cream, apple, and cherry. Despite the very western-looking bar, no alcohol is served, but lots of people bring their own booze.

Open Monday to Thursday from 6 a.m. to 11 p.m., on Friday and Saturday till midnight, and on Sunday from 7 a.m. to 10 p.m.

The **Wrangler Steakhouse,** 1000 Main St. (tel. 796-8852), is an unpretentious local eatery (there isn't one with even any pretensions of being pretentious) with rustic wainscotted cypress walls decorated with a wood-burned mural of old Bandera. It has a big stone fireplace, amber lighting, and alpine-style chunky wood furnishings that look like they came from the cottage of the three bears. The inevitable jukebox plays country music.

For openers, order up a plate of cheese and bean nachos ($2.75), or a guacamole salad with chips ($3.50). Entrees include a ten-ounce tender and juicy rib-eye steak for $10.25, filet mignon wrapped in bacon for $9.95, or a six-ounce top sirloin for $6.95—all served with salad-bar fixings and a baked potato. Chicken-fried steak with cream gravy and a big stack of french fries is $4.95. And there's lots more than steak. A seafood platter (shrimp, oysters, scallops, and fried fish filet) or a dozen fried oysters will cost you $9.45. An order of three enchiladas is $3.95. And if you just want something light, consider an eight-ounce burger with fries for $4.25, a B.L.T. for $2.25, or deep-fried chicken breast filet strips with cream gravy, fries, and salad-bar selections ($4.25). Order pie à la mode for dessert and release the kids to the video game room in the back while you relax over coffee. Open daily from 11 a.m. to 2:30 p.m. for lunch and 5:30 to 10 p.m. for dinner.

**THINGS TO DO:** Most dude ranch guests at one time or another get into town to see the museum, check out the shops on Main Street, and see what life is like in the urban center of cowboy country. There's also horse racing at a nearby track.

If you really want to explore the town in depth, pick up a walking-tour map at the chamber of commerce; it details historic buildings like the 1881 Old Jail, the oldest stone building in Bandera (1855), several 19th-century churches, and other landmarks.

If Kerrville isn't on your itinerary, plan a day's excursion to the Y.O. Ranch from Bandera—a not-to-be-missed experience. Details are in the Kerrville section, below.

## The Museum

The **Frontier Times Museum,** 506 13th St. (tel. 796-3864), came into existence in 1927 as a monument to pioneer days. Founder J. Marvin Hunter, a

Texas history buff and ardent collector, personally knew veterans of Indian wars, pioneer settlers, outlaws, stage drivers and robbers, gamblers, Texas Rangers, and trail drivers. His book, *100 Years in Bandera,* is on sale here and tells many of their stories. Hunter died in 1957, and the museum was acquired by a nonprofit foundation.

The museum is a jumble of hundreds of relics from frontier days, including objects both intriguing and bizarre. In the latter category are displays of "some dried lichee nuts given to Mrs. Charles Montague by a Chinese merchant in Mexico," a pig with eight legs, and centipedes (there's also a boa constrictor) preserved in a jar. Other exhibits include a collection of rare and antique bottles said to have come from Judge Roy Bean's Jersey Lillie saloon; mounted eagles, deer heads, squirrels, birds, a gila monster, a Texas longhorn steer with a spread of eight feet, and a two-headed calf, among other trophies; relics of pre-settler days like flint arrowheads and skinning knives; the shrunken heads of a Jivaro Indian girl and a wild dog of the Ecuadorean jungles; a pair of copper conquistador saddle stirrups; a necklace made of alligator teeth; old buggy whips and walking canes; a collection of 500 bells from all over the world, some of them dating from the 6th century B.C.; clothing worn by Bandera residents in the 1800s; patchwork quilts; a German hand grenade; and knots made by the Fire Boys of the San Antonio Fire Department's Station 5. That's just a representative sampling of the over-30,000 items that make up this unique collection. The artifacts aren't all from Bandera; some, like the shrunken heads, clay idols, a Chinese Han Dynasty gong, and a wooden idol from Easter Island, were donated by Bandera residents who traveled to foreign lands. There's also a Gallery of Paintings of the Old West displaying art depicting scenes ranging from attacks on the Pony Express to buffalo hunts. And the museum building itself is interesting, its walls made of stones from caves, fossils, petrified wood, and stones from historic sites.

This only-in-Texas museum is great fun. Don't miss it! Hours are Monday to Saturday from 10 a.m. to noon and 1 to 4:30 p.m., on Sunday from 1 to 4:30 p.m. only. Admission is $1 for adults, 25¢ for children 6 to 16 (under 6, free).

## Shopping

As the cowboy capital, Bandera has a few Main Street shops you should mosey into. Most colorful of these is Bungy Grant's **Bandera General Store,** 311 Main St. (no phone), housed in a 1910 building, which was the Blue Goose Pool Hall in a previous incarnation. Her wares run a wide western gamut including arrowheads, gold-sprayed cow patties, holsters, spurs, chaps, bandanas, novelty items, antique saddles, Indian headdresses, and hand-woven blankets from Oaxaca. The store's Cowboy Wall of Honor is signed by local, state, and national rodeo champs. And there's a whole room of garage sale items in the back to pick through.

Bungy gives an amusing little talk on Bandera to any interested tourist. She is, by the way, mom of locally renowned country-and-western singer Ballan Grant. Together they run another venture—a beat-up 1961 trailer called the Prairie Schooner, and billed as "Texas's smallest hotel." It's decorated with Ballan's cartoons, pictures of cowboys and their ladies, and paraphernalia from the store. There's a Murphy bed in the dining room, a pink stove and a green refrigerator in the kitchen. It rents for $35 a night; apply at the store.

The **Cowboy Capital Western Art Gallery,** 309 Main St. (tel. 796-3006), is housed in the 1910 First National Bank Building. The bank's safe was blown by professional yeggmen in 1921, but the dynamite charge, which alerted everyone in town, did not penetrate the inner doors. As the entire citizenry made haste with shotguns and pistols, the robbers fled without taking a cent. A posse went after them and a shootout ensued, resulting in the capture of two bandits; the third, badly wounded, escaped for the nonce but was found and taken into custody a few days later. The bank was robbed again in 1932, this time successfully —the robbers netted over $5,000 in cash, checks, and jewelry. They were never apprehended. In 1950 D. W. "Speedy" Hicks, a local rancher, purchased the building, and in 1983 he opened the art gallery. On display is western art from all over the state of Texas.

A cowboy town is the place to buy western wear. So check out the **Diamond T Trading Post,** 303 Main St. (tel. 796-3655). In business for 39 years, it's a mom-and-pop store run by A. B. and Elaine Small. Some of the more interesting items here are boot jacks for removing cowboy boots, a belt buckle with six 357-magnum bullets worked into the design, beaded headbands, buckskin gloves, a glass paperweight with a scorpion inside, and Ken and Barbie dolls dressed by Wrangler in cowboy/cowgirl garb. Of course there's a full line of Levis, Wranglers, Tony Lama boots, and all the rest as well.

There's more of the same—and more—at **Bo's Rodeo and Ranch Shop,** 306 Main St. (tel. 796-4535). Owned by local rodeo promoter Bo Chesson and his wife, Onella, the shop is heated by a wood stove in winter. In the back room, Bo makes skid boots for calf roping, branding irons, muzzles, chaps, saddles, bridles, stirrups, horn protectors for steers, bridle bits, bareback riggings, and other equestrian and rodeo rider gear. The store also carries a good selection of boots, belts, shirts, hats, and buckles. The dressing room is shaped like an outhouse.

You might also want to visit **A-1 Wildlife Taxidermy,** 312 Main St. (tel. 796-3904), where local hunters have their animals stuffed.

## The Track

There's year-round quarterhorse racing at **Bandera Downs,** two miles east of town on Hwy. 16 (tel. 796-3081). The schedule varies from year to year, but there are generally two to three races scheduled each month. The races last all day, and there are generally about 20 races each time; the track is just 550 yards, so a race doesn't take very long.

Nicest place to sit is in the air-conditioned Turf Club, where you can watch the action through big picture windows and catch close-up details on TV monitors. It costs $10 for seats, and you have to call in advance to reserve a table. The food's not fancy—just burgers, fries, hot dogs, and calf fries (them's calf testicles!). If you sit in the stands admission is $2.50 for adults, $1.50 for ages 6 to 12 (under 6, free). There are no betting windows, but people have been known to place bets. Ask a friendly local to direct you to the nearest tout.

**NIGHTLIFE:** In season, there's always plenty happening back at the ranch, and even if you're here off-season, ask at the desk if there are any goings-on at neighboring ranches, which you'd be welcome to attend. Otherwise, your options are the following:

**The Cabaret Dance Hall,** 801 Main St. (tel. 796-8162), is an authentic cowboy palace that's been a dance hall and restaurant for over half a century. In its heyday people came from all over Texas to hear greats like Bob Wills, Hank Williams, Jim Reeves, Faron Young, and Ernest Tubb. It was for many years a well-known spot on the C&W circuit, and people who made it at the Cabaret often went on to Nashville fame. Willie Nelson was a backup musician at the club in the 1960s. And a decade prior to that the Cabaret was headquarters for the annual three-day drunken bash with which local ranch hands would kick off the summer.

Both inside and out, this is your typical western dance hall. It's housed in a low weathered-wood building with a front porch. Inside, the dance floor is the size of a high school gym with a silver ball suspended overhead. It's flanked by long red-and-white-oilcloth-covered tables; a long oak bar is at one end, the bandstand at the other, and a room on the side has pool tables, dart boards, and pinball machines. Food is served all day—at this writing just pizza and salad bar, but steaks are planned for the future. There's live music on Saturday nights, dancing to recorded music the rest of the week. "We play traditional country music," says owner Cal Chapman, "because otherwise we'd get our throats cut." Wear your cowboy duds and don't order a Perrier at the bar.

Open Monday to Thursday from 11 a.m. to 10 p.m., on Friday to 2 a.m., on Saturday from 5 p.m. to 3 a.m., and on Sunday from 5 to 10 p.m.

**Arkey Blue's Silver Dollar Saloon,** 308 Main St. (tel. 796-8826), has been a scene of local revelry since 1921, though not always Arkey's domain. "Saturday nights they frisk for weapons," joked my native guide, Bungy Grant. "If you don't have one, they'll lend you one." But don't let me scare you off. Actually, Arkie's is a friendly place, patronized by everyone in Bandera (except hard-core Baptists) from ages 8 to 80. On a typical weeknight, maybe local songbird Ballan Grant will come by and sing a few songs, and other talented customers will accompany her on fiddle and bass. At intervals Perky will make his railroad noise, and someone will give out with a rebel yell. You'll soon meet everyone in the place. Arkey's band plays on Friday and Saturday nights, and that's when the sawdust-covered dance floor is really mobbed and jumping. Sit down at a long oak table, order a beer, and ask a local to show you where Hank Williams carved his name. Or carve your own—no one will care. People who've worn out boots dancing here have hung them up on the wall. In winter a working fireplace adds to the cozy atmosphere. Pizza and snack food are served.

Arkey's is open daily from 11 a.m. to 2 a.m.

# 2. Kerrville

Kerrville, founded in 1856, represented a coming together of camps of people who were engaged in making hand-hewn shingles from the giant cypress along the Guadalupe River. Some were from Tennessee and Mississippi, others were German immigrants. The town was named for Maj. James Kerr, a soldier in the Army of the Republic of Texas, statesman, surveyor, doctor, and the first American settler on the river.

The picture of shingle-makers in a bucolic riverside setting is a bit deceptive in what it evokes. Kerrville was as beautiful then as it is today—a picturesque setting of rugged cedar- and oak-covered hills and green valleys latticed by clear spring-fed streams and rivers. But its settlers were beset by the same frontier hardships and dangers as were neighboring Bandera pioneers. Bandera Pass, between the two towns, was the scene of many a bloody battle between settler and Indian. In 1732 Spanish troops battled Apaches there; the Spanish won and the Apaches signed a peace treaty and agreed to a retreat northward to their traditional hunting grounds. Apaches abandoned the territory, but in 1841, 1840 Texas Rangers battled several hundred Comanches at the pass, killing over 100 warriors and the Comanche chief. The Rangers' casualties were only five killed and six wounded. The Colt pistol, just invented, turned the tide in favor of the Texans. But many settlers were killed—and scalped—by Comanches, fell victim to wild animal attacks, died of cholera, were set upon by bandits, and otherwise suffered the rigors of frontier life. The Civil War compounded matters by turning neighbor against neighbor and even dividing families into adamant pro-Union and pro-Confederate camps.

It was after the war that Kerrville's most prominent citizen arrived on the scene. Capt. Charles Schreiner, for whom the town might more aptly have been named, came here in 1869 to begin his one-man empire. As one historian put it, Schreiner proceeded to "write his own biography on the whole face of the Hill Country and in the hearts of its people." Schreiner came to Texas with his family from Alsace-Lorraine in 1852 at the age of 14. Two years later he enlisted in the Texas Rangers, and during the Civil War he fought for the South, though one of his own brothers joined up with Union sympathizers and was murdered by Confederate vigilantes. When Schreiner arrived in Kerrville there were few businesses other than saloons and the sawmills that had evolved from shingle making. He opened a general store; set up a bank as part of it that became the Charles Schreiner Bank, still flourishing today; did some ranching on the side; drove over 300,000 head of cattle to northern markets; began raising goats and sheep to supply what became a lucrative wool business; operated a grist mill, sawmill, and cotton mill; started the waterworks and the electric company; donated land for a Presbyterian church; founded a college; and all the while kept acquiring land, eventually amounting to 550,000 acres. Many of Schreiner's businesses—in fact most of them—are still extant today, run by Charles's descendants. You'll meet them if you stay at or visit the Y.O. Ranch or Y.O. Ranch Hilton.

Kerrville is now a prosperous resort area, still a ranching community but one so affluent that its residents are known as "Cadillac cowboys." Tourism is its major industry (followed by agriculture), and people flock here for hunting, recreation, natural beauty, and to experience a bit of the cowboy lifestyle at one of the county's famed dude ranches. It's an art community where 35 nationally known artists (mostly cowboy artists) reside and galleries are numerous. And Kerrville is also the site of some of the nation's most elite children's camps.

**GETTING THERE:** Kerrville, just 26 miles from Bandera, is reachable via Hwy. 16 or Hwy. 173, both wonderfully scenic routes through winding countryside and rolling hills. Hwy. 16 is especially beautiful where it crosses the Guadalupe River. Hwy. 173 is a more direct route. San Antonio is about an hour away, Austin less than two hours.

**Greyhound** and **Kerrville Bus Co.** buses arrive/depart the station at 429 Sidney Baker (tel. 512/257-7451), connecting Kerrville with San Antonio, Dallas, Fort Worth, Houston, and El Paso.

**GETTING ORIENTED:** Make your first stop the **Kerrville Area Chamber of Commerce,** 1200 Sidney Baker, at Holdsworth (tel. 512/896-1155), for maps, brochures, and information on all events and attractions. The chamber is open weekdays from 8:30 a.m. to 5 p.m., on Saturday from 9 a.m. to 3 p.m. You can write in advance for information to P.O. Box 790, Kerrville, TX 78029.

**GETTING AROUND:** There's no getting around Kerrville without a car unless you use your thumb. You'll probably arrive in one; if not, you can rent from **Ford Rent-a-Car,** 400 Sidney Baker South (tel. 257-5553).

Of course, if money is no object you could take taxis. Call **Easy Rider Taxi Company** (tel. 896-3030).

**ANNUAL EVENTS:** Tourism is Kerrville's biggest industry. That always augurs well for an event-filled annual calendar. For details on any happenings listed below, and on additional events during your stay, contact the chamber of commerce (tel. 512/896-1155).

In mid-January young people from five counties vie for prizes in the **Hill**

Country District Junior Livestock Show at the Hill Country Youth Exhibit Center on Hwy. 27 East.

February and March, the **Kerrville Society for the Performing Arts** sponsors a series of **classical concerts** at the Kerrville Municipal Auditorium, 900 E. Main St. (tel. 257-7300), featuring traveling opera companies and symphonies.

If you're in town Easter Weekend, don't miss the **Hill Country Chili Cookoff** in Louise Hays Park. About 5,000 people come to taste the concoctions brewed by 120 teams, enjoy the country-western bands, and watch the five- and ten-kilometer runs that are part of the fun. And it's all free.

The **Kerrville Folk Festival** runs for 9 to 11 days, including Memorial Day Weekend and through the first week in June. A large contingent of Texas songwriters perform their own tunes, and there are dozens of other soloists, duos, and groups, mostly but not all American. Some of the performers are big names —like Jerry Jeff Walker, Josh White, Jr., Gary P. Nunn, Tom Paxton, and Peter, Paul & Mary. The event takes place in an outdoor amphitheater at the Quiet Valley Ranch, nine miles south of town on Hwy. 16. You can buy tickets for the full series (about $65) or for various segments. Write in advance for ticket information to P.O. Box 1466, Kerrville, TX 78029, or call 512/257-3600. You can also buy them at the gate.

Kerrville's biggest event (about 35,000 people attend) is the **Texas State Arts & Crafts Fair,** Memorial Day Weekend and the weekend following at the Fairgrounds out at Schreiner College. There are crafts booths and demonstrations of every kind—pottery, stained glass, woodworking, glassblowing, blacksmithing, woodcarving, leatherwork, doll making, jewelry, weaving, etc. Entertainment includes C&W bands, square dancing, clowns, and yarn spinning; food booths sell everything from fajitas to funnel cakes; there's a petting zoo for children and booths where they can try crafts activities. Tickets are about $5.50 per day for adults, $3.50 for ages 6 to 12 (under 6, free).

Kerrville celebrates an old-fashioned **July Fourth** with a day of activities in Louise Hays Park. There are food concessions, country bands, a military band, canoe races, patriotic speeches, horseshoe pitching, cow-chip throwing, sack races, and apple bobbing—all capped, of course, with a fireworks display.

The **Kerr County Fair** in late July is your archetypical county fair with livestock events (blue ribbons for the best chicken, goat, pig, etc.); competitions for best cakes, quilts, crafts items, and such; helicopter rides; hot-air balloon rides; carnival rides; and Friday- and Saturday-night dances with major C&W stars. It's a four-day, Thursday-to-Sunday event.

In early August the **Heart of the Hills Annual Golf Tournament** takes place at the Scott Schreiner Golf Course, Country Club Drive (tel. 257-4982). Players from all over Texas compete, and there are ladies' lunches and brunches with fashion shows in addition to the goings-on on the greens.

Labor Day Weekend brings the **Kerrville Bluegrass Festival,** a three-day series of bluegrass and gospel concerts featuring major and emerging artists. It's one of the biggest and best bluegrass festivals in the state, with exciting mandolin, banjo, and band competitions, good food, crafts displays, and numerous informal jam sessions. All performances take place in an outdoor amphitheater at the Quiet Valley Ranch, nine miles south of town on Hwy. 16. Advance-purchase tickets for all three days are about $24, single-day tickets are available on request, and children under 12 get in free. Ticket prices are $1 additional at the gate. For advance tickets, write to P.O. Box 1466, Kerrville, TX 78029. For information, call 512/257-3600.

There's usually a small **Renaissance Festival** in Kerrville on Labor Day Weekend as well, sponsored by the Hill Country Arts Foundation (tel. 367-

5121). People dress in period costume, and there are falconers, food booths, reciters of Shakespeare, and dances. Call for details.

Jimmie Rodgers, "the singing brakeman" of the 1920s, was a Kerrville boy, and early in September his birthday is celebrated at the **Jimmie Rodgers Jubilee.** His songs are played, and there are dances, food booths, and an auction. Admission is free.

The **Experimental Aircraft Association Kerrville Fly-In & Airshow** takes place in mid-September at the Kerrville Municipal Airport. A "parade of flight" features home-built, antique, classic, military, and modern aircraft in flight, as well as the newest designs of air recreational vehicles. It's a three-day event; tickets are about $3 for adults, $2 for children 6 to 12 (under 6, free).

The **Kerrville Goodtime Music Festival,** Columbus Day Weekend in October, offers a mix of English and Irish ballads, war songs, children's songs, courting melodies, blues, bluegrass, western swing, and songs of the open road. There are fiddlers, cloggers, square dancing, mountain dulcimers, penny whistlers, banjo and harmonica players, arts and crafts booths too. And you'll get to sing a bit yourself around the campfire after midnight. Be sure to enter the "worst hat contest." It takes place at the Quiet Valley Ranch amphitheater on Hwy. 16. Write in advance for ticket information to P.O. Box 1466, Kerrville, TX 78029, or call 512/257-3600.

December **Christmas in the Hills** activities include house tours, home and business lighting contests, fashion shows, Christmas tree decoration exhibits, a parade, and a Mistletoe Ball at a major hotel.

**WHERE TO STAY:** A stay at the nearby **Y.O. Ranch,** Hwy. 41 between U.S. 83 and I-10 (mailing address is Mountain Home, TX 78058; tel. 512/640-3222), is as exciting as an African safari. In fact it is an African safari, Texas style. Herds of exotic animals run the range on this 100-square-mile property—gemsbok oryx, zebra, ostrich, giraffe, wild turkey, emu, rhea, and several varieties of antelope, deer, sheep, elk, and goat. Some are game animals that can be hunted on guided excursions (this is the largest private hunting area of its type in the world, larger than some of the famous preserves in Africa and India); others are endangered species protected by the ranch's conservation program. They're all viewable on tours and photo safaris, which take place on a daily basis and are open to the public as well as to ranch guests.

The ranch was acquired in 1880 by Capt. Charles Schreiner, who in his heyday drove over 300,000 head of longhorn cattle along the western trail to northern markets. The ranch today maintains the world's largest quality herd of registered Texas longhorns, as well as one of the country's finest herds of registered quarterhorses. And it's still run by the Schreiner family—Charlie III and his four sons (Charlie IV, Walter, Gus, and Louis), and the kids of Charlie IV and Walter. From Kerrville it's about an hour's drive through stunningly scenic creek-crossed ranch country, with an eight-mile drive along a "washboard road" into the property itself. Then you're quite literally in Marlboro country (this is where they shot those commercials), a gorgeous terrain of rolling hills forested with oak, cedar, mesquite, and shinnoak, and rocky fields of tall grasses and cacti. Fifty-two windmills on the property draw water from underground and add to the picturesque vista. And Kerr County's two oldest log cabins are on the property.

In addition to year-round hunting (you can get your license here, and the ranch can provide necessary gear, process, freeze, ship, and arrange for taxidermy), activities include hayrides, campfire cookouts, barbecues, game-viewing outings, horseshoe throwing, racquetball, and hiking wildlife trails. Depending on the season, you might also get to see working ranch activities like branding and sheep shearing. A large swimming pool, poolside bar, sundeck, and outdoor hot tub by a waterfall are near an observation deck enabling guests to watch wildlife while in the pool area. A game room adjoins, and there's also a gorgeous lodge where hunters gather in front of the fireplace at night, play cards, drink brandy, and swap tales of the one that got away.

The ranch can accommodate up to 35 people in a lodge and century-old log cabins (one is an 1852 schoolhouse, another a stagecoach stop) decorated with Texas antiques—perhaps yours will have an old oak dresser, a spinning wheel, an oak ice box, an immigrant's steamer trunk, shelves of copper plates or pottery, Wells Fargo signs, saddles, or mounted hunting trophies. They're all air-conditioned, but have no phones or TVs (the desk takes incoming calls and relays messages). Some baths have shower only. Furnishings run to wagon-wheel headboards and comfortable leather chairs. Some rooms have peaked, beamed ceilings; some have living rooms with working stone fireplaces.

Meals not served around a campfire are eaten at long tables in the rustic Chuck Wagon dining room, a cozy place with a beamed barn ceiling, big stone fireplace, and wood-paneled walls hung with hunting trophies and photographs of ranch activities. You'll see lots of cowboys in spurs and dusty boots at every meal. Ranch meals are hearty. Every day begins with a big cowboy breakfast, and a typical lunch or dinner might include barbecued brisket or pork chops, mashed potatoes, green beans, pinto beans, salad, homemade cornbread and butter, and fresh-from-the-oven peach cobbler, and coffee. Adjoining the Chuck Wagon is the Y.O. General Store where you can buy limited-edition gold Colt six-shooters, jalapeño jelly, and other of life's little necessities.

Per-person rates at the Y.O. are $60 a night for adults, half price for children 6 to 12 (under 6, free). That includes all meals and activities except the 2½-hour wildlife tour ($12 for adults, half price for ages 6 to 12; under 6, free). A full-day photo safari is $150 per person. The Y.O. has exciting two- and three-week summer-camp programs for kids. Hunters also have a variety of packages to choose from. Whether you stay here (and I highly recommend it) or visit for an afternoon or day, don't miss the Y.O. Ranch, a quintessentially Texan experience.

Another magnificent Schreiner family enterprise is the **Y.O. Ranch Hilton,** 2033 Sidney Baker, Kerrville, TX 78028 (tel. 512/257-4440), offering rustic western elegance in the heart of the scenic Hill Country. It opened with a big celebrity-studded bash in 1984, attended by rodeo champions, cowboy movie stuntmen, Amanda Blake (Kitty from "Gunsmoke"), and others, some of whom left handprints and footprints in wet cement à la Mann's Chinese Theatre in Hollywood. Charles Schreiner III has long been collecting Old West memorabilia, and the hotel displays many of these treasures. In the beautiful lodge-like lobby, unique wrought-iron candelabra chandeliers festooned with 350 Chisolm Trail–era branding irons are suspended from a high raftered ceiling. The entranceway is flanked by standing and crouching bears. Persian rugs define cozy sitting areas on the Saltillo-tile floors, much of the furniture is covered in cowhide, and there's a massive limestone fireplace. A 7½-foot-tall sculpture by western artist H. Clay Dahlberg called *Rough Men and Tough Times* is the lobby centerpiece; it depicts a cowboy fighting to stay in the saddle as an enraged longhorn lunges under his horse.

The 200 rooms, housed in eight two-story stone buildings with barn-red roofs, are among the most originally and beautifully decorated in Texas. They're done in subtle earth shades like adobe and mauve, rose-toned brown and grayish blue, or muted green and dusty rose, with Dhurri throw rugs on Saltillo-tile floors, walls hung with framed prints and engravings from *Harpers' Weekly* (an

1800s "Journal of Civilization"), mounted heads and horns, and custom-made knotty-pine furnishings. Suites are especially luxurious, some with fireplaces and all with wet bars. All rooms have direct-dial phones and cable color TVs.

The Sam Houston Dining Room, tastefully decorated in Victorian motif, has oak wainscotted walls covered in period tapestry and hung with photographs and paintings of Sam Houston and members of his family. The ornate oak back bar, Greek revival in style with Corinthian columns (mirroring similar columns throughout the restaurant), comes from a turn-of-the-century Texas pharmacy. Carpeting and tablecloths are rust colored, and lighting emanates from elaborate English brass candelabra chandeliers and gaslight-style wall sconces. The wine cooler here was an abandoned ice box from a grocery store, which Mary Helen Schreiner (Charlie IV's wife) bought for $25 at an auction. The restaurant specializes in exotic game; you might start a meal with a pâté made of Blackbuck antelope and goose liver seasoned with sherry and served on toast points ($4.25) and follow with an entree of venison sautéed in maître d' butter and shallots in bordelaise sauce ($13.25). Of course there are many other options. Appetizers range from nachos ($4.25) to shrimp tempura ($5.75), entrees from country-fried chicken in home-style gravy ($6.95) to filet mignon ($12.95). And since this is an all-purpose hotel restaurant, it also offers hamburgers, fajitas, salads, and sandwiches. The adjoining Boon Bar, named for a famous Y.O. Ranch stud horse, adjoins. Another bar, the Elm Water Hole Saloon, has a late-1800s, 30-foot bar with hand-hewn oak bar stools covered in deerhide. In this classic Old West setting free hors d'oeuvres are served weekdays during Happy Hour, and there's live music for dancing Thursday, Friday, and Saturday nights, DJ-provided music the other nights. A quieter retreat is the Guadalupe Bar, scene of nightly piano-bar or bluegrass entertainment. Additional on-premises facilities include a courtyard pool with swim-up bar, outdoor Jacuzzi, kiddie pool, and barbecue grills, a night-lit tennis court, and the adjoining Schreiner Golf Course. Visits to the ranch can be arranged.

Rates are $50 to $100 single, $20 for each additional adult, free for children of any age traveling with a parent or parents. Weekend packages are available, and sometimes (in summer) a sign out front offers guests the option of paying half the temperature at checkout time. The higher end of the rate scale is for deluxe rooms. Facilities for the disabled are also available.

**Inn of the Hills,** 1001 Junction Hwy. (27W) near Harper Road (tel. 512/895-5000, or toll free 800/528-1234), perches on the banks of the Guadalupe River at a point where it widens into a scenic lakeside setting girded by rolling green hills. The inn offers country-club comforts and amenities. There's a large courtyard pool and beautifully landscaped sundeck, the latter offering a choice of sunning and tree-shaded areas; it's one of four swimming pools on the property. Toddlers can splash around in an adjoining kiddie pool. A tennis court is lit for night play, a miniature golf course and children's playground are on the lawn, and bikes can be rented. And for river recreation, paddleboats, sailboats, and canoes are available. That's all just for openers, because inn guests have full use of the Guadalupe Family Sports Center, right on the property, putting two additional tennis courts, racquetball, bowling (16 lanes), basketball, volleyball, an indoor lap pool, massage, saunas, steam, a hot tub, and an exercise room right at your doorstep. And golf courses are nearby. The Sports Center has its own pool, beautifully situated right on the river, and a river-view restaurant, the only one in Kerrville, with windows all around making optimum use of the vista. It's a lovely facility, furnished with upholstered bamboo chairs at beautifully appointed tables set with dusty-rose cloths. All the food served here is fresh and homemade. At lunch there are scrumptious salads like white meat chicken tossed with apples, oranges, and pecans in a mild curry dressing ($6.25). A typical dinner might begin with mushrooms filled with a spicy crabmeat stuffing ($6), followed by fried-in-batter shrimp with house salad and fresh vegetables ($14.95), and end with Italian walnut cream cake ($2.95) for dessert.

Hotel rooms aren't fancy, but they're reasonably priced and adequate in view of all the attendant amenities here. Some have one stone or wood-paneled wall and barnwood or beamed stucco ceilings. They're equipped with cable color TVs, phones, in-room coffee makers, and in most cases, two-sink bathrooms.

More luxurious are the condominium rooms, all with patios overlooking the river. Decorated in mauve/dusty-rose/pale-peach color schemes, they have ash furnishings and brass lamps. A clock radio is added to the above amenities, and most condo accommodations have full kitchens, equipped with pots, pans, dishes, and silver.

Off the lobby of the main building, itself a cozy setting with sofas before a massive stone fireplace, is the rustic La Fuente Dining Room, paneled in pine, furnished in leather, and lit by wagon-wheel chandeliers and wrought-iron sconces. Walls are adorned with western art. It's open daily for breakfast, lunch, and dinner. An essentially steak and seafood menu is featured, though other options are offered. The adjoining Pub is a popular local spot, offering live country entertainers and dancing nightly. A coin-op laundry for guests is an additional facility.

Rates in regular rooms are $47 to $78 single, $55 to $80 double, the higher end of the scale for larger and better-located accommodations. An extra person pays $6, and children under 10 stay free. Condominium rooms range from $80 to $85 without kitchens, from $115 to $165 a night with, the latter price representing a two-bedroom suite with living room. Parking is free. No-smoking accommodations are available.

The **Lazy Hills Guest Ranch,** eight miles west of Kerrville in nearby Ingram (mailing address is Box G, Ingram, TX 78025; tel. 512/367-5600), is a beautiful 750-acre property with 30 miles of riding trails winding through stream-crossed woods and hills. Guests can pluck catfish and bass from ranch ponds; play tennis (there are two night-lit courts); participate in cookouts, hayrides, breakfast rides, trail rides, and marshmallow roasts; enjoy the putting green and other lawn games (horseshoe pitching, shuffleboard, archery, volleyball, and basketball); play Ping-Pong and video games in an indoor rec room; or do laps in the Olympic-size swimming pool. There are beautiful hiking trails where you'll see many deer and other wildlife; the woods are also great for birdwatching, and hospitable owner/hosts Bob and Carol Steinruck have prepared a list of the hundreds of sparrows, warblers, orioles, grackles, finches, and other birds commonly seen. In season (mid-November to January 1) there's hunting for deer and turkey. At night, guests gather in the Green Room before the fireplace for games and sing-alongs around the piano. Sometimes a resident cowboy sings country ballads out on the patio. And it's also nice to bask in the outdoor hot tub under a starry sky.

Lazy Hills caters largely to a family clientele. Its outdoor pavilion has a well-equipped children's playground and a treehouse. The 25 rooms are country-rustic in style, most containing one wagon-wheel headboarded queen-size bed along with a bunk bed, a twin bed, or sofa beds. All are air-conditioned, have shower baths, and are fronted by porches. Curtained windows and denim bedspreads add a bit of homey quality, but these are not fancy digs. The nicest units are the seven with working stone fireplaces; ask for one when you reserve. There are no phones or TVs, but the desk does take messages.

Meals not eaten outdoors are taken in the large knotty-pine-paneled dining room, decorated with mounted deer heads and offering scenic country views through large windows. A massive stone fireplace makes things cozy. Days begin here with a hearty country breakfast—bacon or sausage (from ranch-grown hogs), hotcakes, french toast, eggs, grits, homemade toasted bread and biscuits, coffee, and juices. At lunch the Steinrucks might serve up seafood salad with fresh homemade bran muffins, fresh fruit, and apple crisp for dessert with your coffee. Dinners are more substantial, like chicken-fried steak with cream gravy and mashed potatoes, green beans, fresh-baked biscuits, salad, and buttermilk pie.

To get to Lazy Hills from Kerrville, take Hwy. 27 west to Ingram, turn right at the light and drive 2½ miles till you see the sign on your right.

Nightly rates are $62 for a single room, $47 per person for two adults sharing a room, $45 for three, $42 for four. Weekly rates are $395, $325, $304, and $290, respectively. Children 12 to 16 pay half price on a daily basis, with further reductions for littler tots and stays of a week or more too complex to go into here; ask when you reserve. Rates include all meals and activities.

The **Quality Inn,** 2124 Sidney Baker, Kerrville, TX 78208 (tel. 512/896-1313, or toll free 800-228-5151), offers a lot of quality for the price. If hotel rooms tend to make you claustrophobic, you'll love these: they're huge, attractively decorated in earth tones, and very nicely furnished. The entire hotel was recently refurnished, recarpeted, repainted, and repapered, so everything is spanking new and fresh. All 97 rooms are equipped with the standard modern amenities, including king-size or double-double beds and cable color TV. Especially nice are the rooms facing the courtyard; they have oak armoires that conceal the TVs and art nouveau lamps on the desks. The courtyard they face is centered on a medium-sized pool and sundeck surrounded by live oaks and other plantings.

A big plus here is the Alpine Lodge, a Swiss-owned, on-premises restaurant with a traditionally cozy decor. Its wood-paneled walls are covered with pictures of the Alps, and there are stained-glass windows, Swiss horns, cuckoo clocks, cowbells, wine racks, and lots of thriving green plants. In addition to lavish buffets Thursday, Friday, and Saturday nights, and all day Sunday priced at $11.50 to $12.50, there's an à la carte menu from which you might compose a meal of traditional French onion soup au gratin ($2.75), followed by wiener-schnitzel with a stuffed potato and vegetable du jour ($10.75), and a homemade dessert of custardy bread pudding with fresh whipped cream ($2.75). Entrees include a terrific salad bar. Lighter fare—burgers, sandwiches, and salads—is also available. There's dancing to live music in the adjoining lounge on Friday and Saturday nights.

Rates are $40 to $49 single, $48 to $57 double, $6 for an extra person (under 16, free). Off-season, December 1 to mid-May, you'll pay about $5 less across the board. The higher end of the price scale is for courtyard rooms. No-smoking rooms are offered as well.

**RESTAURANTS:** As in Bandera, if you stay at a ranch you'll likely take most of your meals there. Kerrville does offer some notably good restaurants, however, and if you get a chance, try some of them. In addition to those listed here, don't forget **Rachel's Table,** mentioned later on in this section under "Shopping." Hotel restaurants like the **Alpine Lodge** at the Quality Inn and the **Sam Houston Dining Room** at the Y.O. Hilton also merit consideration.

Whether you go for cocktail-hour margaritas and delicious Mexican *antojitos* (appetizers) or a full meal, don't miss **Mamacita's,** 215 Junction Hwy., right next to Republic Square (tel. 895-2441), a delightful stucco-walled restaurant with arched Mexican- and Texan-themed stained-glass windows. The decor of the three dining rooms is lovely; tables are topped in terracotta tile, chairs upholstered in striped forest-green fabric, and floors of Saltillo tile or carpeted in rust. One room has a central Mexican fountain. Upstairs is the very comfortable Cantina lounge and adjoining outdoor garden terrace with white wrought-iron umbrella tables, either setting a happy choice for the Happy Hour.

Everything is made from scratch. Start out with an order of queso flameado, seasoned chorizo sausage and melted Monterrey jack cheese rolled in flour tortillas ($4.25); and nachos al carbon, crispy tostada chips piled with cheese, refried beans, char-broiled fajita chunks, guacamole, and jalapeños ($5). There's also very good ceviche ($3.95), and a house specialty is avocado de Mamacita's—avocado filled with cheese, dipped in batter, deep-fried, and topped with ranchero sauce and sour cream ($4.25). Those are appetizers, though you could share a variety of them and make a nice dinner of it. Or forge ahead with entrees like char-broiled jumbo shrimp in garlic/butter sauce ($9.45); tacos al carbón, char-broiled steak rolled in fresh flour tortillas with chile con queso ($5.95); and chile relleño, poblano pepper stuffed with cheese or beef, dipped in batter, and deep-fried ($6.75). All the above come with rice, refried beans, and guacamole. You can also order smaller platters of burritos, tacos, enchiladas, etc., and there's a *niños* menu featuring items like a cheese enchilada with rice and beans served with a Shirley Temple or soft drink for $3.25. If your appetite hasn't flagged (mine never has), try the flan for dessert ($1.65). Mariachi bands entertain on Wednesday, Friday, and Saturday nights.

Open daily from 11 a.m. to 2 p.m. and 5 to 10 p.m. No reservations. Arrive off-hours to avoid long lines.

One of the most charming restaurants in town is **Fara's,** 1201 Broadway (Hwy. 27 East), at B Street (tel. 896-6580), specializing in very good northern Italian cuisine. Iranian owner Fara Farahani has turned an old home into a garden-party setting with green floors, forest-green tablecloths, varicolored globe lights, latticework partitions, and, of course, lots of plants. Antique Italian copper statuary, baskets and racks of wine, and an espresso machine on a sideboard make it a garden party in Roma. During the day it's a sunny garden (there are windows all around); at night it's softly lit and romantic. The food is delicious.

At dinner start off with an appetizer of eggplant parmesan ($5), unless you plan to have it later as an entree ($8)—it's excellent. Other viable beginnings are escargots ($5) and Greek stuffed grape leaves ($4)—Fara's not rigidly Italian in concept. The shrimp scampi here ($10.25), sautéed in lemony butter and white wine and served over spaghetti, is highly recommended. Fara's also does a very good fettuccine with escargots ($11.25); fettuccine Alfredo ($7); veal marsala, sliced baby veal in cream/butter/marsala wine sauce topped with fresh mushrooms and served with broccoli and spaghetti ($10.95); and filetto, tenderloin filet smothered in a scrumptious mixture of eggplant, onions, ham, and melted cheese, also with broccoli and spaghetti ($10.25). All entrees come with salad and rolls and butter. A bottle of soave or lambrusco with your meal is just $10.50, and for dessert there's a homemade cheesecake with pecan crust ($2.75) that could vie with anything New York has to offer. Order it with espresso ($1.35). The lunch menu is the same, but prices are a few dollars lower across the board.

Open for lunch, weekdays only, from 11 a.m. to 2 p.m.; for dinner, nightly from 5:30 to 10 p.m. Reservations suggested.

**WHAT TO SEE AND DO:** Whether you stay there or visit, take a 2½-hour lunchtime tour, or sign up for a full-day photo or hunting safari, the not-to-be-missed Hill Country attraction is the Y.O. Ranch (details in "Where to Stay," above). Second to that in importance is the Cowboy Artists of America Museum, one of the few places where you can see many fine works of western art. But you're mostly here to enjoy the beautiful scenery, crisp, clean air, and blue skies.

## The Cowboy Artists of America Museum

The only museum of its kind in the country, the Cowboy Artists of America Museum, 1550 Hwy. 173 (tel. 896-2553), features the works of the nation's premier artists of Western American realism. It houses an impressive collection of works by its 29 member artists (originally members all had to be working cowboys, and some still are) supplemented by special exhibits. Some members live and work on the property. The museum's objective—to perpetuate the memory and culture of the Old West as typified by the late Frederic Remington, Charles Russell, and others—pays tribute to its spiritual founders. Set on a ten-acre hilltop in Kerrville, an appropriate cowboy country setting, it is housed in an architecturally significant southwestern-style building. The exterior evokes the haciendas of the area's past, and the ceiling within is composed of 18 boveda brick domes, a construction rarely seen outside of old Mexican buildings. All rooms branch off a main courtyard under a jasmine vine. The gallery floors, made of mesquite, are also notable; tree trunks were cut into slices, squared off, glued together with mastic, and polished. Out on the terraced patio is a semicircle of 29 pink-blossoming crape myrtles, and in front of each a CAA artist has left his foot- and handprints in cement and signed his name. The panoramic view from the patio is spectacular.

Western art has become very popular and valuable in the last decade or so, but since so much of the best of it is in private homes and collections, one doesn't get to see a lot of it. This fine museum offers a rare opportunity; its membership standards insist on the highest in quality and authenticity.

Hours are Tuesday through Saturday from 9 a.m. to 5 p.m., on Sunday from 1 to 5 p.m. Admission is $2 for adults, 50¢ for children 6 to 12 (under 6, free). Every fourth Tuesday admission is free. There's a gift/bookstore on the premises that carries many fine books on western art and sells prints and posters of works in the museum. There are also occasional lectures on current exhibits.

## Sports

**Hunting** is very big in Kerrville. You can arrange to hunt at the Y.O. Ranch (they have actual guided safaris) as well as at other ranches. Licenses and equipment are readily available. Among the game hunted here are whitetail deer, a variety of exotic deer, Corsican rams, aoudad sheep, wild turkey, dove, quail, wild boar, and javelina. Contact the chamber of commerce for a full description of hunting possibilities.

There's **canoeing** on the river. Rent canoes at Scenic Valley Sales, 1726 Sidney Baker (tel. 896-6462).

**Pedalboats** can be rented during the summer from the landing in Louise Hays Park off State Rte. 16, south of downtown.

You don't have to be a guest to participate in **trail rides** at the Y.O. Ranch or Lazy Hills (see "Where to Stay" for further information and phone numbers).

The Burkett Ranch, on Hwy. 16N, about ten miles from town (tel. 896-3434), offers **skeet shooting.**

There's an 18-hole **municipal golf course** at 1101 Sidney Baker (tel. 257-4982). And members of any private country club can play at the River Hills Country Club, on Hwy. 173 a mile south of town (tel. 896-1400).

HEB Municipal Center, 1607 Sidney Baker (tel. 896-7955), has public **tennis** courts.

## Shopping

Like Bandera, Kerrville offers a few interesting shopping experiences. For openers, it's headquarters for Texas's most renowned jeweler, **James Avery Craftsman, Inc.**, off Hwy. 783 (Harper Road) about a half mile north of I-10 (tel. 895-1122). Avery started out in 1954 handcrafting religious jewelry of sterling silver, gold, and copper in a garage. As his clientele grew, he moved to a larger garage, then a studio, then into a 125-year-old cabin, and finally into the present vast workshop/showroom you see today, part of a jewelry empire that includes several plants and a chain of retail stores from Louisiana to California. He also expanded his line from religious jewelry to include a wide spectrum of designs. They range from oil derrick tie tacks and Texas-themed charms (spurs, boots, horseshoes, cowboy hats), to modernistic gold and silver bracelets and traditional wedding bands and engagement rings. Many pieces incorporate precious and semiprecious stones. Avery is usually on the premises, and you can discuss made-to-order pieces with him or one of his competent craftspeople. The showroom is open Monday to Saturday from 8:30 a.m. to 5 p.m.

The **Old Camp Verde General Store and Post Office**, 11 miles south of Kerrville on Hwy. 173 (tel. 634-7722), was established in 1857 to serve the nearby Fort Camp Verde and, later, pioneer ranchers. Near Bandera Pass, scene of a major battle between the Comanches and the Texas Rangers in 1841, it is about halfway to Bandera. As the fort it served was the one that used camels for transport (see "Bandera," above), a camel motif is much displayed. It's a beautiful drive to this old-fashioned country store, and there's much to enjoy on arrival. The cherrywood candy cases date to 1875, and the selection of wares includes duck decoys, copper molds, needlework art, hurricane lamps, bowl and pitcher sets, wildflower seed chests, Hill Country honey made from purple sage blossoms, calico goose-shaped doorstops, collector's thimbles, baskets, weather vanes, wind bells, and bird feeders. For the kids there are reproductions of old children's books with marvelous illustrations, calico cats, Raggedy Ann dolls, papier-mâché clowns, and $1 grab bags. You get a dozen fresh country eggs with a $5 purchase. And you can mail letters here. Open Monday to Saturday from 9 a.m. to 5:30 p.m., noon to 5:30 p.m. on Sunday.

**Old Republic Square**, 225 Junction Hwy. (tel. 257-4118), is a quaint collection of 14 shops and galleries in two long knotty-pine buildings with shingled roofs. Some are of the ordinary shopping center variety, but a few are special. Check out western sculptor **Bill Bond's gallery,** built around a pecan tree. His beautiful bronzes of cowboys, Indians, and horses have won numerous awards. **El Buzon** carries imported clothes and jewelry from Mexico, India, Cyprus, Paraguay, and other places. And you'll also want to browse a bit in **County Fair Gifts** and the **Hanging Tree,** the latter a gallery featuring works of southwestern artists.

**Old Ingram** is a historic village seven miles west of Kerrville on the banks of the Guadalupe River that was established in 1897. Today craftspeople in copper, wood, clay, and cloth display their wares where once the founder Rev. J. C. W. Ingram ran a general store and post office and other 19th-century merchants plied various trades. There are two blocks of old stone buildings housing art galleries and shops selling handcrafted jewelry, furniture carved from native Texas woods, Indian rug and wall weavings, antiques, Mexican folk art, hand-carved decoys, vintage clothing, old-fashioned homemade chocolates and candies, patchwork quilts, and Peruvian rugs. There's even a blacksmith shop.

Plan your visit around lunch at **Rachel's Table** (tel. 367-4343), owned by Pat Reed and so named because she always liked the name Rachel. It's a charming place with stone and white stucco walls, rough-hewn beams, shuttered windows, and tables covered in calico and adorned with cloth flower arrangements. There are Persian rugs strewn on the stone floors, and many plants thrive in the sunlight. Country antiques complete the couldn't-be-quainter picture. It's very charming.

All the food on Rachel's Table is home-cooked, healthy, and delicious. There are hearty homemade soups like spicy Texas bean and Portuguese sausage and cabbage ($2 per cup, $3 per bowl), served with homemade corn muffins. Pat cooks up fresh hams and chickens for her sandwiches like chicken salad on whole wheat with homemade cranberry relish ($4.99) and ham with melted Swiss on rye ($4.75). And every day there's a different scrumptious cobbler—peach, blackberry, apple, apricot, or strawberry—with fresh whipped cream ($2.85) for dessert, though a moist, nutty pineapple cake with luscious cream-cheese topping ($2.45) is also tempting.

It's open Tuesday to Saturday from 11:30 a.m. to 2:30 p.m., and on Monday as well in summer.

To get to Old Ingram, go west on Hwy. 27 to Hwy. 39 and follow the signs.

Finally, you might also want to stop in at **Schreiner's,** 1736 Water St. (tel. 896-1212), Charles Schreiner's old general store that has burgeoned over the years into a mini department store. It carries a full line of western wear, hummingbird feeders, hunting supplies, and great kitchenware, along with the more prosaic offerings you'd find in any modern emporium. There's some good browsing, but the real reason to visit is because this is where the Schreiner empire began.

## Classic Showcase

The cars and stars of yesteryear are displayed at this enjoyable little car and wax museum at I-10 and Harper Road, Exit 505 (tel. 895-5655). Classic antique cars are displayed in detailed settings of movies or scenarios they appeared in, peopled by the wax images of stars or other significant principals. Jean Harlow arrives at Hollywood's Clover Club in a classic Brewster; Carole Lombard and Clark Gable are seen at the Paramount lot in a 1948 Lincoln Continental coupe; around a World War II vintage Jeep Generals Eisenhower, Patton, and MacArthur, and Admiral Nimitz compare notes on the European and Pacific theaters; and Henry Ford chats with Dr. George Washington Carver (evidently they were close personal friends) in front of one of Ford's early cars. Other restored cars include a 1932 Model J Duesenberg, a 1938 Lagonda, several Rolls-Royce models, a 1932 Isotta Fraschini coupe roadster made for Rudolph Valentino, a 1924 Bentley that won races at LeMans, a 1935 Aston Martin four-seater, and a 1931 Model A Ford. And additionally depicted in wax are Jackie Gleason and Art Carney, Howard Hughes, Will Rogers, and Jack Benny. Ragtime music helps set an oldtimey mood.

Admission is $2 for adults, $1 for children ages 6 to 11 (under 6, free). The museum is open on Monday and Wednesday to Saturday from 10 a.m. to 5 p.m., on Sunday from noon to 5 p.m.

## The Hill Country Museum

This museum, at 216 Earl Garrett St. (tel. 896-8633), is the turreted Romanesque revival mansion Charles Schreiner built in 1879 and continued adding to through 1897. It was designed by a noted architect of the period, Englishman Alfred Giles. Schreiner brought in expert masons and stone carvers from Germany, imported brass lighting fixtures and a bronze fountain from France, and used ten kinds of wood in the parquet floor. After his death in 1927, a Masonic Lodge was headquartered here and the public library was operated on the lower floor. Today the home has been restored to its 1890s appearance and refurnished in period style. A visit provides the opportunity to learn a bit about the life of this very influential Hill Country pioneer. Upstairs, in period display cases from Schreiner's original general store are pioneer artifacts—clothing, Fiesta costumes, Civil War memorabilia, china and pottery, Indian arrowheads, duck rifles, etc.

It's open for viewing Monday to Saturday from 10 a.m. to noon and 2 to 4:30 p.m. Adults pay $2; children 12 and under, $1; preschoolers are admitted free. Call before you go; the museum sometimes closes unexpectedly.

**NIGHTLIFE:** The **Long Branch Dance Hall**, Harper Road, just south of I-10 (tel. 895-3488), is a big barn of a place featuring live country music Wednesday, Friday, and Saturday nights. It's an authentic redneck beer and dance place where you can let loose and have a good time. Bring the kids if you want, especially on Saturday night; the local ranchers do.

**Crider's Dance Hall**, Hwy. 39 in nearby Hunt, about 16 miles west of Kerrville (no phone), offers dancing under the stars by the Guadalupe River. There's live music—about three country bands a night—and a rodeo show precedes Saturday night's music and dance. Notice the dinosaur tracks (they're real) in the limestone rock behind the dance area. Open in summer only.

At the scenic point where the Johnson Creek and the Guadalupe River meet in Ingram, on Hwy. 39, the **Hill Country Arts Foundation** (tel. 367-5121) has an open-air amphitheater overlooking the water. May through August they put on about five plays; typical productions are *Carousel, The Odd Couple, Our Town, Godspell,* and *The Sound of Music.* There's also an indoor theater where they occasionally do plays the rest of the year. A lovely gift shop and art gallery are on the premises, and the grounds are beautiful—very conducive to a pretheater picnic on the grass. Tickets are about $7 for adults, $4 for children under 12.

In addition to the above, check out nightlife options mentioned above in descriptions of hotels and ranches, and if you're here in March remember the classical concert series (see "Annual Events").

# Chapter IX

# AUSTIN

1. **Austin Basics**
2. **Where to Stay**
3. **Where to Eat**
4. **What to See and Do**
5. **Austin Nights**

AUSTIN WAS A REMOTE frontier village called Waterloo, populated by about four white families and thousands of Indians, when the vice-president of the Republic of Texas, Mirabeau Bonaparte Lamar, came here to hunt in 1838. After bagging a buffalo (no difficult feat, the area was teeming with them), Lamar announced to his hunting buddies, "Gentlemen, this should be the seat of the future Empire." The next year, when he was elected president of the Republic, Lamar exerted influence on his commissioners to select the city, renaming it Austin, as the new seat of Texas government. It wasn't hard to work up enthusiasm for this beautiful area. Even the commissioners waxed poetic, reporting that "the imagination of even the romantic will not be disappointed on viewing the valley of the Colorado, and the fertile and gracefully undulating woodlands and luxuriant prairies at a distance from it. The most skeptical will not doubt its healthiness, and the citizen's bosom must swell with honest pride when, standing in the portico of the capitol of his country, he looks abroad upon a region worthy of being the home of the brave and free." There was ample reason at the time to "doubt the healthiness" of the present capital, Houston, a mosquito-infested swampland where yellow fever and cholera were epidemic. On the other hand, remote Austin was more vulnerable to Indian attack. One early resident lamented, "The Indians are stalking the streets at night with impunity . . . and occasionally they knock over a poor fellow and take his hair."

Nevertheless, in 1839 Lamar and his cabinet arrived with 50 wagons full of government documents and paperwork (government archives accumulated quickly even then) and was welcomed with a 21-gun salute. Edwin Waller laid out the town, put lots up for sale, and became the city's first mayor. By 1840 Austin had almost 1,000 citizens, two newspapers, and a bogus French count in residence representing King Louis Phillipe (France was the first European power to recognize the new nation).

The first capitol building was protected from Indian marauders by an eight-foot stockade. But they weren't the only menace. In 1841, when Sam Houston was reelected for a second term as president of Texas, he cited the danger of Mexican invasion as reason to move the government back to his namesake city. Austin was determined, however, to keep those 50 wagon-

loads of archives (probably double the amount by that time). Houston sent a
secret force of Texas Rangers to retrieve them, but Austin vigilantes over-
took the expedition and brought the archives back. By 1844 the government
was once again in Austin—politicians and papers alike. Soon after, Texas became part of the United States and Austin was officially designated the state
capital. The new stability led to the construction of substantial government
buildings. Governor Elisha Marshall Pease led the procession to a new capitol building (not the present one) on his inauguration day in 1853, and in 1856
he was the first resident of the still-extant Governor's Mansion.

By 1860 Austin was a flourishing city with a number of distinguished
homes, fine churches, theaters, and other urban amenities. Then came the
Civil War. Austin and all of Travis County voted against secession, but Texas
voters went the other way. Governor Sam Houston was ousted from office
for his failure to support the Confederacy. President Lincoln sent Houston a
letter offering 50,000 federal troops to keep Texas in the Union, but the San
Jacinto veteran tossed it in the fireplace of the mansion library, declaring "I
love Texas too well to bring strife and bloodshed upon her." After the war
Gen. George Armstrong Custer came in with federal troops to preserve
order.

In 1871 the railroad came to Austin, replacing the mail coach as the city's
only connection with the outside world. A week of festivities, balls, and excursions celebrated the event. In 1883 with the opening of the University of
Texas, Austin became the educational hub of the state. The present majestic
Capitol building was completed in 1888, the same year as the luxurious Driskill Hotel. And as the 20th century dawned, the 1890s completion of a dam in
Austin, the world's largest, marked a transition from horsepower to electricity. It was a short-lived transition, however. The dam burst in 1900 during a
flood of the Colorado River and was irretrievably damaged. Mule cars replaced the electric trolleys of which Austin was so proud, and progress was
held in abeyance until 1913 when a new dam was constructed. State government and the University of Texas kept Austin relatively affluent during the
1930s Depression. And the 1950s and 1960s brought an influx of new industries such as electronics, computers, and scientific research. But unlike other
Texas cities, Austin has not sacrificed its natural beauty to urban sprawl.

Austin in the 1980s could still inspire the praise of those early commissioners. Crisscrossed by creeks and the winding Colorado River, centered on
a beautiful lake, surrounded by verdant hills, and dotted with over 100 parks,
it is one of the prettiest cities in Texas. It's also one of the most varied and
cosmopolitan—more liberal, less redneck than the rest. What other Texas
city would tolerate a nude beach called "Hippie Hollow"? It has terrific restaurants (a sizable segment of the population knows its way around a nouvelle cuisine menu), a flourishing art and music scene, worthwhile museums,
and a notable symphony orchestra and ballet company. It's home to the biggest university in the South and the seat of state government. And a mild
climate makes Austin the perfect setting for any number of resort activities.
Most visitors will agree with traveler Frederick Law Olmsted's 1854 opinion
that it's the "pleasantest place in Texas."

# 1. Austin Basics

**GETTING THERE:** Thirteen major airlines, including American and Southwest, fly into **Robert C. Mueller Municipal Airport,** centrally located at I-35 and
51st Street.

By **car** Austin is just 80 miles from San Antonio via I-35. Dallas is about 200 miles away, also via I-35, and Houston 162 miles via U.S. 290.

Both **Trailways** (tel. 512/467-7676) and **Greyhound** (tel. 512/458-5267) buses connect Austin with most Texas cities and points beyond; terminals are at I-35 and 49th Street and 916 E. Koenig Lane, respectively.

And **Amtrak** (toll free 800/USA-RAIL) offers rail service a few times a week between Austin and Dallas or San Antonio. The station is near downtown at 250 N. Lamar Blvd.

**GETTING ORIENTED:** The **Austin Convention & Visitors Bureau** in the Chamber of Commerce Building at 901 W. Riverside Dr., between 1st Street and Lamar Boulevard (tel. 512/478-0098), can answer all your questions and provide maps, brochures, and calendars of events. They're open weekdays only, from 8:30 a.m. to 5 p.m. You can write to them in advance at P.O. Box 1967, Austin, TX 78767. They also maintain a center at the airport that is open daily from 9 a.m. to 9 p.m. And there's a **State Highway Department Travel Information Bureau** in the Capitol rotunda (tel. 512/475-2028), open daily from 8 a.m. to 5 p.m.

**GETTING AROUND:** Though parking can be a problem, for the most part Austin is a city best navigated by car. Just about every car-rental company is represented. Good rates are offered by **Budget** at 3330 Manor Rd. and the airport (tel. 512/478-6437). Also consider **National Car Rental** at 800 W. 6th St. (tel. 512/474-7277) and the airport (tel. 512/476-6189).

**Capitol Metro** has a comprehensive **bus system,** but you may spend a considerable amount of sightseeing time waiting for buses to arrive. For routing information, call 474-1200 and tell them where you are and where you want to go. Basic fare is 50¢. Transfers are free. Under Capitol Metro's auspices is the **Armadillo Express** (Dillos), an old-fashioned trolley bus that travels along Congress Avenue through the central business district and connects with free parking lots at the City Coliseum and the Capitol complex. You can pick up a map of its exact route at the Convention & Visitors Bureau (also of all Capitol Metro routes). Fare is 25¢, and you can transfer at reduced rates to other Capitol Metro buses. Regular buses run from 5:30 a.m. to midnight Monday to Saturday, 8 a.m. to 7 p.m. on Sunday. Dillos run Monday to Thursday from 6:30 a.m. to 9 p.m., on Friday to midnight, on Saturday from noon to midnight, and not at all on Sunday. Service is very frequent. Look for "Catch a Dillo" signs.

Most hotels provide shuttle service to and from the **airport.** If not you can take a Capitol Metro bus to, or close to, most hotels for 50¢. A taxi between the airport and downtown hotels is about $5.

**Taxis** cost $1 when the meter drops and $1 per mile after that for up to four people boarding and embarking in the same place. If you need one, call Yellow Cab at 472-1111.

**ANNUAL EVENTS:** The third week in January, the **Austin Boat, Sport, and Motorcycle Show** takes place at Palmer Auditorium, Riverside and South 1st Street (tel. 478-9383). Tickets, available at the door, are about $3 for adults, $1 for children 12 and under.

Sometime late in March there's a **Capitol 10,000-Meter Race** (6.2 miles) sponsored by the Austin *American-Statesman.* One of the nation's five largest races, it starts at the Capitol building and winds through the city to an Auditorium Shores finish line. About 20,000 hopefuls enter each year. Call 445-3500 for details.

Late March or early April also brings the **Austin–Travis County Livestock**

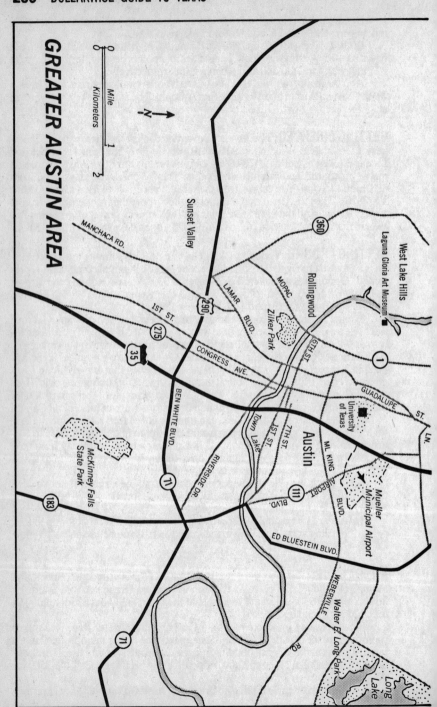

GREATER AUSTIN AREA

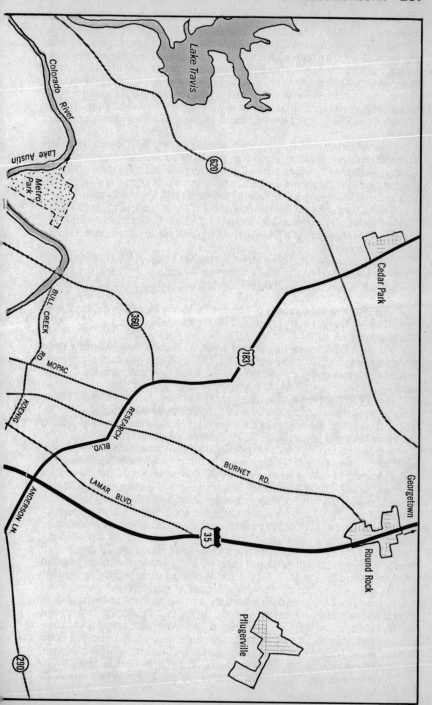

**Show and Rodeo** to the Texas Heritage and Exposition Center, 7311 Decker Lane (tel. 928-3710). The ten-day event includes livestock and agricultural exhibits and judgings, a carnival, cutting horse exhibitions, tractor pulls, a barbecue cookoff, a full carnival with rides and concessions, equestrian events, horse racing, calf scrambles, a non-motorized parade, auctions, and of course, all the rodeo events—bareback riding, calf roping, steer dogging, barrel racing, bull riding, clowns, etc. Following each rodeo performance there's a concert by a major country singer, like Eddy Raven, Moe Bandy, Reba McEntire, Tammy Wynette, Gary Morris, or George Strait. Tickets are available from major ticket outlets.

Two weekends in April there are activities along the 150-mile **Highland Lakes Bluebonnet Trail,** a fabulous opportunity to see the magnificent Hill Country blanketed by wildflowers while enjoying arts and crafts shows, fiddlers' contests, chili and barbecue cookoffs, and other events along the way. For details and a self-guided map, contact the Convention & Visitors Bureau.

**The Legends of Golf Tournament** takes place at the end of April on the Onion Creek Golf Course on I-35 South (tel. 282-4430). Tickets to events are in the $5 to $15 range. Top golf pros compete for $500,000 in prize money. Call for ticket information.

In early May the **Old Pecan Street Spring Art Festival** (tel. 472-4864) takes place on East 6th Street between Congress Avenue and Red River Street. There are street performers, food booths, arts and crafts booths, and children's events.

The first or second Sunday of May the **O. Henry Pun-Off** is held at 2 p.m. on the lawn of the O. Henry Home and Museum, 409 E. 5th St. (tel. 472-1903). Admission is free.

May also brings another rodeo, the **PRCA–Travis County Sheriff's Posse Rodeo** at the Sheriff's Posse Arena on U.S. 183 South (tel. 243-2026). It's a great rodeo, and it kicks off the Austin rodeo season; after it there is a small rodeo somewhere in the county almost every weekend all summer long.

**Fiesta Laguna Gloria,** the third weekend in May, features about 250 arts and crafts booths at the Laguna Gloria Art Museum, 3809 W. 35th St. (tel. 458-8191). Also ethnic foods, children's activities, entertainment, and an auction. Admission is about $5 for adults, $2 for children, payable at the gate.

**July Fourth** is celebrated with a fireworks display over the lake at Auditorium Shores, a free concert by the Austin Symphony, and the **Willie Nelson Picnic,** a big, exciting shindig starring not only Willie but a host of other major stars like Neil Young, David Allan Coe, Faron Young, and Asleep at the Wheel; it varies from year to year of course, as does the location. Call 443-7037 for details. Gates open at 10 a.m. and the concert begins at noon and ends after sunset with fireworks. Tickets are about $20 per person. Call as far in advance as possible for ticket information.

The August **Austin Aqua Festival** is a two-week event (usually the first two weeks of the month) with land and water parades, land and water events, and ethnic nights on the shores of Town Lake. It includes yacht regattas, gymnastic events, an auction, beauty pageants, horseshoe pitching, raft races, swim meets, tennis tournaments, fishing contests, waterski contests, and fireworks. A festival queen and princesses are chosen. Ethnic fest nights include food and music of Czechoslovakia, Germany, Mexico, etc. And there's quite a lot of big-name entertainment. In past years western night concerts have starred Eddy Raven, Tanya Tucker, Charly McClain, the Gatlin Brothers, and Gary Morris. Some events require tickets. For information, call 472-5664 or 472-5699.

On **Halloween** night tens of thousands of costumed revelers jam 6th Street. It's quite a show.

The fall season also brings **UT football games** at Longhorn Stadium. The Longhorns are consistently ranked in the top 20 among college teams, and about 80,000 people attend each home game. If UT wins, the tower is lit up bright orange. Call 471-3333 for information on games, 477-6060 to charge tickets.

**Christmas** is celebrated with the lighting of one of Austin's moonlight towers (billed as "the world's largest man-made Christmas tree") in Zilker Park, usually the first Sunday of the month. Downtown Republic Square becomes a Victorian fairy tale for most of December—a miniature village with toy trains, teddy bears, music, and a Christmas pageant performed nightly. Trees along beautiful Town Lake are also lit for the holiday season, as are those in the Austin Garden Center. The Garden Center offers complimentary hot chocolate and cookies to Christmas-season visitors, has special displays of Christmas trees and poinsettias, sells wreaths and handmade ornaments, and plays Christmas music. Finally, there's the **Armadillo Christmas Bazaar** at Willie Nelson's Austin Opera House, 200 Academy Dr. (tel. 443-7037), a colorful mart of handmade and imported items; shopping is enhanced by live music from Austin's best bands.

For details on any of the above events, and to find out what else will be happening during your stay, call 478-0098.

## 2. Where to Stay

Like most other cities in Texas, Austin is overbuilt, hotelwise. Generally, a room is easy to come by at the last minute—except perhaps during football season in the fall when fans descend on the town. And during the occasional vast convention.

The rather new (1985) **Waller Creek Plaza**, 500 N. I-35, at 5th Street, Austin, TX 78701 (tel. 512/480-8181, or toll free 800/235-8181), is a delight—an expression of the excellent taste and ingenuity of its owners Lloyd and Barbara Hayes and their daughter, Candy. Throughout, it's a personal expression rather than a corporate creation. The exquisite lobby has Portuguese rose marble floors strewn with Chinese rugs, Florentine marble walls, and sofas upholstered in peach and silver raw silk. Rooms are luxuriously residential in feel, with silk-look wall coverings, Drexel Heritage mahogany furniture of 18th-century Italian design, and corniced drapes and bedspreads in pretty cotton chintz fabrics. They're decorated in charming color schemes like soft green and apricot, and they're equipped with dressing room areas, desks, alarm clocks, AM/FM radios, and armoire-concealed cable color TVs with movie channels and other special stations. Some rooms have sofas and comfy armchairs with hassocks. All offer pleasing views of the Capitol, Waller Creek (it meanders through the property), or the atrium, and suites have oversize whirlpool tubs with large one-way windows; while you soak at leisure you enjoy a spectacular view of the Capitol, but don't become one. Floor-to-ceiling windows at each end of the hallways also offer stunning vistas.

The hotel's main dining room is Austin's, a Scottish-decor eatery with plaid carpeting, red leather booths and chairs, and Halaphane lamps overhead. A wall of windows overlooks Waller Creek. The menu, however, does not offer finnan haddie and haggis but American/continental fare.

Picture windows facing the creek are also a feature of the Mezzanine Bar, a stunning lounge furnished with a copper-topped Portuguese marble bar, Italian-tapestry banquettes, French imperial-design chairs, mauve velvet sofas, and an 18th-century Scottish armoire. Piano-bar entertainment is featured from 4:30 p.m. to 2 a.m. daily in this serene setting, along with cocktails and light fare, like raw oysters.

Breakfast and high tea are served in the tenth-floor atrium, ascending seven stories to a skylight ceiling. Room balconies facing the atrium (rooms are on the 10th to 17th floors only; lower floors contain parking space) are festooned with tropical plantings, ferns, and bougainvillea. The room's centerpiece is an Italian fountain complete with ponies, doves, and a cupid, and tables are interspersed with ficus trees. On the 18th floor is Lloyd's of Austin, a jungle-theme nightclub with an exquisite leopardskin-pattern carpet, a zebrawood bar, lush greenery, and a 19th-century Chinese tapestry that somehow harmonizes. Windows all around offer superb views of Austin. Nightly, a trio provides mellow music for dancing.

Guests have use of a beautiful health club with top-of-the-line David equipment, a TV monitor for aerobics tapes, steam, shower, massage, tanning beds, an immense whirlpool, locker rooms, and a bar serving fresh-squeezed juices and other healthful fare. Workout clothing is available. There's a small outdoor pool with a waterfall, deck, and outdoor whirlpool. And enhancing the beauty of the property is Waller Creek itself and rock grotto landscaping with five waterfalls.

Rates are $95 to $105 single, $110 to $120 double, $12 per extra person (children under 18, free). Rooms with king-size beds are $5 additional. The weekend rate (Friday, Saturday, and Sunday night for up to four people) is $80 per night. Valet and self-parking cost $5 a night, and facilities for the disabled are available.

Since its 1886 opening the **Driskill Hotel,** 604 Brazos St., Austin, TX 78701 (tel. 512/474-5911, or toll free 800/228-0808), has served as the state's unofficial capitol—a center of political activity and haunt of visiting legislators and lobbyists. In the late 19th century there were numerous stories of deals here involving the supply of liquor, girls, and gifts. The first gubernatorial ball, for Gov. Sul Ross in 1887, was one of many to follow in the lavish Crystal Ballroom. And more recently Lyndon B. Johnson made the Driskill his headquarters while awaiting election returns, first as JFK's running mate, later in his presidential race against Barry Goldwater. The original five-story Romanesque revival structure, supplemented in 1930 by a 12-story tower, was created before the State Capitol building by cattle baron and supplier of beef to the Confederate Army, Col. Jesse Lincoln Driskill. A life-size oil painting of him hangs in the lobby. In the latter part of the 19th century the Driskill was the finest hotel in the Southwest, offering gaslight, steam heat, mineral water in the taps, and a push-button call system that would bring a bellman to a guest's room.

A $4-million facelift in 1983 has restored much of this historic hostelry's turn-of-the-century grandeur. The traditional entrance, the largest arched doorway in Texas, was reopened, and the colonnade once again became the main lobby. Reaffirming its roots to cattle trail days, the Driskill commissioned a 4,000-pound bronze sculpture from Texas artist Barvo Walker to highlight the lobby bar area; called *The Widow Maker,* it depicts two cowboys on horseback, one in a frantic effort to save the other whose foot is caught in the stirrup and is in danger of being dragged to death. Original archways and balconies that had been obscured by previous renovations were revealed in this renovation, and the lobby was recarpeted in colors that were popular in the 1880s—turkey-red and spinach-green. The upper mezzanine's 35 columns were marbelized by Britisher Malcolm Robson, who has done similar work at Buckingham Palace and the Houses of Parliament.

Rooms at the hotel have been charmingly redecorated in traditional styles and delightful color schemes—some have pale-green walls with a leaf frieze, moss-green cotton chintz curtains with a pink-rose design, forest-green velvet-upholstered armchairs, and pink Laura Ashley–like fabric bedspreads. Others utilize a beige/turquoise/sienna scheme. All are equipped with desks, mahogany-topped dressers, cable color TVs with HBO movies, AM/FM clock radios, and amenities baskets of fine toiletries in the bath. Rooms in the original five-story section are the most attractive, with 14 foot ceilings, and in some cases, immense baths. Ask for them when you reserve. For $15 additional per night, guests can enjoy Driskill Preferred Service; it includes extras like nightly bed turndown with champagne and chocolate-dipped strawberries the first night (milk and chocolate-chip cookies thereafter) and daily newspaper delivery.

There's a very elegant dining room here with Louis XV–style chairs upholstered in ecru velvet at peach-linen-clothed tables lit at night by silver-based frosted-glass candle lamps. Exquisite art nouveau lamps, painted mirror friezes, and shaded wall sconces contribute to the room's luxurious ambience, as does classical background music. Dinner here might start off with an appetizer of baked brie with slivered almonds served with apples and French bread ($6.95) or a wilted spinach salad with hot bacon dressing ($3.95). Classic gourmet entrees include grilled New York sirloin served with a creamy cracked peppercorn sauce ($17.95), baked red snapper with a creamed shrimp and crabmeat sauce ($15.75), and roast duck glazed with fresh fruit and orange liqueur ($16.25). All entrees are served with potato and fresh vegetables. At lunch you can order simpler fare, such as a chicken salad sandwich ($5.25) and a hot-fudge sundae ($3.25).

Another facility is the mezzanine-level Lobby Bar, a popular meeting place of senators and congresspeople from the Capitol. It's lovely to sink into a tufted-leather sofa here and enjoy the piano-bar entertainment offered from 5 to 7 p.m. and 9 p.m. to midnight. In addition to cocktails, light fare (nachos, sandwiches, and raw oysters on the halfshell) is available.

Additional amenities include complimentary transport to/from the airport, a gift shop, a New Mexico art gallery, a top-of-the-line men's clothing store, an American Airlines ticket desk, and a concierge to handle all requests. Guests can use the Supreme Court Health Club just across the street for a minimal charge. Valet parking is $6 a night; self-parking, $10.

Rates are $89 for a standard room, $99 for a medium room, $109 for deluxe. An extra person pays $15, and children under 18 stay free. Higher rates are for larger rooms and higher floors. Weekend rates (Friday, Saturday, and Sunday nights) are just $75, single or double.

The 301-room **Austin Marriott,** 6121 I-35, at U.S. 290, Austin, TX 78752 (tel. 512/458-6161, or toll free 800/228-9290), offers a wide range of resort facilities. On the premises are a medium-size pool, sundeck, and whirlpool, served, spring through fall, by the Barefoot Bar specializing in frozen daiquiris, piña coladas, and suchlike. Room service is also available poolside. And complimentary use of the U.S.A. Fitness Center, just a few blocks away, opens up a full complement of spa activities to guests, including a large indoor lap pool, steamroom, sauna, frequent aerobics classes, massage, tanning room, indoor track, weight rooms, even a babysitting service. The hotel is also within two minutes of Austin's largest shopping mall.

At Diamond Lil's Dining Emporium, a Gay '90s setting with etched-glass windows and gaslight-style chandeliers, breakfast, lunch, and dinner are served daily. Breakfast and lunch offer a choice of buffets or menu meals. The à la carte lunch menu offers items ranging from taco salad ($4.95), to baked lasagne ($5.25), to a cheeseburger with fries ($5.25). Dinners are a bit more elaborate; you might begin with baked onion soup crusted with melted cheese ($3.25); select an entree of roast prime rib of beef au jus with horseradish sauce ($13.95), served with a fresh vegetable and baked potato; and finish up with deep-dish apple pie topped with Häagen-Dazs ice cream ($2.95). There are also full dinners in the $10 range. The adjoining lounge is a cozy living room-like setting with plush sofas and shaded table lamps. Here an abundant spread of complimentary hors d'oeuvres is offered weekdays at Happy Hour (5 to 8 p.m.), and at night it's a popular dance spot where a DJ plays top-40s tunes and oldies.

Another Marriott eatery is the Café de Vin, a tiny French bistro with an outdoor section of umbrella tables. It features premium wines by the glass along with light fare like cheeses, croissant sandwiches, and fresh fruit platters.

Rooms are attractively decorated in rose/pink/turquoise color schemes, with pretty Oriental prints adorning beige-papered walls. Handsome walnut furnishings in traditional styles include a table and two chairs in each room. And among the amenities are cable color TV with HBO and Spectravision movies, digital AM/FM alarm clock radios, and full-length mirrors.

There's a gift shop off the lobby that also sells liquor, sundries, and resort clothing. Complimentary transport is offered to and from the airport. Parking is free.

Rates are $105 single, $120 double, $15 for an extra person (children under 12, free). Weekend rates—Friday, Saturday, and Sunday nights—are about $85, single or double.

Shortly after press time a brand-new Marriott is scheduled to open in Austin, this one boasting an even more convenient location at I-35 and 11th Street. That puts guests within easy walking distance of the Capitol complex. Call the toll-free number above for details.

Built in 1924, the 16-story **Stephen F. Austin Hotel,** 701 Congress Ave., Austin, TX 78701 (tel. 512/476-1061, or toll free 800/531-5048), is an elegant little hostelry in the center of town. A handsome colonnaded façade provides access to an old-world interior, the Caen stone-walled lobby dominated by a stunning floral centerpiece. Here exquisite Oriental rugs define cozy seating areas—plush sofas and high-backed wing chairs of Italian design amid the potted palms. Soft lighting emanates from shaded table lamps and wall sconces. Casement windows are framed by gold-braided rose velour draperies, a grand marble stairway leads to the next level, and a bar nestles in the corner. Afternoon tea (cucumber and tomato sandwiches, pastries, fresh fruits, tartlets, and fresh-baked scones topped with Devonshire cream and strawberry preserves) is served here weekday afternoons. A harpist entertains from 3:30 to 7 p.m., a pianist from 7 to 11 p.m.

Lavish buffets are featured at breakfast, lunch, and Sunday brunch in the charming Austin Garden Room, its trellised walls covered with a very pretty lilac-and-rose-motif fabric that is also used for floor-length tablecloths. The buffet is served from a trellised island at the center of the room. An à la carte menu is also available offering items ranging from a classic salade niçoise ($7.25) to a Reuben sandwich ($7.25), to more serious entrees like veal piccata with marsala and mushrooms ($15.25).

Both lunch and dinner are served in the lavish Remington Room, furnished with plush horseshoe-shaped sienna booths and tapestry-covered banquettes at white-linened, flower-bedecked tables. The room is softly lit by small shaded brass lamps and shaded crystal-ornamented sconces. Etched-glass partitions and planters of greenery add to the room's loveliness. A typical dinner here might include an hors d'oeuvre of fresh scallops and watercress mousseline in buerre blanc ($10.25) followed by an entree of swordfish with ginger and orange sauce ($17.25). It's the kind of place you might opt for a post-entree salad course—perhaps watercress with warm slices of goat cheese ($3.95). And for dessert there are hot soufflés like chocolate and Grand Marnier ($7.25). Luncheon entrees are in the $6 to $12 range for the most part.

Both the hallways and rooms are very residential in feel. The latter are individually decorated, some in art deco style. A typical accommodation might utilize a color scheme like peach/moss green/forest green and have a canopied brass bed with floral chintz spread and throw pillows, white louver-door closets, wicker furnishings, a burgundy velvet sofa, and walls hung with botanical prints. In other words, they're just lovely. All rooms are equipped with cable color TVs concealed in armoires, shoeshine apparatus, AM/FM clock radios, live plants, desks, and fancy toiletries in the bath. Some have wet bars. Guests enjoy the services of a can-do-anything concierge (service is very much highlighted at the Austin), nightly turndown with Godiva chocolates, 24-hour room service, complimentary use of the nearby Supreme Court Health Spa, and complimentary transport to/from the airport. Parking is $5 a night.

Rates are $95 to $125 single, $110 to $135 double, $15 for an extra person (under 12, free). Weekend rates are considerably reduced, and no-smoking accommodations are available.

**The Brook House,** 609 W. 33rd St., just west of Guadalupe Street, Austin, TX 78705 (tel. 512/459-0534), is an exceptionally lovely bed-and-breakfast hostelry run by Englishman David Fullbrook and his American wife, Gwen. Their neat-as-a-pin, white-trimmed gray wood-frame house, fronted by a porch with white wicker furnishings, is charming. Potpourri-scented public areas have dark pine floors strewn with Dhurrie rugs and ten-foot ceilings, some of them white wood beamed in dark pine. Breakfast—fresh-baked croissants (cinnamon/ sugar, strawberry/cream cheese, or apricot/pecan) or blueberry muffins, a rich blend of coffee, dry cereals, orange juice, and fresh fruits—is served in your room or at a turn-of-the-century pickled oak table set with Royal Doulton china. A cozy living room has a sofa and armchairs in front of a working fireplace and Salem-stenciled white walls. There are three guest bedrooms.

The sunny Blue Room has its own porch under the shade of an oak tree. Furnished in Colonial pine pieces, including a double bed, it has pretty floral-print wallpaper, three large windows, and a windowed door. A moss-green carpet provides the theme of the Green Room, its floral-print wallpaper hung with framed pencil drawings of Sturbridge Village. The Green Room bed is a queen-size four-poster mahogany with tobacco leaf and rice motif; it's spread is a Laura Ashley–like cotton chintz strewn with ruffled and eyelet pillows. There's a small sofa, and shelves of knickknacks add to the general feeling of hominess. The Rose Room is furnished in antique oak and pine pieces. It has twin beds with pink-flowered Wedgwood-blue comforters and blush beige wallpaper with a border of pink roses. Live plants are a nice touch.

The Blue and Rose Rooms share a bath, and the Green Room has a large private facility of its own. All baths are supplied with Crabtree & Evelyn soaps, lotions, and bath cubes, and towels are rolled in wicker baskets. You'll also find a selection of books and magazines in your room, and, upon check-in, fresh flowers and gourmet chocolates. The Fullbrooks greet arriving guests with coffee and shortbread. And guests are free to put up tea or coffee in the kitchen throughout the day or use the phone and TV in the living room. "You can make yourself right at home," says Gwen. The Brook House is the B&B one always hopes to find when traveling. Its interior decor is aesthetically impeccable, and the Fullbrooks are hospitable and charming. You'll enjoy getting to know them.

Rates are $50 single, $55 double for the Rose or Blue Rooms; $60 single, $65 double for the Green Room. Reduced rates are offered for stays of a week or longer.

**The Holiday Inn Town Lake,** 20 N. I-35, at the Town Lake exit on the north access road, Austin, TX 78701 (tel. 512/472-8211, or toll free 800/HOLIDAY), consists of an original circular tower overlooking the Capitol, and a newer tower, added in 1985 and overlooking the lake. The original tower was totally renovated in 1985, so both sections are new and spiffy looking. Together the towers comprise 321 rooms, all of them double doubles or king-size. They're smartly decorated in low-key taupe/gray/sienna color schemes and equipped with desks, cable color TVs with movie and other special channels, digital alarm clocks, AM/FM radios, and full-length mirrors. On-premises facilities include a medium-size pool and lake-view sundeck, a small exercise room, a whirlpool, and saunas for men and women. There's an elegant restaurant called the Pecan Tree on the lobby floor specializing in Texas fare such as chicken-fried steak, fajitas, and ribs. Also on this floor is Pistachio's, a comfortable lounge offering live music for dancing on weekends, a large-screen TV for sporting events, and occasional other entertainments ranging from magicians to old movies. A sizable Happy Hour buffet is served at Pistachio's on weekday afternoons. Other pluses: a 12-mile path around the lake, which joggers can enter directly from the hotel, free fresh fruit at the registration desk after your run, and homemade pizza available from room service till midnight to give you a reason for tomorrow's run. Complimentary transport to/from the airport is provided. Parking is free. No-smoking rooms and facilities for the disabled are also offered.

Rates are just $55 single, $65 double, $8 per extra person, free for children under 18. The weekend rate is $55 for up to four people.

The very well-located, four-story **Ramada Inn–Capitol,** 300 E. 11th St., at San Jacinto, Austin, TX 78701 (tel. 512/476-7151, or toll free 800/2-RAMADA), is an excellent choice in the low/moderate price category. A well-run property just a block from the Capitol complex, it has 146 clean and attractive rooms decorated in shades of brown and sienna with polished cotton bedspreads. Cream-colored walls are hung with watercolors of turn-of-the-century Austin. All rooms are equipped with cable color TVs, some housed in oak armoires and all with movie channels and other special stations. Some rooms also have AM/FM radios and/or clocks. Facilities include a nice-size outdoor pool and sundeck (room service is available out here), and a sunny, plant-filled restaurant serving reasonably priced meals. Courtesy transport to/from the airport is offered, valet parking is free, and local phone calls cost only 35¢.

Rates are $52 to $54 single, $59 to $61 double, $7 for an extra person (under 18, free). Weekend rates, subject to availability, are $40 single, $45 double on Friday, Saturday, and Sunday nights. There are also very handsome suites for $115 and up.

In about the same price bracket are four very acceptable **La Quinta Motor Inns,** at 7100 I-35 North, St. Johns Exit, Austin, TX 78752 (tel. 512/452-9401); near Highland Mall at 5812 I-35 North, at the Hwy. 290 East exit, Austin, TX 78751 (tel. 512/459-4381); at 1603 E. Oltorf St., off I-35, Austin, TX 78741 (tel. 512/447-6661); and at 4200 I-35 South, at the Ben White Boulevard exit, Austin, TX 78745 (tel. 512/443-1774). All charge about $47 to $52 single, $53 to $58 double, $5 for an additional person (18 and under, free). The nationwide toll-free number is 800/531-5900. See Chapter I for details on this fine hotel chain.

There are also two **Motel 6** locations, at 2707 I-35 South, between Woodward and Oltdorf Streets, Austin, TX 78741 (tel. 512/444-4842), and 9420 I-35 North, at Rundberg Lane, Austin, TX 78753 (tel. 512/836-0714). The former is a more convenient location. Once again, details are in Chapter I.

## 3. Where to Eat

Some of the California-trendiest restaurants in Texas are found in Austin. It's one of the few places in the state where a sizable part of the population cares about things like sun-dried tomatoes, radicchio, and shitake mushrooms. You're in for some innovative and exciting meals.

Owners Peggy and Ron Weiss and Jeff Weinberger created **Jeffrey's,** 1204

W. Lynn (tel. 477-5584), in 1975, converting a 1930s mom-and-pop grocery store in an unfashionable part of town into a charming country-style restaurant. Now over a decade later they've attracted rave notices from such major publications as *Money, Ultra,* and *Esquire,* and the area has become chic because of their presence. The trio of UT-Austin buddies lived abroad after graduation, cultivating an interest in fine continental cuisine. And Peggy, originally from Louisiana, had a good background in Créole cookery. They decided their old college town was ready for serious food. "What we offer," says Ron Weiss, "is an evolutionary cuisine—more of a fluid process than a set standard way of doing things." Thus the menu changes nightly, in order to make use of seasonal and market specialties and to allow optimum creative expression to chef Raymond Tatum. What the varied and eclectic dishes have in common is a subtle orchestration of spicing and seasonings to enhance the freshest and highest-quality meats, fish, vegetables, and fruits used in preparation. Fish comes from Gulf Coast waters, Boston (mussels, clams, and softshell crabs), and the West Coast (salmon and swordfish); rabbit and quail are raised to the restaurant's specifications at a Texas farm; and Peggy tends an herb garden and grows edible flowers like nasturtiums for garnishes. The food is beautifully presented too, an artistic as well as a culinary pleasure. A meal at Jeffrey's is akin to the discovery of a new and exquisite color in the spectrum.

Since the menu is ever-changing, you probably won't find items I describe listed when you visit. But it will give you some idea of Jeffrey's offerings. One of the most delicious and subtle things I ever ate here was an appetizer of fresh-poached oyster in soy sauce and fresh lemon juice, garnished with grated daikon radish and seasoned with cayenne ($5.25). It tasted like sushi in heaven. Other fond memories are of a crab ravigote—fresh crabmeat tossed in homemade mayonnaise with red and green bell pepper slivers and a soupçon of garlic; it was garnished with avocado slices and lettuce leaves and served with slices of crisp garlic toast ($6.50). And if you've never tried steak tartare, this is the place to experience it in its highest incarnation—delicately spiced with cayenne, paprika, Dijon mustard and soy sauce, and served with capers, chopped red onion, quail egg, and gherkins ($5.50). Those are all appetizers. Lucky you if redfish sautéed in pecan butter ($17.25) is among the entrees when you visit. Ditto the beef filet in beaujolais sauce ($19.95). Portions are large, by the way, in contradistinction to the usual skimpiness that is so in vogue these days. And entrees include fresh vegetables cooked to al dente perfection; a sprightly salad of red leaf and Boston lettuce, thinly sliced radishes, cucumbers, and cherry tomatoes in a cream-based garlicky vinaigrette seasoned with dill and Dijon mustard; and crusty loaves of delicious French bread (black and white) with butter. Of course, there's a carefully chosen wine list to complement your meal. And for dessert there's usually le succès—layers of baked meringue interspersed with almond butter cream studded with toasted almonds, the whole topped with chocolate butter cream icing ($3.25). Chocolate intemperance, a chocolate-mousse-filled brownie crust ($3.25), ain't bad either.

Jeffrey's interior is charming, but not fancy. In spite of the prices, it's okay to come in jeans, and there's no haughty maître d' or "A" table. You don't come here to be seen, you come to eat. Softly lit, it looks like a candlelit country house. White barnwood walls are hung with the blackboard menu and works of contemporary artists, glossy pumpkin pine tables are adorned with small bouquets of fresh flowers, and wine racks are prominently displayed. White-shuttered, café-curtained windows add to the cozy feel.

Open for dinner only, Monday to Thursday from 6:30 to 10:30 p.m., on Friday and Saturday to 11 p.m. No reservations. Come early to avoid a wait. You can park in the grocery store lot on 13th Street.

If Jeffrey's is beyond your budget, try the slightly less expensive **Clarksville Café**, just next door at 1202 W. Lynn (tel. 474-7279), under the same ownership and offering a similarly innovative and adventurous cuisine. The ambience is a little more casual (you'll see more people in jeans) and the offerings a tad more international in scope. It's a charming two-room setting, with works of local artists displayed on pale-gray walls, wicker-seated chairs at candlelit butcher-block tables, lighting fixture fans suspended from a beamed teal-blue ceiling, and a number of green plants here and there. Desserts and wines are displayed in a glass case, and large bouquets of flowers provide splashes of color. The background music is light jazz.

Chefs Mick Vann and Christopher Shirley own a farm about 25 miles from Austin where they grow vegetables, herbs, and fruit and collect the fresh eggs used in their recipes. Another farmer raises Pharaoh quail and New Zealand rabbits to their specifications. Their menu changes nightly, but it usually includes a renowned Thai hacked chicken appetizer—shredded chicken tossed with peanut butter, ginger, sesame oil, cayenne, and soy sauce, served on a bed of grated cabbage and garnished with julienned green and red peppers and cucumber ($5.50). Two soups are offered nightly—they might be a velvety crab and artichoke bisque, and cream of leek, a rich soup of leeks, garlic, cream, and bacon in chicken stock ($2.75 for a cup, $3.25 for a bowl). Other appetizers might include chiles Tesuque, fresh New Mexico green chiles stuffed with Monterrey jack and cream cheese, beer-battered and deep-fried and served with tomatillo sauce ($5.75); a spicy pâté of duck and rabbit liver flavored with a touch of applejack brandy ($4.95); or boucheron goat cheese and sun-dried tomatoes wrapped in grape leaves and grilled ($6.50). Entree choices are equally eclectic, possibly including fresh-grilled gulf redfish served with garlic/jalapeño mayonnaise ($15.25); lasagne made with fresh garlic pasta, layered with ricotta and mozzarella cheeses, pesto, and porcini mushrooms, and topped with béchamel sauce ($9.75); roast Long Island duckling served with a sauce of shallots, fresh cranberries, madeira, and raspberry vinegar ($13.25), and sautéed boneless chicken breast in a sauce of brandy, garlic, lemon, butter, and Créole mustard ($10.25). Presentations are exquisite and portions hearty. All entrees are served with two fresh vegetables, delicious fresh-baked French and whole-wheat breads and butter, and a three-lettuce salad with red onion, carrot curls, and fresh mushrooms in creamy avocado-based vinaigrette. Homemade ice creams are featured every night for dessert, along with offerings shared over at Jeffrey's like the ultra-rich chocolate intemperance ($3.25). There's a sizable wine list featuring French and California brands, mostly in the $15 to $25 range. Some half dozen good wines are offered by the glass each night, and fresh fruits and juices are used in all bar drinks.

Open for dinner only, Monday to Saturday from 6 to 11 p.m. No reservations; arrive early to avoid a wait.

Superb Basque cuisine is featured at **Costa Vasca**, 3437 Bee Caves Rd., between Walsh Tarlton Lane and Westwood (tel. 327-7460 or 327-7472), the creation of Pamplona-born Ernesto Arduz and his Bostonian wife, Claudia. Ernesto, trained in culinary matters from the age of 15 and practically raised in the kitchen of his grandparents' country restaurant, came to the U.S. about 16 years ago and worked at several prestigious Washington, D.C., bastions of haute cuisine, including the renowned Jockey Club. When Elizabeth Taylor was married to John Warner, Arduz catered many dinners at their Fairfax home. The Arduzes then opened their own restaurant in Brazil, near the Bolivian border where many American oil companies are located, and Texas oilmen convinced them to come to the Lone Star State. They opened Costa Vasca in 1983, and have enjoyed a wide success. Both Lady Bird Johnson and Governor White are enthusiastic patrons.

Costa Vasca has a warm and romantic, though not overly formal, ambience. An alluring display of desserts and aged Basque cheeses is set out on a long table near the entrance. Oak-wainscotted white walls are hung with Spanish travel posters, white-linened tables are softly lit by oil candles, and the pillars along a row of colonnaded archways down the center of the room are hung with plants in baskets. Burgundy carpets and draperies add an elegant note, and Spanish music (singers and guitarists) creates the appropriate mood. Wednesday through Saturday nights a flamenco guitarist entertains.

One of the best times to experience Costa Vasca's cuisine is at Sunday brunch, a $15.95-per-person buffet. It is lavish beyond one's wildest expectations. On my last visit there were appetizers of pâtés (rabbit, pheasant, and seafood), smoked trout and smoked salmon, fried escargots in spicy sauce, marinated quails, cured ham, black sausage, veal tongue cooked with fresh vegetables, gazpacho flavored with fresh basil, French lentil soup with chorizo slices, imported French haricots in extra-virgin olive oil tossed with roasted peppers and crabmeat, a cauliflower and carrot salad, marinated pheasant with roast peppers and onions, salad (fresh endive, spinach, and lettuce), new potatoes with anchovies and black olives, and a salpicon de mariscos (shrimp, monkfish, octopus, and scallops marinated in olive oil with capers, black olives, and roast peppers). In addition, seven entrees were offered: seafood sausage with lobster and oyster sauce; salmon croquettes topped with quail eggs; braised beef cooked with onions, endives, and beer; roast lamb marinated with fresh rosemary, garlic, and lemon; rabbit with roast peppers, tomatoes, ar.d white wine; imported escargots cooked with chorizo, paprika, and tomatoes; and whole suckling pig, marinated in lemon juice, cumin, garlic, and olive oil, and baked with beer. Wild rice, flageolet beans with ham, and potatoes with cream and Spanish sheep cheese were the accompaniments. A wide selection of lush desserts was also displayed, like a gâteau Basque, a double-crust tart filled with pastry cream and raisins, flavored with brandy and lemon.

An à la carte dinner is considerably more expensive; appetizers are in the $4.50 to $7 range, entrees run $10 to $15.95, and desserts, from $3.50. A full lunch, however, can be had for about $15—appetizer, entree, and dessert. All entrees are served with crusty bread and alioli, a delicious homemade mayonnaise flavored with garlic and finely chopped roast pepper. The wine list highlights Spanish wines and offers superb sangría—red or white.

Costa Vasca is open for lunch Tuesday to Friday from 11:30 a.m. to 2:30 p.m., for Sunday brunch from 11:30 a.m. to 3 p.m., for dinner Tuesday to Saturday from 6 to 10:30 p.m. and on Sunday, with a reduced menu, to 9:30 p.m.

The German-owned **Courtyard**, 1205 N. Lamar Blvd. (tel. 476-7095), is an elegant restaurant serving "nouvelle Texas cuisine with dumplings." The restaurant's young and talented chefs, Horst Pfeiffer and Jürgen Koch, both in their 20s, have been studying the culinary arts since the age of 15, as is the European tradition. And Jürgen learned many tricks of the trade from his father, master chef at a well-known Stüttgart restaurant. When owner Gert Rausch decided to open a restaurant in Austin, he called and asked Jürgen's father (his own culinary mentor) to send him a good German chef. He sent Horst, and when business boomed, Horst sent for Jürgen.

The Courtyard is a beautiful restaurant. Its balconied stucco walls lit by lanterns and sconces are designed to resemble exterior façades enclosing a Saltillo-tiled courtyard. Trellised room dividers and numerous plants, both suspended from pillars and potted in large wicker baskets, enhance the al fresco illusion. White-linened tables are beautifully appointed with gray napkins, flickering hurricane lamp candles, and scrolled menus tied with burgundy ribbon. Waiters preparing flambé dishes tableside and wine bottles chilling in silver buckets create the air of sophisticated excitement that certain restaurants evoke. Light jazz is the perfect background music for the setting.

The food is superb—as at Jeffrey's, innovative and beautifully presented. Gert has a Kerrville farmer raising axis venison, wild boar, ducks, quail, rabbits, buffalo, and pheasant for the restaurant. He also owns a wholesale seafood business, from which he supplies the Courtyard with the very best fish.

One way to dine here is to order the $35 prix-fixe meal, a multicourse feast that varies nightly but might be something like this: an appetizer of foie gras with snow pea and chopped walnut salad in oil and balsam vinegar dressing; seafood stew of lobster, salmon, oysters, and shrimp in a shallot-flavored saffron/champagne/cream sauce; a palate-refreshing passionfruit sorbet served on a scalloped orange; an entree of buffalo steak in pecan cream sauce made with game stock and brandy; and a dessert of marble (dark and white chocolate) mousse. Another option is to request a *dégustation* or tasting menu featuring small portions of many items; decide the price range with your waiter. And you can also order à la carte. Once again the menu changes nightly, but there are often delicious salmon dumplings studded with pistachio and served with spinach in a creamy lobster sauce ($5.95) and velvety foie gras made with port wine and garnished with spinach ($8.25). Those are appetizers. Entrees might include double lamb chops with montrachet cheese and thyme ($18.25), wild pheasant in sage sauce ($17.25), and Louisiana redfish in pecan lime butter ($17.25). Delicious breads, flavored with sautéed onion, bacon, pecans, or sunflower seeds, is served with entrees. Crêpes filled with butter pecan ice cream, flambéed tableside in Kahlúa and brandy, and topped with butter/caramel sauce ($6.25 for two), is a recommended dessert. The wine list features French, California, and German vintages, many of them available in half bottles. Sorbets are not automatically served between courses, but you can request them.

The Courtyard is open for dinner only, Monday to Saturday from 6 to 10:30 p.m. Reservations essential.

First-rate Mexican fare (not Tex-Mex) is featured at **Tula,** 608 W. 24th St., at Seton (tel. 473-8852), a popular Austin restaurant with a striking contemporary decor. The interior is spare but colorful, with a beautiful gold and turquoise rug from Tamoaya on a wide-plank pine floor, wicker-seated chairs at navy-blue-clothed tables, and stark-white stucco walls with occasional navy, yellow, and shocking-pink panels. Waiters arrayed in various colored shirts (turquoise, yellow, and pink) are part of the decorative scheme. There's additional seating in a covered open-air courtyard enclosed by large potted plants. And the background music is an interesting mix ranging from mariachi and marimba to Spanish rock.

Everything is made from scratch. This is a good opportunity to try authentic dishes from all areas of Mexico. Botanas (light food you can eat as a snack or appetizer) include queso flameado, melted cheese topped with Mexican sausage ($4.75), and arroz Tula, rice baked with corn kernels, white cheese, and sour cream ($3.75), either dish served in a cast-iron bowl. Among the restaurant's specialties are calabacitas, zucchini filled with shrimp, bell peppers, and chopped tomato, topped with melted cheese ($6.95); deboned chicken breast in a rich mole sauce served with tortillas, rice, and beans ($6.95); and carne asada a la Tampiqueña, Tampico-style char-broiled steak served with guacamole, melted mozzarella laced with poblano pepper strips and fried onion, refried beans, and a flour tortilla filled with cheese ($8.25). There are also Mexican "sandwiches" or tacos filled with Mexican sausage and potatoes ($4.25). At Sunday brunch (11 a.m. to 3 p.m.) try the tacos de barbacoa, steamed beef tacos served with refried beans and rich hot sauce. Tula's guacamole is yummy, with discernable chunks of avocado, and refried beans here are also notably tasty. Pata de conejo, a nonalcoholic after-dinner drink made with milk, coffee, vanilla, sugar, and cinnamon, is served gratis at the end of your meal.

You'll probably be stuffed well before dessert time, but loosen your belt and continue; it's worth it. A choice of creamy flan, delicious crêpes in caramel sauce, chocolate cheesecake, and orange pound cake with orange glaze—all homemade, all $2.50—awaits you. Tula's has a full liquor license, and features exotic house specialty drinks like malinche—a 14-ounce concoction of tequila, fresh grated coconut, lime juice, and crème de cacao ($3.25). There are also nonalcoholic fresh-fruit drinks made with strawberries, cantaloupe, or pineapple.

Open Sunday to Thursday from 11 a.m. to 10 p.m., on Friday and Saturday to 11 p.m. During Happy Hour (weekdays from 2 to 7 p.m., weekends to 6 p.m.) there are free botanas and drink prices are reduced. Reservations suggested at dinner.

**Oasis Cantina del Lago,** 6550 Comanche Trail North, a mile off Ranch Road 620 (tel. 266-2441 or 266-2442), offers a view unequaled almost anywhere but Big Sur, California. It consists of 25 wood-decked balconies terraced into the hillside overlooking beautiful Lake Travis and the verdant, forested hills beyond. The uppermost seating is 500 feet above the water on the High Sierra deck. The whole experience of visiting the Oasis is lovely. The drive here (along Loop 360N to FM 2222W to RR 620W) is gorgeous. And the property itself is delightfully landscaped with flower and rock gardens. The traditional hour to arrive is about 5:30 p.m., so you're comfortably positioned in time to experience the magnificent setting of the sun over Lake Travis. When it finally disappears below the horizon everyone in the restaurant applauds. Though al fresco dining is a big attraction here, if it's a little chilly for sitting outdoors, the Oasis also has a very cozy lodge with a massive stone fireplace, mounted deer heads on the walls, and a high beamed knotty-pine ceiling; you can still enjoy "the view" through picture windows. Monday-night football and other sporting events are aired on a large-screen TV in the lodge.

The fare is Mexican (this is a cantina)—not gourmet but adequate. Order 12-ounce margaritas and share an order of fajita nachos ($7.95) to snack on. Or opt for a whole dinner such as the Oasis—a beef taco, one beef and one cheese enchilada, chili con queso, rice, beans, and guacamole salad ($8.50). There's Blue Bell ice cream for dessert ($2.25) and a tasty flan ($2.85). Another good idea is to come for the all-you-can-eat Sunday brunch served from noon to 3 p.m. You won't catch the sunset, but it's always nice watching sailboats glide across the lake.

Spring through fall the Oasis is open from noon to 10 p.m. Sunday to Thursday, till 11 p.m. on Friday and Saturday; closing is an hour earlier in winter.

After your meal, drive down Comanche Trail from the restaurant; it's one of the most scenic roads in Texas. You'll pass Hippie Hollow, a nude sunbathing area, and reach Windy Point Park, a popular windsurfing beach.

Heaping platters of delicious homemade pasta are a great lure at **Basil's,** 900 W. 10th St., at Lamar Boulevard (tel. 477-5576), in every way a delightful restaurant. Both writer James Michener and Texas Gov. Mark White are habitués. Situated in a 1930s white wood frame house, Basil's offers a home-like setting with bare oak hardwood floors; matte gray walls hung with tasteful gilt-framed paintings, prints, and photographs; and lace-curtained windows framed by burgundy draperies. Several intimate dining areas are connected by graceful archways, and classical music helps set an elegant tone.

Owner/chef Alan Lazurus started out flipping burgers in New York City and developed his culinary skills working in restaurants throughout the Southwest and California. He's had recipes published in *Bon Appetit* and catered many important political functions. Everything is fresh and homemade, and crusty fresh-baked wheat bread and butter are served with your meal. Appetizer options include homemade sausage with marinara sauce and sweet peppers ($4.25), calzoni (pasta pies stuffed with feta cheese and spinach, deep-fried, and served with sour cream and horseradish sauce; $4.50), or on a lighter note, a tasty spinach salad ($3.25). Among Alan's pasta specialties are paglia e fieno, spinach and egg noodles with prosciutto, peas, and mushrooms in a cream sauce ($8.50); carrot pasta stuffed with hazelnuts and cheeses in marinara sauce ($8.25); and a traditional lasagne made with spinach pasta and four cheeses ($8.50). Half portions of pasta dishes are available with other entrees for $5. These might include redfish sautéed with artichokes and gulf lump crabmeat in a creamy mustard sauce ($15.25), poached jumbo shrimp atop a fresh filet of fish with a creamy Gorgonzola cheese sauce ($15.25), and scaloppine of veal sautéed with garlic, lemon, capers, and white wine ($13.25). You'll find fresh-grated parmesan cheese on your table. A small, carefully chosen wine list highlights moderately priced California wines while including the requisite French and Italian selections.

Basil's is open daily from 6 to 10:30 p.m. Reservations suggested.

Housed in an 1870 building, the **Old Pecan Street Café**, 310 E. 6th St., between San Jacinto and Trinity (tel. 478-2491), is alluringly simpático. It has a Greenwich Village ambience—a combination of light jazz music and a decor of bare wood floors, exposed brick and limestone walls, flourishing plants suspended from 12-foot ceilings, and candlelit tables covered in variegated colors and adorned with small flower arrangements. A big bouquet atop the bar further prettifies the room. There's additional seating in the stone-paved courtyard out back, a lush tropical garden under a century-old grape arbor. Occasionally a band or pianist performs in the Trinity Room, upstairs.

The cafe's cuisine is homemade and hearty, topped off by great fresh-baked desserts. At dinner you have the option of a light meal, such as a chef's salad, one that has three cheeses, walnuts, raisins, and alfalfa sprouts in addition to the usual ingredients ($6.95). Or you can go for a full gourmet dinner, like an appetizer of mousse truffle pâté ($5.95), an entree of tenderloin filet in a buttery, tarragon-rich béarnaise sauce ($16.95) or seafood crêpes ($10.25), and a dessert of crêpes filled with almonds and bananas in rum ($3.95) or homemade pumpkin cheesecake ($3.95). All entrees are served with soup or salad and a vegetable. In addition to the regular menu, there are always tempting specials like New Zealand venison ($17.50), redfish and crab in Pernod sauce ($16.25), and grilled game hen ($10.50). The lunch menu highlights quiche, crêpes, salads, and sandwiches, with most offerings in the $6 to $10 range. And the Sunday brunch menu is similar, though it additionally offers a three-egg omelet served with fresh fruit and a glass of Codorniu champagne ($8.50). A wine list highlighting French and California wines is available.

Open Sunday to Thursday from 11 a.m. to midnight, on Friday and Saturday to 2 a.m.

Really good Chinese restaurants are few and far between in Texas, which makes **Chinatown**, 603B Brazos St. (tel. 477-3644), all the more of a find. Housed in a century-old stone building, the restaurant has a modernistic three-level interior, the levels along with white screens serving to create intimate dining areas. Most innovative is the use of concealed spotlamps to project Chinese calligraphic symbols on a taupe wall in lieu of more traditional decorative arts. Adding warmth and counteracting the more spartan interior design elements are soft lighting, an exposed original stone wall, and dark-wood Chinese chairs carved with bird and flower designs at elegantly appointed burgundy-clothed tables. It's all quite impressive, and the several levels allow for a no-smoking section.

The fare ranges from eggrolls and pupu platters to more sophisticated offerings. Opt for the latter. A good beginning is the Chinese chicken salad textured with crispy rice noodles and flavored with vinegar, sugar, sesame jam, and spices ($6 for two). An appetizer of six fried or steamed dumplings ($4.95) is also recommendable. Szechuan specialties include various items cooked yu-hsiang style—shredded with garlic, minced water chestnuts, tree ears, and ginger in a spicy hot-and-sour sauce. Shrimp or scallops prepared this way cost $10.95; beef or chicken, $9.50; eggplant, $8.50. Similarly, you can order chicken, beef, or shrimp kung-pao—marinated in five spicy sauces with hot peppers, and stir-fried with peanuts and diced scallions ($9.50, $10.50, and $10.95, respectively). I also like the crispy whole fresh fish deep-fried and smothered in sweet-and-sour sauce ($13.95), bean curd sliced with country-style vegetables ($7.95), and jalapeño chicken with black bean sauce ($10.95). Lunch entrees are in the $5 to $7 range. There's a late-night menu on Friday and Saturday nights from 11 p.m. to 2:30 a.m., including many interesting noodle dishes. And a tea-time menu offered weekdays from 2:30 to 5:30 p.m. features delicious Chinese snack fare with which you might order exotic drinks á la Trader Vic's. There's valet parking after 6 p.m.

Hours are Monday to Friday for lunch from 11 a.m. to 2:30 p.m., for tea until 5:30 p.m.; dinner is served Monday to Thursday nights from 5 to 10 p.m., till 2:30 a.m. on Friday and Saturday nights. Reservations suggested.

A good and quite reasonably priced Szechuan restaurant, **Taiwan,** 420 W. William Cannon Dr., at Bill Hughes Road in the South Ridge Plaza Shopping Center (tel. 445-0677), is not a fancy place, though pleasant and attractive. White vertical blinds block the uninspiring parking lot view, white walls are decorated with Chinese scrolls and paintings, seating is in comfortable taupe velvet-upholstered oak chairs at bare butcher-block tables, there's brown wall-to-wall carpeting, and a number of plants are placed here and there. Chinese chicken salad ($3.25), subtly and interesting flavored, makes a good precursor to the main course, as do a pungent hot-and-sour soup ($1.25) and an order of eight fried dumplings ($4.25). Among the spicier entree recommendables are a delicious stir-fried boneless lamb with broccoli in a hot sauce ($7.50), the chef's special beef, sliced beef tenderloin lightly flavored with orange in hot sauce ($7.50), shrimp and chicken with hot pepper sauce ($6.50), and whole steamed fish with black bean sauce ($7.75). If you prefer milder fare, try the chicken with walnuts ($6.50), moo shu pork served with four pancakes ($6.25), or shrimp sizzling rice ($7.25). An order of a vegetable dish—spicy eggplant and garlic sauce ($5.25) or snow peas and broccoli in oyster sauce ($5.25)—is a good addition to any meal. At lunch there are full meals—soup, eggroll, entree, and fried rice—for $3.95 to $4.75. Taiwan will alter degree of spiciness as per request and/or leave out MSG in preparation. The restaurant's a little off the beaten track, but worth the drive.

Open Sunday to Thursday from 11:30 a.m. to 10 p.m., on Friday and Saturday till 10:30 p.m.

**Dirty's,** 2808 Guadelupe, at Fruth Street, 1½ blocks above 27th Street (tel. 478-0413), has been an Austin institution since 1926. Owner J. C. Pickens has been here 32 years, the chef for 37, and the carhop, 39. A sign out front, bracketed by Coca-Cola signs, reads "Fountain Service/Martin's Kumbak Place."

That's the real name; the original owner was John Martin, and the word "kumbak" meant "come back." G.I.s nicknamed the place "Dirty's" during World War II. You'll see why. Housed in a tumbledown shack, it's an authentic greasy spoon, with Formica tables, orange vinyl banquettes, ancient Coca-Cola and Budweiser clocks at the counter, and a yellowed print on the wall of Custer's Last Stand courtesy of Anheuser-Busch. The TV is always on, and sometimes the jukebox as well. You can drive up and be served in your car, but the best way to do Dirty's—once you've stepped inside to order and soak up the ambience— is to take your grub to the picnic tables just outside.

What do you eat at Dirty's? A double patty cheeseburger (made with good fresh meat) on a sesame seed bun, with tomato, pickle, and mayo ($2.25), delicious homemade skinny french fries (75¢), and a chocolate malted ($1.25). Dirty's is a big college hangout, but you'll see all kinds chomping burgers here— cowboys, blue-haired old ladies who come by after church, families, even Yuppies. It's a tradition.

Open from 11 a.m. to midnight Tuesday to Sunday.

## 4. What to See and Do

Both the Capitol complex and the University of Texas are exciting attractions. And there's quite a bit more for tourists to explore, including the homes of short story writer O. Henry and the state's most famous woman artist, Elisabet Ney.

**THE CAPITOL COMPLEX:** Plan to spend several hours touring the state Capitol, the Governor's Mansion, and other on-site attractions.

### The State Capitol Building

The 309-foot dome of the Capitol, at 11th and Congress Streets (tel. 463-0063), dominates the Austin skyline, much as the Capitol dome dominates Washington's. This being Texas, the former is seven feet higher than the latter. Begun in 1882 and completed in 1888, it is made almost entirely of Texas materials. Its exterior walls are of pink Texas granite, its interior walls of white Texas limestone. The floor of the Capitol, made from terrazzo quarried in Texas, was put down in 1936 to celebrate the state's centennial, replacing the original clay tile, brick, and wood flooring. Walls are wainscotted with seven native Texas woods—oak, ash, cedar, pine, cherry, walnut, and mahogany. The building itself, however—especially the dome—is strikingly modeled on Washington's Capitol. On some 26 park-like acres, it is shaped in the form of a Greek cross, with a rotunda and dome at the intersection of the main corridors on the first floor. So similar are the two buildings, one has an eerie sense of being in the wrong city, a feeling exacerbated after a nighttime stroll on 6th Street, which is so reminiscent of Washington's Georgetown. This is Austin's fourth Capitol.

Free guided tours of the Rotunda, South Foyer, House of Representatives, Senate, and Governor's Reception Room are given daily every 15 minutes between 8:30 a.m. and 4:30 p.m. There's free two-hour parking in the state visitor parking lots at 11th and Congress and 15th and Congress. The Capitol's main entrance faces south, reflecting Texas's southern heritage.

A beautiful design in the **Rotunda** floor depicts seals of the six countries whose flags have flown over Texas—Spain, France, Mexico, Texas, the U.S., and the Confederacy. A bust of Texas's only woman governor, Miriam A. Ferguson, occupies a pedestal here.

The **South Foyer** floor is embedded with the names of 12 battles fought on Texas soil, with crossed torches representing victory—even above the Alamo. Flanking the archway between the two rooms are statues by Elisabet Ney of

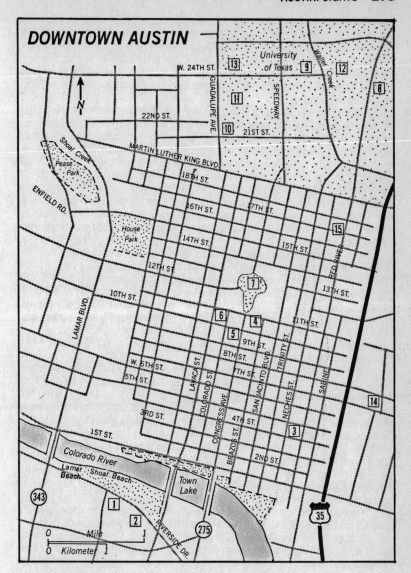

# DOWNTOWN AUSTIN

KEY TO NUMBERED SIGHTS

1. City Coliseum
2. Palmer Auditorium
3. O. Henry Home
4. Old Land Office Building
5. Old Bakery
6. Governor's Mansion
7. State Capitol

8. Lyndon B. Johnson Library and Museum
9. UT Performing Arts Center
10. Harry Ransom Center
11. UT Tower
12. Texas Memorial Museum
13. Littlefield Home
14. French Legation
15. Frank C. Erwin, Jr., Special Events Center

Sam Houston, commander-in-chief during the Texas Revolution, and Stephen F. Austin, the "Father of Texas." There are also two large paintings by W. H. Huddle, one *The Surrender of Santa Anna,* depicting the morning following the Battle of San Jacinto, the other a portrait of Davy Crockett in deerskin jacket, coonskin cap in hand. A tourist information center is located in this foyer, and copies of the 1861 Ordinance of Secession and the Texas Declaration of Independence are on display.

The **Senate** is headquarters for the state's 31 senators, who meet beginning in January of odd-numbered years for 140 days, and during the interim whenever the governor calls a special session. Each senator represents 500,000 Texans and serves for four years. The Senate's presiding officer is called the lieutenant-governor. Two impressive turn-of-the-century paintings by H. A. McArdle grace the Senate Chamber walls: *Dawn of the Alamo,* depicting the last day of that fateful battle, and *The Battle of San Jacinto,* showing the 18-minute skirmish during which Sam Houston and his army won the war for independence. The desks in this room are originals, though microphones have been placed where there were originally inkwells. Senators are allowed the right of filibuster (the record set here is 44 hours).

In the **House of Representatives,** 150 members meet concurrently with the Senate. House members serve two-year terms, and the presiding officer is the speaker of the House. Behind the desk used by the speaker is the original battle flag from San Jacinto. Desks here are also original, but a mechanized voting system has been installed. The chandeliers overhead, weighing 800 pounds each, were originally kerosene and had to be cranked up and down for lighting. Portrait panels show members since the 13th Legislature in 1873.

Visitors can sit in on sessions of the House or Senate; balcony seating is on a first-come, first-served basis.

The **Governor's Reception Room,** in the south wing, is where the governor holds press conferences and signs bills into law. The governor is elected for a four-year term. Here the six flags of Texas are displayed, and most of the furnishings are cherry to match the woodwork. Doors leading off this room are to the governor's and his staff's working offices. The desk currently in use was brought in during the administration of John Connally. On one side of the room is a large Tennessee marble-topped table, a gift to the state from descendants of Davy Crockett. An exquisite mirror on the east wall was a gift from France in 1888. Other notable pieces here are an 18th-century grandfather clock and a portrait of George Washington done by Gilbert Stuart's daughter, Jane, one of many replicas she did of her father's famous portrait.

Not on the tour, but open to public view, is a display on the creation of the Capitol and earlier Texas capitols on the north wing of the third floor.

And every hour on the hour, weather permitting, Capitol Police conduct dome tours leaving from the fourth floor, west wing. Lining the interior of the Rotunda are paintings of governors, provincial governors, and presidents of the Republic of Texas. The dome tour involves a lot of climbing (about 100 steps), but allows you to step outside and enjoy a panoramic 360° view of the city.

## The Governor's Mansion

The oldest building in the Capitol complex, the Governor's Mansion, 1010 Colorado St. (tel. 463-5516), dates to 1854–1856, making it also the fourth-oldest governor's mansion in continuous use in the United States. Governor Elisha Pease and his wife, Lucadia, the first residents of master builder Abner Cook's Greek revival mansion in 1856, deemed it "a pleasant residence and a credit to the taste and liberality of the State." Since that time the only major changes have been a 1914 remodeling, which involved the removal of a servants' wing and the addition of more living space for the governors' families, modern kitchen facilities, and a conservatory. Other than that, alterations largely involved decoration until a $3-million renovation in the years 1979 to 1982 made concessions, for the first time, to modern living. Peeling walls, poor plumbing, and inadequate kitchen space were remedied, and 19th-century American furniture was amassed to augment existing pieces, but basically the effort was toward restoration rather than change. The mansion's colonnaded exterior has been white since Governor Colquitt (1911–1915) decided Texas should have a "White House."

There are numerous anecdotes relating to occupants of the mansion and their families. There have been several children born here, 15 weddings, and a suicide—a love-sick nephew of Gov. Pendleton Murrah (1863–1865) shot himself in an upstairs bedroom, spawning ghost stories for years to come. Sam Houston was in office in 1861 when Texas seceded from the Union. A Union supporter, he was ousted when he refused to sign an oath of loyalty to the Confederacy. During the Civil War the mansion was occupied by Union troops. Its next occupant, the despised pro-Union Texan E. J. Davis, was not reelected after his term but refused to vacate the mansion until he was forced out. And Gov. James Stephen Hogg (1891–1895) drove nails into the banister to keep his sons from sliding down it; the filled holes are still visible today.

Many quality furnishings have been donated as gifts over the years, one of the great benefactors in this regard being James Hogg's daughter, Ima, who gave or loaned numerous fine furnishings and silver pieces up to the time of her death in the late 1970s.

On free tours of the mansion, given every 20 minutes Monday to Friday between 10 and 11:40 a.m., you'll see several rooms.

The cactus-hued **Library,** matched to a paint chip uncovered during restoration, contains a collection of books on Texana. Among its notable furnishings are Stephen F. Austin's Empire walnut desk, a Duncan Phyfe piano stool, an Empire sofa used by the Pease family, and an Elisabet Ney bust of William Jennings Bryan.

The red, white, and blue **State Dining Room** centers on a Sheraton-Regency-style late-19th-century mahogany banquet table set with the official state china and sterling flatware. The 1790 sideboard, a gift from Miss Ima Hogg, is one of the oldest pieces in the house. The set of six Empire side chairs and the Sheraton library table are attributed to Duncan Phyfe.

The **Conservatory,** added in 1914, is used for informal family dining. Its mahogany Empire table and library tables are again Duncan Phyfe pieces, the rug depicts seals of the six flags of Texas and native wildflowers, and cabinets along the walls contain mementoes left by each governor's family.

The **Small Parlor** is notable for its elaborate ceiling cornices and its art and furnishings. The artworks include a painting of Sam Houston that has hung in the mansion since the late 19th century, a Thomas Gainsborough portrait done in 1758, and a *Bluebonnet Landscape* by Julian Onderdonk. The room's handmade rug incorporates Aubusson and Savonnerie patterns.

The **Large Parlor** contains an 1810 Duncan Phyfe sofa, an early-19th-century Hepplewhite mahogany clock, several notable tables, and four oil paintings of Austin scenes by William Henry Huddle, the artist whose paintings of Davy Crockett and San Jacinto grace the Capitol's South Foyer. Chandeliers in both the Small and Large Parlors once hung in the parlor of an Indian sultan.

Many of the furnishings of the first occupants, Governor Pease and his family, are seen in the **Pease Bedroom.** Their portraits are also displayed here.

There's also a **Sam Houston Bedroom** containing San Jacinto Sam's massive four-poster, an Elisabet Ney bust of him, a painted photograph portrait, and a pair of loveseats belonging to the infamous Count de Saligny while he was chargé d'affaires to the Republic of Texas.

The grounds are also included on the tour.

## The Old Land Office Building

Completed in 1857, the Romanesque-style Old Land Office Building, at 11th and Brazos Streets, originally housed maps, deeds, patents, and other state records. It looks like an old German castle, with thick walls and heavy iron doors. Short story writer O. Henry was inspired to set a murder tale in the building (the killer hid the body at the top of the old circular stairway). Today you'll find no hidden bodies, but there are two museums on the premises.

On the first floor is the **Texas Confederate Museum** (tel. 472-2596), run by the Texas Daughters of the Confederacy since 1918. Thousands of relics from Civil War years are here displayed. They include flags of various Confederate companies, soldiers' uniforms and other period clothing, the cane-back chair used by Jefferson Davis, a large statue of Gen. Robert E. Lee, weaponry (guns, swords, cannon balls, bullets from Gettysburg, etc.), surgical instruments, Confederate money, photographs of principals, the last written order of Robert E. Lee, the first baby shoe of a Confederate veteran, flowers from the bier of Robert E. Lee, a necklace made out of a lady's hair, flags, military awards, and more.

Upstairs is the **Daughters of the Republic of Texas Museum** (tel. 477-1822). In the summer of 1891 Hallie Bryan and Betty Ballinger became concerned over the lack of interest Texas evinced in its own history. They formed an organization called the Daughters of the Lone Star Republic, whose motto was "Texas— One and Indivisible." In 1892 they changed to their present name and were subsequently given charge of the Alamo, the Land Office Building, and the French Legation. Exhibits highlight, but are not restricted to, the period 1836–1846. They include a wreath of dyed and natural chicken feathers made by the wife of a San Jacinto veteran, a gavel made from a plank in the floor of Davy Crockett's Tennessee home, portraits of Alamo heroes, a stone from the walls of the Alamo, parts of the Capitol that burned in 1881, replicas of earlier state capitols, Republic of Texas currency, period clothing, weaponry, quilts, and maps. And that's not the half of it.

Both museums are open weekdays only, from 9 a.m. to noon and 1 to 5 p.m. Admission is free, but donations are appreciated.

## The Old Bakery and Emporium

Built in 1876 as a bakery by Swedish immigrant Charles Lundberg, the brick-façaded limestone building at 1006 Congress Ave., between 10th and 11th Streets (tel. 477-5961), remained just that through 1936. Today it's a kind of grandma's house—a senior citizens–run crafts market and tea room. In the back of the store are some tables and chairs where lovely older ladies serve fresh-baked cookies and cakes, sandwiches, and beverages. And on sale are handcrafts made by senior citizens in and around Travis County—rag rugs, homemade jams and relishes, Christmas tree ornaments, wreaths, patchwork quilts, crocheted shawls and blankets, potholders, and the like. Prices are very reasonable; take a cocoa-and-cookies break after touring the Capitol and then do your shopping for next Christmas. The facility also functions as a hospitality center, providing information and brochures on Austin attractions.

It's open weekdays only, from 9 a.m. to 4 p.m., also summer and December Saturdays from 10 a.m. to 3 p.m.

**THE UNIVERSITY OF TEXAS:** As integral a part of the Austin scene as the Capitol and its doings is the famed University of Texas, bounded, more or less, by Guadalupe Streets, I-35, Martin Luther King Boulevard, and 26th Street (tel. 471-1420). It was conceived when Texas was still part of Mexico in 1827, but was not actually established until 1883 when liberal arts and law departments opened their doors to 221 students, eight professors, and a proctor. The UT was designed to be a "university of the first class" open to men and women on an equal basis, not requiring religious qualifications for admission and not offering courses of a sectarian character. It was to a large extent modeled on Thomas Jefferson's University of Virginia. Between 1894 and the present, many departments have been added, some with graduate divisions. There are also affiliate schools such as the Medical Branch (UTMB) in Galveston. In its early years funding was a major problem for the university, but ever since oil was discovered on UT land in 1923 its royalties have contributed greatly to operating expenses. Only Texas would have an oil-endowed university! (You can see Santa Rita No. 1, the first drilling rig to strike oil on UT land, just above 19th Street at San Jacinto Boulevard.)

Today UT is a city within a city with over 50,000 students, a main campus of 321 contiguous acres (and about 1,000 additional acres around town), and 125 major buildings. Approximately 4,000 courses are offered at the university's eight colleges, six schools, and 50 departments. And the current faculty includes 15 members of the National Academy of Sciences, a Pulitzer Prize winner, and two Nobel laureates. Author James Michener maintains an office on campus.

## How to Tour the Campus

I've toured many universities in my years as a travel writer, often wondering as I did so what other line of work I might take up. Not so at UT Austin. Especially not to be missed here is the fascinating Lyndon B. Johnson Presidential Library and Museum. To get to the campus, take I-35 to Martin Luther King Boulevard and look for the Arno Nowotny Building on the southwest corner. A limestone structure with burnt-orange trim, it houses the **Visitor Center** (tel. 471-1420), where changing exhibits are offered and you can get help organizing your campus tour, pick up a map of the campus, and find out anything that will be going on at UT during your Austin stay in the way of speakers, films, special performances, etc. It's open weekdays from 8 a.m. to 5 p.m.; on weekends information is available by phone and at the LBJ Library. Parking is always a problem on campus. You might want to put your car in a garage at Whitis Avenue and 21st Street near many of the buildings you'll want to see. Or you can park free at the LBJ Library lot on Red River Street and take a free shuttle bus around the campus, boarding and debarking at various key points. To find out about athletic events during your stay, call 471-3333. Allow at least four or five hours for your tour. Admission to all museums is free.

## The Lyndon B. Johnson Presidential Library and Museum

An excellent curatorial staff here has created an exciting memorial to the Johnson years that throws light not only on LBJ's life and administration but on his political era, especially the 1960s. Located at 2313 Red River St. (tel. 482-5136), it is open to the public daily from 9 a.m. to 5 p.m. Housed here are 35 million documents, occupying four floors, of Johnson archives. Upon entering, first see the 20-minute orientation film about LBJ's life. This is enhanced by first-floor exhibits on "The Early Years." Lyndon's mother, Rebekah Baines Johnson, contributed so many photographs, scrapbooks, and other memorabilia to this section that one archivist commented, "It's as if she knew from the moment he was born that he was going to be president." If she didn't, Lyndon did, as some of the fascinating, if less than totally flattering biographies of our 36th president reveal. In any case, you'll see myriad photographs, his grade-school report card (all As except for a C in deportment), a letter to his grandmother, etc., and learn about his roots in the Hill Country where residents were beset by poverty and the rigors of frontier life. In other parts of the museum you'll see the chairs in which Johnson and Kosygin sat in 1967, listen to phone recordings of anecdotes about LBJ (told by congressmen, presidential aides, Luci Bird, and others), read the letter Mrs. John F. Kennedy wrote to Johnson after JFK's funeral, and see the missal on which LBJ took the oath of office aboard *Air Force One* after Kennedy's assassination.

Other exhibits include a replica of the "hot line" that transmitted and received messages to and from the Kremlin when LBJ was president, notes for presidential speeches, the 1968 presidential limo, newspaper clippings, political cartoons, intimate family portraits with captions prepared by Lady Bird, Johnson's House and Senate campaign memorabilia, American political memorabilia from George Washington's time to the present, the coat and hat worn by Lady Bird at the 1965 inauguration, secret memos from LBJ advisors on the Vietnam War, and a videotape sampling of LBJ humor.

Special sections of the museum document the Vietnam War, the Great Society (including an Alfred Leslie painting of *13 Americans* the program was designed to help), Lady Bird Johnson's life and contributions, the war on poverty, international affairs during the Johnson years, civil rights, and Johnson's role in the space program. And gifts from heads of state to Johnson and his family—ivory tusks from the president of Cameroon, a gorgeous rug from the Shah of Iran, a ceremonial dagger from the Sultan of Malaysia, a Tang Dynasty sculpture given by Chiang Kai-shek, etc.—in themselves make up an interesting museum. Up on the eighth floor is a replica of the Oval Office used by the president. There's lots more.

As Johnson himself described the museum's contents in his 1971 speech dedicating the library: "It is all here: the story of our time—with the bark off. There is no record of a mistake, nothing critical, ugly, or unpleasant that is not included in the files here . . . in one place for friend and foe to judge, to approve or disapprove."

## Sid Richardson Hall

Located right next to the LBJ Library in Sid Richardson Hall, the **Barker Texas History Center** (tel. 471-1741) contains the most extensive collection of Texana ever assembled, along with holdings on the entire Southwest. This is the building where Michener maintains an office and where he did much research for his book, *Texas*. Collected here are the papers of Moses and Stephen F. Austin, over 120,000 books and periodicals, 2,000 historic Texas newspapers, over 8,000 manuscript and printed maps, and numerous Texas photographs and sound recordings. Most of these are, of course, of interest mainly to serious researchers. But there are also exhibits for tourists—on James Michener's writing of his novel, on Texas music, on women in Texas history, on Texas poster art, the Alamo, etc. You'll also see the desk of Gov. James Stephen Hogg and his over-size chair, the Elisabet Ney casts of her Austin and Houston sculptures, promotion circulars designed to encourage migration to Texas (one calls it the "Garden of America"), a letter from Santa Anna to his Mexican generals in Texas after San Jacinto, and Santa Anna's plan for the assault on the Alamo.

Hours are Monday to Saturday from 8 a.m. to 5 p.m.

In Unit One of Sid Richardson Hall is the **Latin American Collection** (tel. 471-3818), which features changing exhibits such as *Vision of Mexico* highlighting Mexican textiles, paintings, and sculpture.

It is open Monday to Thursday from 9 a.m. to 10 p.m., on Friday to 6 p.m., on Saturday from noon to 5 p.m., and on Sunday from 2 to 10 p.m.

## The U T Performing Arts Center

If you'd like to tour this impressive $41-million, over-4,000-seat entertainment complex, you can arrange to do so by calling 471-2787. Hour-long free tours take you backstage and to props, costume, and scene-painting areas. Details about performances here are in nightlife listings, below. Like Sid Richardson Hall, the Performing Arts Center is close to the LBJ Library, at 23rd Street and East Campus Drive.

## The Texas Memorial Museum

Founded in 1936 for the Texas Centennial, this art deco museum at 2400 Trinity St., next to the Performing Arts Center (tel. 471-1605), covers the fields of "natural and civic history." On the premises are nearly 70,000 animal specimens, 3.5 million fossils, 17,000 ethnographic and historical specimens, and 50,000 rocks, minerals, and gems. There are four floors of exhibit space with displays including walking sticks and canes of Texas governors, gems and minerals, tableaux of birds and animals in the five major geographic regions of Texas, a model of UT in 1885, pre-Columbian pottery of Peru, Navajo sand paintings, firearms, ancient coins, Stone Age skeletons, and a carved stone representing an 1850 treaty between the United States and various Texas Indian tribes. Changing exhibits enhance the permanent collection. A 35-foot-long mosasaur skeleton dominates the Centennial Hall entrance.

Hours are 9 a.m. to 5 p.m. weekdays, 1 to 5 p.m. on Saturday and Sunday.

## The Harry Ransom Center

Over on the other side of campus at 21st and Guadalupe Streets the Harry Ransom Center houses the **Huntington Art Gallery** (tel. 471-7324), after the LBJ Library the most interesting visitor attraction on campus. A notable collection, it encompasses the extremely impressive Michener Collection of 20th-century American Art (about 350 works) and the C. R. Smith Collection highlighting art of the American West in the 19th century. The former includes works by Josef Albers, Tom Wesselmann, William Glackens, Jack Tworkov, Richard Anuszkiewicz, Mark Tobey, Franz Kline, Moses and Raphael Soyer, John Sloan, Stuart Davis, Arthur Dove, Helen Frankenthaler, Ben Shahn, Arshile Gorky, John Marin, and numerous other important artists of our times. The latter features works by Albert Bierstadt, Henry F. Farny, Charles M. Russell, and many other fine artists of this genre. Other holdings include the William J. Battle Collection of plaster casts of Greek and Roman sculpture, a vast print collection ranging from the 15th through the 20th centuries, over 500 works of Latin American art, American decorative arts from the 18th century to the present, and a Gutenberg Bible, one of five complete specimens in the United States. The permanent collection is supplemented by traveling exhibitions ranging from Robert Motherwell graphics to medieval Indian sculpture.

There is also an exciting and extensive program of classic films, films about art, lectures, dramatic productions, and concerts. Be sure to inquire about happenings during your stay.

While you're here, check out the changing photography exhibits (like the works of Lewis Carroll) in the **Humanities Research Center** (tel. 471-9119) on the sixth floor. There's also a permanent display on the early history of photography including the world's first photograph, taken in 1826. Both facilities are open Monday to Saturday from 9 a.m. to 5 p.m. and on Sunday from 1 to 5 p.m. Additional art exhibits are housed in the Art Building at 23rd and San Jacinto Streets.

On the seventh floor of the Harry Ransom Center are an exhibit on Gloria Swanson—costumes, movie stills, etc.; a collection of Republic of Texas porcelain; and paintings of famous authors like Tennessee Williams, C. P. Snow, Shakespeare, Ben Jonson, and Somerset Maugham.

Down on the fourth floor, mystery writer Erle Stanley Gardner's study is re-created, and changing exhibits feature collections from libraries of well-known writers.

## Other Points of Interest

Sites on this side of campus also include the following. The strip of Guadalupe Street between Martin Luther King Boulevard and 26th Street is known as **The Drag,** a popular gathering spot for students, lined with bookstores, boutiques, and eateries.

Six statues and the Littlefield Fountain make up the **Littlefield Memorial Entrance Gate** at 21st Street and University Avenue. The fountain was erected in 1932 in memoriam to the 97 UT students who gave their lives in World War I. The statues are of Texas Sen. John H. Reagan, Texas Gov. James Stephen Hogg, Woodrow Wilson, Robert E. Lee, Confederate Army Gen. Albert Sidney Johnson, and Confederate President Jefferson Davis.

You can tour the **Littlefield Home,** 24th Street and Whitis Avenue (tel. 471-5424). George Washington Littlefield was an early benefactor of UT, a wealthy cattleman and banker who donated hundreds of thousands of dollars to the institution. His brick and sandstone turreted Victorian mansion, built in 1893–1894, is open for touring weekdays from 8 a.m. to noon and 1 and 5 p.m. Its interior wainscotting, plaster friezes, and molded plaster medallions are exquisite, as are the ornate period furnishings.

Also noteworthy is the 606-foot **UT Tower,** its observation deck closed to the public since 1974 when a young man jumped to his death, the ninth suicide in its 50-year history. But an even more tragic event associated with the structure occurred on August 1, 1966, when deranged architectural engineering student Charles Whitman engaged in a shooting spree from the deck, killing 16 people and wounding 32 others. On a less grisly note, the tower clock, with four faces, chimes the quarter hour and a carillonneur plays a ten-minute concert on the tower bells three times a week at 12:50 p.m.

**THE ELISABET NEY MUSEUM:** Located in Austin's historic Hyde Park area, this museum at 304 E. 44th St., at Avenue H (tel. 458-2255), was once the home and studio of one of Texas's most eminent artists. Elisabet Ney was born in Germany in 1833, daughter of a stone carver who made a comfortable living fashioning statuary for churches and cemeteries. She was a liberated woman a century before Simone de Beauvoir penned *The Second Sex.* Iconoclastic even as a child, young Elisabet created her own clothing independent of current styles, and preferred to spend time with her father in his studio rather than in the kitchen with mom learning domestic skills. When at the age of 17 she was refused permission by her parents to study sculpture in Berlin, Ney went on a hunger strike until they relented, agreeing only to the compromise that she begin at age 19 and study in Catholic Munich rather than Protestant Berlin. Her ambitions, which would seem quite normal today, were shocking in her time; there were women artists, but they generally confined themselves (or were confined by the male-dominated art world) to such feminine expressions as painting flowers and miniatures. Ney arrived in Munich in 1852, and after convincing a reluctant academy of art to take her on, she enrolled as the first woman ever in the sculpture department. In 1854, following graduation, she moved to Berlin to study with Germany's most prominent sculptor, Christian Rauch. Once again she defied her parents, who strongly objected to the move. Her training with Rauch was grounded in neoclassicism, the popular art form of the time. Rauch not only influenced her work, but was able to gain her admittance to the Berlin Academy and introduce her to Berlin society. One of her first major works was a bust of philosopher Arthur Schopenhauer, who was impressed despite his well-known contempt for women. The misogynist called her "very beautiful" and "inexpressibly charming" in letters to friends, and to one correspondent wrote, "Perhaps you know the sculptress Ney; if you do not you have lost a great deal." After sculpting Schopenhauer, Ney received commissions from King George V of Hanover and other notables. In 1863 she married her lover since student days, Edmund Montgomery, retaining, in her usual avant-garde fashion, her maiden name. Montgomery was a successful philosopher/physician. They lived for a time on the resort island of Madeira. In 1865 Ney traveled to Italy to sculpt a likeness of Giuseppe Garibaldi, the nation's unifier and liberator. She also did a bust of Baron Otto von Bismarck, chancellor of Prussia and the most powerful man in Germany at the time. And in 1869 she moved into a makeshift studio in the royal palace to sculpt King Ludwig II of Bavaria. However, it is believed her association with so many heads of state somehow resulted in political difficulties, accounting for Ney's and Montgomery's abrupt departure to the United States in 1871. They settled in Thomasville, Georgia, where Elisabet's behavior was considered scandalous. She rode around town wearing bloomers and other outré garments, took an unladylike interest in business affairs, and continued to call herself Miss Ney and Montgomery "my best friend" even when she was obviously pregnant. They were attracted to Texas because the frontier had a large German population and the climate would be beneficial to Montgomery's failing health (he had tuberculosis). They purchased a plantation in Waller County, and for the next 20 years Ney devoted herself to running it and raising her two sons. Arthur, her firstborn, died of diphtheria at the age of 2, but she was passionately devoted to her second child, Lorne. Unfortunately, her preoccupation with him inspired Lorne to rebel, and when, at the age of 20, Lorne married a woman his mother considered beneath him, they became estranged.

Ney's sculpture career was in abeyance until 1890, when she was commissioned to create statues of Sam Houston and Stephen F. Austin for the Texas Pavilion of the 1893 Chicago World's Fair. Both statues are today on view in both the state and national Capitols. The studio on 44th Street is the one she designed and moved into to create these works. She called it Formosa. Here she resumed her artistic career, going on to model busts of many prominent Texas statesmen, of William Jennings Bryan, and, what she considered her masterpiece, of Lady Macbeth.

Ney died in 1907, and in 1908 her Austin studio became one of Texas's earliest art museums. The largest existing collection of her works is housed here, along with photographs of other pieces. The museum is open for self-guided tours Tuesday to Friday from 11 a.m. to 4:30 p.m. and on Saturday and Sunday from 2 to 4:30 p.m. Admission is free, but donations are appreciated. A knowledgeable docent is always on hand to show you around or answer questions.

**THE LAGUNA GLORIA ART MUSEUM:** Clara Driscoll's lakeside Mediterranean-style villa at 3809 W. 35th St., at the end of Old Bull Creek Road (tel. 458-8191), is the setting for one of Texas's most beautiful art museums. Clara Driscoll, born into a wealthy Texas ranching family in 1881, was an all-around gal. A sharpshooter, excellent rider, and expert with a lariat, she once single-handedly captured a group of cattle thieves on the family ranch. But she was more than just a cowgirl. Her education at the finest New York and Paris schools was very cosmopolitan. She spoke Spanish, French, and German, and traveled in Europe and India. She was also a beauty, with dark red hair and creamy skin.

At the age of 22 Clara became a Texas celebrity for her role in saving the Alamo. Herself the granddaughter of two San Jacinto veterans, she bought the property for $75,000 to save it from a hotel syndicate that planned to raze the shrine and build on the site. Later she was reimbursed by the state (which now owns the Alamo and runs it under the auspices of the Daughters of the Republic of Texas).

In her early 20s Clara wrote and published several books. Her comic opera, *Mexicana*, was produced on Broadway in 1906, the same year she married newspaperman Henry Hulme Sevier in New York's St. Patrick's Cathedral. While on their honeymoon in Europe, the young couple conceived the idea of building a home that would eventually become a museum. In 1915 they chose the site at the base of Mount Bonnell, a high mountain bluff overlooking the Colorado River, because it reminded them of Lake Como in Italy. They named their 15-room mansion Laguna Gloria, Spanish for "heavenly lagoon." An enthusiastic gardener, Clara transformed the hillside of rock and wild vegetation into beautifully landscaped Italian gardens surrounded by unspoiled woodlands. The villa stands on the highest of four grassy terraces offering panoramic views of the winding river and distant hills. The formal gardens in the forefront are embellished with a mission bell framed by an arch, a gazebo, birdbath, wishing well, fountain, sundial, and Italian statuary. Be sure to stroll the grounds when you visit.

The stucco house itself, with its wrought-iron-grilled windows, two-story ballroom, balustraded balconies, and four-story square tower, is exceptionally beautiful. A decorative window, carved to resemble the famous rose window of the San José Mission in San Antonio, provides natural light to the residence's main stairway. On the ground floor, large arched double doors open to a patio on the west façade, and an arcade shelters the south end. In the ballroom the wall panel above the fireplace is an old rafter from the Alamo; artist Peter Mansbendel carved a scene, "The Battle of the Alamo," into the wood as a tribute to Clara Driscoll. Beautiful tile floors enhance the first-story rooms.

During the Seviers' 1916 to 1929 residence, the home was a social center of Austin, visited by many notables, among them Franklin D. Roosevelt, Sam Rayburn, and Lyndon Johnson. In 1929 the couple moved to Corpus Christi following the death of Clara's brother so that she could manage the vast Driscoll interests to which she was the sole heir. They included 100,000 acres of land, 16 oil wells, gas wells, banks, cotton gins, and numerous real estate holdings. During the Depression when businesses were floundering, Clara almost doubled the value of the family estate. In 1933 Sevier was appointed American ambassador to Chile by Franklin D. Roosevelt, and the couple lived there from 1933 to 1935.

They were divorced in 1937, and Clara resumed her maiden name the following year. In 1943 she donated Laguna Gloria and its surrounding acreage to the Texas Fine Arts Holding Corporation to be used as an art museum, along with $5,000 as an initial purchasing fund. She died in 1945.

The museum highlights modern American art. It has no permanent collection, but shows changing exhibits of both regional and nationally known artists, among the latter photographer Gordon Parks, Jim Dine, Frank Stella, Buckminster Fuller, Robert Rauschenberg, Christo, Robert Motherwell, and Picasso.

In addition to exhibits, the museum offers a comprehensive schedule of classes, lectures, films, concerts, and workshops. Be sure to find out what's on during your visit.

The third weekend in May the Fiesta Laguna Gloria takes place here, with 250 craftspeople from around the country showing their wares at booths and selling Mexican food.

The museum is open Tuesday to Saturday from 10 a.m. to 5 p.m., on Thursday night till 9 p.m., and on Sunday from 1 to 5 p.m. Admission is free. Call before you go because the museum sometimes closes during exhibit installations.

In 1988 a new city-owned museum operated by the Laguna Gloria Museum will open downtown on 4th Street, offering seven times the present exhibition space, a restaurant, an auditorium, and a permanent children's gallery. Hopefully, the historic home of Clara Driscoll will remain open to the public at that time.

**THE FRENCH LEGATION:** On September 25, 1839, the French government became the first European power to officially recognize the new Republic of Texas. And from that time until Texas was annexed by the United States, King Louis Phillipe maintained a diplomatic agent at the French Legation in Austin, a lesser version of an embassy headed by a chargé d'affaires. This personnage was one of the most colorful characters in Austin's early history, the Count Alphonse Dubois de Saligny. For openers, the title "count" was of his own devising, as was the "de Saligny." Not of noble birth at all, he was the son of a tax collector whose last name was Dubois. (He also presented himself as five years younger than he was, but that seems minor).

Arriving in Austin with a slew of servants, including a personal chef, coachman, and houseman, de Saligny deemed no local dwelling adequate. He stayed for a few days at Bullock's Inn, then rented a place next door to it while a suitably grand house, the Legation, was being built. Beginning with his refusal to pay Bullock's bill, de Saligny's career in America was a farcical litany of misdeeds and an embarrassment to the French. Throughout his stay he neglected bills and paid others with counterfeit money. He exacerbated his problems with Bullock during what came to be known as the Pig War. After moving next door he complained that the innkeeper's marauding pigs were wandering on his property and ruining his garden. He ordered a servant to turn any pigs on his grounds into bacon. This the servant did, and Bullock retaliated by beating the servant. De Saligny, outraged, appealed to the Republic of Texas. When they refused to do anything about the matter, the chargé d'affaires took it upon himself to break off French diplomatic relations with Texas and moved to New Orleans until a compromise was reached.

Actually, even when not in high dudgeon de Saligny often deserted his post and slipped away to New Orleans, a city that afforded more sophisticated diversions to a cosmopolitan Frenchman than frontier-town Austin. One of these diversions involved a New Orleans woman whose husband challenged de Saligny to a duel; he had to go into hiding to escape. De Saligny was also known to have a volatile temper. Charles Wyke, a British colleague, described him as "violent, imprudent, and . . . unscrupulous in his assertions." "He has quarreled with everybody near him," added Wyke.

Nevertheless, de Saligny's hundreds of letters to Paris are a fascinating account of early Texas. He had plenty of criticism for Sam Houston, though he admitted the San Jacinto hero "did not lack a certain dignity, despite the strange attire in which he is always decked out, and the numerous gold, silver, and iron rings that he wears in his ears and on his fingers." He also deplored Houston's "debauched habits," his "laziness," and his "immoderate passion for strong drink." Of Houston's successor, Lamar, de Saligny was more approving politically, but disdainful on a personal level. "He is small, ugly, awkward, ordinary," the count reported to Paris. "Unbelievable efforts are needed to get him to say even a few words, and then his diction is slow and labored."

It's most interesting to tour de Saligny's Louisiana bayou–style Greek revival home, a legacy from the days of the Republic of Texas. In the parlor are his original rosewood sofa and matching armchair (he purchased French imported furniture in Louisiana) and a portrait of his king. Other rooms in the house are furnished in period pieces, though in the study you will see the letterhead press that de Saligny used to print up counterfeit money.

In 1848, since the legation was no longer serving a purpose as Texas was part of the United States, the house was sold to Dr. Joseph Robertson whose family and descendants lived here until 1948. Their furnishings, also from the Texas Republic period, are in the three bedrooms (two downstairs, one upstairs). On the tour you'll also see the kitchen (an outbuilding that is a replica of the original that burned down in 1878), the servant's quarters, and the gardens.

The French Legation, like the Alamo, is run by the Daughters of the Republic of Texas. It's open for continuous docent-guided tours from 1 to 5 p.m. Tuesday to Sunday. Adults pay $2; students, $1; children 10 and under, 50¢. The French Legation is at 802 San Marcos St. (tel. 472-8180).

**ZILKER PARK:** A beautiful and well-used 360-acre park, buffeted by the 50-acre Barton Creek greenbelt, this is one of Austin's treasures. Located at 2100 Barton Springs Rd., just off the MoPac Expressway (tel. 477-8672), Zilker Park centers around Town Lake, which is bordered by an 8½-mile jogging track. There are ample picnic areas with grills and playground areas for children. Canoes (tel. 478-3852) can be rented on the lake, and you can swim at **Barton Springs** (tel. 476-9044) mid-March through the end of October. This natural spring-fed swimming pool is almost the length of a football field and its temperature is a consistent 68°. Adults pay $1.50 to swim here, children 12 to 18 pay 50¢, and under-12s pay 25¢.

On the north side of the park are **Zilker Gardens**, 2200 Barton Springs Rd. (tel. 477-8672), an area of winding trails and special botanical gardens that is open daily during daylight hours. These 22 acres include a biblical garden with a statue of Saint Francis of Assisi and an Oriental garden designed by Isamu Taniguchi with waterfalls, lotus ponds, a teahouse, graceful bridges, and handmade Oriental lanterns. A rose garden contains a cupola from an 1894 schoolhouse and eight columns of climbing Don Juan roses. There's also a fragrance garden with Braille plaques and an azalea garden centered around a goldfish pond. Arbors, fountains, reflecting pools, a wishing well, and an Egyptian sundial from 1500 B.C. are among the embellishments of these lovely gardens, and there are some 1840s buildings—a blacksmith shop, a schoolhouse, and a Swedish immigrant's cabin—to explore as well.

The **Zilker Eagle** (tel. 478-8167) is a mini-train that chugs along the north side of the park (weather permitting) from 10 a.m. to dusk daily, year round. Adults pay 95¢ and children under 12 pay 80¢.

Zilker Park is also much utilized in summer for al fresco entertainment. The **Zilker Hillside Theater** (tel. 477-5824), an amphitheater with grassy hillside seating (bring a blanket and a picnic to performances here), is just across from the Barton Springs swimming pool. During its May-to-September season, three weekends are set aside for musical productions starring local actors. In the past these have included *Jesus Christ Superstar, Guys and Dolls, Man of La Mancha,* and *Pippin.* There's a full schedule of jazz and classical concerts and Shakespeare in the Park plays. And on Sunday nights there are films. Call the above number for details. Admission is always free.

## THE O. HENRY HOME AND MUSEUM:

Writer William Sydney Porter, better known as O. Henry, lived in Austin for over a decade, from 1893 to 1895, in the house, now a museum, at 409 E. 5th St., at Neches Street (tel. 472-1903). Born in North Carolina in 1862, Porter came to Texas at the age of 20 for the climate in hopes of curing a persistent bad cough. When he recovered his health he decided to stay on, working as a ranch cook and handyman for Richard Hall, one of his doctor's sons. Porter fell in love with Austin when he and Hall visited in 1884, and moved there, finding varied work and enjoying the city's social life. In 1887, the year Porter married his wife, Athol, Richard Hall became land commissioner and employed Porter as a draftsman of maps and deeds in the Land Office. When Hall ran for governor in 1891 and lost, he also lost the appointment privilege of Porter's job. Unfortunately, the only job the dreamy Porter could find was that of teller at the First National Bank of Austin, where he had much difficulty keeping his books straight. In his spare time he founded his famed but short-lived newspaper, *The Rolling Stone.* When indicted by the U.S. Grand Jury for embezzlement from the bank, he hopped a banana boat to Honduras, leaving Athol and his daughter in Austin. He had planned for his family to join him in exile, but Athol was ill with tuberculosis and unable to make the trip. Porter returned to her—and to face the music. Athol died in 1897, and in 1898 Porter went to prison for 3½ years. It was in this grim seclusion that he began writing seriously. Not wanting to use his real name, he adopted the nom de plume O. Henry. After leaving prison, he moved to New York where he spent the next eight years, during which time he wrote and published an astounding 381 stories and gained fame as one of America's most noted short story writers. He died in New York in 1910 at the age of 48.

The home O. Henry occupied briefly has been a museum since 1934. There's no actual tour, but a knowledgeable person is always on hand to answer questions. About a third of the furnishings belonged to the Porters; the rest are period pieces similar to what they had.

In the parlor, you'll see photographs of O. Henry at age 22 and of his daughter, Margaret; the piano that Athol played; the writer's dictionary; and a copy of *The Rolling Stone.*

Photographs of O. Henry and Athol also grace the dining room, where you can see the fruit-pattern china Athol painted as a gift for a friend and a complete collection of O. Henry's works. They were all published originally in newspapers and magazines and only later anthologized in books.

A 1903 issue of *Cosmopolitan* magazine in which one of O. Henry's stories appears is on view in Margaret's bedroom, along with a framed fan and needle book (the latter made by Athol), doll furniture, and O. Henry's hat.

The master bedroom contains all the family furnishings, and closeted in the armoire are some of Athol's clothes.

You can purchase many of O. Henry's works, including a frameable copy of *Gift of the Magi,* at a gift shop on the premises—a store that also affords the opportunity to be the first on your block with an O. Henry T-shirt.

An annual event, the O. Henry Pun-off, takes place on the lawn on the first or second Sunday of each May; it's billed as three hours of "pun-ishment."

Open Tuesday to Saturday from 11 a.m. to 4:30 p.m., on Sunday from 2 to 4:30 p.m. Admission is free.

**THE NEILL-COCHRAN MUSEUM:** Designed and constructed by master builder Abner Cook (also responsible for the Governor's Mansion), this Greek revival–style plantation home at 2310 San Gabriel St. (tel. 478-2335), dates to 1855. Like the Governor's Mansion, it has a colonnaded façade reminiscent of a Greek temple, and symmetry is its hallmark. Its six 26-foot-tall Doric columns are made of cypress and painted white. Overhead, the Romeo balcony has a balustrade in Cook's signature design called "bundles of wheat." The house itself is constructed of limestone quarried from the back of the property. Walls are 18 feet thick and begin deep in the ground, floors are made of Bastrop pine, and most of the windows you see today contain the original hand-pressed glass and green shutters.

When the house was built, this was an out-in-the-country location. The property extended west to Shoal Creek, and just across the creek was another Abner Cook creation, Governor Pease's plantation. The house was originally built for a lawyer named Washington Hill, but his East Coast bride, fearing Indian attack, refused to live in so isolated a setting and opted for a town house. For the next 20 years it was a rental property, serving as an asylum for the blind, occupied by federal troops, used as a hospital to treat Union soldiers (many died here and are buried on the grounds), and briefly sheltering Gen. George Armstrong Custer of Last Stand fame. Texas Gov. Andrew Jackson Hamilton lived here while the Governor's Mansion was undergoing repair from 1870 to 1876, purging the property of its Union stigma. The Neills, one of the two families for whom the house is now named, bought the house after that and lived here through the 1890s. Scottish-born Col. Andrew Neill was a lawyer and Texas patriot who had been taken prisoner by Mexicans in the 1840s. Neill escaped and later fought in Indian campaigns and the Confederate Army. People have claimed to see his ghost here, wearing a Confederate uniform and rocking in his chair on the balcony. During the Neill tenancy, major politicians often gathered to discuss affairs of state around the library table.

Judge Thomas Beaufort Cochran, president of the Travis County Bar Association, bought the house around the turn of the century, making extensive improvements without sacrificing the architectural integrity and character of Cook's original structure. Among other things, the Cochrans installed the first indoor bathroom and electric lights. Judge Cochran died in 1913, but his widow lived here until her death in 1953. The Colonial Dames of America bought the property in 1958, restored it, and turned it into a museum with furnishings of the 18th and early 19th centuries, reflecting the spectrum of years under different ownerships.

On a 45-minute tour you'll see the formal parlor, furnished in French pieces from the 1700s. Sèvres porcelain displayed here is complemented by a chandelier, candelabra, sconces, and cache pots by Sèvres. There are also Louis XV and XVI chairs. A portrait over the mantel is of Diane de Poitiers.

The front parlor is furnished mostly in 19th-century English and Victorian pieces. The four mahogany chairs are Hepplewhite shieldbacks, and on the floor is a Royal Kermanshah Persian rug.

Additional Hepplewhite shieldback chairs are seen in the back parlor, where a portrait of Virginian George Mason hangs over the Duncan Phyfe swanback sofa. The Baccarat crystal chandelier overhead is from New Orleans, and the English neoclassic secretary has oval inlay panels of amboyna wood from New Guinea.

In the dining room a 1775 Royal Worcester tea service is displayed in a mahogany Chippendale corner cabinet. Other notable items are a 1790 mahogany Hepplewhite table, a collection of Sheffield silver, and a Waterford crystal chandelier and epergne.

Upstairs in the library are two early Victorian chairs that belonged to Mrs. Stonewall Jackson, bellows that belonged to Dolley Madison's mother, and a Duncan Phyfe sofa. A Copley portrait of George Washington hangs over the mantel.

The southeast bedroom is furnished in 1830 American Empire pieces designed to complement Greek revival architecture. The bed is covered with a popcorn crocheted spread.

A Sheraton four-poster, Hepplewhite armchairs, and a 1608 needlepoint sampler are on view in the northeast bedroom.

The northwest bedroom has a walnut half-tester bed bought in New Orleans in 1846 by Texas Supreme Court Justice Ruben Reeves.

You can also visit the Rock House Dependency, an outbuilding that once served as slave quarters, later a laundry. Its brick floor comes from the Old Ursuline Convent in San Antonio. The upper story is today furnished as a bedroom and features a bed made by early Texas governor, Elisha Pease; the lower story, furnished as an old Texas kitchen, houses domestic tools and implements. There's also a carriage house on the premises.

Guided tours are given Wednesday through Sunday from 2 to 5 p.m. Adults pay $1; children under 6 are admitted free.

**THE LONE STAR RIVERBOAT:** This old-fashioned paddlewheeler docked behind the Hyatt Regency Hotel, 208 Barton Springs Rd., between Congress Avenue and South 1st Street (tel. 327-1388), plies not a river but beautiful Town Lake, a landlocked body of water formed by the Longhorn Dam across the Colorado River. It's seven miles long, and the boat travels past many sights, both scenic and significant. The former include peach orchards, plum and pear trees, ancient cypresses, and dogwoods—not to mention such wildlife as blue herons, cormorants, red-tailed hawks, beaver, muskrats, and possum—and a beautiful wisteria-covered gazebo at the beginning of Zilker Park. Beyond the Barton Creek area are magnificent cliffs and Eilers Park, home to hundreds of ducks. And the Lone Star offers marvelous views of the Austin skyline at sunset. In the latter category, you'll travel past the spot where the Old Chisolm Trail crossed the Colorado (Austin was a focal point for cattle drives) and see many homes and sites that were important in the city's history. The relaxing 1½-hour ride is interestingly narrated, and drinks—beer, wine, and sodas—are available.

The *Lone Star* departs on Friday, Saturday, Sunday, and holidays at 5:30 p.m. from late May to Labor Day weekend. Adults pay $7; children 12 and under, $4.

**THE ARTS WAREHOUSE:** This former warehouse at 300 San Antonio St. (tel. 473-2505) serves as studio space for 38 Austin painters, weavers, sculptors, ceramicists, jewelry makers, and furniture designers, among others. You can see the artists and craftspeople at work here and purchase their creative output. On the whole, the level of work is higher than I've seen at similar establishments. There's also a large gallery where works of nonaffiliated artists are shown.

The premises also contains **Discovery Hall** (tel. 474-7616), a small hands-on science museum with workshops for children on Saturday ranging from frog dissections to laser demonstrations. Admission to these programs are $1.50 for adults, $1 for children 14 and under. Call for details.

The Arts Warehouse itself is open weekdays from 10 a.m. to 5 p.m., on Saturday to 6 p.m. Individual artists' schedules vary; you'll find many of them in their studios on weekday afternoons.

**SPORTS:** Options listed below are in addition to Zilker Park activities already mentioned, which include canoeing, a lakeside jogging trail, and a vast swimming pool.

## Biking

You can rent bicycles at the **Cycology Bike Shop,** 53rd Street and Avenue F (tel. 454-6295); at **University Schwinn Cyclery,** 2901 N. Lamar Blvd. (tel. 474-6696); and at **Cothron's Bike Shop,** 509 Rio Grande (tel. 478-2707). Call ahead to make sure they have what you need and to find out rental terms.

The most popular bike trail is the 8½-mile lakeside loop around Town Lake, but there are many attractive cycling paths; call the **Austin Parks and Recreation Department** (tel. 499-2000) for specifics. They can even send you a free booklet with maps on the bike trail system.

## Caving

The **University of Texas Grotto** is a group of spelunkers who organize expeditions. Call 453-4774 for information.

## Fishing

As a lake district, Austin offers good fishing for white bass, crappie, largemouth bass, catfish, striped bass, and perch. Contact the chamber of commerce (tel. 478-0098) for specifics. Most sporting goods stores sell licenses.

## Golf

There are two municipal 18-hole courses, **Jimmy Clay** at 5500 Nuckols Crossing, near Teri (tel. 447-1938), and the **Lions** at 2910 Enfield, near Exposition (tel. 477-6963).

## Tennis

There are over 100 courts in town, most of them in parks and available for free play on a first-come, first-served basis. For details on locations, call the **Austin Parks and Recreation Department** at 474-9707.

# 5. Austin Nights

College town Austin probably offers more exciting nightlife options than any other city in Texas. For the younger set especially, there's the Old Pecan Street strip, a seven-block section of 6th Street lined with renovated Victorian and old stone buildings that house numerous chic eateries, clubs, art galleries, chocolate-chip cookie outlets, and boutiques. It's so reminiscent of Washington, D.C.'s Georgetown strip that plunked down on one or the other it would take me a minute or two to determine where I was. The strip is mobbed nightly with a lively, action-seeking, bar-hopping crowd. Music spills out onto the street from every club and bar, and street performers vie with street vendors for attention. Even if you've no interest in the music, it's fun to stroll the strip and observe the nightly scene. Parking is difficult; take a taxi or use a nearby lot.

Even aside from 6th Street, there's lots to do here after sundown. A recent week's after-dark doings included headliner concerts by Liza Minnelli, Alabama, Ricky Skaggs, Randy Newman, George Carlin, and James Brown, and theatrical productions of *Noises Off, Vanities, Romeo and Juliet,* Harold Pinter's *Betrayal, Look Homeward, Angel, Ain't Misbehavin', West Side Story, Bus Stop,* and Arthur Miller's *All My Sons.* The Erick Hawkins Dance Company was in town, there were performances by the Austin Symphony Orchestra and Ballet Austin, and Houston's Texas Opera Theatre was doing *Carmen.* That's just the bare bones of it—maybe 5% of your options. And keep in mind that many greats—such as Jerry Jeff Walker and Janis Joplin—were once unknowns playing 6th Street clubs.

A free magazine called *Kaleidoscope,* available at most hotels and at the Convention and Visitors Bureau, tells all, as does the Saturday "Time Out" section of the Austin *American-Statesman.*

**TICKETS:** Tickets to many events are available through the **Shamrock Ticket Service,** with six outlets in Austin. Call 443-7037 for a 24-hour recording listing available tickets. Call 443-2722 to find out the nearest Shamrock location or to charge tickets.

**BIG EVENTS:** The following listings include facilities used for headliner concerts, classical concerts, operas, important theatrical offerings, and other events.

Major doings take place at the **Frank C. Erwin, Jr., Special Events Center,** on the UT campus at 1701 Red River St., between 15th Street and Martin Luther King Boulevard (tel. 471-7744 to find out what's on, 477-6060 to charge tickets). An 18,000-seat arena constructed in 1977 at a cost of $29 million, it annually hosts the Ice Capades, Disney on Ice, Ringling Bros. and Barnum & Bailey Circus, Sesame Street Live, the Muppet Show on Tour, and the Harlem Globetrotters. In addition there are many headliner concerts here, like Tina Turner, Kenny Rogers, Dolly Parton, Liza Minnelli, Alabama, Bruce Springsteen, Sting, and Madonna. And UT basketball games—men's and women's—also utilize the arena, which is bathed in orange light whenever they win. Call to find out what's on while you're here.

A lot of Austin's most notable entertainment takes place at the **UT Performing Arts Center,** 23rd Street and East Campus Drive (tel. 471-1444 to find out what's on, 477-6060 to charge tickets). The facility's major showcase is the 3,000-seat **Concert Hall,** which annually hosts, along with numerous college productions, major symphony and dance companies, touring Broadway musicals, operas, and solo artists. It is also the home of the Austin Symphony and Ballet Austin. In other words, you might catch comedians like George Carlin, Robin Williams, and Rodney Dangerfield; Broadway plays like *Sugar Babies* starring Ann Miller and Mickey Rooney or *On Your Toes* with Leonid and Valentino Kozlov; dance companies like Alvin Ailey, Merce Cunningham, and Paul Taylor; headliners both pop and classical, such as Itzhak Perlman, Leontyne Price, Marilyn Horne, Ella Fitzgerald, Tony Bennett, Burl Ives, and Paul Schaeffer; performances by the Saint Louis Symphony Orchestra, the Tokyo

String Quartet, or the Dresden Philharmonic; the Houston Ballet's production of *Giselle;* the Chinese Golden Dragon Acrobats and Magicians of Taipei; illusionist David Copperfield; the San Francisco Opera Center's *Don Giovanni;* or the Old Vic Theatre's *King Lear.* Then again, perhaps Cary Grant will be here showing film clips of his movies and talking about his career. All the above is just a fraction of the yearly happenings at this superb campus facility.

And the center also houses the 400-seat **Opera Lab Theatre,** presenting chamber operas in English and other productions suitable to a smaller space. The season is basically September to May, but there are occasional summer productions. Convenient parking is available in the lots directly east of the LBJ Library and Sid Richardson Hall (access via Red River Street).

The 44,000-square-foot, 6,000-seat **Palmer Auditorium** and the adjoining 30,000-square-foot, 3,600-seat **City Coliseum,** South 1st Street at Riverside Drive on Town Lake (tel. 476-8231 for a recording of happenings at both facilities, 476-5461 to talk to a human being and find out where to purchase tickets), separately or together host some of the major events in Austin. These include trade shows, car shows, boat shows, tractor pulls, circuses, carnivals, and headliners like Miles Davis, Joan Rivers, KISS, Billy Idol, Huey Lewis, and Rodney Dangerfield.

Touring Broadway shows often play the **Paramount Theatre,** 713 Congress Ave. (tel. 472-5411), a 1,300-seat converted 1915 vaudeville house that has been restored to its original opulence—complete with deluxe opera boxes, a wealth of baroque detail and gilt trim, and a harp-playing angel watching over the stage from on high. In its early years the Paramount hosted all the greats of the era— Sarah Bernhardt, Anna Pavlova, the Barrymores, George M. Cohan, Orson Welles, Helen Hayes, even the Metropolitan Opera. But after the early 1930s it became a mere motion-picture emporium, and by the 1970s, in poor repair, it had sunk to the status of a "B" movie house. Happily, it was then restored rather than razed, and now its grandeur is almost as much an attraction as its first-rate theatrical productions. These have included *Dracula* starring Martin Landau, *Sugar Babies* with Ann Miller and Mickey Rooney, *Mass Appeal* with E. G. Marshall, *Cotton Club Revisited* with Cab Calloway, and *A Coupla White Chicks* with Susan Anton and Elizabeth Ashley. And the Paramount presents a great deal more than Broadway shows. It has featured major dance companies (like Merce Cunningham, Paul Taylor, and Martha Graham); full-scale operatic productions; classical concerts and soloists; comedians like Lily Tomlin, Cheech & Chong, and Rich Little; jazz artists like Dave Brubeck, Herbie Mann, Ramsey Lewis, and McCoy Tyner; and numerous other headliners—Randy Newman, Ben Vereen, Billy Joel, Dolly Parton, Kris Kristofferson, and the Pointer Sisters among them.

Broadway show tickets are generally in the $11 to $25 range. Call the above number to find out what's on; call 477-6060 to charge tickets.

**COUNTRY:** The best little roadhouse in Texas—certainly one of the most authentic—is the **Broken Spoke,** 3201 S. Lamar Blvd., between Ben White Boulevard and Manchaca Road (tel. 442-6189). No slick urban cowboy bar this. Heralded by Coca-Cola signs and an invite to "Dine and Dance Texas Style," it's a down-home, country, honky-tonk dance hall that's been a popular local hangout for over two decades. In the past, the Spoke has hosted such greats as Tex Ritter, Willie Nelson, Ernest Tubb, Roy Acuff, Bob Wills, and George Strait. And when the state legislature is in session, every Tuesday night the speaker of the Texas House of Representatives leads a legion of legislators and lobbyists to the Spoke for some political partying. This is probably the only honky-tonk anywhere to have ever received a citation commending its services from the state legislature in the form of a Senate resolution, reading in part: "Whereas, providing not only sumptuous dining but games, dancing, musical entertainment, and a generous amount of rustic charm as well, Joe Baland, James White and their hardworking families have propelled the Broken Spoke from its humble beginnings on the footsteps of an abandoned lumberyard to its current preeminence among Texas entertainment institutions; now, therefore, be it . . . Resolved, that the Senate of the 65th Legislature of the State of Texas commend the Broken Spoke and its proprietors . . . upon their continuing success in providing the citizens of and visitors to Austin with exceptional food and entertainment in the style which only Texas can offer. . . ."

The "rustic charm" consists of a cluttery front room with torn vinyl booths at Formica tables and neon beer sign adornments; the back room, where the bands play, has tables on either side of the dimly lit dance floor. As a reviewer described it, "No one who has ever spent a night in the Spoke . . . has ever come away wondering what a Texas honky-tonk is 'really like.'" There's live music—pure country, no crossover—Wednesday, Friday, and Saturday nights from 9 p.m. to 1 or 2 a.m. Other nights there's the jukebox, and people come by to eat what Annetta White calls "one helluva chicken-fried steak" ($3.65) and shoot a little pool. In fact you could do a lot worse than have dinner here—good, cheap, real Texas food. And since 1984 the Spoke has had a full liquor license, ending a long brown-bag era. Admission is usually $3.50 to $4.50 on music nights, depending on the night and the entertainment, no admission charge otherwise.

Willie Nelson, when not "on the road again," lives in Austin and owns a club here, the 1,700-seat **Austin Opera House**, 200 Academy Dr., between Riverside Drive and Congress Avenue (tel. 443-7037). It has a year-round season featuring headliner entertainers (about four or five shows a month). In the past Neil Young, Spyro Gyra, Bonnie Raitt, James Brown, Randy Newman, Dire Straits, and Rosanne Cash have played the Opera House. And of course, sometimes Willie takes the stage himself. It's not all country—jazz, English new wave, and heavy metal artists have also played here. Tickets are usually in the $10 to $15 range. They're available three to four weeks in advance from Shamrock Ticket Outlets (tel. 443-2722).

**Austin City Limits** is not a club but a live TV show taped at the KLRU studio on the UT campus, at the intersection of Guadalupe and 26th Streets (tel. 471-4811). ACL showcases both established and new country entertainers, and when big-name artists are being taped, Austinites have a chance to enjoy a free concert. It does take a little persistence, though. The studio only seats about 400 people, and tickets are distributed on the day of the performance only, on a first-come, first-served basis. People start lining up at about 8 a.m. Seating is also "first come," so the line begins again at about 5 p.m. But country music fans find it all worthwhile to see stars like Neil Young, Loretta Lynn, Waylon Jennings, Ricky Skaggs, Eddy Raven, Juice Newton, the Gatlin Brothers, Merle Haggard, Ray Charles, and David Allan Coe. Performances take place between August and January.

**COMEDY:** Any college town is sure to have a comedy club these days. Austin has two. There's the **Comedy Workshop**, 1415 Lavaca St., between 14th and 15th Streets (tel. 473-2300). Except on Monday (local talent night), the workshop features major rising stars of comedy—the guys who appear on the Carson and Letterman shows and in movies, like Bill Hicks, Jay Leno, and Franklyn Ajaye. A show consists of three comics, always including a headliner. There are two shows nightly on Friday and Saturday, one show Sunday to Thursday. Tickets are $1.50 on Monday nights, $6.50 to $8 the rest of the week. On Tuesday nights the club often offers a two-for-one admission. Drinks are available, but there's no minimum. You can buy tickets at the door, but it's a good idea to call ahead and reserve, since they sometimes sell out.

And since university kids love comedy clubs, they support a second establishment, a **Laff Stop**, 8120 Research Blvd., at Anderson Square (tel. 467-2333). They also feature the national-circuit comics, and some big names have played here—Shirley Hemphill, Pete Barbutti, the Smothers Brothers, Gabe Kaplan, Steve Allen, and Waylon Flowers and Madame, among them. Tuesday to Thursday nights the club offers one show with three comics (though sometimes one of them is a ventriloquist, hypnotist, impressionist, or magician). On Friday and Saturday nights, there are two shows. Admission is $5.50 weeknights, $7.50 on Friday and Saturday nights, though admission sometimes goes up to $15 for top performers. There's a full bar, and snacks are available. On weekends, Laff Stop has a two-drink minimum.

**Esther's Follies**, at the Ritz Theater, 320 E. 6th St., between Trinity and San Jacinto Streets (tel. 479-0054), is a satirical musical revue that has been playing to an enthusiastic audience since 1977. An Austin *American-Statesman* reviewer described it pretty well as "a mad-hatter's pastiche of songs, skits, dances, and even oddball opera." There are also campy film clips worked into the productions from movies like *Zombies from Peoria*. It changes every few months, because the largely collegiate audience comes again and again. Many of the skits are UT or Austin oriented, so you may miss a few insider jokes. It's kind of like *Saturday Night Live* with a Texas/university slant, and like that show some parts are hilarious, some fall flat. On the whole it's a pretty entertaining evening, and the cast of 12 is a talented crew. Tickets are $6, with occasional two-for-one admissions offered on Friday evenings. There are shows on Friday at 9 p.m. and on Saturday at 9 and 11 p.m. After the Friday shows live bands come on stage and there's dancing. Live bands also perform during the week. Seating is on a first-come, first-served basis, so arrive early to get a good seat.

**LIVE MUSIC:** Perched 65 feet above ground, **The Treehouse**, 502 Dawson Rd., at Barton Springs Road (tel. 477-1198), has picture windows all around to provide panoramic views. It's quite attractive inside as well, with a beamed pine ceiling and Breuer chairs at butcher-block tables. Walls are hung with works of Austin artists. In fact, it would be a very romantic setting if the music were at a lower decibel level; it's just not the same shouting sweet nothings at your date as whispering them. There's live entertainment nightly from 9:30 p.m., usually well-known regional jazz, rhythm-and-blues, country, or mellow rock bands. If you come by weekdays between 4 and 8 p.m. you can skip dinner, order a reduced-price drink or two, and indulge in the lavish complimentary Happy Hour buffet—fresh-made tortilla chips, refried beans, chile con queso, jalapeños, fresh fruit, crudités with dip, boiled shrimp, barbecued chicken wings, and cheeses on my last visit. A snack menu is available later on. The folks on the dance floor are Yuppie types, mostly in the 25 to 40 age group. Valet parking is free. There's a $2 cover Tuesday to Thursday nights, $3 on Friday and Saturday nights, no cover on Monday or Tuesday.

Even higher up is the **Foothills Piano Bar Lounge**, on the 17th floor of the Hyatt Regency Hotel, 208 Barton Springs Rd., between Congress Avenue and 1st Street (tel. 477-1234). It's quite elegant. You'll sit in comfortable upholstered chairs at marble-topped tables, all of which offer marvelous vistas, via floor-to-ceiling windows, of the downtown skyline. There's excellent piano-bar music here Tuesday to Saturday from 6 p.m. through 1 a.m. You might consider dining first at the adjoining restaurant (same views) on entrees like duckling rubbed with fines herbes and spices, spit roasted, and served with raspberry sauce and wild rice ($16.50), then stepping next door for after-dinner drinks and piano bar. Snack fare is available at Foothills itself, ranging from escargots en croûte spiked with Pernod ($5.95) to a fresh fruit and cheese plate ($7.25). Delicious desserts and specialty drinks, like Bailey's Irish Cream with Finlandia vodka ($4.75), are also available, as are fine wines and champagnes. There's no cover charge.

One of the most happening places on the Strip is **Anchovies,** 503 E. 6th St., at Neches Street (tel. 474-6602), with nightly live music attracting a crowd ranging from college kids to still-boogeying Big Chillers. There's a nice-sized dance floor, where you can twist again to the oldies-only music—'50s, '60s, and '70s rock tunes, heavy on the Motown. Most of the entertainers are local groups, but occasionally big names like Three Dog Night and The Association (remember "Cherish"?) play here. One of Anchovies' lures is its valet-attended rest rooms, equipped with colognes, hair brushes, mouthwashes, mints, Visine, hand lotions, blow dryers (great when it's raining), and curling irons. A Cajun menu is offered. Weekdays from 5 to 8 p.m. well drinks are $1.75 and Wednesday to Friday there's a complimentary Happy Hour buffet. Cover charge is $1 Sunday to Wednesday, $3 on Thursday, $5 on Friday and Saturday, sometimes more if a well-known performer is playing.

Then there's **Maggie Mae's Lime Street Station,** 325 E. 6th St., at Trinity Street (tel. 478-8541), an attractive bar with bare pine floors, candlelit tables covered in green-and-white-checkered cloths, and big windows adorned with stained-glass hangings from a pub in Oxford, England. There's live music for dancing Tuesday through Saturday nights from 9 p.m.—rock, jazz, funk, and fusion. Sunday and Monday nights sporting events are aired on a large-screen TV. A "food court" offers diverse cuisines—Friar's Feast purveys deli sandwiches with old-world names like the corny king's beef, Tony Zapata's has fajitas and nachos, the China Dragon serves eggrolls, and Frank's Coney Island, hot dogs. It's all very inexpensive. On Friday and Saturday nights the entertainment takes place upstairs in a more elegant room with swagged forest-green draperies and an ornate chandelier overhead. There's no cover or minimum any night. The crowd is mostly post-college age, the music is good, and the decibel level allows for conversation if you're not sitting right next to the band.

Next door is the original **Maggie Mae's,** 323 E. 6th St. (same phone), a funkier club that opened in 1978 and is still going strong. It built its reputation on folk music, which it still offers Sunday, Monday, and Thursday nights, occasionally alternating with acoustic jazz. It's a long, narrow space with graffiti on the walls and a 50-foot bar at which you can order 80 kinds of imported beer. No cover or minimum here either.

Housed in a converted roller rink, **South Bank,** 312 Barton Springs Rd., at Riverside Drive (tel. 472-0661), caters to a crowd that likes it loud. The decor is bistro-like, with bentwood chairs at café tables and art à la Lautrec. The floors are still roller-rink wood. Music varies from rock to R&B, country, new music, and even gospel on occasion. There's live entertainment seven nights a week from 9:30 p.m. till about 1 a.m., Wednesday and Thursday nights generally bringing the most ear-splitting bands. A full restaurant menu with entrees like fettuccine carbonara ($5.95) and pork chops ($9.50), the latter served with baked potato, salad, and vegetable, is offered nightly till 9 p.m., a snack menu till midnight. You can also choose from about 100 international varieties of beer. Admission ranges from free to $4, depending on who's playing.

**MUSIC OUTDOORS:** Symphony Square, 1101 Red River St. (tel. 476-6064), is a complex of four late-1800s limestone homes and buildings centered around a 350-seat outdoor amphitheater, the scene of many a festive summertime concert. June through August, there's something happening every Friday, Saturday, and Sunday night at 8:30 p.m.

Friday's programs come under the heading "Moon over Waller Creek," an eclectic selection that might include comedy, jazz, gospel, folk, or reggae—anything but classical music. Performers are all local talent, and tickets are about $2.50 to $5.

Saturday-night shows are in the "Catch a Rising Star" series. They feature 6th Street club bands—usually rock, but sometimes jazz or country. Admission is $4 or $5.

Sunday nights are given over to "Classical Sunset" concerts—chamber music, string quartets, ensemble works, and soloists. Tickets are $2.50 to $3.

And there are children's concerts and activities on Wednesday at 9:30 a.m. in summer—fables, mimes, clowns, and music geared to young people. Most people bring a picnic lunch to enjoy under the "magic oak tree" after the show. Lemonade is sold on the premises. Admission is 50¢ for children, free for adults accompanied by a child.

Tickets to all performances are available at the door on a first-come, first-served basis. Arrive early to avoid disappointment.

There are also special holiday events here, such as a candlelit Christmas concert and an Easter egg hunt.

**THEATER:** The Mary Moody Northen Theatre, 3001 S. Congress Ave., between Woodward and Oldorf Streets (tel. 448-8484), is part of St. Edward's University, but is also an Equity house featuring frequent guest artists. Summer shows feature national performers; the rest of the year actors are students and faculty. The theater seats 200 in an arena stage setting. A recent season's productions included *The Music Man, Bus Stop, The Prime of Miss Jean Brodie, Born Yesterday, Cat on a Hot Tin Roof,* and *Grease,* among others; they do about 11 different shows a year. You can charge tickets at the above number.

Housed in a converted 1880s grocery warehouse, the Capitol City Playhouse, 214 W. 4th St., between Colorado and Lavaca (tel. 472-2966), offers a year-round theater season for adults and children. There's always a musical production around Christmastime (like *A Funny Thing Happened on the Way to the Forum*). The New Theatre Festival every year features new scripts that have been chosen from national entries and gone through a year-long process of readings and critiques. Five fully mounted festival plays are chosen from an original 12 to 16; three are presented in spring and two in the fall. A Black Theatre Program every spring features works like *For Colored Girls . . .* and *Ain't Misbehavin'.* Every April there's an Opera Program, in which a full operatic production is presented in conjunction with the Austin Civic Symphony. In summer you can see a contemporary drama or musical, running concurrently with, or just after, its appearance on Broadway. And the rest of the year the Playhouse puts on a mix of dramas, musicals, and new works, along with a full schedule of children's shows. All performers are local actors. Tickets are usually in the $7 to $9 range ($15 on opening night), $4 to $5 for children's shows.

**MUSIC AND DANCE:** The Austin Dance Umbrella (tel. 444-8698), a nonprofit educational institution, sponsors year-round dance concerts at locations all over town, both local and national performers and troupes running the gamut from folklorico to ballet to modern. If you're interested in dance, call to find out what's on during your stay.

A similar organization, the **Music Umbrella of Austin** (tel. 476-1324), sponsors musical events, songfests, and songwriter's and composers' competitions. Like Dance Umbrella, they act as a clearinghouse for information about what's on in town. You can call up to find out, or to ask where you can go to hear a hot country group, a string quartet, reggae band, or whatever else you're in the mood for.

# Chapter X

# THE METROPLEX: THE DALLAS/FORT WORTH AREA

### 1. Dallas
### 2. Grand Prairie and Arlington
### 3. Fort Worth

THE AREA ENCOMPASSING Dallas, Fort Worth, assorted suburbs, and the "mid-cities" in between (most notably Grand Prairie and Arlington), is referred to as the Metroplex. It's an alliance only geographically. Residents of cowtown Fort Worth disdain sophisticated Dallas as "just as bad as New York," and Dallasites view Fort Worth condescendingly, about the way New Yorkers view New Jersey. For example, a Dallas columnist recently considered moving to Fort Worth, because "that town's dull social season would at least save on our dry-cleaning bills." And humorist Will Rogers once said, "Fort Worth is where the West begins and Dallas is where the East peters out." As for the mid-cities, Grand Prairie and Arlington, they're mostly of interest to children; like Anaheim, California, and Orlando, Florida, they're jam-packed with theme parks and amusement parks.

Regional allegiances and disparities notwithstanding, as a tourist you'll do well to consider the Metroplex an entity, because for purposes of exploring its attractions you can set yourself up in any part of it and use it as a base to visit the rest. Dallas and Fort Worth are only about 30 miles apart.

## 1. Dallas

Dallas was founded by John Neely Bryan, a Tennessee lawyer who established a trading post on the banks of the Trinity River in 1841. His sole companions were his horse and his dog, Tubby. Choosing his location with an eye to steamboat transport (which never materialized), Bryan laid out a town of 20 grid-like streets on the riverbank and set up trade with the Indians and westbound wagons. A year later he convinced two families who were living 20 miles away to join him and married one of their daughters, Margaret Beeman. He built a cabin for his bride on what is today Dealy Plaza, and it, or one like it, is still there (it's a matter of some controversy whether this is the actual Neely cabin). Bryan named his city Dallas, after a friend, an ironic choice since its county, created in 1846, was also named Dallas but in honor of Vice-President

George Mifflin Dallas (it was popular in the early statehood years to name Texas towns for nationally prominent figures). If Bryan had been more egotistical, the city today might be a more-alliterative Big B.

In 1852 Bryan sold the townsite to capitalist Alex Cockrell for $7,000. Cockrell built a bridge over the Trinity River, started a sawmill and a brickyard, and began constructing a hotel. When he was shot in a quarrel in 1858, his wife, Sarah, an early women's libber, continued running all Cockrell's enterprises while raising six children.

Meanwhile the city had been incorporated in 1856, about the same time that a group of several hundred European socialists set up a Utopian colony across the river. They called it La Réunion because, though it was French led, its members included Germans, Swiss, Poles, and Belgians. The experiment failed, and the colony was absorbed by Dallas, its European sophisticates adding a cosmopolitan flavor to the frontier town. They brought French cuisine, haute couture, art, and culture, and they attracted other cultivated European immigrants to the area. Then as now, there were people in Dallas who breakfasted on croissants and café au lait.

As the Civil War approached, Dallas had a courthouse, hotel, newspaper, brewery, and whisky distillery. Its population was 755. And its citizenry was divided over the issues that would soon lead to war. Dallas wasn't a large slaveholding city, and many European immigrants were fervent Union supporters. Nonetheless, in 1859 the city issued a strong pro-slavery statement. When Dallas burned to the ground a year later, the populace believed the destruction was the work of northern sympathizers, and there were hangings and other vigilante reprisals. In 1861 Dallas approved secession by a three to one margin. During the war the city served as a general quartermaster and commissary headquarters for the Confederate Army, and though it saw no action, it lost many men on the battlefields. The major effect of the war, however, was a large influx of freed slaves who moved west and vastly increased the city's black population.

Dallas quickly rallied from the war and the fire, but its continued existence wasn't assured until 1872–1873 when the townspeople, having pressured, bribed, tricked, and otherwise cajoled railroad officials, routed the north-south Houston & Texas and the east-west Texas & Pacific lines through the heart of Dallas. Since Dallas never had a viable river (Will Rogers once suggested paving it over), a navigable harbor, or any other noteworthy natural resources, there was no real reason for the railroad to come through, no real reason for the town to continue prospering and eventually become the nation's seventh-largest city. But it did.

By 1876 the population had more than doubled, land values skyrocketed, and speculators and entrepreneurs converged on the city. Overnight, Dallas was commercialized. Public improvements followed rapidly—streetcars, telegraph, streetlights, electricity, paved roads, telephones, and modern buildings. Railroads made Dallas a sophisticated metropolis and a distribution center for the south. Even agriculture became big business as farmers began exporting cotton and wheat by rail. By the turn of the century, Dallas streets were filled with "horseless carriages," necessitating traffic laws forbidding speeds in excess of seven miles an hour. The State Fair was an annual event. Wealthy tycoons had built mansions in Highland Park. And Herbert Marcus and Al Neiman were about to open a store.

In the 20th century Dallas has evolved into one of America's largest and most important cities. Transportation center of the Southwest, it contains the nation's largest commercial airport. It's a leading center of banking, insurance, film production, conventions and trade shows, wholesale merchandising, fash-

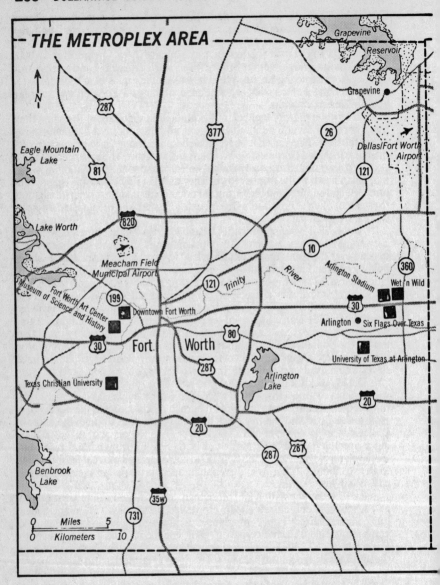

THE METROPLEX AREA

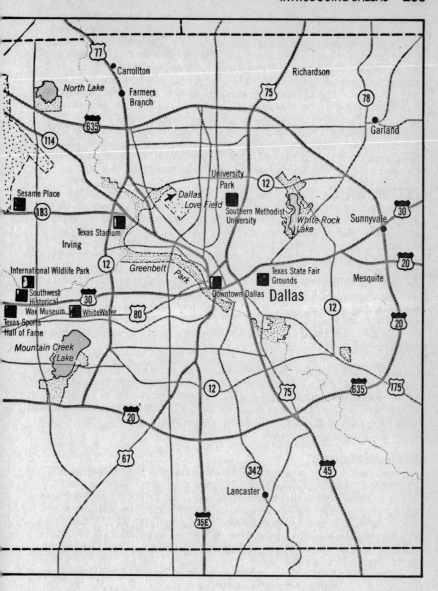

ion, petroleum, computer technology, and electronics. It has the third-largest concentration of million-dollar-company national headquarters in the country. And it supports a vibrant cultural scene, including an important art museum, a symphony orchestra, an opera company, and excellent theater. Its hotels and restaurants are world class. And its hub is a cluster of freeway-girded, steel-and-glass skyscrapers rising from a vast low-lying prairie suburb. In the '60s a local wag remarked, "This is going to be one helluva town if they ever get through building it." That comment is still apt. Cranes and construction sites remain a constant on the Dallas landscape, as new office buildings and housing proliferate in line with predictions that the population will be doubled by the year 2000. Some doomsayers claim overbuilding will lead to economic disaster. But Dallas has always survived, and more than that, flourished. My bet is that the 21st century will find people wondering still when its development will ever halt.

**GETTING THERE:** The very impressive **Dallas/Fort Worth International Airport,** larger than the island of Manhattan, is served by over 35 airlines, including all the major carriers. It is 18 miles from downtown. In addition, a few airlines (Southwest, Muse, Air Midway, and Texas Airline) route flights in and out of the smaller Love Field, about half as far from downtown.

Both **Trailways** and **Greyhound** connect downtown Dallas with the rest of the country. The Trailways terminal is at 1500 Jackson St. (tel. 214/655-7000), the Greyhound terminal close by at Commerce and Lamar (tel. 214/741-1481).

And limited passenger service is available via **Amtrak** to/from Union Station, also downtown at Young and Houston Streets. For information, call 214/653-1101, or toll free 800/872-7245.

By **car,** other than Fort Worth, the closest major city is Austin, 203 miles south via I-35.

**ORIENTATION:** Like any big Texas city, Dallas requires map study. The city is ringed by a loop that is I-635 north and east, I-20 on the southern arc, and Loop 12 to the west, the latter veering off to form a concentric inner loop. I-30 bisects the city horizontally, and other major arteries radiate star-like from its downtown center. During rush hours it doesn't matter which ones you take—you'll crawl along in jam-packed traffic.

### Information Sources

Before you arrive, write to the **Dallas Convention & Visitors Bureau,** 1507 Pacific Ave., Dallas, TX 75201, and request brochures, maps, a quarterly events calendar, and a hotel weekend package guide. Of course, they can also answer all your travel questions. And upon arrival visit their helpful office at the above address (it's on the corner of Akard Street, third floor; tel. 214/954-1482). On the premises you'll find a vast array of informative brochures, and knowledgeable staff members are on hand to help. The bureau is open Monday to Friday from 8:30 a.m. to 5 p.m.

The CVB also maintains a booth in the main lobby at Love Field, open seven days a week (hours are subject to change).

A third office is conveniently located downtown in Union Station, at Young and Houston Streets (tel. 214/747-2355). It's open weekdays from 9 a.m. to 5:30 p.m., weekends to 5 p.m.

**GETTING AROUND:** Like Houston, Dallas requires wheels. All major **car-rental companies** are represented, both at the airports and other convenient in-town locations. **Budget,** for instance, has offices both at the International Airport (tel. 214/574-4141 or 574-4800) and Love Field (tel. 214/357-0288), as well as in town at 3127 W. Mockingbird Lane (tel. 214/357-1574), downtown at 2122 Olive St. (tel. 214/741-6843), in the Valley View Mall at 5803 LBJ Freeway (tel. 214/233-7609), and at 505 S. Central Expressway (tel. 214/231-3126). Also well represented is **National,** at the International Airport (tel. 214/574-3400), at Love Field (tel. 214/357-0478), downtown at 2400 Commerce St. (tel. 214/939-0544), in North Dallas at 12816 Coit Rd. and LBJ Freeway (tel. 214/233-0855), and at a Holiday Inn at 4099 Valley View Lane (tel. 214/387-8966).

Of course, if you must, you can get around by bus. **Dallas Area Rapid Transit (DART)** does provide transport throughout the entire metropolitan area with 24-hour service on major routes. Fares are based on a zone system, beginning at 50¢ for the first zone. Weekdays only **DART Hop-A-Bus** service provides transportation on three downtown routes for just 25¢. And you can save on astronomical downtown parking garage rates by utilizing **Park & Hop;** you park at Reunion Arena all day for just $1 and receive a Hop-A-Bus coupon good for one round trip. For routing information throughout the system, call 979-1111 or 826-2222.

**Taxi** fares in cities like Dallas can do you in. It may be cheaper to rent a car for a day than take a taxi from point A to point B. Fares are $1.30 for the first tenth of a mile, 10¢ for each additional tenth of a mile, 10¢ for every three-fifths of a minute waiting time (those add up quickly in Dallas's usually tied-up traffic), 50¢ for each additional passenger from 7 a.m. to 7 p.m., $1 for each additional passenger from 7 p.m. to 7 a.m. From the International Airport to downtown, your taxi fare will be about $20, $10 from Love Field. If you need a taxi, call Yellow Cab (tel. 426-6262).

## Airport Transfers

Some major hotels offer free transport to/from the airports, but most rely on the **Link,** a bus service connecting both airports with numerous hotels throughout the metropolitan area. And hotels not directly on the Link route usually offer free shuttle service to/from the nearest hotel that is. Fare is $8 one way, $15 round trip. You'll travel in air-conditioned comfort and be provided with a complimentary Dallas newspaper or *Wall Street Journal* to read on the way. The Link operates from 6 a.m. to 10 p.m. daily. Call 790-0441 for details.

**ANNUAL EVENTS:** There's always a lot happening in Dallas. Major annual events are listed below, but you should also write in advance to the **Dallas Convention & Visitors Bureau,** 1507 Pacific Ave., Dallas, TX 75201 (tel. 214/954-1452), for a calendar detailing happenings during your stay. Also check local papers when you're in town.

## January

Dallas gets the New Year off to a rousing start with the **Cotton Bowl Parade** on January 1—a morning procession of beautiful floats, clowns, bands, etc.—along Commerce Street. Call 565-9931 for details. Of course, the parade's not the only event of the day; it's followed by the nationally televised **Cotton Bowl Classic**—an exciting game between the Southwest Conference champion and another nationally ranked college team. For ticket information write to CBAA, P.O. Box 47420, Dallas, TX 75247, or call 214/638-2695.

## March

**Virginia Slims of Dallas,** in the early middle of the month, draws some of the biggest names in women's tennis. Will Martina and Chris go to the finals again, or will someone new finally rise from the lower ranks? You'll find out at the Moody Coliseum on Southern Methodist University campus. For ticket information, call 214/750-8362.

Another athletic event is the **NCAA Basketball Final Four,** in which the nation's top college teams compete for the national title at Reunion Arena. Call 214/651-1986 for details.

## April

It's the biggest, oldest, and bestest chili cookoff in the Dallas/Fort Worth area—the **Prairie Dog Chili Cook Off & World Championship of Pickled Quail Egg Eating.** Close to 100,000 people attend the two-day free weekend event. They enjoy not only great (and less-than-great) chili, but a parade, continuous live entertainment, dancing, a junior cookoff for chefs 8 to 18, games and competitions (an anvil toss, lemon roll, tobacco spitting, beer drinking, eat-and-run stewed-prune-spitting contest, and the selection of a Miss Prairie Dog Hot Stuff). A highlight is the pickled-quail-egg-eating contest (the record is 36 in a 30-second time limit). Sometimes chilihead weddings are part of the festivities. It all takes place at Traders Village, 2602 Mayfield Rd., off Hwy. 360 in Grand Prairie. For details, call 214/647-2331.

There's also a **Western Days Celebration and Rodeo** at Traders Village in April.

Like the cookoff, early in the month, **World Championship Tennis Finals** at Reunion Arena, draw the biggest names in men's tennis. For information, call 214/969-5556; to charge tickets, 214/787-1500.

Later in the month the **International Bazaar** takes place on the City Hall Plaza, a three-day event in which over 35 countries are represented with booths in the shape of Moroccan tents, Chinese pagodas, and classical Greek temples. Each nationality features its indigenous food, folk dancing, and crafts. Admission is free. For details, call 214/720-2232.

Late April through about mid-June, for seven weekends you can attend an Olde English Renaissance festival called **Scarborough Faire** in nearby Waxahachie, 30 miles south of Dallas. The pageantry includes Maypole dances, puppet shows, falconry displays, living chess matches, royal processions, feasts, jousting, musical and theatrical entertainment, games like axe throwing and gag the dragon, jugglers, jesters, musicians, and mirthmakers. There are food vendors offering everything from Scotch eggs to "trollhouse" cookies and hundreds of craftspeople retailing stoneware whistles, wind chimes, unicorn boxes, kaleidoscopes, chain mail, handmade brooms, tin soldiers, you name it. Tarot card readers and palmists too. Admission is $9.50 for adults, $4.50 for children 5 to 12 (under 5, free). For ticket information, call 214/937-6130.

Every Friday and Saturday, April through September, the **Mesquite Championship Rodeo** takes place about 15 miles east of downtown Dallas at the 6,400-seat Mesquite Arena, I-635 at Military Parkway (tel. 214/285-8777). It's a full professional rodeo, with bull riding, steer wrestling, calf roping, bareback riding, a kids' calf scramble, saddle bronc riding, barrel racing, rodeo clowns, and more. The show starts at 8:30 p.m. Tickets cost $5 for adults, $3 for children 12 and under, $7 for box seats. Don't miss it if you're in town.

## May

Early May brings the **Cinco de Mayo Fiesta** (celebrating Mexico's freedom from France) to Traders Village in Grand Prairie, 2602 Mayfield Rd., off Hwy. 360 (tel. 214/647-2331). Folkloric dancers, mariachi groups, and Latin bands provide free entertainment. And there are guest appearances by Mexican movie and recording stars. Plenty of tacos too.

The **Swiss Avenue Tour of Homes** comes next, a walking tour focusing on the Georgian, Spanish, Mediterranean, Victorian, English Tudor, and Prairie School–style homes along the tree-lined streets of a 140-acre Historic District just north of downtown. In addition to house tours, activities include an antique show, a quilt display, refreshments, musical entertainment, and an old-fashioned neighborhood parade. Tickets are about $6. Call 214/824-6603 for information.

The **Byron Nelson Golf Classic,** an annual tournament on the Professional Golfer's Association Tour, is held every May at Las Colinas Sports Club in Irving; call 214/742-3896 for details.

And the month winds up with **Artfest** on Memorial Day Weekend—over 200 arts and crafts booths in Fair Park. Admission is about $3. Call 214/361-2011 for details.

## July

A mammoth fireworks display with old-fashioned patriotic band concerts takes place every **July Fourth** at the Cottonbowl. Call 214/565-9931 for information. There are also July Fourth activities in **Old City Park**—a parade, a speech by a local notable, children's games, square dancing, music, and pie-eating contests. Call 214/421-5141 for details. Check the local papers and contact the Dallas Convention & Visitors Bureau to get the full scoop on Independence Day activities.

Late July through early August the **Ringling Brothers and Barnum & Bailey Circus** comes to the Reunion Arena each year. Call 214/658-7068 for information.

## September/October

The weekend after Labor Day weekend, dozens of Indian tribes converge on Traders Village, 2602 Mayfield Rd., off Hwy. 360 (tel. 214/647-2331), for a giant **Indian Pow-wow** with dance competitions in full regalia, an immense arts and crafts show, food booths, and tepees.

Late September through mid-October, Dallas hosts the **State Fair of Texas,** the largest state fair in the country. It has everything you could ask for in an event of this kind—amusement park rides, a large area of livestock exhibits, circus acts, fireworks displays, headliner performances, parades, numerous free outdoor concerts, wrestling, a high-dive show, rodeo, crafts booths, cooking demonstrations, an ice show, a Broadway musical, international exhibits, every kind of carnival food from cotton candy to corn dogs, even a side show. And one of the best attended State Fair events is a gridiron clash between the Universities of Texas and Oklahoma. That's not the half of it. Admission is $4.50 for adults, $1.50 for children 5 to 12 (under 5, free; senior citizens admitted free on Tuesdays). Parking costs an additional $3 per car. It all takes place at Fair Park, of ourse. For further information, call 214/565-9931. Check the papers for details.

Almost contiguous with the State Fair is **Cityfest,** a five-week downtown event featuring jazz concerts, lectures, street dancing, fashion shows, crafts, bands, Oktoberfest activities, aerobics, children's performances, art exhibits, a Victorian afternoon tea, theatrical events, and more. Call 214/720-2232 for details.

## October

There's a full **Oktoberfest** at Traders Village, 2602 Mayfield Rd. in Grand Prairie (tel. 214/647-2331), with a biergarten tent, oom-pah bands, German dance, and the best of the wurst *mit* sauerkraut.

Late October through early November is the **Neiman-Marcus Fortnight,** an annual salute since 1957 to a foreign country. The original downtown Neiman's at Main and Ervay Streets (tel. 741-6911) features the foods, fashions, furnishings, art, crafts, and thematic decorations of the chosen country. And there are special guest appearances by such notables as the Queen of Thailand, Princess Margaret, Sophia Loren, and Irene Papas and Anthony Quinn.

A weekend in late October is also set aside for the **Vineyard Fair** featuring some 600 artisans, live entertainment, and food booths along Routh, Fairmount, Boll, Worthington, and McKinney. Sometimes it is internationally themed in conjunction with the Neiman-Marcus Fortnight.

## December

The Dallas County Heritage Society features **Candlelight Tours of Old City Park** during the holiday season. The celebration begins with the tree lighting at City Hall, a festivity enlivened by choir and band music. From the tree lighting, there's a parade to the park joined by horse-drawn carriages, bell ringers, carolers, strolling minstrels, holiday revelers, and Santa himself. The historic buildings are decorated in period Christmas themes and lit by hundreds of candles. There are guided tours, fresh-baked breads and cakes for sale, crafts demonstrations, musical entertainments, games, and melodrama. Brent Place, the park's 1876 farmhouse restaurant, serves holiday fare, and sleigh rides, carriage rides, and children's activities are part of the fun. It's all designed to acquaint visitors with the ways in which Christmas was celebrated in North-Central Texas between 1840 and 1910. Call 421-7800 for information.

There are also special Christmas tours of the **DeGolyer House** at the Dallas Arboretum and Botanical Gardens (tel. 327-8263). The house is decorated for the season, and bell ringers, church choirs, and carolers fill the house with holiday music.

**HOTELS:** Like Houston, Dallas is overbuilt, which means you can almost always get a room, weekend rates are substantially reduced, and on the whole your hotel dollar goes pretty far. The only time a room might be difficult to obtain is during a major sporting event, like the Texas/Oklahoma Football Weekend at the Cotton Bowl in October. And even then, when my parents decided at the last minute to come visit me that particular weekend, I didn't really have trouble making reservations; it just took a few more phone calls. Do reserve in advance any time of year to give yourself optimum choice.

Listings begin with $100-and-up deluxe and upper-bracket categories, the former a tad more luxurious and expensive than the latter. Hotels designated moderately priced are in the $50 to $85 range. And below that, these days, we're talking budget.

## Deluxe Choices

The celebrated **Mansion on Turtle Creek,** 2821 Turtle Creek Blvd., at Gillespie Avenue, Dallas, TX 75219 (tel. 214/559-2100, or toll free 800/527-5432), is the premier choice of the royal (King Olaf of Norway, Queen Sirikit of Thailand, Princess Margaret) and the recognizable (Victoria Principal was married in the Garden Room, most of the cast of "Dallas" stays here during filming in summer, and other notable guests have included Frank Sinatra, John Travolta, Givenchy, Saudi billionaire Adnan Khashoggi, Ralph Lauren, and President Gerald Ford). For all that, the Mansion's not glitzy. Under the ownership of oil heiress Caroline Hunt Schoellkopf, it achieves instead an air of old-moneyed establishment. Built by cotton baron Sheppard King in the 1920s, an era when no display of wealth was considered too ostentatious, it was designed to evoke a

16th-century Italian country mansion. The son of a later owner, oil billionaire Freeman Burford, once described his magnificent 23-room home as an "F. Scott Fitzgerald fantasy." And indeed it was the scene of many a Gatsby-esque party. Guest Tennessee Williams retreated here to write in the 1940s and may have incorporated the high-living Burfords into his lexicon of southern characters.

Ms Schoellkopf purchased the estate in 1979 and spent $21 million converting it to a deluxe hotel and relandscaping its 11½ surrounding acres to lush gardens that have been featured in *Architectural Digest*. The ivied pink stucco building overlooks a fountain courtyard and circular drive, the kind that is used as background in Cadillac commercials. Its canopied entrance is a 32-foot-high rotunda with a grand staircase and floor-to-ceiling arched windows. And the interior, highlighted by Italian marble and Spanish tile flooring, is lavishly adorned with custom chandeliers, valuable antiques, museum-quality artworks, and jardinières filled with thousands of dollars of fresh-cut flowers, exquisitely arranged. In the lobby, Louis XVI–style chairs and ecru velvet sofas, set off by Chinoiseries and black lacquer tables, face a working fireplace, one of several in the hotel's public areas.

Tremendous effort is made to treat every guest like a VIP. Staff members will address you by name, and guest histories are taken and frequently consulted. Your birthday or anniversary may be acknowledged with champagne or flowers, your preferences will be remembered, and returning guests are likely to find a special treat in their rooms—perhaps a box of homemade chocolate truffles or a basket of fruit. That's all in addition to such niceties as a concierge who can procure a Learjet at a moment's notice or get your tux cleaned in the middle of the night, 24-hour room service, complimentary overnight shoeshine, twice-daily maid service, nightly bed turndown with imported chocolates, and complimentary limousine service for trips in a two-mile radius.

The 129 guest rooms are large and luxurious, decorated in soft romantic colors like gold/ochre, peach, or champagne. They're very residential in feel, with cable color TVs (with remote control) concealed in handsome walnut armoires that double as pull-out desks, shelves of books and selections of coffee table magazines, AM/FM radios, four-poster beds triple-sheeted in Belgian linen and made up with oversize down pillows and silk moiré spreads, sofas and ottomans, and three phones (bedside, bath, and living area). Baths have rose marble vanities with makeup mirrors and full-length mirrors, and they're furnished with Hermès hand soaps and other customized toiletries, oversize bath towels, hair dryers, and terry robes.

Limousine transport is offered to the nearby Crescent Club, a deluxe superspa offering exercise, dance, and aerobics classes; every imaginable kind of workout equipment (Nautilus, CAM III, free weights, jump ropes, etc.); massage, herbal wraps, saunas, hot and cold plunges, facials, whirlpool baths, mineral baths, saunas, steam rooms, lockers, workout clothing, a juice bar, and all the equipment and cosmetics (from curling irons to colognes) you need to get yourself back together after a workout.

The hotel's major dining room merits a separate recommendation in the restaurant section of this chapter. Additional food and beverage facilities include the delightful cove-ceilinged Promenade, where sunlight from large arched windows illuminates the workings of many a briefcase breakfast at the Italian rose marble tables. It's a delightful setting with yellow-print upholstered seating, crystal chandeliers, and marble flooring, made 18th-century garden-like by a trellised ceiling, ficus trees, and large floral arrangements. It's the kind of place you can breakfast on fresh raspberries and cream or lunch on chilled poached salmon with cucumber dill salad. High tea is also served at the Promenade.

The Lower Bar, reminiscent of Washington's Jockey Club with its brown tufted-leather sofas, beamed ceiling, blazing fireplace, and forest-green walls hung with hunting prints, is the place to see and be seen in town at cocktail hour and late-night piano bar. Hors d'oeuvres are served in the adjoining Upper Bar, a few steps up, at tables lit by brass candle lamps.

Other facilities include an outdoor heated pool and sundeck. Some rooms open on the pool and have private garden patios. And no-smoking rooms and facilities for the disabled are also available.

Rates are $170 to $225 single, $25 per extra person, $8.50 a night for parking. Inquire about weekend packages incorporating special features like champagne on arrival and room-service breakfast.

Built by a beer baron with champagne taste, Adolphus Busch, in 1912, and recently renovated to the tune of $48 million, the **Adolphus**, 1321 Commerce St., between Field and Akard Streets, Dallas, TX 75202 (tel. 214/742-8200, or toll free 800/227-4700), is as opulent as a Fabergé egg. A 22-page booklet is required to detail the wealth of art and antique treasures housed in its plush precincts. And its mansard-roofed beaux arts exterior, with Louis XIV wrought-iron grillwork, is as striking a landmark in Dallas's chrome-and-glass modern downtown as it was in the early 20th century when contrasted with Commerce Street's humble wooden storefronts. The Adolphus has always been a social hub of the city, a setting for debutante balls, society weddings, and other grand events. Caruso sang here in the '20s. In the '30s Benny Goodman and Harry James played big-band music in the Century Room, and famous guests included President Franklin D. Roosevelt and Amelia Earhart. And the '40s and '50s added entertainers like Liberace, Sophie Tucker, and Eddie Cantor to the list of luminaries who performed for Adolphus guests.

Headliners no longer entertain at grand hotels, but celebrities and notables do stay here—everyone from Jimmy Carter to Gloria Vanderbilt. Guests are cosseted with every service and luxury—a 24-hour, can-do-anything concierge; complimentary overnight shoeshine; a *Wall Street Journal* and/or Dallas paper delivered to your door each morning; 24-hour room service; and nightly bed turndown with gourmet chocolates, to name a few.

Rooms are exquisitely furnished with Queen Anne and Chippendale reproductions, carpeting is English Axminster, and beds are covered with plump French country-style down comforters with matching ruffled pillow shams. Lace-curtained windows and live plants add to the residential feel. Most rooms offer large walk-in closets, and all feature sitting areas with sofas and armchairs, fully stocked mini-bars, full-length mirrors, two or three phones, cable color TVs with movie stations, and AM/FM radios. And marble-walled baths contain terry robes, scales, thick oversize towels, and fine imported toiletries.

The Adolphus is impressive in every nook and cranny, beginning with the Main Lobby where mahogany-paneled walls are hung with 17th-century Flemish tapestries (they're part of a set; the others are displayed at the Metropolitan Museum of Art in New York). In the grand-hotel tradition, the Lobby Lounge occupies an entire floor. Afternoon tea and cocktails are served here amid the potted palms and Chinoiseries while a pianist entertains on the ornately carved antique grand piano. It's lovely to while away an afternoon here over tea and scones with whipped cream and raspberry preserves, or perhaps champagne and caviar, to say nothing of sinfully rich chocolate truffles. The hotel's main dining room is one of Dallas's premier restaurants, the magnificent gilt and rococo French Room (it is fully described in the next section of this chapter). Lunch and complimentary afternoon hors d'oeuvres are served in the pubby New York–style, burgundy and marble Palm Bar; deli sandwiches and salads are featured. And a more all-around dining facility is the Bistroquet, a delightful

French country setting with floral-print-cushioned Windsor chairs, mahogany-paneled walls adorned with framed botanical prints and china plates, and candlelit tables with checkered cloths. It's open for all meals; a highlight is the champagne brunch served here on Saturday and Sunday.

Additional guest facilities include a Clark Hatch Physical Fitness Center offering extensive workout equipment, aerobics classes, steam and sauna, massage, tanning booths, and a whirlpool bath. Guests can also use a nearby pool and jogging track.

I could really go on forever describing this hotel; there are $2\frac{1}{2}$ million worth of stunning antiques in the lobby alone. And it has been aptly described as "the most beautiful building west of Venice."

Rates are $140 to $180 single, $155 to $195 double, $20 for an extra person (children under 16 stay free). Weekend rates are reduced to $129, single or double. Parking (valet only) is $7.50 a night.

Right in the heart of downtown Dallas, the **Fairmont,** at Ross and Akard Streets, Dallas, TX 75201 (tel. 214/720-2020, or toll free 800/527-4727), has always been a glittering hub of local events. In 1968, the year the hotel opened, the Dallas Opera began its season with a parade of elephants (for *Aïda*) through the Fairmont's lobby and ballroom. And speaking of opera, gourmet guest Luciano Pavarotti has taken over the kitchen to prepare his own meals. Additional excitement emanates from the hotel's Venetian Room, a lavish supper club decorated with murals of the famed canals, where headliner entertainers like Joel Grey, Carol Channing, Ella Fitzgerald, and Tina Turner perform. The Venetian Room is also used for sumptuous Sunday buffet brunches (more about this facility in nightlife listings, farther along in this chapter).

The Fairmont's marble-walled lobby sets the grandiose tone for the entire establishment. Hung with immense crystal chandeliers, carpeted in burgundy and gold, and decorated with ornately gilt-framed mirrors and a 24-foot-square Aubusson tapestry of Cabeza de Vaca, it contains a plush lobby bar, scene of afternoon piano entertainment. Also off the lobby are exclusive shops (you *can* purchase a Hermès tie on the spur of the moment) and galleries, and the Brasserie, a 24-hour, garden-decor restaurant with white shuttered windows, ficus trees, and street lamps evoking, ostensibly, a French café. In addition to a regular continental/American menu, it features international dishes in conjunction with frequent mini-festivals for which the restaurant is redecorated and waiters and waitresses are appropriately costumed. For Oktoberfest, for instance, the staff was attired in Bavarian garb, and sauerkraut-garnished, paprika-sauced dishes and German wines and beers were added to the dining options.

The Pyramid is the Fairmont's haute-cuisine French restaurant, a setting dominated by an inverted pyramid of glass and brass set off by sienna suede walls and comfortable, high-backed upholstered chairs. The fare in this deluxe room has garnered many awards. At dinner you can order à la carte or opt for a table d'hôte meal at $39.50—like fresh mussels stuffed with crabmeat mousse in a light mustard cream sauce, followed by a chilled avocado soup with salmon caviar, an entree of baby pheasant braised en casserole with truffle and foie gras sauce, a salade de saison, a dessert of hot lime soufflé with a light lemon sauce, chocolates and petit fours, a raspberry liqueur, and coffee. Wine, of course, is extra. At lunch, though fancier choices are offered, you might dine on a simple hot sandwich of roast beef, Swiss cheese, avocado, and onion served with coleslaw and steak fries for $7.75. The adjoining Pyramid Lounge is a popular nightspot featuring live entertainment (a vocalist and piano or a trio) for dancing nightly.

Fairmont rooms are decorated in a variety of styles, some contemporary, some traditional, but all attractive and residential in feel. They have large walk-in closets, full-length mirrors, cable color TVs with HBO, AM/FM radios, alarm clocks, and shoe polishers. Bath amenities include extra phones, Irish linen hand towels, terry robes, scales, makeup mirrors, and large white scallop seashells filled with exclusive toiletries. *U.S.A. Today* and one or both of the Dallas papers are delivered to your door each morning, and a chocolate mint is left on your down pillow at nightly turndown. There's a complimentary limo for guests to use when shopping, dining, or theater-going (reserve it in advance), room service is round the clock, a concierge is on hand to accede to any requests, and there's a car-rental desk in the lobby. For a small fee, guests can use the nearby Brookhollow Country Club (tennis, golf, swimming) and the adjacent Metropolitan Fitness Center offering an indoor Olympic-size pool, a one-twelfth-mile jogging track, Cam II and Nautilus equipment, whirlpool, sauna, steam, massage, basketball, racquetball, squash, volleyball, and more. In addition, on the Terrace Level of the hotel itself is an outdoor Olympic-size pool and flower-bordered sundeck with adjoining kiddie pool; room service is available poolside.

Rates are $156 to $210 single, $185 to $240 double, $25 for an extra person, including children. Greatly reduced weekend rates are available. Parking is $8.50 per night.

The **Mandalay Four Seasons,** 221 E. Las Colinas Blvd., between O'Connor Road and Wingren Drive, Irving, TX 75039 (tel. 214/556-0800, or toll free 800/268-6282), nestles in a peaceful lakeside setting on beautifully landscaped grounds just 15 minutes by car from downtown and 10 minutes from the Dallas/Fort Worth International Airport. It's a bit like a country club, complete with four indoor and eight outdoor tennis courts, seven racquetball courts, two squash courts, three separate training and exercise rooms featuring Nautilus equipment, large indoor and outdoor swimming areas, whirlpools, saunas, a one-eighth-mile jogging track, the 18-hole Hackberry Creek Golf Course, and the Las Colinas Equestrian Center—all of the above on the premises or very close by and easily accessible to guests. And that's not to mention such spa services as massage, herbal wraps, facials, etc., and the availability of lessons in tennis, golf, riding, aerobics, etc.

Like all Four Seasons hostelries the Mandalay offers numerous frills—24-hour concierge and room service, complimentary newspaper delivered with room service, nightly bed turndown, overnight shoeshine, and a willingness to accede to almost any guest request. Rooms are stunning, decorated in taupe, rose, or soft Wedgwood-blue color schemes. Wall coverings that look like watered silk are hung with beautiful artworks—Chinese embroideries, framed botanical prints, old lithographs, and such. Your beautiful marble bath will have a phone, hair dryer, scale, and luxury toiletries. Full-length mirrors, cable color TVs, and AM/FM clock radios are, of course, provided, and complimentary Aretesia and Mountain Valley water are distributed daily.

The hotel's main dining room is the Café D'Or, its drapes, walls, and carpeting all of an exquisite floral pattern of roses on a cream-and-green trellis-like background. The garden ambience is enhanced by flower boxes, flowers on every table, ficus trees, and lavish flower arrangements. Large windows look out over Lake Carolyn.

The oak-paneled Enjolie is the gourmet room, much acclaimed for its first-rate nouvelle cuisine. It's also one of Dallas's prettiest restaurants. An immense flower arrangement in a beautiful Oriental vase graces the entranceway, tables are clothed in wheat-color linen and elegantly appointed with Lenox china and fine silver, lighting emanates from shaded sconces and ornate chandeliers, and chairs are upholstered in silk and leather. Classical background music further heightens Enjolie's delightful atmosphere. A typical Enjolie dinner might include an hors d'oeuvre of stuffed quail with mushrooms and truffle sauce ($12.25), an entree of paupiette of salmon with lobster mousse and caviar ($22.75), a salad course of Boston lettuce, spinach, radicchio, and endive with warm goat cheese and croutons ($4.75), and one of the pastry chef's raved-about desserts. A distinguished wine list is, of course, available, and Enjolie, like all Four Seasons restaurants, offers a full low-calorie menu with three or four courses (including desserts) totaling just 800 calories at dinner, 500 at lunch.

Another facility here is Rhapsody, a lake-view bar/lounge offering piano-bar music and dancing nightly as well as meals. In summer there's a poolside eatery called the Pavillion for refreshing salads and strawberry daiquiris. Afternoon tea and piano entertainment are offered at Les Jardins, a lushly planted lobby bar with a marble and brass fountain and ficus trees growing toward a skylight ceiling. And complimentary hors d'oeuvres are served afternoons at Apéritif, another lobby bar/lounge. In addition to a sundry shop, the hotel houses Haftar Boutique where you can find anything in the way of gifts from a plush stuffed panda bear to a French doré clock.

Rates at the Four Seasons range from $155 to $185 single, $180 to $210 double, $25 for an extra person (under 18, free). Weekend rates are very much reduced, and excellent packages are available. Valet parking is complimentary. Facilities for the disabled and no-smoking accommodations are also available.

## Upper-Bracket Hotels

The glittering 1,000-room **Hyatt Regency,** 300 Reunion Blvd., Dallas, TX 75207 (tel. 214/651-1234, or toll free 800/228-9000), combines an excellent downtown location with a host of facilities. The hotel shares a ten-acre park with historic Union Station, the 50-story Reunion Tower, and the 19,200-seat Reunion Arena, center for numerous sporting events and headliner concerts. It may be the most architecturally dramatic hostelry in town, from its gleaming silver glass exterior to its futuristic interior centered on an immense atrium lobby—an indoor park, complete with cascading waterfall, under an 18-story skylight. Glass elevators lit by tiny lights whisk guests through the atrium level and beyond, providing scenic views en route.

Or you could ride the escalator to the extraordinary second floor centered on a stunning fountain of water cascading over a glass dome (it looks like some kind of mystical symbol) and using lovely indoor pools adorned with flowering plants to separate facilities. These include the Park Place Bar, lit by marquee lights and offering seating amid a small forest of ficus trees. A wall of windows look out on Reunion Tower. The Park Place is a simpático setting for afternoon cocktails, enhanced by the music of a jazz trio on weekdays from 5 to 8 p.m. Also on this floor is the Hyatt's main restaurant, the Café Esplanade, with poolside tables lit by charming small brass lamps with shell-shaped shades. Open daily from 6 a.m. to 2 a.m., it features lavish buffets, a beautiful salad bar, and a menu highlighting regional specialties like fajitas, chicken-fried steak, and mesquite barbecue. Next to the Esplanade is Fausto's, the hotel's gourmet dining room, centered on a lotus fountain under a stained-glass skylight. Fausto's offers piano-bar entertainment from 6 to 10 p.m. Monday to Saturday, and the door and walls surrounding its baby grand are of stained glass in a musical motif. They're gorgeous, as is everything in this plush restaurant, decorated in soft shades of mauve, rose, and cocoa. Tables are clothed in silver-gray linen and adorned by fresh roses in crystal holders. A haute-cuisine Italian seafood menu is featured, but you can enjoy the piano music at the oyster bar/wine bar as well. And during cocktail hour Fausto's is popular for pizza. Of course, guests also use dining and drinking facilities over at Union Station, and Reunion Tower has a revolving restaurant and cocktail lounge at 550 feet. The former, Antares, is open daily for lunch/brunch and dinner, including a complete evening prix-fixe meal for $21. All seats offer spectacular views. (More about the cocktail lounge in nightlife listings, later on in this chapter.) Finally, the second floor houses an extensive gift and sundry shop retailing everything from designer clothing to the usual drugstore necessities.

Hyatt rooms are attractive, modern accommodations, decorated in trendy mauve and teal blue and equipped with cable color TVs with Spectravision and HBO movies, full-length mirrors, AM/FM radios, alarm clocks, and live plants. You'll find French-milled soaps and other fine toiletries in the bath, and you'll also enjoy nightly bed turndown with a gourmet chocolate. The 17th floor of the hotel is given over to the Regency Club, complete with plush private lounge and personal concierge service. Regency Club guests are pampered with upgraded room decor and amenities (designer sheets, terry robes, hair dryers and mineral water in the bath, and daily newspaper delivery) plus complimentary continental breakfast and evening cocktail hour with "upscale hors d'oeuvres" like sushi and steak tartare.

The Hyatt's third floor contains a small swimming pool surrounded by a comparatively vast sundeck with a whirlpool bath and umbrella tables. Also on this floor are a well-equipped health club, two tennis courts, a one-tenth-mile jogging track, and saunas for men and women. And rounding out facilities are a lobby concierge, and, at Union Station, a florist, car-rental desk, and a branch of the Dallas Convention & Visitors Bureau.

Rates at the Hyatt range from $110 to $140 single and $130 to $160 double; an extra person pays $20, and children under 18 stay free. Regency Club rates are $160 single, $190 double. Valet parking is $6.50 per night and self-parking $4, though you can park for about $1 per night adjacent to Reunion Arena. Facilities for the disabled are also offered.

In the booming North Dallas area (some say it's becoming a second hub of the city) is the **Marriott Quorum,** 14901 Dallas Parkways just south of Belt Line Road, Dallas, TX 75240 (tel. 214/661-2800, or toll free 800/228-9290). A multifacility property, it offers a lot in its price category. There's complimentary transport to/from the nearby Galleria and 170-shop Prestonwood Mall; on-premises shops and services include airline and car-rental desks; and there's even a coin-op laundry for guest use. On request, all guests are offered nightly bed turndown with a chocolate. An indoor-outdoor swimming pool, sauna, and exercise room are provided. The hotel's all-purpose restaurant is Chicory's, an attractively decorated facility with forest-green walls, rose furnishings, and etched-glass lily-motif windows. Lavish buffets are featured at breakfast, lunch, and Sunday brunch in addition to an American/continental menu. The adjoining Chicory's Lounge is a plush setting for nightly entertainment and dancing, Monday night football aired on large-screen TV, and bountiful complimentary Happy Hour buffets. Guests can also relax in the lobby bar while enjoying afternoon piano music.

Marriott rooms are Oriental in feel, with bamboo and wicker furnishings and gilt bamboo-framed Chinese prints on the walls. They're equipped with full-length mirrors, alarm clocks, AM/FM radios, and cable color TVs with Spectravision and HBO movies. The 11th floor is given over to the concierge level, complete with plush lounge, a private concierge on duty, complimentary breakfast and Happy Hour hors d'oeuvres and cocktails, and upgraded room decor and amenities. Guests on this level get free newspapers delivered each morning, shoeshine machines, live plants, sofas and easy chairs with hassocks, bathrobes, and bathroom scales, among other perks.

The hotel's gourmet restaurant is Mesquite's, an intimate and elegant setting for fresh seafood, ribs, and prime cuts of beef, grilled over mesquite wood. It's open for lunch and dinner.

Rates at the Marriott Quorum are $110 single, $125 double, $15 for an extra person (under 12, free). Concierge-level guests pay $125 single, $140 double. Self-parking is free; valet parking, $4 per night. There are family-plan rates and super-saver weekend rates that can reduce room tariffs as much as 50%. In addition, no-smoking rooms and facilities for the disabled are available.

The 11-story art deco **Stoneleigh Hotel,** 2927 Maple Ave., at Wolf Street, Dallas, TX 75201 (tel. 214/871-7111, or toll free 800/255-9299), dominated the Turtle Creek landscape when it was built in 1923. In its heyday it attracted such celebrities as John Wayne, Bob Hope, Marlene Dietrich, and Judy Garland, and it was the first hotel in Dallas to install a swimming pool and the first to offer that marvelous invention, air conditioning. Its red neon sign is a registered historical landmark. Today the Stoneleigh offers gracious residential charm rather than startling innovation, and it is still a hideaway for some limelight-shunning stars like Shirley Jones, Robert Duvall, and Gavin McLeod. It's been efficiently and lovingly run by the Corrigan family since the 1940s.

Since rooms are individually decorated, it's impossible to describe them; they're comfortable and homey, and equipped with all the modern amenities. Guests are pampered with twice-daily maid service and nightly bed turndown, and the *Dallas Morning News* is delivered to your door each morning. And a courtesy van offers transport to/from Love Field and stops at theaters, shops, and restaurants within a two-mile radius of the hotel. Other on-premises facilities include a large and lovely heated swimming pool nestled in a forest glade (don't worry, there's plenty of room for sunning). Adjoining the pool are a charming rock garden with flower beds and lotus ponds and a small stone bridge leading to a children's playground. The pool area also contains two night-lit tennis courts, and just next door to the hotel is a coin-op laundry.

The Stoneleigh Dining Room is an old-fashioned resort-style restaurant with burgundy leather chairs and a marvelous pastoral-themed mural on the wall. Very good continental fare—like fettuccine with sautéed gulf shrimp in a sauce of heavy cream, Romano cheese, and garlic butter ($9.75)—is served at dinner; a full lunch can be had for $10 or less. In an adjacent lounge called the Den, guests enjoy Happy Hour buffets, nightly entertainment, and Monday-night football on large-screen TV with $1 beer and free hot dogs.

Rates are $92 to $115 single, $105 to $125 double, $13 for an extra person (children under 16, free). Inquire about competitively priced weekend packages. Parking is free.

## Moderately Priced Accommodations

Up in the North Dallas area, the **Best Western Inn LBJ,** 8051 LBJ Freeway (I-635), at Coit Road, Dallas, TX 75251 (tel. 214/234-2431, or toll free 800/528-1234), is a neat and clean property in a good neighborhood just a 15- to 20-minute freeway ride from downtown. There's coffee brewing throughout the day in the lobby, and though there's no on-premises restaurant, an adjoining 24-hour Jojo's (that's a pretty good Texas coffeeshop chain) offers room service, and McDonald's, Arby's, and Denny's are right across the street. Better yet, you're a few minutes' drive from Bagelstein's (see restaurant recommendations) where you can have fresh-baked bagels with cream cheese and whitefish salad for breakfast.

There are 205 rooms housed in a six-story building. They're attractively furnished in oak pieces (including a cabinet that conceals the cable color TV with movie channel) and decorated in pretty sienna/Wedgwood-blue color schemes. White walls are hung with landscape paintings. A small outdoor swimming pool and sundeck complete the facilities at this pleasant but unpretentious property. Parking is free.

Rates are $45 single, $52 double, $5 for an extra person, free for children under 18.

The **Park Cities Inn,** 6101 Hillcrest Ave., at Binkley Avenue (four blocks north of Mockingbird Lane), Dallas, TX 75205 (tel. 214/521-0330), offers one of the best locations in the moderately priced category—just across the street from S.M.U. and near all the campus-oriented restaurants and nightspots in the area. Built in 1963 and privately owned, it is pleasant, clean, and well run. Coffee is served throughout the day in an inviting lamp-lit lobby where comfortable couches and chairs are placed amid potted plants, and a wide choice of newspapers and magazines are spread on the coffee table. Rates include a continental breakfast—sweet rolls, blueberry muffins, toaster waffles, buttered toast, and juices with coffee or tea—served in a pristinely contemporary breakfast room on the second floor. Decorated in earth tones, it offers seating in upholstered chrome chairs at butcher-block tables, and overhead gallery lights illuminate well-chosen artworks on the walls.

Guest rooms are also done up in earth tones; they're vaguely Spanish in feel, with sienna carpeting, white stucco walls hung with southwestern-themed art, and dark furnishings. All have cable color TVs with HBO movies, AM/FM radios, and full-length mirrors. King-size sitting rooms are larger than the standards and add cream-colored velvet sofas and small refrigerators to your amenities. Even larger are executive rooms, which have desks as well.

Rates are $52 single, $60 double in a standard room; $56 and $64, respectively, in a king-size sitting room; $65 and $75 for executive rooms. An extra person pays $5 per night; children under 12 stay free. Parking is free.

Though the Market Center area is not the most scenic in Dallas, it's not an unsavory neighborhood and it is just a five-minute drive from downtown. A good choice here is the **Quality Inn,** 2015 Market Center (Industrial) Blvd., just off I-35, Dallas, TX 75207 (tel. 214/741-7481, or toll free 800/228-5151). An attractive and well-run property, it houses 280 rooms in an 11-story cream stucco building entered via a charming Mexican-style, plant-filled Saltillo-tile lobby centering on a fountain. Afternoons and evenings, piano-bar entertainment is offered in the cozy lobby lounge. Out back is a nice-size pool and sundeck, and 50 of the rooms open out to it. All rooms at the Quality have been recently refurbished and refurnished; they're quite nicely decorated in shades of burgundy and beige and offer double or king-size beds, tables with two chairs, and color TVs with special cable channels.

A restaurant called Tivoli Gardens serves breakfast only—à la carte or buffet, depending on the number of guests in residence. Lunch and dinner are served at the very pretty Brandi's, where walls are adorned with floral prints and beige-linened tables are set amid potted palms. A lavish dessert display table here doubles as the setting for a big floral centerpiece. At night Brandi's tables are lit by candles in crystal holders. The reasonably priced menu gives diners a choice of light fare (burgers, salads, sandwiches), Texas specialties (barbecue, chicken-fried steak), and continental cuisine (for example, escalopes of veal glazed with hollandaise and served with rice pilaf for $8.50).

The Quality has a concierge floor (the 11th) where guests are pampered with brandy at nightly turndown, free newspaper delivery each morning, special bath amenities, a private lounge, and the services of a concierge. Rates here include complimentary continental breakfast and a nice spread of Happy Hour hors d'oeuvres. A gift shop and a small workout room with exercise equipment and a tanning bed round out the facilities. Free transport is offered to/from Love field, and transport to/from the International Airport is available at reasonable cost. Parking is free.

Rates are $65 to $70 for one person, $10 for each additional person, $10 extra across the board for concierge-floor rooms (remember that includes breakfast and afternoon hors d'oeuvres, along with other frills), and children under 16 stay free. Weekend rates are considerably reduced if you reserve far enough in advance. No-smoking rooms are available.

Just across the street is the **Rodeway Inn,** 2026 Market Center (Industrial) Blvd., Dallas, TX 75207 (tel. 214/748-2243, or toll free 800/228-2000), a prim-looking two-story brick motel with white shuttered windows and white-trimmed gray doors. It offers 82 clean and pleasant standard motel units decorated in earth tones with bamboo-motif bedspreads and drapes, brown wall-to-wall carpeting, tub/shower baths with dressing areas, and cable color TVs with movie channels. A small pool/sundeck is out back, and a 24-hour Denny's restaurant is just next door. Parking is free.

Rates are $45 to $50 single, $55 to $60 double, $5 for an extra person, free for children under 18.

**Days Inn,** 2753 Forest Lane, at Grissom (two blocks east of Harry Hines Boulevard), Dallas, TX 75234 (tel. 214/620-2828, or toll free 800/325-2525), greets visitors in friendly fashion with fresh-baked chocolate-chip cookies at the registration desk. Its Northwest Dallas location puts you in proximity to both airports and in a 10- to 15-minute freeway drive of downtown. There's only one drawback; it's surrounded by freeways, and if highway noise stops you from sleeping you'd best stay elsewhere. If that isn't one of your sensitivities, I heartily recommend the place. Its 100 rooms are clean and attractive in the standard hotel/motel mode, furnished with oak pieces, decorated in shades of beige and brown, and sporting Oriental prints on grasspaper-covered walls. Your color TV offers HBO and other cable stations. There's a medium-size pool out back, a small game room for the kids, and a coin-op laundry just down the road. A pleasant on-premises pine-paneled restaurant called Tastyworld serves low-priced meals, like a full turkey dinner with cornbread dressing, mashed potatoes, cranberry sauce, and honey wheat rolls with butter for $5.65. Room service is available from 6 a.m. to noon. Parking is free.

Rates are $45 to $50 single, $50 to $55 double, $5 for an extra person; children under 18 pay $1. And facilities for the disabled and no-smoking rooms are available as well.

You'll easily know when you've arrived at the **Greenwood Inn,** 6950 N. Stemmons Freeway, between Commonwealth Drive and Mockingbird Lane, Dallas, TX 75247 (tel. 214/631-6660). Bright-green trim, railings, stairways, and awnings give it a year-round St. Patrick's Day verdancy. Though it seems a bit out of the way, the Greenwood is actually close to (and provides free transport to/from) Love Field, Market Center, the Convention Center, the Medical Center, and sports arenas. The International Airport bus stops here, and downtown is just a five- to ten-minute drive, depending on traffic. Though it's not a fancy place, the Greenwood does have a certain cachet; Willie Nelson sometimes stays here when he wants to avoid fanfare, as do some of the Dallas Cowboys.

Rooms are clean and adequate. All have one exposed brick wall and are decorated in shades of brown, tan, and rust. They're equipped with all modern amenities, including cable color TV with HBO and AM/FM radio. The nicest are those on the upper floor (it's a two-story building) with high, beamed ceilings. There's a small pool and sundeck out back, and a comfortable bar/lounge called the Greenwood Door, decorated with photographs of Bogart and Gable, opens to an outdoor patio with umbrella tables. The garden-decor Greenhouse

Restaurant has Saltillo-tile floors, caned bentwood chairs, latticework partitions, and many, many ferns and other plants suspended from an overhead trellis. Solid American fare—from blueberry pancakes in the morning to lunchtime chiliburgers to fried chicken/apple pie dinners—is served here throughout the day and available poolside via room service. A coin-op laundry and small game room for children are additional facilities. Parking is free.

Singles pay $44; doubles, $47; an extra person, $3 (children under 12, free). Special facilities for the disabled are available.

Other good low-moderate-cost choices include a **La Quinta Motor Inn** at 10001 N. Central Expressway (U.S. 75), between Meadow Road and Walnut Hill Lane, Dallas, TX 75231 (tel. 214/361-8200, or toll free 800/531-5900). It's a particularly well-run property in a good central location, and it offers a medium-size pool and sundeck, complimentary van service to/from anywhere within a three-mile radius, free parking, and a pot of coffee always brewing in the lobby. A 24-hour Jojo's restaurant adjoins, and Greenville Avenue's restaurant row is less than a mile away. If highway traffic noise bothers you, request a room in the back when you reserve. Details on the La Quinta chain are in Chapter I.

Rates are $50 single, $55 double, $5 for any number of additional people (within reason, of course), free for children 18 and under. Parking is free. Weekend rates offer further reductions, subject to availability. No-smoking accommodations and facilities for the disabled are also offered.

There are about a half dozen additional La Quintas in the Dallas area. Details are available via the above 800 number.

### Budget Choices

**Motel 6,** as always, is your best bet in the rock-bottom category (details and rates are in Chapter I). The chain has two Dallas locations—at 4610 South R. L. Thornton Freeway (Hwy. 35E) just north of Ledbetter Drive, Dallas, TX 75224 (tel. 214/372-1456); it's about a ten-minute drive from downtown. The other is at 9626 C. F. Hawn (U.S. 175), at St. Augustine Road, Dallas, TX 75217 (tel. 214/286-5206); it's about a half-hour drive from downtown.

A conveniently located **Rodeway Inn,** 4150 N. Central Expressway (U.S. 75), at the Fitzhugh Avenue exit (just five minutes from downtown), Dallas, TX 75204 (tel. 214/827-4310, or toll free 800/228-2000), is another good budget choice. A neat, two-story brick building with white doors and shutters, it contains 84 rooms and offers an outdoor pool and sundeck, a 24-hour restaurant called the Pit Grill just next door, and a coin-op laundry within easy walking distance. Rooms are pleasant, clean, and well maintained. Walls are white stucco (though in some cases one is exposed brick or wood paneled), and color schemes utilize teal blue polished-cotton bedspreads and drapes and tan carpeting or vice versa. All rooms are equipped with full tub/shower baths and adjoining dressing rooms, cable color TVs with movie stations, in-room coffee makers, and the other expected modern amenities. King-size rooms have recliner chairs as well.

Rates are just $39 single, $41 for two people in a double-bedded room; $45 for two people in two beds or a king-size; an extra person pays $5; and children under 17 stay free. Parking is free.

### Bed-and-Breakfast

Ruth Wilson's **Bed & Breakfast Texas Style,** 4224 W. Red Bird Lane, Dallas, TX 75237 (tel. 214/298-5433 or 298-8586), matches travelers with home-away-from-home accommodations that are carefully inspected for cleanliness, comfort, and hospitality. Requirements also include locks on bedroom doors, and hosts are encouraged to prepare full breakfasts. Ruth's Dallas offerings range from a bedroom with sunny, plant-filled patio in a modern condo near the downtown area, to rooms in suburban homes with swimming pools, to an antique-furnished room with canopied bed in a Victorian mansion.

Rates range from about $25 to $45 single, $30 to $65 double, always including a breakfast that might be anything from croissants and coffee to a full Mexican or bacon-and-egg meal. Reserve at least two weeks in advance, even farther ahead to get the optimum choice of accommodations. There's a $5 surcharge for one-night stays.

Ruth also has listings in other Texas cities, so you can make additional B&B reservations at the same time.

## Long-Term Stays

Like Houston, Dallas is a sprawling city with numerous multi-unit apartment dwellings that can be rented furnished on a long-term basis (minimum is usually three months) and offer many on-premises facilities. For instance, **Oak Run Apartments** in North Dallas (tel. 214/386-8844) has efficiencies and one- and two-bedroom furnished apartments starting at about $375 a month at 5801 Preston Oaks Rd., just off Preston Road. Some have wood-burning fireplaces, and all offer kitchens with dishwashers. On the premises are a swimming pool/sundeck, volleyball court, and laundry facilities.

This is just one of several Dallas properties managed by a firm called **Fox & Carskadon;** you can call them collect at 214/934-0050 to discuss all area rental options.

# RESTAURANTS: Sophisticated Dallas is fast becoming a formidable contender for top-restaurant-city status, with haute-cuisine haunts rivaling the bicoastal bastions. You can dine sumptuously or in nouvelle simplicity. And you can also enjoy wide-ranging ethnic diversity and all the Texas traditionals like great barbecue, chicken-fried steak, Tex-Mex, and the Lone Star State's best chili. A university town (S.M.U.), Dallas also offers a lot of eateries priced for student budgets.

The following are Dallas's most exclusive dining rooms serving French and nouvelle American cuisines. Two are in hotels, not surprising these days as there's a national trend toward superb restaurants in the finest hostelries. After this category, everything is moderate or low-priced and listed alphabetically by type of cuisine.

## Luxury Establishments

One of the fewer-than-a-handful of restaurants to receive a four-star rating from the *Dallas Times Herald,* the **Routh Street Café**, 3005 Routh St., at Cedar Springs Road (tel. 871-7161), is a certain contender for best little restaurant in Texas. In fact it's garnered more than local raves; everyone from *Vogue* to *Bon Appétit* has lavished praise on co-owner/chef Stephan Pyles, and not only celebrities (like the cast of "Dallas") but major chefs visiting from other parts of the country are frequent patrons. Pyles's cuisine is southwestern American (or American nouvelle), but his passion for food derives from a postcollege stay in Europe, and his training includes three years on staff at the Mondavi Winery in Napa Valley working with three-star French maîtres like Roger Vergé, the Troisgros brothers, and Michel Guérard. Their influence shows, both in food preparation and in presentation; it's mostly the ingredients like buffalo meat,

Gulf Coast redfish, and Hill Country axis venison that smack of *les États Unis*. And then, the excellent and reasonably priced wine list is all American—90% of it representing California wineries and the rest including wines from about 20 states, even Texas. All of Routh Street's waiters are trained in the ways of wine, which means there's no need to deal with that oft-intimidating personnage, the sommelier. And four premium wines (two reds, two whites) are always offered by the glass.

The menu at Routh Street, a five-course prix-fixe meal (with four to six choices for each course) at $45 per person, changes nightly. I'll save myself a lot of superlative adjectives by saying right here that every morsel of every course was exquisite, original in conception, and otherwise heavenly. Routh Street proffers the exalted culinary experience one hopes for in a haute-cuisine, haute-tab restaurant. On a recent visit I began with a first course of catfish grilled over apple wood and served in Créole mustard sauce with grits baked in maple syrup. Other possible choices were grilled quail with warm goat cheese, tomatillo chutney, and marinated black-eyed peas or linguine with smoked duck, herbed mayonnaise, and jicama (an exotic tuber fruit that tastes like an appley turnip). The second course is a palate refresher—perhaps a garden salad of radicchio, lamb's lettuce, and white chicory or an extraordinarily delightful grapefruit-clove ice. It's all leading up to the big moment, the entree—perhaps grilled chop and loin of lamb with roast garlic custard and pecan sauce served with potatoes in a lightly herbed cream sauce and fresh al dente vegetables. Or roast partridge and squab in port wine with cranberries and young leeks. Or roast loin of veal with herbed fresh ricotta and tangerines. The fourth course is a repetition of the second, an ice or salad. I would recommend the ice after the appetizer and the salad after the entree. And finally, you come to the sumptuous desserts, such as a magnificent lemon/macadamia nut/meringue pie that *Cook's Magazine* described as combining "a creamy-textured filling with the crispness of a praline in a rare marriage of clear lemon and buttery nut flavors."

And what of the setting? Routh Street is a converted 1920s wood-frame house, the interior of which has been razed to create a pristine art deco ocean-liner decor that still retains its residential warmth. Carpeting and seat upholstery is gray, walls impeccably smooth peach lacquer, and table linens a harmonizing apricot hue; white lattice grids, brushed stainless-steel railings, and porthole-like air vents add a soupçon of hi-tech. Some very fine artworks, baroque and Renaissance background music, and lovely flower arrangements complete the picture.

Routh Street Café is open nightly from 6 to 10:30 p.m. Reservations are essential, and on weekends you might even need to make them a few weeks in advance.

Good news for the champagne-taste/beer-budget crowd: Pyles and co-owner John Dayton are planning to open a second, lower-priced, more casual eatery, also on Routh Street, called The Courtyard. It may be open by the time you read this.

As in Houston, some of the city's premier restaurants are hotel dining rooms. Most lavish of these is the famed **French Room** at the Adolphus, 1321 Commerce St., between Field and Akard Streets (tel. 742-8200). A rare Louis XV mahogany architect's table serves as the stand for the maître d's reservations book. Behind it is a 19th-century painting of *Venus and Cupid,* one of many impressive gilt-framed oil paintings adorning the rich walnut paneling. A 19th-century English Chippendale mahogany mantel graces a working black marble fireplace, its fretwork housing a collection of Chinese porcelain *blanc de chine* figurines. Then there are the bronze doré lamps, the marble-columned walls and high vaulted ceilings painted with rococo murals of cherubs strewing flowers amid fleecy white clouds, the 17th-century hand-blown Venetian glass chandeliers, and the Savonerrie-reproduction carpets—all combining to evoke an opulent European palace salon.

Your gilt-edged menu, proffered by a tuxedoed waiter, lists classic French cuisine specialties prepared by award-winning chef Pascal Vignau. You could get things extravagantly underway with an *hors d'oeuvre froid* of beluga caviar ($55), in contrast with which a cream-rich scallop mousse with vegetables and lime butter ($11) seems a spartanly frugal choice. Or you may want to experience a soup as unique as quail consommé with Chinese enoki mushrooms ($7.50). Tantalizing entrees include a ragoût of fresh lobster with noodles and basil ($36.50), veal medallions with eggplant and sorrel cream ($28.50), and butterfly of turbot with ratatouille and garlic cream ($24.50). The extensive French-dominated wine list is distinguished, and Edward Schulten was named the most knowledgeable sommelier in the Southwest in a French-government-sponsored competition. Be sure to finish your meal with one of the exquisite selections from the dessert cart—perhaps a feuilleté de framboises, a flaky pastry filled with fresh raspberries and butter cream, topped with powdered sugar, and served in a pool of hot caramel sauce marbelized with raspberry ($5.50).

The French Room is open for dinner only, from 6 to 10 p.m. Monday to Saturday. Coats and ties are required for men. Reservations are essential. Free valet parking is offered to diners.

The restaurant at the **Mansion on Turtle Creek** (see hotel recommendations, above), 2821 Turtle Creek Blvd., at Gillespie Avenue (tel. 526-2121), is among Dallas's most prominent see-and-be-seen precincts; you might espy anyone from Lady Bird Johnson to Larry Hagman and Linda Gray at the next table. But it's more than just a trendy gathering place of glitterati; Wolfgang Puck of Los Angeles was involved in its culinary conception, and young chef de cuisine Dean Fearing (who once led a rock band called Escoffier and the Sauciers) is one of Dallas's most talented *artistes. Food & Wine* magazine recently named him an "Up and Coming Young Chef of America," and every restaurant he has been associated with has garnered five stars from food critics.

Like the rest of this ultraluxurious hotel, the dining room reflects the 16th-century Italianate style of the original King mansion. Its several dining areas incorporate an oak-paneled library with an intricately carved plaster ceiling, a richly ornamented German stone manteled fireplace, and stained-glass windows displaying the coat-of-arms of the Barons of Runnymede (Mrs. King was a descendant of King Edward III of England). The magnificent main dining area was designed by great French architect M. Jacques Carée, director of the École des Beaux-Arts de Fontainebleau. It has an elaborate carved wooden ceiling embellished with *putti,* walls hung with museum-quality gilt-framed paintings, and a fireplace that is a reproduction of one from Bromley Castle in England. There's also a sunny plant-filled veranda with old Spanish tile floors, the corner insets depicting the life of Don Quixote. This very charming room has vaulted ceilings and a row of arched windows overlooking a garden.

The menu changes seasonally and incorporates many regional specialties into a nouvelle French format. Presentations of food are artistic triumphs, and everything is as good as it looks. A recent menu offered such varied beginnings as smoked salmon with warm new potato salad and chive sour cream ($11.50), rabbit and venison sausage with green bell pepper pasta and Cajun sauce ($9.50), South Carolina quail with stir-fried autumn squash in a spicy fried pumpkin crêpe ($10.25), and a hearty Texas black bean and jalapeño jack cheese soup with stuffed Anaheim chili ($5). As for entrees, there were such choices as sautéed New Zealand venison with spicy golden pear sauce and wild rice compote ($25), roast California pheasant with Burgess chardonnay-orange mint sauce and speckled pepper pasta ($23), rack of lamb breaded with Texas pecans in roasted garlic sauce ($25.50), and in contrast, an almost austerely Oriental grilled swordfish steak with sushi vinaigrette and sesame asparagus ($21.50). Selections from the distinguished wine list are de rigueur, as is one of the exquisite dessert offerings, perhaps the crème brûlée with raspberry sauce. Dinner is easily a $100-per-person affair with wines, tips, etc. Lunch can be managed for a bit less, since there are salads and omelets, and several other entrees are under $15.

Lunch is served daily from noon to 2:30 p.m., dinner from 6 to 10:30 p.m., and late supper Monday to Saturday from 10:30 p.m. to midnight. Coats and ties are required for men. Reservations essential.

**Calluaud's**, set in a small frame house at 2619 McKinney Ave., at Routh Street (tel. 823-5380), has gleaned national attention for its classic Gallic fare, with even esteemed critic Craig Claiborne ranking it "with the finest French restaurants in the country." The *Wall Street Journal* took another tack; they cited it as a hub for Dallas power lunches. Chef Guy Calluaud, trained in the European tradition from his earliest years, comes from a family of passionate chefs. Both his parents, three brothers, and a sister are also *cuisiniers*, and his great-grandmother was chef to Napoléon III. Guy still uses some of her recipes hand-written on sheepskin parchment.

The intimate setting is elegant and refined. Wainscotted textured-silk, wheat-colored walls are hung with impressionistic gilt-framed oil paintings; tables are clothed in white linen over pale-peach underlays and exquisitely appointed with Villeroy and Boch china, English silver, and single-rose vases; soft classical music is played; and the room centers on a small skylit garden atrium. Do note the stunning Venetian glass chandeliers overhead. Artistic food presentations begin with a basket of bread wrapped in lace-fringed white linen and accompanied by butter in a floral-motif china dish stamped with the words "bon appétit." Guy usually emerges from the kitchen to greet diners.

The menu changes every four months, but it always offers classic dishes (with some nouvelle innovations) prepared with the finest and freshest ingredients.

A typical lunch might begin with a terrine of chicken livers with truffles and port ($6) or perhaps escargots in garlic butter sauce ($7.50). After that a salad might suffice (particularly with all that good crusty bread and butter), perhaps a mix of chicken, roasted almonds, and heart of lettuce with a walnut/chervil dressing ($12.50) or a lobster salad with green beans, mushrooms, and rémoulade of celery root ($12.50). A tangy hot apple tart with fresh whipped cream ($4) is the perfect ending. An ecstasy-inducing Calluaud dinner I recently enjoyed began with a pheasant pâté en croûte with pistachios ($8), continued with a fresh salmon served with wild mushrooms, tomato, basil, and madeira sauce ($21), went on to a salad course of tender greens with walnut dressing and fried cheese ($8), and culminated in a fluff of hazelnut soufflé topped with rich, thick whipped cream ($6). One must order wines with such meals; Calluaud's fine list highlights French and California vintages. Returning for a minute to the important subject of desserts, soufflés (available at dinner only) are the house specialty, but the dessert cart is not to be lightly dismissed. A lemon meringue tart ($4) and a panier of red berries with zabayon sauce and sponge sugar ($6) were also extremely memorable.

Open for lunch weekdays only, from 11:30 a.m. to 2:30 p.m., and for dinner Monday to Saturday from 6 to 10:30 p.m. Reservations essential.

Guy Calluaud and his charming wife, Martine, also own the delightful **La**

**Bonne Auberge,** 6306 Greenville Ave., at Caruth Haven Lane (tel. 692-6920). Country cousin to Calluaud's, it looks very much the French provincial inn, complete with ivied brick exterior, shingled roof, and dormer windows. Guests are welcomed by the warmth of a blazing fire at the entrance, and the interior features rough-hewn beams on whitewashed wooden ceilings and barnwood-wainscotted walls covered in a lovely floral fabric. Crisply white-linened tables are adorned by vases of country flowers, and seating is in hunter's-green Windsor chairs or comfortable booths. Bare wood floors, lots of plants, and soft lighting from brass chandeliers with tiny fluted shades and matching wall sconces complete this pretty picture.

The menu, like the decor, is country French, highlighting seafood dishes. Lunch might consist of a salad of bay scallops in lemon pesto over a julienne of crisp vegetables ($8.50), a lobster salad sandwich on fresh croissant ($9), or an omelet stuffed with shrimps sautéed in garlic and garnished with parsley ($5.50). Scrumptious homemade rolls and butter are served with these simple meals, and a glass of wine is de rigueur. It's still a light meal, so do order a dessert such as the irreproachable puits d'amour (similar to crème brûlée and served in a pool of raspberry sauce). At dinner, commence with a kebab of escargots and bacon in spicy basil sauce ($6) or a French-style oyster chowder ($4). Broiled fresh fish—salmon filet ($15), Dover sole ($15), brook trout ($9.50), or an assorted seafood grill ($12)—is offered with a choice of such sauces as hot-and-spicy diable, poivre vert, Dijon mustard, and beurre blanc. More complex entrees include a red snapper grenobloise with capers, lemon, croutons, and butter sauce ($10.50), a classic paella made with saffron rice ($13), fresh noodles with seafood and cream sauce ($9.50), and in the nonseafood category, duckling in fresh peach sauce ($14.50) and broiled spring baby chicken seasoned with herbs and lime ($9). The wine list once again highlights French and California wines, and the famed Calluaud soufflés are a dessert option. You might adjourn after dinner to the charming candlelit bar/lounge for a cognac, especially if it's Friday or Saturday night when piano-bar entertainment is offered.

Open for lunch weekdays from 11:30 a.m. to 2:30 p.m., for dinner Monday to Saturday from 6 to 10:30 p.m. Reservations essential.

The most exciting of the restaurants in the chic West End Historic District is **La Touraine,** 1701 Market St., at Ross (tel. 749-0080), a beautiful bistro housed in a century-old building. Though the fare is country French, the decor is Parisian elegant. Rich oak-paneled walls display gilt-framed mirrors and oil paintings; 1930s French frosted-glass lighting fixtures with bird designs create soft amber lighting; windows are curtained in antique lace; white-linened, candlelit, and flower-bedecked tables are most beautifully appointed with monogrammed napkins and fine china; and a lavish floral arrangement graces the bar. French music—Edith Piaf, Brassens, etc.—enhances the Gallic ambience, as does the mostly French staff of smartly attentive waiters. Fourteen-foot rough-hewn beamed ceilings provide the one note of rusticity in these posh precincts.

The romantic setting is a delight, and it's matched by the delectable dishes prepared each night by chef François Grandjean, who the owners lured from a fashionable Clichy seafood restaurant. Speaking of the owners, they are, with additional Parisian partners, the same people who operate Dallas's favorite *boulangerie,* La Madeleine; all the restaurant's delicious fresh-baked breads derive from that sublime source (details about La Madeleine later in this chapter).

At La Touraine dinner starts off with hors d'oeuvres like grapefruit stuffed with crabmeat ($6.50), a velvety chicken liver pâté ($5.75), or a traditionally hearty soupe à l'oignon topped with thick melted Gruyère over garlicky croutons ($5). Country dishes include a classic coq au vin stewed in vin rouge and served with fresh noodles ($10.50) and boeuf bourguignon ($10.50) with steamed potato. Grandjean's seafood creations also merit attention, such as a coquilles Saint-Jacques, pan-sautéed scallops in a champagne sauce over Créole rice. One should always consider a salad course after a French entree—here perhaps a salade Solognote of curly lettuce with bacon, mushrooms, and crunchy croutons tossed in hazelnut oil and sherry vinegar ($4.95). And in Dallas, where diners generally must drive after a meal, I applaud La Touraine's offering of premium wines by the glass, in addition, of course, to a well-chosen wine list highlighting French and California burgundies. It can be difficult to choose a dessert here: the tangy tarte tatin, a hot upside-down apple pie ($5.45), is certainly a temptation, but it does mean forsaking the white-chocolate mousse ($3) and the crêpes soufflées au Grand Marnier ($5.75). Happily, there's a solution to this dilemma—an assiette gourmande ($6.75), which is a tasting platter of five different desserts. The lunch menu offers some inexpensive options such as a croque monsieur—grilled ham and cheese sandwich—served with a salad ($5.25) and a salade niçoise ($5.50), in addition to heartier entrees in the $10 range.

Open for lunch Tuesday to Friday from 11:30 a.m. to 2 p.m., for dinner nightly from 6:30 to 10:30 p.m. Reservations essential at dinner. A piano bar is in the works for the future.

## American

A pubby, laid-back S.M.U. hangout, **Snuffer's,** 3526 Greenville Ave., half a block north of McCommas Boulevard (tel. 826-6850), is the kind of place where good rock'n roll is always playing on the jukebox, the bar is always mobbed, and the food is simple but satisfying. Like most college-crowd haunts, it doesn't stint on atmosphere. Soft lighting emanates from amber-bulbed fixtures suspended over bare oak tables, walls are plastered with old family photos owner Pat Snuffer bought at an estate sale, seating is in oak pews garnered from an old Dallas church, and numerous hanging plants add the jungle touch. The front room is quieter, the back room more attractive with Saltillo-tile floors and white spruce walls. An outdoor café area with umbrella tables is planned for the future.

Snuffer's menu is small, but everything on it is homemade from quality ingredients. The restaurant cooks up fresh chickens daily to make its marinated chicken breast sandwiches with cheese ($4.45) and chicken salads ($4.50). Another popular choice is a half-pound cheeseburger with mustard, pickle, red onion, lettuce, and tomato ($3.50, $3.75 with cheese), best enjoyed with an order of yummy, gooey bad-for-you, cheddar french fries ($2.50). Other offerings include salads, nachos, and boiled shrimp; nothing's over $5.50, and there are no desserts.

Open Monday to Saturday from 11 a.m. to 2 a.m., on Sunday from 11:30 a.m. to 2 a.m.

## Barbecue

Everyone told me that some of the best barbecue in the state was at **Sonny Bryan's Smokehouse,** 2202 Inwood Rd., at Harry Hines Boulevard (tel. 357-7120). But the first time I visited, its rundown, greasy spoon funkiness (I mean this place goes way beyond rustic) daunted me. You don't expect ambience at a Texas barbecue joint, but on the other hand one can do without flies. I left without eating, and felt this could not be a recommendable. That night, I happened to mention the experience to Stephan Pyles, chef of Dallas's premier restaurant, the Routh Street Café. "Well, you'll just have to go back," he said. "It's great.

You can't leave Sonny's out of your book." So, dutifully, back I trekked, braving the mob patiently waiting at lunch for one of the uncomfortable, sardine-packed schoolroom arm desks in the cement-floored, fluorescent-lit "dining area." The one with the flies. And darned if it wasn't worth it! Sonny's barbecued beef ($2.30 a sandwich) *is* the best, his coleslaw the creamiest and chunkiest. His great-grandfather, Elijah H. Bryan, started the business in 1910 across the Trinity River; his father, Red Bryan, moved to the present location; and Sonny's been the power behind the pit since 1958. The place is a legend. Even the Hunts ask Sonny to cater parties.

If the weather is good, try for one of the seats at the single outdoor picnic table, grab a tree stump, or sit out on the lawn in front of the Salvation Army Thrift Shop next door. But don't pass Sonny's up because it's too cold to go out; the camaraderie and the food make up for the lack of atmosphere. A full beef, ham, or rib dinner with beans and coleslaw is $4.85; a bigger dinner, $5.55; a canned or on-tap beer, $1.35.

Sonny's is open Monday to Saturday from 10 a.m. to 3 p.m., on Sunday from 11 a.m. to 2 p.m. No credit cards. Arrive early (a little before 11) to avoid waiting for a seat. Very late arrivals risk having food run out.

## Best Breakfasts Plus

None of the following is open just for breakfast, but they're all extremely popular for that meal. However, you will want to visit Bagelstein's at later hours for pastrami and rye, the Vickery for its overstuffed hero sandwiches, Good Eats for mesquite-grilled specialties, and La Madeleine for afternoon tea.

New Yorkers homesick for matzoh ball soup and chopped liver have a spiritual home in Dallas. It's **Bagelstein's**, at 8104 Spring Valley Rd., at Coit Road, in the Northwood Hills Shopping Center (tel. 234-3787). Owners Larry and Susan Goldstein started out with a little bagel factory in 1976, and in a decade have blossomed to major Gothamite deli proportions. What a treat is breakfast at Bagelstein's, on Sunday complete with the *New York Times*. As soon as you snuggle into one of the navy-blue leather booths, a gratis basket of fresh-baked cheese strudel and danish is placed before you. You nibble on this as you sip coffee and peruse the menu, and by the time your waitress arrives you've really eaten enough breakfast. But it would be bad form not to order, so you go ahead and get a toasted pumpernickel bagel with cream cheese, Nova, tomato, and Greek olives ($4.75) or Larry's fabulous whitefish salad ($5.25). Not even 10 a.m. and you've already put away about 1,000 calories. Soon you won't snuggle into a booth, you'll squeeze in.

Lunch or dinner, a bit more moderation is possible but not probable. There are well over 100 items to choose from, including New York pastrami or Chicago corned beef piled high on rye bread ($4.35), a smoked fish platter of whitefish salad, lox, and sable, served with bagels, cream cheese, and fresh vegetables ($8.95), cheese blintzes with sour cream ($4.50), or perhaps an appetizer of stuffed cabbage ($2.95) followed by sliced brisket ($7.65). The latter comes with a cup of soup (like mushroom barley), salad, mashed potatoes, and a vegetable. There's New York–style cheesecake ($1.95) for dessert, one of several fresh-baked offerings (many of them swimming in whipped cream) on display in the revolving glass case. That's to say nothing of waffles topped with ice cream and hot-fudge sundaes.

In appearance, Bagelstein's looks much like its New York counterparts. One wall is covered with a collage of restaurant menus from around the world, including renowned Big Apple delis. A large appetizer display case of smoked fish, borscht, matzohs, egg noodles, schmaltz, halvah, and other Jewish soul foods nestles in a corner of the dining room. And the front room is given over to the bakery. Bagelstein's is renowned. Larry sends sandwiches over to the set of "Dallas," caters movie productions and ABC Sports when they're in town, and kept comedian Shecky Greene from pastrami withdrawal when his daughter was at S.M.U. A no-smoking section is yet another plus.

Bagelstein's is open on Monday from 6 a.m. to 3 p.m., Tuesday to Sunday to 9 p.m. Arrive early on Sunday morning if you can to avoid a wait for seats.

**La Madeleine French Bakery,** 3072 Mockingbird Lane, a block west of U.S. 75 (tel. 696-6960), is the creation of Francis Holder, a professional baker from Lille who owns 75 boulangeries in France and decided Americans too would appreciate his authentic croissants and baguettes. He brought along partner Patrick Esquerré, a PR rep for Young & Rubicam in Paris (one of his clients was the now-defunct Giscard d'Estaing government) and, on the advice of Stanley Marcus (of Neiman-Marcus), they debuted in Dallas. They opened at the above address in 1983 and were so successful that another location (3906 Lemmon Ave., at Oak Lawn; tel. 521-0182) followed a year later, and a third outlet was soon installed in Fort Worth. It's one of the city's favorite breakfast nooks, especially on weekends when people cheerfully share tables and spend hours over coffee and croissants, perusing the papers and chatting with strangers.

A charming French country decor is part of La Madeleine's appeal. The front room houses the glass display case filled with moist, buttery croissants (plain, cheese, almond, apricot, chocolate, etc.), brioches, palmiers, beignets, petit fours, petit pains, and sourdough rolls that are delicious buttered and dunked in big cups of café au lait, and luscious tartes, gâteaux, chocolate meringues, and eclairs. A cheese croissant or most any breakfast pastry—with unlimited cups of rich French coffee—will cost $2.50 or less. The dining area is furnished with wicker-seated chairs at oak tables of varying shapes and sizes. French baskets, breads, baking equipment, and photographs of Paris boulangeries adorn exposed brick walls, ceilings are beamed, and floors bare oak. China plates are displayed in a pine sideboard.

Though many people come by for continental breakfasts and afternoon tea/coffee/pastry breaks, La Madeleine also serves traditional Gallic fare throughout the day—salade niçoise, croissant sandwiches, croque monsieurs, quiches, and soups. Almost everything is under $5, and wines are available by the glass.

The Mockingbird Lane Madeleine is open daily from 7 a.m. to 9 p.m.; Lemmon Avenue, daily from 7:30 a.m. to 9:30 p.m. No credit cards.

Is this Dallas? The **Good Eats Café,** 3531 Oak Lawn Ave., at Bowser (tel. 521-1398), with its ultra-contemporary black-and-white diner decor, looks like a transplant from a trendy New York neighborhood. The floor is covered in black-and-white checkerboard linoleum tile, white walls are hung with neon signs and movie posters (including a still of Ronald Reagan as a cowboy), and white enamel lamps and fans are suspended from high ceilings. During the day sunshine streams in through large windows, and at night the café is cozy by candlelight.

This is one of Dallas's most popular breakfast spots, especially on weekends when everyone comes to schmooze over frittatas, open-face omelets served with hash browns and toast ($3.95); stacks of thick buttermilk pancakes dripping with butter and topped with homemade whipped cream, maple syrup, and fresh strawberries or pecans ($3.25); or slabs of french toast flavored with vanilla and cinnamon and served sprinkled with powdered sugar ($3.40). There's fresh-squeezed orange juice, too. At other meals, mesquite grilling is featured—chicken, brisket, sausage, pork ribs, or a variety of fish that might include salmon, snapper, redfish, shrimp, sea bass, or tuna, grilled crisp outside, tender inside, and served with herbal butter and two fresh vegetables. Daily specials are listed on a blackboard over the open kitchen window in bright colored chalk. A barbecued brisket sandwich is $4.25; an order of mesquite-grilled shrimp with mashed potatoes and corn on the cob, $10.25. Everything is made from scratch, all veggies and fish are fresh, and desserts like four-layer chocolate cake and strawberry cake with cream cheese icing ($2.50 for either) are baked on the premises.

Open Sunday to Thursday from 7 a.m. to 11 p.m., on Friday and Saturday to 11:30 p.m.

The **Vickery Feed Store,** 6918 Greenville Ave., at Park Lane (tel. 363-9198), dates back to the early 1900s when Vickery was a suburb of Dallas and its rustic residents viewed the encroaching city with alarm. The owner of an adjoining meat market built it as a home for his mother-in-law (who was living with him and driving him crazy). In 1947, two years after the town of Vickery was incorporated into Dallas, the home was converted to a feed store. And so it remained until 1981, when Jerry Oliverie, maintaining some of the rough-hewn feed store ambience, opened his restaurant. It's a mix of funky '40s decor and '80s slick, with bare pine floors, a glossy black bar with chrome stools, enamel lamps and fans overhead, and pine-paneled walls hung with an exhibit of photographs depicting old Vickery. Seating is in shiny red leather booths and banquettes at black matte tables, and beer is stored in an antique refrigerator. The Feed Store is always mobbed and tends to be kind of noisy; it's not the place for intimate rendezvous.

The lure is fresh, homemade food served in hefty portions. The breakfast club regulars come for ham and cheddar omelets with homemade hash browns and a toasted bagel ($4.45) or the V.S.F. special—a fried egg on rye toast with cream cheese and pastrami, also served with hash browns ($2.95). The rest of the day there are gargantuan sandwiches like a baguette stuffed with grilled Italian link sausage, bell pepper, onion, and provolone cheese in rich tomato sauce ($4.15), or a California-like sandwich on marble bread of Muenster and Swiss cheeses, cucumber and tomato slices, avocado wedges, black olives, and spinach leaves, slathered with bleu cheese dressing ($3.75). Drink it down with fresh-squeezed lemonade ($1.25), imported beer (there's a wide selection), or Soave Bolla ($2.65 the glass). Sandwich listings are supplemented by items like homemade beef stew ($2.95), a rich cheese/broccoli soup ($2.25), and a few serious entrees such as steamed king crab legs served with drawn butter ($10.25). Homemade desserts include rich chocolate decadence cheesecake ($2.50) to cap your Vickery feed.

Open Tuesday to Friday from 6 a.m. to 2 a.m., on Saturday from 8 a.m. to 2 a.m., and on Sunday from 8 a.m. to midnight. Arrive off-hours if you want to avoid the crowds.

## Cafeteria

For good, old-fashioned home-cooking, there's nothing like a first-rate cafeteria. One of the best of the genre is Dallas's **Highland Park Cafeteria,** 4611 Cole Ave., at Knox Street (tel. 526-3801), a family operation started by Dewey and Carolyn Goodman in 1925. Today their daughter, Gloria, and her husband, Edmund Yates, are in charge, and Carolyn comes by frequently to see that everything is *comme il faut.* As cafeterias go, this one's quite elegant, with comfortable booths, soft lighting emanating from graceful brass chandeliers, brown wall-to-wall carpeting, large plants and ficus trees, and cream-colored walls hung with Persian rugs and watercolors of flowers done by Mr. Goodman's sister-in-law. A large oak cabinet is used to display family china. The walls along the serving line are lined with presidential portraits and biographies. Upstairs, in the buffet area, decorations include English posters depicting Shakespearean characters with commentaries about them from writers like Tolstoy and Auden (Edmund Yates is an aficionado of the Bard).

All the food is fresh and homemade, with baked items (cakes, breads, and pies) emerging hot from the oven throughout the day. A huge soup-to-nuts meal can be had for $6 or less: a bowl of cream of mushroom or curried broccoli soup; an entree of meat loaf, fried chicken, or turkey with dressing; side orders of macaroni and cheese and baked squash; buttered biscuits, jalapeño muffins, or garlic toast; coffee, and rich sour cream cheesecake. Of course, there's no need to eat all that, but it won't cost much if you do. Upstairs, large all-you-can-eat buffet meals are $8.95 at lunch (11:30 a.m. to 2 p.m.) or dinner (5:30 to 8 p.m.), $3.95 for children 4 to 12 (under 4, free). There are nonsmoking areas, and you can take food out if you like. The vast array of items—everything from stuffed peppers to a hot dog and mashed potatoes—means that everyone will be happy. Great salads here, too.

Open Monday to Saturday from 11 a.m. to 8 p.m. There's another location at 5100 Belt Line Rd., at Dallas Parkway (tel. 934-8800). It's open Monday to Saturday from 11 a.m. to 8 p.m., and on Sunday from 10:45 a.m. to 3 p.m.

### A Chicken Shack

Authentic down-home cooking makes **Bubba's,** 6617 Hillcrest Ave., at Rosedale, in the Snider Plaza Shopping Center (tel. 373-6527), a big hit with diverse Dallasites—fashionably attired Yuppies, families, blue-haired old ladies, business people, and S.M.U. students among them. They come for fried chicken, fresh-baked buttermilk biscuits, and country gravy, reputedly like mama used to make (mine didn't). For a chicken shack named Bubba's, it's downright trendy looking: glossy white enamel walls are hung with framed Louis Icart art deco prints, a mirrored wall is adorned with neon tubing from an antique Wurlitzer, seating is at chrome-edged black pedestal tables in fire engine–red leather chrome-frame chairs, and the floor is covered in black-and-white checkerboard linoleum tile. Background music is 1930s jazz. Windows all around make for lots of sunny daylight; otherwise lighting is recessed in a cove ceiling. Trendy or not, you still have to wait in line, cafeteria style, to get your eats, and they're served in sectional styrofoam dishes on plastic trays. In good weather you can take your meal to one of the streetside tables out front.

A hearty meal at Bubba's might consist of three pieces of crispy-on-the-outside, juicy-on-the-inside fried chicken, with two vegetables (they change daily, perhaps black-eyed peas and mashed potatoes with homemade cream gravy), and a fresh-baked hot yeast roll, all for $4.29. Jars of honey on every table are the only condiment. With two pieces of chicken only, the same meal is $3.79. Other options are chicken-fried steak ($4.89), a half dozen chicken livers ($3.69), and fried catfish ($4.89). A much-needed towelette comes on your tray. Bubba's is popular for breakfast too, like two fried eggs with sausage, biscuits, and cream gravy for $3.29. And there's always a homemade peach, cherry, apple, or apricot cobbler on the menu for just 99¢.

Open daily from 6:30 a.m. to 10 p.m. No credit cards.

### Chili

Texans are always raving about chili—their official state food—but it's not so easy to find a restaurant serving this dish in its purest manifestation. **Tol-**

bert's, 4544 McKinney Ave., at Knox Street (tel. 522-4340), is practically a shrine to chili. Founder Frank X. Tolbert was the author of the definitive work on the subject, *A Bowl of Red,* and the motivating force behind the famed annual world championship chili cookoff at Terlingua. He died in 1984, but his chili lives on and the restaurant is still run by Tolbert family members. How serious are Texans about chili? A 1982 letter from Texas Gov. William P. Clements, Jr., designates November 6 as official Chili Day. "One cannot be a true son or daughter of the State," says Clements, "without having his [*sic*] taste buds tingle at the thought of the treat that is real, honest-to-goodness, unadulterated Texas chili." And the menu encourages diners to intone the final verse of Bones Hooks's "Chili Eaters Prayer" before dipping spoon into bowl: "Chili eaters is some of your chosen people. We don't know why you so doggone good to us. But, Lord, God, don't never think we ain't grateful for this chili we about to eat." Does that inspire you or what?

A bowl of the best Texas red is $2.35 small, $3.35 large, and though grated cheese, onions, and pinto beans are available, give them a miss and eat your chili the way God intended. Of course the menu features more than chili. There are excellent half-pound burgers (with chili, onions, and cheese for $4.10), a very authentic chicken-fried steak platter served with thick Texas toast, salad, homemade fries, and country-style cream gravy ($5.65), and a Texas-size hot dog smothered in Texas red with mustard, onions, and grated cheddar ($3.55). Salads and Tex-Mex fare are also offered. Everything is made from scratch. There are no desserts, but there is a full bar featuring specialty drinks like the Terlingua Kicker—gold tequila, pineapple and orange juice, sour mix, and 151-proof rum ($2.75).

Tolbert's sunny interior (light streams in through a wall of windows) is appropriately rustic, with bare pine floors, exposed brick, and rough-hewn wainscotting. In pristine contrast are stark-white Levolor blinds, hanging enamel lamps, overhead beams, and walls. The latter are primarily decorated with neon beer signs and photographs from chili cookoffs. The background music is progressive country. Off in the corner are some video games for the kids. Note the hundreds of catchy-phrase buttons displayed behind the bar; if you bring one in that they don't have, a free draft beer is yours.

Tolbert's is open Monday to Thursday from 11 a.m. to 11 p.m., on Friday and Saturday to midnight, and on Sunday from 11:30 a.m. to 11 p.m.

## Chinese

Every August in China, when the moon is at its fullest, brightest, and most spectacular, families come together, lovers court, and all give thanks for the bounties of the harvest season. It is for this joyful celebration that owners Sam and Tim Tsay named their beautiful restaurant **August Moon,** 15030 Preston Rd., at Beltline (tel. 385-7227). The large interior is divided into intimate dining areas, each of them uniquely exquisite. They're decorated primarily in shades of coral and pine-tree green, enhanced by Ching Dynasty vases, a fountain with water flowing from a maiden's vessel into a plant-bordered pool, a delicate mural of a Chinese landscape, a replica of a famed 17th-century Chinese painting of the Yangtze River, and other noteworthy artworks and artifacts, all softly lit by Chinese lanterns and candlelight.

Sam Tsay, from Taiwan, started out chopping cabbage in a Chinese restaurant in Missouri to support himself during college. Impressed by his skill with a chopping knife, the owner told him he should open his own restaurant. Somehow the idea took hold in his mind, and he talked his brother, Tim, who had always loved cooking, into studying Chinese culinary arts in Taiwan. After apprenticing in one of Taiwan's top hotel restaurants, Tim came to the U.S. and the brothers opened their first restaurant in Quincy, Illinois. Their lavish Dallas establishment dates to 1980. Tim Tsay today oversees a staff of eight chefs, among them experts in Szechuan, Hunan, Mandarin, and Cantonese specialties.

The extensive menu offers a vast number of options. I like to begin with the delicately wrapped pot stickers served in a bamboo steamer with ginger soy sauce, vinegar, and hot pepper ($4.25 for six). And a unique appetizer choice is Sam's king crab, wrapped in wonton dough with water chestnuts and Swiss cheese and fried ($5.25). For an entree (remember steak is always a good choice in Texas), there's sesame beef, U.S. flank-steak cubes sautéed to rosy juiciness with orange peels and hot sauce, sprinkled with sesame seeds, and served on a bed of Chinese vermicelli with seasonal vegetables ($13.25). Other delicious recommendables are five-flavor shrimp—gulf shrimp marinated in dry sherry and sautéed with crisp green pepper and snow peas in a delicately spiced sauce studded with candied walnuts—($10.25); and crisp, deep-fried whole red snapper, coated with spicy Hunan sauce, and topped with finely shredded pork, snow pea pods, bamboo shoots, and Chinese mushrooms ($14.95). Chinese desserts usually leave Westerners wistful, but not Sam's fresh-baked macadamia chocolate mousse ($3.25), mandarin cheesecake ($3.25), and even Häagen-Dazs ice cream ($1.75)! Large parties (ten people minimum) ought to inquire in advance about multicourse Imperial banquets featuring stunningly presented dishes of various regions for about $25 per person. Free Chinese hors d'oeuvres are served in the bar weekdays from 4 to 7 p.m. And dim sum can also be arranged. There's a full bar. Luncheon entrees are in the $5 to $6 range.

Open Sunday to Thursday from 11 a.m. to 10:30 p.m., on Friday and Saturday till 11 p.m. Reservations suggested.

## Ethiopian

One doesn't expect such exotica as Ethiopian restaurants in Texas, but not only does Dallas have such, it has one of the best in the country, the **Queen of Sheba**, 3527 McKinney Ave., at Lemmon Avenue East (tel. 521-0491). The setting is ethnic and festive. I especially like the private booths along either wall— bamboo and trellis enclosures lit by rattan-shaded globe lamps and candles in red glass holders. Burlap-covered beams in the center of the room double as planters for philodendrons, and decorations include Ethiopian art and artifacts, basketry, and travel posters. Native music helps create the right mood. About half the clientele is Ethiopian.

If you've never tried this cuisine, you should know that it is eaten with the hands. Food is served on a large, thin pancake-like bread called injera, and an additional platter of injera comes on the side. You use it in place of utensils to scoop up the various dishes. This being Texas, you'll do very well to order a beef entree like lega tibs—Ethiopian-style shish kebab fried with onions, peppers, and hot spices, and served with a delicious tangy salad ($7.25). If you're not dining alone, your companion's entree might be the yatakelt wott plate of green beans, onions, carrots, potatoes, and other steamed vegetables seasoned with garlic, ginger, and green pepper ($5.95)—it's one of the tastiest vegetable dishes I've ever had, similar to the veggies served in Parisian Algerian restaurants with couscous. Since all the food is served on one large platter, sharing is easy. Another good alternative is the six-entree combination, including the vegetables, minchet abish (a highly spiced stew of ground beef cooked with onions, red pepper, butter, and assorted herbs, and served with cottage cheese), ke'y yesega wott (spicy beef stew served with salad and yogurt), doro wott (a piquant chicken stew served with spiced egg), a lentil stew with mixed vegetables, and azifa (fresh cold lentil salad flavored with spices and lemon juice). Dishes tend to be hot and spicy, so if you prefer milder preparations be sure to specify. Lunch entrees are all under $5. There's a full bar, and tej (Ethiopian honey wine) is available.

Open from 11 a.m. to 11 p.m. Monday to Thursday, from noon to midnight on Friday and Saturday, and noon to 11 p.m. on Sunday. *Melkam Migib!* (That means "hearty appetite" in Amharic.)

## Indian

**Sahib,** 9100 N. Central Expressway (U.S. 75), at Park Lane, in the Carruth Plaza Shopping Center (tel. 987-2301), is a very elegant restaurant serving authentic Indian cuisine in a stunning setting. It was, until recently, owned by the prestigious Taj International, owners of some of the finest hotels and restaurants in India. And though under new management, it has retained the superb chefs who reigned in the kitchen during the days of the Taj. Beautifully decorated, Sahib has set off its tan-linened tables with forest-green napery, fresh flowers, and hurricane lamp candles. Indian music, sculptures, and carved brass trunks, along with photographs from British raj days, help create a suitably exotic mood, helped along by lush plantings. Subdued pink lighting casts a romantic glow over it all. There's an open kitchen, where you can see the white-hatted chef tending his tandoori oven.

A Sahib dinner might begin with vegetable samosas—deep-fried pastries made with a yogurt-based dough and stuffed with spiced potatoes and green peas ($2.95)—or with an appetizer of barbecued lamb rolled in fresh-baked unleavened bread with chopped onions, mint, ginger, and herbs ($4.75). Tandoori (clay oven) specialties are featured; a good bet is the mixed grill of chicken, lamb, and shrimp ($10.50), served with Indian rice and salad. Or you might opt for the surf grill of tandoori shrimp, lobster, and fish marinated in yogurt and freshly ground spices, cooked in the clay oven, and served with roast bell peppers, onions, and mushrooms ($15.25). Other than tandoori, I love Sahib's lamb biryani, a rice casserole studded with chunks of tender lamb and flavored with saffron and other herbs ($9.75); ask for a side order of hot sauce, a flavorful accompaniment if you like spicy fare. Other enhancements to any of the above entrees might include raita, a cooling dish of whipped homemade yogurt with diced potatoes, cucumbers, and tomatoes, seasoned with roast ground cumin and garnished with cilantro ($2.75); chewy tandoori-baked nan, an Indian bread ($1.75); or sweet mango chutney ($2.25). For dessert there's an incredible saffron- and cardamom-flavored homemade ice cream sprinkled with pistachio ($3.50), a refreshing and satisfying conclusion to your meal and an exciting new taste sensation.

Great treats at Sahib, by the way, are the lavish all-you-can-eat lunch and Sunday brunch buffets, the former for $8.50, the latter at $10.50. They provide an opportunity to try a great variety of Indian dishes. All bar drinks are available.

Sahib is open for lunch Monday to Saturday from 11:30 a.m. to 2:30 p.m., for Sunday brunch to 3 p.m., for dinner Sunday to Thursday from 5:30 to 10 p.m. and on Friday and Saturday until 11 p.m. Reservations suggested on weekends.

## Italian

**Campisi's "Egyptian Restaurant,"** 5610 E. Mockingbird Lane, between Greenville and McMillan Avenues (tel. 827-0355), has been around since 1945 when Sicilian Carlo Campisi took over the old Egyptian Lounge but neglected to change the sign. Today it's achieved cult status, and if Carlo's son, Joe (now in charge with his son, Corky, and daughter, Marie) ever tried to remove that old sign, he'd probably run into considerable flak from customers. Campisi's is a Dallas tradition. Morgan Fairchild cited it on "Lifestyles of the Rich and Famous" as offering "the greatest Italian food in the world." *D Magazine* gives it the "best pizza" award. And the restaurant is a second home to dozens of sports stars and other notables whose pictures line the walls of the VIP Room—Lee Trevino, the Dallas Cowboys, Tom Lasorda, Burt Reynolds (Joe and Corky had small roles with Burt in the movie *Semi-Tough),* and Steve Wynn (Joe won the Las Vegas Golden Nugget's first golf tournament), among others.

Campisi's interior is no Yuppie peach and chrome, hi-tech affair. A bold color scheme utilizes Italian-flag red, green, and white. Walls are green, lighting is very low (even at lunch, tables are lit by candles in red glass holders), and the red leather booths are the old-fashioned kind with jukeboxes on the walls and coathooks. A large oil portrait of Carlo Campisi overlooks the action in the dining room. No need to worry about the action in the kitchen; chefs Linzell Briggs, Elishus Sanders, and Ben Price have all been back there preparing Mama Campisi's old family recipes for three decades.

One thing you can't go wrong ordering here is the pizza; it's great! Pies come small ($3.25), medium ($4.95), and large ($6.25), with a surcharge for each extra item. For $9.95 you can get a large pizza with the works—Italian sausage, hamburger, salami, mushrooms, onions, green peppers, olives, garlic, jalapeño, and meatballs! Though you don't usually think of ordering bread with pizza, Joe's special garlic toast ($1.75) shouldn't be missed for any reason. You might try some with a small antipasto ($3.50) prior to your pizza. Most other entrees include a salad and garlic toast, like ravioli with butter sauce ($5.95), spaghetti and Italian sausage ($5.95), baked lasagne ($6.25), or a combination plate of all three ($7.25). Veal picante in butter and lemon sauce comes with fettuccine and salad for $7.95. This is hearty Sicilian cooking, prepared with quality ingredients. Joe even grows sweet basil and other herbs in his garden for restaurant use. There's a full bar.

Open Monday to Friday from 11 a.m. to midnight, on Saturday to 1 a.m., and on Sunday from 11:30 a.m. to midnight. Arrive off-hours to get a booth and a parking space. No credit cards.

### Japanese

**Fuji-Ya,** 13050 Coit Rd., a block north of I-635 (tel. 690-8396), is a pleasant little restaurant, its glossy gray walls decorated with Japanese prints. There's a pine-paneled sushi bar up front, rows of navy-cushioned booths along the walls are divided by rice-paper screens, and a row of red paper lanterns at the entrance adds a cheerful note. Owner/chef Naoshi Iida, a sumo wrestler in his younger days (one often sees his burly pals here), had retired to cheffing in Chiba, Japan, when a family friend asked him to come work at a Dallas restaurant. Naoshi planned to stay only a year to see a bit of the U.S., but met his wife, Fusako, liked Dallas, and decided to set up on his own in 1978.

The Iida's offer very high-quality and authentic fare, a fact attested to by the large number of Japanese diners patronizing the place. Sushi, prepared with the freshest of fish, is a specialty. You can select it from the chart (two pieces to each order) or opt for the $12.50 assortment that includes a bowl of delicious miso soup. Also fabulous are the shrimp tempura ($9.95) and salmon teriyaki ($8.75), both served with rice, soup, salad, and tea. Children under 12 can order a $4.95 dinner of shrimp tempura, gyoza (fried meat dumpling), rice, and soup or salad. And full lunches are in the $4.25 to $7.25 range. Enjoy a bottle of sake

($2.95) with your meal, and try Fusako's scrumptious homemade pound cake ($1.75) for dessert with your tea. All bar drinks are available.

Open for lunch Monday to Saturday from 11:30 a.m. to 2 p.m., for dinner Sunday to Thursday from 5:30 to 10 p.m., on Friday and Saturday to 11 p.m.

## Mexican

**Chiquita,** 3810 Congress Ave., at Oak Lawn Avenue (tel. 521-0721), serves some of the best Mexican fare in Dallas in charmingly festive surroundings. White stucco walls are hung with large bunches of colorful paper flowers in wicker baskets, tables are set with cantaloupe-colored napery, café-curtained windows add a homey warmth, and candles in hand-blown glass holders overhead create a magical glow at night. It's all very inviting, and owner Mario Leal takes immense pride in his culinary offerings, which are more Mexico City in conception than Tex-Mex.

Start off with an appetizer of rajas con crema—strips of chile poblano wrapped with cream cheese, onions, and zucchini in flour tortillas ($5.25). Other fortuitous beginnings are a ceviche and avocado plate ($3.95), tortilla soup ($2.95), and chorizo flameado—melted Monterrey jack cheese mixed with spicy chorizo sausage and served in flour tortillas ($5.05). Chiquita does excellent fajitas, juicy, tender, and flavorful, served with pico de gallo and refried beans ($7.95). Another superb steak dish here is the carne asada Tampico style —sliced filet mignon broiled over a hickory fire, served with sautéed onions and green peppers, soft tacos, and a triangle of grilled Linares cheese ($8.75). And then there's hickory-broiled chicken *à la parrilla* served with broiled tomato, lemon butter, and salad ($7.95). Shrimp dishes here are also very good choices. Everything is totally fresh and made from scratch. All bar drinks are available. And for dessert there's a tempting Kahlúa pie ($2.25).

Chiquita is open Monday to Thursday from 11:30 a.m. to 10:30 p.m., on Friday and Saturday till 11 p.m.

Under the same ownership and offering an identical menu and similarly delightful decor is **Mario & Alberto,** 425 Preston Valley Shopping Center, corner of Preston Road and I-635 (tel. 980-7296). Hours are also the same. Reservations are essential.

The **Mercado Juárez Café,** 1901 W. Northwest Hwy., at Spangler Road (tel. 556-0796), is more than just a restaurant—it's a festive evening's entertainment. Housed in a huge old warehouse, it contains a vast on-premises Mexican mercado (market) purveying everything you might find south of the border— panchos, piñatas, papier-mâché items, sombreros, blankets, Yucatán hammocks, Mexican foods and spices, you name it. And while you dine, you're serenaded tableside by talented musicians. They're not just mariachi bands, they'll perform any song you request. Quaff a few margaritas and sing along. The decor is colorful. Tables lit by candles in red glass holders are covered with alternating red, white, or green cloths, there are striped awnings, gaily painted Mexican ladderback chairs, crêpe paper flowers, and piñatas.

Not only is the atmosphere great, the food's good too. You might start out with a Mexican-style shrimp cocktail garnished with avocado slices ($4.25); whitefish ceviche marinated with lemon, spices, tomatoes, onions, cilantro, and peppers, also served with avocado ($3.25); chorizo sausage and cheese nachos ($4.95); or queso adobado, melted Monterrey jack cheese served over strips of pork tenderloin marinated in mild red peppers and spices ($4.50). The house specialties are mesquite-broiled meats and seafood, such as shrimp, baby goat, steak, or chicken ($11.50, $11.50, $9.50, and $7.50, respectively), grilled with onions and peppers and served with Spanish rice, bean soup, pico de gallo, and guacamole. Also excellent is camaron Juárez—large shrimp stuffed with white cheese and bacon, egg battered, deep-fried, and served with rice, refried beans, tartar sauce, pico de gallo, and guacamole ($9.25). There are under-$3.50 *platos para los niños* and inexpensive enchiladas, tacos, and tortas (Mexican sandwiches) for lighter meals. All bar drinks are available, and for dessert there's praline ice cream pie ($2.25) or a rich and gooey concoction of empanadas filled with caramel and pecans and topped with whipped cream and strawberry sauce ($2.25). Saturday and Sunday brunch features dishes like eggs scrambled with potatoes, chorizo sausage, onions, and cheese served with refried beans, pico de gallo, flour or corn tortillas, tostados, fresh fruit salad, coffee or tea, and Mexican pastries—all for $5.25.

Open Monday to Thursday from 11 a.m. to 10 p.m., on Friday and Saturday to 11 p.m., on Sunday from noon to 10 p.m.

## Pizza

Great pizza does not abound in Texas, but there is one Dallas chain where I've enjoyed many a mozzarellaed masterpiece. **Rockyano's,** with ten Dallas-area locations, including 115 Medallion Center, on Northwest Hwy. at Skillman Street (tel. 692-8412), bakes up scrumptious and crusty round or deep-dish pizzas topped with fresh, natural ingredients. Prices are terrific too. At lunch (11 a.m. to 3 p.m.) you can have all the pizza you can eat with unlimited salad-bar items (macaroni salad, potato salad, lettuce, tomatoes, mushrooms, grated cheddar, canned peaches, sliced cucumbers) and chocolate pudding for dessert, all for $3.99. A large (10- by 14-inch) deep-dish pie with the works—extra cheese, pepperoni, mushrooms, green peppers, black olives, Canadian bacon, ground beef, and Italian sausage—is $8.60 ($8.20 for a round pie). Or you can order a large deep-dish pie with any two toppings for $6.95 ($6.50 round).

The atmosphere is quintessential pizza parlor—low lighting, neon beer signs, Formica tables, stained-glass lighting fixtures, video games, and a large-screen TV to which everyone's eyes are always glued. A nice touch are the wainscotted stucco walls plastered with pages from Italian magazines. Eat in, or if the TV din disturbs you, bring a pie back to your hotel room.

Check the phonebook for the closest location. The above is open Sunday to Thursday from 11 a.m. to midnight, on Friday and Saturday to 1 a.m. No credit cards.

## Steak

The quintessentially Texan **Trail Dust Steak House,** 10841 Composite Dr., just south of Walnut Hill Lane and a block east of I-35 (tel. 357-3862), serves notice to city slickers: "This ain't no country club and no neckties are allowed on these here premises." If you do wear one, you'll set off "a gall-darned commotion of bell-ringin' and hollerin' " and you'll have to take it off or they'll cut it off and hang it with thousands of others on the wall (with your business card if you like). Since many patrons wear ties with the object of having them snipped off, this tie collection is certainly one of the world's ugliest. Other interesting features here are a large sliding pond for kids in the middle of the room (there are video games too), and a nice-size dance floor where you can Texas two-step to live country music at night. The entirety is housed in a big red barn of a place. Inside, rough-hewn pine-paneled walls are decorated with ranching tools, steer horns, cowboy movie posters, and other western paraphernalia; long rows of tables flanking the dance floor are lit by hurricane lamp candles and covered with red-and-white-checkered oilcloth; and floors are littered with peanut shells.

Mesquite-broiled steaks are the featured item: $12.25 for a 24-ounce porterhouse T-bone, $8.25 for a "dainty" 14-ounce club T-bone, $17.95 for the "bull shipper"—a 50-ounce porterhouse steak! All entrees come with salad, ranch bread, and country-style beans. Corn on the cob or a baked potato is $1.05 additional. Mesquite-grilled chicken ($7.25) and barbecued pork ribs ($8.25) are also options, and for under-12s there are under-$5 listings. There's homemade fudge pecan pie topped with ice cream ($2.25) for dessert, and all bar drinks are available.

An inexpensive lunch menu features items like mesquite-broiled chicken with western fries, salad, and grilled bread for $4.25; an eight-ounce sirloin steak with the same accompaniments for $5.25. And all the draft beer you can drink at lunch will cost just $1.75.

Open for lunch weekdays from 11 a.m. to 2 p.m., for dinner Monday to Thursday from 5 to 11 p.m., on Friday and Saturday to midnight, on Sunday from noon to 11 p.m. Arrive early to beat the crowds; there are no reservations except for large parties. Music begins between 7 and 8 p.m.

## Thai

**Sawatdee**, 4503 Greenville Ave., at Yale (tel. 373-6138), is a cozy, almost lodge-like Thai eatery, run by Paul Boon with brother and sister, Chai and Neuk. Among them, they have several decades of experience turning out exotic fare at Trader Vic's where all were trained. Their own eatery is quite pleasant, with redwood-stained pine walls, brown carpeting, and tan curtains and table-cloths. Prettifying elements include *Casablanca* fan chandeliers overhead, a red carnation in a vase on each table, a few Thai artifacts, a painting of a Siamese palace, and a number of plants here and there. Many of the diners are S.M.U. students.

There are several very recommendable appetizers. Crispy spring rolls stuffed with barbecued pork, cucumber, bean sprouts, and egg, and served with plum sauce ($4.25), are delicious, as is mee krob, a dish of crispy hot rice noodles tossed with pork and shrimp and topped with sweet-and-sour sauce and shredded egg ($4.25). And you can't go wrong with moo satay, skewers of pork served in spicy peanut sauce with cucumber salad ($4.25). An excellent soup is the tom ka gai, made with chicken, mushrooms, and coconut milk ($5.75 for two). For an entree I like the sizzling seafood platter (actually it's served from a hot pan) of shrimps, scallops, crab claws, and calamari cooked with straw mushrooms and asparagus in chili sauce ($10.95). A chicken dish prepared with sweet basil and hot green chili ($7.95) and tiger cry steak (sliced char-broiled steak with salad and spicy sauce; $8.95) are also among my favorites. If you're in the mood for something light, Sawatdee does interesting salads. And for dessert there are fried bananas with shredded coconut and powdered sugar ($1.95). Lunch entrees are in the $5 to $6 range, and a full lunch (like lemon chicken with soup, fried rice, and fried wonton) can be had for just $3.75. There's a full bar.

Sawatdee is open for lunch weekdays from 11 a.m. to 2:30 p.m., for dinner Sunday to Thursday from 5 to 10:30 p.m., till 11 p.m. on Friday and Saturday. Reservations accepted.

**WHAT TO SEE AND DO:** For such a big, important city, Dallas doesn't have quite as many major sightseeing attractions as you might expect. It does have some unique ones, though, like a biblical sound-and-light show, a public square dedicated to Thanksgiving, and Southfork, television home of the Ewing family. Plan your sightseeing agenda to encompass Fort Worth, Arlington, and

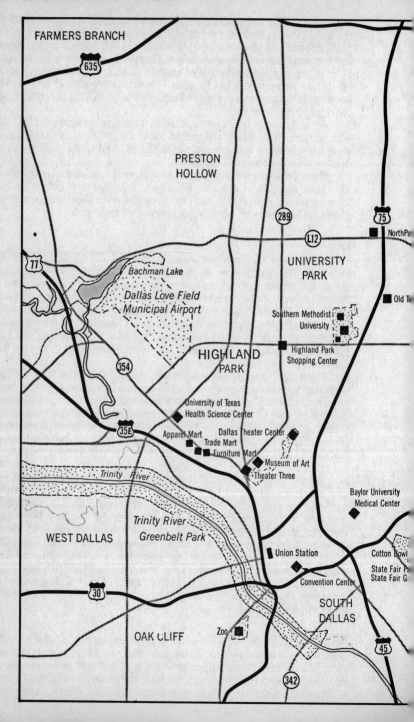

FARMERS BRANCH

PRESTON
HOLLOW

Bachman Lake

Dallas Love Field
Municipal Airport

UNIVERSITY
PARK

Southern Methodist
University

Highland Park
Shopping Center

HIGHLAND
PARK

University of Texas
Health Science Center

Apparel Mart
Trade Mart
Furniture Mart
Dallas Theater Center
Museum of Art
Theater Three

Trinity River

Baylor University
Medical Center

Trinity River
Greenbelt Park

WEST DALLAS

Union Station

Cotton Bowl
State Fair P
State Fair G

Convention Center

SOUTH
DALLAS

OAK CLIFF

Zoo

NorthPa

Old To

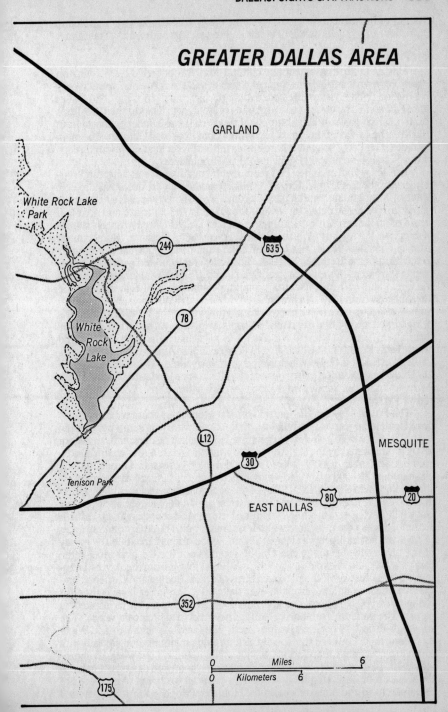

# GREATER DALLAS AREA

GARLAND

White Rock Lake
Park

White
Rock
Lake

Tenison Park

MESQUITE

EAST DALLAS

244

635

78

L12

30

80

20

352

175

```
0              Miles           6
0           Kilometers         6
```

Grand Prairie attractions, all of which are easily visited while you're based in Dallas and enjoying its excellent hotels and restaurants and exciting nightlife.

## Fair Park

This 277-acre amusement and cultural complex, bounded by Washington Street, Pennsylvania Avenue, Second Avenue, and Parry Avenue, attracts over five million annual visitors. It's been a major fairground since the 1886 Dallas State Fair and Exposition, and much of its present form dates to the 1936 Texas Centennial Exposition celebrating 100 years of Texas's independence from Mexico. The 24-day State Fair of Texas takes place here each October. The main entrance is on Parry Avenue where during the State Fair flags representing each of the 50 states are flown. Highlights of Fair Park include:

**The Texas Hall of State:** This monumental building, the architectural centerpiece of the Centennial Exposition, is considered an art deco masterpiece. Made of Texas granite, marble, and Cordova cream limestone, it is situated on a raised terrace and fronted by six 80-foot columns and a bronze and gold-leaf statue of an Indian warrior. Inside, the circular Hall of Heroes displays statues of Stephen F. Austin, William Barrett Travis, Sam Houston, Mirabeau B. Lamar, Thomas J. Rusk, and James Walker Fannin, all important contributors to the birth of the Republic of Texas. The walls are decorated with a frieze depicting the battles of the Alamo and San Jacinto. The Hall of Heroes opens into the Great Hall of Texas, its murals, under a 46-foot skylight ceiling, depicting Texas history from 1519. An immense gold-leaf medallion represents the six nations whose flags have flown over Texas. At this writing the West Texas Room is being turned into a library and reading room, with archival materials and books focusing on Texas in general and Dallas in particular. The East, North, and South Texas Rooms house changing regional exhibits. And on the lower level is the Dallas Fashion Gallery featuring changing costume exhibits ranging from Dallas designer clothing to frontier outfits. Hours are Monday to Saturday from 9 a.m. to 5 p.m., on Sunday from 1 to 5 p.m. Admission is free. For information, call 421-5136.

**The Dallas Museum of Natural History:** Housed in another beautiful art deco Centennial Exposition building, the natural history museum provides an overview of the state's wildlife, vegetation, and natural resources. Its first-floor lobby is dominated by the skeleton of a 40-foot mosasaur, a sea serpent discovered in East Dallas in 1979. It lived some 75 million years ago. Throughout the museum are 250,000 plant and animal specimens, including just about every species known to exist in Texas. The permanent collection includes birds, mammals, fossils, wild game, reptiles, fish, insects, gems and minerals, shells, porcelain wildlife art, and rare books on natural history. And countless fossil seashells are embedded in the museum's walls. Mountains, prairies, deserts, and swamps of Texas are portrayed in wax in over 50 first-floor dioramas, inhabited by grizzly bears, bald eagles, jaguars, etc. On the second floor are the bird gallery, the earth science gallery exploring prehistoric Texas (fossils from the Age of Dinosaurs and the Ice Age), the porcelain birds of artists Boehm and Doughty, and exhibits on game animals from all over the world. The lower level is used for changing exhibits of photographs, illustrations, and other art forms inspired by nature. The museum's temporary exhibits have included, in recent years, "The Insects of Texas," "The Texas Prairie," and "The Plains Apache Way and Wichita Memories." Look for the Touch Cart, a rolling mini-museum stocked with touchable specimens that docents will elucidate upon; it's out weekday mornings at 10, 10:45, and 11:30 a.m. On Sunday afternoon you can take a behind-the-scenes tour observing labs, taxidermy, etc.; call for hours. And there are usually lectures and films on weekends. Hours are Monday to Saturday from 9 a.m. to 5 p.m., on Sunday and holidays from noon to 5 p.m. Closed Thanksgiving and Christmas. Admission is free. For information, call 670-8457.

**The Dallas Aquarium:** Opened in 1936 and expanded in 1964, this very manageable attraction is conveniently housed on a single floor, yet it is one of the oldest and largest aquariums in the Southwest. The collection, which numbers 3,500 specimens representing about 300 species, consists of native freshwater fishes from both cold and warm waters, tropical freshwater and marine fishes from the Texas Coast and the Atlantic and Pacific Oceans, and various reptiles and amphibians, freshwater and marine invertebrates. There's an extensive collection of small, exquisitely colored tropical fish, electric eels from the Amazon, piranhas, African lungfish (they can burrow in mud and lie dormant until rainy season when a pond grows dry), Hawaiian and Australian barrier reef tanks, seahorses, alligator snapping turtles native to East Texas, and an "amazing but true" exhibit of the glass catfish (you can see through it), the four-eyed fish, and other interesting types. Look for the Touch Cart, a docent-operated, hands-on exhibit, on weekends. Hours are Monday to Saturday from 9 a.m. to 5 p.m., on Sunday and holidays from noon to 5 p.m. Closed Christmas and Thanksgiving. Admission is free. For information, call 670-8441.

**Science Place I and Science Place II:** Expanded in 1986 to encompass two buildings, Science Place I and II offer hands-on scientific exhibits and live demonstrations relating to energy, health, future human environments, and other subjects scientific. Science Place II houses a planetarium offering three shows every weekend. Hours are Tuesday to Saturday from 9 a.m. to 5 p.m., on Sunday and holidays from noon to 5 p.m. Closed Monday, Christmas, and Thanksgiving. Admission is $1 for adults, 50¢ for children under 12. Call 428-8351 for hours and further details. Planetarium shows are enhanced by exhibits on astronomy.

Science Place I contains major exhibits on the physical sciences and on light, among other things. It also offers intriguing traveling exhibits like "Chips and Changes," about the impact of the microchip on everyday life. A large science store carrying exciting educational toys for children is on the premises. Hours and the telephone information number are the same as for Science Place II. And if you're wondering why I've listed II before I, it's because I is the second or newer building. In fact, it's not even completed as I write. So please forgive if there are any changes by the time you're reading this.

**The Dallas Civic Garden Center:** Rooted, so to speak, in the 1936 Centennial, this was the Horticulture Building of the fair. Today it occupies 2½ acres and an additional 7,000 square feet under a 40-foot skylight, a simulated rain forest with a 25-foot waterfall and a catwalk so you can observe the entire tropical environment—ferns, hibiscus, orchids, and all—from the treetops. Outside, winding paths meander through herb and scent gardens designed for the blind with labels in Braille, a labyrinth of hedges, a Shakespeare garden, a miniature rose garden, crape myrtle groves, a wishing well garden, water gardens, and seasonal flower displays of mums, camellias, roses, etc. Future plans call for expansion to seven acres and 26 garden areas by 1989. The center offers frequent lectures on subjects of botanical interest, and every Sunday afternoon in July there are free concerts in the garden auditorium at 3 p.m. under the heading of "Basically Beethoven" (they always include some works by Beethoven along with other classical selections). Hours are Monday to Saturday from 10 a.m. to 5 p.m., on Sunday and holidays from 12:30 to 5 p.m. Closed Christmas and Thanksgiving. Admission is free. For information, call 428-7476.

**The Age of Steam Railroad Museum:** A joint venture of the State Fair and the Southwest Railroad Historical Society since 1964, this is one of 152 railroad museums throughout the country. Its eight display cars include a sleeper, club coach, dining car, and baggage car, as well as a private car built in 1900 for the use of the president of the Fort Worth and Denver Railroad. Other exhibits include a 1903 Dallas railroad station, a New Orleans trolley car, the Union Pacific *Big Boy* (one of the largest locomotives ever made), and an extensive collection of railroad memorabilia. Hours are 11 a.m. to 5 p.m. on Sunday only. Admission is $1.50 for adults, 75¢ for those 16 and under. For information, call 421-8712.

In addition, Fair Park contains the famed **Cotton Bowl** and the **Music Hall,** both detailed elsewhere in this chapter, and it is the scene of the yearly State Fair of Texas (see "Annual Events") and frequent antique and art shows, usually at the Grand Place. You'll also enjoy looking at other buildings and statuary around the park. Plan to make a day of it. You can dine on traditional Texas fare at the park's Old Mill Inn on the corner of First and Grand.

## Old City Park

Like Houston, Dallas has a bit of its past preserved in the shadow of downtown skyscrapers. At Old City Park, 1717 Gano St., at Ervay (tel. 421-7800), the Dallas County Heritage Society maintains 36 authentically restored and fully furnished North-Central Texas buildings dating from 1840 to 1910. There are costumed docents stationed in buildings throughout the park, and on weekends there are crafts demonstrations and an old fiddler entertains. The park itself dates to 1876, when ten acres were set aside on an old Cherokee camping site during the country's centennial celebration. For almost a century it was an oasis where old oak and pecan trees provided shade for strollers and picnickers. It was the site of the city's first zoo, and there were greenhouses, concerts, flower shows, weiner roasts, and square dances. It wasn't until the late 1960s that the first historic building was brought to the park and the idea of an architectural heritage program evolved. The park's landscaping is meant to evoke the 19th century.

Begin your tour at the turn-of-the-century **railroad depot,** a park information center where you can purchase tickets and see a 15-minute multimedia presentation on Dallas history. Near the depot is the **section house,** where a local foreman lived (at one time a family with six children occupied this tiny two-room house) and kept five to seven miles of local track in good repair.

Smelling deliciously of spices and potpourri, **McCall's Merchandise,** a one-room country store, sells reproductions of what it sold in Snow Hill, Texas, in the early 1900s—*McGuffey's Readers,* hand-milled soaps, penny candy, patchwork hangings, etc. A second **general store,** also one room, is furnished with period dry goods tables, plate-glass showcases, and a bench and chairs where the regulars hung out around the pot-bellied stove—gossiping, telling jokes, playing checkers, chewing tobacco, and arguing politics. Stores like this operated on the barter system, with payments made in farm produce, and it was not unusual for overextended farmers to end up as tenants on land ceded to pay the storekeeper. You could buy almost anything in the general store, from whisky (the word "grocery" derived from "groggery") to hardware, from horse blinders to hair ribbons. It also contained the post office.

**Millermore,** the first historic house brought to the park, was built in 1850s by a prosperous farmer, William Brown Miller. His daughter, Minnie, lived in the house until her death in 1960. Furnishings reflect the last quarter of the 19th century. Adjacent to Millermore are the oak and cedar **log house** the Millers first lived in when they came to Texas in 1847 and a **log playhouse** built for Miller's granddaughter in 1907 that is patterned after the original log house. In the same area are a late 1800s barn, today housing a pottery workshop, and a cellar house used as a storm cellar, root cellar, and cool storage room for milk and

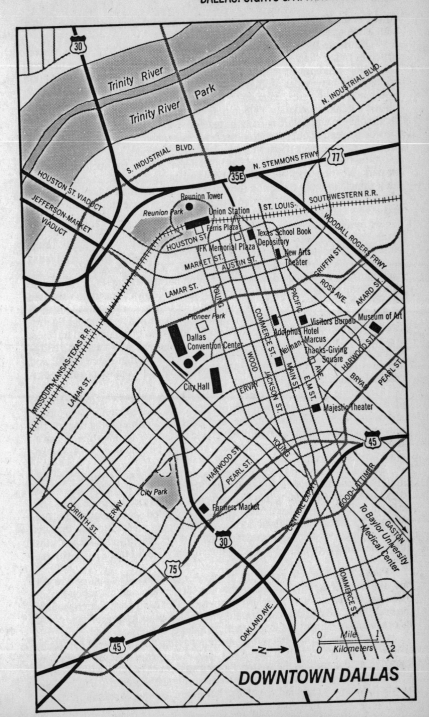

**DOWNTOWN DALLAS**

butter. A short walk brings you to another cluster of structures—a pottery shed, kiln, granary, and windmill.

The ornate 1880s **bandstand** is the only structure in the park that is a reconstruction rather than a restoration. Near it is the **print shop,** one of the most interesting buildings to visit; a docent gives demonstrations of 19th-century printing and newspaper production methods and you can examine early linotype machines, presses, composing tables, and other tools. And next door is **Citizen's Bank,** founded in 1905, a time when many Texans preferred to keep their money in empty lard cans in the general store. Banks often earned a bit on the side by renting out space to other businesses, here exemplified by the dentist's office in the back room with a pedal-operated drill.

Of similarly grisly interest is the 1890s **doctor's office and apothecary** across the park. No long years of medical school and internship were required to hang out a shingle in those days, and the sawbones operated on his hapless patients without anesthesia. This Victorian-furnished Queen Anne cottage belonged to one of the wealthier and better-educated doctors of the period, the latter evidenced by a large collection of medical books. The only consolation of medicine in this era was its affordability: office visits were $1; house calls, $2.50. In the same area of the park is **Drummer's Hotel** (1904), so named because traveling salesmen, called drummers, were the mainstay of its business. When they arrived in town, they banged on a drum to announce their presence (hence the phrase "drumming up business"). Typical of small-town Texas hotels situated by railroads, Drummer's had a dining room (the original was removed in a 1942 remodeling, but another room is so furnished) that town residents also patronized. They enjoyed the lively patter, news, and jokes of commercial travelers over all-you-can-eat 25¢ meals. A guest often shared a room—and even a bed—with a total stranger, summers were stifling, winters often bitterly cold, and there were bedbugs to boot. The "bath" consisted of a chamber pot and washstand. Not quite the Hilton.

One of the most notable structures is the Queen Anne–style **George House,** a typical 1900 middle-class dwelling from Plano, Texas. Its exterior is characterized by bay windows, turrets, gables, and gingerbread ornamentation, and the house was built by hardware merchant David C. George for his bride. It has 11 rooms (six downstairs, five upstairs) and three outbuildings—a privy, smokehouse, and storm cellar.

Before 1900 schooling was a catch-as-catch-can affair for many Texas children. Farm chores came first. The **Renner School,** founded in 1888, was a two-story Greek revival building that also served as a town meeting place. Boys and girls entered through separate doors and were seated separately; grades one through five occupied the lower floor, while the upper grades used the upstairs room or "high school." Punishments included the switch, a smack with the ruler, the dunce cap, and, most humiliating for boys, being made to sit with the girls.

**Pilot Grove Church** represents all pioneer churches. The church was the hub of a frontier community, used not only for services and marathon prayer meetings, but picnics and other social activities. This Methodist church, built in the mid-1890s, is a one-room clapboard structure housing its original pine pews. Its organ and bell tower are from other churches of the period.

**Gano House,** built in 1845–1846 and purchased a decade later by Dr. Richard M. Gano, is basically a two-room log cabin with a covered breezeway known as a "dog trot" in the center. Pioneers did much of their work, visiting, and even sleeping out of doors; rooms were merely shelters used in bad weather or when danger threatened. Near the house are another windmill, a curing shed, a log-cabin kitchen, and the **Lively cabin,** built in 1856 as a very primitive one-room home.

Tours of the park buildings are given Tuesday to Friday from 10 a.m. to 4 p.m. (last tickets sold at 3 p.m.), weekends from 1:30 to 4:30 p.m. (last tickets sold at 3:30 p.m.). Prices are $4 for adults, $2 for senior citizens and children 12 and under. The park itself is open free to the public from sunrise to sundown every day except Thanksgiving, Christmas Eve, Christmas Day, New Year's Eve, and New Year's Day.

Plan your day around lunch at **Brent Place,** a quaintly charming restaurant in a gabled 1876 farmhouse with lace-curtained windows, walls covered in period floral papers and hung with framed needlepoint samplers, an old wood stove, and brick-red wooden ceilings. There are three luncheon seatings Tuesday to Sunday, at 11:15 a.m. and 12:15 and 1:15 p.m. Reserve in advance by calling 421-3057. Meals are table d'hôte, priced around $8 per person. A typical Brent Place bill of fare might offer Jerusalem artichoke salad, roast loin of pork with baked apricots and fresh asparagus, fresh-baked yeast rolls and bran muffins, and maple layer cake for dessert. Everything is homemade and prepared from recipes from the restaurant's library of early Texas cookbooks.

## Dallas Arboretum and Botanical Gardens / DeGolyer House

Just 12 miles from downtown Dallas, you can leave the glass-and-concrete city behind and take time to smell the roses. The Dallas Arboretum and Botanical Gardens, 8525 Garland Rd., at Whittier Street (tel. 327-8263), comprise 66 acres of gardens and forested land, the latter in a ten-year development program that will eventually be highlighted by tens of thousands of flowering trees along the shores of 1,250-acre White Rock Lake. By 1995 the springtime display is expected to rival Washington, D.C.'s cherry blossoms. Though much is in the works, there's plenty to thrill flower and garden enthusiasts even now. During the mid-March to early-April Spring Festival each year over 140,000 tulips bloom, along with daffodils, crocus, hyacinths, and azaleas. And spring is also heralded by strolling musicians, dance groups, symphonic music, and other weekend entertainments. Labor Day there's Art on the Lake, a big crafts fair with booths, entertainment, and food concessions. And the Chrysanthemum Show comes in late October—a vibrant display of mums, dahlias, late summer annuals, and fall foliage, also enhanced by entertainment (usually strolling guitar and dulcimer players). But even when no special event is taking place, the gardens are a treat to visit. Pick up a walking-tour brochure at the gate, which will direct you to wildflower areas, the perennials, formal gardens, the kitchen garden, a wisteria arbor, seasonal displays, entertainment, picnic groves, etc. There's also a hiking/jogging/biking trail around the lake (enter on Lawther Drive off Garland Road).

In addition to exploring the gardens and arboretum, visitors can tour the hacienda mansion built in 1939–1940 by oil-millionaire Everette DeGolyer and wife, Nell. Originally called Rancho Encinal, and encompassing 13 rooms, the house was built in the Spanish Colonial revival style and surrounded by 43 acres of formal English gardens and woodlands. The mansion was the first in Dallas to have central air conditioning.

The immense library, lined with floor-to-ceiling oak bookcases that once contained 15,000 volumes, is the heart of the house. DeGolyer was a noted rare book collector, whose books (many of them about the Southwest) went to major university libraries after his death. In this room you'll see a portrait of him in the robes of Princeton University, as well as his 17th-century desk; most of the other furnishings are 15th- and 16th-century English and Spanish pieces.

Some library shelves conceal a secret compartment where the most valuable books were kept.

The octagonal dome-ceilinged entry foyer houses a 14th-century English baptismal stand and is lit by a seven-foot, solid-silver chandelier from an 18th-century Spanish monastery.

The dining room, under a baroque barrel-vaulted ceiling, contains a very valuable 18th-century antique Persian carpet, 17th-century Italian silk velvet-upholstered chairs, a ceramic Della Robbia representing the family crest, and a 17th-century English sideboard atop which are bowls of Chinese influence flanked by Persian lamps.

The pueblo-style Indian Room has a remarkable herringbone-pattern ceiling made of rough-hewn California redwood and stripped saplings of pine. The family used it as a den and displayed Spanish, Columbian, and Indian artifacts in its wall niches. A videotape shown in this room describes developmental plans for the Arboretum and Botanical Gardens.

A large collection of 17th-century English antiques are on display in the baronial living room, also notable for its exquisite 20-foot Italian Renaissance plaster ceiling with classical coffers, its pegged oak floors, its mammoth fossilized stone fireplace, and its 16th-century Flemish tapestry.

The parlor, built in the English 18th-century Adam style, was the family gathering place. It is hung with lovely Irish Waterford cut-glass chandeliers.

You'll also see the master bedroom, adjoining Mrs. DeGolyer's large dressing room that overlooks a *putti* fountain in the garden, and the charming oak-paneled breakfast room with bull's-eye stained-glass bay windows and a redwood-beamed ceiling. There are photos of the rooms not on view, and the rooms that are toured contain photos depicting them as they were when the DeGolyers lived here.

Probably the best time to see the house is early in December when it's decorated for an old-fashioned Christmas and there are carolers, bell choirs, and dulcimer players.

The gardens are open Tuesday to Sunday year round (except Christmas and New Year's Days), from 9 a.m. to 5 p.m. November 1 to the end of February, 10 a.m. to 6 p.m. the rest of the year. Gates are shut an hour before closing time. Admission is $2 for adults, $1 for children 6 to 12 (under 6, free). Tuesday admission is free for all. House tours are included in the admission price; they're given on Tuesday at 1, 2, and 3 p.m., Wednesday to Friday on the hour from 10 a.m. to 3 p.m. Allow a minimum of two hours to see everything.

## The Dallas Art Museum

Any big city would be proud of a facility like the Dallas Museum of Art, 1717 N. Harwood St., just south of the Woodall Rogers Freeway (tel. 922-0220) —especially now with its new $6-million Decorative Arts Wing housing the $35-million Wendy and Emery Reves Collection. The 15,000-square-foot wing recreates the entry hall, great hall, library, salon, bedroom, dining room, and patio of La Pausa, the Reves villa in the south of France. The benefactors' furnishings form a unique backdrop for their collection, which includes important works by impressionist and post-impressionist painters (Van Gogh, Cézanne, Renoir, Gauguin, Manet, Pisarro, Monet, Bonnard, and Toulouse-Lautrec) and decorative art spanning five centuries and many nations. Among other items, there are 363 pieces of Chinese export porcelain, Spanish and Middle Eastern carpets, Renaissance iron and woodwork, Venetian glass, and European furniture from the Renaissance through the Victorian period. And a small gallery is devoted to Winston Churchill memorabilia.

Which is not to say that the Reves wing is the whole story. The museum has been around since 1903, and its current holdings include significant collections of pre-Columbian art; African sculpture; textiles; late-19th- and early-20th-century Americans like Homer, Eakins, Sargent, and Hassam; abstract expressionists (Gorky, Kline, Tobey, Pollock); and Mondrian, including earlier representational works. There's a lovely sculpture garden with reflecting pool and waterfalls, a peaceful enclosed oasis amid downtown skyscrapers. And in addition to the permanent collection, the museum of course offers an ongoing program of temporary exhibits such as "Lone Star Regionalism," "Primitivism in 20th-Century Art," "The Art of the European Goldsmith," "Textile Traditions of Guatemala," and "Naum Gabo: Sixty Years of Constructivism," to name some fairly recent examples. The museum's Gateway Gallery is especially geared for children, featuring hands-on exhibits, a blackboard with colored chalk, and an adjoining kiddie gift shop. A full and exciting schedule of lectures, workshops, demonstrations, concerts, gallery talks, and classic and art-related films complements the museum's other offerings. Pick up a calendar when you visit. Do consider lunching at the museum restaurant, offering homemade fare at lunch, brunch, and Thursday-night dinner, as well as afternoon tea and cocktails. It's worth coming up here even if you don't eat to see the exquisite Frank Lloyd Wright leaded-glass windows.

The museum is open Tuesday to Saturday from 10 a.m. to 5 p.m., on Thursday till 9 p.m., and on Sunday from noon to 5 p.m. Admission is free except for the Decorative Arts Wing ($3 adults, $1 for children under 12). Guided docent tours are offered daily; call for hours. One-hour parking is free if you validate your ticket in the gift shop; after that, parking costs $1 per half hour with a maximum of $5.

## The Dallas Zoo

The beautifully landscaped, 50-acre Dallas Zoo in Marsalis Park, 621 E. Clarendon Dr. (take I-35 south to the Ewing exit; tel. 946-5155), is home to 2,000 animals, including one of the world's largest collections of American and Chilean flamingoes and a superb reptile collection. A delightful park setting, the zoo will be even more wonderful when an expansion to 105 acres is completed in 1990 and a simulated African savannah will allow for herds of elephants, giraffes, lions, jackals, hyenas, zebras, rhinos, antelopes, and gazelles to run free in a natural plains setting with waterfalls, streams, and striking rock formations. Birds will also abound in these grasslands—storks, pelicans, egrets, hornbills, cranes, even vultures. The Wild Africa concept is in line with the latest zoo philosophies that put animal breeding and concern for animal welfare first, creating natural habitats instead of animal prisons.

Already extant highlights of the zoo are the aviary of pheasants, water birds, and peacocks; great apes; hoofed animals including African wild sheep, zebras, oryx, antelopes, gazelles, Congolese okapi (the only living relatives of the giraffe, they look like a cross between that animal and a zebra), and Siberian saigas; camels and llamas from South America, India, Africa, and the Middle East; baboons and monkeys; small mammals like raccoons, porcupines, and prairie dogs; bears; and big cats. You can take a one-mile train ride around the perimeter of the zoo from the station east of the entrance. Trained African elephants perform in front of the Large Mammal Building at 2 p.m. daily April through September. There's a primate feeding at 3 p.m. daily. And in summer there's a children's zoo (June 1 through mid-August, open from 10 a.m. to 6 p.m. weekends, to 5 p.m. Monday to Thursday, to 2 p.m. on Friday) with petting areas. A thunderous "monsoon" occurs at noon on Saturday and Sunday in the tropical rain forest. Strollers can be rented and souvenirs purchased at the zoo's Novelty Shop, and there are food concessions and picnic areas.

The zoo is open April 1 to September 30 from 9 a.m. to 6 p.m., till 5 p.m. the rest of the year. Admission is $2 for adults, $1.25 for ages 6 to 11 (under 6, free).

## Southfork Ranch

If Friday nights find you glued to the tube, you'll likely want to join the throngs traipsing through the Southfork Ranch (tel. 231-2088), setting for the world-famous TV show, "Dallas." You'll recognize it immediately—the patio where Miss Ellie and the Ewing family members currently speaking to each other often breakfast, the swimming pool around which Lucy's wedding took place, the tree-lined drive, the horse pastures where Donna and Ray converse. Southfork was originally a ranch owned by, coincidentally, a J. R. Duncan.

Gawking tourists eventually took their toll on the Duncan family who, having lost all semblance of privacy, sold the property to Terry V. Trippet. And Trippet turned the home and surrounding acreage into a giant entertainment/convention-center complex that draws over a quarter of a million tourists a year. He added to the thrill of being at Southfork by offering 15-minute house tours (they depart continuously throughout the day), stagecoach and surrey rides around the property ($1 per person), comedy and magic shows at various locations, food outlets serving up barbecue sandwiches and margaritas, and a regulation-size rodeo arena, actually built for various episodes but also used for professional rodeos every Saturday and Sunday between 2:30 and 4:30 p.m. (admission is $2). Country music is played over loudspeakers and audible throughout the property. And kids will enjoy seeing the resident horses, longhorn cattle, bulls, buffalo, and donkeys. There are two gift shops where you can buy Southfork T-shirts, ashtrays, hats, glasses, silk jackets, you name it. And everything in the house is also for sale, from the crystal chandeliers to the gilded bombé chest of drawers. In fact, you can, as many honeymooners do, stay overnight in the house. It costs $2,500, but the bedroom is gorgeous and adjoins a lavish bath with bidet and oversize tub with a wall of windows overlooking the pasture. You can also lease the Southfork limousine for $60 per hour with a three-hour minimum.

In June, July, and August, when the most filming is going on here, call before you go; the ranch is occasionally closed to visitors. Those are, however, the months when you're most likely to get a glimpse of Pam, Donna, Clayton, J.R., Sue Ellen, Miss Ellie, and the rest of the Ewings. Weekends and holidays draw the biggest crowds, so come during the week if you want to avoid the crush; on the other hand, the weekend rodeos are fun.

The ranch is open 365 days a year from 9 a.m. to dusk, with house tours departing from 9:30 a.m. to a half hour before dusk. Take the house tour first; it's a good orientation to the rest. Even if you're not a "Dallas" fan, you'll enjoy the very scenic countryside drive to the ranch. Take U.S. 75 north to Plano (Exit 30, Parker Road), go east for six miles to FM 2551 and make a right; there's no sign. Admission is $5 for adults, $3 for children 4 to 10 (3 and under, free).

## Thanks-Giving Square

Plumb in the middle of downtown Dallas, Thanks-Giving Square, actually a triangle bordered by Bryan and Ervay Streets and Pacific Avenue (tel. 969-1977), is a place for quiet meditation in the eye of the storm. Dallas businessman Peter Stewart conceived the idea of a square to commemorate Thanksgiving and the concept of being thankful in a nondenominational way. It was designed by architect Philip Johnson and completed in 1977. About 17 feet below street level, the square is effectively removed from city hubbub, and cascading waterfalls obscure traffic noise. The water, not just in falls but tranquil pools, symbolizes life and cleansing, as an incline bridge symbolizes man's quest for higher meaning. At each entrance are marble plaques engraved with quotes from Scripture. And French bells that toll every day at noon are inscribed with quotations from Psalm 136 ("O give thanks unto the Lord for He is good"), 150 ("Let every thing that hath breath praise the Lord"), and 98 ("O sing unto the Lord a new song").

The white marble Chapel of Thanksgiving, modeled after a Russian mosque built in A.D. 847, is a place for silent meditation and prayer, its ascending "spiral of life" asparkle with 67 stained-glass windows. There are chairs around a sort of marble altar, atop which a candle is lit and a bowl placed for special Thanksgiving thoughts. Visitors write down what they're most thankful for and put it in the bowl.

Beneath the chapel, in the Hall of World Thanksgiving, are the original 1777 declaration of national Thanksgiving and special Thanksgiving proclamations issued by all 50 state governors in 1977, the holiday's 200th anniversary. Also displayed here are the flags of all nations that celebrate a day of thanksgiving.

The chapel garden is shaded by sweetgums, live oaks, cedar elms, and crape myrtles. It's an extremely popular spot.

There are frequent events at the square ranging from choir and band performances to visits by such varied religious leaders as the Dalai Lama, Cardinal Arinze of the Vatican, rabbis, and Indian gurus. There are also photographic and other exhibits.

Hours are Monday to Friday from 9 a.m. to 5 p.m., on Saturday, Sunday, and holidays from 1 to 5 p.m. There's no admission charge.

## The Biblical Arts Center

One of the most unusual attractions in Dallas, or anywhere, is the Biblical Arts Center, 7500 Park Lane, at Boedeker Street (tel. 691-4661). It all began in the 1950s with artist Torger Thompson who taught Sunday school classes using chalk renderings (he called them "chalk talks") to illustrate Bible stories. From this activity he was inspired to do something more lasting and monumental, and feeling that few artists had attempted to depict the Day of Pentecost, he chose that event for his masterpiece. He began researching it and sketching, and over a period of ten years he developed the plans for *The Miracle at Pentecost*, a portrayal of the day the apostles received the power of the holy spirit. An addition to his home was required as the sketches grew larger and larger. At this juncture, Thompson realized financial backing would be necessary to complete his vision of the project.

Mattie Caruth Byrd, a religious woman and wealthy art patron, heard about Thompson's plight and set up a foundation to fund the project in 1966. Thompson and assistant Alvin Barnes spent three years completing the 124- by 21-foot mural, and the site of the warehouse in which they worked became the site for a building to house the mural and other works of religious art—all of it funded by Ms Byrd. The present building was completed in 1981.

The highlight of the center is a 30-minute sound-and-light show where the world's largest oil painting is used to elucidate the story of *The Miracle at Pentecost*, shown once an hour on the half hour. (The Pharisee in the blue robe, it might interest you to know, is Stanley Marcus of Neiman-Marcus fame.) Not since the days of Cecil B. DeMille, said *Texas Highways* magazine, has anyone assembled such a biblical cast. And there is something Hollywood-like about the way Thompson brings the Bible to life. It's enhanced by stereophonic music, gusts of wind, and circles of light pinpointing characters as their stories are dramatically told. It isn't Michelangelo, but we live in the 20th century, not the Renaissance.

Other areas of the museum display Judeo-Christian art and artifacts on loan from other museums and from its own collections. And some exhibits document the development of the mural itself. In the Founder's Gallery, Ms Byrd's art collection—not all of it religious—is displayed. It includes Chinese and French provincial furnishings, tapestries, Japanese ivory carvings, decorative arts pieces, and Baccarat crystal chandeliers. The colonnaded atrium of the museum (its central feature is a replica of the Garden Tomb of Christ at Calvary, believed to be the actual burial place of Jesus) was planned as a place for quiet reflection. And there's also a performing arts theater where Bible-related plays, lectures, and concerts take place.

The building itself is Romanesque in design, evocative of Holy Land structures with its massive stone columns, soaring vaulted ceilings, and natural stone floors.

Open Tuesday to Saturday from 10 a.m. to 5 p.m., on Sunday from 1 to 5 p.m. Admission to the galleries is free. To see the presentation of *The Miracle at Pentecost,* adults pay $3.50; senior citizens, $3; children 6 to 12, $1.75 (under 6, admitted free).

## City Hall

Aficionados of architect I. M. Pei will want to take a look at Dallas's striking City Hall, on Young Street between Akard and Ervay Streets (tel. 670-3957). The ten-level trapezoid-shaped building is cantilevered outward at an angle of 34°, giving the impression it might fall on top of you. *Dallas Times Herald* columnist Jim Schultze suggested that artist Christo wrap it and leave it wrapped. These jabs notwithstanding, it is, as Ada Louise Huxtable commented, "undeniably among the most interesting urban constructions of the 20th century." A monumental sculpture by Henry Moore graces the plaza, along with a circular pool with two rotating red shapes donated by Stanley Marcus in memory of his late wife. There are tables and chairs for picnicking and seating for the many events that take place on the plaza: the International Bazaar in April and Christmas-tree lighting in December, a beach party every summer (the plaza is covered with sand, and there's swimming, volleyball, tanning contests, and music), concerts, protest rallies, evangelists, demonstrations, and so on.

The lobby offers changing exhibitions that run the gamut from dinosaur bones to flower shows to children's art. The building houses 1,400 city employees and the mayor's office (he's one of the few to rate more than a cubicle). Go up to the sixth floor to get a good look at the interior; all the cubicles have glass walls, so workers are on a constant display. The Council Chamber is also on the sixth floor, and its Wednesday 1 p.m. meetings here, and the City Planning Commission's Thursday 1 p.m. meetings, are open to the public. You're free to wander around the building. There are long- and short-term art exhibits throughout; ask at the lobby desk for details. Call the above number to find out if any special events are on.

## The Kennedy Memorial and Nearby Sights

There's really not all that much to see in the downtown area bounded by Commerce, Market, Record, and Main Streets, yet this site of the John F. Kennedy assassination draws vast numbers of tourists. A tomb-like **memorial** designed by architect Philip Johnson has been erected on the site. A block away is the cedar-log **John Neely Bryan Cabin** (not the cabin the 1841 Dallas founder actually lived in but one very much like it). And also in the area is the ornate

Romanesque revival-style **Old Red Courthouse,** built in the early 1890s, complete with eight circular turrets.

## Participant Sports

There are five **public golf courses** in Dallas where greens fees are $5 to $8. They are **Cedar Crest,** 1800 Southerland Ave., at Old Bonnie View (tel. 943-1004); **Grover C. Keeton,** 2323 Jim Miller Rd., at Bruton Road (tel. 388-4831); **L. B. Houston,** 11223 Luna Rd., at Royal Lane (tel. 869-1778); **Stevens,** 1005 Montclair, at Colorado Boulevard (tel. 946-5781); and **Tenison,** 3501 Samuell Blvd., at East Grand Road (tel. 823-5350).

**Tennis** is a big sport in Dallas. As a recent issue of the *Dallas Observer* noted, there are 288 public courts, one for every 3,140 citizens, but luckily "not all of those people are trying to get on a court at any given time." Municipal courts are listed in the Blue Pages under "Dallas, City of, Park & Recreation Department." For reservations and additional information, call 428-1501.

**Biking** is not the way to get around this freeway-routed metropolis. But there are bicycle trails such as the three-mile route on Bachman Lake, 3500 Northwest Hwy., and the nine-mile White Rock Lake trail. For bike-trail maps, call 670-4029.

Want to go out on **bird-watching** expeditions? Call the Audubon Society at 223-2857.

There's **horseback riding** at the Diamond J Corral on Hwy. 380 and FM 1385 (tel. 733-4514). Rentals are about $10 an hour. Call for reservations.

**Ice skating** rinks are located in the Galleria, at Dallas Parkway and LBJ Freeway (tel. 387-5533), and the Prestonwood Ice Capades Chalet, also in a mall at Belt Line Road and Preston Road (tel. 980-8988).

Any major hotel these days either has its own **jogging** course or can direct you to the nearest one. White Rock and Bachman Lakes are the two most popular sites, not only for joggers but rope jumpers, skaters, skateboarders, breakdancers, and whatever else.

A few **information sources:** Call the **Dallas Park & Recreation** 24-hour hotline, 670-7070, to find out about park activities. Also check the *Dallas Morning News*'s Friday "Guide" and the *Dallas Times Herald*'s "Weekend," both offering comprehensive, up-to-the-minute sports listings on everything from croquet to parachuting.

## Spectator Sports

In addition to the choices listed below, check out the annual events calendar earlier in this chapter; if something occurs every year, as major athletic competitions usually do, it's listed there.

The **Dallas Cowboys** play at least 11 home games at the 65,000-seat Texas Stadium, 2401 E. Airport Freeway (Hwy. 183) in Irving, between August and December. Tickets to individual games are about $20, available through Rainbow Ticketmaster (tel. 787-1500). You can also write in advance to the Dallas Cowboys Football Club Ticket Office, 1 Cowboy Parkway, Irving, TX 75063 (tel. 214/556-9900)—not a bad idea, since tickets are hard to come by. The Texas Stadium also hosts the **S.M.U. Mustangs** (college football) who play five or six home games between September and November; for information or to charge tickets, call 692-2902. And high school football playoff games take place here mid-November through mid-December. Call 438-7676 for information. Forty-five-minute guided tours of the stadium are given weekdays at 10 a.m. and 2 p.m., weekends and holidays at 11 a.m. and 12:20 and 2 p.m. Adults pay $2.50; children under 12 pay $1.50. Call 438-7676 for details and information about other sporting events (track, wrestling, etc.) here.

Finally, it might be helpful to know that the Dallas Transit System operates a "Cowboy Flyer" bus to all regularly scheduled Texas Stadium games; for information, call 826-2222.

Reunion Arena, 777 Sports St., next door to the Hyatt Regency Hotel, a 19,200-seat facility, is home to the **Dallas Mavericks** (NBA), who play 41 home games during their November-to-mid-April season here, one or two preseason games, and, hopefully, postseason playoff games. Tickets range from about $5 to $30, and they're hard to get; call as far in advance as possible. Early in April the ten top-seeded men in tennis compete in the **World Championship Tennis Tournament,** a major celebrity-attended event (they even serve strawberries and cream à la Wimbledon). Tickets range from $5 to about $10,000 (for best box seats for the entire tournament). They go fast, so get them far in advance. **MISL (Major Indoor Soccer League)** teams play in the arena November to April. And in early March there's the **Southwest Conference Post-Season Basketball Classic.** Tickets for all the above can be charged at 787-1500. For event information (there are also wrestling and boxing matches here, rodeos, etc.), call 745-1540.

Major athletic competitions at the **Cotton Bowl** are listed in "Annual Events." Call 421-8703 for additional information.

And the **Texas Rangers** of the American League West play about 81 home games at Arlington Stadium, 1500 Copeland Rd., at I-30, during the April-through-October season. Tickets range from about $4 to $9 ($2.50 for children 13 and under). Games are enhanced by Diamond Vision, a 40- by 30-foot TV monitor for airing instant replays and audience closeups. In summer there are about six postgame headliner concerts starring country singers like Loretta Lynn, the Oak Ridge Boys, and Conway Twitty. Tickets for concerts are $3 additional. For information, call 817/273-5222.

**SHOPPING:** The most impressive shopping in Dallas is at its futuristic mammoth malls. In addition to the places listed below, also keep museum shops in mind; they always offer interesting inventories, and you help support them when you buy. Old City Park's old-fashioned general store is particularly noteworthy.

### Books

The Southwest's largest bookstores are branches of a chain called **Taylor's,** here at 5455 Belt Line Rd. (tel. 934-1500) and 4001 Northwest Parkway (tel. 363-1500). Both carry vast inventories on subjects as diverse as aging, art history, calligraphy, etiquette, genealogy, hypnotism, the oil business, the occult, public speaking, weight lifting, and World Wars I and II. Of course, there's an immense fiction section, and if you'd rather read the Cliff Notes, they're here too. I'd say you're likely to find just about anything you're looking for. There are about 200 categories.

Discount books are offered at the **Bookstop,** 5400 E. Mockingbird Lane (tel. 828-4210), and the nearby **Century Bookstore,** 3032 Mockingbird Lane (tel. 691-8157), with another location at 3428 Oak Lawn Ave. (tel. 521-0582). Both Centurys are marvelous for hard-to-find magazines (which in Dallas includes most of them).

### Department Stores

Everyone knows **Neiman-Marcus** stores. The original, founded in 1907 and moved to its present location at 1618 Main St., at Ervay (tel. 741-6911), is here in downtown Dallas. Many unique promotions are offered. For one thing, charge-card customers receive points for all merchandise charged, one point for one dollar, and these are redeemable in prizes ranging from gourmet chocolates to a week in England including hotel and air fare! Of course, you have to spend $100,000 in a year to get that, but I'm sure there's them that has (a Lalique figurine here, a Galanos fur there, and you're well on your way). Even if you can't afford Neiman's exclusive merchandise, it's fun to browse, especially during the October/November Fortnight when lavish decorations, celebrity guests, museum exhibits, fashions, food (several restaurants are created just for the occasion), furnishings, and entertainment celebrate a chosen country. The store's Christmas catalog, offering such whimsical his-and-hers gifts as $2,000 Chinese Shar-Pei puppies or matching Jaguars (his an XKE for $5,559, hers a mink-trimmed jaguar coat for $5,975), is also famous. And there are frequent celebrity appearances by people like Bill Blass and Oscar de la Renta.

## Factory Outlets

Big savings can be had at **Outlet Malls of America's** 54 stores at 1717 E. Spring Creek, off Central Expressway (U.S. 75), Exit 31 (tel. 578-1591). It's in Plano, about 15 minutes west of Southfork. Most are factory outlet stores, though some are just low-priced retailers. It's all conveniently under one roof. You can shop here for bargains in every kind of men's, women's, and children's shoes and apparel, jewelry, paintings, leather goods, gifts and party goods, western wear, brassware, imports, bedding, china, cookware, eyeglasses, books, handbags, plants, toys, and more.

## Farmers Market

Though as a tourist you're not likely to be shopping for produce, you will enjoy a stroll through the colorful open-air **Farmers Market**, 1010 S. Pearl Expressway, just north of I-30 (tel. 670-5879). It takes up a few blocks with its four big tent-like, corrugated-roof structures (orange, green, red, and yellow) filled with booths of over 200 vendors selling farm-fresh eggs, a cornucopia of fresh fruits and vegetables in bushel baskets, honey, nuts, garden plants, peppers, etc. Saturday is the best time to come; that's when the selection is largest. It all smells and looks delicious. Often there's entertainment, fresh-cut flowers are sometimes available, and during holidays like Christmas, Easter, and Halloween you can buy seasonal decorations and gift items.

On Taylor Street between Pearl and Harwood is an annex called the **Bazaar,** a large collection of stalls selling unrelated items that included, on my last visit, pickled vegetables, umbrellas, plants, garden furnishings, lingerie, fresh herbs and spices, kitchen gadgetry, crafts, jewelry, canning supplies, handbags, and homemade chowchow. Some good bargains here, and it does make for enjoyable browsing.

Old City Park is close by, so you might combine a morning at the market (it opens at 6 a.m. daily) with a tour of the park—and possibly with a hot-croissant-and-coffee breakfast at La Madeleine on Lemmon Avenue (see restaurant recommendations) as well.

## Olla Podrida

The most colorful complex of shops in Dallas is Olla Podrida, 12215 Coit Rd., between the LBJ Freeway (I-635) and Forest Lane (tel. 239-8541). A white stucco, terracotta tile-roofed converted warehouse, it originated in 1972 as studio space for a group of potters. Word spread to other artisans looking for workspace, and little by little it evolved into a "stew pot" of various craftspeople—a distinctive marketplace where artists maintained studios and shops. The group decorated the interior with architectural salvage: wrought-iron grillwork, stained-glass windows from old mansions and churches, a bench from an old Denver saloon, hotel chandeliers, old signs and posters, etc. They added a skylit roof to let in natural light, hung a bell with a sign reading, "If you're happy and you know it, ring the bell" (it rings a lot), and created a Mexican façade complete with fountain.

Today Olla Podrida has numerous art studio/shops: a custom metal sculptor, photographer, painters, potters, a candlemaker, custom shoemaker, stained-glass artist, clockmaker, tarot card reader/palmist, and voice teacher, among others. And there are shops selling hand-knit sweaters, Texana, kites, stationery, western apparel, antiques, toys, bed and bath items, Indian artifacts, Christmas decorations, belly-dancing accessories, wine-making supplies, and various and sundry other things. There are several places to eat on the premises. Shopping here is good fun.

## Resale

Those wealthy Dallas matrons who wouldn't dream of wearing the same designer duds twice don't necessarily give their discards to the maid. Many of them turn up at **Champagne Taste,** 1106 Preston Royal Plaza (tel. 368-8935), where you can pick them up for a song. Oh, how I love those discounted Diors and cut-rate Cardins.

## Western Wear

**Boot Town,** 5909 Belt Line Rd., at Preston Road (tel. 214/385-3052 or toll free 800/22-BOOTS), has everything in the way of western wear, including famous brand boots—Tony Lama, Acme, Nocona, Justin, Dingo, Lucchesi, etc.—at 20% to 50% below list price. Also top names in belts, buckles, hats, scarves, jeans, etc. It's one of the biggest western-wear dealers in Texas.

## Malls

There's a **Galleria** mall, complete with ice skating rink, on the Dallas Parkway between the LBJ Freeway (I-635) and Alpha Road (tel. 458-2600). It's anchored, to use mall terminology, by three major department stores—Macy's, Marshall Field, and Saks Fifth Avenue—and a deluxe hotel, the 440-room Westin. Other facilities include a posh private tennis and racquetball club and five movie theaters. The retail part includes 160 shops in two architecturally striking towers. Among the well-known notables: Gump's, B. Dalton, Benetton, The Gap, Elizabeth Arden, Georgette Klinger, Godiva Chocolatier, Laura Ashley, Scandia Down, Tiffany & Co., Louis Vuitton, Banana Republic, Radio Shack, F.A.O. Schwarz, Pappagallo, and Charles Jourdan. And there are over a dozen eateries, including Vie de France (great croissant sandwiches), Uncle Tai's, and the very nice Zucchini's at the Westin for fresh healthful fare.

Raymond Nasher, owner of **NorthPark Center,** a 150-shop upscale mall at North Central Expressway (U.S. 75) and Northwest Hwy. (tel. 363-7441), is an art aficionado and one of the major private collectors in the country. To share this passion with shoppers, he displays pieces from his collection throughout the mall. While you're checking out Laura Ashley's latest line you'll also be enjoying works by artists like Lichtenstein, Mark DiSuvero, Henry Moore, Warhol, Oldenburg, Rodin, Picasso, Arp, and Matisse, among others. What a treat! Major department stores at NorthPark include Neiman-Marcus, Lord & Taylor, J. C. Penney, and Joske's. Other well-known emporia are Crabtree & Evelyn, a Doubleday bookstore, The Gap, Gucci, I. Miller Shoes, a James Avery jewelry outlet, Rizzoli International, and Hoffritz for Cutlery. There are quite a few restaurants, among them a Fuddrucker's for fab burgers (see Houston restaurants recommendations for details on this chain).

**Prestonwood Town Center,** 5301 Belt Line Rd., off Dallas Parkway (tel. 980-4275), is yet another major mall. This one has 170 shops and boutiques, including Neiman-Marcus, Lord & Taylor, J. C. Penney, Joske's, and Montgomery Ward. An ice-skating rink, five movie theaters, and a play area for children are pluses, and in addition to five major restaurants you can pig out here on Mrs. Field's fab chocolate-chip cookies, the best anywhere. Prestonwood is a little less high-toned than some of the above-mentioned; forget Charles Jourdan, here's Thom McAn. It's not bargain-basement or anything (there is a Neiman's after all), but you'll find more of a choice pricewise.

**AFTER DARK:** Dallas has a glittering nightlife scene, including an impressive line-up of ballet, opera, symphony, and theater options, and an equally exciting roster of let-loose clubs offering everything from rock to reggae. And there are always a couple of headliners in town as well. Lower Greenville Avenue is the city's nightclub mecca, conveniently close to S.M.U. And the burgeoning Dallas Arts District, a 60-acre historic section just west of downtown, is shaping up as the city's Greenwich Village or Left Bank. The new Dallas Symphony Orchestra concert hall, designed by I. M. Pei, will be its core upon completion in 1988. No matter how long your stay in Dallas, you won't lack for nighttime thrills.

To find out what's happening utilize the following sources:

The *Dallas Morning News,* in conjunction with the Dallas Arts Combine, operates **Artsline,** a 24-hour recording that will keep you abreast of everything happening in town relating to the fine arts. That includes plays, operas, jazz and pop concerts, classical music performances, films, museum shows, and more. The number to call is 385-1155.

At hotels, restaurants, and theater lobbies around town, you may come across a free weekly newspaper called the **Dallas Observer.** It's a comprehensive source for all events—nighttime and otherwise—and it also contains amusing and interesting articles. Pick it up and peruse.

Check out, too, the *Dallas Morning News* **"Guide"** to dining, nightspots, theater, and movies in every Friday's paper, and the *Dallas Times Herald*'s similar **"Weekend"** section, also every Friday. **D Magazine** also has complete listings.

## Tickets

Like many big cities, Dallas has a half-price/day-of-performance ticket outlet. **TKTS/KVIL,** Suite 260 of the Corner Office Center Building, 9850 N. Central Expressway (U.S. 75), at Walnut Hill Lane (tel. 369-8500), offers tickets on this basis for almost all major Dallas productions, including operas and some Fort Worth events. Radio Station KVIL (103.7 FM) announces what's available throughout the day. Tickets for evening performances are sold Tuesday to Saturday between noon and 7 p.m.; for matinees, 9 a.m. to noon Wednesdays and weekends. It's not a bad idea to call before you go, since the service is sometimes mysteriously closed. Tickets must be paid for in cash.

If discount tickets aren't available, call **Rainbow Ticketmaster** to charge (via MasterCard or VISA) tickets for all major Dallas sports, music, and theatrical events. Dial 263-6102 for a listing of available tickets, 787-1500 to charge tickets.

## Mixed Bags

It would be nice if theaters and other performance arenas each stuck to one kind of entertainment—nice when you're categorizing at any rate. However, the excitement of variety I'm sure outweighs the obsessive/compulsive delights of neat labeling. Hence, the following mixed bags.

**The Music Hall:** The 3,420-seat Music Hall at Fair Park (tel. 565-1116) is the setting for numerous cultural attractions. It has been in continual operation since 1925.

The **Dallas Opera** presents its fall season (four productions, four performances each) here in November and December. All operas are sung in their original languages with English captions. A recent season included *Otello, La Bohème,* Wagner's *Götterdämmerung,* and Donizetti's *L'Elisir d'Amore.* Ticket prices range from $4 to $60. They can be charged at 871-0090.

It's also the home of **Dallas Summer Musicals,** June through August, featuring major stars like Carol Burnett, Debbie Reynolds, Ginger Rogers, and Carol Channing. A recent season included *La Cage aux Folles* with Peter Marshall and Keene Curtis, *My One and Only* with Sandy Duncan and Tommy Tune, *Zorba* with Anthony Quinn, and *Jesus Christ Superstar* starring Anthony Geary, among others. There's also a major musical production in October in conjunction with the State Fair. Ticket prices range from about $10 to $45. Call 565-1116 for information.

The theater has also served as home for the **Dallas Civic Opera Company** since its inception, and showcases the annual visit of the Metropolitan Opera each spring. The Metropolitan has recently stopped touring, but future plans call for the presentation each May of other major opera companies from around the world along with major soloists. For details, call 979-0123 or 661-9750.

The **Dallas Symphony Orchestra** (tel. 692-0203) also has a September-to-May season here; see their listing elsewhere in this chapter for details.

And a variety of **headliner** artists, representing every facet of the entertainment world, perform on the Music Hall stage during winter months. In the past the diverse talents of Bette Midler, Hal Holbrook, Anne Murray, Lola Falana, Gordon Lightfoot, Lena Horne, and Johnny Mathis have attracted capacity audiences here.

**The Majestic Theatre:** The 1,589-seat Majestic Theatre, 1925 Elm St., between Harwood and St. Paul Streets (tel. 880-0137 for information), originally opened in 1921 and hosted acts like Houdini, Jack Benny, Burns and Allen, and Mae West. When movies replaced vaudeville, it became a lavish cinema palace, scene of scores of celebrity-studded premières. Totally renovated in 1983, it is, though lacking some of the old features like a merry-go-round and a petting zoo, a spectacular setting for dramatic productions. The bronze-trimmed marble entrance, richly paneled and carved plaster foyer hung with gilt-framed mirrors, Italian fountain, massive crystal chandeliers and gold-crowned Corinthian columns, and ceiling painted with twinkling stars have all been restored. The theater is indeed majestic once again.

Fall through spring, the Majestic hosts a **Broadway Series** of about five productions with major stars, such as Noel Harrison in *Noises Off,* the world première of James Kirkwood's *Legends* featuring Mary Martin and Carol Channing, the female version of *The Odd Couple* with Sally Struthers and Rita

Moreno, and *A Coupla White Chicks* with Elizabeth Ashley and Susan Anton. Tickets are available through major ticket outlets.

The **Dallas Black Dance Theatre** (tel. 371-1170) also performs here. They do three major productions, about four or five performances of each, in December, February, and May. DBDT is Dallas's first (since 1976) and only black professional dance company; they've performed at New York's Brooklyn Academy of Music and received excellent notices in the *New York Times* and other publications. The company's style is lyrically modern, but does include some jazz and classical choreography in its repertoire. Single tickets are in the $5 to $30 range, and you can charge them via Ticketron or the above number.

The **Dallas Ballet** (tel. 744-4430 to charge tickets) does six productions here each year between the end of October and the end of March under the artistic direction of Flemming Flindt (Flindt was for 12 years artistic director of the Royal Danish Ballet). A recent season included Stravinsky's *Petrouchka,* Chopin's *Les Sylphides,* the dances from Borodin's opera *Prince Igor,* the Spanish masterpiece *The Toreador,* and guest artist Alvin Ailey in a production of *The River,* choreographed to music by Duke Ellington. The point is, you can always count on an exciting Dallas Ballet season, incorporating both classical and contemporary works. Tickets range from $5 to $40 for individual performances.

And April of each year the **Dallas Opera** performs small, less-frequently performed works here. A recent season's offerings included Monteverdi's *La Favola d'Orfeo, The Mother of Us All* with libretto by Gertrude Stein, and Mozart's *The Abduction from the Seraglio.* Tickets, $7 to $50, can be charged at 871-0090. The Dallas Opera also offers a Recital Series here featuring a singer and pianist during September and February.

**The Plaza Theatre:** At 6719 Snider Plaza, one block west of Hillcrest Avenue and three blocks south of Lovers Lane (tel. 363-7000), the Plaza presents a variety of entertainments, including three summer (June and July) productions, seven performances each, of the **Public Opera of Dallas.** These works are always performed in English, with the aim of attracting a new opera audience. And the company promotes new American talent, along with international guest stars from major opera companies. A recent season included productions of Rimsky-Korsakov's *Mozart and Salieri* (the original *Amadeus*), *The Mikado,* and Donizetti's *Don Pasquale.* For ticket information and reservations, call the above number or 231-6566.

**Dancers Unlimited,** a highly acclaimed six-member modern dance company, performs at the Plaza in November, March, and May. For ticket information and reservations, call the above number or 742-7821.

The remainder of the season is given over to traveling shows from around the country—a marvelous production of *A Woman of Independent Means* starring Barbara Rush; *Palace of Amateurs,* a new play starring Mariel Hemingway; *The Dining Room;* and *Crimes of the Heart.* Call the above number for ticket information and reservations.

The theater itself has been renovated in 1920s art deco style at a cost of $2 million; the original theater dates to 1929 and was originally called the Varsity.

## The Dallas Symphony Orchestra

The Dallas Symphony Orchestra (tel. 692-0203 for information or to charge tickets) is the 6th-oldest and 11th-largest orchestra in the country. A new $75-million home for the orchestra, the I. M. Pei–designed **Morton H. Meyerson Symphony Center,** is scheduled for completion in 1988. In the meantime, its offerings are as follows:

A wide array of **classical series** take place at the Fair Park Music Hall during a September-to-May season. There are performances every Thursday, Friday, and Saturday night, and Sunday matinees, often featuring acclaimed guest artists like Itzhak Perlman, Luciano Pavarotti, and Leontyne Price.

A variety of top guest artists perform in the **SuperPops** series, also in the Music Hall, from January to late April or early May. These stars have included Joel Grey, Rita Moreno, Robert Goulet, Henry Mancini, and even Jerry Lewis.

In June and July the DSO presents **Starfest** at Park Central, near the LBJ Freeway (I-635) and Coit Road. It's an outdoor pavilion with 1,600 reserved seats (chairs at tables for four) sold on a subscription-only basis and seating for an additional 8,400 people on the sloped lawn. Everyone brings picnic dinners to these concerts under the stars. The music is an eclectic mix of classical, country, show tunes, gospel, etc., and there are even comedy nights. Ticket prices vary with the artist; in the past Starfest concerts have featured Kenny Loggins, the Pointer Sisters, the Everly Brothers, Bill Cosby, Sammy Davis, Jr., Crystal Gayle, John Denver, and Gladys Knight and the Pips, among others. Concerts begin at 8:30 p.m. Arrive early to get a good lawn seat.

Twelve free **Youth Concerts** take place during a January-to-May season, 12 of them (in May) outdoors in the parks, the others downtown at noon on Pacific Avenue and Akard Street.

The **Discovery Series** takes place each June and July at the beautiful Majestic Theatre, 1925 Elm St., between Harwood and St. Paul Streets. Featured presentations can be anything from soloists to full orchestral productions, including such notable classical performers as pianist/conductor Leon Fleisher; Igor Kipnis, who's been called the world's greatest harpsichordist; and pianist Dmitris Sgouros.

Finally, there are 7 p.m. **lectures** presented by S.M.U. faculty member/composer/conductor Simon Sargon prior to winter classical concerts about the music to be heard.

For further details, write to the Dallas Symphony Association, Inc., P.O. Box 26207, Dallas, TX 75226.

## The Dallas Opera

The Dallas Opera (tel. 979-1023), a world-class company that has been bringing performances of grand and chamber opera, operatic concerts, and recitals to Dallas since 1957, is renowned for its musical artistry and imaginative productions. For several seasons its stage was the only one in America on which Maria Callas would perform.

In addition to its offerings described elsewhere in this chapter (see Fair Park Music Hall and the Majestic Theatre), the company sponsors **Opera on the Go,** a touring ensemble that performs operatic scenes throughout the Metroplex area (in parks, malls, etc.) between late August and mid-October. There's no admission charge. Call the above number for a performance schedule.

## Theater

Like New York and other cities, Dallas has that wonderful institution, a summer **Shakespeare Festival** (tel. 987-1993) with free productions in State Fair Park (it has a 3,500-seat outdoor amphitheater) from mid-July through early August. Performers include some nationally known actors and actresses like Sigourney Weaver and Ron Leibman, along with lesser-known but very experienced troupers. They do some innovative productions, like *Hamlet* in the manner of Edwin Booth's 1886 version, a *Shogun Macbeth,* and *Much Ado About Nothing* set in the 1930s. Tickets are on a first-come, first-served basis, and though gates open at 7:15 p.m., people start lining up by 6:30. Picnicking at your seat before the show is a festival tradition. One reviewer aptly described Shakespeare in the park as "a midsummer night's delight."

The 215-seat **Dallas Repertory Theatre,** 150 NorthPark Center on Central Expressway (U.S. 75), between Park Lane and Northwest Hwy. (tel. 369-8966), has been producing current and past (mostly Broadway) dramas and musicals since 1969 under the competent artistic direction of founder/producer Ed DeLatte. A professional Equity house, its shows are cast locally but employ actors from all over the country. Their year-round season usually includes about eight shows; for example, in 1986, *Greater Tuna, Evita, Our Town, Joseph and the Amazing Technicolor Dreamcoat, Crimes of the Heart, Pump Boys and Dinettes, A Chorus Line,* and *The Gingerbread Man,* a children's musical fantasy from London. In addition, DRT offers special small-scale matinee productions like *Meet Mark Twain,* an original one-man show starring the theater's general manager, Don Cowan. These are part of the theater's "DR Tea" program of intimate afternoon productions followed by English teas, complete with finger sandwiches and scones, served in the lobby and picture gallery. Regular shows are in the $11 to $14 range (afternoon tea shows, $15), with discounts available for students and seniors.

The **Dallas Theater Center** (tel. 526-8857), a repertory company since 1958, presents plays on two stages, the Frank Lloyd Wright Theater, 3636 Turtle Creek Blvd., between Blackburn and Lemmon Avenues (it was designed by Wright), and the Arts District Theater, 2401 Flora St., just east of Pearl Street. Their September-to-May season offers about six productions, with five-week runs at either facility (sometimes overlapping) plus an annual holiday showing of *A Christmas Carol.* A recent season included an adaptation of Richard Wright's *Native Son, Glass Menagerie,* Vinnette Carroll's *The Ups and Downs of Theophilus Maitland,* Thorton Wilder's *The Skin of our Teeth, All the King's Men,* and Eugene O'Neill's *Moon for the Misbegotten.* That's a pretty impressive roster! Ticket prices range from about $11 to $22. There's also a Teen/Children's Theater program, geared to preteens and younger, offering about four productions a year at the Frank Lloyd Wright Theater. Tickets are $4.50.

**Theatre Three,** in the Quadrangle at 2800 Routh St., between McKinney and Cole Avenues (tel. 871-3300), established in 1961, is an Equity theater presenting about six or seven quality productions each year. A typical season runs quite a theatrical gamut, including such diverse productions as Molière's *School for Wives* and *For Colored Girls . . . ,* and another year ranging from Cole Porter's *Anything Goes* to the award-winning feminist revue *A . . . My Name is Alice.* Performers comprise both local and national talent. Tickets are $12.50 to $14.50 ($8.50 to $9.50 for previews), and once a month there's a "miser's matinee" for just $5.

The **New Arts Theatre,** 702 Ross Ave., at Market Street (tel. 761-9064), is a professional theater group, founded in 1975, offering seven productions a year, primarily contemporary in nature. The casts are largely local actors, "fleshed out," a publicist explained, "by New York and West Coast people." The 1986 season featured productions of *The Rocky Horror Show, Clouds* by Michael Frayn (he also wrote *Noises Off*), *Gemini, Extremities, Dog Days* by Simon Gray (he also wrote *Otherwise Engaged*), *Master Harold and the Boys,* and Caryl Churchill's *Top Girls.* It's the kind of line-up for which any serious theater-goer would crave a season ticket. Individual tickets are $8.50 to $14.25.

## Headliners

Vegas-caliber headliners play the deluxe **Venetian Room** at the Fairmont Hotel, 1717 N. Akard St., at Ross (tel. 720-2020), an opulent supper club with brown velvet walls and draperies, gold moldings, ornate seven-foot candelabra chandeliers, and murals in gilt-framed arches of the canal—all of it designed to evoke an 18th-century Venetian palace. Among the stars who've appeared here are Tony Bennett, Carol Lawrence, Mel Torme, Joel Grey, Bernadette Peters, and Ella Fitzgerald. Tickets are $15 to $25, depending on the performer, and you can dine here as well, either à la carte or from a table d'hôte menu (salad, grilled fresh salmon with green peppercorn sauce, garden vegetables, potatoes du jour, and strawberry cheesecake with coffee for $23). That's in addition to your ticket price, of course. In between sets, there's big-band music for dancing.

Other stages offering frequent headliner concerts include the 19,200-seat **Reunion Arena,** 777 Sports St. (tel. 745-1540 for a recording of events, 658-7070 to talk to a human being), which has hosted Kenny Rogers, Frank Sinatra, and Bruce Springsteen, among other superstars; **Texas Stadium,** 2401 E. Airport Freeway (tel. 438-7676 to find out what's on, 556-9900 for ticket information), the 65,000-seat arena used by Michael Jackson on his Victory Tour; and the mammoth 72,000-seat **Cotton Bowl** stadium in Fair Park where the Rolling Stones, Willie Nelson, and Elvis have electrified audiences (tel. 421-8703 for event and ticket information).

## Live Music

One of the most elegant settings for Dallas nights is the **Jazba** at Ratcliffe's, a restaurant at 1901 McKinney Ave., at St. Paul (tel. 748-7480). You needn't dine here to enjoy the high-quality jazz acts in this sleek and stunning club (it's separate from the dining area), with plush black armchairs at white-linened cocktail tables, exquisite calla lily–motif carpeting, marble-topped bar, and art deco lighting fixtures. The music is straight-ahead, 1950s-style bebop, not avant garde. Dress to the nines. Admission is $5, and the average drink is $3.50. Of course, you might just order up a bottle of Dom Perignon for $115, perhaps accompanied by such light fare as a seafood cocktail of crabmeat, shrimp, oysters, clams, and gulf shrimp ($11.95) or smoked Scottish salmon stuffed with herbed cheese, capers, and red onion ($13.99). There are tasty desserts like double chocolate (white and dark) mousse as well ($5.50). Open Tuesday to Saturday from 9 p.m. to 1:15 a.m.

**Redux** (pronounced "Redo"), 1827 Greenville Ave., at Alta Street (tel. 823-9524), is a glittery new art deco club, so named because it's been a nightclub twice before, so it's a nightclub redux. The owners designed it to have the feel of a deluxe old movie palace, and very attractive it is, with leaded-glass panels, wonderful paintings on the walls, and big flower arrangements on the bar. You have to be reasonably dressed to get in: no jogging gear, and classy jeans are only minimally acceptable. You do see people here, though, in outfits ranging from furs and tuxedos to slick urban cowboy garb. Style aside, it's a great club for music lovers, featuring talented local and regional groups and possessed of an excellent sound system. The owners' music philosophy is no country and no heavy metal, but everything in between. In the lull between sets a 12- by 18-foot screen comes down and rock videos are aired. There's live music every Tuesday to Saturday from 9 p.m. to 1:30 a.m. And should you want to get away from the band for a few minutes of quiet conversation, it's possible up on the balcony. Admission is $3.50 to $10, depending on the act.

**Rick's Casablanca,** 1919 Greenville Ave., between Ross and Belmont Avenues (tel. 824-6509), is a high-energy club decorated in tropical motif with murals of palm trees and flamingoes, and, of course, pictures of Bogie. It's always mobbed with a young, party-till-you-drop crowd; the owner looks for music acts which make dancing irresistible. Some of Rick's frequently appearing groups have a large local following, such as a funk band called Ultimate Force and the R&B band, Robert Lee Kolb and the Local Heroes. There's no dance floor, but everyone boogies a bit in between the tables. You can get away from it all for a breath of fresh air on a patio with palms and tropical plants. Usually, though, there are people dancing right out on the street, since the show inside is televised on a screen over the door. There's live entertainment seven nights a week from about 8 p.m. to 2 a.m. Cover charge is $3.50 to $5.50, depending on who's playing.

**Poor David's Pub,** 1924 Greenville Ave., three blocks south of Belmont Avenue (tel. 821-9891), is one of the most popular spots on this club-dotted strip. Opened in 1977, it has outlasted numerous other Lower Greenville enterprises by offering very good music in comfortable, unpretentious surroundings. Owner David Card books all kinds of music acts as long as they're top-quality, so the Pub might be featuring rock, country, folk, reggae, acoustic guitar, or blues, depending on the night you show up. On Monday nights, Anson and the Rockets, considered by many to be Texas's best blues band, always takes the stage. And there are occasional big names like Mary Travers, the Four Freshmen, Jerry Jeff Walker, Riders in the Sky, Tom Paxton, and John Sebastian. The Pub is casual—you can wear your jeans, and they needn't be designer. It has the feel of an old New York Greenwich Village club. Admission is $3.50 on Monday night and $1.50 on Tuesday, Songwriters Sounding Board night (when local songwriters and singers perform their own material). The rest of the week you'll pay $3 to $12, depending on the act. There's no drink minimum. Light fare is available.

## Dancing

The most chi-chi club in town is without a doubt the **Starck Club,** 703 McKinney Ave., in the Brewery (tel. 720-0130), partially owned by rock singer Stevie Nicks and named for its famous designer, Philippe Starck (also responsible for the interiors of major Paris nightclubs). Prince, WHAM, and Tears for Fears are a few of the celebs who have thrown private parties here, and a slew of visiting royals and rock luminaries have made the scene. The club has 20,000 square feet of black marble flooring, the chairs are the same as those in President Mitterrand's bedroom, and even the bathrooms are special—the taps in the sink are laser activated! More important perhaps, the current DJ, who plays mostly European dance music, has been rated one of the top five in the country by *Billboard* magazine. It's the kind of place you can order caviar and champagne in between dance numbers. Open nightly; till after hours Monday to Saturday, till 2 a.m. on Sunday. Admission is $5 Thursday to Sunday, $10 on Friday and Saturday.

**In Cahoots,** 8796 N. Central Expressway (U.S. 75) at the Park Lane exit (tel. 692-5412), is a sleek hi-tech club with art deco furnishings, exposed pipes and steel beams, glass brick, and neon tubing. There are three ten-foot video screens over the sunken dance floor, two more flanking the DJ booth, and eight smaller video monitors around the room. The music (top-40s danceable) is further enhanced by a state-of-the-art laser light show and dancers in sexy leotards performing on stages. Weekends especially, the place is wall-to-wall Yupscales, 35 and under, and there's lots of pickup action. A game room in the back offers blackjack and video games. In Cahoots lures 'em in with Monday-to-Friday Happy Hour buffets 5 to 8 p.m. Admission is $4 on Friday and Saturday nights, Sunday to Thursday there's no cover, and valet parking is always free. The club is a mite hard to find. Go east on Park Lane and look for the North Park East sign on your right; turn in and follow the road till you see the club.

Don't ask me what the **Acapulco Bar,** 5111 Greenville Ave., a block south of Lovers Lane (tel. 692-9855), looks like—I've never been here when it wasn't too mobbed to tell. What you will see is a crowd of good-looking, well-dressed people (though garb varies from Yuppie to urban cowboy, the former predominating) actively involved in picking each other up. One good reason for the Acapulco's popularity is its fabulous free dinner buffets, Tuesday to Friday from 5 to 9 p.m., on Saturday from 7 to 9 p.m., typically featuring fajitas, tacos, nachos, salads, fresh fruits, and international entrees. The club's award-winning margaritas are also noteworthy. Music is top-40s. If you tire of dancing you can adjourn to the blackjack table. Open Tuesday to Saturday. Admission is $1 Tuesday to Thursday, $4 on Friday and Saturday. Valet parking is $2.

At Reunion Tower's **Top of the Dome,** Reunion Boulevard at Stemmons Freeway (tel. 651-1234), you can dance to a band playing top-40s tunes 550 feet up. The Dome is a rotating cocktail lounge making a full revolution every hour. The band plays nightly from 9 p.m., and the nighttime view of downtown and beyond is spectacular. All the plush seats here offer full views. Come by for the lavish Happy Hour buffet, weekdays from 5 to 7 p.m., and stay to dance. The Dome serves hors d'oeuvres and drinks, but if you want a full meal you can have it at an adjoining restaurant called Antares (tel. 741-3663) where a complete soup-to-mousse dinner costs $20.25 and à la carte entrees are in the $15 to $20 range.

## Comedy

**Comedy Corner,** 8202 Park Lane, at Greenville Avenue (tel. 361-7461), is the Dallas representative of the ubiquitous comedy clubs that have sprung up around the nation in recent years. Like others of its ilk, it presents the circuit comics you see on Carson and Letterman, along with occasional big names like Waylon Flowers, Shirley Hemphill, and Gabe Kaplan. It's open nightly. On Monday nights the Dallas Comedy Workshop, a local improv group, performs at 8:30 p.m. and admission is $3.50. Tuesday nights there are both amateurs and professionals on stage; shows start at 8:30 p.m. and admission is $5.50. On Wednesday, Thursday, and Sunday you can see three acts (basically an M.C., newcomer, and headliner), once again at 8:30 p.m. and with an admission of $5.50. And on Friday and Saturday nights there are two shows a night, at 8:30 and 10:30 p.m.; admission is $8 on Friday, $9 on Saturday. There's always a two-drink minimum, and drink prices begin at about $3.

## Film

The **USA Film Festival** (tel. 692-2573) is a nonprofit organization that has been offering Dallas a year-round program of themed film festivals and series since 1970. Films are usually shown at the Inwood Theatre, 5458 Lovers Lane, at Inwood Road (tel. 352-5793), or at two theaters at the Loews Anatole Hotel, 2201 Stemmons Freeway (I-35E) in Market Center, (tel. 748-1200). Its offerings always include a spring (March or April) five-day festival of Southwest Premières of major Hollywood studio movies, works of new and independent American filmmakers, and short films and videos. Individual tickets are $5 to $10, and you can also get tickets for the full series.

Sometime each year, USAFF presents KidFilm, a three-day festival of the best international animation and live-action films for children of all ages. It's usually accompanied by symposiums for adults, with experts discussing the effects of movies on children.

Once a year a Master Screen Artist & Gala Tribute honors a notable in the field with an award dinner and dance; past winners have included Shirley MacLaine, Gregory Peck, Charlton Heston, Kirk Douglas, and Jack Lemmon. The tribute includes film clips, celebrity appearances, readings of telegrams from other actors and directors, etc., and over the weekend there's a retrospective of the winner's works, after which he or she discusses them with the audience. The tribute dinner-dance costs about $250 per ticket; the retrospective with discussions, a more affordable $5 or so per film.

Similar is the annual Great Director Award, followed by two or three days of the chosen director's films and postfilm discussions. The bash itself is less expensive; films, once again, are about $5 per.

In addition, the Festival presents several four-week film series throughout the year with themes like "Musicals of the Fifties," "A Salute to Columbia Pictures," and "Best of Texas." And occasionally there are premières with guest artists.

Call 692-2573 to find out what's happening during your stay.

The **Dallas Museum of Art,** 1717 N. Harwood St., just south of Woodall Rogers Freeway (tel. 922-0220), also offers terrific classic and art-related films. You might catch a Hitchcock series, a Charlie Chaplin retrospective, Russian film classics, or a film interview with Frank Lloyd Wright. Wouldn't you rather pay $2.50 to see *All the King's Men* or *Camille* than $6 to see the latest Spielberg-factory production?

## Some Electronic Evening

Here's something a bit out of the ordinary. **Photon,** 12630 E. Northwest Hwy., at Shiloh Road (tel. 681-9083), brings video games one step further. Instead of controlling intergalactic battles with joysticks, you become an electronic outer-space warrior with armor consisting of a helmet with stereophonic headphones, coding lights and sensors, a powerpack belt, a chest control module housing a sophisticated microprocessor, and a phaser energizer. The battle, in which you are joined by up to ten team members, is fought on the planet Photon, a two-level, heavily mazed extraterrestrial territory of tunnels, secret passageways, bunkers, and battlements, enhanced by futuristic lighting, music, sound effects, and swirling fog. Your mission is to penetrate your opponents' defense and destroy their base goal, all the while scoring as many points as possible and avoiding getting "zapped." Games last 6½ minutes each. Photon games are the latest thing in hi-tech nightlife—the "ultimate fantasy-like, space-age experience," according to its inventor. If you've always wanted to engage in Space Age warfare or vaporize your pals, this is your chance; it does make a change from catching the local movie, doesn't it? And if you'd rather watch than play, there's a spectators' deck overlooking the planet and an electronic scoreboard to keep track of the action. Hours are 4 to 11 p.m. Monday to Thursday, to 1 a.m. on Friday, noon to 1 a.m. on Saturday, and noon to 11 p.m. on Sunday. There's an initial one-time charge of $4.50 for your Photon ID card, and games cost $3 each.

## 2. Grand Prairie and Arlington

Head west from Dallas on I-30 and you'll come to every child's favorite part of Texas. Grand Prairie and Arlington have, among other attractions, a major theme park, one of the nation's largest water parks, an immense wax museum, and a safari park. Not to mention a 106-acre flea market for mom and dad to explore, and Arlington Stadium, home of the Texas Rangers baseball team (here you munch nachos, not hot dogs, during the game). Grand Prairie is 13 miles from Dallas, 17 from Fort Worth; Arlington is 15 miles from either city.

One word of caution. Don't try to squeeze too much into one day. Six Flags, especially, is a full day's entertainment.

**INFORMATION SOURCES:** The **Grand Prairie Convention and Visitors Bureau** 900 Conover Dr., at Republic Parkway (tel. 214/264-1558), can answer all your questions about local attractions and provide maps and brochures. You can write to the bureau in advance at P.O. Box 531227, Grand Prairie, TX 75053. Hours for visiting are Monday to Friday from 8 a.m. to 5 p.m.

In Arlington, the same services are provided by the **Arlington Convention and Visitors Bureau,** 1908 E. Randol Mill Rd., at Stadium Drive (tel. 817/265-7721, or toll free 800/433-5374). Or write to them at P.O. Box A, Arlington, TX 76010. The bureau is open Memorial Day to Labor Day from 8 a.m. to 5 p.m. weekdays, from 9 a.m. to 6 p.m. on Saturday, from noon to 4 p.m. on Sunday. The rest of the year, hours are 8 a.m. to 5 p.m. weekdays only.

**WHERE TO STAY:** You can, of course, stay in Dallas or Fort Worth and make day trips to the mid-cities attractions. If you'd like to stay in the entertainment mecca itself, some suggestions follow. Reserve well in advance during the busy summer season.

**Sheraton CentrePark,** 1500 Stadium Dr. East, between Copeland and Randol Mill Roads, Arlington, TX 76011 (tel. 817/261-8200, or toll free 800/325-3535), nestles conveniently between Six Flags and Arlington Stadium. It's a shiny, new 19-story hostelry (opened 1985) on beautifully landscaped grounds with waterfalls, lagoons, and tropical plantings retained from the Seven Seas Sea Life Park, previously occupying the site. Another remnant is a fully masted 18th-century pirate ship by the pool. The 320 rooms are decorated in low-key mauve-with-cocoa/gray color schemes and feature attractive art on the walls. They're equipped with full-length mirrors, cable color TVs with Spectravision movies, digital alarm clocks, and baths with shower massage and high shower heads so that tall people needn't stoop; there are high shelves for soap and shampoo too.

The 18th-floor is a concierge level with the usual cozy lounge and extra room amenities and services, including terry robes, nightly bed turndown with a Godiva chocolate, upgraded bath toiletries, a live plant, daily newspaper delivery, and Perrier water in your room. Concierge-level guests also enjoy complimentary continental breakfast and cocktail hour hors d'oeuvres.

The Café in the Park, a pretty peach-and-cream reasonably priced eatery overlooking a waterfall, serves all meals, in addition to which there's a lavish Sunday brunch buffet in the lobby. Other facilities include a very large pool, poolside refreshment stand, and outdoor Jacuzzi; Legends (as in sports legends), a comfortable bar/lounge where a large spread of complimentary hot and cold hors d'oeuvres is served weekdays at Happy Hour; Jetts, a plushly attractive disco; a concierge desk (ask about tickets, sometimes discounted, to local attractions); airline and car-rental desks; Water's Edge, a beautiful sunken lobby bar with a 24-foot waterfall and a border of marble planters filled with calla lilies; and a gift shop. One other plus is that from higher floors you can watch the games at Arlington Stadium.

Rates are $85 single, $95 double, $10 for an extra person, free for children under 16. Concierge-level rates are $105 single, $115 double. Parking is free. Weekend rates (Friday, Saturday, and Sunday) are $74, single or double. And no-smoking rooms and facilities for the disabled are available.

At the **Amberly Suite Hotel,** 1607 N. Watson Rd., at Brown Boulevard half a mile north of Six Flags, Arlington, TX 76011 (tel. 817/640-4444, or toll free 800/227-7229), also opened in 1985, you'll enjoy apartment living at moderate hotel prices. Amenities in mini- and two-room suite accommodations include full-size refrigerators, built-in microwave ovens and coffeemakers. The two-room suites have living/dining room areas and fully equipped kitchens, and the refrigerators are filled with complimentary soft drinks. If you don't need all these homey amenities, regular rooms with king-size bed are also available, and even these have small refrigerators. All the rooms and suites are very tastefully decorated in coral and misty-green color schemes; they have cable color TVs with movie channels, AM/FM radios, full-length mirrors, and hair dryers in the bath.

Many facilities are offered. There's a pleasant guest laundry with coin-op washers and dryers, chairs and a TV, even an ironing board and folding table. Free transport is offered to/from Dallas/Fort Worth Airport. There's a small outdoor pool and sundeck. You can buy tickets to all the area attractions at the desk, avoiding lines at the parks. Watson's, a very pretty little restaurant off the lobby, offers very low-priced breakfast, lunch, and Sunday brunch buffets, as well as à la carte lunches and dinners and gourmet take-out fare. And the adjoining Fireside Lounge is a pleasant place to relax over cocktails and complimentary hors d'oeuvres in the afternoon (as the name suggests, it has comfortable sofas in front of a working fireplace). There's also a fitness center, open 24 hours, with an exercise room, gym equipment, a sauna, and a whirlpool bath. The whole setup is just delightful—neat as a pin, charmingly decorated, and very well run.

Rates begin at $60 single, $75 double, for a conventional king-size room; $65 single, $80 double, for a mini-suite; $75 single, $87 double, for a two-room suite. An extra adult pays $12 a night, and children under 18 stay free. Parking is free. Friday- and Saturday-night weekend rates are considerably reduced: $55 per night for single or double occupancy. Facilities for the disabled are offered.

In a lower price bracket, you'll find a **La Quinta,** at 1410 N.W. 19th St., off I-30, Grand Prairie, TX 75050 (tel. 214/641-3021, or toll free 800/531-5900). A 24-hour Denny's restaurant adjoins, there's a swimming pool, and rates are just $43 to $53 single, $49 to $57 double. An extra person pays $5 a night, and children under 18 stay free. No-smoking accommodations and facilities for the disabled are available. See details on the La Quinta chain in Chapter I.

Other inexpensive and reliable chain accommodations can be found at the **Days Inn,** a mile from Six Flags at 1195 N. Watson Rd., Arlington, TX 76011 (tel. 817/649-8881, or toll free 800/325-2525). It has 124 rooms with cable color TVs offering HBO movies, a swimming pool, a guest laundry, and a restaurant. Rates vary seasonally from about $42 to $50 single, $47 to $55 double. Children under 18 pay $1, and an extra adult pays $5.

And **Motel 6** has properties at 2626 Randol Mill Rd. East, just off Hwy. 360, Arlington, TX 76011 (tel. 817/649-1101), and 406 E. Safari Blvd., Grand Prairie, TX 75050 (tel. 214/642-3497). See Chapter I for details.

**WHERE TO EAT:** Most people visiting the area just dine at the attractions they're visiting, though "dine" is a rather highfalutin word to describe most theme-park fare. I always like to leave the parks for lunch and get away from the crowds and excitement; it's restful, and I find it helps recharge everyone's batteries for the action-packed afternoon. If you do that, just make sure you get your hand stamped so you can get back in again without paying.

Just adjacent to Six Flags is **On the Border,** 2011 Copeland Rd. East, between Collins Street and Hwy. 360 (tel. 817/460-8000), where many tables look out on a waterfall and a stream. Inside, it has a striking forest-green and terracotta decor, with lots of cacti (especially under the skylight), big wagon-wheel chandeliers overhead, and tables inlaid with antique maps of the border area. White stucco walls are hung with stuffed fighting cocks and mounted deer heads

—in other words, no lack of ambience here. Mesquite-broiled fare is a specialty. Try the chicken parrilla—mesquite-broiled boneless chicken breast that has been marinated in a tangy sauce, served on Mexican rice with pico de gallo and guacamole ($8.50). Beef, chicken, or pork fajitas ($7.95) are also an excellent choice, served up on a sizzling platter with flour tortillas, marinated onions, and a pastry shell filled with guacamole, sour cream, and pico de gallo. The same fixings with mesquite-grilled shrimp are $10.50. For a less expensive lunch, try a mesquite-grilled chicken or steak sandwich ($4.50), a cheddar-and-bacon burger ($3.95), or a fajita salad ($6.50). An order of homemade steak-cut fries is just 65¢ with sandwiches. As for the kids, they can get a full meal—hot dog, burger, or Mexican fare with fries, soft drink, and ice cream for dessert—for just $3.50.

Hours are Sunday to Thursday from 11 a.m. to 11 p.m., on Friday and Saturday till midnight. There's a full bar.

The **Antique Sampler,** 2100 W. Pioneer Parkway (Hwy. 303), between Fielder and Bowen Roads (tel. 817/861-4747), is really more of a visitor attraction than a place to eat. A 30,000-square-foot converted Coca-Cola factory, it is primarily a vast antiques mall housing the wares of over 200 dealers. However, owners Jim and Gerry (his wife) Heth also maintain the little **Apple Sampler Tea Room** on the premises. Under a canvas awning and lit by street lights, the tea room is a charming place with little bunches of flowers on every table. And all the food is fresh and delicious. You can come by for a continental breakfast (10 to 11 a.m.) of fresh-baked rolls, muffins, and coffee or hot mulled apple cider. At lunch (11 a.m. to 3 p.m.) the blackboard menu lists items like quiche ($3.50), broccoli cheese soup ($2.35), and chicken salad ($4.25), all homemade and accompanied by selections from a terrific salad bar. There are oven-fresh desserts too, like apple dumplings with orange sherry sauce ($2.25). And from 3:30 to 5 p.m. there's a full afternoon tea with pastries, scones, and tea sandwiches for $3.95. Everything here is made from scratch.

Before or after you eat, plan a browse or some serious shopping. Jim and Gerry exercise stringent quality control, so the selection is excellent, and prices are very reasonable. "Everything is priced to sell," says Gerry. "These people aren't in the museum business." You'll find a large selection of English and American antiques and collectibles, dolls, Chippendale, carousel animals, china, glassware, Victoriana, quilts, and much more.

Hours are Wednesday to Sunday from 10 a.m. to 6 p.m.

**WHAT TO SEE AND DO:** Because Grand Prairie and Arlington are so close together, I've grouped their attractions in one lump as well. All of the below-listed are in easy driving distance of one another.

### Six Flags Over Texas

The nation's first regional theme park (originally they were going to call it "Texas Under Six Flags," but one planner protested that "Texas ain't never been under nothing"), Six Flags Over Texas, just off I-30 at Hwy. 360 in Arlington (tel. 817/640-8900), offers a full day of family fun. There are dozens of rides including thrillers like Shock Wave (the world's largest double-loop roller coaster), the Air Racer (a biplane that takes you 100 feet aloft and travels at 36 miles per hour), the Texas Cliffhanger (a free-fall ride likened to stepping off a ten-story building), Roaring Rapids (a rafting trip on a raging river; you *will* get soaked), a Runaway Mine Train, a Coney Island–style parachute, and a terrifying new bobsled ride with "out-of-control" cars navigating hills and hairpin turns.

For the less death-defying among you, there are antique car rides, ferris wheels, and an old-fashioned carousel. And there's lots in between. Over in Looney Tunes Land, the younger set can enjoy a ball crawl, kiddie rides, and netting to climb. Your park hosts are costumed characters Bugs Bunny, Daffy Duck, Sylvester, and the rest of the Looney Tunes bunch.

When feet get weary, you can recoup at one of the park's air-conditioned shows: a full-scale rousing musical production with elaborate sets and costumes, a country music show, a high-dive show, a costumed-character revue, an Old West gunfight, a wide-screen thrill cinema, and a puppet show starring a Don Rickles–like (but milder) snake named Jim Bob Buzzard.

There's no lack of interesting shops and diverse eateries, plus a picnic area. In summer, there are frequent headliner concerts starring people like the Beach Boys, Lionel Ritchie, Willie Nelson, Ronnie Milsap, and Crystal Gayle (in addition to park admission, you pay a supplementary charge of a few dollars). There are also nighttime fireworks displays.

There's a month-long Christmas festival every year with strolling carolers, lavish decorations including 600 Christmas trees and thousands of twinkling lights, a parade, holiday foods, arts and crafts exhibits, special shows, and Santa on hand to greet guests. Shops throughout the park are stocked with special gift items, and even Bugs and his pals are decked out in holiday garb. A snow machine creates a sledding area. Admission during the holiday month is just $5.50, and parking is free. Call ahead for hours.

Other than that, the Six Flags season is from early March to Thanksgiving. The park is open weekends only in spring and fall, daily in summer. Admission, including all rides and shows, is $15.50 for adults, $8.50 for children under 42 inches tall (under 3, free). Two-day tickets are available. Parking is $3. Hours vary seasonally.

A few helpful suggestions for park visiting: dress appropriately; shorts, a T-shirt, and sneakers are the ideal garb, and though jeans might seem a good idea, they're not. Flume and river-rafting rides get you soaking wet, and wet denim is not comfortable. Do pick up a show schedule and park map when you arrive, and take a few minutes to plan out your day. Arrive at show areas about ten minutes early to be sure of obtaining seats. Don't miss the Six Flags shows; they're great, and most provide an opportunity to sit down in a cool place. Don't leave your pet in the car; there are free kennels. If your kids are the "buy-me" types (whose aren't?) it's a good idea to specify a dollar-limit to be spent in souvenir shops and put off shopping until the end of the day. And, finally, remember where you parked.

## International Wildlife Park

It's a drive-through safari with over 2,000 animals roaming free on 360 lushly planted acres. It's an animal breeding and conservation center. And its an amusement park with rides, wild animal shows, and circus acts. It's International Wildlife Park, 601 Wildlife Parkway, just north of I-30 and Belt Line Road in Grand Prairie (tel. 214/263-2201). There are over six miles of roadway meandering through this natural-habitat preserve populated by zebras (including very rare white zebras), tigers, elephants, rhinos, chimps, Arabian oryx, hippos, ostriches, gazelles, Watusi cattle, antelope, elk, camels, giraffes, Cape buffalo, and more. And pools of water teem with birdlife, not just the resident swans, wattled cranes, and herons, but freeloading flocks of ducks and geese. Animal food is available for each vehicle, and "close encounters of the safe kind" are encouraged. After the safari, kids can ride elephants and camels, hop aboard the Wildlife Express train, go on a Mombosa Riverboat Adventure to view exotic birds and alligators, see trained bear shows and parrot shows at the

Afri-Theater, navigate paddle and bumper boats on Lake Victoria, and take in circus shows with animal acts, jugglers, and clowns. Or hail the world's slowest taxi (a giant turtle ride). There are plenty of food stands, indoor and outdoor restaurants, and a picnic area.

The Wildlife Preserve is open daily March to November; Entertainment Village (that's all the rest, except for the circus), daily during summer and weekends in spring and fall. The circus acts are Memorial Day to Labor Day only. Admission is $10.50 for the whole park, $7.95 on spring and fall weekdays when only the drive-through safari is open, free for children under 3. Hours are from 9:30 a.m. daily, with the last car admitted between 4 and 6 p.m., depending on the time of year.

### Wet 'n Wild

You've been traipsing around the area's theme parks in the blazing Texas sun. Everyone's sticky and cranky. Now's the time to cool off at Wet 'n Wild, just off I-30 across from Six Flags at 1800 E. Lamar Blvd. in Arlington (tel. 817/265-3013), the nation's "newest and largest" family water recreation theme park. Its 35 attractively landscaped acres sparkle with splashy attractions. There's Banzai Boggan, a water roller coaster that you ride in a plastic sled down a 45° chute and then skip porpoise-like across 150 feet of flat water. The Corkscrew Flume starts you at a height of 60 feet and accelerates you through twists and turns leading to a vertical drop into a 100-foot-long mystery tunnel with water spray jets and strobe lights, ending in a splashdown. You can ride an innertube along Raging Rapids through eddying whirlpools and over slippery waterfalls. Romp in a giant water playground. Plunge down the 70-foot slides of Shotgun Falls or the 300-foot-long Kamikaze Waterslide. Float along the Lazy River soaking up Texas rays. Jump ocean-size waves in the Surf Lagoon. Free-fall 76 feet down *Der Stuka,* named for a German World War II dive bomber. Or do laps and practice dives in a vast swimming pool. There are gift shops, food concessions, and picnic tables. And swimmers enjoy live poolside entertainment. Bring your bathing suit and towels. Coin-op lockers and shower facilities are on the premises.

The park is open mid-May through mid-September: weekends through early June and after Labor Day, daily the rest of the season. Hours vary seasonally; call ahead. Admission is $11.75 for adults, $10.25 for children 3 to 12 (under 3, free). Parking is free.

### Traders Village

Morocco has its souks, Paris its *marché aux puces,* and Texas has Traders Village, a 106-acre complex at 2602 Mayfield Rd., off Hwy. 360 in Grand Prairie (tel. 214/647-2331), where every weekend over 1,600 dealers sell everything from auto parts to Zuni turquoise. You can buy a new (or used) set of hubcaps here, probably even a whole car. There are arcade games and amusement park rides to keep the kids entertained, not to mention frequent events like rodeos, chili and barbecue cookoffs, Oktoberfest celebrations, Mexican fiestas, auto swap meets, and Indian pow-wows. (Since some of these are major area happenings see the Dallas annual events calendar for details.)

Once a cotton field, Traders Village came into being in 1973, the brainchild of Irving L. "Tag" Taggart who envisioned a flea market of Disney-esque proportions. Over the years he's attracted dealers of every stripe, selling everything under the sun (except, says Tag, "pornography and drug paraphernalia"). Other than that, you'll find Texana and Mexicana, priceless antiques and handcrafts, toys, bicycles, hardware, furniture, pottery, records, political memorabilia, shoes, clothing, fruits and nuts, plants, western wear, neon beer signs, even someone who will take your picture with a boa constrictor. And some of the most enjoyable concessions are one-timers using the facility for garage sales.

On the premises is an RV and camping park with a grocery store, picnic areas, full hookups, laundry, gas station, playground, showers, rec hall, and swimming pool. Call 214/647-8205 if you're interested in staying there. And, of course, there is no lack of on-premises food vendors at the village, offering stuffed baked potatoes, German sausages, funnel cakes, pizza, fried chicken, deli sandwiches, tacos and nachos, Cajun fare, and corn dogs.

Traders Village is as much a sightseeing attraction as a market. Over 52,000 people attend each weekend. Hours are 8 a.m. to dusk. Admission is free; parking in the 1,000-car lot costs $1.25.

## The Wax Museum of the Southwest

Meet the waxen heroes, stars, and villains of today and yesteryear at the Wax Museum of the Southwest, 601 E. Safari Parkway, off I-30 in Grand Prairie (tel. 214/263-2391), one of the nation's largest wax figure collections. Its tableaux are the usual mix of glamor, gore, and glory. They include Warren Beatty and Faye Dunaway in *Bonnie and Clyde,* Newman and Redford in *The Sting,* country music great Johnny Cash, astronauts on the moon, a haunted house (Jack the Ripper, Frankenstein, Dracula, etc.), a re-creation of Da Vinci's *The Last Supper,* and Old West heroes and outlaws (Jesse James, Wyatt Earp, Wild Bill Hickock, Buffalo Bill Cody, Belle Starr, Calamity Jane, and Judge Roy Bean, among others). Of course, the Alamo is depicted. Of course, John Wayne is represented. Of course, Elvis and Michael Jackson are here. Ditto President Reagan. Then there are the Kennedys and the Connallys arriving in Dallas on November 22, 1963. And a new exhibit of 54 figures called "America's Road to Freedom" features 54 people instrumental in shaping the nation—George Washington, Betsy Ross, Ponce de Leon, John Hancock, Francis Scott Key, and others—in historical sequence from Columbus in 1484 through the 1960 Summit Conference.

Also on display is a $2-million antique gun collection featuring guns owned by people like Billy the Kid and Bat Masterson. You'll see exhibits of barbed wire, pre-Columbian art, Indian artifacts, western art, and early transportation. And the museum is also headquarters of the American Cattle Breeders Hall of Fame.

The wax museum is housed in a re-creation of a turn-of-the-century Old West opera house. It has food outlets, souvenir shops, and video arcade games. It's open daily from 9 a.m. to 9 p.m. Memorial Day to Labor Day; the rest of the year from 10 a.m. to 5 p.m. weekdays, to 6 p.m. weekends. Admission is $6.50 for adults, $5.50 for children 4 to 11 (under 4, free).

## Caelum Moor

A totally unexpected thrill is Caelum Moor, on I-20 at Matlock Road in Arlington. You'll likely drive past it while you're in the area, and you may wonder if you took a wrong turn and wound up at Stonehenge or if Arlington has a little-known conclave of ancient Druids among its residents.

Commissioned to create a work to grace the 340-acre grounds of Kelton Mathes Development Corporation's commercial development center, the Highlands, California sculptor Norm Hines created a five-acre environmental piece of seven separate free-standing pink granite stone forms that refer back to megalithic sites in Ireland and Scotland. The original concept came from company chairperson Jane Kelton (the Keltons are a Scottish family), who specified that the stones ought to look "like God put them there." It was her inspiration for a hi-tech, 21st-century city-within-a-city to be rooted in the traditions and feelings of the ancient past. Caelum Moor is the name of a small constellation in the southern skies; it means "the sculptor's tool."

Each of the massive stone pieces, the largest soaring 30 feet, has symbolic significance (one represents water rushing over stones, another sacred fire, a third the great mother, etc.). They're also texturally exciting, with highly polished surfaces contrasting to rough rock. And the setting itself is appropriately evocative; gentle verdant hills are planted with cedar elms, hawthorne, red oaks, and spring-blossoming plum trees. From one of the stones, water cascades into a 2½-acre man-made lake, and in spring the grounds are covered with wildflowers. A grassy amphitheater overlooking the lake is used for concerts, theater, and other entertainments.

Aesthetics, of course, are subjective, but I think Hines has created a masterpiece—a hauntingly beautiful, awe-inspiring work redolent of Celtic mysteries. For details on amphitheater activities, call the Arlington Visitors Bureau (tel. 817/265-7721).

## Other Attractions

The above-listed are the mid-cities' major draws. A few other points of interest are:

The **Fielder Museum,** 1616 W. Abram St., at Fielder Road (tel. 817/460-4001), is a 1914 two-story brick home that has been converted into a museum of Arlington history. Here you'll learn that after the Civil War Arlington, originally Hayterville, was renamed for Robert E. Lee's Virginia home. Housed in the basement, originally a root cellar and food storage area, is a transportation display with replicas of a 1920s railroad and station. Other permanent exhibits include a general store wherein you can peruse penny candy, tobacco, an antique cash register, bolts of material, shoe hooks, butter churns, nutmeg grinders, old sewing machines, and other paraphernalia of yesteryear. Upstairs, the permanent exhibits are an early 1900s barbershop complete with rotating pole, towel-warming apparatus, old-fashioned barber's chair, razor and strop, and a case full of men's collars; a large exhibit of historic Arlington photographs (political rallies, a cotton sale on Main Street, a demonstration of women for Prohibition, etc.); and a turn-of-the-century Victorian bedroom and library. Changing exhibits ranging from artifacts pertaining to Sam Houston and Santa Anna to a display of handmade Texas-themed quilts supplement the museum's regular offerings.

Admission is free. Docents in period costumes lead guided tours on a continual basis throughout the day. Hours are Tuesday to Friday from 9:30 a.m. to 4 p.m., on Sunday from 1:30 to 4:30 p.m.

Then, of course, there's **Arlington Stadium,** 1500 Copeland Rd., at I-30 (tel. 817/273-5222), home of the Texas Rangers baseball team. They play about 81 home games here during the season. See Dallas "Spectator Sports" for details. In summer, games are sometimes followed by headliner concerts, usually featuring country stars.

**General Motors** has an immense plant in Arlington at 2525 E. Abram St., one block west of Hwy. 360 (tel. 817/649-6211). It turns out as many as 700 cars per day! And almost all stages of the process are open to view on hour-long free guided tours. However, the tours are geared more to automotive students than to tourists. The factory workings are very noisy, and it's difficult to hear the guide. This isn't for everyone—only the most passionately interested will enjoy it. Reservations are required. Tours are given weekdays only, between 11 a.m. and 1 p.m.

You might want to stop in at **Sheplers,** 2500 Centennial Dr., at Hwy. 360, just north of Six Flags (tel. 817/640-5055), the largest western-wear store in Texas, and peruse their 50,000 pairs of jeans, 15,000 pairs of boots, barbecue aprons, Cherokee war bonnets for kids, belts, buckles, one-of-a-kind cowboy hats, western-themed books and greeting cards, bandanas, turquoise jewelry, shower curtains depicting Texas sunsets, wagon-wheel chandeliers, chili fixings, western paintings and sculptures, horseshoe clocks, steer horns—the works.

Finally, take a gander at **Skymark Tower,** I-30 and North Cooper Street, an eight-story pink-granite-and-glass art deco office building that is local entrepreneur Hugh Moore's answer to New York's Trump Tower. In fact, the exquisite Erte statue, *Liberty, Fearless and Free,* that graces the building's front lobby was unveiled in a 1985 ceremony at Trump Tower. Galleries on every floor showcase art treasures like Lalique crystal, Steuben glass, and other paintings, sculptures, and Gatsby-era decorative art objects. A chauffeur-driven 1937 Cadillac Imperial Cabriolet, the longest car ever made in the U.S. and one of a small fleet of antique cars owned by Hughes, is available for tenant use. It will also pick up hotel guests who wish to dine at the building's exclusive Café Erte or a 1920s speakeasy/jazz club called Hernando's Hide-a-way. These facilities are nearing completion as we go to press, so you might want to call the Arlington Visitors Bureau (tel. 817/265-7721) for details. In the back lobby by the restaurant is a stunning 7½-foot golden harp that will be played during lunch and cocktail hour.

This is the first of an enclave of five buildings Moore has planned. The others will be art nouveau, Victorian, Italian renaissance, and postmoderne. It's definitely worth stopping by for a look.

# 3. Fort Worth

In 1841 Jonathan Bird became the first Anglo-American settler in what would shortly become Fort Worth. He constructed a citadel on the banks of the Trinity River but was unable to protect his small colony from Comanche attack or the ravages of hunger. The settlement was soon abandoned, but two years later Texas military leaders met with chiefs of nine Indian tribes at the site and signed Bird's Fort Treaty separating Indian lands from territory open to colonization.

It wasn't quite the end of Fort Worth's Indian troubles, but the city did begin to take shape in 1849 when Maj. Ripley Arnold and a group of U.S. Dragoons founded Camp Worth on a high bluff overlooking the river (a better vantage point than Bird's for observing approaching Indians). A lonely army outpost on the Texas frontier, it was named for Gen. William Jenkins Worth, a Texas war hero.

From the 1860s Fort Worth's economy has been closely linked to the cattle industry. A vital stopover point on the Chisolm Trail that connected South Texas with Kansas railheads and points north, it was the last town where cowboys could stock up on supplies and run riot in local saloons before venturing into the wilderness. Fort Worth was about as rowdy and rambunctious as the Wild West ever got. The action centered on Hell's Half Acre, a vice-ridden 14 block district of saloons, dance halls, brothels, and gaming establishments. The Sundance Kid was one of many outlaws who hid out there to escape the clutches of the law. Hell's Half Acre was rife with violence: gunfights were quite ordinary occurrences, and not the worst of its manifestations (one particularly grisly incident involved the crucifixion of a lady of the evening on an outhouse door!) The arrival of Texas & Pacific Railway Co. Engine No. 20 on July 19, 1876, was cause for jubilant celebration, as the city's ultimate survival depended on it. It was the end of trail drives from Fort Worth, but the beginning of a meat-shipping, and later a meat-packing, industry. Fort Worth was moving toward Victorian respectability, as new homes, schools, and churches replaced saloons and brothels . . . at least some of them. The last of Fort Worth's legendary gun-fights took place on Main Street on February 8, 1887. Former marshal and Indi-an fighter "Long Hair" Jim Courtright was gunned down by Luke Short, owner of the White Elephant Saloon and previous owner of the storied Long Branch Saloon in Dodge City, depicted on the TV series "Gunsmoke." Courtright was a crack marksman, both left- and right-handed, more skillful with a six-shooter than Short. He used to bet people $10 that if they faced a tree and he faced away from it, he could turn and fire at it faster than they could. No one ever saw him lose. But Short tricked him, pretending to be unarmed so that the draw came as a surprise. Even so, Courtright would probably have emerged victorious had a cylinder of his gun not failed to rotate.

Today there are no gunfights on the streets of Fort Worth, except for occa-sional staged reenactments of the above. But the city still has a tremendously authentic western feel, its stockyards and other areas peopled with real (not urban) cowboys. Fort Worth promotes itself quite accurately as "the way you want Texas to be." It probably has more saloons featuring live country music than any other Texas town. You can attend a cattle auction or a rodeo here, catch a Willie Nelson concert at Billy Bob's, or buy a pair of cowboy boots at an Exchange Avenue establishment that's been in business since the turn of the century.

But Fort Worth is much more than the state's "Texasmost" city. It can rival just about any Texas city for culture, offering a mini-Smithsonian district of high-ly acclaimed art and science museums, along with first-rate theater, ballet, and symphony options. It has sophisticated nightlife, exclusive French restaurants, revitalized historic districts, and high-toned shops. The heart of Hell's Half Acre is now a beautiful water garden designed by Philip Johnson. In short, Fort Worth is one of Texas's most exciting cities from a tourist's point of view. A very good case can be made for using Fort Worth as a base to explore all Metroplex attractions.

**GETTING THERE:** Once again, the **Dallas/Fort Worth International Airport** (see Dallas, above) is your air destination. It's 26 miles from downtown.

By **car** you're just 30 miles from Dallas via I-30.

Both **Greyhound** and **Trailways** have downtown terminals, the former at 1005 Commerce St. (tel. 214/263-1181), the latter at 901 Commerce St. (tel. 817/332-7611).

Limited service is also available via **Amtrak** to/from downtown Fort Worth. The station is at 1501 Jones St. (tel. 817/332-2931, or toll free 800/USA-RAIL).

**ORIENTATION:** For the lowdown on all Fort Worth attractions and events, write, call, or visit the **Fort Worth Convention & Visitors Bureau,** 700 Throck-morton St., Fort Worth, TX 76102 (tel. 817/336-8791). They're well supplied with maps, brochures, events calendars, etc., and can answer any questions you have about the area. Hours are Monday to Friday from 8:30 a.m. to 5 p.m.

A smaller office serving the same function is the **Visitor Information Center** at 123 Exchange Ave., just east of Commerce, in the Stockyards (tel. 817/624-4741). It's open Monday to Saturday from 10 a.m. to 5:30 p.m., on Sunday from noon to 6 p.m.

**GETTING AROUND:** As always in Texas, a car is convenient, but Fort Worth sights are concentrated enough that you *could* make do without one. April through October, **City Transit Service of Fort Worth (Citran)** operates "Jolly Trolleys" to and from downtown, Sundance Square, cultural complex museums, the Stockyards, and the zoo. And Citran buses can also take you farther afield. Call 870-6200 for routing information, or inquire at your hotel.

A taxi between the airport and downtown hotels will cost about $30. Happily, there's the **Fort Worth Airporter** (tel. 817/334-0092), providing transport to/from Dallas/Fort Worth International Airport for a mere $6 one way, $10 round trip. It connects with all the major downtown hotels. **Taxis** in town charge $1.30 for the first quarter mile, $1 for each additional mile, 50¢ for each additional passenger. If you need one, call Yellow Checker Cab (tel. 332-3137).

As for **car rentals,** see the phone numbers in the Dallas section, above. Downtown there's a **Budget** office at 924 Henderson St. (tel. 336-6600), a **National** office at 615 Commerce St. (tel. 574-3400).

**ANNUAL EVENTS:** These are the biggies. Check local papers and inquire at the Convention & Visitors Bureau (tel. 817/336-8791) to find out about additional happenings during your stay.

### January

The **Southwestern Exposition and Fat Stock Show** (tel. 322-7361), a two-week event beginning late in January and spilling over into early February, is almost a century-old tradition (since 1896). It's a big whoop-de-do with hundreds of farming and ranching exhibits in the Amon G. Carter, Jr., Exhibits Hall and elsewhere, over 40 acres of livestock exhibits, the nation's most significant rodeo (with about 22 action-packed performances) and largest horse show, a huge carnival with midway rides, special children's activities and exhibits, live entertainment, auctions, and a great deal more.

### February

About 250 amateur boxers compete for regional titles in 12 weight classes at the **Fort Worth Regional Golden Gloves Tournament** (tel. 336-9271), mid-month, at the Will Rogers Memorial Center.

### March

Some 5,000 runners gather early in March every year in the Stockyards district to compete in the **Cowtown Marathon and Ten-Kilometer Run.** Call 870-5248 for details.

Mid-March, the winners of the above boxing tournament and other regional winners come together at Will Rogers Memorial Center once again, this time to compete in the **Texas State Golden Gloves Tournament.** Call 336-9271 for information.

Cowtown goes green for **St. Patrick's Day,** with events including a parade, Irish games, a liar's contest with an authentic Blarney Stone (that may or may not be true), a dance, athletic events, and traditional Irish games. Call the visitors bureau for details.

### April

The **National Cutting Horse Association Super Stakes** takes place late April through early May, with a purse of about $2 million! If you're not familiar with the cutting horse sport, it's something like this: a herd of cattle is held at one end of an arena, about three to four head per participating cutter. The cutter moves in and tries to separate one or more cows from the herd in 2½ minutes. The cast of characters includes assistants to the cutter, herd holders, and "turnback" men who keep the cows positioned for the cutters. Various elements of form come into it. It's quite exciting to watch, testing the skill of both horse and rider. The guy sitting next to you will no doubt be able to explain the intricacies of the sport better than I have. This is the world's most important cutting horse event! Call 244-6188 for details.

## May

The first weekend in May cowtown celebrates **Mayfest,** a spring festival of art, entertainment, folk dancing, crafts booths, food booths, and games by the river in Trinity Park. For information, call 332-1055.

Also early in the month, around May 5, there's a **Cinco de Mayo Celebration,** with a Mexican rodeo, folkloric dances, ethnic foods, games, etc., all in the Stockyards district. For details, call 626-3055.

A major golf tournament, the **Colonial National Invitational,** a nationally televised event featuring the finest P.G.A. golfers on the challenging Colonial Country Club course, takes place in mid-May. Call 927-4280 or 927-4277 for details.

## June

The second weekend in June, excitement centers in the Stockyards area with the **Chisholm Trail Round-Up,** a vast western heritage event with trail drives, parades, rodeos, chuck-wagon dinners, barbecue and chili cookoffs, street dances, gunfight reenactments, stampede races, cowboy skills contests, etc. If you want to join the trail ride, contact the Visitors Bureau months in advance (it's not really set up to accommodate tourists, but with persistence you might get in on it). If you plan to stay at the Stockyards Hotel, and/or go to Billy Bob's, advance planning is also essential; reserve both as far in advance as possible.

Like many cities, Fort Worth offers free **Shakespeare in the Park** performances, here two productions a year throughout the summer, beginning in June. The park in question is Trinity Park. Arrive early to get a good spot on the grass, and bring a blanket and picnic dinner. There's usually a third non-Shakespearean play performed at the end of summer. Call 924-3701 for information.

## July

The annual **Fourth of July** fireworks celebration takes place in Heritage Park on the banks of the Trinity River.

And in mid-July there's the **Miss Texas Pageant** at the Tarrant County Convention Center; the state's Miss America contestant is chosen. Call 244-6345 for details.

## September

Another big western heritage celebration, **Pioneer Days,** takes place on a weekend late in the month, once again with activities centered in the Stockyards area. Events are similar to the Chisholm Trail Round-Up, but there are also pioneer-skills contests such as quilting and log-cabin building. Once again, make early reservations for Billy Bob's and the Stockyards Hotel. Call 625-6349 for details.

## October

The Fort Worth Symphony Association sponsors an annual **Oktoberfest** celebrating Texas's German heritage, with music, dance, ethnic foods, and games. For details, call 924-8622.

## November

Late November/early December brings another major equestrian event to town, the **National Cutting Horse Association Futurity,** once again with a purse of about $2 million. See above (April) for an explanation of this sport. Call 244-6188 for details.

The **Parade of Lights** in late November ushers in the Christmas season with the lighting of downtown skyscrapers, lavishly decorated floats, entertainment, a Christmas tree lighting, and numerous activities in Sundance Square.

**WHERE TO STAY:** The first two listings here are my top recommendations, both uniquely wonderful. Make reservations for either of these deservedly popular hostelries as far in advance as possible, especially during big Fort Worth happenings (see "Annual Events"). The rest are brief takes—good value for your money in less-rarefied price categories.

The **Worthington,** 200 Main St., in Sundance Square, Fort Worth, TX 76102 (tel. 817/870-1000, or toll free 800/433-5677), is, quite simply, one of the best-run and most attractive hotels in the state. It's the kind of place where service is swift and friendly and great care is taken with every detail, both aesthetically and operationally. You'll know you're someplace special the moment you enter the sunny lobby where waterfalls cascade from the mezzanine into Italian marble ponds bordered by planters of palms and calla lilies. And the refreshing sound of splashing waters is often enhanced by music played on a concert grand piano. Atop the registration desk are a large silver bowl of fresh fruit and an exquisite floral arrangement. "We try to appeal to all the senses," a hotel spokesperson explained.

The Worthington's 509 rooms are very tastefully decorated in subtle earth-tone color schemes with striking accents of clear red, orange, green, or blue. Gallery-white walls are hung with fine art prints from Fort Worth's museums. Every room has a comfortable sitting area with two armchairs at a table and a small sofa; furnishings are light oak, and beds are covered with pretty cotton spreads and made up with fluffy down pillows. The suites have private studies (author Dan Jenkins wrote *Baja Oklahoma* in one of them), and many accommodations have balconies or terraces. Guests are cosseted with numerous frills: fresh roses in the bath and bedroom; in the bath, a scale and luxury toiletries; nightly turndown with gourmet chocolates and twice-daily maid service; a newspaper and a rose with room-service breakfasts; bedside remote control of your cable color TV; 24-hour room service (they call it private dining); and full concierge services (they'll even provide you with an umbrella if it's raining).

The hotel's very elegant gourmet dining room, open for dinner only, is the multilevel Reflections, its ceiling gilded with over $1 million worth of gold leaf! If you make a reservation, your name will be printed on the matchbook at your table. The fare is first-rate American nouvelle. Also lovely is the Brasserie La Salle, on the mezzanine, with 15-foot windows and walls hung with works of artists like Matisse, Vuillard, and Ingres. When you come down to breakfast you'll find a rack of newspapers at the entrance, and the niceties include a choice of unsalted and lightly salted butter and freshly squeezed orange juice.

The hotel's second level is called the Athletic Floor. It offers an aerobics room (there are classes and video workout tapes), massage, indoor pool and whirlpool, sauna, sundeck, a full complement of Kaiser workout equipment, two outdoor tennis courts, and a plush lounge. All necessary workout gear and clothing can be purchased or borrowed, and locker rooms are equipped with all the necessary toiletries.

Sunday brunch and afternoon tea (with crumpets, scones, and tea sandwiches) are served in the mezzanine Bridge Area, a French bistro setting where the pianist entertains. The Bridge has a wall of windows offering terrific vistas of downtown Fort Worth. Also on the Bridge level is Lite Bite, a weekday lunch eatery serving overstuffed deli sandwiches, soups, salads, and other "lite bites."

The Worthington's nightspot, Ricochet, is plush and living-roomy with comfortable velvet furnishings. Monday to Saturday nights, live bands play for dancing, except during football season when Monday-night games are shown on a large-screen TV. Lavish cocktail-hour buffets are served weekday afternoons should you prefer roast beef from the carving table and oysters Rockefeller with a 46-ounce margarita to the mezzanine high tea.

Rates for a standard room (double double) are $107 single, $122 for two or more people. King-size rooms are $110 and $125, respectively; balconied rooms with king-size beds, $115 and $130; executive parlors (with Murphy beds), $105 and $120. Inquire about packages and discount weekend rates. Self-parking is $3.50 a night; valet parking, $5. Facilities for the disabled are available.

If you're traveling with the kids, your accommodation of choice is definitely the **Stockyards Hotel,** in the heart of the Stockyards area at 109 E. Exchange Ave., just off Main Street (tel. 817/625-6427, or toll free 800/423-8471). Built in 1907 and restored to its original frontier-town appearance, the Stockyards offers "classic cowboy comfort." This isn't Disney-esque Old West, it's the real thing. Bonnie and Clyde stayed here in 1933, and her gun is on display in a glass case in the room they occupied. And the hotel is furnished in authentic period antiques or quality reproductions. The lobby, entered via massive oak doors with etched-glass windows, is decorated in "cattle baron baroque," with cowhide-upholstered chairs, fan lamps suspended from pressed-tin ceilings, overstuffed genuine leather sofas, and many western paintings and sculptures.

Rooms are done up in four motifs—Indian, mountain man, western, and Victorian. They all have old-fashioned water closets with oak pull-chain toilets, stunning antique-reproduction oak armoires (they conceal anachronistic color TVs with AM/FM radios), porcelain and brass bath fixtures, and old-fashioned ceiling fan chandeliers. Victorian rooms add burgundy carpeting, brass beds, white wicker armchairs, mauve curtains with lace valences, and fringed lampshades to this basic setting; mountain man rooms have deerskin headboards, rustic shutters made of centuries-old wormwood on the windows, upholstered oak rocking chairs, and western art and steer skulls as wall decorations . . . and so on and so forth. Most luxurious accommodation is the $350-a-night Celebrity Suite that houses stars like Johnny Cash and the Gatlin Brothers when they play Billy Bob's; it has a private patio with whirlpool, a stereo, bar, and working fireplace, among other luxuries. However, even if you're not a country star, as a Stockyards guest you'll enjoy frills like nightly turndown with chocolate "nuggets" and a poem called "Cowboy's Heaven" on your pillow, Artesia water, and luxury bath toiletries and potpourri.

An important facility here is the famed Booger Red's Saloon, named for a legendary bronco buster and rodeo star who started his career offering $500 to anyone who had a horse he couldn't ride. Booger is honored in the Cowboy Hall of Fame. I'm sure he would have loved his namesake saloon: it has a massive oak bar (it was featured in the TV miniseries, "The Blue and the Gray") with saddle-topped bar stools, lace café-curtained windows, pine-wainscotted walls hung with western art and mounted buffalo heads, and a reproduction wrought-iron wood-bladed pulley fan suspended from the pressed-tin ceiling. Tables are lit by gaslight-style candles at night. It's a setting that almost forces people to start acting like John Wayne or Annie Oakley within its precincts. At dinner, barbecued specialties are featured, like a sparerib or beef brisket platter ($12.25 and $11.25, respectively) with red beans, baked potatoes, steak fries, home-made jalapeño cornbread, and salad. Everything here is made from scratch, including the peach cobbler for dessert. Wednesday through Sunday nights there's honky-tonk piano music.

Rates are $95 single, $105 double, $15 for an extra person, special rates offered on weekends subject to availability. Parking (valet only) is $4 a night. The Stockyards only has 52 rooms, and it's deservedly popular. Reserve as far in advance as possible.

**La Quinta Motor Inns** (details in Chapter I) has two Fort Worth locations: at 7920 Bedford-Euless Rd., a few blocks east of Grapevine Hwy., Fort Worth, TX 76118 (tel. 817/485-2750), and at 7888 I-30 and Cherry Lane, Fort Worth, TX 76108 (tel. 817/246-5511). To reserve at either you can dial toll free 800/531-5900. Both properties adjoin 24-hour restaurants and offer swimming pools, along with all the expected modern amenities. The latter is a slightly more convenient location, nine (as opposed to ten) miles from downtown. Rates at both are about $42 to $48 single, $50 to $55 double, $5 per additional person, free for children under 19.

**Motel 6** (see Chapter I for details and rates) is also well represented in Fort Worth with three locations: 3271 I-35, just below East Long Avenue, Fort Worth, TX 76106 (tel. 817/624-8476); 6600 South Freeway (Hwy. 81/I-35), between Highland Terrace and Sycamore School Road, Fort Worth, TX 76134 (tel. 817/551-5266); and 8701 I-20/30, at Las Vegas Trail, Fort Worth, TX 76116 (tel. 817/244-6060). The first is the closest to downtown, just a few minutes by car.

**WHERE TO EAT:** Don't think just because Fort Worth promotes itself as the Wild and Woolly West that all its residents are hicks. This is a town as conversant in sauce bordelaise as sauce barbecue.

The most exquisitely elegant of Fort Worth's French restaurants is **Michel,** 3851 Camp Bowie Blvd., at Madeleine Place (tel. 732-1231), its romantic dining rooms occupying a gracious, turn-of-the-century wood-frame house (once a brothel, owner Michel Baudouin informs me). The interior decor is a delight. Walls are covered in a charming country French fabric (also used for tie-back curtains) and hung with ancient maps, prints, and mezzotints. Beautiful stained-and leaded-glass windows, a wall of exposed wine racks, and a fireplace help create a cozy setting. Soft lighting emanates from Georgian pewter chandeliers and candles in silver holders (copies of 14th-century *bougeoirs*) on rose-clothed tables. And taped classical music completes the Elysian ambience. Upstairs is additional dining space, a plush, living roomy bar/lounge, and a plant-filled patio that offers superb downtown views.

Chef Louis Chalut, one of the new breed of young maîtres, did his apprenticeship with the Troisgros brothers and later worked at Le Grand Véfours in Paris. This impressive résumé is well evidenced in his superb culinary creations, not to mention artistic (but not fussy) presentations of food on large white platter "canvases." There are two menus, an à la carte listing that changes every four to six weeks and a nightly table d'hôte or menu de dégustation. The latter is priced at $42 and might typically offer a lobster bisque, followed by fresh asparagus en feuilleté dribbled with butter sauce, grilled salmon béarnaise, medallion of veal in tarragon cream sauce, and a dessert of white and dark chocolate mousse. The wine list features about 150 French and California vintages, and the bread, served with a custard-like swirl of butter, is sliced from a fresh-baked baguette. À la carte entrees are mostly in the $16 to $21 range.

If $100-and-up dinners for two are beyond your budget, take heart; Michel plans to open a moderately priced wine bar/bistro serving French café fare (what could be better?) called Le Chardonnay, at Forest Park Boulevard and Park Hill Drive. It will very likely be completed by the time you read this. Call the other restaurant for information.

Michel is open for dinner only, Tuesday to Saturday from 6 to 10 p.m. Reservations essential.

*D Magazine* calls **Saint-Emilion,** 3617 W. 7th St., at Montgomery Street (tel. 737-2781), "Fort Worth's premier restaurant." This charming country French restaurant, housed in a quaint-looking brick building with a pointy pitched roof and flower boxes in the windows, is the creation of Bernard Tronche (who grew up in the Saint-Emillion region near Bordeaux) and his American wife, Karen. Tronche worked with chef Jean-Claude Rosset, who presides over the glassed-in open kitchen, when they were respectively manager and sous-chef at Calluaud's, one of Dallas's most noted French restaurants. Rosset describes his Saint-Emilion cuisine as "a blend of fancy and family," arrived at by adding nouvelle sophistication to classic French cuisine prepared from old family recipes. He's been behind the scenes in famous French kitchens since the age of 14.

The menu changes several times a year to make optimum use of seasonal specialties. A full prix-fixe dinner is a very reasonably priced $25, with several choices for each course. A recent *menu d'automne,* for example, listed hors d'oeuvres of country-style duck pâté studded with pistachios, fresh mussels in a white wine and shallot sauce, and traditional escargots bourguignons. Next course was a mixed salad of tender Boston lettuce and walnuts dressed in a light vinaigrette with just a soupçon of mildly pungent cheese. Eight entrees, categorized poetically as *de la forêt* and *de la vallée,* included, among the former, a roast quail stuffed with veal and almonds and garnished with Belgian endives and, among the latter, a roast breast of chicken stuffed with apricots and prunes. From *la table des desserts* you might have selected plump fresh strawberries lightly tossed in custard on a tartlet crust, a darkly rich chocolate mousse, or a superb crème caramel. All is beautifully presented, entrees accompanied by firm, subtly flavored al dente vegetables and crusty, delicious French bread served with butter in a French crock. The French/California wine list is small but *recherché,* and at least half a dozen premium wines are offered by the glass at both lunch and dinner. Lunch, by the way, is à la carte, with entrees like omelette niçoise ($5.25), a Bayonne ham sandwich on baguette ($4), and roast breast of chicken basquaise with tomatoes, onions, and bell peppers ($6.50). A side order of classic pommes frites is $1.75.

Saint-Emilion's charming interior is a delightful setting in which to enjoy these delectable offerings. Lithographs of the French countryside and Riviera and pottery from Provence adorn burlap-covered walls, crisply white-linened tables are set with sturdy white china and fresh flowers, multipaned windows are curtained in provincial French fabrics, and classical music is played in the background.

Open for lunch weekdays from 11:30 a.m. to 2:30 p.m., for dinner Monday to Saturday from 6 to 11 p.m. Reservations essential.

Another excellent gourmet eatery is **Tours,** 3429B W. 7th St., at Clifton

Street in the Chicotsky Shopping Center (tel. 870-1672), owned by Craig Kuy-kendall and his wife, Julie Shaw. They first met in Austin where Craig owned a restaurant and Julie worked in the kitchen. After they married in 1982, they went to France for six months where Julie studied at the prestigious cooking school, La Varennes, and Craig took courses at L'Academie du Vin. They wound things up with a culinary tour of France and decided to give Fort Worth the benefit of their new-found expertise. Like many of today's most innovative young chefs, Craig and Julie have adapted French methods to American and regional specialties, creating a uniquely haute U.S.A. cuisine. Their dinner menu changes weekly to give full reign to creativity in the kitchen, and they grow their own herbs, fresh vegetables, and even the flowers that adorn the coral-clothed tables. Fresh seafood comes from the Gulf Coast.

A Tours dinner might begin with anything from Mexican quesadillas ($5.75), to fried brie with cranberry relish ($5.75). All entrees come with a choice of a marvelous house salad (a mixture of leaf lettuce with almonds, sesame seeds, pumpkin seeds, grated parmesan, and carrots with a light bleu cheese dressing) or totelots (fresh pasta squares tossed with a creamy sauce that gets its tang from mustard, shallots, parsley, and parmesan). Both are so good that I feel the best move is to pay a supplement and get both. A typical entree might be Cornish hen diablé ($12.50) in a hot butter-mustard sauce seasoned with fresh-cracked black pepper, cayenne, shallots, garlic, tomato, and parsley. It's served with new potatoes tossed in butter and fresh steamed snow peas. Delicious dinner rolls accompany it all. Tours specializes in sumptuous chocolate desserts, and they're among the best I've ever had. The pièce de résistance is a boule de neige ($4.25), the recipe for which has appeared in *Bon Appetit*. It's an ultra-rich semi-sweet chocolate boule on a brownie-like crust topped with extra-thick whipped cream and garnished with candied violets. Thus described it sounds a bit prosaic, but believe me, it's as memorable as your first kiss. Craig's expertise is evidenced in the small but very carefully chosen wine list, which is always supplemented by a selection of premium wines available by the glass. Luncheon here is a much more affordable affair, with all entrees well under $10.

Tours is an unpretentious but attractive restaurant, with a contemporary decor—slate-gray walls hung with art deco–like prints of flowers in vases, caned bentwood chairs, gallery lighting, and exposed wine racks. At night tables are lit by tall white tapers. The background music is classic jazz played at a low decibel level. The food is haute, but the ambience is casual. It's okay to come in jeans.

Tours is open for lunch weekdays from 11:30 a.m. to 2 p.m., for dinner Tuesday to Saturday from 6 to 10 p.m. Reservations are essential.

**Juanita's**, in Sundance Square, at 2nd and Houston Streets (tel. 335-1777), is partly owned by June Jenkins, wife of sports scribe/novelist Dan Jenkins (*Semi-Tough*), who first opened a Tex-Mex restaurant in Manhattan of the same name and then opened a *branch* in Fort Worth! Only famous Fort Worth natives with impeccable Texas credentials like the Jenkinses (June herself was a Texas Christian University homecoming queen) could get away with this coals-to-Newcastle maneuver. The couple live half the year in Fort Worth and half in New York. "We're semi-coastal," says June. The restaurants, by the way, are named for a country-singing waitress in another of Jenkins's books, *Baja Oklahoma*, which Dan wrote across the street in a Worthington Hotel suite.

Juanita's is a gorgeous restaurant with a turn-of-the-century saloon decor. Dark oak-paneled walls and mirrored columns, a cocoa pressed-tin ceiling, and bare oak floors create an appropriately western backdrop, but most notable is the use of a variety of lovely and cheerful polished cotton fabrics for tablecloths, chair upholstery, napkins, and café curtains. And a symbolic yellow rose in a cut-glass vase graces each table. A more opulent floral arrangement adorns the

Victorian bar, which is lit by gaslight-style fixtures. And there are ficus trees here and there bordered by planters of colorful flowers. When the weather warrants, you can also dine on the canopied cobblestone patio under a trellis of wisteria vines.

Juanita's fare is authentic Tex-Mex seasoned with a pinch of Big Apple culinary sophistication. Start out with botañas (appetizers) of deep-fried, cheese-stuffed jalapeño peppers ($3.75) or macho nachos topped with chili beef, refried beans, melted cheese, and guacamole ($4.75). Proceed to specialties like boneless breast of chicken basted with butter and coarsely ground chopped jalapeños, served with green rice and tossed salad ($8.25), quail braised in tequila, also served with green rice and salad ($9.50), or shrimp sautéed with new potatoes, red, green, and yellow peppers, onions, and hot spices ($9.50). You can also order more conventional items like a taco al carbón topped with chili con queso ($4, $7 with rice and beans), and from 11 a.m. to 4 p.m. and after 9 p.m. there are "light fare" listings such as ceviche stuffed avocado ($7), a chili/cheese omelet ($5.25), and a Mexican salad bowl ($7.25). For dessert the ultimate indulgence is a fried flour tortilla topped with vanilla Häagen-Dazs, mango slices, and Grand Marnier ($4). On the other hand there are also Dove bars ($2.50).

Open Sunday to Thursday from 11 a.m. to 1 a.m., till 2 a.m. on Friday and Saturday. Reservations essential.

One of the prettiest restaurants in Sundance Square is the elegant **Lombardi**, 300 Main St. (tel. 877-1729), a country-look Italian restaurant housed in a turn-of-the-century brick building. Its interior is extremely charming, with wicker-seated chairs at ecru-clothed, candlelit tables, forest-green carpeting, a trellised wood ceiling, and brick-wainscotted stucco walls hung with traditional fruit and flower prints and decorative plates. A brick fireplace is filled with plants, furnishings include lovely antique English sideboards, and there's a beautiful table used for the display of pastries, pastas, and breads. Additional seating is provided at wrought-iron garden tables on a brick terrace and shaded by a white canvas awning.

Northern Italian fare is featured, highlighting fresh fish and seafood (note the lobster tank that doubles as a gurgling fountain), fresh-baked breads and pastries, and homemade pastas. A dinner at Lombardi's will get off to an excellent start with antipasti caldi of garlicky crab claws sautéed in white wine or a combination of fried mozzarella, scampi, and calamari ($6.25 for either). Entrees are served with soup or salad. There is, of course, steamed or grilled lobster served with lemon butter sauce (priced per pound). Another excellent *specialita di pesce* is filet of sole sautéed with tomatoes, mozzarella, and fresh basil ($13.25). Lombardi's veal specialties like scaloppine sautéed with brandy, mushrooms, and cream sauce ($13.95) are also highly recommendable. And you can't go wrong with a plate of pasta—perhaps fettuccine sautéed with smoked salmon and cream sauce ($10.25), or green and white thin noodles sautéed with ham, mushrooms, cream, and parmesan ($10.25). Ideally, I like to order a nonpasta entree and split a pasta dish with my dining partner (few are reluctant to join in this scheme). Side orders of pasta notwithstanding, to say nothing of the amount of delicious bread and butter one has consumed, as the meal draws to a close attention must still be paid to the dessert dolci—especially the soufflés that come in an array of flavors including raspberry, Grand Marnier, and Bailey's Irish cream ($4.50). Chocolate mousse cake and key lime pie ($3.25) are also tempting. A good selection of French, Italian, and California wines is available, with the inexpensive option of a carafe of Sebastiani mountain burgundy for $10. At lunch, entrees are in the $8 to $10 range.

Lombardi is open for lunch weekdays from 11 a.m. to 2 p.m., for dinner

Monday to Thursday from 5:30 to 10 p.m., on Friday and Saturday till 11 p.m. Reservations essential.

A branch of the very popular French-owned Dallas croissanterie, **La Madeleine,** can be found in Fort Worth at 6140 Camp Bowie Blvd., at Winthrop Avenue (tel. 732-4655). Like its Dallas counterpart, it abounds in French country charm, with bare oak floors, wicker-seated chairs, a rough-hewn beamed ceiling, and antique French farm implements displayed on the white stucco walls. Fresh flowers grace every table. Come by for breakfast or afternoon tea and make your selections from the glass counters (they're adorned with ceramic tiles depicting French bakers) filled with croissants, raspberry tarts, gâteaux, baguettes, meringues, pâtisseries, brioches, chaussons de pommes, and other such. Other times of the day, there's more substantial fare such as croissant sandwiches, soups, quiche Lorraine, a salade niçoise, or a plat du jour like chicken Dijon with authentic pommes frites and buttered baguette. The latter is $4.75, and everything else is less.

Hours are 7 a.m. to 9 p.m. daily.

Finally, in a town whose slogan is "where the West begins," you're bound to find first-rate barbecue. Just mosey on over to **Angelo's,** 2533 White Settlement Rd., at Vacek Street (tel. 332-0357), where Fort Worth native Angelo George has been turning out juicy ribs etc. since 1958. Angelo's has all the earmarks of authenticity—bright-orange vinyl booths at Formica tables, walls paneled in artificial wood and hung with mounted moose, deer, and buffalo heads, dim lighting, a full standing stuffed bear or two, and bare cement floors. It's huge, but that doesn't mean you can easily get a seat; during the peak lunch and dinner hours the place is packed. Until 3:05 p.m. there's cafeteria service only; after that you can beckon a waitress. Hard to beat, the barbecued sliced beef sandwich comes on a bun with chopped onions, pickles, mustard, and barbecue sauce ($2.95), best when accompanied by Angelo's slightly sweet homemade coleslaw spiked with celery seeds and/or his creamy potato salad jazzed up with bits of pimiento egg, pickle, and seasonings (75¢ for either). Wash it all down with a humungous frosted mug of beer ($1.35). The chili here is great too, ditto the Polish sausage. Available after 5 p.m. only is a rib and beef combo plate with beans, potato salad, coleslaw, pickles, chopped onions, barbecue sauce, and bread ($7.75).

Open Monday to Saturday from 11 a.m. to 10 p.m.

Also consider a meal at **Booger Red's** in the Stockyards Hotel, and check out some of the restaurants in the Stockyard area generally; you'll find some real authentic chicken-fried steak and chili.

**FORT WORTH ATTRACTIONS:** A mini-Smithsonian district of first-rate museums (the Kimbell, Museum of Science and History, Fort Worth Art Museum, and Amon Carter), a major cattle-trading market where the Old West lives on (the Stockyards), an awesomely beautiful botanical garden, a renovated early-1900s restored historic district (Sundance Square), and a museum of ancient Israeli, Canaanite, and Philistine artifacts. Those are just a few of the exciting options awaiting the Fort Worth visitor.

### The Fort Worth Stockyards

The Stockyards area, centered at Main Street and Exchange Avenue, and extending north as far as Stockyards Boulevard, east to the railroad tracks, west to just beyond Ellis Avenue, and south to 24th Street, is the real heart of Fort Worth. It's because of the cattle industry that Fort Worth is "where the West begins," and this is its hub. The city is home to six major livestock associations

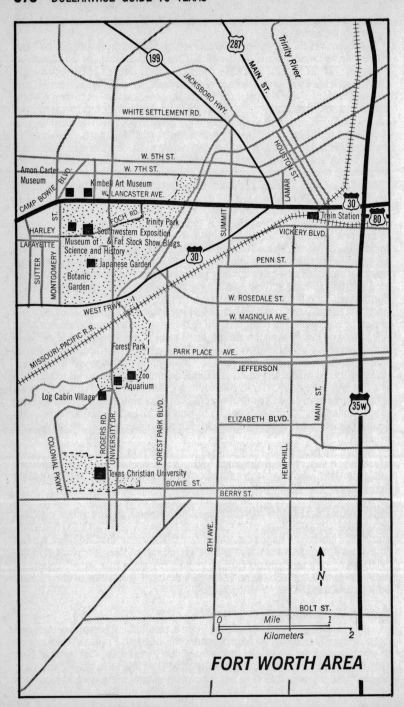

FORT WORTH AREA

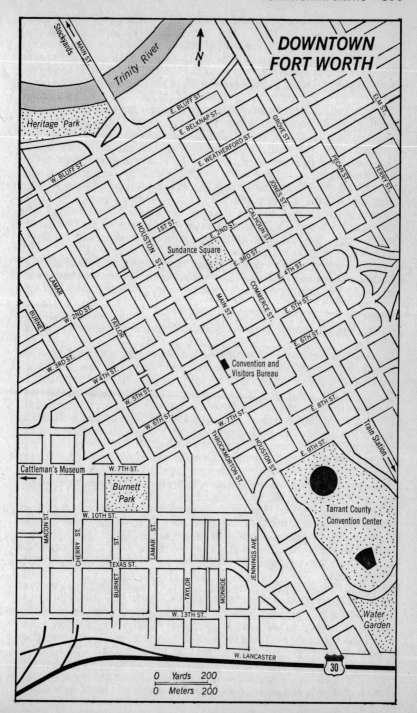

## DOWNTOWN FORT WORTH

N

Stockyards

MAIN ST.

Trinity River

Heritage Park

E. BLUFF ST.

E. BELKNAP ST.

W. BLUFF ST.

E. WEATHERFORD ST.

GROVE ST.

PECAN ST.

ELM ST.

TERRY ST.

HOUSTON ST.

1ST ST.

E. 2ND ST.

JONES ST.

CALHOUN ST.

Sundance Square

E. 3RD ST.

E. 4TH ST.

LAMAR

TAYLOR

MAIN ST.

COMMERCE ST.

E. 5TH ST.

W. 2ND ST.

BURNE

W. 3RD ST.

E. 6TH ST.

W. 4TH ST.

■ Convention and Visitors Bureau

W. 5TH ST.

E. 8TH ST.

W. 6TH ST.

Train Station

W. 7TH ST.

THROCKMORTON ST.

HOUSTON ST.

E. 9TH ST.

Cattleman's Museum

W. 7TH ST.

Burnett Park

Tarrant County Convention Center

MACON ST.

W. 10TH ST.

CHERRY ST.

BURNET ST.

TEXAS ST.

LAMAR ST.

TAYLOR

MONROE

JENNINGS AVE.

W. 13TH ST.

Water Garden

W. LANCASTER

30

| 0 | Yards | 200 |
| 0 | Meters | 200 |

and the oldest stockyard (founded in 1893) in the country in continual operation. It all started in the 1860s, when Fort Worth was a convenient R&R (rest and revelry) stop along the rugged Chisholm Trail. It soon became a leading market for trading cattle. Thousands of cowboys drove their longhorn herds up Main Street, and as cowtown was born and boomed they went on to become cattle barons. Then the railroad came to town, signaling the end of the cattle-drive era. Now cattle could be shipped direct from Fort Worth, instead of being driven farther north. Permanent stockyards were built and a livestock exchange commission came into being. When two major meat-packing plants, Swift and Armour, were lured to the area in 1903, the success of this venture was assured.

Still a vital cattle-trading market today, the Stockyards are in the midst of a revitalization, with investors (led by Billy Bob Barnett, owner of the famed honky-tonk) contributing over $30 million to preserve the area's authentic western character and historic structures. The Stockyards may be more Old West than the Old West ever was (though I kind of doubt it), but like Sundance Square, this is a serious attempt at recapturing a part of Texas heritage. The area's old brick streets are lined with swinging-door saloons, saddle and boot shops, chili parlors, and other uniquely western-flavor enterprises. It's easy to spend a full day exploring here.

A good place to begin is at the **Visitor Information Center,** 123 Exchange, just east of Commerce (tel. 817/624-4741). It's open Monday to Saturday from 10 a.m. to 5:30 p.m., on Sunday from noon to 6 p.m. There you can pick up a map highlighting all attractions of the Stockyards Historical District and get answers to any questions you might have about them. The office can also provide information about other Fort Worth attractions. There's free parking on the premises.

The old mission-style **Livestock Exchange Building,** just next door at 131 Exchange (tel. 624-1301), houses livestock commission companies and buyers. Visitors are welcome at beef cattle auctions every Monday (and sometimes on Tuesday) from 10 a.m. to 1 or 2 p.m. Monday is the best day to go. You may recognize the place; it's been featured on "Dallas" a number of times. In the Stockyards' heydey these auctions handled about two million head a year; today a mere quarter of a million head pass through. You won't understand a darned thing that's going on; just don't make any funny movements like touching your hat or lifting your program unless you want to end up owning a cow. It is interesting, though, to watch the ranchers wheeling and dealing, and you can usually find some cowboy who will explain everything to you. (I've had it explained dozens of times and never grasped a word of it.)

The Exchange Building also houses some western stores and art galleries, and you can have breakfast or lunch with the cowboys in the **Cattle Car Café** (tel. 624-2241), open weekdays only, from 8 a.m. to 3 p.m. Step outside and stroll along the overhead walkway where you can see the 20 acres of pens, Sunday through Tuesday filled with cattle. Until the 1950s there were about 100 acres of pens.

The streets of the district are lined with shops, which can offer a good hour or two of browsing. Don't miss the **Stockyards Drug Store,** in a 1910 building at Main and Exchange (tel. 624-1626), the oldest continuously operating drugstore in the county. In addition to western wear and souvenirs (the largest selection of the latter in town), and the usual drugstore items like aspirin and cold tablets, it has some fascinating exhibits such as an 1895 safe with a big hole blown in the door by Butch Cassidy and his gang; a 1903 post office from Jermyn, Texas; and the largest pair of U.S. Army boots ever issued—size 22 (to a Texan, of course, Benjamin "Foots" Fowler). The best western-wear shop in town, also at Main and Exchange, is **M. L. Leddy & Sons** (tel. 624-3149). And while you're at that intersection, the **General Store & Trading Post** (tel. 625-4061) is also rather fun.

**Rodeo Drive:** Billy Bob is, at this writing, in the process of converting the stretch of Commerce between his club and Main Street into a pedestrian walkway with western-themed shops, restaurants, and children's play areas. To show the folks in Los Angeles a thing or two, he's calling it Rodeo (pronounced *row-*dee-oh) Drive. Says Billy Bob of the Beverly Hills Rodeo (row-*day*-oh) Drive, "they don't even know the meaning of the word, much less how to pronounce it." His plans call not for Gucci and Cartier but for a major equestrian center offering riding lessons, horse boarding, and an arena for riding competitions and horse shows. A bar called the Wild Horse is also contemplated; you'll be able to ride in on your horse and get a drink. Another area will be set aside for special events like chili cookoffs. In conjunction with this project the Cowtown Coliseum, built in 1908, is being refurbished (air-conditioned and heated for the first time) and will be used for rodeos and horse shows. Much of this will be completed by the time you read this.

Meanwhile, there are a number of eating places in the area already. Do have at least one meal at the **Booger Red Restaurant** (see Stockyards Hotel recommendations above). Light fare is also offered at the **White Elephant Saloon,** a must on your Stockyards tour (see the nightlife listings). The Information Center map lists several other choices for Tex or Tex-Mex meals. Come back at night and go bar-hopping along Exchange Avenue between Ellis and Main; it's lined with places offering country music and dancing. Of course, **Billy Bob's** is *the place* to go at night (details in the nightlife section).

Over at 2406 Main is the **Bob Wills Museum** (tel. 624-7442), honoring the man of whom Waylon Jennings sings, "It don't matter who's in Austin, Bob Wills is still the king." Leader of one of the most popular country dance bands in history, Bob Wills and the Texas Playboys, he appeared in over a dozen cowboy movies of the 1940s and wrote the super-hit tune "San Antonio Rose." In 1945 *Time* magazine said Wills was the highest paid bandleader in the country, outgrossing even such notables as Benny Goodman and Harry James. The museum is run by Wills's widow, Betty, and daughter, Diane Wills Malone, and one or both are usually on the premises and happy to chat with visitors. Inside the museum you'll see a video about Wills's personal and musical history, along with numerous photographs, artifacts (his fiddle, movie memorabilia and clips, Betty's musically themed needlepoint creations), and much more. And of course you can buy just about every record or cassette Bob Wills ever made, not to mention songbooks and sheet music. The museum is open Tuesday to Thursday from 11 a.m. to 4 p.m., on Friday and Saturday to 6 p.m., and on Sunday from 1 to 5 p.m. Admission is $3 for adults, $2.50 for seniors, $1 for children 5 to 12 (under 5, free).

Finally, the Stockyards has a lovely riverwalk called **Saunders Park** along Marine Creek that flows diagonally through the area. You can enter it at Main and 25th Streets or from the White Elephant's rear beer garden. Lined with terraced stone walls and rock gardens, it makes a pretty and peaceful walk. There are waterfalls along the way, and you'll also pass a historical marker honoring the Thomas B. Saunders family who have been actively involved in cattle ranching since the 1850s.

## The Amon Carter Museum

Opened in 1961, the Amon Carter Museum, 3501 Camp Bowie Blvd., at West Lancaster Street (tel. 738-1933), houses (in a Philip Johnson building) an impressive collection of American paintings, prints, watercolors, and photographs. Founder Amon G. Carter, Sr., a Fort Worth newspaper publisher and philanthropist, collected paintings and sculpture by the premier artists of the American West, Frederic Remington and Charles M. Russell. Upon his death in 1955 he left his collection and funding for a museum in Fort Worth to house and expand it. This museum today owns one of the nation's finest collections of American 19th- and 20th-century American photographs, including daguerreotypes documenting the Mexican-American War of 1846–1848, some 100 photographs documenting the Civil War, 3,000 photographs of Plains Indians and American military figures, and works of Thomas Eakins, Ansel Adams, Alfred Stieglitz, Laura Gilpin, Walker Evans, Dorothea Lange and many others. In 1979 the museum commissioned Richard Avedon to produce a series of photographs of people in the American West, 120 works of which were exhibited here in 1985.

The museum's holdings of paintings include major works by Albert Bierstadt, Winslow Homer, and Georgia O'Keeffe. Also represented are Stuart Davis, Grant Wood, Ben Shahn, George Catlin (a large collection), Marsden Hartley, and Arthur Dove. Of course there's a large nucleus collection of Remington and Russell bronzes and paintings, and a few modern artists like Warhol, Poons, and Ad Reinhardt are also represented. An extensive print collection features numerous Audubon bird prints, George Bellows lithographs, and works by Currier & Ives. Works from the permanent collection are displayed in the main gallery, while changing exhibits occupy the mezzanine and upstairs galleries. There's an excellent bookstore on the ground floor, video programs on the collection are shown throughout the day, there are docent tours at 2 p.m., and there's an ongoing program of lectures and films, both classic and art related. In other words, you might catch a film on the architect Palladio and his influence on America or *Drums Along the Mohawk*. Pick up a calendar of events when you visit.

The museum is open Tuesday to Saturday from 10 a.m. to 5 p.m., on Sunday from 1 to 5:30 p.m. Admission is free.

### The Kimbell Art Museum

Fronted by a grove of yaupon holly trees and a reflecting pool, the Kimbell Art Museum, 3333 Camp Bowie Blvd., between Arch Adams (that's where you park) and Montgomery Streets (tel. 332-8451), is a gem—a mini-Metropolitan that is one of the finest art museums in the Southwest. The Kimbell's comprehensive holdings comprise the full spectrum of art history from Sumerian sculpture of 3200 B.C. to major 20th-century artists like Picasso, Matisse, Vuillard, Derain, Rouault, Miró, Mondrian, and Maillot. Ancient art areas include archaic and classical Greek, early Roman, Egyptian, Syrian, Persian, and pre-Columbian works. There are also medieval French frescoes and paintings by Hogarth, Reynolds, Gainsborough, Turner, Hals, Rembrandt, Rubens, Van Dyck, Dürer, Bellini, Tintoretto, El Greco, and Goya. The collection is rich in French art of all periods (Lorrain, Fragonard, Boucher, Géricault, Courbet, Ingres, Boudin, Corot, Monet, Pissarro, Sisley, Degas, Cézanne). Also substantially represented are the Orient—China, Japan, Korea, India, Southeast Asia—and Africa. And the travertine and concrete building itself, designed by architect Louis I. Kahn, is a work of art, noted for its imaginative use of natural light and subtle articulation of space; its interior is admirably designed for its function—viewing art.

The North Gallery, upstairs, is used for the presentation of important and very diverse loan exhibitions such as the *Forbes* magazine Fabergé collection, "Henri Matisse: Sculptor/Painter," "Manifestations of Shiva," and "The Inscribed Rugs of Armenia." In conjunction with exhibitions, the Kimbell offers a full schedule of lectures, artist talks, films, theatrical productions, classical concerts, and workshops. Free docent tours are given at 2 p.m. Tuesday through Friday and at 2 and 3 p.m. on Sunday.

Plan to lunch at the Buffet Restaurant when you visit. It's a charming restaurant with indoor tables in a room adorned with 5th-century Syrian mosaics and outdoor seating in a flower garden centered on a Maillol sculpture. A typical meal here is a $6.50 prix fixe of Hungarian paprika soup, salad-bar offerings, fresh-baked bread and butter, a beverage (coffee, tea, or lemonade), and homemade German chocolate cake.

The museum is open Tuesday to Saturday from 10 a.m. to 5 p.m. and on Sunday from 11 a.m. to 5 p.m. Admission is free.

## The Fort Worth Museum of Science and History

Housing more than 100,000 artifacts and scientific specimens from around the world ranging from fossils to Texana, the Museum of Science and History, 1501 Montgomery St., at Crestline Road (tel. 732-1631), is a fascinating place indeed. There are four permanent exhibit areas on the main floor. In Medical Hall you'll see displays on Neolithic skull surgery (it had a 66% success rate), an Indian medicine man's pouch of healing herbs and amulets, and a mummified baby crocodile from King Tut's tomb, along with such 20th-century displays as computer centers dealing with various parts of the body. In Man and His Possessions, exhibits run the gamut from an Eskimo's animal-skin bag for carrying game to Alan Bean's spacesuit, from Greek lamps of 400 B.C. to modern lightbulbs. Another area deals with Calculators and Computers, with exhibits on their history and many hands-on activities. Also on this floor are Rocks and Fossils, including skeleton replicas of dinosaurs in combat. The lower-level Hall of Texas History houses tableaux of period rooms from the second half of the 19th century—a blacksmith shop, barber, Victorian parlor, schoolroom, log cabin, etc. Here you'll also see letters of Davy Crockett and Stephen F. Austin and exhibits on Texas Indians and explorers, on pioneer medicine, oil, cattle—the works. Regular holdings are enhanced by an ongoing series of changing exhibits such as "Women in Science," "Wolves and Humans," and "Genetic Engineering." It's all wonderfully innovative; the curatorial staff has worked hard to make information interesting and accessible to adults and children alike.

While you're here, be sure to see the current **Omni Theater** show. If you've never seen an IMAX film, combining state-of-the-art multi-image projection and sound equipment with oversize 70-mm film and a concave screen, you're missing the greatest cinematic thrill of the era. Via IMAX, viewers are plunged into the depths of the ocean, travel through space, and hang-glide over Hawaii in a hot-air balloon. It's dazzling. There are about 30 shows a week, with each film playing for a six-month period. If your visit coincides with the debut of a new film, it may be hard to get tickets. To avoid possible disappointment, reserve in advance via Ticketron (tel. 214/265-0789) or Rainbow Ticketmaster (tel. 214/787-1500). Tickets cost $5 for adults, $3 for children 12 and under and senior citizens.

Also on the premises is the **Noble Planetarium,** offering weekend shows fall through spring, shows daily (except Monday) in summer. In addition to the regular fare dealing with comets and the time continuum, there are also nighttime and matinee presentations of *Laser Magic,* a laser light show with a musical score ranging from classical to contemporary rock. Ticket prices vary.

The museum is open Tuesday to Thursday from 9 a.m. to 5 p.m., on Friday and Saturday to 8:30 p.m. and on Sunday from noon to 5 p.m. It may be open on Monday as well (call before you go). Admission is free.

## The Fort Worth Art Museum

Though the current Fort Worth Art Museum at 1309 Montgomery and W. Lancaster Sts. (tel. 738-9215) dates to 1954, it traces its beginnings to the turn of the century when Andrew Carnegie funded space for an art gallery and library set up by culturally minded citizens. The museum's collection of international 20th-century art has been growing ever since. Today its holdings include some 2,000 works in all media, among them Andy Warhol's *Twenty-five Colored Marilyns;* major works by Picasso, Rothko, Stella, and Ellsworth Kelly; 20 recently acquired Jackson Pollock paintings and prints, and 10 Robert Motherwells. Other artists represented here are Albers, Davies, Kandinsky, Eakins, Lichtenstein, O'Keeffe, Avery, Oldenburg, Grooms, Cornell, and Shahn. In fact you'll find almost all the well-known—and several lesser-known—moderns here.

All the galleries are on one floor, a comfortable viewing situation. Displays always comprise a changing exhibit from the permanent collection and about three temporary shows such as "Calder Animals," "Artists and Studios" (Alexander Liberman's photographs of leading 20th-century artists in their studios), and "Surrealist Prints from the Collection of the Museum of Modern Art." There are occasional lectures and a full schedule of films (art related and classic), concerts, and other events. Inquire at the desk when you come in. There are also docent tours of the permanent collection; call ahead for hours.

The Fort Worth Art Museum is open Tuesday to Saturday from 10 a.m. to 5 p.m., on Sunday from 1 to 5 p.m. September to May the museum stays open till 9 p.m. on Tuesday. Admission is free.

## The Fort Worth Botanic Garden

The first seeds for the Fort Worth Botanic Garden, 3220 Botanic Garden Dr., off University Drive (tel. 870-7686), were planted in 1912 when the city purchased 37½ acres for the purpose of creating "an outdoor library of plants." Today the Botanic Garden encompasses 114 beautifully landscaped acres and is still in the process of further development. Stop in at the **Garden Center** at the entrance for a map of the premises.

The highlight is the 7½-acre **Japanese Garden,** a setting of exquisitely tranquil beauty. From the massive feudal stone "gate of heaven," winding pathways meander through bamboo groves, over arched stone bridges, and past waterfalls splashing into serene pools filled with golden Imperial koi. Spring flowers include wisteria and azaleas, complemented by blossoming dogwood, plum, crabapple, and cherry trees. In fall, colorful chrysanthemums cascade from a marble bridge and Japanese maples blaze scarlet. There are many other trees— weeping willows, pecans, mesquite, and dark groves of evergreen. Bamboo-railed steps lead to a moon-viewing deck, also used for dance performances. There are pagodas, tea houses, pitch-roofed Shinto-style structures, stone lanterns, and statuary. And the meditation garden is a replica of a centuries-old Zen temple in Kyoto, its rock formations representing a tiger leading her cubs across a mountain stream. A Japanese garden is designed to mirror nature in a controlled form using asymmetry to reflect untouched surroundings. Nature here is honored and revered. If I had time for just one sight in Fort Worth, this timeless garden would be my choice.

In other parts of the facility are an oval rose garden with a wisteria-covered stone colonnade leading to a fountain pond in the lower rose garden; it's patterned after European formal gardens. You can also stroll through a fragrance garden, a camelia garden, azalea plantings, a perennials garden, a greenhouse, and a conservatory. Octagonal display gardens are planted with annuals that grow well in this region. The grounds are beautifully designed, with flagstone walks and terraces, waterlily ponds, and lush forested areas. The Botanic Garden is the setting for several events each year. Most notably, in mid-November and early spring there are Japanese Garden Festivals with folk dancing, food, tea ceremonies, and demonstrations of origami, Japanese calligraphy, flower arranging, bonsai, and martial arts. There's also an ongoing series of one-day workshops in subjects like pruning and identifying spring wildflowers.

The Botanic Garden is open daily from 8 a.m. to 11 p.m. The Japanese Garden hours are Tuesday to Sunday, 9 a.m. to 7 p.m. April 1 to the end of October; the rest of the year the same days from 10 a.m. to 5 p.m. Admission ($1 for adults; children under 12, free) is charged only to the Japanese Garden.

## Sundance Square

A charming historic district of restored turn-of-the-century Fort Worth buildings, many of them architecturally significant, Sundance Square occupies two square blocks in the heart of downtown bordered by Commerce, Houston, 2nd, and 3rd Streets. Tree-lined red-brick sidewalks lit at night by period street lamps further the nostalgic ambience, and Richard Haas, an artist who specializes in trompe l'oeil effects, has painted realistic re-creations from Fort Worth's past business enterprises on store windows at identical sites. During the renovation process, buildings within the Square were restored as much as possible with original bricks, trim, and other architectural elements. Only those deemed structurally unsound were replaced by replicas. The project is part of a larger development plan called City Center, which expands the area to include two vast office towers, the magnificent Worthington Hotel, and other revitalization efforts radiating from the Square's hub.

In the Square itself, 12 buildings have been restored, including the **Knights of Pythias Building** (1881), at 3rd and Main Streets, the first Pythian temple erected in the world. The three-story turreted structure resembles both a medieval guild and a northern European city hall. Other particularly interesting edifices are the 1908 **Plaza Hotel** at 301 Main, the **City National Bank Building** (1886), designed by one of the leading architectural firms of the day, and the **Weber Building,** 302 Main, which is one of the oldest existing structures in Fort Worth, dating to the early 1800s; it is fronted by cast-iron columns. Despite Haas's whimsical creations, this is, on the whole, a serious renovation effort, not a manufactured quaint district making a grab for the tourist market. It is named for the Sundance Kid.

There are several things to do in Sundance Square. It's a hub of art galleries, fine restaurants, courtyard cafés, and exclusive boutiques, as well as a setting for many public events, especially around holiday times. Some of the most notable shops are: **Second & Main,** named for its address (tel. 332-1743), for exquisite holiday gifts ranging from fall harvest decorations to old-fashioned Christmas tree ornaments, depending on the season. The store also functions as a downtown source of information on the arts; they keep a computerized listing of everything going on in town and can arrange tickets for all performing arts events. **Metro,** at 302 Main (tel. 877-5550), is an ultra-chic boutique selling a wide variety of art deco and other exquisitely designed objects and wares, including Italian cookware and espresso machines, neon art, designer phones, Lucite radios from France, and other contemporariana. Under the same ownership is **Trouvé,** 317 Main (tel. 332-4084), for exclusive women's and children's wear, including many French designer labels—all *très, très joli et cher.* So lovely are the arrangements at **Flowers on the Square,** 311 Main (tel. 870-2888), it's like visiting a flower show. Also very nice is **Fort Worth Books,** 400 Main (tel. 877-

1573), a refined bookshop where classical music and jazz are played and a vast selection of periodicals, including international fashion magazines, can be obtained.

There are several restaurants in Sundance Square, some of which are detailed above. Stop in at the **Houston Street Bakery,** 300 Houston (tel. 870-2895), for scrumptious pastries. Or relax over a glass of wine and a plate of oysters at **Winfield's '08,** 301 Main (tel. 870-1908), an opulent turn-of-the-century-style restaurant and bar.

**Fire Station No. 1,** at 2nd and Commerce Streets (tel. 732-1631), is the city's first fire station, constructed in 1907. Now part of the City Center Towers, it houses a historic exhibit called *150 Years of Fort Worth,* a display of over 200 objects ranging from Plains Indian artifacts to cowboy gear, correspondence, photographs, paintings, pioneer possessions, and period costumes. It's open daily from 9 a.m. to 7 p.m. Admission is free.

You can also take a romantic moonlight **horse-and-carriage ride** from Sundance Square. Twenty-minute excursions run by Brainard Farms Carriage Livery (tel. 870-1464) depart nightly from 8 p.m. to 1 a.m. The cost is $15 for one to three people, $5 for each additional.

One final Sundance Square attraction is so important it merits a separate listing. It is the . . .

### Sid Richardson Collection of Western Art

If, like me, you're an admirer of the works of premier western artists Frederic Remington and Charles M. Russell, you'll be thrilled to visit the Sid Richards Collection of Western Art, 309 Main St., between 2nd and 3rd Streets (tel. 332-6554). It houses a permanent display of 52 of their works from the collection of the late oilman and philanthropist Sid W. Richardson. The museum opened in 1982. Remington (1861–1909) was instrumental in creating the Wild West of the popular imagination. Born in New York, he was intrigued by his father's tales of the West during the Civil War and at age 19 traveled to Montana. He spent a year running a sheep ranch in Kansas, then returned east and spent a lifetime painting and sculpting scenes of the West—some of them from observation and memory, but mostly drawing on his poetic imagination. So vivid was his vision that it is hard to realize he did not paint and sculpt everything from life. Russell (1864–1926), originally from St. Louis, was, like Remington, early fascinated by the West. He also traveled there as a young man and worked as a sheepherder in Montana. In 1882 he joined a cattle drive as a wrangler and spent many years on the trail, always sketching along the way. He was over 35 when he began dedicating himself to art, but he soon became one of the most successful artists of his day. Though Russell worked from observation and Remington from fantasy, both men painted a romantic picture of the Old West.

The museum is open Tuesday to Friday from 10 a.m. to 5 p.m., on Saturday from 11 a.m. to 6 p.m., and on Sunday from 1 to 5 p.m. Admission is free. Pick up a gallery guide at the desk; it gives a bit of information about each painting.

### Fort Worth Nature Center and Refuge

Over 20 miles of beautiful hiking trails traversing varied terrain and vegetational habitats are among the attractions at the Fort Worth Nature Center and Refuge, nine miles northwest of downtown via Hwy. 199 to Buffalo Road (tel. 237-1111). This 3,500-acre refuge offers cross-timbers forest (mostly post and blackjack oak), western prairie, marsh, lake, and river-bottom habitats, providing a haven for a wide variety of plant and animal species. Whitetail deer, coyote, fox, bobcats, ringtail cats, flying squirrels, and mink are among the frequently seen animals. There are thousands of species of plants and birds; a checklist is among the materials available at the Hardwicke Interpretive Center (park headquarters), where you'll also find nature exhibits. En route to the center you'll pass (or rather, you shouldn't pass; park your car and get out) a buffalo herd and a prairie dog town. Hiking trails range from about 600 feet to 7½ miles. A highlight is the boardwalk out over the marsh with a viewing station.

In spring the Refuge is blanketed with wildflowers, and there are guided nature walks every Sunday afternoon. It's spectacular. Occasional weekend programs are offered the rest of the year as well. Do inquire; they're always well worth joining. Don't forget to slather on mosquito repellent.

The Refuge is open weekdays from 8 a.m. to 5 p.m. and weekends from 9 a.m. to 5 p.m. Admission is free. There are picnic tables.

## Fort Worth Zoo

Like just about every Texas city, Fort Worth has a zoo. It's in Forest Park at University Drive and Colonial Parkway, just south of I-30 (tel. 870-7050). And a very nice zoo it is, with natural woodsy landscaping and several noteworthy exhibits. A creek runs through the 40-acre, tree-shaded park, and animals live in moated environmental-habitat enclosures amid bamboo groves, rock waterfalls, and limestone bluffs. The Herpetarium, with more reptile and amphibian residents than any other zoo in the country, is world famous. It's won awards for breeding rare lizards, snakes, and crocodiles in natural settings (like the Amazon River or a simulated desert). Also rather special is the James R. Record Aquarium, one of the largest in the Southwest. Its 150 exhibits include over 2,000 freshwater and marine, vertebrate and invertebrate, aquatic and semi-aquatic creatures.

Another unique facility is a 3.6-acre elephant breeding area, a setting in which you can see not only cute little baby elephants but rarely-viewed-in-zoos male (or bull) elephants. The reason is that male elephants go through an uncontrollable period of wild frenzy every so often (it's called "musth"), which causes difficulty in zoo management. This facility has been designed to allow an elephant to go berserk without damaging the zoo or injury to zookeepers.

Baby elephants aren't the only wee animals you'll see here; there's an infant-care section full of cute, fuzzy little things. There's also a sizable free-flight, mixed-species aviary, and shore birds, cranes, flamingos, swans, and birds of prey are displayed in various sylvan and lagoon-like areas of the park. And of course there are the usual cast of lions, hyenas, ostriches, gazelles, springboks, zebras, chimps, gorillas, giraffes, tigers, bears, etc.

There's a fast-food restaurant with outdoor seating, where picnicking is also permitted; it's in the center of the zoo near the gift shop. Weekends, there are special programs and touchcarts at the aquarium and elsewhere; inquire at the information station by the main gate. And daily multimedia programs are presented in the Education Center, on weekdays at 1 and 3:30 p.m., on weekends every half hour from 1 to 4 p.m.

The zoo is open daily from 9 a.m. to dark (closing time varies seasonally). Admission to the zoo is $2 for adults, $1.50 for children 3 to 1 (2 and under, free).

On the premises is the **Forest Park Train Ride,** entrance just next to the zoo (tel. 923-8911). It's the world's longest miniature train ride, a very pleasant 45-minute excursion. In summer the train departs weekdays between 10 a.m. and 5 p.m., weekends to 6 p.m. The rest of the year it runs weekends only, from 10 a.m. to 4 p.m. Admission is 75¢.

And just across from the zoo is **Log Cabin Village,** at Log Cabin Village Lane, off University Drive (tel. 926-5881), a 7.6-acre woodland setting where seven pioneer log cabins have been restored, refurnished in period pieces, and opened to view. Inside each cabin is a docent who gives a little talk to visitors and demonstrates such colonial skills as candlemaking, quilting, spinning, and fireplace cooking. There are also corn-grinding demonstrations at a grist mill on the property.

The most elaborate of the structures is the two-story log home of the Foster family, built with timbers from oaks and cedars that were hand-hewn by Foster slaves. It was built in the early 1850s, and a Mississippi friend of the Fosters called it "the finest log house I saw in all of Texas." The others are not quite as grand, but all have interesting histories involving Comanche attacks and family lore. An informative brochure is provided, but to get the most out of the experience, I suggest purchasing the more complete guide in the gift shop before you start your tour. It costs $3.95.

One other hint to enhance your visit: wear comfortable walking shoes. The wooded paths are not easily managed in high heels.

The village is open weekdays from 8 a.m. to 4:30 p.m., on Saturday from noon to 4:30 p.m., and on Sunday from 1 to 4:30 p.m. Adults pay $1 admission; children under 12 pay 35¢.

## The Cattleman's Museum

An imaginatively presented historical overview of the cattle industry—from the evolution of the first American beef animal, the Texas longhorn, to the present—is offered at the Cattleman's Museum, 1301 W. 7th St., between Ballinger and Collier Streets (tel. 332-7064). Operated by the 100,000-member Texas & Southwestern Cattle Raisers Association (TSCRA), whose headquarters are in the same building, it is fronted by a bronze sculpture, *The Brand Inspector*, dedicated to "the lawmen known as 'range detectives' who placed their lives in danger to capture rustlers and recover stolen livestock." A self-guided tour is enhanced by creative use of video displays, blowups of old photographs, and period artifacts. You'll learn how Mexican ranchers fled south after Texas won independence in 1836, leaving large herds of free-roaming longhorns behind. Prior to this time, America's favorite meat was pork. Texans began rounding up herds, and, within a few decades, driving them northward to a beef-hungry America. The heyday of the long trail drives—the heart of cowboy legend and lore—was from 1865 to the mid-1880s; during those years over five million head of cattle were moved to Kansas and Missouri railheads, the Rocky Mountains, and Canada.

The Chisholm and other famous cattle trails are described, and you'll learn a lot about early ranching life and its cast of characters—cattle barons, villains, and ranch families. Women were outnumbered ten to one by men in 19th-century Texas, a nice change from today, though I doubt many modern women would exchange lots with these hard-working ladies. Also covered is the history of cattle thievery, from the days when rustlers were lynched by vigilantes to the present. A "breed wall" displays the many breeds of cattle existing today and elucidates, via computer data bank, on their various characteristics. There are displays of tools of the cowboy trade like branding irons, bridles, barbed wire, revolvers, and spurs, and a "branding wall" shows over 2,000 different cattle brands. Other exhibits deal with the effect of drought on cattle raising, cattlemen's opposition to federal aid ("federal interference" in these parts), and the history of fencing and barbed wire.

Memorial Hall honors industry giants—men and women whose contributions were so significant they caused the industry to change direction. There's a video theater where you can view cassettes on famous cattle ranches and other relevant subjects. And, finally, some exhibits focus on the TSCRA itself, which was founded in 1877 and has always been active in combatting cattle thievery. In 1883 the association paid rewards of $250 to those who rustled up the outlaws. Handguns used in the killing of two TSCRA inspectors are among the museum's displays.

This is a truly fascinating museum, covering an aspect of Texas history essential to any real understanding of the state. Don't miss it. Knowledgeable people are always on hand to answer questions.

Open Monday to Friday from 8 a.m. to 5 p.m. Admission is free.

## The Fort Worth Water Garden

Once the heart of Fort Worth's notorious Hell's Half Acre, the Water Garden, at Houston and 13th Streets, is a refreshing oasis centered on a cascading terraced waterfall that spills into a pool below. Designed by Philip Johnson and John Burgee, it also has fountains and a wet wall, from which water flows "sheet-like" into a moat at the base. And you can walk on concrete steps from top to bottom of the waterfall. The grounds are landscaped with live oak, sweet gum, and white wisteria trees, a grove of Japanese ginkgos, and thousands of plants including snow azaleas, emerald zoysia, and blue asters. At night the Water Garden is illuminated by special "moon" lighting from high steel poles.

It's open daily from 10 a.m. to 10 p.m.

## The Charles D. Tandy Archaeological Museum

Exhibits from a Bible-oriented excavation at a site in Tel Batash-Timnah, Israel, are on display at this small museum at the Southwest Baptist Theological Seminary Campus, 2001 W. Seminary Dr. (tel. 923-1921). The ongoing excavation, started in 1977 by archeologist/seminary professor Dr. George Kelm and his wife, Linda, deals with an area called the Sorek Valley wherein 11 civilizations, most of which ended in tremendous destruction, are buried. The Kelms' primary focus is on the transition from the Canaanite period of history to the Israelite period (14th to 12th centuries B.C.), and they hope to use their discoveries to enhance understanding of the Bible through understanding the people who lived in the biblical era. In ancient times, the valley stood as a kind of buffer zone between warring Israelites and Philistines. The story of Samson originates here. The Kelms have uncovered a succession of gates to the city from various periods and walked into old Canaanite storerooms. Outlines of streets and houses have been clearly revealed.

On display here are over 100 Canaanite, Israelite, and Philistine artifacts dating from about 1850 to 500 B.C., including pottery, stone rollers used to crush wine and olives, weapons, household utensils, tools, spear points, skeletons, beads, carbonized wheat and almonds, and vessels. Guided tours are available on request if you call ahead. Other exhibits elucidate the history of the site and the development of the excavations.

The museum also contains the Heritage Room of rare books, mission artifacts, and memorabilia related to the history of the seminary.

Open Monday to Saturday from 8 a.m. to 5 p.m., except on holidays. Admission is free.

**NIGHTLIFE:** From the world's biggest honky-tonk to a contemporary jazz palace, from weekend rodeos to Broadway shows, there's plenty to keep you busy after dark. Plan to spend at least one evening saloon-hopping in the Stockyards district.

**Billy Bob's Texas,** at Stockyards Boulevard and Commerce Street (tel. 429-

7270), is a cowboy's dream, an immense honky-tonk housed in a two-acre, early-1900s livestock holding pen. It's the creation of rancher/oilman/ entrepreneur/good ol' boy Billy Bob Barnett, an ex-football player for the Chicago Bears and a bit of a bear himself at six foot five and 250 pounds. Every weekend the club books the biggest names in country music—people like Willie Nelson, Merle Haggard, Waylon Jennings, Johnny Cash, and Crystal Gayle. Even rival club owner Mickey Gilley has played here. And there are occasionally noncountry acts as well. Bob Hope once rejected a weekend invitation from the Reagans when Billy Bob invited him to perform on New Year's Eve. "I don't know about 'invited,' " deadpanned Hope. "I still have lariat burns on my neck." You can get tickets for headliner concerts via Ticketron outlets nationwide, and it's a good idea to do so. Seating capacity is 6,000, but that's not really so much when a big star takes the stage. The rest of the week up-and-coming and well-known regional acts perform.

There's more to Billy Bob's than just entertainment and Texas two-steppin', though. Among other things, there are eight pool tables, a big shooting gallery, a casino with blackjack and craps tables, 46 bar stations, a gallery of western art sculpture (two more, including the impressive *Texas Gold,* are outside the club), carnival midway games, bootshine stands, a have-your-photo-taken-in-western-costume outlet, video and pinball games, and an electronic gunfighter to draw against. You can stay the pangs of hunger at any of three eateries; try the chili at the Texas Cafe—it's great. And every Friday and Saturday night daring bull riders perform in the 500-seat rodeo arena (tickets are $2). Finally, be sure and visit the vast emporium where you can buy anything from Billy Bob underpants to a "bullie bag"—a little pouch also known as a *saco de toro* that used to be attached to a bull (guess where?). A full line of western clothing here too.

Though Billy Bob's is in the Stockyards' tradition of raucous Fort Worth clubs where outlaws and cowboys let loose, it's perfectly okay to bring the family. Everyone will enjoy this Texas-style extravaganza.

Billy Bob's is open nightly till 2 a.m. Admission is $3.50 Sunday to Thursday, $8 to $30 on Friday and Saturday nights, depending on the entertainer. There's free self-parking; valet parking costs $3.

One of the world's most beautiful nightclubs is Fort Worth's lyrically named **Caravan of Dreams,** in Sundance Square at 312 Houston St. (tel. 877-3000). Housed in a converted early-1900s warehouse, it's a multilevel affair. The downstairs club/restaurant seats 350 in a beautiful room decorated with murals depicting the development of musical instruments in Europe and the evolution of jazz from New Orleans to contemporary manifestations. It ends cleverly right at the stage where live jazz is performed Wednesday through Sunday nights. Top national artists are featured, people like McCoy Tyner, Betty Carter, Mose Allison, Stan Turrentine, and Carmen McRae. Admission is about $5 to $12, depending on the performer, and you can charge tickets in advance at the above number. Inexpensive fare is available, ranging from chicken yakitori to Black Forest ham sandwiches with homemade potato salad.

In addition to jazz, the Caravan features art exhibits, national and regional dance companies, theatrical productions, art films, and poetry readings, much of it taking place in a 212-seat theater upstairs. Ascending farther, you'll come to a two-level grotto-like rooftop bar with waterfalls and cactus gardens, one of the nicest places in Texas for al fresco cocktails. And finally, atop the roof, is a geodesic dome housing four distinct desert ecological systems. The dome's neon light shows can be seen all over downtown Fort Worth.

Caravan of Dreams offers some of the most exciting performances and cultural entertainment in Texas. The club is closed Monday and Tuesday. Be sure to find out what will be happening here during your stay.

The **White Elephant Saloon,** 106 Exchange Ave., just off Main Street (tel. 624-1887), was originally located in the notorious Hell's Half Acre and owned by Luke Short, a gambler, saloon owner, and gunfighter with at least ten notches on his six-shooter. The gunfight between Short and former marshal "Long Hair" Jim Courtright has already been described in this chapter, and you'll find out more about it on the back of the Saloon's menu.

Legends abound about the place; it's rumored that Teddy Roosevelt recruited his Rough Riders here. One thing's for sure. Like the original in the 1880s, the reincarnated White Elephant is one of Fort Worth's most popular nightspots, offering live country music seven nights a week. *Esquire* magazine calls it one of the 100 best bars in America. It's a very authentic-looking western saloon. Bright-red walls are lined with photos of old Fort Worth, and there are gartered barmaids, pool tables, and a long wooden bar with brass footrail. The requisite nude over the bar is a little unusual though; it's a sexy white elephant in the buff.

Light fare is available—chili, nachos, and such. Upstairs is a 100-seat performance space where old-fashioned western melodramas are performed on Friday and Saturday nights in summer and concerts (country, folk, and bluegrass) take place the rest of the year. The Hip Pocket Theatre (details later in this chapter) also does 12 shows a year up here every spring. April through October there's also live entertainment and dancing in the outdoor Beer Garden every Thursday, Friday, and Saturday night; it has picnic tables and benches under a dozen-or-so chinaberry trees, and there's balcony seating designed to look like the Stockyards walkway.

All in all, there's always something going on at the White Elephant, including reenactments of the famous shootout every February 8 at 7 p.m. Hours and admission vary; call ahead for details.

The **Fort Worth Symphony Orchestra** and **Fort Worth Chamber Orchestra,** in existence for about 60 years, have a September-to-May concert season at various performance spaces around town. There are also occasional concerts in June. Call 921-2676 for concert information, 335-9000 to charge tickets. There are three major series, all of which run the full season. The Masterpiece Series presents noted classical artists performing with the entire symphony at the Tarrant County Convention Center. The Chamber Orchestra Virtuoso Series features smaller musical groups from the orchestra at the Ed Landreth Auditorium on the Texas Christian University campus. And the Pops Series features the full orchestra, once again at the Convention Center, with artists like Roberta Flack, the Smothers Brothers, Chuck Mangione, Judy Collins, and the Captain and Tennille. Every year there's one "premier event," a season highlight featuring such luminaries as Isaac Stern or Itzhak Perlman.

Broadway impresario Billy Rose was one of the founders of **Casa Mañana,** 3101 W. Lancaster Ave., at University Drive (tel. 332-6221), a longtime Fort Worth institution. It began in 1936 as Fort Worth's contribution to the state's Centennial celebration. Forty acres of pasture were transformed into the world's largest revolving stage and café, accommodating 4,000 dancers and diners. Broadway musicals were presented. Today the Casa is still presenting Broadway musicals but in a 1,816-seat geodesic dome/theater-in-the-round erected in 1958. The theater has a (June through early September) season of six summer musicals, some with well-known performers like Noel Harrison in his dad's *My Fair Lady* role and Van Johnson in *Showboat.* A typical season combines old favorites and recent hits like *Best Little Whorehouse . . . ,*

*South Pacific, Camelot, Jesus Christ Superstar, My One and Only,* and *Porgy and Bess.* There are performances Monday to Saturday night and on Saturday afternoon. Tickets are in the $12 to $16 range.

The rest of the year the Casa is for *bambinos,* with two-week runs of children's shows like *Winnie the Pooh, Cinderella,* and *Charlotte's Web.* Performances are on Friday night and Saturday afternoon. Tickets are $5 for all.

The **Hip Pocket Theatre** (tel. 927-2833) has been presenting a year-round season of varied drama since 1977. Its primary aim is to showcase and première original works by regional playwrights and to introduce Texas audiences to works rarely seen in this area, such as plays by Sam Shepard and Federico García Lorca. Music, dance, mime, and puppets are often used by the company to create an imaginative and innovative theater experience. And many of the works presented are written or adapted by co-founder and artistic director Johnny Simons. You never know what this whimsical group will be up to. They've done an operatic version of *Tarzan,* a commedia dell'arte version of *A Funny Thing Happened on the Way to the Forum,* an adaptation of '60s cult cartoonist R. Crumb's *Zap Comix, A Date with Judy* based on the '50s TV series, a full-scale production of the rock musical *Tommy,* and Molière's *Tartuffe.*

The theater maintains a 275-seat outdoor performance space, the Oak Acres Amphitheatre at 1620 Las Vegas Trail North, just north of Hwy. 820. A barbecue dinner is served prior to the show (by reservation) and a band plays music before and after. There are about five productions here each June-through-October season, with performances on Friday, Saturday, and Sunday nights at 9 p.m. The last show of the season is always on Halloween night, and everyone comes in costume. In spring (March through early June) the Hip Pocket performs upstairs at the White Elephant Saloon, 106 Exchange Ave., just off Main Street, the same days and hours. And in December and February there are performances on selected weekends (Saturday nights and matinees and Sunday nights) at the Kimbell Art Museum, 3333 Camp Bowie Blvd. These are sometimes related to current exhibits. For example, during a show of 17th-century French paintings the company performed La Fontaine's fables. Tickets are always under $10, and reductions are offered to seniors and students.

A local acting group called the **Fort Worth Theatre** produces five or six shows a year at the Wm. Edrington Scott Theatre, 3505 W. Lancaster Ave., at Montgomery Street (tel. 738-6509). A recent season's offerings included *On Golden Pond, Moby Dick Rehearsed* (adapted from the Melville novel by Orson Welles), *Private Lives, Mame,* and *Witness for the Prosecution.* Tickets are in the $7.50 to $8.50 range.

**Johnnie High's Country Music Revue,** at the 3,000-seat Will Rogers Auditorium, 3301 W. Lancaster Ave., off University Drive (tel. 481-4518), bills itself as the "second-largest country music stage show in the world." It's a fast-paced, foot-stompin', hand-clappin', evening of music, clog dancing, singing, and comedy, presented by a troupe of 30 talented, elaborately costumed performers. This is good, clean family entertainment, so take the kids. There are performances every Saturday night at 7 p.m. Tickets cost $7 for balcony seats, $8 downstairs. Children under 12 pay $4 anywhere in the house.

The **Cowtown Coliseum,** 123 Exchange Ave., at Commerce Street (tel. 624-1101), was the largest show arena of its day when it opened in 1908. Ten years later it housed the world's first indoor rodeo. Major entertainers from Caruso to Elvis Presley have performed here. Today it is used for Friday- and Saturday-night professional rodeos featuring bull riding, calf roping, steer wrestling, barrel racing, bronco riding, equestrian events, and calf scrambles. Admission is $6 to $8. There are also occasional headliner concerts, Wild West shows, and lumberjack contests.

There's usually something happening at the **Tarrant County Convention Center,** 1111 Houston St. (tel. 332-9222). In the past they've presented headliners like Melba Moore, Barry Manilow, and Al Green; Broadway road shows like *Annie;* symphonies, ballets, and operas; and even the Harlem Globetrotters. Check it out.

*Chapter XI*

# EL PASO: A TWO-NATION VACATION

**1. El Paso Particulars**
**2. Hotels**
**3. Restaurants**
**4. What to See and Do**
**5. After Dark**
**6. Juárez**

EL PASO'S COLORFUL HISTORY spans over 400 years, beginning in 1581 when a small band of Spanish soldiers and priests ventured north in search of the legendary Cities of Gold and heathen souls to convert, respectively. Instead, the "heathen" converted the Spanish—they murdered them. Nevertheless, Spain's interest in colonizing the area remained, and in 1598 conquistador Juan de Oñate led a colony of 400 settlers and 6,000 head of livestock through the pass that separates the Franklin and Juárez mountain ranges. He named the new land El Paso del Río del Norte (pass to the river of the north) and claimed it for Philip II of Spain. El Paso developed as a caravan station on the Camino Real, and in 1659 the Mission Nuestra Señora de Guadalupe was built by Christianized Indians on the south bank of the Rio Grande.

The bloody Pueblo Indian Revolt of 1680 in New Mexico forced the Spanish to flee Santa Fe along with bands of Tiwa Indians who may have been reluctant voyagers. They settled at the pass and built Mission Ysleta del Sur, which can still be seen today at the Tigua Indian Reservation (details later in this chapter). The presidio of El Paso del Norte was founded in 1683 near the Guadalupe Mission.

By the mid-1700s about 5,000 people lived in and around this desert oasis, including Tigua (the former Tiwas), Piro, and Suma Indian tribes. A dam across the Rio Grande and a series of canals supplied water for fields of wheat, corn, and beans, and there were vineyards producing highly acclaimed wine and brandy. However, El Paso was by no means a serene settlement. Apache raids went on until 1879, and the area had all the vices of a typical western town, including gunfighters, gamblers, cattle rustlers, and dance-hall girls.

The early 19th century brought the first Anglo settlers. In 1821 Mexico became independent, and El Paso was incorporated into the state of Chihuahua. The city was too far west (it's closer to San Diego than to Houston) to be considered part of Texas when the republic was established in 1836. But soon after the 1848 Treaty of Guadalupe-Hidalgo between the United States and Mexico fixed the Rio Grande as the boundary between the two nations, El Paso became a Texas county and part of the U.S. of A. It was a boom time, the arrival of the Forty-Niners en route to the California gold fields bolstering the town's economy. During the Civil War, Confederate troops occupied Fort Bliss until 1862, after which the citadel fell into Union hands for the remainder of the war. After the war, cowboys driving cattle farther west replaced the Gold Rush crowd in the local scheme of things. The arrival of the railroad in 1881 assured the town's survival and set in motion the beginnings of a civilized society with schools, courts, and churches. It didn't come all at once, of course. In the 1890s notorious outlaw John Wesley Hardin was gunned down in an El Paso saloon (the local newspaper reported his demise by stating, "except for being dead, Hardin looked remarkably well"). And smuggling and bootlegging were rampant through Prohibition years.

In 1968, Presidents Lyndon B. Johnson and Gustavo Díaz Ordaz met to settle a century-long border dispute between the United States and Mexico arising from the meandering channels of the Rio Grande. A concrete channel was constructed to keep the river in place and a 55-acre park, Chamizal National Memorial, was established on the site.

Today El Paso, the state's fourth-largest city, is a modern metropolis in the desert, so uniformly sunny that groups booked into the Convention Center are not charged if it rains! Its population (480,000) is a mix of Spanish (65%), Anglo, and Indian, and residents tend to be bilingual. And the city's economy rests on natural gas, oil refining, copper, agribusiness, and clothing and boot manufacturing. Fort Bliss, larger than Rhode Island, also plays a role, as does tourism. El Paso's rugged mountain ranges and unspoiled cactus-studded desert scenery are a not-to-be-missed Texas attraction. There's much to do, and much that you can't do elsewhere in the state—like getting acquainted with desert flora and fauna, viewing ancient Indian pictographs, and visiting a modern Indian reservation. And of course a big lure is Juárez, right across the river, where you might attend a bullfight, peruse Mexican arts and crafts in the marketplace, and dine on authentic south-of-the-border fare. More about Juárez later in this chapter.

## 1. El Paso Particulars

**GETTING THERE:** The **El Paso International Airport,** at the eastern end of town, is served by about eight major carriers, including American, Southwest, Eastern, Delta, and United.

**Amtrak** trains come into Union Depot at 700 San Francisco Ave. (tel. 915/545-2247, or toll free 800/872-7245).

You can take a **Greyhound** bus to the terminal at 111 San Francisco Ave. (tel. 915/544-7200) or **Trailways** to 200 W. San Antonio Ave. (tel. 915/533-5921).

Chances are you won't drive into town unless you're doing an extremely comprehensive tour of the state. By car, the closest major cities covered in this book are San Antonio (571 miles southeast via I-10) and Lubbock (298 miles northeast via U.S. 62/180).

**GETTING ORIENTED:** For a complete rundown on El Paso hotels, sights, restaurants, etc., contact the **El Paso Convention and Visitors Bureau**, 5 Civic Center Plaza, at Santa Fe Street and San Francisco Avenue, El Paso, TX 79999 (tel. 915/534-0696, or toll free 800/351-6024). It's housed in the sombrero-shaped Civic Center. Hours are Monday to Friday from 8 a.m. to 5 p.m. There's also an information booth at the airport staffed by volunteers and open approximately the same hours.

**GETTING AROUND:** A **car** is a must to see El Paso's widespread sights. **Budget** has an office at the airport, 1329 Airway Blvd. (tel. 915/778-5287), and also on the west side of town at 4024A N. Mesa St. (tel. 915/532-3435). **National** is also represented at the airport, 6500 Convair Rd. (tel. 915/778-9417), and at 5700 Trowbridge Dr. (tel. 915/772-4056).

If need be, there are **buses** stopping at sights in El Paso and Juárez. For routing information, call **Sun City Area Transit** at 533-3333.

A **taxi** costs 90¢ when the meter drops, $1 per mile thereafter, 50¢ for each additional person over age 6. Fare from downtown to the City Market in Juárez is about $4, $8 to the ProNaf market. Fare between the airport and downtown hotels is about $10. Many El Paso hotels provide free airport transfer. If you need a taxi, call Yellow Cab (tel. 533-3433).

**ANNUAL EVENTS:** As always, check with the **El Paso Convention and Visitors Bureau** (tel. 915/534-0696) to find out what's happening during your stay and for details on the events listed below. The city's **Arts Resources Department** (tel. 915/541-4481) is another good source. Annual highlights include the following:

The year gets under way with the **Southwestern International Livestock Show and Rodeo,** a major nine-day event since 1929, highlighted by professional national P.R.C.A.-circuit rodeo performances, all the usual livestock competitions and exhibits (about 3,000 animals are shown), auctions, a parade, a cutting horse competition, barbecue, and concerts by top country performers. It takes place in late January and early February at the El Paso County Coliseum at Boone Street and Paisano Drive. For details, call 532-1401.

In late February and early March El Paso enjoys two weeks of Spanish classical drama at the **Siglo De Oro Festival** at Chamizal National Memorial, 800 S. San Marcial St. (tel. 541-7880). Celebrating the "golden age" of Spanish drama (the late 16th through mid-18th centuries), it offers classic plays in Spanish and English followed by round-table discussions and symposia. Professional theater troupes from the U.S., Mexico, Spain, Portugal, Venezuela, and Puerto Rico participate. Admission is free.

May brings **bullfight season in Juárez** (tel. 915/593-6760 from El Paso) with events every Sunday from Easter through Labor Day. The bullfights take place at the Plaza de Toros Monumental (details in the Juárez section). There's also a **Cinco de Mayo** (May 5) Parade in Juárez, celebrating the overthrow of French rule.

June through August there are free **Music Under the Stars** concerts at Chamizal National Memorial every Sunday night at 8 p.m. The music might be mariachi, big band, country, jazz, patriotic, classical, folk, Dixieland . . . or something else altogether. Call 541-4481 or 541-7880 for details.

There's a big fireworks display **July Fourth**, once again at Chamizal. Call the El Paso Convention and Visitors Bureau (tel. 915/534-0696) to find out what else is on.

The **El Paso Street Festival,** a four-day event in early July featuring food booths, country music headliners, and arts and crafts at the Civic Center, will probably be discontinued, but since it's still a possibility, I'll mention it. Call 533-1700 for details.

The **Fiesta de Las Flores,** a celebration of Hispanic culture, takes place Labor Day Weekend in Washington Park. Activities include folkloric dancing, food booths, and a traditional Mexican rodeo. Call 592-7130 for details.

Another Hispanic happening—the **Diez y Seis de Septiembre Parade,** held every September 16 in Juárez—celebrates Mexican independence from Spain. The revelry begins the night before.

Every Wednesday afternoon at 11:45 a.m., October through December, the City of El Paso Arts Resources Department presents **Art à la Carte,** a series of free outdoor concerts at San Jacinto Plaza. Cal 541-4481 for details.

Under the same auspices, the El Paso **Kermezaar** is held the second week of October at the Civic Center, an arts and crafts festival featuring works by regional artists. Call 541-4040 for details.

And the **El Paso Pro Musica,** a professional chamber choir and orchestra, presents an October-through-April concert series at various locations around town. Call 532-9139 for details.

There's still more in October. The **Border Folk Festival,** the first weekend of the month at Chamizal, features crafts, rodeo events, bluegrass, Cajun music, Norteño, ballet folkloric, western swing, country music, Irish storytelling, Polynesian dancers, Middle Eastern belly dancers, and much more. Participation is international, and all events are free. Call 541-7780 for details.

Also early in the month is the **Amigo Airsho** at Biggs Army Airfield, featuring all kinds of precision flying, parachute feats, and air acrobatics. Tickets are about $5.50 for adults, $2.50 for children under 12. Call 545-2864 for details.

The superbowl of rodeos, the **North American Rodeo Commission Coors World Finals,** takes place late in October at the El Paso County Coliseum. Don't miss it if you're in town. Rodeo stars from the U.S., Australia, Canada, and Mexico compete. Call 546-2161 for details.

There's lots to be thankful for if you're in El Paso around **Thanksgiving.** There's a big parade on Thanksgiving Day complete with lavish floats, bands, and a parade queen. There are art shows and athletic competitions later in the day. The parade kicks off the **Sun Carnival,** a two-month festival of winter events. From Thanksgiving to Christmas there are performances by Ballet El Paso of *The Nutcracker* at Magoffin Auditorium on U-Tech Campus (tel. 533-2200 for details).

The highlight of the Sun Carnival though is the **Sun Bowl** football game between two college teams at the end of December; call 533-4416 for ticket information.

## 2. Hotels

For the most part, getting a hotel room is no problem in El Paso, but it is a popular convention town. Though you'll never encounter a no-room-at-the-inn situation, it's best to reserve in advance to be sure you get your first choice.

The **Westin Paso del Norte,** 105 S. El Paso St., at West San Antonio Avenue, El Paso, TX 79901 (tel. 915/533-4646, or toll free 800/228-3000), a majestic grande-dame hotel, is currently being restored to its former opulence at a cost of $59 million. (By the time you read this it will be complete.) Built in 1912 on a no-expense-spared basis, it was the dream hotel of multimillionaire Zach T. White. In its heyday, handshakes in the lobby settled huge cattle deals, stray bullets from Pancho Villa's riders pocked the red-brick walls, and celebrities who signed the guest roster included Caruso, Amelia Earhart, Charles Lindbergh, Presidents Taft and Hoover, Tom Mix, Clark Gable, Buster Keaton, and

Will Rogers. The Paso del Norte's peerless elegance is underscored the minute you step into the gracious chandeliered lobby with its ornate scagliola marble columns capped by a magnificent Tiffany-glass dome. Westin has restored all the splendor of the original ten-story edifice, while adding a 17-floor tower to accommodate a greater number of guests.

Rooms are exquisitely decorated in plush residential motifs, utilizing three appealing color schemes—rose/beige, peach, and forest green. The beautiful mahogany furnishings are Italian Renaissance and French reproductions, walls are adorned with stenciled borders and botanical and bird prints, and though the decor and comforts (including down pillows) are old world, amenities are up-to-the-minute. They include AM/FM radio, alarm clock, and color cable TV with a remote-control device. Guests will be cosseted with nightly turndown, luxury bath toiletries, terry robes, full concierge service, and 24-hour room service.

Afternoons, a pianist will play the grand piano in the lobby during cocktail hour/afternoon tea. Two lobby restaurants, the casual Café Rio and the (jackets required) Dome Bar & Grill, are in the works. Nightly entertainment will be offered as well. That's all I can tell as yet, having toured the property in a hard-hat; further details will be forthcoming in the next edition. Other facilities will include a penthouse swimming pool with steamroom and Jacuzzi and a small health club. I am quite sure that this hotel will become El Paso's premier accommodation.

Rates are $90 to $130 single, $100 to $140 double, $13 for an additional person (children under 18, free). Self-parking is free; valet parking, $3 per night. Weekend rates are considerably discounted. No-smoking accommodations and facilities for the disabled are available.

The **El Paso Marriott,** 1600 Airway Blvd., at Montana Avenue, El Paso, TX 79925 (tel. 915/779-3300, or toll free 800/228-9290), has created a suitably southwestern setting. Its Spanish colonial-style terracotta-tiled lobby centers on a Mexican fountain under a skylight, and its walls are hung with Peruvian tapestries. The 300 attractively furnished rooms utilize desert color schemes—rusts, tans, and burnt oranges—and have Mexican paintings on the walls. Each is equipped with cable color TV with Spectravision movies, alarm clock, and AM/FM radio, and poolside rooms have upgraded bath amenities, including hair dryers.

A very nice on-premises restaurant, La Cascada, is decorated in similar motif. Stucco walls are hung with copperware and mirrors framed in dark wood, and lighting comes from ceramic gaslight-style fixtures. Reasonably priced Mexican/American/continental fare is featured, both à la carte and in lavish buffet meals. A more elegant steak and seafood restaurant here specializes in tableside flambé preparations. It adjoins a comfortably furnished lounge where a complimentary Happy Hour buffet is served weekday afternoons and there's dancing nightly to DJ music (oldies and top-40s). Additional facilities include a large indoor/outdoor pool, sundeck, sauna, whirlpool, small exercise room, and table tennis. There's also a coin-op laundry (on the second floor) for guests.

Rates at the Marriott are $89 single, $102 double, $10 for an additional person (children under 17, free). Weekend rates (Friday and Saturday nights) are almost 50% lower. Parking is free, and no-smoking rooms and facilities for the disabled are available as well.

**Embassy Suites,** 6100 Gateway Blvd. East (I-10), between Geronimo Drive and Trowbridge Drive, El Paso, TX 79905 (tel. 915/779-6222, or toll free 800/EMBASSY), is a conveniently located hostelry offering a lot in its rate category. For the price of a luxury room you get a full suite with a living room, bedroom, and fully equipped kitchen, and rates also include an all-you-can-eat breakfast served daily in a delightful atrium dining area with Cinzano umbrella café tables amid trees and potted plants under an eight-story skylight ceiling. A tiered Mexican fountain is its centerpiece. This is no continental croissant-and-coffee affair; you can wade into pancakes, eggs, french toast, bacon, sausage, the works.

The suites have all been recently refurbished and they're looking lovely, with handsome oak furnishings, attractive wallpapers, lace-curtained windows, velvet-upholstered sofas, and ruffled polished-cotton bedspreads. I like the three color schemes the decorators used here: turquoise/adobe, rose/cream, and Wedgwood-blue/dusty rose. There are cable color TVs in the bedroom and living room.

A restaurant/bar lounge occupies the eighth floor (in El Paso that's a dining room with a view). The former offers continental fare, the latter nightly entertainment and complimentary Happy Hour hors d'oeuvres. Off the atrium is a nice-size indoor swimming pool surrounded by tropical plantings and adjoining an outdoor sundeck. A whirlpool, sauna, and steam room can also be found in this area. Complimentary cocktails are served in the atrium nightly between 5:30 and 7:30 p.m., while a singer (usually country) entertains. There's no concierge, but the front desk offers such guest services as making restaurant and tour reservations, appointments, etc. Complimentary transport is available to/from the airport and downtown, subject to availability. Finally, there are three coin-op laundries on the premises, and should you wish to stock your kitchen, a Safeway is just across the street. The hotel will do your shopping for you if you leave a list at the desk.

Rates are $87 single, $97 double, $10 for an extra person, free for children under 12. Parking is free, and no-smoking accommodations are available. Weekend rates are available, and sometimes reduced rates are offered during the week if occupancy is low. Ask.

Less expensive lodgings include the 121-room **La Quinta Motor Inn** at 6140 Gateway Blvd. East (I-10), at the Geronimo Drive exit, El Paso, TX 79905 (tel. 915/778-9321, or toll free 800/531-5900). It's close to the airport (free transfer is provided), two 24-hour restaurants (a Denny's and a pancake house) adjoin, there's a swimming pool, and local phone calls, coffee in the lobby, and parking are all free. The motel is just five miles from downtown. Rates are $40 single, $45 double, $5 for additional adults (children under 18, free). Rooms with king-size beds are $5 additional across the board. Facilities for the disabled and no-smoking rooms are available.

A second 130-room **La Quinta** is at 7550 Remcon Circle, at the junction of Mesa Street and I-10, El Paso, TX 77912 (tel. 915/833-2522, or toll free 800/531-5900), on the west side of town. Rates and facilities are about the same.

Another good choice in this price category is the **Rodeway Inn** at 6201 Gateway Blvd. West (I-10), between Geronimo Drive and Airway Boulevard, El Paso, TX 79925 (tel. 915/778-8611, or toll free 800/228-2000). Right across the street from El Paso's largest shopping center and practically within walking distance of the airport, it offers clean, modern motel rooms with all the expected amenities, an on-premises restaurant and lounge, and courtesy airport transfer. Rates are $40 to $50 single, $45 to $55 double, $4 for an additional person (children under 17 stay free). Parking is free.

Finally, El Paso has two **Motel 6** locations, at 7840 N. Mesa St., El Paso, TX 79932 (tel. 915/584-3485), and 11049 Gateway Blvd. West (I-10), at Lomaland Drive, El Paso, TX 79935 (tel. 915/591-6600). See Chapter I for details and rate information.

## 3. Restaurants

In addition to the restaurants described here, you'll want to have a meal at the Tigua Indian Reservation and the Cattleman's Steakhouse at Indian Cliffs Ranch (see "What to See and Do"). There are also dining choices in the Juárez section of this chapter.

**Del Valle,** 403 Executive Center Blvd., just off I-10 (tel. 545-4935), is a pleasant, unpretentious family-run restaurant owned by Perry and Gerry Vandervort, their daughter, Elizabeth, and son, Bruce. It's decorated with Mexican artifacts and works of local artists, and humorous mottoes such as "Man should come with an instruction booklet" are posted on a blackboard by the entrance. There are fans and stained-glass lighting fixtures overhead, cream-colored stucco walls, and many plants.

Decor is beside the point at Del Valle (it means "of the valley," as Vandervort does in Dutch). The point here is the fabulous food, made from scratch and in many cases prepared from unique recipes. Start off with an appetizer plate ($3.75 for two) of fried jalapeños, chili con queso, nachos, and quesadillas. Excellent entree choices are a casserole of chicken with white cheddar cheese and green chiles served with Spanish rice and refried beans ($4.50); a salad in a crisp flour tortilla "bowl" filled with beef, beans, lettuce, tomatoes, and onions, and smothered with guacamole dressing ($3.75); or stacked red beef enchiladas served with Spanish rice and pinto beans ($4.50). There are also daily specials, such as charolitas—grilled steak and onions with a pile of flour or corn tortillas, pico de gallo, pinto beans, and guacamole ($5.75 at lunch, $7.75 at dinner). None of the above is expensive, but there are lower-priced entrees for children and senior citizens. The kids might also want to inquire about the "mile-high" ice cream dessert. Thursday and Friday nights a pianist entertains. There's a full bar.

Open Sunday to Thursday from 11 a.m. to 9 p.m., on Friday and Saturday till 10 p.m.

**Cooper's,** 508 N. Stanton St., between Franklin Street and Missouri Avenue (tel. 546-9378), is a charming California-like eatery frequented by local politicos. You're likely to see the mayor or county judge at a nearby table. The decor features barnwood and stucco walls hung with paintings and ink drawings of cowboys and Indians, a rustic version of a coffered wooden ceiling, stained-glass windows and hangings, and numerous plants. Seating is in comfortable high-backed booths at glossy knotty-pine tables. That's the main room; there are four very pleasant additional dining areas, plus a beer garden out back under the shade of two mulberry trees. And that's not to mention the bar under a log eave with historic newspaper clippings ("Japan Accepts Terms," etc.) lining exposed brick walls.

Everything served here is fresh and homemade. You might opt for an avocado/bacon cheeseburger ($4.25) served with fresh fruit and beans or slaw, a turkey and Swiss cheese sandwich on rye with lettuce, tomato, and the same accompaniments ($4.25), a bowl of chili ($3.25), quiche with spinach salad ($4.50), or an eight-ounce char-broiled ribeye steak with chili, salad, and fruit ($8.25). Homemade desserts include scrumptious apple cheesecake ($2.75) and southern pecan pie ($2.50). There are always drink specials, like a $1.50 Bloody Mary. Monday-night football is aired on the TV over the bar, and there are free franks and $3.50 pitchers of beer, and weekday Happy Hours Cooper's puts out complimentary munchies.

Open Monday to Saturday from 11 a.m. to 8 p.m. for dining, till 10 or 11 p.m. for drinks and light fare.

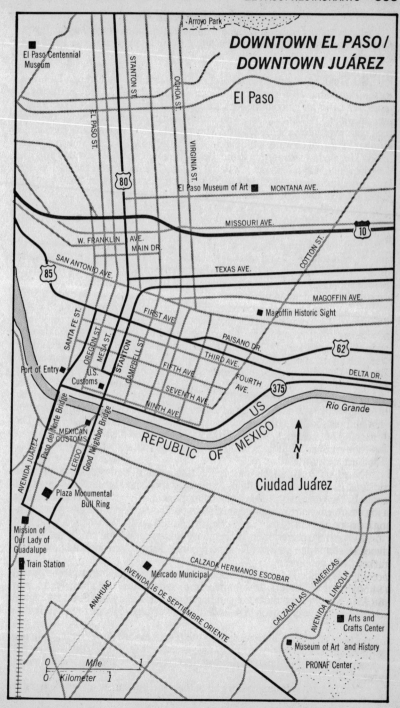

**DOWNTOWN EL PASO/
DOWNTOWN JUÁREZ**

El Paso Centennial Museum

Arroyo Park

El Paso

STANTON ST.

OCHOA ST.

EL PASO ST.

VIRGINIA ST.

80

El Paso Museum of Art ■ MONTANA AVE.

MISSOURI AVE.

10

W. FRANKLIN AVE.

MAIN DR.

SAN ANTONIO AVE.

85

COTTON ST.

TEXAS AVE.

MAGOFFIN AVE.

■ Magoffin Historic Sight

SANTA FE ST.

FIRST AVE.

PAISANO DR.

62

OREGON ST.

MESA ST.

STANTON ST.

CAMPBELL ST.

THIRD AVE.

FIFTH AVE.

FOURTH AVE.

DELTA DR.

Port of Entry ■

U.S. Customs

SEVENTH AVE.

NINTH AVE.

375

Rio Grande

US

N

Paso del Norte Bridge

MEXICAN CUSTOMS

LERDO

Good Neighbor Bridge

REPUBLIC OF MEXICO

AVENIDA JUÁREZ

■ Plaza Monumental Bull Ring

Ciudad Juárez

Mission of Our Lady of Guadalupe

Train Station

ANAHUAC

AVENIDA 16 DE SEPTIEMBRE ORIENTE

■ Mercado Municipal

CALZADA HERMANOS ESCOBAR

CALZADA LAS AMERICAS

AVENIDA LINCOLN

■ Arts and Crafts Center

0    Mile    1

0    Kilometer    1

■ Museum of Art and History

PRONAF Center

## 4. What to See and Do

El Paso offers some of the most unique attractions of any city in Texas, ranging from ancient Indian desert lands to bullfights across the border in Juárez.

**HUECO TANKS:** About 30 miles east of El Paso in the Chihuahuan Desert is **Hueco Tanks State Historical Park,** Ranch Rd. 2775 (tel. 857-1135), 860 acres of mountain caves and incredible rock formations comprising an outdoor "museum" of some 5,000 ancient to 17th-century Indian pictographs. Some of these rock paintings date back 6,000 years! The mountains are also notable for a large number of *huecos* or water-holding cavities (Hueco Tanks literally means "tank tanks") formed by weathering in the rock, which for centuries provided an oasis that drew animal and human life to the region. The mountains themselves are lava formations that welled up some 35 million years ago when Texas was still under the sea. Over centuries they jutted up from the desert plain, and erosion caused natural reservoirs in the hills that filled with clear, potable rainwater. One hueco here holds 150,000 gallons of water, others as much as 10,000 gallons.

Paleo Indian projectile points found in the vicinity indicate the presence of man here as long as 10,000 years ago. These first inhabitants hunted bison and other now-extinct animals, but didn't draw on the rocks. Later, Desert Archaic Period nomadic hunting and gathering groups took refuge in the hills. The oldest surviving pictographs are attributed to them—simple red-and-yellow figures and zigzag lines believed to convey information such as game trails and water locations. (Keep in mind that, to some extent, all interpretations are conjectural.) Later rock art was done by the Jornada branch of the Mogollon Indians who arrived here around A.D. 1000. Cave and underground pit-house dwellers, they were advanced enough to do some farming, planting corn, squash, and beans. By A.D. 1200 they had advanced to multiroom pueblo villages, which were, for some unexplained reason, abandoned in the 1400s. They painted the majority of the figures here—animals, Kachina-like figures, and stylized designs which archeologists believe had a religious significance, perhaps involving prayers for rain and prosperity. Other more complex pictographs date to the 1700s. The Lipan and Mescalero Apaches and the Kiowa depicted men on horses, soldiers, ten-foot snakes, mythological figures, dancing Indians, masks, and lizards. Their art told stories.

Needless to say, all this is incredibly fascinating. The desert scenery is magnificent, its variegated mountains of jumbled rock and jagged peaks creating a majestic backdrop to the desert grasslands punctuated by cactus, creosote, mesquite, tarbush, yucca, and oak-juniper woodlands. When it rains (not often, only about eight inches a year), brightly colored wildflowers offer a vivid contrast. Over 150 species of birds, including golden eagles and prairie falcon, can be observed in the area, and animal life includes gray fox, bobcats, mountain lions, and porcupines.

The question is, how best to see it all and experience the awesome beauty and quiet of the desert. In summer, free guided tours are given Wednesday through Sunday, and there are slide programs on Friday and Saturday nights. Other times of year you might be able to set up a ranger-guided tour if you call in advance.

There are about 20 campsites on the premises for RVs or tents, equipped with water and electricity, picnic areas, grills, and showers. Cost is about $10 a night. People spending the day are also welcome to use the shaded picnic areas.

You can drive through quite a bit of the park, but you won't see pictographs unless you do some exploring on foot. Stop at the office on the way in, pick up a map, and look at a model of the park. Unfortunately, the pictographs aren't marked in any way, so if you're on your own, finding them is a needle-in-the-haystack affair. And really, park programs are not sufficiently comprehensive for the most interested visitors. If you want to explore in depth, call far in advance and see if some special arrangement can be made. Either way, be sure to dress and equip yourself properly—good walking boots, jeans, a sunhat, sunblock lotion, mosquito repellent, and a canteen are essential.

The park is open daily from 6 a.m. to 10 p.m., the office from 8 a.m. to 5 p.m. There's a $2 entry fee per vehicle. To get here, take Montana Avenue east following it as it becomes U.S. Hwy. 62/180, make a left on Ranch Rd. 2775, and proceed for eight miles.

**THE TIGUA INDIAN RESERVATION:** The oldest identifiable Indian group in Texas, the Tiguas (pronounced *tee*-wahs), live on a reservation 15 miles southeast of downtown El Paso at 119 S. Old Pueblo Rd. (tel. 859-7913), at a site they settled in 1681. They were originally part of the Tiwa Pueblo Indian tribe of New Mexico, whose culture can be traced back as far as 1500 B.C. Many of the Tiwas were converted to Christianity during the Spanish occupation of New Mexico, and during the Great Pueblo Revolt in 1680 the Spanish forced some of the tribe to flee northward with them. They established a mission at Ysleta Del Sur in 1682, the church of which is still standing on its original foundation and in continuous use since the 17th century. It is the oldest extant mission church in Texas.

The tribe was granted 36 square miles around the mission by King Charles V of Spain in 1751, but that grant was later revoked by the American government. A claim for restitution of lost land, including Hueco Tanks park, a traditional Tigua hunting ground, is still pending before the U.S. Indian Claims Commission. The reservation was organized as a tourist attraction in the 1960s with the help of the Texas Indian Commission and interested El Pasoans. Today tribal elders are attempting to teach the younger generation the Tiwa language and culture and pass on medicinal knowledge using herbs, roots, and plants. The reservation operates under a form of tribal government, and ceremonial dances and other old customs are practiced.

Visitors can take a guided or self-guided tour of a replica of an authentic mid-1800s Indian pueblo and see demonstrations of Indian crafts. If you arrive in the morning you'll see delicious Indian bread being baked in outdoor adobe ovens. There's a large Arts and Crafts Center where you can buy pottery, weavings, jewelry, bells, moccasins, and other Indian handicrafts. It shares the premises with the Tigua restaurant serving Indian and Mexican fare. It's very attractive, with a high thatched log-beamed ceiling, white stucco walls and columns hung with Indian artifacts and prints by native American artist Woody Crumbo, Saltillo-tile floors, and candlelit, burgundy-clothed tables. Among other items, the restaurant offers terrific fajitas served with pico de gallo, guacamole, grated cheese, sour cream, and corn or flour tortillas ($7.25). Other choices are red enchiladas (corn tortillas smothered in red chile sauce topped with onions and cheese and served with rice, beans, and salad; $5), and gorditas (cornmeal patties stuffed with spicy ground beef, topped with lettuce, cheese, and fresh tomatoes, and served with rice and beans; $5.50). Even if you've chosen an entree that comes with tortillas, get a side order of that fresh-baked Indian bread. Wine and beer are available. Light jazz or traditional Indian music is played. The restaurant is open Wednesday to Saturday from 11 a.m. to 9 p.m., Sunday through Tuesday to 6 p.m. Dining here is part of the experience of visiting the reservation. The crafts store is open daily from 8 a.m. to 6 p.m. June through September, till 5 p.m. the rest of the year. Adjacent to the Arts and

Crafts Center, in a mid-1700s house, is a museum of Tigua artifacts and exhibits tracing the history of pueblo culture.

During the summer on Saturday and Sunday at 11 a.m., 1 p.m., and 3 p.m. there are Indian dance performances on an outdoor stage with seating under thatched roofs. Admission is $1.50 for adults, 75¢ for children.

To get to the reservation, take I-10 east to Zaragosa Road, go south to Alameda Avenue, and east to Old Pueblo Road. It's open daily. Call ahead for tour times.

**WILDERNESS PARK MUSEUM:** At the eastern slopes of the Franklin Mountains, the 17-acre Wilderness Park Museum, 2000 Trans Mountain Rd. at Gateway Boulevard South (tel. 755-4332), deals with the prehistoric inhabitants of El Paso and their adaptation to a desert environment. Exhibits housed in an adobe brick building include five major dioramas. A replica of Olla Cave in the sierra of Chihuahua depicts Paleolithic Mogollon cliff dwellers. Across from Olla Cave, mammoth hunters are represented, and a mastodon sinks slowly into the mud, pierced by spears. A third tableau shows a hunter-gatherer group living in *jacales* (small brush huts). The next represents pithouse dwellers of a later era when extended families lived together and agriculture made its first appearance. And a long diorama on the east wall shows Hueco Tanks, for centuries an Indian spiritual meeting place and hunting ground. Additional exhibits display artifacts of southwestern tribes—projectile points, chipped-stone tools, grinding slabs, jewelry, gourds, baskets, pottery, etc. Others deal with how Indians made the colors used in pictographs and plants used for medicines and fibers. These are complemented by changing exhibits such as objects used in everyday life, a display of masks, and southwestern art shows.

After you've explored these fascinating indoor exhibits, walk the mile-long nature trail leading from the museum through the foothills of the Franklin Mountains. It will be more interesting if you first purchase a small book in the gift shop identifying desert plants. You'll see agave, from which Indians made needles and thread; yucca, with edible buds and a green stalk that tastes like sugarcane (its roots were also used for soap and shampoo); coyote melon, its seeds grindable into flour; deadly nightshade (consult Agatha Christie); hemlock (ditto); squaw tea, said to cure hangovers; flowering cactus, poppies, and wildflowers, among other vegetation. You may also see quail, rabbits, golden eagles, and hawks. And the trail takes you past a pithouse (an example of a 2,000-year-old subterranean residence with a roof of branches, twigs, and adobe mud); a pueblo such as was used in this area until about A.D. 1400; a kiva, or subterranean chamber, which Pueblo Indians used for religious and ceremonial purposes; and a ramada or lean-to made of yucca stalks with stones to sit on. It's an easy walk through magnificent unspoiled desert and mountain scenery. Wear comfortable walking shoes though.

The museum is open Tuesday to Saturday from 9 a.m. to 5 p.m. and Sunday from 1 to 5 p.m. Admission is free. There are no scheduled tours, but you might try calling to see if one can be arranged by appointment.

**RANGER PEAK AERIAL TRAMWAY:** You'll see right away that El Paso has fantastic mountain scenery. For an eagle's-eye view of it, take a ride on this aerial tramway (tel. 566-6622), from the foothills of the Franklin Mountains to Ranger Peak, 5,632 feet above sea level. From this exalted location you'll enjoy a 7,000-square-mile vista—the majestic Hueco and Guadalupe Mountains to the east, the Organ Mountains to the north and New Mexico in the background, the Florida Mountains to the west, and Mexico to the south. You won't be disappointed in this magnificent 360° panorama at any hour, but the most extraordinary time to visit is just before sundown, remaining just long enough to see the lights go on in the Rio Grande cities. And in spring and summer the cactus on the mountain are in bloom. *Magnifico!*

In summer the tram runs daily from noon to 9 p.m.; the rest of the year it runs Monday, Thursday, and Friday from noon to 6 p.m., to 9 p.m. on weekends. Adults pay $2.25; children under 12 pay $1.25. To get there, take McKinley Avenue west until you reach the tramway station.

**INDIAN CLIFFS RANCH:** Just 35 miles east of downtown El Paso (take I-10 to the Fabens exit and proceed north for 4½ miles) is Indian Cliffs Ranch (tel. 544-3200), a 40,000-acre spread offering a variety of western activities. These include buggy rides around the property and chuckwagon dinners and overnights at an 1850s citadel called Fort Misery, complete with bunkhouse, lookout tower, and jailhouse. All of these outings are largely designed with groups in mind, but if you call far in advance, you might be able to work something out. I think it's worth a try, because sleeping under the stars in the desert and waking to a campfire breakfast is a terrific experience.

If you can't manage any of that, however, you should at least come out to dine at the **Cattleman's Steakhouse** and enjoy the scenery and facilities, especially if you have kids in tow. There are stalls where horses are boarded, and occupants usually include a burro and some farm animals as well. Antique wagons are on display near the stalls. There are buffalo, prairie dogs, and longhorns to see; a children's play area called Fort Apache offers tire swings, a stagecoach, slides, a rustic playhouse, and nets to climb; and there's a small zoo with goats, ducks, and pigs. There's also a video game room, but I just hate the idea of kids ignoring the wonders of nature for this ubiquitous and hypnotic activity.

The steakhouse is a gorgeous restaurant housed in an adobe building with thatched mesquite ceilings and a rustic interior. White stucco walls are hung with Indian rugs, copper pots, steer horns, and other western paraphernalia. Most of the dining areas have large windows offering stunning vistas of the desert, mountain peaks, and cliffs, as does the bar/lounge with its lake-view veranda. Plan your arrival to include cocktails or dinner at sunset. Two tables are built into a surrey with a fringe on top, and another is in an old-fashioned sled. There's also a garden room with lush tropical plantings and palms around a fountain centerpiece. Strolling country musicians entertain while you dine. All the fare is homemade, meat is butchered and aged on the premises, and baked goods are oven fresh. A 14-ounce sirloin steak is $14.75; 12 ounces of juicy prime rib, $13.75; barbecued ribs or beef, $10.25—all served with ranch beans, a baked potato, coleslaw, and fresh-baked bread and butter. If beef's not your thing, you might order scampi ($17.25) or steamed flounder in lemon butter ($8.95). And the kids can tackle an eight-ounce ranch burger with fries and a peach half ($4.75). There's a full bar, and desserts include homemade apple pie à la mode ($3) and Bavarian chocolate cream pie ($2.10).

The restaurant is open weekdays from 5 to 10 p.m., on Saturday from 4 to 10 p.m., and on Sunday from 1 to 9 p.m. Reservations essential. On Sunday afternoons there are complimentary hayrides for restaurant customers (call for hours).

**THE MAGOFFIN HOME STATE HISTORIC SITE:** Built in 1875 by El Paso pioneer Joseph Magoffin, this 19-room mansion at 1120 Magoffin Ave. and Octavia Street (tel. 533-5147), displays a uniquely regional architectural style. It's built of sun-dried adobe brick with Greek revival details such as pedimented and pilastered doors and windows and a scored plaster façade meant to suggest marble. Magoffin's family were movers and shakers in the area, having settled in what is now El Paso in 1849 and established a community called Magoffinsville. Though they were very successful traders and accumulated a fortune, Joseph's father, James, went through some hard times. He was once arrested by Mexicans and spent nine months in jail (he later claimed that it took 2,900 bottles of champagne to buy his freedom). Because he sided with the Confederacy during the Civil War his property was confiscated at the war's end. And at about the same time his mansion was washed away when the Rio Grande flooded.

Joseph Magoffin retrieved the family fortune and went on to enlarge it. The home he built is a re-creation of the one that washed away. In the 1870s it was a "magnificent country seat" on 40 acres of land; today it is ten blocks from downtown and 1½ acres remain, though they are restored to their 1880s appearance. A social and civic leader, Magoffin served as county judge, alderman, Customs inspector, county commissioner, and justice of the peace; was elected mayor of El Paso four times; and served as vice-president of the State National Bank for 40 years and as an officer of several prominent civic enterprises. He and his wife, Octavia, entertained lavishly at their elegant home.

Forty-minute tours of the house (except for the parts still occupied by Magoffin's granddaughter) are given throughout the day. The house is built without nails, and its exterior walls are at least three or four feet thick, its interior walls two or three feet. Its raftered matchboard pine ceilings are 14 feet high. All the principal rooms have adobe fireplaces with Greek revival detail. The formal parlor served as City Hall from 1892 to 1898 (prior to that they used local saloons). It's the most elegant room in the house, used to entertain special guests. The living room, in which the family congregated, is much less fancy and quite a bit more comfortable. All the rooms are furnished with original family pieces and there are oil portraits and photographs of family members throughout. Most of the rugs are Wilton carpets imported from England. The Magoffins kept a dining room table, which, with leaves, could seat 48, not an unusually large dinner party for them.

The estate is open for tours Wednesday to Sunday from 9 a.m. to 4 p.m. Admission is $1 for adults, 25¢ for children 6 to 12 (under 6, free).

**THE EL PASO MUSEUM OF ART:** Located at 1211 Montana Ave., between Brown and Noble Streets (tel. 541-4040), this delightful museum is housed in the 1908 Greek revival home of one-time Texas state Sen. W. W. Turney. It became a kind of catchall museum in 1947 and was converted into an art repository in 1960 when two wings were added to house the Kress Collection, a gift of 57 paintings and two sculptures by European masters from 1300 to 1800, displayed in areas designated as Early Renaissance, High Renaissance, and Baroque-Rococo. Included in this collection are works by Lippi, Tintoretto, Van Dyck, Vecchio, Murillo, Botticelli, Bellini, and others. A rather interesting aspect is a number of works done by followers of the masters.

The rest of the permanent collection highlights American painters of the 19th and 20th centuries, including Andrew Wyeth, Remington, Rembrandt Peale, Peter Hurd, and Childe Hassam; colonial American art; and Mexican folk art and *retablos* (religious paintings on metal sheets). The latter are displayed downstairs, along with reproductions of famous sculptures by Rodin, Michelangelo, and others, which visitors can touch, and a collection of French, Spanish, and Italian fans. New exhibits on Hueco Tanks and El Paso Indians are in the works at this writing. And there is an ongoing schedule of changing exhibits such as "Indian Paintings from the Los Angeles County Museum of Art," "Mexican Iconographic Art," and "The Rowdy London of William Hogarth." The ex-senator's home is a beautiful setting in which to view art, with its plush Victorian furnishings, crystal chandeliers, stained-glass windows, and exquisite carpets. There are occasional concerts and frequent lectures in the ornate parlor or the downstairs auditorium. Note the Tiffany window at the top of the stairs. Porcelain Boehm birds are on display in the West Wing foyer.

The museum is open Tuesday to Saturday from 10 a.m. to 5 p.m., on Sunday from 1 to 5 p.m. Admission is free.

**CHAMIZAL NATIONAL MEMORIAL:** This 55-acre park at 800 S. San Marcial St. (tel. 541-7880) was created to mark the 1968 settlement of a century-long border dispute. The flags of both border nations fly here, and there's usually quite a bit going on in the way of special programs, festivals, and theatrical events. A museum on the premises (in the Memorial Building) houses exhibits on the history and exploration of the 2,000-mile boundary between the United States and Mexico. There are changing art exhibits, and a 30-minute film about border history, narrated by Ricardo Montalban, is shown in English or Spanish upon request. In addition there's an ongoing series of educational films on American and regional subjects ranging from *Victory at Yorktown* to *Tigua Indians: Our Oldest Texans.* In fact, you might catch anything at Chamizal, from a Mexican rodeo to a performance of *A Chorus Line.* Call the above number when you arrive in town to find out what will be on during your stay. Also check the annual events calendar.

Directly across the river, the Mexican section of Chamizal Park offers 700 acres of shade trees, rose gardens, fountains, and a museum of Aztec art. Every June there's a trade fair on the Mexican side with displays of arts and crafts from all over Mexico.

**FORT BLISS:** The "largest air-defense center in the free world," and training camp for missilemen, artillerymen, and air-defense units from 22 Allied countries, Fort Bliss, entrance at Pershing Drive and Sheridan Boulevard (tel. 568-2121), at 1,125,000 acres, is bigger than the state of Rhode Island. Its roots go back to 1848 when infantry units were dispatched to the area to protect ranchers from Indians and bandits. One would expect the fort to be a top-security operation closed to public scrutiny; however, many parts of it are open to public view. These include Memorial Circle (plaques commemorating the fort's 100th anniversary and its war dead around a 96-foot flagpole); a Japanese garden; Pershing House (home of the famous general, who lived here and commanded the fort from 1914 to 1916); Officers Row; the Old Barracks; the Bliss Monument, honoring William Bliss, Zachary Taylor's chief-of-staff in the Mexican War; the old stables used to house the garrison's mounts until 1943 when horses were discontinued; and the Fort Bliss National Cemetery.

Most interesting are two museums on the premises. The **Fort Bliss Museum,** known as the Replica Museum (tel. 568-2804), focuses on the military campaigns in which the fort has been involved from 1848 to 1948. Housed in four adobe buildings that are replicas of mid-19th-century fort buildings, it contains paintings, photographs, and prints of battles; weaponry displays; artifacts from various campaigns; audio-visual displays; and an 1855 chapel, quartermaster store, and barracks. Exhibits also tell the story of the explorers, missionaries, conquistadors, traders, and frontiersmen who settled El Paso. Sometimes there are living-history programs and crafts demonstrations (call for hours). And the plants surrounding the museum are examples of local desert fauna that might have been here in the mid-1800s.

The **U.S. Army Air Defense Artillery Museum** (tel. 568-5412) documents the history of air defense from its earliest manifestations to its present sophisticated weaponry. Visitors are greeted by "Willie the Doughboy," an animated figure who recounts the World War I beginnings of air defense from his bunker near the front in France as bombs and shells explode in the background. Period music enhances other exhibits. Displays include a tableau of prisoners-of-war in Japan, antiaircraft artillery, a model of a Civil War observation balloon, machine gun mounts, a 1941 German V-1 jet-powered bomb, World War II submachine guns, modern missiles and defense systems, the propeller of a shot-down World War II German fighter plane, and audio-visual explanations of the operations of rockets and missiles. In the lobby's Mini Theatre, 12-minute films related to military history are shown throughout the day. In addition to the 10,000-square-foot building housing the above, there's an outdoor weapons-display area. There's also a gift shop on the premises where you might pick up an album of military music or *An Army Wife's Cookbook*.

Both museums are open daily from 9 a.m. to 4:30 p.m. Admission is free. Stop in at the Headquarters Building near the entrance and pick up a map.

**THE EL PASO ZOOLOGICAL PARK:** El Paso has a nice little 5½-acre zoo at Paisano Drive and Evergreen, in Washington Park (tel. 541-4601), a tree-shaded oasis that serves as home to over 200 animals. Highlights are Spider Monkey Island, a natural habitat with waterfalls, rocks, and trees; the Biome Building, housing tropical rain forest and southwestern desert environments; a good reptile collection (a rattlesnake den with over 20 rattlers hiding in the cacti illustrates how difficult they are to spot); and an aquarium. South American parrots, macaws, and peacocks fly and roam freely around the zoo, and there are four types of flightless birds—ostriches, cassowarys, rheas, and emus—on display. Other inhabitants include giraffes, zebras, cheetahs, rhinos, elephants, gorillas, waterfowl, lions, leopards, gazelles, Barbary sheep, bears, antelope, baboons, elands, jaguars, Bengal tigers, pumas, bobcats, and sea lions. The zoo is due for a major expansion, which will probably be well under way by the time you read this. There are picnic areas in Washington Park.

Hours are 9:30 a.m. to dusk Monday to Friday, 10 a.m. to dusk on Saturday, Sunday, and holidays. Adults pay $1.25 admission and children 6 to 12 pay 75¢ (under 6, free).

**SPORTS:** El Paso's baseball team, the **Diablos,** are a top-notch minor-league team. They play at Dudley Field, 3931 Findley Ave., near Boone Street (tel. 544-1950), April through September to a passionate standing-room-only crowd. There are all kinds of promotions; you'll enjoy 10¢ hot dogs, a free comic T-shirt, water pistol, seat cushion, or some such at every game.

A number of intercollegiate athletic events take place at the **University of Texas El Paso** (UTEP). Call 747-5330 to find out what's on during your stay.

Just ten minutes from downtown El Paso via I-10 is **Sunland Park Race Track** in New Mexico (tel. 505/589-1131; it's a local call). During a mid-October to early May 90-day season, it features thoroughbred and quarterhorse races at 12:30 or 1 p.m. on Friday, Saturday, and Sunday. Big-name races include the $275,000 Sun Country Futurity, the $225,000 West Texas Futurity for quarterhorses, and the $400,000 Riley Allison Futurity for thoroughbreds. There's a glass-enclosed, air-conditioned Clubhouse with restaurant, and the entertainment includes prerace aquatic performances on the infield lake. General admission is $1, reserved grandstand seats are an additional $2, and Clubhouse admission and seating, $5. It's a good idea to call ahead and reserve first-tier seating at the Clubhouse. A meal at the Clubhouse can be anything from a bowl of chili ($3) to a ten-ounce steak with baked potato and salad ($11.25).

For further sports listings, see "Annual Events" and "Juárez," in other sections of this chapter.

## 5. After Dark

**DANCING:** There are plenty of places to dance away the desert nights. **Dallas,** 1840 Lee Trevino Dr., at Montwood Drive, in the Vista Hills Shopping Center (tel. 598-1548), is a slick urban cowboy bar offering live country and rock music (a 60/40 ratio) Monday to Wednesday nights, disco the rest of the week. The club has a circular dance floor, six pool tables, a video game room, and three ten-foot video screens. Its decor is red-and-blue neon, including a row of blue neon Lone Stars lining the bar.

Under the same auspices is **Phoenix,** 1461 Lee Trevino Dr., at Vista del Sol Drive, in the Lee Trevino Center (tel. 598-6545), its walls adorned with neon scenes of tropical beaches, a panther stalking a rabbit, etc. Other attractions are a big, rectangular, trilevel dance floor, state-of-the-art lighting equipment, three ten-foot video monitors, roulette, video games, a bar for exotic drinks made with Häagen-Dazs ice cream, and a complimentary buffet offered all night long. Music is top-40s rock played by a DJ.

Both clubs charge $3 admission all night on Friday and Saturday after 9 p.m.; other nights admission is free. Both are open till 2 a.m. Sunday to Thursday, till 4 a.m. on Friday and Saturday.

Another popular spot, **Teddy's,** on the 17th floor of the Holiday Inn at 113 W. Missouri Ave., between El Paso and Oregon Streets (tel. 544-3300), offers a panoramic view of city lights and top-40s disco music. Free hors d'oeuvres are served weekdays from 5 to 8 p.m. during Happy Hour. There's a game room with backgammon tables, and in addition to drinks, sandwiches and snack fare are available.

Open Monday to Saturday till 2 a.m.

**SYMPHONY:** The **El Paso Symphony Orchestra** has a September-through-April season at the Civic Center, Santa Fe Street and San Francisco Avenue (tel. 532-8707), often featuring guest artists like Lorin Hollander and Dutch *lieder* singer Elly Ameling. The orchestra was founded in 1930, and is under the direction of Abraham Chavez, Jr.

**MISCELLANY:** An ongoing schedule of theatrical, musical, and dance programs, among other entertainments, is offered at **Chamizal National Memorial Park** (details above). Call 541-7880 to find out what's on during your stay.

Headliners play **UTEP;** call 747-5265, the university's Special Events Center number, to find out about big concerts and other happenings on campus. You can also catch classic films at UTEP.

Another source of local happenings is **Ticketmaster.** Call 915/532-4661 to find out what's on and purchase tickets.

## 6. Juárez

El Paso has three border crossings into Juárez. The most convenient is the Santa Fe Bridge, which takes you into town four blocks from the City Market (Mercado Juárez). You can park on the Texas side and walk across. Cordova Bridge is closer to ProNaf, another major shopping center, but you can't walk across it, you have to drive or take a taxi. There are shopping-tour buses from all major hotels, but I think it's more fun to shop at your own pace. It's easy to spend three or four hours browsing in Juárez's colorful marketplaces. On the other hand, the tours are fine for attending greyhound and horse races and bull-fights. The major operator is **Golden Tours** (tel. 779-0555); inquire at your hotel desk.

Juárez is the fourth-largest city in Mexico, with a population of over a million.

**SHOPPING:** The most impressive shopping area in Juárez is **ProNaf,** a government-sponsored complex near the Cordova Bridge on Avenida Lincoln just north of Avenida 16 de Septiembre. **Centro Artesanal,** ProNaf's biggest shop, occupies three floors housing an array of vendors under one roof selling quality arts and crafts from all over Mexico. You can't bargain here; prices are fixed and reasonable. Other ProNaf stores adjoining sell leather, clothing, etc. There's free parking in an immense lot.

City Market, at Avenidas 16 de Septiembre and Progreso, is a more colorful shopping environment, probably because in addition to a full roster of Mexican craft items it also stocks produce, spices, and Mexican candies. And sometimes there are strolling mariachis. Dozens of shops nestle under one roof here, offering everything from taco molds to piñatas to portraits of Julio Iglesias on velvet.

A third popular shop is the **Glass Factory,** 1500 Avenida 16 de Septiembre at Brasil, where you can observe glassblowers heating molten glass in brick furnaces and shaping it into fish, birds, vases, bulls, glasses, etc.

If you're not yet sated, check out the shops along **Avenida Juárez** between the Santa Fe Bridge and Avenida 16 de Septiembre.

**BULLFIGHTS:** Between Easter Sunday and Labor Day there are bullfights on selected Sunday evenings at the 17,000-seat **Plaza de Toros Monumental Bullring,** Avenida 16 de Septiembre (tel. 915/593-6760). Some of these are major bullfights featuring top matadors, some are lesser matches. The matador must kill the bull to complete the fight, after which he is awarded an ear, two ears, two ears and a tail, or the ultimate—all the above plus a hoof! It's a three-act drama, and some women in the crowd fling roses at the matador.

A **Golden Tours** bus (tel. 779-0555) costs $6.50 per person round trip, $3.50 for children 5 to 12. The matches begin at 5 or 6 p.m.

If you want to learn more about bullfighting, you might visit the **Bullfight Museum,** back across the border in El Paso at the Del Camino Motor Hotel, 5001 Alameda Ave. (tel. 772-2711); manager and enthusiast Jorge Bate will show you around and explain the intricacies of the sport. It's quite interesting.

**JUÁREZ RACE TRACK:** Year round, Wednesday through Sunday at 8 p.m., there are greyhound races at **Juárez Race Track,** Rte. 45 and Avenida Vincente Guerrero (tel. 915/778-6322). It costs under $1 to sit in the best seats—the Blue Section of the air-conditioned Jockey Club—and you can dine up here very inexpensively as well. There's also horse racing at the track on Sunday at 1:30 p.m. from May to September. You can place your bets in American currency.

Once again, **Golden Tours** (tel. 779-0555) provides round trip transportation from major hotels (same price as above).

**DINING IN JUÁREZ:** My favorite Juárez restaurant is **Casa del Sol,** right in the ProNaf complex (tel. 36509), a plush eatery with terracotta tile floors, exposed brick archways, wrought-iron amber lanterns suspended from a dark-beamed ceiling, and white stucco walls adorned with charming murals of Mexican scenery. A blazing fire in the stucco and stone hearth further enhances the ambience in winter. If you come in for a margarita and nachos break from shopping, plop yourself down in one of the comfortable armchairs around the tiered fountain in the plant-filled bar/lounge. Or sit down for a full meal and make selections from the immense menu; try an appetizer of netskies, deep-fried pastries filled with goat cheese and minced turkey ($3.75), followed by shrimp fiesta, shrimp stuffed with green chili and cheese, wrapped in bacon, broiled in brochette, and served over rice with a baked potato ($11.75). It's all extraordinarily delicious. A less expensive meal might center on the Casa's superb spaghetti cooked with oil, garlic, fresh jalapeño peppers, onions, and tomatoes, and topped with white Chihuahua cheese and fresh coriander ($3.95). For dessert, the flan ($1.75) is the optimum in creamy wonderfulness.

Open Sunday to Thursday from noon to 11 p.m., on Friday and Saturday until 1 a.m. At night mariachi bands entertain. Reservations suggested.

There's also a restaurant in **Decor,** one of the ProNaf Center shops, a pristinely pretty one with Saltillo-tile floors, black wrought-iron furnishings and chandeliers, amber lighting, and big bouquets of colorful paper flowers on every table. Lots of light streams in through a wall of windows. It's a good place to rest up over snacks and cocktails during lengthy shopping excursions. Prices are very low: a guacamole salad with chips is $2.50; an order of three enchiladas with rice and beans, just $2.25; a margarita, a mere $1.25.

Hours are 10 a.m. to 6 p.m. daily.

And for something a little different, try **Shangri La,** 133 Avenida de las Americas, at Zaragosa (tel. 30033), an attractive burgundy-carpeted Chinese restaurant with white-linened tables, gold foil cherry-blossom-motif wallpaper, and plum banners with gold Chinese letters overhead. The fare is very Americanized, but sometimes shrimp fried rice and eggrolls hit the spot. And though it's not on the menu, and not particularly Chinese, Shangri La makes a fabulous tomato salad appetizer; ask for it. You can have a full wonton-soup-to-lichee-nuts meal here for about $5, including a glass of wine.

*Chapter XII*

# THE PANHANDLE

### 1. Lubbock
### 2. Amarillo

THE TABLE-FLAT NORTHERNMOST SECTION of West Texas is called the Panhandle for obvious reasons: it is the handle of the great skillet of the state. One of the last parts of Texas to be settled by Europeans (Indians have lived here for 12,000 years), it lies in the southernmost portion of the Great Plains of the United States. The first white men to explore the region were Coronado and his army, who passed through in 1541 searching for the legendary Seven Cities of Gold. They found a veritably treeless wasteland. (It is actually known, in fact, when the first tree was planted; Thomas Cree, a pioneer settler, planted a bois d'arc sapling in the city of Panhandle, about 20 miles northeast of Amarillo, in 1888. The stump bears a historical marker today.) Coronado called the Panhandle the Llano Estacado or "staked plains," because the Spanish drove wooden stakes (some say they used buffalo bones) into the ground to serve as guideposts along the featureless prairie terrain. It wasn't until the 1860s that European settlers began to arrive, first to hunt buffalo, which they did with great assiduity. By 1880 the 60 million head that once roamed the plains was in danger of total annihilation! However, by that time other settlers had arrived to graze cattle here.

Even today the Panhandle plains are largely unspoiled. The region's rugged canyons and vast grasslands are the topography we think of when we conjure up images of the West—sprawling cattle ranches, oil derricks and windmills rising from treeless plains, spacious skies, and amber waves of grain.

## 1. Lubbock

Lubbock, though it didn't exist at the time as such, was along the route followed by Coronado in 1541. He found Comanches, buffalo, antelope, prairie dogs, and coyotes, but no gold and no earthly reason to stay on or explore further. For over three centuries thereafter, except for buffalo hunters and trail drivers, no one else much bothered with this lonely expanse of grassland either. It was considered uninhabitable. It wasn't until 1879 that a group of Quakers first settled here, realizing the potential for raising cattle where feeding grasses grew in such abundance. They formed the nucleus of what would become a vast cattle empire, centered on two towns that merged in 1890 to form Lubbock, named for former Texas Ranger, signer of the Texas Declaration of Independence, and Civil War hero Tom S. Lubbock. By the turn of the century Lubbock had a population of about 300 and a thriving cattle economy. The first Santa Fe Railroad car pulled into town in 1909, and Lubbock, despite difficult early years marked by drought, prairie fires, and sandstorms, continued to grow and prosper.

Today it is a clean and pleasant American town of tree-lined streets and manicured lawns, its economy still largely based on agriculture. Lubbock produces 30% of the U.S. cotton crop and large amounts of wheat and sorghum. Some 27% of the nation's crude oil also emanates from the area. And one of the Southwest's leading universities, Texas Tech, is based here. If Coronado could see Lubbock today, perhaps he'd hang up his saddle and stay a spell.

**GETTING THERE:** The **Lubbock International Airport,** in the northeast part of town on Quirt Avenue, is served by American, Southwest, and Delta airlines.

**By car,** once again, we're talking vast distances from most Texas cities. You're closest to Amarillo, 120 miles north via I-27. Both Dallas and El Paso are 298 miles away, the former via I-20 and U.S. 84, the latter via U.S. 62/180.

**By bus.** Lubbock is served by the **Texas, New Mexico, and Oklahoma** bus company (called **T.N.M.&O.)** (tel. 806/765-6641).

**GETTING ORIENTED:** Your information source is the **Lubbock Visitors and Conventions Bureau,** 14th Street and Avenue K, Lubbock, TX 79408 (tel. 806/763-4666). Hours are Monday to Friday from 8 a.m. to 5 p.m. Write ahead for maps, calendars of events, and any other information you require.

**GETTING AROUND:** You can rent a car at the airport from **Budget** (tel. 806/763-6471), **National** (tel. 806/762-2161), or **Avis** (tel. 806/763-5433). It's really the only way to go.

But there is a **city bus system.** Call 762-0111 for routing information.

A **taxi** between the airport and downtown hotels will cost about $8. Taxi rides cost $1.50 when the meter drops, $1 a mile thereafter. If you need one, call Yellow Cab at 765-7777.

**ANNUAL EVENTS:** The **Lubbock Visitors and Convention Bureau** (tel. 806/763-4666) can fill you in on all events taking place during your stay. Important annual happenings include the following:

Late April or early May, a three-day weekend is set aside for the **Lubbock Arts Festival** at the Memorial Civic Center, 1501 6th St. An annual celebration of the arts, it features gallery shows of local and nationally recognized artists, crafts booths and demonstrations, and performing artists ranging from flamenco dancers to chamber music to oom-pah bands. Ethnic food booths serve up baklava, Polish sausage, tacos, you name it. And there are special creative activities for children. Thousands of people participate. It's quite something.

September is the most event-filled month in Lubbock. The **South Plains Fair,** in Mackenzie State Park at Avenue A near East Broadway (tel. 744-9557 for information) is one of the biggest in Texas, second only to the Dallas State Fair. It takes place late in the month, sometimes running into October, and features livestock exhibits and judgings, parades, live music, fiddler's contests, carnival midway rides and attractions, acrobats, jugglers, animal acts, ventriloquists, crafts exhibits, and a flower show. And there's a headliner show every night of the fair, starring artists like George Strait, the Statler Brothers, Nitty Gritty Dirt Band, and Ricky Skaggs. General admission is about $2.50 for adults, $1 for children under 12. Concert tickets are an additional $4 to $12, depending on the performer. The fair has been taking place since 1917.

A newer September event (since 1984) is the **Texas International Wine Classic,** also late in the month at the Memorial Civic Center and elsewhere in town. Celebrating the state's emerging wine industry, the Classic features wine tastings, champagne brunches, cooking-with-wine seminars, a gourmet dinner with selected wines, and lectures by noted wine makers and other experts. It's an opportunity to learn a lot about wine and get a little tipsy in the bargain. You can sign up for one, some, or all of the events, the latter costing somewhere around $100. Call the Visitors and Conventions Bureau for ticket information and other details.

**HOTELS:** Lubbock is one of the few Texas towns that isn't overbuilt when it comes to accommodations. During Texas Tech football season, September to January, it's sometimes difficult to get a room on weekends. And occasionally conventions fill up the town. You can almost always squeeze in someplace, but for optimum choice, reserve in advance.

A top hotel choice is the **Lubbock Plaza,** 3201 Loop 289 South, off Indiana Avenue, Lubbock, TX 79423 (tel. 806/797-3241, or toll free 800/448-8228), offering a great deal in its price range. Its 202 rooms have ivy-hung, wrought-iron balconies overlooking a vast, lushly planted, skylit atrium. Said atrium contains the Fountain Court Lounge (for piano-bar entertainment, complimentary hors d'oeuvres weekdays from 5 to 9 p.m., and lavish Sunday brunches), a flower-bordered fountain, a sizable indoor swimming pool, children's wading pool, sauna, video game room, exercise/weight room, and 1.2-mile jogging track. There are umbrella tables and garden chairs on the balconies where you might enjoy the illusion of an al fresco breakfast.

Rooms are large and lovely, decorated in subtle color schemes such as pale coral/gray or pale mauve/silver blue. King-size rooms have sofa beds and coffee tables; the rest contain plush oversize velvet recliners with reading lamps. All offer cable color TVs with HBO, desks with two upholstered chairs, AM/FM clock radios, full-length closet mirrors, and makeup mirrors and shower massages in the bath. The Plaza features special "lady traveler" rooms; these are in the hotel's most secure locations and offer hair dryers (curling irons are available on request) and upgraded bath toiletries.

One of the reasons I love to stay here is the hotel's policy of playing classical music (in lieu of Muzak) in the public areas and restaurants. There are two dining rooms. Recipes is a pleasant 24-hour eatery with a garden motif, its tables amid planters of flowers and potted palms. Excellent American/continental fare is served. Beethoven's is a little gem of a formal dining room, agleam with crystal glassware and chandeliers reflected in mirrored walls. A pianist entertains on a white baby grand while you dine. Beethoven's menu offers traditional French/continental haute cuisine. After dinner the action is at the Plaza's lively disco/video lounge, Oliver's, where a DJ spins top-40s, country, and oldies, and rock videos are aired on five monitors. Major sporting events are also shown here.

Additional Plaza pluses: complimentary airport transfer, free parking, a florist and gift shop on the premises, concierge service, and 24-hour room service.

Rates are $60.50 single, $6 for each additional adult (children under 18, free). Discounts are offered on weekends. Parking is free. No-smoking rooms and facilities for the disabled are also available.

Another fine atrium-centered hostelry is the **Grenada Royale,** 5215 Loop 289 South, at Slide Road, Lubbock, TX 79424 (tel. 806/794-5353, or toll free 800/222-1122). It's very Spanish in feel, as you'll realize upon entering the Saltillo-tile lobby with its plush leather furnishings and large wrought-iron candelabra chandeliers suspended from a coffered dark-wood ceiling. The Grenada's stucco-walled, skylit atrium evokes a Spanish courtyard, with palms, lush greenery, and globe streetlights.

The rooms—all of which are actually suites—are furnished with dark Mediterranean pieces. Each has a fully equipped kitchen, living room, and bed-room, with phones and remote-control cable color TVs in both the latter rooms. They're attractively decorated accommodations, comfortably residential in feel. All open on the atrium, and many have balconies.

The atrium itself, a beautifully landscaped area (two full-time gardeners tend its plantings), is the setting for complimentary buffet breakfasts that are included in rates at the Granada—not just coffee and muffins but a full meal of eggs, bacon, hash browns, pancakes, toast, fruit, fresh-squeezed orange juice, and tea or coffee. Afternoons, complimentary cocktails are served and a pianist entertains.

The atrium also houses an indoor swimming pool, whirlpool, steam room, sauna, and video game room. An adjoining outdoor flagstone terrace is used as a sundeck. Guests can use the nearby Supreme Court Racquetball Club for a small fee. Other amenities include a coin-op laundry and free transportation to/from the airport and a nearby shopping mall. There's no restaurant on the premises, but you can purchase frozen dinners, sandwiches, light fare, and Häagen-Dazs ice cream at the gift shop.

Rates are $79 single, $89 double, $10 for an additional person, free for chil-dren under 12. Weekend rates (Friday, Saturday, and Sunday nights) are just $65, single or double. Parking is free and facilities for the disabled are provided.

The 147-room **Lubbock Inn,** 3901 19th St., at Brownfield Road, Lubbock, TX 79410 (tel. 806/792-5181), is a locally owned property, unimpressive from the outside but quite nice within and offering good value for your money. Homey rooms are furnished in sturdy oak pieces and decorated with western art. And they offer luxurious extras like phones and TV speakers in the bath, remote-control color TVs, double sinks, and bedside switches for all room lights. King-size rooms have tufted-leather armchairs. And a very attractive king-size suite with a full living room and a refrigerator is priced at just $75 a night for up to four people. The hotel's Recovery Room lounge on the second floor is a pleasant venue for afternoon cocktails. Its oak-paneled walls are hung with turn-of-the-century photographs of Lubbock, and its large windows over-look the Texas Tech campus. A complimentary buffet is served weekday after-noons. Additional facilities include a large swimming pool enhanced by waterfalls, free use of washers and dryers in an on-premises laundry room, com-plimentary transport to/from the airport and anywhere else nearby, and a pleas-ant, reasonably priced coffeeshop open daily from 6 a.m. to 11 p.m.

Rates are $44 single, $50 double, $6 for an additional person, free for chil-dren under 12. Parking is free, and no-smoking rooms are available.

There's also a **La Quinta** in Lubbock (see Chapter I for details), conve-niently located at 601 Avenue Q, Lubbock, TX 79401 (tel. 806/763-9441, or toll free 800/531-5900). It adjoins a 24-hour Denny's, has a nice-size courtyard pool and sundeck, doesn't charge for local phone calls, and serves complimentary coffee all day in the lobby. Airport transfer is also provided gratis. All in all, it's a very good deal for just $43 a night for singles, $48 for doubles, $5 for an extra person (under 18, free). Parking is free. No-smoking accommodations and facil-ities for the disabled are available.

And Lubbock's **Motel 6** (see Chapter I for details and rates) is at 909 66th St., off Avenue H, Lubbock, TX 79413 (tel. 806/745-6666). It has 178 units and a swimming pool.

**WHERE TO EAT:** Little Lubbock has no lack of varied and worthy restaurants, but the best of them all is a funky barbecue joint that may just be the best mes-quite mecca in Texas. And that's saying a lot.

Whatever you do, don't miss **Jug Little's,** 1514 E. Broadway, between Pine and Oak Avenues (tel. 762-8374), especially if you can make it for Friday or Saturday lunch when live country bands play down-home fiddle music on a stage in the center of the room. I daresay Jug's is responsible for a great deal of Friday-afternoon absenteeism in local offices; it's just so downright cozy and comfy, and so hard to leave. Owner Alton "Jug" Little, a former Texas Tech footballer, has created the archetypical Texas rib shack here. He's covered every inch of the pine-paneled walls with rusty antique farming tools, mounted buffalo and deer heads, horns, photographs of Lubbock locals, barbed wire, steer skulls—you name it. Stirrups and cowboy boots are hung from the rafters. A two-headed calf that was "born in Paris, Texas and lived for four hours" graces the eave over the bar. There's a full horse-drawn stagecoach with two passengers, an Indian and a skeleton. And wedged into the remaining spaces here and there are stuffed boars, bears, rattlesnakes, and wooden Indians.

Lots of for-real cowboys eat at Jug's, including All American rodeo champ Jim Shoulders. When Reagan came through town on his presidential campaign, his lunch was catered from Jug's. And George Bush has been in a number of times. You never know what's going to happen when you drop by this place. Occasionally "Jug" gets up a rattlesnake show, a live monkey show, or brings in some wolverines. And he once rode a brahma bull through the restaurant to promote a Texas Tech rodeo!

Even if nothing special's happening, the bill of fare is an ample draw. The mesquite-grilled ribs ($4.25 for a sandwich, $6.50 a plateful) are outrageously good. And you can't go wrong with a combination plate of ribs, beef, and sausage for $7.75. It's all served with homemade bread and beans, and I'd suggest an order of chili—all that chili should be—on the side. There's a full bar, a component in those cozy take-that-job-and-shove-it Friday afternoons.

Hours are Monday to Saturday from 10 a.m. to 3 p.m.

A totally different atmosphere characterizes another Lubbock barbecue eatery, the **Road House,** FM 2641, about a quarter mile west of Amarillo Road (tel. 763-6001), set on 12 verdant acres overlooking a creek, with ducks, chicken, geese, and peacocks roaming the grounds. It's a beautiful, rather romantic setting. In good weather you can enjoy apéritifs or after-dinner drinks on a creekside terrace under lofty elms or take a hayride around the property. The cozy interior, with three fireplaces, a beamed ceiling, and lots of hanging plants, has a 1940s motif. Walls are plastered with period sheet music and advertisements, there are magazine racks by every booth stocked with World War II–era copies of *Life* magazine, and big-band music emanates from an old Wurlitzer.

There's a simple menu, featuring large platters of smoky barbecued ribs ($10.50), beef ($9.50), sausage ($8.50), a combination of all three ($9.50), or chicken ($8.50)—all served with coleslaw, potato salad, and beans. A child's plate is $5.50. Possible extras include a loaf of homemade bread for $3.25 (go for it), mushrooms cooked in butter and red wine ($2.50), and a baked potato ($1.75). There's homemade ice cream for dessert ($1.75), and all bar drinks are available.

The Road House is open Monday to Thursday from 5 to 9 p.m., on Friday and Saturday to 10 p.m., and on Sunday from 4 to 9 p.m. They don't take reservations. Come early to avoid a wait.

Only in the flat plains of Lubbock could a sixth-floor restaurant like **Giorgio's,** 1901 University Ave., in the Texas Financial Center (tel. 747-2583), provide far-reaching panoramic views. This "lofty" dining room is one of the most elegant in town, not only the best vantage point for watching the sun set over Texas Tech, but a sophisticated setting for French and Italian haute-cuisine fare. The gray-and-mauve color scheme, chrome-framed chairs, and track lighting combine to create a handsome contemporary decor. I like to come on Thursday night when jazz artists perform in the lounge. Sunday through Wednesday taped classical music or light jazz is played during dinner, and weekends a DJ plays top-40s tunes for dancing.

For appetizers, there are escargots in mushroom caps drenched with garlic butter ($5.95) and warm spinach salad tossed with bacon and onion dressing and grated egg ($4.50). Entree choices include sautéed chicken breast Oscar topped with asparagus, crabmeat, and tomato-flavored béarnaise ($11.75), an eight-ounce filet au poivre in creamy cognac sauce ($15.75), veal marsala sautéed in garlic butter with fresh mushrooms ($15.75), and beef Stroganoff ($11.75). All are served with fresh vegetables and a choice of steamed rice, buttered noodles, or potatoes. Local wines supplement the usual French and California offerings on the restaurant's wine list. And there are rich desserts like mocha chocolate-chip cheesecake ($3.95) and ice cream–filled crêpes topped with Kirsch-flavored dark cherries, whipped cream, and grated chocolate ($3.50). Or you might opt for an ice cream drink, like chambord (a raspberry liqueur) mixed with Cointreau and vanilla ice cream ($3.95). At lunch Giorgio's is much less expensive, featuring entrees like fettuccine with red clam sauce and a salad ($5.75) and a triple-decker sandwich with soup ($6.25).

Open for lunch weekdays from 11 a.m. to 2 p.m.; for dinner Monday to Thursday from 6 to 10 p.m., on Friday and Saturday to 11 p.m.; and for Sunday brunch from 11 a.m. to 2 p.m., the latter a table d'hôte meal featuring appetizer and entree for $11.50. Reservations suggested at dinner.

A pleasant surprise in Lubbock is **Asahi**, 6502 Slide Rd., at Loop 289, on the top floor of the Sentry Savings Building (tel. 794-3117), a very good Japanese restaurant featuring teppanyaki cooking. Diners sit around large, grill-centered tables while a chef in a tall red hat chops, cooks, and serves meat, fish, and vegetables with samurai-like swiftness. Everything here is fresh and home-made. Full dinners, including soup, salad, hibachi vegetables, flambéed shrimp, steamed rice, and green tea might feature an entree of hibachi New York strip steak ($13.50), beef sukiyaki ($12.50), sesame chicken ($9.50), shrimp or scallops with butter and lemon ($13.50), or even lobster tail ($17.50). A bottle of sake ($3.50) is a most recommendable accompaniment, and for dessert there's an untypically Japanese, but nevertheless scrumptious, feather-light home-made cheesecake topped with fresh strawberries and real whipped cream ($2.95). Full lunches are in the $5.95 to $6.95 range, except for the lobster which is $9.95. Everything here is first rate, and my only reservation is the chef's tendency to oversalt (if you don't like salty food, ask him to go easy). The setting is quite nice. Walls are decorated with Japanese art and kites, there are paper lanterns overhead, and kimonoed waitresses enhance the suitably Oriental ambience.

Open for lunch weekdays from 11:30 a.m. to 3 p.m., for dinner Monday to Thursday nights from 5:30 to 10 p.m., on Friday and Saturday to 11 p.m., and on Sunday from 5 to 10 p.m. Reservations essential at dinner.

**The Depot**, 19th Street and Avenue G (tel. 747-1646), is housed in an actual 1928 Spanish Renaissance revival train depot for the Fort Worth & Denver South Plains Railway. It's lavishly decorated inside. The mauve-walled bar/lounge has a working fireplace, a 1940s Wurlitzer jukebox, a handsome reproduction turn-of-the-century oak bar, and plush furnishings. You can have cocktails and hors d'oeuvres at Cinzano umbrella- or tree-shaded tables on a brick-floored beer garden out back. And the elegant main dining room is vaguely Victorian with lace-curtained bay windows framed in burgundy velvet, stained-glass fixtures, and exposed brick walls. A beautiful 1890s oak hutch rests against one wall, and others are decorated with turn-of-the-century railroad-themed murals. Gray-linened tables are lit by candles in cut-glass holders.

Steak and seafood are featured. A Depot meal might begin with a salad of hearts of palm and artichoke hearts marinated in a tangy vinaigrette ($5.50), and proceed to an entree of filet mignon ($12.50), 12 ounces of prime rib ($14.50), deep-fried butterfly shrimp on a bed of rice ($10.50), or mesquite-grilled flounder stuffed with crabmeat dressing ($10.50). All entrees include a trip to the salad bar (displayed on period steamer trunks) and rolls and butter served with hot cheese. Additional accompaniments can be ordered à la carte, like fettuccine Alfredo ($2.50); a baked potato stuffed with grated cheddar, bacon, onions, and spices ($2.50); or steamed broccoli with melted cheese sauce ($2.45). Desserts change nightly, but the homemade hot rum cake with vanilla ice cream ($3.25) is usually featured and a good bet. The Depot offers a nice selection of French and California wines, along with full bar options. At lunch the menu lists a wide array of sandwiches, burgers, salads, and heartier entrees, most in the $4.50 to $7 range. Monday-night football and other important sporting events are aired on a large-screen TV in the lounge.

The Depot is open for lunch weekdays from 10:30 a.m. to 2 p.m., for dinner Monday to Thursday from 5:30 to 10 p.m., on Friday and Saturday till 11 p.m. Reservations essential.

José Ramirez, his wife, and two daughters offer first-rate homemade Mexican fare at **José's,** 5029 Avenue H, just south of 50th Street (tel. 744-3784). This mom-and-pop operation has been a going concern for two decades, and Ramirez is a Lubbock civic leader for whom a local elementary school is named. Though the restaurant has attracted its share of celebrity diners—from George Bush to Ricky Ricardo—it's an unpretentious setting with Formica tables, brick-patterned linoleum floors, colorful plastic chairs (yellow, turquoise, red, green, and orange), and walls plastered with photographs and caricatures of Texas Tech footballers, local politicians, the Lions Club, and other local groups. A large oil painting of José himself dominates. Sporting events and afternoon soap operas are aired on the TV over the bar.

A good choice here is an order of nachos ($3.95) followed by fajitas ($6.95) served with rice, beans, guacamole salad, and corn or flour tortillas. A children's plate for $2.55 includes rice, beans, and a choice of a taco, enchilada, or tamale. And sopapillas are served gratis for dessert.

José's is open Tuesday to Saturday from 11 a.m. to 2 p.m. and 5 to 9 p.m., on Sunday from 11 a.m. to 2 p.m.

**WHAT TO SEE AND DO:** There's quite a bit to see in this college-cowboy town. Not-to-be-missed attractions include an outdoor history-of-ranching museum, a prairie dog town, and a tour of Texas's largest winery.

### The Ranching Heritage Center

One of the most intriguing of Lubbock attractions, the Ranching Heritage Center at Texas Tech University, 4th Street and Indiana Avenue (tel. 742-2498), is a 15-acre outdoor museum of 25 buildings and other structures demonstrating frontier ranching lifestyles and architecture of the 19th and early 20th centuries. The buildings have been brought here from ranches throughout the state, and historians and architects examined old records and diaries, talked to living former occupants or their descendants, and worked with archeologists to gather precise and detailed data for restorations. Timber, rock, and other components used in repair work were gleaned from the buildings' original sites and all work was done with tools of the era (shingles were made with froes and mallets, beams shaped with adzes). Berms (earthen mounds) and hillocks were built around the grounds to isolate the area from the modern environment, and each building's landscaping is indigenous to its original locale.

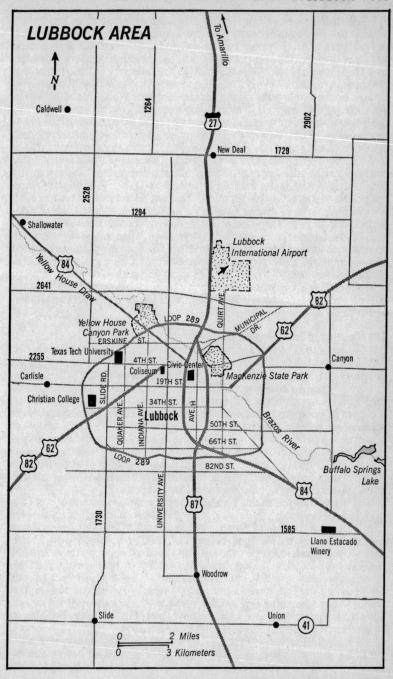

## LUBBOCK AREA

To Amarillo

Caldwell

1264

2902

27

New Deal 1729

2528

1294

Shallowater

Yellow House Draw

84

Lubbock
International Airport

2641

Yellow House
Canyon Park
ERSKINE ST.

LOOP 289

QUIRT AVE.

MUNICIPAL DR.

82

2255 Texas Tech University

4TH ST.
Coliseum Civic Center

62

Canyon

Carlisle

SLIDE RD.

19TH ST.

MacKenzie State Park

Christian College

QUAKER AVE.

INDIANA AVE.

34TH ST.

AVE. H

Lubbock

50TH ST.

Brazos River

62

66TH ST.

82

LOOP 289

82ND ST.

Buffalo Springs
Lake

84

1730

UNIVERSITY AVE.

87

1585

Llano Estacado
Winery

Woodrow

Slide

Union

41

0          2 Miles
0          3 Kilometers

The structures range from primitive log cabins erected when Texas was a republic to a turn-of-the-century Victorian mansion that had indoor plumbing and gas lighting. An 1875 stone house is a veritable fortress with rifle slits on the walls, a reminder of the ever-present frontier danger of Indian attack. The Matador Half-Dugout (circa 1890) shows a style of architecture dictated by the lack of timber in Texas; a hole is scooped into the side of a hill, with flour-sack-covered earthen walls reducing lumber requirements. And some of the homes use such unlikely environmental building materials as yucca stalks nailed to cedar posts. All are furnished in appropriate period style. A tour of the buildings provides an overview of the development of ranching from a small-time operation to a big business. And in addition to homes, there are windmills, a coal-burning steam locomotive, a bunkhouse, schoolhouse, commissary, office building, blacksmith shop, barn, carriage house, granary, depot, cattle shipping pens, and a cooling house for preserving milk and meat. A Spanish/Mexican component that will elucidate the late-1700s era of Texas history is nearing completion at this writing. And an operational general store sells all kinds of wonderful old-fashioned things—potpourri, period cookbooks, lace, dolls, etc.

The best time to come is on Sunday afternoon, when costumed docents are on hand and guided tours are offered. Other times you're given a self-guided tour brochure and a radio receiver with recordings for each structure. The center is open Monday to Saturday from 9 a.m. to 4:30 p.m., on Sunday from 1 to 4:30 p.m. Allow about two hours and wear comfortable shoes; there's about a mile of walking. Admission is $1.25 for adults, 75¢ for children 12 and under, with a family discount available.

### The Museum of Texas Tech University

Adjacent to the Ranching Heritage Center is the University Museum (tel. 742-2490), a multipurpose facility with a general educative purpose and exhibits in history, art, science, and technology. Murals, paintings, artifacts, and dioramas trace the area's development from 12,000 years ago to the present, beginning with mammoth hunters and proceeding to early Indian tribes (there's a replica of a Comanche camp), Coronado staking the plains, Spanish and Anglo settlers, the growth of towns, military campaigns, and the development of ranching, agriculture, and the petroleum industry. A Food and Fiber exhibit deals with the Lubbock region's agricultural products—cotton, cattle, and wool —including displays on cowboy culture and the processing of cattle from the open range to the gas range. Dinosaur and mammoth skeletons, rocks and minerals, make up the bulk of the Natural History section.

A particularly interesting feature is the museum's documentation of Lubbock Lake, a nationally significant archeological site a mile north of town on the Clovis Highway. Lubbock Lake excavations go back to man's earliest existence in North America, the Paleoindian Period of 12,000 to 8,000 years ago. The remains of mammoths and extinct horses, camels, bears, bison, and giant armadillos have been found on the site. The bears would have been about three times larger than a modern grizzly, and the armadillos, six feet long and three feet tall! Other interesting finds have included a 5,000-year-old oven, puebloan pottery sherds, many Comanche and Apache artifacts, and evidences of later Anglo European occupation. There are sometimes tours of the actual site on Saturday in summer; if you're interested, inquire at the museum.

Finally, this university museum offers some excellent—mostly regional— art shows such as photography exhibitions of works by Ansel Adams and Edward Curtis, collections of American glass, current Texas painters, and Mexican artworks. The Moody Planetarium is on the premises.

Museum hours are Tuesday to Saturday from 9 a.m. to 4:30 p.m., on

Thursday night till 8:30 p.m., and on Sunday from 1 to 5 p.m. There are planetarium shows weekdays at 11 a.m. and 2 p.m., on Thursday and 7:30 p.m., and weekends at 2 and 3:30 p.m. Admission to the museum is free. Planetarium admission is $1 for adults, 50¢ for children under 12.

## Texas Tech University

While you're in the area, you might want to tour the rest of the 1,800-acre campus, which is bounded by 4th and 19th Streets north and south, University and Quaker Avenues east and west (tel. 742-2136). It's a beautiful campus—the kind you see in the movies—with lots of trees (every one of which has been planted and lovingly nurtured by the university) lining the walkways and terracotta-roofed Spanish-style buildings. A highlight is the internationally recognized **Textile Research Center** in the Engineering Quadrangle, with exhibits of cotton from all over the world, showing the processing operation from a bale of cotton, wool, or mohair to a finished piece of material. About 95% of all American-grown mohair, 35% of all wool, and 30% of all cotton is produced in Texas. The center serves as a liaison between farmers and industry.

The university also houses the world's premier livestock and nutrition center, a working/teaching hospital, a law school, and a business school, among other facets. It's the most academically diverse campus in the state. Call 742-1480 to arrange a guided tour tailored to your specific interests, or write ahead to the News and Publications Office, Texas Tech University, P.O. Box 4640, Lubbock, TX 79409. Tours can be arranged for weekdays from 9 a.m. to 4:30 p.m., on Saturday to noon. Among other things, you can arrange to view the stars through the Observatory telescope, tour a garden run by the Horticultural Department featuring plants that thrive in the region, and check out some interesting art and architecture.

## The Llano Estacado Winery

Wine is a burgeoning industry in Texas ("The Next Big Thing from Texas" is the slogan of the Texas Wine Growers Association), and Lubbock's Llano Estacado Winery, FM 1585, 3¼ miles east of U.S. 87 (tel. 745-2258), is at its hub. Starting in 1976 they staked the plains with vineyards and began producing premium-quality wines. Utilizing about 80% locally grown grapes, they've produced about a dozen wines and garnered a few dozen awards—not just in Texas but in national and international competitions. And haute-cuisine restaurants in Dallas and Houston have begun adding these fine Texas wines to their recherché French and California lists. (Llano Estacado is putting an end to snob jokes about the "Yellow Rosé of Texas" and "Château Alamo.")

The Winery gives very comprehensive tours, followed by tasting sessions of course, on Saturday from noon to 6 p.m. and on Sunday from 1 to 6 p.m. The most exciting time to come is late July or early September, when harvesting and grape crushing takes place. But any time of year it's most interesting to see the facilities—the crusher/stemmer machines, the wine press, stainless-steel fermentation tanks, various oak casks for aging red and white wines, the bottling process, and the laboratory. You'll learn a great deal about the process of wine making before adjourning to the tasting room. Guides are very knowledgeable and happy to answer your questions. You can also purchase the winery's output on the premises. Admission is free.

## Sports and Recreation

**Buffalo Springs Lake,** nine miles southeast of Lubbock (take 50th Street all the way out; tel. 806/747-3353), is a delightful 1,225-acre wildlife refuge for buffalo, racoons, bobcats, possums, fox, and Canadian geese. In summer you can rent paddleboats, rowboats, and canoes to take out on the 225-acre man-made lake, or take a Buffalo Gal Excursion Boat tour, a one-hour narrated trip on a 15-passenger boat (fare is $2.60). For all water-activity information, call 744-6977. You can also angle for catfish, bass, walleye, crappie, perch, and other lake fish; a state license—available at the park's concession for a minimal fee, along with bait—is required. You have to supply your own fishing gear, however.

The Llano Estacado Audubon Society has established a three-mile hiking trail in the park, a beautiful rustic route amid yucca, sage, sunflowers, and hackberry trees. Several hundred species of birds can be observed here. There are campsites and picnic areas with tables and grills. And in summer trail rides are offered on the south side of the canyon. This is beautiful country, especially in spring and summer when the wildflowers are in bloom and every evening when the sun sets over the canyon. If you come in spring, you may catch the Country Western Music Festival, a noon-to-sundown event that takes place here every year. A water park and swimming area are being considered for the future.

Admission is $1.50 for adults June through the end of September, $1 the rest of the year, 75¢ for children year round. Mosquito repellent is advisable spring through fall.

Right in town is **Mackenzie State Park,** Avenue A near East Broadway (tel. 762-6411), a large greenbelt offering swimming, golf, camping, picnicking, fishing (there are four man-made lakes), amusement-park rides, and biking and hiking trails. But the highlight for most people is the park's **Prairie Dog Town,** where pint-sized rodents (relatives of the groundhog) put on a round-the-clock show busily digging the L-shaped, 15- to 20-foot tunnels they call home. Prairie dogs once populated the plains in vast numbers; a colony of 400 million occupied an area of 37,000 square miles. However, cute as they are, they're agricultural pests, so they're now confined to this large field enclosed by a two-foot-high concrete wall. Most people, adults and children alike, can sit spellbound watching their antics for at least an hour. Don't miss it.

Contact the **Visitors and Conventions Bureau** (tel. 806/763-4666) for information about other sports facilities and activities, including Texas Tech games and occasional celebrity golf and tennis tournaments.

## The Buddy Holly Statue and Walk of Fame

A "heroic-size" eight-foot bronze statue of Lubbock's most famous native son, Buddy Holly, is the central feature of the downtown Walk of Fame at 8th Street and Avenue Q, honoring West Texas–area natives who have made significant contributions in the entertainment industry. Buddy Holly was born in Lubbock on September 7, 1936, and attended school here. He went on to organize the famed Crickets and become a major rock star, recording nine top-ten hits before his death in a plane crash (along with Richie Valens and the Big Bopper) in 1959. Surrounding the monument are bronze plaques honoring other local music stars like Waylon Jennings, Mac Davis, and Jimmy Dean.

**NIGHTLIFE:** The local "country club" is **Cowboys,** 7301 S. University Ave., at Loop 289 (tel. 745-9727), offering live country music on Thursday, Friday, and Saturday nights with a variety of entertainment the rest of the week. The country acts are sometimes regional groups, sometimes big names like Gary Morris and John Conlee. Every other Tuesday, live rock groups play Cowboys. On Wednesday night the club is for women only until 9:30 p.m. and a sexy male dance revue takes the stage; after 9:30 men are allowed in and a DJ plays top-40s tunes for dancing. Sunday night is teen night; no alcohol is served and the crowd is very young. Cowboy's has a 40-foot-square dance floor enhanced by state-of-the-art sound equipment and a 12-foot-square matrix neon light show. The decorations are neon beer signs, mirrored cowboy boots suspended over the dance floor, and murals of rodeos and other western scenes. A cozy game room contains eight pool tables, video games, and a working fireplace.

Admission is $3 on Friday and Saturday nights, $2 the rest of the week. Open Tuesday to Sunday till 2 a.m.

The Texas Tech crowd hangs out at the **Willow Hill Diner,** 4413 82nd St., in the Center Building (tel. 794-6036), where a DJ plays top-40s tunes, a little country, and occasional oldies for dancing. The setting is slick, with black-and-white tile floors, black lacquer tables, and shiny tufted black leather booths. Four video monitors and the requisite amount of neon lights complete the picture. A full menu is offered: sandwiches, salads, and entrees like barbecued chicken ($5.55) and meat loaf ($4.95), both served with two vegetables (like mashed potatoes and fresh green beans) and homemade cornbread. In good weather you can eat on the outdoor patio, a pleasant retreat from the diner's wall-to-wall-people interior.

Open nightly till 2 a.m. Dinner is served until 10 p.m. Sunday to Thursday, till 11 p.m. on Friday and Saturday. No admission charge.

Just across the street is **82nd St. Live,** 4414 82nd St., at Quaker Avenue (tel. 793-8833), a comedy club featuring both Texas and national headliners. There are 8:30 p.m. shows on Wednesday and Thursday night, 8:30 and 10:30 p.m. shows on Friday and Saturday night. Each show consists of an emcee introduction and two full comedy acts. Admission is $5.

The **Lubbock Symphony Orchestra** (tel. 762-4707) has a September-to-May six-concert season at the Lubbock Memorial Civic Center, 1051 6th St. Guest artists and conductors usually perform with the orchestra, and in its 40-year history these have included such notables as Arthur Fiedler, Van Cliburn, Leonard Warren, and Henry Mancini. Informal, half-hour talks about the evening's music precede some of the concerts. Tickets are in the $10 to $12 range.

**Ballet Lubbock** (tel. 793-9107) also has a September-to-May season at the Civic Center. Call for program and ticket information.

**Texas Tech University** is a cultural and activities center in Lubbock offering concerts (both classical and rock), lectures (anyone from Henry Kissinger to Allen Ginsberg), classic movies, athletic events, theater, opera, etc. An on-campus facility, the **Lubbock Municipal Auditorium and Coliseum** (tel. 762-4616) has featured rodeos, tractor pulls, major boxing matches, out-of-state symphony orchestras, and such headliners as John Denver, Rick Springfield, Alabama, Wayne Newton, and Bob Hope. Call to find out what's on during your stay. To find out about theater productions and films, call 742-2136. Or call 742-1480 for an overview of all campus happenings during your stay.

## 2. Amarillo

Unlike other Texas cities whose continued existence in the late 19th century depended on the coming of the railroad, Amarillo didn't exist until the railroad came. A miscarried plan put the Fort Worth & Denver City Railroad 20 miles off course in the middle of nowhere. It was easier to start a city there than to move the tracks, and in 1887 Amarillo, named for the yellowish Amarillo Creek (*amarillo* means "yellow" in Spanish), came into being. Oldtimers say that early settlers fairly ached for the sight of a tree or the sound of a bird. But in no time they planted trees and put up a courthouse, post office, hotel, stores, windmills, and the inevitable saloons where only grass had been before.

The town quickly developed into one of the world's greatest cattle-shipping markets. At times 50,000 head could be seen at prairie water holes waiting to be herded into railroad cars. Even today, cattle outnumber people in Amarillo about 20 to 1, and there's a big livestock auction once a week. For many years cattle raising, trading, and shipping was about all that went on in Amarillo. A steer could be raised on the open range for the price of a chicken, so why bother with anything else? The advent of barbed wire marked the beginning of other agricultural pursuits—first wheat and later cotton, sorghum, and other crops, all of which still play a large part in Amarillo's agribusiness economy. Natural gas and petroleum were discovered in the area in 1918 and 1921 respectively, and the extraction of helium from natural gas began in 1928, with Amarillo emerging as a "Helium Capital" supplying 90% of the world's helium from within a 250-mile radius.

In spite of the presence of some large energy-related corporations, a symphony orchestra, nightclubs, a superb French restaurant, and a few other trappings of sophistication, Amarillo has retained the flavor of a small western town where many of the folks you meet are farmers, cattle ranchers, cowboys, and oilmen. Over 50 tree-studded parks attest to continued local efforts toward the greening of Amarillo.

**GETTING THERE:** The **Amarillo International Airport,** at the eastern end of town, is served by American, Southwest, and Delta airlines.

Both **Greyhound** (tel. 806/376-9841) and **Trailways** (tel. 806/374-5371) have bus service into Amarillo, the former coming into a terminal at 816 Taylor St., the latter at 700 S. Tyler St.

**By car,** Amarillo is a very long drive from anywhere except Lubbock, 120 miles to the south via I-27. Unless time is no object, flying is your best bet.

**GETTING ORIENTED:** Write ahead or visit the **Amarillo Chamber of Commerce,** 1000 Polk St., at Tenth Avenue (P.O. Box 9840), Amarillo, TX 79105 (tel. 806/373-7800). Hours are Monday to Friday from 8:30 a.m. to 5 p.m., except for major holidays. They can supply brochures, maps, and information of all kinds.

**GETTING AROUND:** You must have a car in Amarillo. Several firms are represented at the airport, among them **Budget** (tel. 806/335-1696), **National** (tel. 806/335-2311), and **Avis** (tel. 806/335-2313).

A **taxi** from the airport to your hotel will cost $10 or $15. Most hotels in town offer complimentary airport transfer. Taxi fare is $1.30 for the first fifth of a mile, 20¢ for each additional fifth of a mile. If you need a cab, call Yellow Checker Cab (tel. 374-5242).

There is **city bus service** operating throughout Amarillo, but it may not take you where or when you want to go. For routing information, call 378-3094.

**ANNUAL EVENTS:** Contact the **Amarillo Chamber of Commerce** (tel. 806/373-7800) for a full rundown on what's happening during your stay.

The **Amarillo Stock Show and Rodeo** takes place every January at Fairpark Coliseum on the Tri-State Fairgrounds, 10th and Grand (tel. 376-7767), featuring quarterhorse and Appaloosa shows, livestock exhibits, and rodeo events.

Another important local rodeo takes place at **Cal Farley's Boys Ranch Rodeo Arena** on Labor Day Weekend. Boys who live at the ranch, ages 5 through 19, compete in rodeo events. The ranch, a marvelous facility for boys in need of a caring home, is described at some length later in this chapter. Call 372-2341 for information on the ranch rodeo.

An old-fashioned country fair, the **Tri-State Fair,** is another September event, once again at the Tri-State Fairgrounds (tel. 376-7767). It gets under way with a parade and features midway rides, livestock and agricultural exhibits, homemaking exhibits, and concerts by major country music stars.

Finally, in November, usually the first weekend, you can attend the **National Cutting Horse Association Finals** at the Fairgrounds (tel. 372-9186), an exciting riding-cowboy-skills exhibition.

**WHERE TO STAY:** My favorite Amarillo hotel is not its most luxurious or expensive accommodation, but it is a sightseeing attraction in its own right.

The **Big Texan Inn,** 7701 E. I-40, off the Whittaker Street exit, Amarillo, TX 79101 (tel. 806/372-5000), is the fanciful creation of the Lee family, and a totally original and delightful hostelry it is. The Lees are R.J., wife Mary Ann, and eight grown kids, most of whom are involved in the family business. Their 52-room hotel is fronted by an 88-foot statue of a "big Texan" and an 11½-foot-tall steer. Its exterior façade uses a variety of facings (shingles, wood, stucco, etc.) painted in cheerful colors to give the impression of a row of buildings (it's actually one long building) in a western town, complete with hitching posts embedded in wooden tubs filled with flowering plants. Above each room is the sign of a famed western hotel like Denver's Brown Palace. Room interiors are also Old West, with steer horn reading lamps, log-framed murals of western motifs on pale-yellow walls (stagecoaches, oil wells, buffalo hunting, etc.), brass beds, and swinging saloon-style doors separating bedrooms and dressing room/baths. Speaking of baths, some have whirlpool and steam/sauna adjustments (request one when you reserve if you wish), and all have good strong showers. All rooms are equipped with cable color TVs with HBO and other pay stations, AM/FM radios, and digital alarm clocks.

On the premises is Amarillo's most famous dining room (about which more in the restaurant section of this chapter). Adjoining the restaurant is the Trading Post gift shop, where you can purchase such western whimsicalities as a taxidermy-preserved rattlesnake or grizzly bear, boot-shaped drinking glasses, and dance-hall-girl garters. There's also a big shooting gallery and a video game room. Other amenities include a large Texas-shape swimming pool in front of a building that looks like the Alamo (it houses additional rooms that are furnished in Mexican motif), a liquor store (the only one between here and Dallas!), and a coin-op laundry room with ironing facilities. Free transport between the inn and the airport is offered, local phone calls are free, and you can call collect to make a reservation.

Rates at the Big Texan are surprisingly low: singles pay $35 to $46.50; doubles, $40 to $48.50; $5 for an extra person (under 12, free). Those prices include continental breakfast, and parking is free. Facilities for the disabled are available.

A more conventional choice is the **Sheraton Amarillo Hotel Towers,** 3100 I-40 West, at the Georgia Avenue exit, Amarillo, TX 79102 (tel. 806/358-6161, or toll free 800/325-3535), the town's most luxurious hostelry. As such, it has hosted many notables who've had reason to stay in Amarillo, including such various types as John McEnroe, Pat Boone, Wolfman Jack, and LadyBird Johnson. The Sheraton is in the current vogue of atrium-lobby hotels. Here the lobby's quite something, with a meandering waterway, lush plantings, fishtanks, and cockatoos in fancy birdcages. Under the atrium skylight are a medium-size indoor heated pool, whirlpool, and exercise room. There are video games for kids, and an outdoor sundeck adjoins. A lounge called the Amarillo River Yacht Club, on the banks of the lobby's "river," is a delightful setting for weekday afternoon Happy Hour with piano entertainment and complimentary hors d'oeuvres. And breakfast is served in a sunny, plant- and flower-filled atrium nook—a $5.95 buffet of everything you could possibly desire for the morning meal.

Sheraton rooms sport western motifs, achieved in the choice of art and patchwork-quilt-like bedspreads. They're equipped with cable color TVs offering HBO and Spectravision movies, AM/FM radios, alarm clocks, full-length mirrors, plus special toiletries and Water Pik shower massages in the bath. There's a concierge floor (the tenth) featuring all the usual extras—upgraded room decor and amenities, terry robes, desks, bathroom scales, hair dryers, bottles of Perrier, etc. A personal concierge, nightly turndown with a mint and a cordial, complimentary continental breakfast and cocktail-hour hors d'oeuvres in a private lounge, and fresh flowers in your room every day are additional perks.

The gourmet dining room is Gabriel's, serving French/continental cuisine at lunch and dinner. In the adjoining lounge rock bands play nightly for dancing and Happy Hour features a free fajita bar. Rounding out the hotel's facilities are a gift shop, unisex hair salon, and a car-rental desk. Room service is available around the clock, and free transport is offered between the airport and the hotel.

Rates are $65 to $75 single, $75 to $85 double, $20 additional across the board for concierge-level accommodations, $10 for an extra person (children under 18, free). Parking is free. No-smoking accommodations and facilities for the handicapped are offered.

The above-mentioned Big Texan Inn can't be beat in the low-moderate price category, but should it be full you'll do nicely at **Days Inn,** 1701 I-40 East, at the Ross-Osage exit, Amarillo, TX 79105 (tel. 806/379-6255, or toll free 800/325-2525), or a close by **La Quinta,** 1708 I-40 East, Amarillo, TX 79103 (tel. 806/373-7486, or toll free 800/531-5900). Both have swimming pools, are adjacent to Denny's, offer all the modern amenities, and are equipped for handicapped guests. The Days Inn charges $38 single, $43 double, $5 for an extra person, $1 for children under 18. La Quinta's rates are $40 single, $45 double, $5 for an extra person (under 18, free).

And finally there's a **Motel 6** at 3930 I-40 East, at Bolton Street, Amarillo, TX 79103 (tel. 806/372-6318). It too, has a swimming pool.

See Chapter I for details on La Quinta and Motel 6.

**WHERE TO EAT:** For openers, you can eat absolutely free in Amarillo . . . if you can eat enough! Read on.

The **Big Texan Steak Ranch,** 7701 E. I-40 (tel. 372-6000), is world famous for its only-in-Texas promotion. It's "the home of the free 72-ounce steak dinner!" That's right. If you can wolf down a 72-ounce steak, a big baked potato, shrimp cocktail, salad, and roll—in one hour—it's yours free. So far, since the offer was first made in 1963, 19,940 men have tried and 3,481 have succeeded; the women's ratio is 1,844 to 382. Successful aspirants have ranged from a 385-pound wrestler to a 68-year-old grandma, and one man actually ate it raw! What happens if you try and lose? You shell out $29.95 and get a doggy bag and a tall Texas tale to tell the folks back home. Part of the fun of dining here is keeping an eye on someone trying to polish off 4½ pounds of sizzling sirloin at a nearby table; announcements are always made.

But that's not the only attraction. Strolling C & W fiddlers and guitar players entertain while you dine. And the restaurant itself is quite something—a vast two-story affair decorated in unrestrained western motif. The Lees have spent years collecting the paraphernalia that lines the walls: old campfire cooking implements, farm tools, bearskins, steer horns, hunting trophies, bullfight posters, western paintings, rattlesnake hides, etc. Two Indian mannequins "dine" at one table, steaks are displayed on ice in an old stagecoach, the salad bar is in a covered wagon, and lighting emanates from wagon-wheel fixtures and 1890s dangling-crystal chandeliers. It's great. And so is the food.

The Lees serve up their own ranch-raised grain-fed prime beef steaks grilled on lava rock, and even if you don't go for the big one, portions are "Texas size." You can start off with an order of fresh crayfish in red sauce ($4.25), but more adventurous diners might want to try fried rattlesnake chunks ($10.95) or breaded calf fries known as mountain oysters (guess what part of the calf they really are; $6.25). Steaks are served with salad-bar fixings, fresh-baked sourdough buns and butter, and cowboy beans. A ten-ounce sirloin is $12.25; a seven-ouncer, $9.50. Another very recommendable choice is the Chuckwagon Dinner for two or more—a sizzling platter piled high with barbecued beef, chicken, spareribs, and Texas sausage served with potatoes, corn on the cob, carrots and onions, salad bar, cowboy beans, and sourdough buns ($9.95 per person). Seafood entrees, buffalo steak, and fried Texas rabbit are additional options, and for "light grazing" you might consider potato skins stuffed with chunks of chicken, pineapple, and broccoli in a tangy cheese sauce topped with slivered almonds ($4.50) or a half-pound steakburger with ranch fries ($4.50). There's a full bar, and desserts run the gamut from homemade strawberry shortcake ($3.25) to fresh strawberries topped with apricot yogurt, laced with rum, and topped with brown sugar.

Open daily from 10:30 a.m. to midnight.

**Maison Blanche,** 2740 Weasthaven Village, at 34th and Georgia (tel. 353-3523), is named not for its famous Washington, D.C., counterpart but for an airfield in Algiers where Earl Smith once landed in World War II. It's Amarillo's most beautiful restaurant. A flower arrangement graces a stunning Lalique table in the entranceway, an area where Venetian glass chandeliers are suspended from a carved plaster ceiling—a superfluity of elegance before you've even entered the dining room. There's no letdown when you do. Gilt-framed mirrors and oil paintings are hung on walls swagged in coral satin, lighting emanates from candles in cut-glass holders and multi-shaded, crystal-dripping wall sconces, seating is in Louis XVI–style chairs at elegantly appointed tables, and the floral-motif rose carpeting is lovely.

Chef Mark Cheffins has a distinguished culinary career; he's been the genius in the kitchen of some of San Antonio's and Dallas's premier restaurants. His Maison Blanche menu changes seasonally. On my last visit I had a superb hors d'oeuvre of spinach pasta tossed with Texas goat cheese and fresh basil ($9.25) followed by an entree of New Zealand lamb chops with Roquefort butter ($25.95). My companion opted for an appetizer of thinly sliced duck breast with raspberry sauce and fresh mint ($7.95) and an entree of filet mignon grilled with pistachio butter and baby vegetables ($16.25). Our dessert choices were a lemon Bavarian cream with raspberry sauce ($3.95) and a white and dark chocolate mousse ($4.50), both eminently satisfying.

If all that is too rich for your palate or pocketbook, La Maison Blanche offers another option—a plant-filled dining area called the Greenhouse where bougainvillea vines climb white-trellised walls and furnishings are lacy green wrought-iron and bamboo. Here lighter fare is featured, like a tricolor (spinach, red pepper, and egg) pasta salad with ham, tomato, artichoke hearts, fresh basil, and olive oil ($8.75); a grilled New York sirloin sandwich with straw potatoes ($10.25); or an omelet filled with chicken, Swiss cheese, ham, and green pepper ($6.25). The same lush desserts and well-chosen wine list obtain. In good weather you can also sit outside on the Greenhouse patio at Cinzano umbrella tables. A combo—guitarist/flutist/drummer—plays nightly except Monday at the Greenhouse. And there's a beautiful lounge on the premises where a pianist entertains; the antique mahogany bar in this room is from an English castle.

Maison Blanche is open for dinner only, Monday to Thursday from 6 to 10 p.m., on Friday and Saturday till 11 p.m. Weekday afternoons complimentary hors d'oeuvres are served in the lounge between 4 and 7 p.m. Reservations suggested.

**Sutphen's,** 620 W. 16th, at Madison, just off I-40 (tel. 373-0726), is a renowned Texas barbecue restaurant operated by the same family since 1950. It's absolutely great. In the main dining room, beamed ceilings, shuttered windows, tufted-leather booths, and a large working brick fireplace combine to create a cozy/comfy atmosphere. The other dining room has only a gas fireplace, but eight skylights overhead make it a lot sunnier. Order up a combination plate of pork spareribs, barbecued beef, and German sausage ($6.25); it's served with the best coleslaw you ever had, chunky homemade potato salad like mom used to make, thick Texas toast, sliced pickles, sweet onions, and apricots. A draft beer to wash it all down is $1. And of course there are variations of the above—sandwiches, individual meat platters, and even a few other items like chicken-fried steak. Sutphen's catered the christening of the battleship *Texas* and sends Texas "Care" packages to oil marketeers when they're lobbying in Washington (I only wish they'd send them to me).

Open Monday to Thursday from 11 a.m. to 9 p.m., on Friday and Saturday to 9:30 p.m.

**Gardski's Loft,** 1619 S. Kentucky, in Wellington Square at the corner of Georgia Street and I-40 (tel. 353-6626), is a very pleasant garden-like setting with seating at checkered-clothed tables amid dozens of hanging and potted plants. You've seen it before: a big oak bar, brass railings, stained-glass fixtures and panels, planters of yellow mums, and lots of exposed brick—all adding up to a casual rusticity. At night the Loft is lit by candles in amber glass holders.

Everything is made from scratch, and the menu caters to a wide array of dining moods. You might start out with an appetizer of nachos grande topped with beef, beans, cheese, guacamole, lettuce, tomatoes, sour cream, jalapeños, and black olives ($5.35), or a crock of French onion soup topped with toast and a slab of bubbling melted cheese ($2.50). From there you could proceed to a half-pound char-broiled burger topped with cheese, chili, and onions ($3.85) and an order of homemade fries ($1.35). On the other hand there are chicken or beef fajitas served with grilled onions and bell peppers, pico de gallo, guacamole, and sour cream ($6.95); or chicken teriyaki served with salad and rice pilaf ($6.20); or shrimp parmesan ($8.95). Then there are steaks, sandwiches, salads, and chicken-fried steaks. For dessert go for mama's hot apple spice pie topped with ice cream ($2.35). There's a full bar. Nightly (except Monday) a live band plays country music and rock oldies. And during the day crayons are provided for children.

Open daily from 11 a.m. to 1:30 a.m. The full menu is served till 11 p.m. or midnight, after which lighter fare is offered until closing.

Every Texas town has a favorite Tex-Mex eatery. In Amarillo it's the **Santa Fe Restaurant & Bar,** 3333 Coulter Dr., at 34th Avenue (tel. 358-8333), a large, comfortable stucco-walled place with Saltillo-tile floors, ceramic-tile-topped tables, a garden centerpiece under a skylight, and shelves of cactus and Mexican artifacts here and there. Start out with an order of cheese nachos ($3.25) or guacamole salad ($1.95). There's a wide choice of entrees, but about 80% of his clientele, the owner informs me, orders fajitas—charbroiled chicken or beef served with flour tortillas, pico de gallo, and sour cream ($7.25). There are several children's plates for $3. Beer, wine, and all bar drinks are available. At night, Santa Fe is always mobbed, so arrive early to avoid a wait or leave your name at the door and adjourn to the cozy lounge for margaritas until your table is ready.

Hours are Sunday to Thursday from 11 a.m. to 10 p.m., on Friday and Saturday to 10:30 p.m. No reservations.

**WHAT TO SEE AND DO:** Several local attractions involve 30 to 45 minutes of driving time, but they happen to be the most interesting, and in any case, the drives are scenic. Don't miss Cal Farley's Boys Ranch, Palo Duro Canyon, or the Panhandle-Plains Historical Museum.

### Palo Duro Canyon State Park

Twenty-seven miles south of Amarillo on Hwy. 217 is Palo Duro Canyon State Park (tel. 488-2227), 15,743 of the most awesomely beautiful acres in Texas. The park is centered on an abyss 1,000 feet deep and 100 miles long—a dramatic gash across the grassy plains landscape tinted varying hues of pink, red, and orange by the Red River waters that carved it. Colors also reflect the layered sedimentary rocks of major periods in the canyon's 230-million-year-old geological history. The oldest Permian beds, from an era when the sea still covered much of West Texas, consist of brick-red shales and mudstone veined with white gypsum, known locally as "Spanish Skirts." Also very colorful is the Tecovas Formation rock, its varied shades including purple, brown, orange, green, white, and gray. Along with the gray and brown ledge-forming sandstone of the Triassic period, these sections were created 180 to 200 million years ago by meandering rivers and streams flowing from highlands in Central Texas. In the Late Triassic Epoch there were swamps, ponds, and lakes inhabited by crocodile-like reptiles, and small dinosaurs also roamed the region. The uppermost cliffs of the Tertiary period are chalky pinkish tan, deposited two to ten million years ago by rivers and streams flowing east from the Rocky Mountains. At that time great herds of animals roamed the grassy plains (a setting much like Kenya today). The spectacular sand-castle-like rock formations of the canyon are as intriguing as its variegated colors. The Spanish called the canyon Palo Duro (hard wood) because of the juniper and cedar woodlands lining the rim. The Indians made bows and arrows from the cedar.

There are several ways to see the park. In good weather you can take a 30-minute, two-mile narrated miniature train ride on the Sad Monkey Railroad ($2 for tickets). And there are paved roads where you can take scenic drives. But best of all are hiking (there are caves to explore) or horseback riding along the park's many trails. There's lots of wildlife to see (deer, longhorns, aoudad sheep, pronghorn antelope, 190 species of birds), and you might even find evidence of the canyon's long history as an Indian hunting ground. Ancient stone projectile points found here suggest that nomadic peoples hunted mammoths and other Ice Age animals in the canyon as early as 12,000 years ago. There are also camping areas and picnic grills.

Before entering the canyon, you should stop at the park's interpretive center, which houses exhibits on the geology, prehistory, natural history, and human history of the area. A general store, snackbar, and riding stable are also found at the entrance. Dress properly. Sturdy walking boots and mosquito repellent are particularly recommendable.

The canyon is open daily from 8 a.m. to 10 p.m. Admission is $2 per car. In summer make advance reservations for camping by calling the above number.

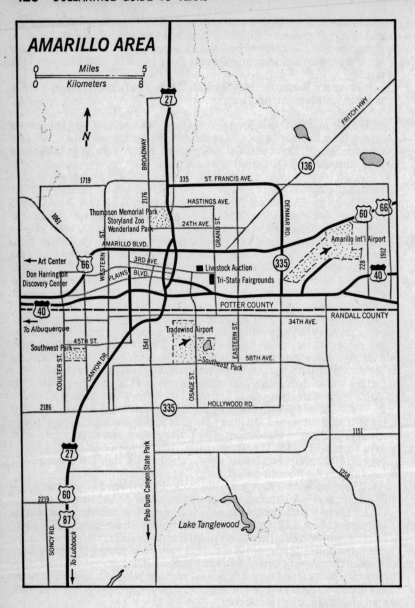

# AMARILLO AREA

Miles
Kilometers

N

27 BROADWAY

FRITCH HWY

136

1719 335 ST. FRANCIS AVE.

2176 HASTINGS AVE.

DENRAR RD.

60 • 66

1061 Thompson Memorial Park
Storyland Zoo 24TH AVE.
Wonderland Park

WESTERN ST.

GRAND ST.

Amarillo Int'l Airport

AMARILLO BLVD.

← Art Center

66 3RD AVE.

Don Harrington
Discovery Center

PLAINS BLVD.

Livestock Auction

Tri-State Fairgrounds

335

228

1912

40

POTTER COUNTY

40

← To Albuquerque

34TH AVE. RANDALL COUNTY

45TH ST.

Southwest Park

COULTER ST.

CANYON DR.

1541

Tradewind Airport

EASTERN ST.

Southeast Park 58TH AVE.

OSAGE ST.

2186 335 HOLLYWOOD RD.

1151

27

1258

60

2219

SONCY RD.

87

To Lubbock

Palo Duro Canyon State Park

Lake Tanglewood

*Note:* The musical extravaganza *TEXAS* is performed nightly except Sunday in the canyon amphitheater (details later in this chapter).

## The Panhandle-Plains Historical Museum

Also in Canyon, 17 miles south of Amarillo, is the Panhandle-Plains Historical Museum, U.S. 87 and Fourth Avenue (tel. 655-7191). The oldest state museum in Texas, it houses exhibits on the history of the state with particular emphasis on the West Texas region. Displays begin with Paleozoic fossils from the age of reptiles and proceed chronologically through Indian, Spanish, Mexican, and Anglo-American eras. There's a Hall of Southern Plains Indians featuring a fine collection of artifacts from Comanche, Kiowa, Arapaho, Apache, and Cheyenne tribes. A visual history of the development of the cattle industry on the Southern Plains is presented in the Hall of Ranching. And you can follow a board sidewalk through a turn-of-the-century Pioneer Village complete with stable, barber, blacksmith, printing office, saloon, doctor's office, bank, dressmaking shop, general store, hotel, pioneer cabins, a schoolroom, and the home of an affluent settler. The museum has natural history displays, a chuckwagon campfire is re-created, and there are changing exhibits of art, antique furnishings, and fashions.

In the annex is a Transportation Hall of wagons, buggies, ox carts, and a 1903 Model A Ford, the first to come off the Ford assembly line. The latest addition to the museum is the Petroleum Wing, housing a 32-foot-tall wooden oil derrick and exhibits enhanced by audio-visual displays and photographs elucidating the petroleum industry. Wars that Texas has fought are also comprehensively covered—the Alamo, the Mexican Wars, the Civil War, etc. And the 1934 art deco building with its Texas historical murals is itself noteworthy. Make a stop here on your way out to Palo Duro Canyon.

The museum is open Monday to Saturday from 9 a.m. to 5 p.m. September to May, till 6 p.m. Monday to Saturday the rest of the year. On Sunday, year round, hours are 2 to 6 p.m. Admission is free.

## Cal Farley's Boys Ranch

Amarillo is the home of one of the most wonderfully inspiring places I've ever visited, Cal Farley's Boys Ranch, 36 miles northwest of downtown in Tascosa (tel. 806/372-6627). Founded in 1939 by world-champion wrestler and successful businessman Cal Farley, the 10,600-acre ranch provides a warm and loving home to about 400 boys of all races and religions whose families are unable to care for them. Some have been behavior problems, and about 50% have had run-ins with the law. Boys Ranch gives them "affectionate discipline, training, and supervision in a family-oriented, long-term, structured program with the opportunity for both academic and vocational education."

Boys ages 5 to 15 are accepted from all over the country, and very fortunate boys they are. They're lovingly cared for by a dedicated staff, with a ratio of one staff member to each boy. Boys live in "families" of 24 under the guidance of a deeply committed married couple. There's nothing institutional about these homes. All have lounge areas with TVs, pool tables, and Ping-Pong; awards cases to display trophies the boys have won; and spacious bedrooms (four boys share a room) personalized with posters and private possessions. Many of the boys are engaged in agricultural or other kinds of training. They run a full farming operation with about 250 head of cattle, chickens, pigs, horses, and other animals; an auto mechanics and body repair shop; and a food-processing plant where milk is pasteurized and cartoned, and honey prepared. And boys learning construction trades have built staff homes and other on-premises structures.

From a very young age the boys are taught how to run a business—a kind of schooling that would benefit youngsters everywhere. A boy might get started in livestock by purchasing a cow or pig with a low-interest loan from the ranch "bank." He raises and cares for the animal and can realize a profit on it and go on to purchase additional animals. By the time a boy is ready to leave the ranch, he not only has a marketable skill but has amassed some capital and learned to be a responsible human being. He's also received a sound academic education, and if he has the aptitude he can go on to college.

But it's far from "all work and no play" on the ranch. The boys learn to ride and participate in an annual Labor Day rodeo, there are lakes for fishing, lots of sports activities, pets, games, trips, and holiday and birthday celebrations. And the Panhandle plains setting is idyllic—some of the most beautiful scenery in Texas. This is old Apache land, little changed since Indian days except for ranch fencing and telephone poles.

The ranch is open to visitors by appointment (call the above number or write to P.O. Box 1890, Amarillo, TX 79174). Visitors are given a tour of the facilities and invited to lunch with the boys. Part of the reason the ranch is open to the public is, of course, financial. Though the boys raise and grow much of their own food, it costs $18,000 a year to provide each one with a home, education, medical care, and guidance. So to some extent the ranch hopes visitors will become contributors. No pressure is put on you to make a donation, but the operation is so inspiring, you'll probably want to help support it. I very much urge you to include a morning and lunch at Boys Ranch on your Texas itinerary. It's a poignantly moving experience to see hundreds of boys who might have drifted into crime being guided to meaningful, productive lives.

To get to Boys Ranch from Amarillo, take FM 1061 northwest to U.S. 385 north.

## The Amarillo Livestock Auction

The Amarillo Livestock Auction, the largest in the country in terms of receipts, takes place every Monday from about 9 a.m. to 5 p.m. at 3000 E. Third Ave. and Manhattan Street (tel. 373-7464). About 4,000 head of cattle are sold here every Monday—everything from calves to full-grown bulls. Pen space on the premises can accommodate 20,000 head of cattle. Visitors are welcome, and you can usually find a friendly cowboy to explain what's going on. Or call in advance and arrange for a free guided tour of the stockyards and auction room. If there are a lot of animals to be sold, the auction sometimes runs over till Tuesday. And there are video auctions the third Thursday of every month at 1 p.m. Buyers view the cattle on a large-screen TV; it's not quite as colorful.

If you really want to get into the spirit of things, have breakfast or lunch at the Stockyard Café on the premises. A T-bone steak with homemade rolls and fresh-cut french fries is $7.25. There's not much ambience, but the people are for real. The café is open from 6 a.m. to 2 p.m. Monday to Saturday.

## Don Harrington Discovery Center

A wonderful little science museum filled with fascinating hands-on exhibits, the Don Harrington Discovery Center, 1200 Streit Dr., in the Medical Center Complex (tel. 355-9547), presents a comprehensive overview of the sciences. An exhibit called "The Human Life Story" takes you through all the stages of a fetus. You can also walk inside a kaleidoscope here, look into infinity, find out your weight on the moon by stepping onto a lunar scale, and roll a coin down a gravity well that illustrates the gravitational pull of the sun on the planets of our solar system. Additional exhibits include an aquarium and a computer learning center. There are frequent planetarium shows in the **Ecosphere** (admission is $2 for adults, $1.50 for children 6 to 12; under 6, free) and in **Theatre 360** where thrilling IMAX films like *To Fly* and *Living Planet* are shown (admission is $3 for all). The **Discovery Theatre** features a solar telescope exhibit and energy- and water-management simulators; the **Family Life Theatre** offers puppet shows on health, nutrition, and drugs; "Man in Space" focuses on our explorations of the moon with interpretive exhibits and lunar rock samples; and "Helium: A Gas for All Reasons" features the story of this rare gas and its use by industry and the U.S. space program (helium is a big business in Amarillo).

The center is open Monday to Friday from 9 a.m. to 5 p.m., on Saturday from 11 a.m. to 5 p.m., and on Sunday from 1 to 5 p.m., with supplemental hours from 7:30 to 9 p.m. Thursday to Sunday night for planetarium and IMAX shows. Admission to the museum is free.

## The Helium Monument

Just outside the center, the Helium Monument, dedicated in 1968, celebrates the 100th anniversary of the discovery of helium in the spectrum of the sun. It has four sealed stainless-steel columns representing the two protons and two neutrons of the helium-4 atom. But the most fascinating thing about the monument is that it is an above-ground time capsule (the only one in the country) containing the flotsam and jetsam of contemporary culture—a "Tonight Show" videotape, dehydrated foods, a Sears catalog, the Amarillo phonebook, cigarettes, restaurant menus, clothing, and seeds for corn, cotton, wheat, and (don't ask me why) crabgrass—among other items, 4,000 altogether. A savings account passbook from an Oklahoma City bank represents a deposit that will ostensibly be worth one quintillion dollars when the column is opened in 2968! The monument also functions as a sundial. Helium was discovered during the solar eclipse of August 1868 by British astronomer Norman Lockyer. Amarillo's helium production is so high, the city is known as the Helium Capital of the World.

## Thompson Park

A full day of family fun can be had at 600-acre Thompson Park, at 24th Street and U.S. 87 (tel. 378-3036).

There's a charming **Storyland Zoo,** complete with a "Hickory, Dickory Dock" clock, baby animal petting area, playground, Snow White's cottage, and sliding pond in a big cowboy boot. Animal residents are sheep, goats, calves, peacocks, rabbits, buffalo, bears, deer, monkeys, raccoons, porcupines, geese, and ducks. It's open from 10 a.m. to 6 p.m. daily. Admission is free.

The park's sports facilities include a 36-hole **golf course,** three **tennis courts,** a **softball** field, and a **swimming pool.**

And the highlight is **Wonderland Park** (tel. 383-4712), an amusement park within a park offering 21 rides and 32 attractions. Rides include a double-loop roller coaster, a flume ride called the Big Splash, a simulated run-the-rapids ride, bumper cars, a merry-go-round, a few other coasters, and kiddieland rides. And there are arcade games, miniature golf, and a shooting gallery, plus food concessions and a picnic pavilion within Wonderland. It's open mid-April through Labor Day, weekdays from 7 to 10:30 p.m., weekends from 1 to 10:30 p.m. From Labor Day to the end of September and mid-March to mid-April the park stays open weekends only. Admission is $7.95 weekdays, $9.95 weekends. You can get your hand stamped, leave to use other park facilities, and return.

The entire park is a shady lakeside oasis with grill-equipped picnic groves.

## Cowboy Morning

This is the kind of thing that brings people out west. Cowboy Morning, at the Tom Christian Ranch, a vast cattle spread, is a 25-minute horse-drawn wagon ride along the most scenic areas of the Palo Duro Canyon. It's a four-hour excursion, departing from major hotels at 7:30 a.m. mid-May through mid-September. At the canyon, cowboys cook up a Texas-size breakfast of eggs, rangeland sausage, homemade sourdough biscuits with gravy, coffee, and orange juice. They give demonstrations of roping, branding, and other cowboy skills, and show the kids how to ride a horse. You'll have some time to explore the canyon and take pictures as well.

Cost is $18 for adults, $13.50 for children 3 to 12 (under 3, free). Reserve in advance by writing or calling the Convention and Visitors Bureau, P.O. Box 9480, Amarillo, TX 79105 (tel. 806/373-7800, or toll free in Texas 800/692-1338).

## Cadillac Ranch

Amarillo's most dubious attraction—though it's one that has received oodles of publicity—is the so-called Cadillac Ranch out on I-40 West, between Soncy and Helium Road. That's where eccentric millionaire Stanley Marsh III has planted a "bumper crop" of ten Cadillacs in a row, front end down with their tail fins up in the air. Talk about staking the plains! They range from 1949 to 1963 models. Tourists have parked right on the freeway and beaten a path through the wheatfields to get a better look. I don't advise this, but if you do park, be sure you're well off the road.

**NIGHTLIFE:** You'll find plenty to do at night in Amarillo. If you're here in the summer, the show *TEXAS* is a must!

The Palo Duro Canyon, off I-40 on Hwy. 217 (details above), is the spectacular outdoor setting for the **Pioneer Amphitheatre** (tel. 655-2181), where a musical extravaganza called *TEXAS* has been playing nightly (except Sunday) during summer months since 1965. The 1,600-seat theater sits at the base of a 600-foot cliff. Though the show changes a bit from year to year, it re-creates, with considerable pomp and western pageantry, the history of the Panhandle and its settlers in the 1880s. It begins with a cowboy astride a magnificent white stallion riding onto the vast stage holding a Lone Star flag aloft. Lavish special effects contribute to the drama—the canyons reverberate with rolls of thunder, lightning streaks across the cliff walls, and there are dust storms, flash floods, and prairie fires. It's great entertainment for the whole family.

This isn't just some amateurish local production. It was written by Pulitzer Prize–winning playwright Paul Green, and it's been reviewed by publications nationwide and seen by over 1.7 million people. Reserve tickets in advance; sellout audiences are common. And bring a jacket or sweater; even on summer nights the canyon can be quite chilly. A big barbecue dinner is available for $5 prior to the show; ask about it when you reserve tickets.

*TEXAS* runs from mid-June to late August. Curtain is at 8:30 p.m. Park admission is free to ticket holders. Tickets cost $6 to $10 for adults, $3 to $10 for children under 12.

The **Amarillo Little Theatre**, 2019 Civic Circle, just off I-40 at Wolfin and Georgia (tel. 335-9991), is a community theater almost as old as Amarillo itself. During a September-to-May season, with occasional shows in summer, it presents a wide variety of dramatic productions. Some recent examples: *Peter Pan* (Peter Foy, who arranged flight for Mary Martin, came and did it here too), *The*

*Elephant Man, Arsenic and Old Lace, Crimes of the Heart,* and *Carousel.* Tickets are about $10.

The **Amarillo Symphony** (tel. 376-8782) also has a September-to-May season. It's at the Civic Center, 4th and Buchanan, and it includes about 65 concerts, usually featuring noted guest artists like Van Cliburn, Marilyn Horne, Ferrante and Teicher, Lorin Hollander, and Shirley Jones. There are classical and pops concerts, children's concerts, and four Christmas-season performances of *The Nutcracker* with the Lone Star Ballet Company.

And while I'm on the subject of the **Civic Center** (tel. 378-3096), it's the setting for many events—tractor pulls, Ice Capades, rodeos, the circus, and headliner concerts starring people like Motley Crue, George Strait, Ronnie Milsap, Amy Grant, Tom Jones, and Alabama, among others. Call to find out what's on during your stay.

The **Country Squire Dinner Theatre,** 135 Sunset Market Town, at Western Street and Plains Boulevard (tel. 358-7486), features relatively famous actors and actresses in their theater-in-the-round productions. For instance, Carol Lynley starred in *A Dash of Spirits,* Patrick and Ethan Wayne (John's sons) in *Come Blow Your Horn,* and Mary McDonough (Erin from "The Waltons") in *Angel on My Shoulder.* They do about eight plays in a year-round season. Ticket prices of $15.95 to $19.95 include a full buffet dinner Tuesday to Saturday nights. At Sunday matinees there's no meal and tickets are $10.50. Monday nights Roger and David Otwell (from the old "Lawrence Welk Show") sing at a $12-per-person dining and dancing show. And Saturday afternoons there are hot dog matinees for children.

The Big Texan Inn runs a full-blown casino operation over at a club called **Monopoly's Boardwalk,** 2600 Linda Circle, at Paramount Boulevard (tel. 359-4101). The place is decorated in Parker Bros. motif, complete with a section called "jail" (housing the DJ and cashiers), Monopoly board tables (all the pieces are available if you want to play), and a 19-foot "Foodwalk" of complimentary hors d'oeuvres. In the Boardwalk Casino you can play blackjack or craps. For $7.50 you get $2,000 worth of chips. No, you can't win—gambling is not legal in Texas—but it's fun to play. A camaraderie quickly develops at the gaming tables, and since nothing is at stake people often share their chips with you if you're on a losing streak. When your chips are gone, you can dance to top-40s, oldies, and country tunes played by a DJ.

There's an admission charge of $2 for men Wednesday to Saturday only; women always get in free. You have to be 23 to gain admittance. Open Monday to Saturday till 2 a.m., on Sunday till midnight.

**Cheers,** 2600 Paramount Blvd. (tel. 358-2151), is a glitzy disco decorated with neon tubing, balloons, and streamers. A sleek white 1947 Studebaker is on display, there are video monitors placed around the room, and pool tables can be found in the VIP room. The DJ plays a mix of country, rock, and oldies. Come by weekday afternoons for lavish Happy Hour Mexican or prime rib buffets. Admission is $1 Sunday to Thursday, $2 on Friday and Saturday night. Open nightly until 2 a.m.

**Willie's,** 2511 Paramount Blvd. (tel. 358-0126), features live bands—mostly country, but some top-40 groups—on Thursday, Friday, and Saturday nights. A few times a month pretty big names play here, people like Roy Orbison, B. B. King, and David Allan Coe. Willie's has a 1,000-square-foot dance floor with a 12-foot video screen overhead, a big working fireplace, and a full casino setup with blackjack, poker, and craps tables. Complimentary hors d'oeuvres are served from 4 to 7 p.m. Music starts at about 9 p.m. Admission is $2 to $10, depending on the performer.

Nearby is **Jolly's,** a comedy club at 2311 Paramount Blvd. (tel. 359-3432), open Tuesday to Sunday nights with three-act shows at 8:30 p.m., 8:30 and 10:30 p.m. on Friday and Saturday nights. On Sunday nights you get an amateur-night format plus the regular show. Generally, performers are the comedy-club-circuit crowd who play the Carson and Letterman shows. Admission is $5 on weeknights and Sunday (except Tuesday when you can get in for half price). On Friday and Saturday admission is $6.

17my88